Multi-Stakeholder Governance and the Internet Governance Forum

Multi-Stakeholder GOVERNANCE and the Internet Governance Forum

Jeremy Malcolm

TERMINUS PRESS
PERTH 2008

For Dominica

Published in Australia by Terminus Press

First paperback edition 2008

10 9 8 7 6 5 4 3

Cover design by Lisa Emmanuel
Cover illustration by Matt Britt

This book was typeset using the $\LaTeX$ typesetting system.
The body text is set in 9 on 11pt Palatino type.

National Library of Australia Cataloguing-in-Publication entry

Author:	Malcolm, Jeremy.
Title:	Multi-stakeholder governance and the Internet Governance Forum / Jeremy Malcolm.
ISBN:	9780980508406 (pbk.)
	9780980508413 (online)
Notes:	Includes index.
	Bibliography.
Subjects:	Internet–Government policy.
	Internet–Management.
	Internet–International cooperation.
Dewey Number:	004.678

Contents

List of Figures

List of Tables

Table of Statutes and International Instruments

Table of Cases

Table of Abbreviations

2LD	Second Level Domain
AACS	Advanced Access Content System
AAP	Alternative Approval Process (*see ITU*)
AARNET	Australian Academic Research Network
AC	Advisory Committee (*see ICANN*)
ACCC	Australian Competition and Consumer Commission
ACCI	Australian Chamber of Commerce and Industry
ACICA	Australian Centre for International Commercial Arbitration
ACLU	American Civil Liberties Union
ACMA	Australian Communications and Media Authority
ACTU	Australian Council of Trade Unions
ADMA	Australian Direct Marketing Association
ADNA	Australian Domain Name Administration
AGIMO	Australian Government Information Managment Office
ALAC	At-Large Advisory Committee (*see ICANN*)
ANSI	American National Standards Institute
AOL	America Online
APC	Association for Progressive Communications
APDIP	Asia-Pacific Development Information Programme (*see UNDP*)
APEC	Asia-Pacific Economic Cooperation
APNIC	Asia-Pacific Network Information Centre

APRA Australian Performers Rights Association

APRALO Asia-Pacific Regional At-Large Organization (*see ICANN*)

ARIA Australian Recording Industry Association

ARIN American Registry for Internet Numbers

AS Autonomous System

ASEAN Association of South East Asian Nations

ASF Apache Software Foundation

ASIC Australian Securities and Investments Commission

ASO Address Supporting Organization (*see ICANN*)

ASRB Accounting Standards Review Board

ASRG Anti-Spam Research Group

ASTA Anti-Spam Technical Alliance

ATM Asynchronous Transfer Mode

auDRP .au Dispute Resolution Policy

AUP Acceptable Use Policy

AURSC Australian Root Server Consortium

AusCERT Australian Computer Emergency Response Team

auWG dot-AU Working Group

B2B Business to business

BASIS Business Action to Support the Information Society

BDFL Benevolent Dictator For Life

BGP Border Gateway Protocol

BIND Berkeley Internet Name Daemon

BOF Birds of a Feather (*see IETF*)

C-CAICE Canadian Coalition Against Internet Child Exploitation

CA Certification Authority

CAC Consumer Advisory Council

CAMDUN Campaign for a More Democratic United Nations

CCBI Coordinating Committee of Business Interlocutors (*see WSIS*)

CCNSO Country Code Names Supporting Organization (*see ICANN*)

ccTLD Country-code Top Level Domain

CDT Center for Democracy and Technology

CEB Chief Executives Board (*see UN*)

CEN European Committee for Standardization

CERT Computer Emergency Response Team

CERT.br Centro de Estudos, Resposta e Tratamento de Incidentes de Segurança no Brasil

CGI.br Comitê Gestor da Internet no Brasil

CMC Computer-Mediated Communication

CNSA Contact Network of Anti-Spam Enforcement Authorities

CoE Community of Expertise (*see GAID*)

CONGO Conference of Non-Governmental Organizations in Consultative Relationship with the United Nations

COO Chief Operating Officer

CoR Committee of the Regions (*see EU*)

CORE Council of Registrars

CPA Certified Public Accountant

CS-IGC Civil Society Internet Governance Caucus

CSB Civil Society Bureau

CSD Civil Society Division (*see WSIS*)

CSR Corporate Social Responsibility

CSS Content Scrambling System

CSTD Commission on Science and Technology for Development

DARPA Defence Advanced Research Projects Agency

DCOS Dynamic Coalition on Open Standards

DDoS Distributed Denial of Service

DEMOS Delphi Mediation Online System

DKIM Domain Keys Identified Mail

DMCA Digital Millennium Copyright Act

DNS Domain Name System

DNSSEC DNS Security Extensions

DOT Force Digital Opportunities Task Force

DRM Digital Rights Management

DSF Digital Solidarity Fund

DVD Digital Versatile Disk

EBITT E-Business, IT and Telecoms (*see ICC*)

EC European Community

ECOSOC Economic and Social Council (*see UN*)

ECSC European Coal and Steel Community

EEC European Economic Community

EESC Economic and Social Committee (*see EU*)

EFA Electronic Frontiers Australia

EFF Electronic Frontiers Foundation

ENISA European Network and Information Security Agency

ENSTA École Nationale Supérieure de Techniques Avancées

ETNO European Telecommunications Network Operators' Association

EU European Union

EUROLINC European Languages Internet Conference

FIRST Forum of Incident Response and Security Teams

FLOSS Free/Libre/Open Source Software

FNC Federal Network Council

FOSS Free/Open Source Software

FSC Forestry Stewardship Council

FSF Free Software Foundation

FTA Fair Trade Agreement

FTC Federal Trade Commission

FTP File Transfer Protocol

G77 Group of 77

GAC Governmental Advisory Committee (*see ICANN*)

GAID Global Alliance for ICT and Development

GATT General Agreement on Tariffs and Trade

GBDe Global Business Dialogue on Electronic Commerce

GFDL GNU Free Documentation License

GIC [1] Global Internet Council (*see WGIG*)

GIC [2] Group for the Internationalization of the Cyberspace

GIFT Global Internet Freedom Taskforce

GIPC Global Internet Policy Council (*see WGIG*)

GKP Global Knowledge Partnership

GNSO Generic Names Supporting Organization (*see ICANN*)

GNU GNU's Not Unix

GONGO Government-Organised Non-governmental Organisation

GPL General Public License

GRASS Group Report Authoring Support System

GSM Global System for Mobile Communications

gTLD Generic Top Level Domain

gTLD-MOU Generic Top Level Domain Memorandum of Understanding

HLSOC High-Level Summit Organizing Committee

HOD Heads of Delegation (*see WTO*)

HTML HyperText Markup Language

HTTP HyperText Transfer Protocol

I18N Internationalisation

IAHC Internet International Ad Hoc Committee

IAIS International Association of Insurance Supervisors

IAL International Law Association

IATA International Association of Transport Airlines

ICA Institute of Cultural Affairs

ICANN Internet Corporation for Assigned Names and Numbers

ICAO	International Civil Aviation Organization
ICC	International Chamber of Commerce
ICCB	Internet Configuration Control Board
ICJ	International Court of Justice
ICPEN	International Consumer Protection and Enforcement Network
ICRA	Internet Content Rating Association
ICRC	International Committee of the Red Cross
ICSID	International Centre for the Settlement of Investment Disputes
ICT	Information and Communication Technologies
ICT4D	ICT for Development
IEC	International Electrotechnical Commission
IEEE	Institute of Electrical and Electronics Engineers
IESG	Internet Engineering Steering Group
IETF	Internet Engineering Task Force
IFWP	International Forum on the White Paper
IGF	Internet Governance Forum
IGO	Inter-Governmental Organisation
IGP	Internet Governance Project
IIA	Internet Industry Association of Australia
IIC	International Internet Council (*see WGIG*)
IIL	Institute of International Law
ILO	International Labour Organization
ILPF	Internet Law and Policy Forum
IMF	International Monetary Fund
IMO	International Maritime Organization
INTA	International Trade Mark Association
InterNIC	Internet Network Information Centre
IOSCO	International Organization of Securities Commissions
IPC	Intellectual Property Committee

IPR	Intellectual Property Rights
IRC	Internet Relay Chat
IRP	Independent Review Panel (*see ICANN*)
IRSG	Internet Research Steering Group
IRTF	Internet Research Task Force
ISFT	Internet Societal Task Force
ISI	Information Sciences Institute at the University of Southern California
ISO	International Organization for Standardization
ISP	Internet Service Provider
ISTF	Internet Societal Task Force
ITAA	Information Technology Association of America
ITR	International Telecommunications Regulations
ITS	Incompatible Time-sharing System
ITU	International Telecommunications Union
IWA	International Workshop Agreements (*see ISO*)
IWF	Internet Watch Foundation
JPA	Joint Project Agreement
JPEG	Joint Photographic Experts Group
JTC 1	Information Technology Joint Technical Committee (*see ISO*)
K4D	Knowledge for Development
LAP	London Action Plan
LDAP	Lightweight Directory Access Protocol
MAAWG	Messaging Anti-Abuse Working Group
MAC	Membership Advisory Committee (*see ICANN*)
MAG	Multistakeholder Advisory Group (*see IGF*)
MBCA	Mutually Beneficial Collective Action
MDG	Millennium Development Goals
MEP	Member of the European Parliament

MIME	Multipurpose Internet Mail Extensions
MINC	Multilingual Internet Names Consortium
MIPI	Music Industry Piracy Investigations
MIT	Massechusetts Institute of Technology
MMWG	Multistakeholder Modalities Working Group
MNC	Multinational Corporation
MOTU	Masters of the Universe
MOU	Memorandum of Understanding
MPEG	Moving Picture Experts Group
MSP	Multi-stakeholder partnership
NACPEC	North American Consumer Project on Electronic Commerce
NATO	North Atlantic Treaty Organization
NGO	Non-Governmental Organisation
NIR	National Internet Registry
NOIE	National Office of the Information Economy
NRO	Number Resources Organization
NSF	National Science Foundation
NSI	Network Solutions Incorporated
NTIA	National Telecommunications and Information Administration
NWG	Network Working Group
OECD	Organization for Economic Cooperation and Development
OHCHR	Office of United Nations High Commissioner for Human Rights
OIC	Organization of the Islamic Conference
OPM	Open Policy Meeting (*see APNIC*)
ORDIG	Open Regional Dialogue on Internet Governance
OSDL	Open Source Development Labs
OSI	Open Systems Interconnection
P2P	Peer-to-Peer
P3P	Platform for Privacy Preferences

PAB [1]	Policy Advisory Body (*see gTLD-MOU*)
PAB [2]	Policy Advisory Board (*see auDA*)
PDP	Policy Development Process (*see ICANN*)
PFIR	People For Internet Responsibility
PGP	Pretty Good Privacy
PICS	Platform for Internet Content Selection
PIR	Public Interest Registry
PNG	Portable Network Graphics
POC	Policy Oversight Committee (*see gTLD-MOU*)
PPP	Public-private partnership
PSTN	Public Switched Telephone Network
PTT	Postal Telegraph and Telephone
QUANGO	Quasi-Autonomous Non-governmental Organisation
RALO	Regional At-Large Organization (*see ICANN*)
RDF	Resource Description Framework
RFC	Request For Comment
RIAA	Recording Industry Association of America
RIPE NCC	Réseaux IP Européens Network Coordination Centre
RIR	Regional Internet Registries
RSS	Really Simple Syndication
RTF	Rich Text Format
SABDFL	Self-Appointed Benevolent Dictator For Life
SAG	Special Advisory Group (*see IGF*)
SC	SubCommittee (*see ISO*)
SEC	Securities Exchange Commission
SET	Secure Electronic Transactions
SGML	Standard Generalised Markup Language
SIA	Satellite Industry Association
SIDN	Stichting Internet Domeinregistratie Nederland

SIG Special Interest Group

SMF Simple Machines Forum

SMTP Simple Mail Transport Protocol

SNMP Simple Network Management Protocol

SO Supporting Organization (*see ICANN*)

SPI Software in the Public Interest

SPIN Segmentary, Polycentric, Integrated Network

SRS Shared Registry System (*see gTLD-MOU*)

SSL Secure Sockets Layer

TAG Technical Advisory Group (*see W3C*)

TC Technical Committee (*see ISO*)

TCCC Telstra Consumer Consultative Council

TEL Telecommunications and Information Working Group (*see APEC*)

TFFM Task Force on Financing Mechanisms

TIO Telecommunications Industry Ombudsman

TLD Top Level Domain

TLG Technical Liaison Group (*see ICANN*)

TLS Transport Layer Security

TRIPS Trade Related Aspects of Intellectual Property

TSB Telecommunication Standardization Bureau (*see ITU*)

UDRP Uniform Domain Name Dispute Resolution Policy

UN United Nations

UNCITRAL United Nations Commission on International Trade Law

UNCTAD United Nations Conference on Trade and Development

UNDP United Nations Development Programme

UNESCAP United Nations Economic and Social Commission for Asia and the Pacific

UNESCO United Nations Educational, Scientific and Cultural Organization

UNGIS United Nations Group on the Information Society

UNICEF United Nations Children's Fund

UNICTTF United Nations ICT Task Force

UNIDROIT International Institute for the Unification of Private Law

UNMSP United Nations Multi-Stakeholder Partnerships

UPU Universal Postal Union

VGT Virtual Global Taskforce

VoIP Voice Over IP

VPN Virtual Private Network

W3C World Wide Web Consortium

WAP Wireless Application Protocol

WCIT World Conference on International Telecommunication

WG Working Group (*see ISO*)

WGCIG Working Group on Constitutional Internet Governance

WGIG Working Group on Internet Governance

WHATWG Web Hypertext Application Technology Working Group

WIPO World Intellectual Property Organization

WITSA World Information Technology and Services Alliance

WLL Wireless Local Loop

WSIS World Summit on the Information Society

WSIS-SCT Civil Society Subcommittee on Content and Themes

WTO World Trade Organization

WTSA World Telecommunications Standardization Assembly

XML Extensibile Markup Language

YSEI Youth Social Enterprise Initiative

Preface

Like many watershed moments, the establishment of the Internet Governance Forum (IGF) in 2006 went unnoticed by most Internet users. But by providing an integrated forum for deliberation on Internet public policy issues, the IGF has the potential to begin to legitimately address some of the Internet's biggest challenges—such as spam, cybercrime, privacy and freedom of expression online that have proved intractable for its current governance regime (an odd patchwork of United States government fiat, decentralised private action and *ad hoc* national and international regulation).

This book explores the potential for the IGF to act as a democratically legitimate and effective body within which for all concerned stakeholders, including those largely excluded from the Internet governance regime until now, to collaborate on the development of public policy concerning the Internet, following a model that draws from the decentralised governance exercised by organisations involved in the development of the Internet's technical standards, but which also recognises the need to interoperate with other sources and subjects of international and transnational (non-state) law.

The principle that the governance of transnational public policy issues is most legitimately exercised through a network of affected stakeholders has much broader application than to the Internet governance regime alone. It is therefore hoped that this book will also be useful to scholars, practitioners and activists in other fields such as environmental governance, sustainable development and trade policy, and that it may stimulate further research on the application of multi-stakeholder governance principles in these issue areas.

The book is based on my PhD thesis in law, which was submitted in March 2008. It has been revised and updated to take account of some of the developments leading up the third IGF meeting in Hyderabad, India, which is to take place in December 2008. The manuscript has also been expanded to include additional material throughout, and several entirely new sections including one in the Introduction on the replication of the Internet's culture.

I would like to extend my sincere gratitude to all those who have supported me in this endeavour, which I commenced before the Internet Governance Forum even existed. In particular, I must thank the supervisors and examiners of my PhD thesis, though the time scale for production of the manuscript did not allow for the consideration of any comments from my examiners (and in any case the errors and deficiencies of the manuscript are mine alone). I must also thank my parents Ian and Kaye and my wife Dominica for their love and support, without which the production of this book would not have been possible.

April 2008 *Jeremy Malcolm*

Chapter 1

Introduction

> I don't wish to offer an opinion about how the net should be run; that's like offering an opinion about how salamanders should grow: nobody has any control over it, regardless of what opinions they might have.
>
> Brian Reid, DEC

Innumerable colourful metaphors have been used to describe the Internet. On one judicial account, it is a "never-ending worldwide conversation."[1] If so, then the concept of "governing" the Internet seems inappropriate, as how is a conversation governed, other than by the participants themselves and the social norms to which they subscribe?

Other descriptions of the Internet focus on its technical attributes, defining it as "the publicly accessible global packet switched network of networks that are interconnected through the use of the common network protocol IP,"[2] or to use a more succinct and celebrated metaphor, "the information superhighway." Following that characterisation, governance of such a highway is arguably the right and responsibility of those whose sovereign jurisdiction it passes through or affects.

Other descriptions again focus on the Internet's unique sociological attributes, calling it "cyberspace" or "a civilisation of the Mind,"[3] as for

[1] *ACLU v Reno* (1996) 929 F Supp 824, 883 per Dalzell J, aff'd, (1997) 21 US 844.

[2] Houlin Zhao, ITU and Internet Governance ⟨URL: `http://www.itu.int/ITU-T/tsb-director/itut-wsis/files/zhao-netgov01.pdf`⟩, 7

[3] John Perry Barlow, A Declaration of the Independence of Cyberspace ⟨URL: `http://homes.`

them the technology that underlies the Internet is far less important than the social interactions that take place upon it. Considered in this way, as a "virtual nation state" if you will, the question of who should exercise governance over it presupposes that it should not govern itself.

Clearly, each of the characterisations exemplified above has quite different repercussions for the way in which the Internet is to be governed, if at all. This goes some way to explaining the gulf that separates regulators who claim the right to exercise governance over the Internet, and those who decry such incursions of the offline world into online territory as being illegitimate.

As a socially constructed artifact, the Internet is whatever we think it is. For a flag-waving Internet pioneer such as John Perry Barlow of the Electronic Frontiers Foundation (EFF), who thinks of the Internet as the last bastion of personal liberty and independence in an increasingly intrusive and corporatised world, that is what it is, and no external governance of that outpost is morally acceptable.

For a bureaucrat such as Haolin Zhou, former Director of the Telecommunications Standardization Bureau of the International Telecommunications Union, the Internet is directly analogous to the telephone network, and hence the historical exclusion of governments from Internet governance has been nothing more than a historical accident, to be rectified without delay:

> People say the Internet flourished because of the absence of government control. I do not agree with this view. I argue that in any country, if the government opposed Internet service, how do you get Internet service? If there are any Internet governance structure changes in the future, I think government rules will be more important and more respected.[4]

It is in this context, with much polarisation on both sides of the debate, that the Internet Governance Forum was established in 2005. The Internet Governance Forum, or IGF, is a forum formed under the auspices of the United Nations, to provide "a transparent, democratic, and multilateral process, with the participation of governments, private sector, civil society and international organisations, in their respective roles,"[5] for dialogue on Internet Governance policy.

But what are "their respective roles"? The agreement calling for the IGF's inception (the "Tunis Agenda") draws a distinction between "inter-

---

eff.org/~barlow/Declaration-Final.html⟩

[4]Declan McCullagh, The UN Thinks About Tomorrow's Cyberspace ⟨URL: http://www.news.com/The-U.N.-thinks-about-tomorrows-cyberspace/2008-1028_3-5643972.html?tag=nefd.lede⟩, and see Zhao (as in n. 2 on the preceding page), 2–3

[5]WSIS, Tunis Agenda for the Information Society ⟨URL: http://www.itu.int/wsis/docs2/tunis/off/6rev1.html⟩, paragraph 61

national public policy issues pertaining to the Internet," which are to be developed "by governments in consultation with all stakeholders," and "the day-to-day technical and operational matters, that do not impact on international public policy issues," which are to be dealt with by "relevant international organisations" with "no involvement" by government.[6]

The distinction is, however, a simplistic one, as technical and policy issues are not so cleanly separated. For example, the decision of ICANN (which, as will be explained below, is the authority responsible for the administration of the root of the Internet's Domain Name System) to approve in principle a new top-level domain .xxx to be used for hosting sexually explicit Web sites, was seen by governments as a public policy issue, to the extent that they called for the decision to be reversed.[7]

Say that the domain coca-cola.xxx were to be registered and that The Coca-Cola Company were to object; immediately more public policy issues, relating to trademark protection, would arise. Thus, there is a web of interrelation between technical and public policy issues, that makes it difficult for any stakeholder included in technical a forum such as ICANN or a policy forum such as the IGF to be disengaged from involvement in their governance.

The IGF's output is explicitly "non-binding," which means that the participation of states in the IGF process does not involve the use of coercive power as is a typical feature of government regulation. In fact since the process is to be "multilateral, multi-stakeholder, democratic and transparent" with "full involvement" of "all stakeholders involved in this process," governments do not, at least in principle, enjoy any position of preeminence in policy formation through the IGF.[8] Neither should they, if the IGF's legitimacy and effectiveness are to be assured.

1.1 The hacker ethos

This last statement may seem bold, in that it could be asked what greater legitimacy the IGF could require than its affiliation with the United Nations. But the United Nations is composed of states. The Internet, on one construction, owes nothing to and indeed is antithetical to the "old" state system—which is why it was so important for the IGF to be constituted as a multi-stakeholder rather than an intergovernmental body. John Perry Barlow, in his *Declaration of the Independence of Cyberspace*—note the metaphor—wrote with characteristic hubris over a decade ago:

[6] WSIS, Tunis Agenda for the Information Society (as in n. 5 on page 2), paras 68, 69, 77

[7] Declan McCullagh, Bush Administration Objects to .xxx Domains ⟨URL: http://www.news.com/Bush-administration-objects-to-.xxx-domains/2100-1028_3-5833764.html⟩

[8] WSIS, Tunis Agenda for the Information Society (as in n. 5 on page 2), paras 29, 73, 77

> Governments of the Industrial World, you weary giants of flesh and steel, I come from Cyberspace, the new home of Mind. On behalf of the future, I ask you of the past to leave us alone. You are not welcome among us. You have no sovereignty where we gather.
>
> We have no elected government, nor are we likely to have one, so I address you with no greater authority than that with which liberty itself always speaks. I declare the global social space we are building to be naturally independent of the tyrannies you seek to impose on us. You have no moral right to rule us nor do you possess any methods of enforcement we have true reason to fear.
>
> Governments derive their just powers from the consent of the governed. You have neither solicited nor received ours. We did not invite you. You do not know us, nor do you know our world. Cyberspace does not lie within your borders. Do not think that you can build it, as though it were a public construction project. You cannot. It is an act of nature and it grows itself through our collective actions.
>
> You have not engaged in our great and gathering conversation, nor did you create the wealth of our marketplaces. You do not know our culture, our ethics, or the unwritten codes that already provide our society more order than could be obtained by any of your impositions.
>
> You claim there are problems among us that you need to solve. You use this claim as an excuse to invade our precincts. Many of these problems don't exist. Where there are real conflicts, where there are wrongs, we will identify them and address them by our means. We are forming our own Social Contract. This governance will arise according to the conditions of our world, not yours. Our world is different.[9]

But why is it so different, and how? On one view, the distinctive culture of the Internet is an historical artifact arising from its development amongst engineers and enthusiasts—colloquially, hackers. Much has been written about the psychology of hackers, but they have been self-described in an Internet standards document identified as RFC 1983, the "Internet Users' Glossary,"[10] as:

Hacker A person who delights in having an intimate understanding of the internal workings of a system, computers and computer networks in particular. The term is often misused in a pejorative context, where "cracker" would be the correct term. See also: cracker.

---

[9] Barlow (as in n. 3 on page 1); however compare Roshni Jayakar, What Stops Free Flow of Information is Dangerous ⟨URL: `http://www.india-today.com/btoday/20001206/interview.html`⟩.

[10] IETF, Internet Users' Glossary ⟨URL: `http://www.ietf.org/rfc/rfc1983.txt`⟩

This definition alone however does not convey a full understanding of the ethos of a hacker and of the culture of his community.[11] A hacker's delight in tinkering with the internal workings of computer systems is realised most fully in an environment where access to computing resources and information is unrestricted. Thus, most hackers believe "that information-sharing is a powerful positive good, and that it is an ethical duty of hackers to share their expertise by writing open-source code and facilitating access to information and to computing resources wherever possible": this is the first principle of one formulation of the so-called Hacker Ethic.[12] (The reference to "open-source code" refers to software for which the source code is made freely available, and which can be distributed and modified without limitation;[13] modern-day hacker culture is in fact largely coincident with open source culture.[14])

Some of the early hackers who were fortunate enough to work in environments that fostered (wittingly or otherwise) such open use of computing resources are now amongst the folk heroes of hacker culture. These include Ken Thompson and Dennis Ritchie, who began development of the operating system Unix at AT&T Bell Labs in 1969, originally because they wanted a faster system on which to run their computer game, "Space Travel,"[15] and Richard M Stallman, President of the Free Software Foundation (FSF), at MIT's Artificial Intelligence Laboratory.

Hackers who were not as fortunate as Thompson, Ritchie or Stallman had two choices: to gain access to third party computer systems or data by stealth, or to create communities of their own such as ham radio, phreaking (telephone hacking), model railroad or amateur rocket groups, in which their freedom to hack would be unimpeded.[16]

1.2 Genesis of the Internet

Amongst such hackers were the architects of the Internet.[17] This is not to say, however, that the Internet began as a hacker project. On the contrary;

[11] In this instance, the use of the male pronoun is not simple sexism, since hackers are overwhelmingly male: Rishab A Ghosh, *Perspectives on Free and Open Source Software* Cambridge, MA: MIT Press, 2005, chap. Understanding Free Software Developers: Findings from the FLOSS Study, 30.

[12] Eric S Raymond, The Jargon File ⟨URL: `http://www.catb.org/~esr/jargon/html/`⟩

[13] For a fuller definition, see Bruce Perens, The Open Source Definition ⟨URL: `http://www.opensource.org/docs/definition.php`⟩.

[14] Christoph Engel, Governing the Egalitarian Core of the Internet, IJCLP 10 2005, 10

[15] Dennis M Ritchie, The Evolution of the Unix Time-sharing System ⟨URL: `http://cm.bell-labs.com/cm/cs/who/dmr/hist.html`⟩

[16] See generally Steven Levy, *Hackers: Heroes of the Computer Revolution* London: Penguin Books, 2001.

[17] References for this section are Robert H Zakon, Hobbes' Internet Timeline ⟨URL: `http://www.zakon.org/robert/internet/timeline`⟩, Christos J P Moschovitis, *History of the Internet: A Chronology, 1843 to the Present* Santa Barbara: ABC-CLIO, Inc, 1999, Barry M Leiner et al., A Brief

it grew out of the ARPANET, a network that began its development in 1969 by DARPA, the Defence Advanced Research Projects Agency, of the US Department of Defense. Nodes of this nascent network were progressively installed at university campuses around the United States, with the size of the network numbering four nodes (or "hosts") in 1969, 13 by 1970, and 23 by 1971. In 1972, email was developed, and became the first "killer application" of the Internet; one that was more than just a cool hack, but was a unique practical application of the new network. During the following year the network expanded overseas, with new nodes in Hawaii, Norway and England.

Over the succeeding years ARPANET expanded further by interconnecting with other wide area computer networks such as Usenet, BITNET and CSNET, a network of the National Science Foundation (NSF). It 1983 the DARPA split the military nodes of ARPANET into a separate network known as MILNET, with the balance eventually connecting into a new network NSFNET, established in 1986 by the NSF, who essentially took the place of DARPA. The Australian Academic Research Network AARNET connected with NSFNET in 1989, by which time there were over 100 000 hosts on the network. In March 1991 NSFNET and its connected networks, together known as the Internet, were opened by the NSF to commercial usage for the first time. The following year there were over a million hosts on the Internet. Today there over 350 million.

One of the innovations of the ARPANET was that its switching technology—that is, the way in which communications were directed from sender to recipient—utilised "packets" of data, rather than a dedicated circuit established between sender and recipient, as for example in the case of the telephone network.

Packet switching had several advantages, including greater efficiency, and greater robustness in the event of a network failure, as packets could take several alternate routes to the same destination. The architecture of a packet-switched network is also less hierarchical than that of a circuit-switched network, in that every node in the network is a peer to every other node, with potentially as critical a role in passing a packet towards its destination. By the same token, a packet-switched network is also intrinsically less secure than one that is circuit-switched.

The network protocols that respectively control the division of information into packets and their transmission from sender to recipient are known as TCP (Transmission Control Protocol) and IP (Internet Protocol). The TCP/IP protocol pair has comprised the basic network communications standard for the Internet since 1983, and laid the foundation for various other network protocols that were to follow.

History of the Internet ⟨URL: `http://www.isoc.org/internet/history/brief.shtml`⟩, IETF, FYI on "What is the Internet?" ⟨URL: `http://www.ietf.org/rfc/rfc1462.txt`⟩ and Idem, The Internet Activities Board ⟨URL: `http://www.apps.ietf.org/rfc/rfc1160.html`⟩.

Another important foundation of today's network services on the Internet is the Domain Name System (DNS), which was introduced in 1984. The DNS enabled Internet servers to be accessed by means of easily-memorable names rather than numbers, and for the names to be stored in a distributed database to which all Internet hosts had access. The names were arranged in reverse-hierarchical order separated by dots, usually with the name of the server first (such as "remus" or "www"), followed by the name of the institution (such as "rutgers" or "ibm"), followed by the institution's type (such as "edu" for an educational institution and "com" for a company).

A further important foundation of today's Internet is BGP, the Border Gateway Protocol. Until BGP was introduced in 1994, NSFNET provided a backbone or central network that linked the various smaller networks of the Internet together. Although IP packets might have traversed several networks en route from source to destination, they always did so via NSFNET at at least one point. BGP rendered this redundant and allowed Internet routing (that is, the process by which IP packets are directed from sender to recipient across potentially numerous autonomous networks) to be decentralised. This allowed for the decommissioning of NSFNET in 1995. From that point, realising the vision of the Internet pioneers from DARPA, whilst there were a number of important constituent backbone networks, there was no single "core" of the networks of the Internet.

On top of the flexible TCP/IP network protocols, utilising the DNS for addressing and BGP for routing between autonomous systems, numerous Internet services were, and indeed continue to be, added. These so-called application layer protocols (in contrast to the lower-level transport and network layer protocols TCP/IP)[18] include the Internet email protocol called SMTP, a file transfer protocol FTP, the protocol that supports the World Wide Web, known as HTTP, and hundreds of others. The most widely used of these services have become Internet standards, and may be identified as such by the use of the number of the "Request for Comment" document (or "RFC") assigned when their specification was first proposed to the Internet community.

The detail of the RFC process will be discussed in more depth in the following chapter, but key is the fact that a document proposed for an RFC may in principle be drafted by anyone, regardless of their affiliation. In this there are echoes of another precept of the Hacker Ethic that one author has identified; "Hackers should be judged by their hacking, not bogus criteria such as degrees, age, race, or position."[19] The acceptance of a new Internet standard proposed in an RFC is predicated upon the achievement of consensus that it should be so accepted, from members of the Internet community who participate (freely) in an unincorporated forum known as

[18]This terminology derives from the OSI networking model discussed at section 2.2 on page 57, under which seven layers of a network were defined—though TCP/IP networking has no equivalent to two of these seven theoretical layers (the session and presentation layers).

[19]Levy (as in n. 16 on page 5), 43.

the Internet Engineering Task Force (IETF).

1.3 Technical and social architecture

Although it has already been observed that the Internet is more than a technical artifact, but also (and perhaps more importantly) a social phenomenon, the reason for the technical focus of the preceding introduction to the Internet's early structure and protocols is that the technical and social are closely interrelated. After all, the architecture of the Internet—the physical design of the network and the manner in which communications traverse it—was shaped by the ethos of the hackers who developed it. They created an Internet that featured:

- decentralisation (a flat, peer-to-peer network topology that distributed network intelligence, and resisted centralised monitoring and intervention—reflecting its designers' preference for decentralisation and autonomy over hierarchy and control);
- interactivity (a default policy of unrestricted bidirectional access between hosts through design principles such as "end-to-end connectivity," thus maximising its capacity for the exchange of information, in line with the Hacker Ethic);[20]
- openness (the use of freely available tools and protocols that empowered the individual Internet user to communicate and publish information without the intermediation of third parties such as media outlets or governments);[21]
- anonymity (the absence of built-in authentication mechanisms either in the transport or network layer (eg. in TCP/IP) or the application layer (eg. in SMTP), which were not only unnecessary within a mutually trusting community, but also fostered anonymity and privacy);
- cosmopolitanism (addressing and routing protocols that cut across boundaries of geography and politics, as its founders collaborated across state and later national boundaries when designing the network);
- egalitarianism (the absence of any framework for certain users to be assigned elevated rights or privileges on the network); and

[20] This can also be, but is not universally, conveyed by the term "net neutrality": Milton Mueller, Net Neutrality as Global Principal for Internet Governance ⟨URL: http://www.internetgovernance.org/pdf/NetNeutralityGlobalPrinciple.pdf⟩.

[21] See further section 4.2 on page 211 for a disambiguation of the meaning of "free" in this context.

- resilience (routing intelligence built into the network that impeded attempts at censorship, in accordance with its designers' iconoclasticism and distrust of authority). As John Gilmore of the EFF is attributed as saying, "The Net interprets censorship as damage and routes around it."[22]

The Internet promoted these values not merely through its culture, but through its very design, which embedded engineering principles that reflected the values of its designers, who had "hardwired their way of life in the Internet architecture."[23] This produced an innate congruence between the technical and the social architecture (or culture) of the Internet.[24]

Shaking the architecture's foundations

However, in the forty years since the Internet's earliest years, the Internet's architecture has not proved unmalleable. Laurence Lessig famously made this point in describing the architecture of the Internet as "West Coast Code," and claiming that it could enable the inherent freedoms of the Internet to be subverted at the behest of commercial interests just as could "East Coast Code"—legislation—at the behest of governments.[25]

It is true that the design features noted above have been affected by a variety of factors, including not only commercial interests, but also technical limitations and political or public policy pressures (since, after all, it has been noted above that technical and public policy management of the Internet are inextricably linked). Some of the architectural limitations upon each of the seven features identified above respectively include the following:

- Despite the intentions of its designers, the Internet was never fully decentralised, and the respect in which it currently most falls short of decentralisation is the DNS. In contrast to the network topology of the Internet, the domain name system is hierarchical. Thus, only the administrator of the "murdoch.edu.au" domain may add subdomains underneath it such as "www," only the administrator of "edu.au" may add new domains at that level for new universities, and only ICANN as the administrator of the root of the DNS may (with the approval of the United States government, at present) add new domains at the top level.[26]

---

[22]See `http://www.toad.com/gnu`.

[23]Engel (as in n. 14 on page 5), 9

[24]For a more comprehensive list of the architectural features of the Internet, see IETF, Architectural Principles of the Internet ⟨URL: `http://www.ietf.org/rfc/rfc1958.txt`⟩.

[25]Lawrence Lessig, *Code and Other Laws of Cyberspace* New York: Basic Books, 1999, 43–44

[26]But see section 4.1 on page 191.

Whilst this arrangement for most purposes creates an efficient division of authority, and sensibly reflects the principle of subsidiarity (that governance should be exercised at the lowest practical level), its does also concentrate authority at its apex. It is therefore no coincidence that it is through ICANN that regulators have most commonly sought to gain a purchase upon Internet governance, nor that control over administration of the DNS root was one of the main bones of contention that gave rise to the establishment of the IGF.

- The Internet's interactivity has been hampered by the loss of end-to-end connectivity caused by a shortage of unique IP addresses.[27] Every Internet host that wishes to be directly accessible to any other Internet host must be assigned a public IP address as a unique identifier. Under the current IP addressing addressing system called IPv4, there is a shortage of IP addresses for all of the hosts that require them. This problem can be circumvented by various techniques such as "network address translation," that hide multiple Internet hosts behind a single IP address, but this comes at the cost of breaking end-to-end connectivity. One concrete effect of this on the Internet's interactivity is that it makes it more difficult to establish Internet telephony calls directly between two hosts using standard Voice over IP (VoIP) protocols.[28]

- Although Internet standards must be published openly, there is nothing to constrain the private sector from introducing proprietary services onto the Internet that are not intended for the Internet standards track and the specifications for which are kept closed. This can reduce the openness and accessibility of those parts of the Internet that make use of those services. For example, the "source code" of a standard Web page may be viewed in any Web browser, and reference material describing how to edit or write such source code using a standard text editor is freely available. If the Web page is constructed using Macromedia Corporation's Flash technology, however, the source code cannot be viewed, or indexed by standard search engines, and the page itself cannot easily be viewed or edited other than using Macromedia software.

- Anonymity and privacy on the Internet are being challenged on several fronts. Lessig identifies three: the increasing requirement that unique identifiers and passwords be used to access Web resources, the use of "cookies"—small text files that Web sites can create on a user's computer to track their activities on that Web site and which can be accessed on the user's subsequent visits, and digital signatures, with which users can be required to identify themselves before

[27]See IETF, Internet Transparency ⟨URL: `http://www.ietf.org/rfc/rfc2775.txt`⟩.

[28]See also generally Idem, The Rise of the Middle and the Future of End-to-End: Reflections on the Evolution of the Internet Architecture ⟨URL: `http://www.ietf.org/rfc/rfc3724.txt`⟩.

using certain services;[29] an Australian example is that the Australian Taxation Office requires Australian businesses to authenticate their assertions of identity using a digital signature when submitting their Business Activity Statements online.

Since Lessig wrote, another prominent limitation on the privacy and anonymity of Internet users has been the use of records of IP addresses allocated to users as evidence of illegal conduct alleged against them. Such records are maintained by ISPs (Internet Service Providers) and have in numerous instances been the subject of discovery orders and subpoenas against those ISPs by copyright owners who allege that a user allocated a particular IP address by the ISP has downloaded copyright material, or made it available for download, without authority of the copyright owner.[30]

- Although the Internet's architecture is cosmopolitan in most respects, since 1985 the DNS has included ccTLDs for the identification of the country of origin of Internet servers. With the characteristic disregard of the Internet's founders for national authority, control of these ccTLDs was originally delegated not to governments, but to whoever within the jurisdiction in question[31] volunteered to take on the task of administering sub-delegations—in Australia's case, the au ccTLD was delegated to Robert Elz of the University of Melbourne.

  Since then, however, governments have claimed the sovereign right to administer "their" ccTLDs as a strategic national resource, and the incumbent root DNS manager ICANN has effectively acceded to these claims.[32] Another incursion upon the architectural cosmopolitanism of the Internet is the technique of "content negotiation" based on the user's projected physical location. This is used by some Web sites to deliver customised content to users thought to be resident in a given country, but can also be used to restrict users from that country from accessing a site's content.[33]

- Whilst the protocols on which the Internet is constructed may be intrinsically egalitarian, the means by which a user gains access to the Internet in practice may entail limitations being imposed upon her access to the network by her ISP, the nature of which limitations she may not even know about. If the ISP is subject to the laws of a country such as China, Vietnam or Saudi Arabia that has an Internet

[29] Lessig, *Code and Other Laws of Cyberspace* (as in n. 25 on page 9), 34-35

[30] The first round of 261 lawsuits against individual Internet users at the suit of the Recording Industry Association of America (RIAA) were filed in 2003: Liane Cassavoy, Music Labels Declare War on File Swappers ⟨URL: `http://www.pcworld.com/article/id,112364-page,1/article.html`⟩.

[31] And even that was not a formal requirement until 1994: IETF, Domain Name System Structure and Delegation ⟨URL: `http://www.ietf.org/rfc/rfc1591.txt`⟩.

[32] See section 2.1 on page 40.

[33] See section 2.3 on page 79.

content regulation regime in place requiring the ISP to filter Internet content before it reaches the user, it may be effectively impossible for the user to participate on the network on the same level as a citizen of a country without such laws.

Such filtering techniques also limit the Internet's resilience in being able to "route around" censorship. The hardware used by ISPs to route Internet traffic is now being specifically designed to facilitate the imposition of such restrictions on users.[34] As the techniques by which ISPs transparently filter their users' access to the network are not specified in any Internet standard, these decision decisions are not subject to broad community review.

The above examples can be claimed as evidence that the architecture of the Internet no longer quite so closely reflects the values of its founders as it once did. Even so, practice has also shown it to be difficult to fundamentally change the Internet's underlying architecture. Attempts by commercial interests, governments or even the Internet technologists themselves, to work against the grain of the network's original design, incur a countervailing cost and are often ineffective in achieving their objectives. Taking in turn once again the seven features of the Internet originally identified above:

- Decentralisation carries an evolutionary advantage on the Internet. Actually, a distributed or decentralised design possesses advantages in any network, such as speed (as it reduces the average distance between a node and the network services it needs to access), reliability (as the duplication of network services makes the network more resistant to failure or attack) and scalability (as growth of the network is not constrained by the capacity of centralised choke-points). It also allows innovation to flourish on the edges of the network, rather than being propagated outward from the core, where it can be more easily controlled or stifled.

  An example is found in the case of the original Napster software, which provided access to a peer-to-peer (P2P) file sharing network over which MP3 music files could be exchanged by its users. When downloading an MP3 file using this service, a user's copy of the Napster software would look up the file's location in a central directory maintained by Napster Inc. By maintaining this central directory, Napster Inc was found to be complicit in breaches of copyright held in music that was transferred using the service. The same charge failed against the publishers of the Kazaa, Grokster and Morpheus file sharing software that used a decentralised directory of files (al-

[34] Steven Cherry, The Net Effect ⟨URL: `http://www.spectrum.ieee.org/jun05/1219`⟩

though they were found liable on the alternate ground that they actively induced acts of infringement by users of the software).[35]

- The impact of the shortage of IP addresses on the Internet's interactivity well illustrates the difficulty in instituting architectural change on the Internet. The solution to the shortage has long been available for implementation, in the form of the next generation IP addressing scheme, IPv6, which was first proposed in 1998.[36] Hardware vendor Cisco projected in 2002 that the adoption of IPv6 by ISPs, alongside legacy support for IPv4, would be complete by 2005, with popular adoption by consumers and enterprise commencing from 2003.[37]

  Yet as at the date of writing, the adoption of IPv6 on Internet-connected networks still runs at less than 1%, with almost no measurable adoption by consumers. One of the few large networks that has announced concrete plans to transition to IPv6 is the US Department of Defence.[38] Considering that this change to Internet architecture is considered to have been urgently required to overcome a demonstrable shortage of IP addresses, it should not be surprising that fundamental changes proposed to other Internet protocols without the same urgency, including proposals to institute improved replacements for the DNS, the email protocol SMTP and the Web protocol HTTP, have been given even shorter shrift.[39]

- Openness in Internet protocols and services also seems to provide them with an evolutionary advantage over closed alternatives. Microsoft Corporation is often criticised for its policy to "embrace and extend" Internet standards by adding its own proprietary features to standards, such as the proprietary markup tags <marquee> and <bgsound> it added to the Web's HTML markup language in 1996.[40] More often than not however, these proprietary extensions will fail

---

[35] See *MGM v Grokster* (2004) 380 F 3d 1154 for the decision in the defendants' favour, *MGM v Grokster* (2005) 545 US 913 for the decision on appeal which succeeded on different grounds, and Pamela Samuelson, Legally Speaking: Did MGM Really Win the Grokster Case?, Comm ACM 48:10 October 2005 for commentary.

[36] IETF, Internet Protocol, Version 6 (IPv6) ⟨URL: `http://www.ietf.org/rfc/rfc2460.txt`⟩

[37] Cisco IOS Learning Services, The ABCs of IP Version 6 ⟨URL: `http://www.sixxs.net/archive/docs/Cisco%20IPv6%20ABC.pdf`⟩, 39.

[38] It was required along with all other US federal agencies to upgrade its network infrastructure to support IPv6 by 2008, and has since established a five-year plan to begin using the new protocol across its network: Jason Miller, DOD to Allocate its IPv6 Addresses ⟨URL: `http://www.gcn.com/print/26_03/43045-1.html`⟩.

[39] See respectively `http://www.handle.net/`, `http://amtp.bw.org/`, and Ihor Kuz et al., Beyond HTTP: An Implementation of the Web in Globe ⟨URL: `http://www.nlnet.nl/project/sirs/200004-report/`⟩. On the other hand, a very significant fundamental change to the Internet's architecture was successfully introduced in the transition of the ARPANET host protocol from NCP to TCP/IP in January 1983, when the network was very much smaller than it is today.

[40] For another example, see A Michael Froomkin, Habermas@discourse.net: Toward a Critical Theory of Cyberspace, Harv LR 116 2003, 837.

to gain acceptance; the markup tags previously mentioned are deprecated by the Web standards body, the World Wide Web Consortium (W3C) and are not supported by non-Microsoft Web browsers.

Microsoft's proprietary Internet server software has also failed to gain dominance over open source alternatives. In particular the open source Apache Web server remains the most popular Web server software, well ahead of Microsoft's Internet Information Server, despite Microsoft's dominance in the market for desktop software.[41]

Lessig has argued that the reason is that the use of open source code sabotages attempts at regulation of the Internet by governments,[42] but a more prosaic reason for the success of open source software on the Internet is that Internet standards are published openly, which takes away the competitive advantage that a proprietary product might enjoy in deploying a proprietary standard.

- For most purposes, anonymity remains Internet users' natural state, because although there are methods by which they can be made to identify themselves, the fact that these methods have to be grafted onto the Internet's basic architecture makes them expensive and difficult to enforce. There has been a spate of recent lawsuits against users alleged to have infringed copyright through the use of P2P file sharing software. In response, many users have simply switched their P2P software of choice to one of the newer applications that better protects their privacy, such as BitTorrent, which divides the shared files across multiple hosts on the network, so that seldom does any user upload or download a complete file to or from a single host.[43] This has made it much more difficult for copyright owners to allege large-scale infringement of copyright against those using BitTorrent to exchange files.

  For anonymity in conducting other activities on the Internet, the Tor project is an one of a number of services that facilitates anonymous Web browsing and publishing, instant messaging and other activities.[44] One of the techniques used by the Tor project is digital cryptography, which ironically is also the cornerstone of many of the techniques used to authenticate users' identities on the Internet. Tor also draws inspiration from the technique of anonymous remailing, which has been used for many years to disguise the origin of Internet email.[45]

- Although national governments have been keen to seize control of the ccTLDs applicable to their jurisdictions, this can never operate as an

---

[41] See `http://news.netcraft.com/archives/web_server_survey.html`.

[42] Lessig, *Code and Other Laws of Cyberspace* (as in n. 25 on page 9), 100.

[43] Interestingly this is done for reasons of technical efficiency, not to frustrate the attentions of copyright owners, which is merely a side-effect.

[44] See `http://www.torproject.org/`.

[45] See also section 4.1 on page 183.

effective constraint on the cosmopolitanism of the Internet, because the generic TLDs (gTLDs) remain available to all Internet users, regardless of their country of origin (in fact, so do many ccTLDs, depending on the policies of the ccTLD administrator). In other words, there is nothing that can be done to prevent a person who is refused registration of a domain underneath their country's ccTLD from registering a similar domain under a gTLD such as com, net, org, biz or one of over a dozen others that are available to registrants worldwide and outside the direct control of any national government.

- Filtering of Internet access, when effective, can impact on both the Internet's egalitarianism and its resilience. However once again because this works against the grain of the Internet's design, it tends to be either costly, ineffective, or both. For example whilst China has perhaps the most sophisticated content filtering regime in the world, there are products that allows China's citizens to very easily bypass their government's filtering.[46] Other methods by which filtering may be evaded include the use of international telephone calls to dial up to foreign Internet providers, or less expensively, the use of "proxy servers" located outside the jurisdiction. Access to known proxy servers is blocked by countries such as China, but it is still possible (if not legal) for knowledgeable users to gain access to them through an encrypted tunnel, using freely-available software such as Tor.

The above examples illusrate that whilst the Internet no longer quite so closely reflects the values of its founders as it once did, endeavours by commercial interests, governments or even the Internet technologists themselves to work against the values implicit in its design meet with resistance or expense that work against change, and reinforce the status quo. To make this point is not necessarily to assert that it is a positive feature of the Internet; indeed, it poses considerable difficulties to those who, in accordance with near-universally-accepted public policy norms, seek to battle such evils as cybercrime, spam (unsolicited commercial email) and trafficking in child pornography and copyright material. On one view, Internet governance as it stands is out of balance in favour of egalitarian hacker values.[47]

However it remains the case, for good or ill, that unless the Internet's architecture is re-engineered from the ground up to build compulsory identity management and cryptography into its core protocols[48]—and the experience of IPv6 demonstrates how difficult this will be—the values

[46] The CustomizeGoogle extension for the Firefox Web browser is one example: see `http://www.customizegoogle.com/zh-CN/` for the extension itself, and `http://yro.slashdot.org/article.pl?sid=05/10/31/1414203&tid=217&tid=17` for some discussion on it.

[47] Engel (as in n. 14 on page 5), 23

[48] Such network protocols do exist. Kerberos is the best known network authentication protocol with strong cryptography. See `http://web.mit.edu/kerberos/www/`.

of its founders will remain to a large degree intrinsic to the Internet's architecture.

Internet culture

Given that the Internet does still bear the relics of its founders' values in its technical architecture, it might nevertheless be argued that those values are no longer reflected in its social architecture or culture. After all, it has been some time since the Internet was principally the province of hackers. Surely, it could be said, the observations made earlier about hacker ethos were more applicable in the pioneering days of the Internet than they are today. In fact the "first war of cyberspace," which pitted the hierarchical power of elites against the largely anarchistic ordering of the Internet's grass roots, was declared last century.[49]

Reflecting this, the Tunis Agenda correctly states that "the Internet, a central element of the infrastructure of the Information Society, has evolved from a research and academic facility into a global facility available to the public."[50] Indeed, it is the greatest achievement of the Internet's developers that their network has become commonplace. It is now used as a forum for e-business, e-government and civil networking, no longer just for exchanging Unix software and Star Trek trivia. Why then should the culture of today's Internet users bear any resemblance to that of their forebears?

The answer to this charge is that just as it has been shown above that the development of the Internet's architecture reflected the hacker ethos, so that ethos, still embedded in its architecture, continues to be imprinted onto today's users of the Internet and their communities—even those who have never so much as programmed their VCR, let alone any software. In essence, hacker culture has developed into Internet culture. And Internet culture replicates itself memetically.[51] Cultural memes[52] are replicated over the Internet even more efficiently than they are offline, due to the suitability of the Internet as a medium for the unimpeded transmission of information. The result is that the culture of today's Internet users tends to reflect similar values of interactivity, openness, egalitarianism, anonymity, cosmopolitanism and so on as are inherent in the Internet's architecture.

Why does Internet culture replicate itself so successfully? In short, users' attitudes are shaped by their usage of the Internet.[53] In particular, users

[49]Tim Jordan, *Cyberpower: The Culture and Politics of Cyberspace and the Internet* London: Routledge, 1999, 214–217

[50]WSIS, Tunis Agenda for the Information Society (as in n. 5 on page 2), paragraph 29.

[51]Garry Marshall, Internet and Memetics ⟨URL: `http://pespmc1.vub.ac.be/Conf/MemePap/Marshall.html`⟩

[52]A meme is a replicable "unit" of culture analogous to a genetic gene; see generally R Dawkins, *The Selfish Gene* Oxford: Oxford University Press, 1976.

[53]M Anandarajan, C Simmers and M Igbaria, An Exploratory Investigation of the An-

are constrained by the architecture of the Internet to behave in accordance with the Internet's values, and due to the psychological inter-relationship between users' behaviour and their attitudes, their attitudes then tend to be shaped by that behaviour.

To give an example, a new user of the Internet will find herself immersed in a community in which thousands of her peers adopt online identities using screen names and avatars, publish their views to the world using blogs (ie. Web logs, or personal online journals), debate these views on innumerable newsgroups and Web-based discussion fora, join new communities of interest that transcend national boundaries, freely exchange cultural objects such as music and video clips, and many other activities that reflect the Internet's values.

In order to effectively use the Internet, the new user herself will have to start using the same tools and employing the same communication strategies as her peers. For a user who did not previously communicate in this way—for example, a user who never before in daily life engaged in discourse with people from overseas, or whose communications in daily life were always characterised by an imbalance of power, or by the spectre of official censorship, or by the exchange of money for cultural objects—there will be a disconnect between her attitudes and her behaviour, which will give rise to cognitive dissonance.

When cognitive dissonance arises, it requires either the user's behaviour or her attitudes to undergo modification. In the case where the user's behaviour is constrained by architecture—and indeed even when it is not—it is more common that the user's attitudes rather than her behaviour will change.[54] It is for this reason that there is a tendency for the values of new users of the Internet to be reshaped into greater conformity with the Internet's cultural norms. Certainly, this does not happen to every new user of the Internet. But it does not need to, in order for the Internet's culture in general to be resilient against change (much as its technical architecture is), and for this culture to be replicated to some degree from one generation of users to the next.

The point could be taken even further. Not only has hacker culture produced Internet culture, and not only does Internet culture tend to survive as new users enter the network, but some have argued that Internet culture is escaping the borders of cyberspace to form a globally shared ideology or "world culture."[55] This can be seen as part of the broader process of cultural globalisation, but whereas the most infectious memes

tecedents and Impacts of Internet Usage: An Individual Perspective, Behaviour & Information Technology 19 2000; T J Johnson and B K Kaye, *It's Show Time! Media, Politics, and Popular Culture* New York: Peter Lang, 2000, chap. Democracy's Rebirth or Demise? The Influence of the Internet on Political Attitude

[54] L Festinger and J M Carlsmith, Cognitive Consequences of Forced Compliance, Journal of Abnormal and Social Psychology 58 1959

[55] Francis Heylighen, Evolution of Memes on the Network: from Chain-Letters to the Global Brain ⟨URL: `http://pespmc1.vub.ac.be/Papers/Memesis.html`⟩

of the global culture were previously carried through the mass media, the Internet now acts as a mutagen and further accelerant to that process.

A global cultural shift which incorporates the egalitarian and cosmopolitan values of the Internet has the potential to be not only culturally, but also politically highly subversive. Already users/citizens interact online in fora beyond the state's control,[56] forming their own supra-territorial networks of relations.[57] In the broader context of economic globalisation, in which national governments are helpless to control the flows of capital across their borders, and multi-national corporations relocate their operations across the world as cost movements dictate—and political globalisation, reflected in the rise to power of supranational bodies such as the European Union—this could come to threaten the institution of the state itself.[58] It could in fact presage the emergence of a new world state, as the old nation states fade into irrelevance.[59]

1.4 Governance mechanisms

The fact that the Internet does not respect geopolitical boundaries, and in a sense transcends them as the vanguard of a new cosmopolitanism, would on the face of it seem to pose a serious obstacle to those who would seek to regulate the Internet, as legal systems as we know them are innately bound to such boundaries. In this way, regulation of the Internet is quite different to regulation of the public switched telephone network (PSTN). The PSTN has both a logically, and also a physically, hierarchical design, in which calls are routed between parties using centralised signalling intelligence. It is possible to predict how a call will travel physically across the PSTN and therefore what governments will have jurisdiction over the terms of its carriage. In contrast, Internet services operate on top of telephony networks (but also other networks), and their geography is dynamic and unpredictable.

Yet it is clear that some form of governance of the Internet—even if only self-governance—is necessary if we are to manage those public policy issues that are left unaddressed by, or even run counter to, the constraints of the Internet's architecture. As Biegel puts it:

> The question is no longer whether cyberspace as a whole can or should be regulated, but whether and to what extent

[56] See Gordon Graham, *The Internet: A Philosophical Enquiry* London: Routledge, 1999, 87.
[57] Jan Aart Scholte, Global Capitalism and the State, International Affairs 73:3 1997
[58] See section 3.2 on page 129.
[59] But see section 4.3 on page 272.

individual problem areas within particular cyber spaces can or should be addressed via regulation.[60]

The purpose of the IGF as stated in the Tunis Agenda is to address such issues: "We further recognise that there are many cross-cutting international public policy issues that require attention and are not adequately addressed by the current mechanisms."[61]

Accepting the jurisdictional constraints that will impede governance of the Internet by conventional legal means, there are nonetheless various other ways in which human affairs are governed. The principles that we have above been describing individually as "values" or "memes," and collectively as "ethos" or "culture," are clearly not of the same status as legal rules, and yet they have a powerful effect on the behaviour of Internet users.[62] Neither does the Tunis Agenda seem to be speaking only of legal rules when it describes the IGF as a forum for the "development of public policy,"[63] yet surely it is intended that the IGF's output will have some practical impact on Internet governance, or the forum would service only a symbolic purpose.

This illustrates the fact that governance is a broader term than government,[64] and that it can be accomplished through a broader variety of mechanisms than the legislative, executive and judicial acts that government performs. A closer synonym for governance is "management," and in the literature of public administration Rhodes has isolated three mechanisms by which governance may be exercised: hierarchies, markets and networks.[65]

The reference to hierarchies as a form of governance includes the use of laws and bureaucratic regulation to control behaviour. Markets are a mechanism of governance in that the behaviour of consumers can be regulated by the basic economic laws of supply and demand. Networks are a more complex hybrid form of governance which involves partnerships of trust between governments, the private sector and the community, and collaborative decision-making procedures such as will be examined in detail in Chapter 4. Pal has suggested that governance by network is epitomised by the emergent forms of governance found on the Internet.[66]

---

[60]Stuart Biegel, *Beyond Our Control? Confronting the Limits of Our Legal System in the Age of Cyberspace* Cambridge, MA: MIT Press, 2001, 119

[61]WSIS, Tunis Agenda for the Information Society (as in n. 5 on page 2), paragraph 60.

[62]Marshall (as in n. 51 on page 16).

[63]WSIS, Tunis Agenda for the Information Society (as in n. 5 on page 2), paragraph 68.

[64]James N Rosenau, *Governance Without Government: Order and Change in World Politics* Cambridge: Cambridge University Press, 1992, chap. Governance, Order and Change in World Politics, 4

[65]R A W Rhodes, The New Governance: Governing Without Government, Political Studies 44 1996

[66]Leslie A Pal, Virtual Policy Networks: The Internet as a Model of Contemporary Gover-

But more particularly for our purposes, the template for the IGF in the Tunis Agenda embodies the concept of governance by network well.

From a parallel but slightly broader perspective, Lessig has identified four mechanisms by which governance can be exercised: laws, markets, social norms and code (the last of which he also describes as architecture or technology,[67] and which Reidenberg described as the *lex informatica*[68]). The first two of these are largely synonymous with Rhodes' hierarchies and markets, and the effect of the third and fourth are respectively the social and architectural forces of the Internet that guide users' behaviour online.

There are a number of other models of governance that have been specifically developed in relation to the Internet. Biegel, for example, in writing on the governance of Cyberspace, considered three regulatory mechanisms: legal frameworks within individual countries, international cooperation, and changes in the architecture of the Internet itself.[69] The first is clearly a type of governance by rules, the second could also be a type of governance by network, and the third is equivalent to Lessig's code and Reidenberg's *lex informatica.*

Norms appear to be missing from Biegel's model, but they are added in the very similar model of Weber, in the form of governance through self-regulation[70] (which Biegel had excluded on the grounds that it is simply the "default position").[71] Kooiman also begins his tripartite typology with self-governance, recognising also co-governance (which includes governance by network) and hierarchical governance.[72]

Expanded further into five regulatory models (one of which, again is the *status quo*), Caslon Analytics subdivides governance by rules into national law or the "digital ring fence" approach, international law or the *lex informatica* (not to be confused with Reidenberg's usage of that phrase, which Caslon Analytics terms "code as law"), and the creation of a new global body.[73]

Similar too are Vedel's four models of Internet governance: community governance (which is largely governance through norms within a relatively culturally homogeneous community), market governance, hierarchical or state regulation, and associative regulation. Associative regulation is Vedel's closest equivalent to governance by network, being based upon vol-

---

nance? ⟨URL: `http://www.isoc.org/inet97/proceedings/G7/G7_1.HTM`⟩

[67] Lessig, *Code and Other Laws of Cyberspace* (as in n. 25 on page 9), 87

[68] Joel R Reidenberg, Lex Informatica: The Formulation of Information Policy Rules Through Technology, Tex LR 76 1998

[69] Biegel (as in n. 60 on the previous page), 124

[70] Rolf H Weber, *Regulatory Models for the Online World* The Hague: Kluwer Law International, 2002, 80

[71] Biegel (as in n. 60 on the preceding page), 221

[72] Jan Kooiman, *Governing as Governance* Thousand Oaks, CA: Sage Publications, 2003

[73] Caslon Analytics, Cyberspace Governance ⟨URL: `http://www.caslon.com.au/governanceguide.htm`⟩

untary agreements between stakeholder groups (though Vedel asserts that "it rarely exists autonomously, and generally requires state intervention either in its design, or its application").[74]

A slightly modified synthesis of all these typologies of control would then suggest that governance can be exercised by means of rules (that is, laws or hierarchies), norms, markets, architecture (that is, the broadest sense of code) and networks. Each of these will be examined again in turn with reference to their suitability as tools for governance of the Internet.

Rules

The most common typology of rules divides them into moral rules and legal rules. To the legal positivist, legal rules have no necessary or inevitable relationship with moral rules. A legal rule is simply a binding and enforceable obligation, regarded as law, that has been posited through a political process by a body politic, to whom obedience to the legal rule is owed.[75] This position is too stark for the natural lawyer, who argues that there are also certain rights and duties that exist as legal rules whether or not they are recognised by the state (for example, fundamental human rights); and similarly that there may be purported legal rules that contravene natural law on substantive or procedural grounds, and thus do not qualify as law at all.

The relevance of this is that there is some debate as to whether rules of international law actually constitute legal rules, or whether they are simply principles of positive morality. This question is raised largely because international society lacks the means to enforce the rules that it makes.[76] One way of accommodating this fact, without granting the status of law to the natural lawyer's supra-legal moral rules, is to accept a division between "hard law" and "soft law," whereby hard law is binding, and soft law is not strictly binding but is generally complied with in practice.[77] But without needing to impugn the status of unenforceable international legal rules as law, the question remains that if they are not enforced, are they of any use in exercising governance over the Internet? What good is an international law proscribing traffic in child pornography, if the law hangs in space as it

[74] Thierry Vedel, Four Models for Internet Governance ⟨URL: `http://www.oii.ox.ac.uk/collaboration/specialevents/20050505_governance_position_papers.pdf`⟩, 65

[75] Anthony Clark Arend, *Legal Rules and International Society* New York: Oxford University Press, 1999, 22. The author adds three other types—rules of etiquette, rules of the game (essentially informal, tacit agreements), and descriptive rules—but for present purposes these will be treated as norms, and discussed below.

[76] Anthony D'Amato, The Neo-Positivist Concept of International Law, Am J Int'l Law 59 1965; A Claire Cutler, *Private Power and Global Authority: Transnational Merchant Law in the Global Political Economy* Cambridge: Cambridge University Press, 2003, 75

[77] Arend (as in n. 75), 24. See section 3.3 on page 136.

were, unsupported by either police or judiciary?[78]

Domestic regulation is not a sufficient mechanism of governance for the Internet either, because as alluded to above, the Internet's cosmopolitanism works against it. When the Australian *Broadcasting Services Amendment Act* 1999 was passed, with the effect that it became illegal to host X-rated pornography in Australia, and became necessary to provide an age verification system when hosting material that would have been rated R or MA if it were a film, the outcome was that some Web sites were simply relocated off-shore.[79]

Similarly, following passage of the Federal Government's *Interactive Gambling Act* 2001 which prohibited online gambling services being offered to Australians, Australian online casino operators have continued to offer the same services to foreigners, and foreigners to Australians.[80] Such legislation effectively has no more than rhetorical value, and even if replicated in a handful of like-minded countries, hardly makes for a global Internet governance regime.

Another problem associated with the use of legal rules, if another is needed, is that the imposition of hierarchical control sits poorly with the Internet's decentralised and egalitarian culture, generating such resistance as has widely emerged online over issues such as the US Digital Millennium Copyright Act.[81] For this reason and those expressed previously, legal rules alone will rarely be the most appropriate mechanism for exercising governance over Internet public policy issues.

Norms

One way in which norms can be distinguished from rules is that norms are "standards of behavior defined in terms of rights and obligations," whereas rules are "specific prescriptions for action."[82] Many of the norms of behaviour on the Internet are those that fall into the category of "netiquette." The principles of netiquette are the subject of RFC 1855,[83] which explains that it is considered rude in online communications to TYPE IN ALL CAPITALS (as this is equivalent to shouting), that one should not send

---

[78] In answer, it might still have normative effect, but this is the subject of the next mechanism of governance to be discussed below.

[79] For both an example of such a site, and an explanation of why it was moved, see `http://www.efa.org.au/Publish/PR991221.html`.

[80] See `http://www.lasseters.com.au/help/lassfaq.jsp` and `http://www.australia-casino.com` respectively.

[81] See for example the resources of the EFF at `http://w2.eff.org/IP/DMCA`.

[82] Stephen D Krasner, Structural Causes and Regime Consequences: Regimes as Intervening Variables, International Organization 36 1982

[83] IETF, Netiquette Guidelines ⟨URL: `http://www.ietf.org/rfc/rfc1855.txt`⟩. This is an informational rather than a standards-track RFC, and is now somewhat technologically dated.

chain letters by email, and that messages posted to a newsgroup or mailing list should be restricted to the topic of that forum.[84]

When Internet norms are disregarded, the consequences can extend offline. The first large-scale commercial senders of spam, a law firm, Canter and Siegel, found their telephone and fax numbers being tied up day and night by automated junk messages from disgruntled Internet users.[85] More recently, one unfortunate spammer is even alleged to have been murdered by by angry spam recipients.[86] Whether or not this is true, it illustrates a danger with reliance on norms as a mechanism of governance: that there is no rule of law to guide their enforcement, with the result that unrestrained vigilantism can take over.[87]

Another problem is that the norms of Internet culture do not always coincide with public policy norms, as for example in the case of intellectual property protection, and that reliance on norms as a mechanism of governance of such issues will therefore be palpably ineffective. Even in cases where the two sets of norms do coincide, the social mechanisms by which norms tend to be enforced may be too weak to make it an effective mechanism of governance of antisocial conduct.[88]

Markets

The free market is an important feature of the modern liberal democratic state. In general the free market is a far more efficient mechanism of regulating an economy than central planning, because the market processes information more efficiently. The closer a market is to the classical model of a "perfect market," the more efficiently it functions in balancing supply and demand, ensuring that prices are set at the optimum level for both suppliers and consumers. The assumptions made in the model of a perfect market are numerous, but amongst the most important are that consumers are rational and seek to maximise their utility (roughly, their happiness), that producers are numerous and seek to maximise their profit, that the product sold in a particular market is uniform and has no perfect substitutes, that

[84] Interestingly, this particular codification of the principles of netiquette also specifies that copyright should be respected, which is a principle inherited from the wider norms of international society rather than from those of Internet culture. See also Ramon Barquin, The Ten Commandments of Computer Ethics ⟨URL: `http://www.cpsr.org/issues/ethics/cei/`⟩.

[85] K Campbell, A Net Conspiracy So Immense ⟨URL: `http://w2.eff.org/legal/cases/Canter_Siegel/c-and-s_summary.article`⟩

[86] David A Utter, Did Anti-Spam Gang Kill Russian Spammer? ⟨URL: `http://www.webpronews.com/topnews/2005/07/25/did-antispam-gang-kill-russian-spammer`⟩

[87] See Richard H McAdams, The Origin, Development, and Regulation of Norms, Mich LR 96 1997, 412; Mark Lemley, The Law and Economics of Internet Norms, Chi-Kent L Rev 73 1998; Froomkin, Habermas@discourse.net: Toward a Critical Theory of Cyberspace (as in n. 40 on page 13), 825–830

[88] For other problems with the reliance on Internet norms as a mechanism of governance, including the potential volatility and the heterogeneity of such norms, see Lemley (as in n. 87).

all participants are perfectly well-informed, and that no transaction costs are incurred in shopping around.

Remarkably, e-commerce conducted over the Internet allows for many of these usually unrealistic assumptions to be satisfied: producers are indeed numerous, search engines such as Google and online discussion fora such as newsgroups provide consumers with near-perfect knowledge, and transaction costs are low—even approaching zero in the case of markets for intangible goods such as Internet domain names, sold using online shopping cart technology. Thus it has been said that e-commerce over the Internet is one of the closest approximations our society has to a perfect market.[89] For this reason the free market can be a useful mechanism for exercising governance over such things such as the allocation of domain names.

However there are other areas in which markets are manifestly insufficient as a mechanism of governance, for any of three reasons. Firstly, the market is often less efficient than it should be due to the presence of externalities (that is, costs or benefits of a party's consumption or production decision that accrue not to that party, but to others).[90] A good example is in the case of spam. More spam email is sent than would be economically efficient, because its cost is borne largely by the recipient rather than the sender, in the form of negative utility—annoyance—as well as the pecuniary cost of the Internet bandwidth taken up by receiving spam, that is eventually passed on to consumers by their ISPs. Unless there was a market mechanism to pass these costs back onto spammers, other methods of governance would be required to tackle this problem.

Secondly, efficiency is not the only criterion of the effectiveness of a market. There are also social considerations to be borne in mind, as was noted in the Tunis Agenda, which observes "that market forces alone cannot guarantee the full participation of developing countries in the global market for ICT-enabled services"[91] (ICT being Information and Communications Technologies, including Internet networks).

Third, there are some problems of Internet governance in which markets are not really involved at all. For example, the protection of users' privacy on the Internet is not an issue which it is particularly useful to analyse in terms of market forces.[92] Other mechanisms of governance are required to manage such issues.

---

[89] Tina Hasenpusch, Does an Economist's Dream Come True—The Internet as a Perfect Market? ⟨URL: `http://citeseer.ist.psu.edu/hasenpusch00does.html`⟩

[90] R Coase, The Problem of Social Cost, J L & Econ 3 1960

[91] WSIS, Tunis Agenda for the Information Society (as in n. 5 on page 2), paragraph 18.

[92] Ruchika Agrawal, Why is P3P Not a PET? ⟨URL: `http://www.w3.org/2002/p3p-ws/pp/epic.pdf`⟩

Architecture

As discussed above at section 1.3 on page 9, the architecture of the Internet is a powerful constraint on how Internet users behave, and even plays a role in shaping and reinforcing the norms of Internet culture. As a method of governance, it is most effective when the public policy goals that are desired to be furthered are in alignment with the Internet's architecture.

To take privacy as a public policy issue, the architecture of the Internet is quite supportive of users who wish to conceal their identity from the owners of Web sites, because it allows them to surf the Web with a fair degree of anonymity; this is both a technical and social feature of the Internet's architecture. In comparison, the owner of a shared resource on an office network is likely to have greater capacity to determine the identity of any particular user who has accessed that resource, because the architecture of an office computer network is designed to place a much higher premium on security, and less on privacy.

By the same token however, the Internet's architecture is a very poor governance mechanism indeed when it comes to the furtherance of public policy that is at odds with the Internet's implicit values. The Internet's characteristic resilience against censorship is of no assistance at all to those who would seek to impose content regulation on Internet users, and neither is its architectural inclination towards anonymity of benefit to those who wish to enforce intellectual property rights online. Architecture is of its very nature, therefore, only an effective tool of governance in those areas in which governance is least needed.

Networks

In a way, networks are an amalgam of all of the other methods of governance. This mechanism can be employed either within a single stakeholder group, or across groups. As an example of the former case, so-called "government networks" are often formed between national regulators.[93] Compared to formal intergovernmental organisations that are formed by treaty, such networks provide more a flexible and inclusive mechanism through which for governments to coordinate their regulatory activities.[94] Similarly within the private sector, the "network organisation"[95] is one

[93]See Annie-Marie Slaughter, *The Role of Law in International Politics* Oxford: Oxford University Press, 2000, chap. Governing the Global Economy through Government Networks and Idem, *Democratic Governance and International Law* Cambridge: Cambridge University Press, 2000, chap. Government Networks: the Heart of the Liberal Democratic Order. Examples include the International Organization of Securities Commissions (IOSCO) (see `http://www.iosco.org/`), the International Association of Insurance Supervisors (IAIS) (see `http://www.iaisweb.org/`), and the Joint Forum (see `http://www.bis.org/bcbs/jointforum.htm`).

[94]Ibid., 215–217

[95] Also variously known as the boundaryless, virtual or post-bureaucratic organisation, and described by being organised by principles of adhocracy, technocracy or heterarchy: Janet

that replaces hierarchical authority with a geographically dispersed collection of business units, horizontally coordinated through information technology.[96]

However this book will focus on multi-stakeholder networks, involving governments, within whose power it is to create domestic and international legal rules, the private sector whose involvement is key to the operation of markets, and civil society which has a role in articulating and developing norms. Networks that include governments and at least one of civil society and the private sector are also known as public–private partnerships or PPPs,[97] and networks of three or more stakeholder groups can also be known as multi-stakeholder partnerships or MSPs,[98] although in this book the term "network" will encompass both variants.

Even prior to the IGF's formation, multi-stakeholder networks had proved one of the most promising mechanisms for bridging the gap between cyberspace and national legal systems. On the issue of spam, for example the Australian Communications and Media Authority (ACMA) has entered into a number of Memoranda of Understanding (MOUs) with its counterparts in other countries, in which the signatories undertake to coordinate their efforts to combat the spam problem.[99] One of these MOUs, the London Action Plan, includes signatories from executive agencies of 38 countries, and 25 private sector signatories.[100]

Another example is the Global Knowledge Partnership (GKP),[101] which contains amongst its over 100 organisational members, stakeholders from all three main groups: governments, the private sector and civil society, from over 40 countries.[102] The GKP's activities include the development of materials and the hosting of events for ICT capacity building and knowledge sharing, the facilitation of partnerships between its members and investment in ICT for Development (ICT4D) and K4D (Knowledge for Development) initiatives, and involvement in public policy development.

Like the other mechanisms of governance, the use of networks comes with its own limitations. One of these is that their legitimacy and effective-

---

Fulk and Gerardine DeSanctis, Electronic Communication and Changing Organizational Forms, Organization Science 6:4 1995, 338–339.

[96] Martin Parker, Post-modern Organizations or Postmodern Theory?, Organization Studies 13:1 1992

[97] Chris Skelcher, Navdeep Mathur and Mike Smith, The Public Governance of Collaborative Spaces: Discourse, Design and Democracy, Public Administration 83:3 2005

[98] See section 5.4 on page 407.

[99] See `http://www.acma.gov.au/WEB/STANDARD/pc=PC_310313`.

[100] See section 2.3 on page 74.

[101] See `http://www.globalknowledge.org/`.

[102] Along with the OECD and WGIG (which are to be discussed below at sections 2.3 on page 72 and 5.1 on page 335 respectively), the GKP was suggested as a possible model for the future IGF at a conference in Malta held by Diplo Foundation in February 2006: DiploFoundation, The Malta Discussions on Internet Governance ⟨URL: `http://www.diplofoundation.org/Conferences/IG/presentations/Conference_Summary.pdf`⟩, 1–2.

ness may be prejudiced by the imbalance that very often exists between the power of one stakeholder group within the network, such as governments or the private sector, as against that of the other groups.[103] Regrettably, this is an error that the Tunis Agenda has perpetuated, in asserting that "[p]olicy authority for Internet-related public policy issues is the sovereign right of States. They have rights and responsibilities for international Internet-related public policy issues."[104]

As will be further demonstrated in following chapters, to so restrict authority for the development of international public policy, particularly where related to the Internet, is short-sighted and fallacious.[105]

It so happens that the network model of governance quite faithfully mirrors the manner in which the Internet has been governed from the beginning. The IETF, W3C and ICANN are amongst those institutions of Internet governance that describe their processes as being based around "consensus" between all interested stakeholders. We will examine these existing Internet governance processes in more detail in the next chapter.

---

[103] Jens Martens, Multistakeholder Partnerships: Future Models of Multilateralism? ⟨URL: `http://globalpolicy.igc.org/eu/en/publ/martens_multistakeholder_partnerships_online_version.pdf`⟩

[104] WSIS, Tunis Agenda for the Information Society (as in n. 5 on page 2) para 35, derived from the earlier Idem, Geneva Declaration of Principles ⟨URL: `http://www.itu.int/wsis/docs/geneva/official/dop.html`⟩, para 49.

[105] Rhodes (as in n. 65 on page 19), 657.

Chapter 2

Internet governance as it was

> Trying to make the [gTLD-]MoU democratic is like trying to teach a goat to sing. It wastes your time and it annoys the goat.
>
> Ken Freed

As noted in the Introduction, governance is a broader term than government, and non-hierarchical mechanisms and institutions, such as norms and markets, can be involved in the governance of social systems. But what specifically is *Internet* governance? The Working Group on Internet Governance (WGIG),[1] which was established by the Secretary-General of the United Nations to report to WSIS on this question, offers the following definition:

> Internet governance is the development and application by Governments, the private sector and civil society, in their respective roles, of shared principles, norms, rules, decision-making procedures, and programmes that shape the evolution and use of the Internet.[2]

This definition is broad enough to encompass every type of governance from the rule-making of nation states, to the market forces of e-commerce, and the standards activities of the IETF. In fact, the definition is perhaps too broad to be particularly useful. It can be narrowed by drawing a distinction

[1] See http://www.wgig.org/.

[2] WGIG, Report of the Working Group on Internet Governance ⟨URL: http://www.wgig.org/docs/WGIGREPORT.pdf⟩, 4

between what I will call technical coordination, standards development, and public policy governance.[3]

In essence, technical coordination is conducted by the institutions that manage the Internet's technical architecture and resources. Some of these institutions have been alluded to above, but their history and structure will be described below in greater detail. The principal mechanisms of technical coordination tend to be the use of norms and markets.

Standards development will be defined as the processes by which technical standards are developed for the operation of the Internet. This chapter's overview of standards development will focus on the work of the IETF, but will also make comparisons and draw contrasts with other standards bodies. In standards development, the dominant mechanisms of governance are norms and architecture.

Public policy governance is potentially the broadest category of all, and yet until recently the most overlooked. It relates to the development of international public policy for the Internet. One way in which to usefully distinguish it from technical coordination and standards development is that the problems engaged by public policy governance are more likely to be problems of regulation, rather than coordination.[4]

To date the mechanism of governance that has predominated in the public policy sphere has been that of rules at the domestic level, however the establishment of the IGF heralds the possibility of a more consistent, network-based model of governance being applied to manage international public policy issues on the Internet.

As both the focus of this book and the mandate of the IGF are limited to public policy governance, discussion of the other two spheres of Internet governance will serve mainly to exemplify processes that may be adapted for use in public policy governance or which illustrate pitfalls to avoid. But since there is not always a clear division between the practice of technical coordination or standards development on the one hand, and the develop-

[3]The Internet Governance Project also divides Internet governance into three distinct functions that are similar to those isolated here; technical standardization (which corresponds to standards development), resource allocation and assignment (technical coordination), and policy formulation, policy enforcement, and dispute resolution (legal governance): John Mathiason et al., Internet Governance: The State of Play ⟨URL: `http://dcc.syr.edu/miscarticles/MainReport-final.pdf`⟩, 9. Sadowsky, Zambrano and Dandjinou identify two functions; Internet administration (incorporating technical coordination and standards development) and Internet governance: G Sadowsky, R Zambrano and R Dandijinou, Internet Governance: a Discussion Document ⟨URL: `http://pws.prserv.net/sadowsky/papers/unintgov.pdf`⟩, 11.

A third, slightly different approach adopts a layered model akin to that of the OSI networking stack, in which the lowest or "infrastructure" layer would largely cover issues such as interconnection and universal access, the intermediate "logical" layer most other issues of technical coordination and standards development, and the highest, "content" layer, public policy governance: Akash Kapur, *Internet Governance: A Primer* New Delhi: Elsevier, 2005, 4.

[4]Marc Holitscher, Internet Governance Revisited: Think Decentralization! ⟨URL: `http://www.itu.int/osg/spu/forum/intgov04/contributions/holitscher-presentation.pdf`⟩, 1

ment of public policy on the other, the formation of the IGF also provides those practising technical coordination and standards development with a venue in which to engage in the explication of international public policy norms that impact their activities.

After surveying each of the three spheres of Internet governance in turn, this chapter will conclude by explaining in more detail why governance by network is a more appropriate mechanism by which for public policy governance to be conducted than any of the other mechanisms alone, which will in turn set the scene for the following chapter's examination of how governance by network fits in with the existing international system.

2.1 Technical coordination

It was noted above that the principal mechanisms for technical coordination of the Internet are norms and markets, and historically it has indeed proved to be in that sequence that reliance on those mechanisms has emerged. Whilst originally the administration of the Internet's architecture was carried out on the basis of informal arrangements and voluntary service, increasingly it is the subject of contracts between bodies such as ICANN and those such as TLD registries with whom it deals. It is again necessary to go back in history to paint a clear picture of how this trend has come about.

Historical development

When the first node of the ARPANET was brought online at UCLA in September 1969, shortly followed by three others by the end of the year, the administration of its technical architecture was shared between the researchers who maintained each of its nodes.[5] These researchers styled themselves the "Network Working Group." They communicated with each other, not by email—because that was not to be invented until 1972—but by the exchange of printed memoranda which they titled "Requests for Comment." The earliest of these RFCs, published in 1969, was a memorandum of the design of the ARPANET's "HOST" software.[6] RFC-3 states:

> The Network Working Group seems to consist of Steve Carr of Utah, Jeff Rulifson and Bill Duvall at SRI, and Steve Crocker

[5] References for this section are Daniel J Paré, *Internet Governance in Transition: Who is Master of this Domain?* Lanham, MD: Rowman & Littlefield Publishers, 2003, IETF, The Internet Activities Board (as in n. 17 on page 6), Idem, The Tao of IETF: A Novice's Guide to the Internet Engineering Task Force ⟨URL: `http://www.ietf.org/tao.html`⟩ and Idem, The Internet Standards Process—Revision 3 ⟨URL: `http://www.ietf.org/rfc/rfc2026.txt`⟩.

[6] Idem, Host Software ⟨URL: `http://www.ietf.org/rfc/rfc1.txt`⟩

> and Gerard Delocheat UCLA. Membership is not closed.
>
> The Network Working Group (NWG) is concerned with the HOST software, the strategies for using the network, and initial experiments with the network.
>
> Documentation of the NWG's effort is through notes such as this. Notes may be produced at any site by anybody and included in this series.[7]

It was not until ten years later that DARPA established the Internet Configuration Control Board (ICCB) under the leadership of Vinton Cerf to guide the evolution of the network's protocols. Coinciding with the introduction of TCP/IP as the network's core protocol pair in 1983, the ICCB became the IAB (Internet Activities Board, subsequently renamed the Internet Architecture Board) and still later in 1989 it spawned two main task forces; the Internet Engineering Task Force (IETF) and the Internet Research Task Force (IRTF). The IETF will be discussed in greater detail below, whereas the IRTF does not directly take part in Internet standards development and can be left aside.

Having formed a body to guide the development of the Internet's standards, DARPA was still left to delegate the responsibility of assigning Internet resources. The best known such resources are IP addresses and domain names, but there are also various other parameters that may be required for use by Internet protocols, and these too are required to be uniquely assigned.

For this purpose DARPA (through an interagency committee, the Federal Network Council or FNC) contracted the University of Southern California's Information Sciences Institute (ISI). The individual at the ISI who handled this task was Jon Postel, a research scientist and manager in the Networking Division of the USC Information Sciences Institute. Although DARPA did not specify a title for the office that Jon held, it soon became known by the name that Postel came to use to describe it; the Internet Assigned Numbers Authority (IANA).[8] The holder of the IANA office operated under the oversight of the IAB, which claimed the authority to approve its appointment.[9]

In 1992 a third organisation was formed as an umbrella body having oversight of both the IAB and IANA. This was the Internet Society (ISOC). ISOC is chartered as a professional society concerned with the growth and evolution of the Internet. Its dual purposes are to provide corporate support for the IETF (for example, legal and insurance coverage, and funding for the RFC Editor), and to promote the responsible and effective use of the Internet through education, discussion, and contributions to

[7] IETF, Documentation Conventions ⟨URL: `http://www.ietf.org/rfc/rfc3.txt`⟩

[8] Idem, IAB Official Protocol Standards ⟨URL: `http://www.ietf.org/rfc/rfc1083.txt`⟩

[9] Idem, Charter of the Internet Architecture Board (IAB) ⟨URL: `http://www.ietf.org/rfc/rfc2850.txt`⟩

public policy.[10] IANA also once described itself as having been "chartered" by ISOC and the FNC, though that is not literally possible since ISOC was formed subsequently.[11]

The inception of ICANN

Although IANA retained oversight of the allocation of IP addresses and domain names, the daily conduct of these tasks was soon delegated to the Stanford Research Institute Network Information Centre (SRI-NIC), which had also managed the centralised database that was the technological predecessor of the DNS.

In 1993, on the recommendation of the FNC, the IP address allocation function was redelegated by IANA to a number of non-profit regional Internet registries or RIRs, which although now expanded in number, continue to operate today.[12]

The DNS registration function on the other hand was transferred in 1992 to a private company Network Solutions Inc (NSI). At this point, the function performed by NSI had acquired a name—it was known as the InterNIC—and it was no longer being performed under contract to DARPA, but to the NSF which by then was the core Internet backbone operator. The contract between NSI and NSF, which was to expire in September 1998, explicitly provided that domain registration services were to continue to be provided pursuant to RFC 1174,[13] the terms of which confirmed IANA's oversight role.

By 1995, the Internet had well and truly exploded into public awareness, with the number of connected hosts having more than doubled to nearly 5 million since the previous year—and before the year was out, it was destined to double again. The demand for registration of domain names had undergone a similar spike, with the number of Web sites increasing tenfold during the year, mostly within the com gTLD. As if that were not enough, NSI for the first time found itself caught in the crossfire between domain name registrants and trademark owners who claimed that domains were being registered in breach of their trademark rights—quite a novel proposition in the light of the received wisdom that domain names were merely an addressing mechanism.

In the wake of these developments, NSI's grant from the NSF soon proved insufficient to cover its mounting costs. NSI accordingly negotiated an amendment to its agreement with the NSF allowing it to charge $100

---

[10] ISOC, Annual Report ⟨URL: `http://www.isoc.org/isoc/reports/ar2004/index.php`⟩

[11] IETF, Assigned Numbers ⟨URL: `http://www.ietf.org/rfc/rfc1700.txt`⟩

[12] Idem, Guidelines for Management of IP Address Space ⟨URL: `http://www.ietf.org/rfc/rfc1466.txt`⟩

[13] Idem, IAB Recommended Policy on Distributing Internet Identifier Assignment ⟨URL: `http://www.ietf.org/rfc/rfc1174.txt`⟩

for domain registrations and $50 for annual renewals—previously, no fees had been charged. It also newly required registrants to warrant that the registration of their domain name would not infringe any third party intellectual property rights, and to indemnify NSI, the NSF and IANA against any claims alleging otherwise. In the event of a third party bringing a claim, NSI had power to suspend the registration of the domain, and to require registrants to submit to an arbitration process.

Predictably, these changes sparked an immediate furore. In the ensuing debate, perhaps only one point was in wide consensus: that the introduction of competition into the market for registration of domain names was essential. Accordingly, a number of reforms to this end were debated the following year, with leadership from ISOC. At first, ISOC backed an early proposal of Jon Postel's in June 1996 ("draft-postel") which would have seen 150 new top-level domains managed by a number of new registrars in competition.[14]

Other proposals continued to circulate however, and so in November ISOC convened a panel called the Internet International Ad Hoc Committee (IAHC)[15] to discuss these in depth. Included on the committee were representatives of ISOC, IANA, IAB, the FNC, the ITU, the International Trademark Association (INTA) and the World Intellectual Property Organization (WIPO).

The IAHC eventually produced a series of recommendations that would have seen only seven new domains created, but with the separation of the function of registry and registrar—allowing multiple registrars to compete at the retail level underneath a monopoly non-profit registry. Key to this proposal was the development of an MOU on gTLDs, which would represent the consensus of a broad group of stakeholders on the administrative arrangements to apply to the new regime.

This uncreatively-named gTLD-MoU[16] expanded upon the final report of the IAHC by providing for a new Council of Registrars (CORE) (which still exists today[17]), a non-profit Shared Registry System (SRS) to administer the gTLDs in which those registrars would offer domain names for registration, a Policy Oversight Committee (POC) to administer the new regime, and a Policy Advisory Body (PAB) to provide a representative policy development organ open to participation by all interested stakeholders.

The gTLD-MoU was signed by Jon Postel of IANA and by Donald Heath of ISOC in March 1997, and subsequently by 224 others including signatories from the private sector such as Australia's Telstra and Melbourne

---

[14] Jon Postel, New Registries and the Delegation of International Top Level Domains ⟨URL: http://www.higgs.com/archive/internet/drafts/draft-postel-iana-itld-admin-02.txt⟩—this is a later revision; the earlier one is no longer available.

[15] See http://www.iahc.org/.

[16] See http://www.gtld-mou.org/.

[17] See http://www.corenic.org/.

IT, from civil society such as APNIC (Asia Pacific Network Information Centre) and INTA, and from intergovernmental organisations such as the ITU, the Universal Postal Union (UPU) and WIPO.

It is notable that the promoters of the gTLD-MoU took care to foster a consensus not only from within but also from outside the traditional "Internet community," and particularly from the trademark owners who had caused so much difficulty for NSI. On the other hand, the gTLD-MoU was criticised for being *too* compliant to the interests of trademark owners. For example, it provided them with a 30-day period within which to pre-screen domain names for infringements before the registration of those names would take effect, and required registrants to submit to the compulsory arbitration of disputes with trademark owners by WIPO member arbitrators.[18]

Criticism was also forthcoming from those of the "old school" of the Internet who saw the involvement of the ITU and WIPO as an unwelcome grab for power on the part of the established telecommunications and IPR bureaucracies.[19] Further criticism emanated from the incumbent monopolist NSI, which perhaps predictably warned of the destabilisation that the gTLD-MoU plan would inevitably wreak.

Last but not least, the gTLD-MoU was criticised in various circles, including the United States Congress, for lacking any significant government participation; and this observation was accurate in that the ITU had not formally consulted its member governments before signing the gTLD-MoU, and that Albania was the only individual government that had signed it.[20]

Of all the critics, it was the United States Government that ultimately held the power to undermine the gTLD-MoU process, as NSI's client for the operation of the registry function. This it comprehensively did in August 1997,[21] when the National Telecommunications and Information Administration (NTIA) of the United States Department of Commerce (as the successor to the NSF) released a Green Paper soliciting comments from the public on the issue of administration and management of the DNS,[22] which did not even so much as acknowledge the gTLD-MoU or the work of the IAHC.

The Green Paper was followed in January 1998 by a White Paper incor-

[18]Ellan Rony and Peter Rony, *The Domain Name Handbook: High Stakes and Strategies in Cyberspace* Lawrence: R&D Books, 1998, 534–543.

[19]Nick Patience, Internet Stumbles Towards Domain Name Consensus, Network Week Aug 15 1997; Rony and Rony (as in n. 18), 535–540

[20]Eric T Fingerhut and P L Skip Singleton, The gTLD-MoU: a Yellow Flag for Trademark Owners on the Information Superhighway, IDEA 38 1998, n33

[21]After having earlier signalled its disapproval of the process in May: Milton Mueller, *Ruling the Root: Internet Governance and the Taming of Cyberspace* Cambridge, MA: MIT Press, 2002, 157.

[22]NTIA, A Proposal to Improve Technical Management of Internet Names and Addresses ⟨URL: `http://www.ntia.doc.gov/ntiahome/domainname/dnsdrft.htm`⟩

porating the comments received,[23] amongst which were those of Australia's National Office of the Information Economy (NOIE) which were critical of the US bias of the Green Paper.[24] The White Paper proposed the formation of a new private non-profit corporation incorporated under United States law to carry out the IANA function, including the DNS administration role IANA had delegated to NSI. In common with the gTLD-MoU proposal, the White Paper recommended the separation of registry and registrar functions, but with each gTLD (and any new gTLDs that the new corporation might form) to be operated by a separate registry.

Otherwise, the White Paper was not prescriptive about the operations of the new organisation: for example, it did not specify a list of new gTLDs that the organisation should oversee, as both the Green Paper and the gTLD-MoU had done, and neither did it prescribe a particular process for resolving disputes between domain name registrants and trademark owners (though it did call upon WIPO to recommend such a process). It stressed however that any new system would have to be constructed in accordance with four guiding principles:

- stability;
- competition;
- private, bottom–up coordination; and
- representation.

Out of the ashes of the gTLD-MoU, a loose group known as the International Forum on the White Paper (IFWP) arose, to develop an organisation based on these four principles.[25] It sponsored a series of international meetings and electronic mailing lists through which all interested stakeholders were encouraged to develop a new consensus on the formation of the corporation described by the White Paper.

IANA interceded early in this process by presenting to IFWP attendees in July 1998 a draft set of bylaws, and inviting IFWP participants to use these as the basis for their discussions. In so doing, it followed much the same process as that of its sibling the IETF in developing Internet standards by RFC. The IFWP participants, however, were not the same body of broadly like-minded engineers with which the IETF was accustomed to deal, and they proved not nearly so compliant. They rejected IANA's invitation to use its draft bylaws as a basis for discussion, on the ground

---

[23] NTIA, Management of Internet Names and Addresses ⟨URL: http://www.ntia.doc.gov/ntiahome/domainname/6_5_98dns.htm⟩

[24] See http://www.ntia.doc.gov/ntiahome/domainname/130dftmail/Australia.htm.

[25] See http://www.ifwp.org/, though the version archived at http://web.archive.org/web/19981206105122/http://www.ifwp.org/ presents a better historical account of the organisation.

that it pre-empted the achievement of consensus that the discussion was designed to forge.

Unperturbed, IANA continued to develop its draft bylaws, amending them to accord with its perception of the broad consensus that had taken shape within the IFWP by about September 1998.[26] Just prior to a scheduled final meeting of IFWP at which the members had intended to reduce their points of consensus into a set of bylaws equivalent to those of IANA, IANA announced its intention to boycott that meeting, as it had already obtained the agreement of NSI to its own revised bylaws purporting to reflect the IFWP consensus. IFWP's final meeting was cancelled, and IANA submitted a further revised version of those bylaws to the NTIA in October 1998.

IANA's high-handed circumvention of the IFWP process caused significant dissent. A group of core IFWP participants, styling themselves the Boston Group,[27] hastily formed to draft their own revision of IANA's bylaws, stating, "It is our considered opinion that the IANA/NSI proposal is neither a product of the IFWP process nor does it conform to the IFWP consensus points." One of the most notable differences between the IANA proposal and the Boston Group submission was the inclusion in IANA/NSI's proposal of a list of interim members of the board of directors of ICANN. In contrast the Boston Group called for the initial board to be elected by vote of participants in the IFWP.

Despite the Boston Group's concerns, of the two submissions (and a third submission received from the Open Root Server Confederation, also critical of the IANA process[28]), it was the IANA proposal, recommending the establishment of a corporation to be called ICANN, that was accepted by the NTIA. However, the NTIA conditioned its acceptance with the following cautionary remarks:

> public comments received on the ICANN submission reflect significant concerns about substantive and operational aspects of ICANN. We strongly recommend that you review and consider the many thoughtful and constructive comments posted at www.ntia.doc.gov. The submissions of the Boston Working Group and the Open Root Server Confederation, among others, articulate specific concerns, many of which we share. As you refine your proposal, we urge you to consult with these groups and others who commented critically on your proposal to try to broaden the consensus.[29]

[26]See http://cyber.law.harvard.edu/ifwp/consensuslist.asp.

[27]See http://www.cavebear.com/bwg/.

[28]See http://www.ntia.doc.gov/ntiahome/domainname/proposals/orsc/ORSC_PRO.htm.

[29]J Beckwith Burr, Media Advisory: Letter to ICANN ⟨URL: http://www.ntia.doc.gov/ntiahome/press/icann102098.htm⟩

Following revisions made to the bylaws in November which mandated the new organisation to establish a membership structure to elect nine of its directors, the DNS root management functions of NSI under the oversight of IANA (together with IANA's other lower-profile resource assignment functions)[30] were thus transferred to ICANN,[31] formally under the oversight of the IAB.[32] This accomplished, IANA was subsumed into the new corporation,[33] and NSI became its first registry operator.

NSI still remains the registry for the com and net gTLDs following its purchase by Verisign Inc in 2000. The org gTLD has since been transferred to the Public Interest Registry (PIR) hosted by ISOC, and ICANN has, through an at times *ad hoc* discretionary approval process, introduced various new gTLDs (aero, asia, biz, cat, coop, info, jobs, mobi, museum, name, pro, tel and travel) now operated by a variety of other registries.[34]

Current arrangements

Between the inception of ISOC in 1992 and the resolution of the Tunis Agenda in 2005, the Internet changed immeasurably: it grew more than four hundred times larger, and entire industries rose and fell around it. Yet formally, comparatively little changed over that period in the institutions by which it was governed. For example its peak body was still the non-governmental, non-profit civil society association, ISOC, and its technical standards were still primarily developed by one unincorporated technical body, the IETF, subject to the oversight of another, the IAB.

In general, the interrelationships between these organisations were not lines of authority but merely of informal oversight or "guidance," mostly as posited in RFCs rather than in agreements or international instruments.

---

[30] But not disturbing the delegation of the role of IP address assignment to the RIRs.

[31] See its Memorandum of Understanding/Joint Project Agreement with U.S. Department of Commerce at `http://www.icann.org/general/icann-mou-25nov98.htm`.

[32] Historically see IETF, IAB Recommended Policy on Distributing Internet Identifier Assignment (as in n. 13 on page 33). Although contemporary references to the IAB's continuing oversight are fewer, the Department of Commerce noted in the appendix to Idem, Management Guidelines & Operational Requirements for the Address and Routing Parameter Area Domain ("arpa") ⟨URL: `http://www.ietf.org/rfc/rfc3172.txt`⟩ that ICANN was to perform the IANA function "in cooperation with the Internet technical community under the guidance of the IAB." Further, in recent correspondence to the NTIA the IAB has stated its own position that at least the protocol parameter assignment functions of IANA are performed for the IETF pursuant to an agreement with ICANN that the IAB is entitled to terminate irrespective of ICANN's arrangments with the NTIA (see `http://www.iab.org/documents/correspondence/2006-07-09-IAB-NTIA-NOI-Response.pdf`). Therefore, although neither of ICANN's current agreements with the NTIA for the performance of the DNS administration and other IANA functions make mention of the IAB's oversight role, the preferable view is that this continues at least in respect of the protocol parameter assignment functions.

[33] See Idem, Memorandum of Understanding Concerning the Technical Work of the Internet Assigned Numbers Authority ⟨URL: `http://www.ietf.org/rfc/rfc2860.txt`⟩.

[34] See `http://www.icann.org/registries/listing.html`.

Figure 2.1: Internet governance organisations

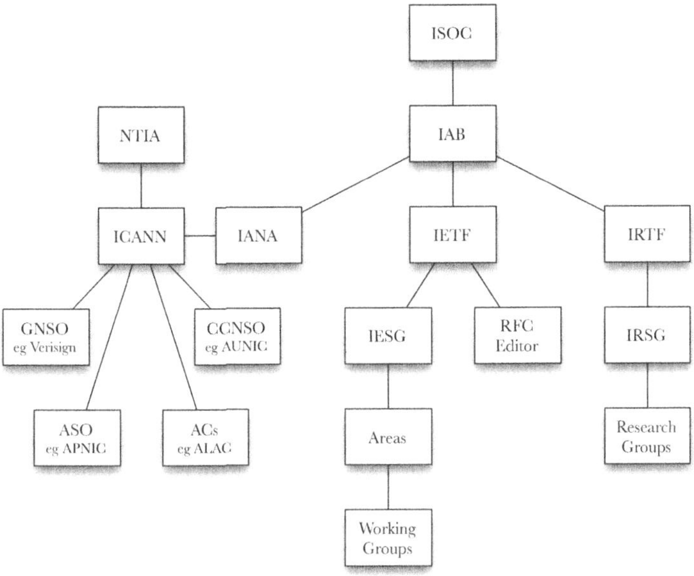

The exceptions are the more recently-formed arrangements: ICANN's with the NTIA, with its gTLD registries, and most recently—only since 2008[35]—with the largest of the root server operators (whose role will be explained below). The concentration of effective power within the network of organisations, and its fluidity, may therefore be very different from what their formal arrangement suggests. With that proviso, a diagram summarising the various organisations and their relationships appears in Figure 2.1.

Whilst most of the organisations illustrated have been described above, a few more words must be said about ISOC, the IAB and ICANN—all of which operate on an international level—before the organisations exercising governance of the Internet's technical coordination on a regional and a national level are examined.

[35]ICANN, Milestone Agreement Reached Between ICANN, and F Root Server Operator, Internet Systems Consortium ⟨URL: `http://www.icann.org/announcements/announcement-04jan08.htm`⟩

International

ISOC is a non-profit organisation incorporated in the United States with offices in Washington, DC and Geneva. It has members in over 180 countries, divided into individual and organisational constituencies, and Chapters which are regional ISOC groups such as ISOC-AU, the Internet Society of Australia. ISOC is governed by a Board of up to twenty Trustees holding office for three years, most of whom are elected by ISOC's members, but with three nominated by the IETF and up to five by the incumbent Board. The panel of candidates for election by members includes those nominated by a seven-member Nominating Committee, and those who are petitioned for candidacy by at least seven percent of the members in a given constituency. ISOC is the "organisational home" of the otherwise unincorporated IAB, IETF and IRTF.

The IAB is constituted both as a technical advisory group of ISOC, and as a subcommittee of the IETF. The members of the IAB, and its Chair, are nominated by a voluntarily-convened nominating committee of the IETF (the Nomcom),[36] and these nominations are approved by ISOC's Board of Trustees. The IETF Chair also sits as an ex officio member of the IAB. The Chairs of both the IETF and IRTF and their Steering Groups (respectively the Internet Engineering Steering Group or IESG, and the Internet Research Steering Group or IRSG) are appointed by the IAB. Membership of the Steering Groups is by nomination of Nomcom, subject to the approval of the IAB. The IAB also acts as an appeal board for complaints of improper execution of the standards process by the Steering Groups. The IAB's own decisions are published by RFC.

The third and best known international body involved in technical coordination of the Internet is ICANN. ICANN is a non-profit California corporation currently contracted to the NTIA to manage the DNS root and to perform related functions of the formerly-independent IANA. The MOU pursuant to which these services are performed (described in its latest revision as a "Joint Project Agreement" or JPA) is due to expire in September 2009.[37] Following its expiry, it is planned that the Department of Commerce will pass most of those functions on to ICANN for it to perform on a fully privatised basis, though in November 2005—just prior to the second session of WSIS—the NTIA matter-of-factly noted that the United States intended to "maintain its historic role in authorizing changes or modifications to the authoritative root zone file."[38]

The board of ICANN is composed of fifteen voting members: eight selected by a Nominating Committee (also known as NomCom, but dis-

---

[36]See IETF, IAB and IESG Selection, Confirmation, and Recall Process: Operation of the Nominating and Recall Committees ⟨URL: `http://www.ietf.org/rfc/rfc3777.txt`⟩.

[37]See `http://www.icann.org/general/JPA-29sep06.pdf`.

[38]NTIA, US Principles on the Internet's Domain Name and Addressing System ⟨URL: `http://www.ntia.doc.gov/ntiahome/domainname/USDNSprinciples_06302005.htm`⟩

tinct from the IETF committee of the same name), two each by ICANN's three Supporting Organisations, and the President who sits ex officio. The ICANN NomCom is required to ensure that the directors it nominates display diversity in geography, culture, skills, experience, and perspective, which includes ensuring that the board contains at least one director, but no more than five, from each geographical region as defined in ICANN's bylaws.[39] Officials of national governments or intergovernmental organisations are disqualified from serving as directors.

The ICANN NomCom itself comprises seventeen voting members, plus a chair and up to five other non-voting associates, advisers and liaisons. Nine of the NomCom's voting members are selected by ICANN's Supporting Organisations by reference to various criteria, with five others being nominated by ICANN's At-Large Advisory Committee described below, and one each of the remainder being designated by the Board to represent academia, by the IETF, and by the Technical Liaison Group also referred to below.

ICANN's three Supporting Organisations (SOs), along with five self-organised Advisory Committees (ACs), serve to advise the ICANN board. Each of the Advisory Committees, and the IETF, appoint a non-voting liaison to the board. An Ombudsman is also appointed to carry out internal review of contested decisions of the board.

The three Supporting Organisations are the Address Supporting Organization (ASO), the Generic Names Support Organization (GNSO), and the Country Code Names Support Organization (CCNSO), which respectively provide policy support to ICANN in the areas of IP addressing, gTLDs and ccTLDs.

The five Advisory Committees are the Governmental Advisory Committee (GAC), the Root Server System Advisory Committee, the At-Large Advisory Committee (ALAC), the Security and Stability Advisory Committee and the Technical Liaison Group. Of these, the first three are of particular note. They are ICANN's liaisons respectively with DNS root server operators, governments and the Internet community at large. Being Advisory Committees, they have no direct vote on ICANN's board, though as noted above ALAC does appoint five voting members to the ICANN NomCom.

The DNS Root Server System Advisory Committee, firstly, is formed of the operators of the DNS root servers. ICANN itself does not actually control these root servers, and never did. The root servers act as the authoritative source of DNS data for the TLDs. When ICANN makes a policy decision to add a new TLD to the root, and this decision is authorised by the NTIA, it is an entry in the DNS configuration files of one of the root servers that actually effects the change. There are thirteen classes of root

[39] ICANN, Bylaws ⟨URL: `http://www.icann.org/general/bylaws.htm`⟩, article VI, section 5.

server distributed throughout the world, under the control of a number of independent operators.[40]

As for the GAC, its mission is to

> consider and provide advice on the activities of ICANN as they relate to concerns of governments ... including matters where there may be an interaction between ICANN's policies and various laws and international agreements and public policy objectives.[41]

Membership of the GAC is open to representatives of any national government. Unlike ICANN's board, some of whose meetings are open to the public and all of which are minuted online, the GAC has resolved to meet behind closed doors. As well as advising the ICANN board directly, the GAC may recommend that the board seek external expert advice, including reference of "issues of public policy pertinent to matters within ICANN's mission to a multinational governmental or treaty organization."[42] Since 2002, the GAC has also been the only Advisory Committee whose advice may not be rejected by the Board without providing written reasons.

One of the GAC's first actions was to draft *Principles for the Delegation & Administration of Country Code Top Level Domains*, which strongly reinforced the newly prevalent conception of the ccTLD as a national resource rather than a simple network identifier as had originally been intended.[43] The Principles state in part:

> The relevant government or public authority ultimately represents the interests of the people of the country or territory for which the ccTLD has been delegated. Accordingly, the role of the relevant government or public authority is to ensure that the ccTLD is being administered in the public interest, whilst taking into consideration issues of public policy and relevant law and regulation.[44]

The NTIA has since acknowledged "that governments have legitimate public policy and sovereignty concerns with respect to the management of

[40] See `http://www.root-servers.org/`.

[41] ICANN Governmental Advisory Committee, GAC Operating Principles ⟨URL: `http://gac.icann.org/web/home/GAC_Operating_Principles.doc`⟩

[42] ICANN, Bylaws (as in n. 39 on the previous page), Article XI-A.

[43] Marcus F Franda, *Governing the Internet: The Emergence of an International Regime* Boulder: Lynne Rienner Publishers, 2001, 70

[44] ICANN Government Advisory Committee, Principles for Delegation and Administration of Country Code Top Level Domains ⟨URL: `http://www.icann.org/committees/gac/gac-cctldprinciples-23feb00.htm`⟩

their ccTLD,"[45] and the same principle was enshrined by governments in the Tunis Agenda.[46]

Finally, and at the other end of the spectrum from the GAC, ALAC's mission is to represent the interests of individual Internet users at large to the ICANN board. It is comprised of fifteen members; five selected by the ICANN NomCom, and two by each of five Regional At-Large Organizations (RALOs). The RALOs are umbrella organisations of Internet user groups, one in each geographic region as defined in the ICANN bylaws. APRALO is the RALO for the Asia-Pacific region including Australia, and ISOC-AU is one of its constituent sub-groups.[47] ALAC has also established an open online forum[48] and, informally, a wiki[49] (a Web site that any visitor can edit and add to), to allow members of the public to directly express their views.

Regional

Apart from the RALOs, the other organisations involved in technical coordination of the Internet on a regional level are the RIRs such as APNIC. These are non-profit organisations responsible for the administration of IP address allocations to ISPs or sub-regional Internet registries, under the coordination of ICANN. Although the RIRs set their own policies, in 2003 they formed a Number Resources Organization (NRO)[50] to deal with issues of joint concern, from which membership of ICANN's ASO is drawn.

The RIRs presently in operation are ARIN (American Registry for Internet Numbers) serving North America, RIPE NCC (Réseaux IP Europeéns Network Coordination Centre) which covers Europe, Central Asia and the Middle East, APNIC which covers most of Asia, plus Oceania, LACNIC (Latin America and Caribbean Internet Addresses Registry) whose coverage is as its name suggests, and AFRINIC, which covers Africa.

APNIC[51], much like the other RIRs, is constituted as a non-profit membership organisation. Since 1998 it has been registered as a corporation in Queensland, Australia. The majority of members are ISPs and large corporations from the Asia-Pacific region who receive resources from APNIC, such as allocations of IP addresses or Autonomous System (AS) numbers. The members elect APNIC's seven-member Executive Council from an

[45] NTIA, US Principles on the Internet's Domain Name and Addressing System (as in n. 38 on page 40)

[46] WSIS, Tunis Agenda for the Information Society (as in n. 5 on page 2), para 63

[47] See http://www.apralo.org/.

[48] See http://atlarge-lists.icann.org/mailman/listinfo/alac_atlarge-lists.icann.org.

[49] See http://www.icannwiki.org/.

[50] See http://www.nro.net/.

[51] See http://www.apnic.org/.

open panel of nominees. The Executive Council elects APNIC's Director General who heads its General Secretariat.

Much like the Areas of the IETF (to be discussed in greater detail below), APNIC has a number of Special Interest Groups (SIGs) which specialise in particular policy areas. SIGs devise their own charters and procedures for reaching and recording consensus. Each SIG's work takes place on public electronic mailing lists which are open to all interested participants, not only to APNIC members. A SIG may also create short-term Working Groups to tackle specific projects on the SIG's behalf.

Two Open Policy Meetings per year are held by APNIC at which the members present ratify any policy proposals developed by the SIGs since the preceding meeting. The proposals are then subjected to a final period of public comment on the SIG mailing list before they are endorsed by the Executive Council.[52] BOF (Birds of a Feather) sessions are also held at Open Policy Meetings, and it is at these sessions that new SIGs may be formed if sufficient interest exists from within the membership.

National

On a national level, the most prominent organisations involved in technical coordination of the Internet are ISOC chapters such as ISOC-AU, and ccTLD registries such as auDA, which administers the au ccTLD.

auDA is a non-governmental organisation established in 1999 to take over administration of the au ccTLD from an individual, Robert Elz.[53] There are a startling number of historical parallels between the transfer of administration from Elz to auDA and the transfer of administration of the DNS root from IANA and NSI to ICANN.

Most obviously, both transfers were the product of the explosion in popularity of the Internet during the mid 1990s, which overwhelmed the resources of the incumbent administrators. In Elz's case, his initial response was to sub-delegate control of the edu.au and gov.au second-level domains (2LDs) in 1990, then net.au and asn.au in 1994. Finally in October 1996 Elz awarded Melbourne IT Ltd a five year contract to administer com.au. Much like NSI, the new monopolist immediately began charging for registration of com.au names amidst widespread dissent from the Australian Internet community.

Echoing the efforts of the gTLD-MoU, there were attempts to regulate Melbourne IT's lucrative monopoly over the most popular Australian 2LD by establishing a ground-up organisation to be called the Australian Domain Name Administration (ADNA), which was incorporated in May

---

[52] For more detail on the APNIC policy development process, see section 4.4 on page 307.

[53] See generally Caslon Analytics, auDA Profile ⟨URL: `http://www.caslon.com.au/audaprofile.htm`⟩.

1997. However mirroring the opposition to the gTLD-MoU mounted by incumbents such as NSI, ADNA's position became untenable when it failed to win support from most of the 2LD administrators.

To resolve this impasse, ADNA's board requested NOIE (now AGIMO; essentially the NTIA's counterpart in Australia) to hold a summit on the future of administration of the au ccTLD. The result of this was the formation of Australia's equivalent to the IFWP: a dot-AU Working Group (auWG) containing public sector, private sector and civil society representatives. Following community consultation, the auWG recommended the creation of auDA, a non-profit corporation, to act as the new ccTLD administrator. Reflecting the view of ICANN's GAC (whose secretariat at the time was NOIE), auDA's constitution accepted "that the Internet Domain Name System is a public asset, and that the .au ccTLD is under the sovereign control of the Commonwealth of Australia."

In November 1999 Elz transferred control of the com.au 2LD to auDA, but retained control over the au root and its other 2LDs. Once again recalling international events, the nascent auDA was criticised by Elz and the incumbent com.au monopolist Melbourne IT, as not having demonstrated its capacity and representativeness sufficiently to justify receiving control of the ccTLD. ICANN proceeded to redelegate the au ccTLD to auDA regardless of these objections in 2001.[54]

Much as the NTIA has retained ultimate authority of the DNS root, the Commonwealth was careful to assert ultimate control over the ccTLD management function through Division 3 of Part 22 of the *Telecommunications Act 1997* (Cth), which provides for the regulation of "electronic addressing" by ACMA and the ACCC (Australian Competition and Consumer Commission). This provision was passed as a precursor to the request of the Australian Government through the Minister for Communications, Information Technology, and the Arts, to ICANN to effect the transfer of control over the au ccTLD to auDA,[55] and reserves to ACMA and the ACCC the power to take over management of the au ccTLD.

In July 2002 AusRegistry Ltd was appointed by auDA as wholesale registry operator for all of the 2LDs that were open for registrations by the general public (then com.au, net.au, org.au, asn.au and id.au), a role akin to that of Verisign in respect of the com and net gTLDs. Melbourne IT was thereby relegated to the status of one of numerous registrars accredited by auDA to accept such registrations.

auDA is a corporation limited by guarantee, containing two classes of members: supply-side (that is, those who supply domain names to the public) and demand-side (that is, consumers of domain names). Each class

---

[54]See IANA, IANA Report on Request for Redelegation of the .au Top-Level Domain ⟨URL: `http://www.iana.org/reports/2001/au-report-31aug01.html`⟩.

[55]See `http://www.iana.org/reports/2001/au-redelegation/alston-to-lynn-04jul01.html`.

of member elects four directors to auDA's board from a panel nominated by that class. The CEO is an additional non-voting member, and the board itself may appoint an additional two independent directors, a prerogative first exercised in 2000.[56]

auDA draws upon the work of a number of *ad hoc* advisory and review panels and committees staffed by volunteers drawn from within and outside auDA's membership. Nominations for membership of a panel or committee are approved by auDA's Chief Policy Officer, an unelected staff position. There have to date been nine such panels and committees, the next of which to sit will be the 2008 Industry Competition Advisory Panel. The panels and committees generate proposals and recommendations which are released for public comment on auDA's Web site before being submitted to the board for its approval.

auDA's public policies are reviewed on a cyclical basis. During policy reviews, public submissions are received and published on auDA's Web site. auDA also had an active mailing list, open to non-members, on which issues of policy were (often very robustly) publicly discussed and debated, but in 2003 it disassociated itself from that list which is now hosted independently.[57]

Criticisms

ICANN has been the most-criticised of all institutions of Internet governance from the moment of its inception. Those criticisms may be grouped into four common categories, all of which, bar perhaps the first, are instructive in their broader application for other entities engaged in Internet governance:

- criticisms of the manner of ICANN's formation;
- objections to the legitimacy of its assumption of public policy authority;
- disputes as to its ability to operate by consensus; and
- criticisms of its failure to act in accordance with the consensus principles by it claims to operate.

The Machiavellian circumstances surrounding its incorporation, as described above at section 2.1 on page 33, sowed the seeds for the first barrage of criticism ICANN received, particularly over the opaque process by which its initial board was appointed. IANA's pedigree notwithstanding, the IFWP process more closely adhered to the Internet's values of openness

[56]See `http://www.dotau.org/archive/2000-12/0014.html`.
[57]See `http://www.dotau.org/`.

and egalitarianism than the IANA process that trumped it by presenting the ICANN bylaws and board of directors as a *fait accompli*.[58]

The second common criticism of ICANN is that it has exceeded its mandate by straying into areas of national and international public policy. A good example of this is found in ICANN's UDRP or Uniform Domain Name Dispute Resolution Policy, which was established in 1999 in response to the report that the US Government's White Paper solicited from WIPO setting out a procedure for the resolution of claims by trademark owners that a registered gTLD infringed their rights.[59]

Complainants in UDRP proceedings who seek to have a registered domain name cancelled or transferred to them must prove that the disputed "domain name is identical or confusingly similar to a trademark or service mark in which the complainant has rights," that the registrant has "no rights or legitimate interests in respect of the domain name," and that the domain name "has been registered and is being used in bad faith."[60]

Academic response to the UDRP has ranged from describing it as "a tremendous achievement in a key aspect of Internet governance"[61] to a "significant threat to free and robust expression on the Internet."[62] Those critical of the UDRP have been so on both substantive and procedural grounds.

Substantively, it is undeniable that domain names, once a simple semantic identifier for IP addresses, have become a strongly-protected form of expression of trademarks and personal names of their proprietors.[63] The opposing interests of the public in free expression have been accorded comparatively less weight. This has been attributed to the fact that UDRP panellists are overwhelmingly intellectual property law practitioners whose practices are predominantly in the service of trademark owners.[64]

One of the most cogent procedural criticisms of the UDRP is that complainants are granted the right to choose which dispute resolution provider should hear their complaint, which generates inappropriate incentives for providers to find in favour of complainants. Sure enough, of the original four accredited providers, those with the greatest propensity to find in favour of complainants, apparently because they steered their caseloads to-

---

[58]See Milton Mueller, ICANN and Internet Governance: Sorting through the Debris of Self-Regulation, Info 1 1999.

[59]See http://www.wipo.int/amc/en/processes/.

[60]ICANN, Uniform Domain Name Dispute Resolution Policy ⟨URL: http://www.icann.org/dndr/udrp/policy.htm⟩

[61]Douglas Hancock, An Assessment of ICANN's Mandatory Uniform Dispute Resolution Policy in Resolving Disputes Over Domain Names ⟨URL: http://www2.warwick.ac.uk/fac/soc/law/elj/jilt/2001_3/hancock⟩

[62]Milton Mueller, Success by Default: Domain Name Trademark Disputes Under ICANN's UDRP ⟨URL: http://dcc.syr.edu/markle/markle-report-final.pdf⟩, 27.

[63]Ibid., 18

[64]See eg Ibid., 23.

wards their most complainant-friendly adjudicators,[65] gained the majority of case references.[66]

There are numerous other areas of public policy outside the UDRP into which ICANN has also been criticised for stepping. For example its agreements with new registries[67] contain non-technical specifications relating to intellectual property infringement, privacy of registrant data, fees the registries may charge, competition policy (prohibiting them from acting as registrars) and so on. As ICANN is performing these policy functions under contract to the US Commerce Department, Froomkin has argued that this amounts to a private delegation of power to ICANN that is unconstitutional and contrary to United States federal law.[68]

But ICANN's assumption of policy authority outside of US borders has been even more conspicuous, particularly for those who would characterise ccTLDs as a national resource, as advanced by the GAC and subsequently accepted by the NTIA and WSIS.[69] In that context, ICANN has taken on a role akin to that of an intergovernmental organisation in transferring control of ccTLDs to governments or governmental nominees such as auDA. auDA's is not the only case in which such a transfer was made in disregard of the wishes of the domain's incumbent non-governmental administrator, even—as in the case of Kazakhstan—when that administrator was formed from the local Internet community.[70]

That ICANN in fact makes national and international public policy decisions is no longer seriously disputed. Indeed, at least until the formation of the IGF, it was probably the best-placed body to do so, sitting at one of the Internet's only chokepoints, the root of the DNS. As much as the existence of such a centralised point of authority may be an aberration from the Internet's culture, the fact is that the issues that ICANN addressed (for example, balancing the interests of domain name registrants against those of trademark owners) were issues that needed addressing, and that it was well placed to address. The reason why it ICANN is criticised for doing so however is that it lacked the legitimacy, democratic or otherwise, that an organ of public policy ought to have.

Weinberg analyses ICANN's response to this charge as at 2000 in the following terms:

---

[65] Michael Geist, Fair.com?: An Examination of the Allegations of Systemic Unfairness in the ICANN UDRP, Brook J Int'l Law 27:3 2002

[66] Milton Mueller, Rough Justice: An Analysis of ICANN's Dispute Resolution Policy (Version 2.1) ⟨URL: `http://dcc.syr.edu/miscarticles/roughjustice.pdf`⟩

[67] See `http://www.icann.org/tlds/agreements/`.

[68] A Michael Froomkin, Wrong Turn in Cyberspace: Using ICANN to Route Around the APA and the Constitution, Duke LJ 50 2000

[69] See section 2.1 on page 40.

[70] Kieren McCarthy, 2005: The Year the US Government Undermined the Internet ⟨URL: `http://www.theregister.co.uk/2005/12/29/us_undermines_internet/`⟩

> First, it has invoked what one might call the techniques of administrative law: it has, in important respects, structured itself so that it looks like a classic US administrative agency using, and bound by, the tools of bureaucratic rationality. Second, ICANN has invoked the techniques of representation: it has adopted structures and procedures that make it look more nearly like a representative (that is to say, an elective) government body. Finally, it has invoked the techniques of consensus: it has asserted that it derives its authority from its ability to manifest the consensus of the larger community through discussion.[71]

However in dismissing each of these responses,[72] Weinberg goes on to make what is the third main criticism of ICANN, which is as to its capacity to operate by consensus (which as noted above is more than a mechanism of governance for ICANN,[73] but a plank of its legitimacy). He claims that because the decisions that ICANN makes often involve competing claims of right (such as between competitive applicants for a registry tender), they are not susceptible to resolution by consensus;[74] and that even for those issues which can be resolved by consensus, ICANN lacks the means to determine that a consensus exists.

A more apt criticism is that ICANN lacks not so much the means (which its SOs and ACs are designed to provide),[75] but rather the will to survey and interpret the community's consensus. In other words, even given that ICANN would gain legitimacy in its policy-making functions if it acted by consensus, and assuming that it has the means to do so, it does not in fact use them. This is the fourth and most persistent criticism of ICANN, for which there is a litany of documented wrongs to convict it.[76]

To take just one example, it is unclear that the board of ICANN acted upon the consensus of the community in adopting the WIPO report that recommended the establishment of the UDRP, particularly since in doing so it did not even comply with its own procedures set down for the development of a so-called "consensus policy."[77] It is all the more ironic that one

[71]Jonathan Weinberg, ICANN and the Problem of Legitimacy, Duke LJ 50 2000, 224–225 (footnotes omitted).

[72]For reasons some of which will be examined further at section 4.4 on page 302.

[73]By this book's typology, it is a consensual form of governance by network: see section 4.4 on page 297.

[74]Ibid., 252. This criticism is addressed at section 4.4 on page 291.

[75]Though they are an excessively blunt instrument for this purpose: see section 6.3 on page 444.

[76]Michael Froomkin David Post and David Farber, Elusive Consensus ⟨URL: http://www.icannwatch.org/archive/elusive_consensus.htm⟩

[77]A Michael Froomkin, ICANN's "Uniform Dispute Resolution Policy"—Causes and (Partial) Cures, Brook L Rev 67:3 2002, 652, n139; and see http://www.icann.org/general/consensus-policies.htm for the list of consensus policies.

of ICANN's grounds for declining to review the UDRP in 2003 was that this was "likely to be contentious; there are not many (if any) areas that are obviously amenable to achieving consensus."[78]

In comparison to the pillorying that ICANN has received from numerous quarters, criticism of other institutions involved in technical coordination of the Internet has been considerably more muted. On a regional level, criticism of APNIC has mostly been limited to the suggestion that its regional monopoly on the allocation of IP addresses should be opened to competition.[79]

On a national level, criticism of auDA's transparency and accountability has only flared outside the bounds of its discussion mailing list in respect of one issue; its handling of the transfer of the au ccTLD from Robert Elz.[80] However, an echo of the disingenuous claims of the early ICANN that "ICANN is nothing more than the reflection of community consensus"[81] is heard in auDA's Chief Executive Officer's claim that "auDA and its 'incumbent administration' does not create policy, it implements policy."[82]

In fact, auDA's Board has considered actions such as the introduction of renewal fees and periods for domain registrations, and even the introduction of the auDRP—its equivalent to the UDRP[83]—as "an administrative change, not a policy change."[84] Whilst some public input was, nevertheless, received on the broad outline for these "administrative changes," the underlying issue that remains is that technical coordination of the Internet inherently engages issues of public policy, and that unless the governing board of a body engaged in technical coordination reflects the consensus of its constituents in an accountable and transparent fashion, the board cannot wash its hands of responsibility for the policy development it undertakes.

2.2 Standards development

Governments have tended to take a back seat in the development and promulgation of technical standards in general, and ICT standards in

[78]ICANN, Staff Manager's Issues Report on UDRP Review ⟨URL: http://www.icann.org/gnso/issue-reports/udrp-review-report-01aug03.htm⟩

[79]Milton Mueller, Competition in IPv6 Addressing: A Review of the Debate ⟨URL: http://internetgovernance.org/pdf/igp-v6.pdf⟩

[80]Jeremy M Malcolm, Who Owns .org.au? Where Domain Name Policy and Law Collide ⟨URL: http://www.ilaw.com.au/public/dnsarticle.html⟩

[81]See David Post and Farber (as in n. 76 on the previous page)

[82]See http://www.dotau.org/archive/2001-11/0068.html, and the author's response at http://www.dotau.org/archive/2001-11/0082.html.

[83]auDA, .au Dispute Resolution Policy ⟨URL: http://www.auda.org.au/policies/auda-2002-22/⟩

[84]See http://www.auda.org.au/minutes/minutes-08052001/.

particular.[85] Thus the Internet's technical standards are not, in general, mandated by law. In this they contrast with the technical standards for international telephony, which are set out in the International Telecommunications Regulations (ITRs), a binding treaty instrument which is developed and periodically updated by the ITU's World Conference on International Telecommunication (WCIT).

Internet standards are complied with not because Internet users are compelled by hierarchically-imposed authority to do so, but because they are of high quality, are timely, widely supported, and represent a high level of technical consensus amongst a broad group of experts and users. Thus, the *de facto* standards of the Internet are a form of governance by norms, whereas the *de jure* standards of international telephony are a form of governance by rules.

The term "Internet standard" is used in two senses. The narrower sense is a specification produced by the IETF that has progressed through its standards development process to the final stage. Whilst the importance of the IETF to Internet standards development can hardly be overstated, the term will be used here more broadly to encompass specifications developed by any standards body that are intended for deployment on the Internet.

Standards bodies

Although Internet standards may not be the sole province of the IETF, as the body responsible for the development of a large majority of such standards, it is unquestionably the Internet's pre-eminent standards development body, and will be the focus of this section. Although it will not be possible to describe all of the dozens of other standards organisations that have played a part in Internet standards development, a discussion will also be made of three other particularly significant bodies: the W3C, the ITU and the ISO. Following this, a brief overview will also be given of a number of standards bodies that can be grouped in the category of industry consortia.

Amongst the standards groups that will not be described in detail, but should be briefly mentioned here, are the IEEE (the Institute of Electrical and Electronic Engineers) and ETSI (the European Telecommunications Standards Institute). The contributions of the IEEE and ETSI to standards development include the IEEE 802.11 wireless networking standard, and the ETSI GSM (Global System for Mobile Communications) standard for digital mobile telephony networks. The Technical Liaison Group of ICANN (TLG) includes ETSI amongst its members, along with the IAB, W3C and ITU.

[85] Andrew Updegrove, The Role of Government in ICT Standardization ⟨URL: `http://www.consortiuminfo.org/bulletins/feb07.php`⟩

IETF

The IETF's standards development process aims to provide a "fair, open and objective basis for developing, evaluating and adopting Internet Standards" by pursuing goals of:

- technical excellence;
- prior implementation and testing;
- clear, concise and easily understood documentation;
- openness and fairness; and
- timeliness.[86]

There is no formal membership of the IETF. It provides an inclusive technical forum for anyone who wishes to participate in Internet standards development. At each stage in the development of a proposed standard, it is discussed and debated on public electronic mailing lists and at three open meetings held each year. Whilst fees are payable for those who attend meetings, none are required to participate on the public mailing lists where most of the IETF's work takes place. Those participating in the IETF do so in their capacity as individuals, not as representatives of their employers.

A macroscopic view of the unique structure of the IETF has already been given above.[87] Here the internal operations of the organisation will be described in more detail.

The IETF is currently divided into eight technical Areas. Work in each of these Areas is managed by an Area Director who is appointed by IETF's Nomcom to the position for two years. The Area Directors and the Chair of the IETF make up the IESG, which bears overall responsibility for the technical management of the IETF's activities.

Within each of the Areas are numerous short-term Working Groups established to work on specific projects, usually the development of specifications for a proposed Internet standard. Each Working Group has a Chair, and may have a number of subcommittees known as "design teams" which often perform the bulk of the work in drawing up the specification.

The charter of a Working Group, detailing its preliminary goals and schedules, is developed before its formation at a BOF (for "Birds of a Feather") meeting, which is called upon application by interested parties to the relevant Area Director. If the BOF so resolves, the Area Director will be requested to recommend the IESG to formally establish the Working Group. Each Working Group establishes its own operating procedures, which are

---

[86] IETF, The Internet Standards Process—Revision 3 (as in n. 5 on page 31)

[87] At section 2.1 on page 38.

generally not legalistic, and may vary its own charter as circumstances require.

The outcome of a Working Group's deliberations are usually eventually published in the form of one or more RFCs. However, this is not to say that all RFCs are destined to become Internet standards. In part this is because the position of RFC Editor is not exclusively an IETF function, being overseen by the IAB and predating the IETF by two decades. Most RFCs in fact are simply informational, and are identified as such in their document header and by the use of an identifying "FYI" code.[88] Amongst the informational RFCs are documents on the IETF itself, such as RFC 3233 which provides a definition of the IETF, and RFC 3716 which is a report on its recent administrative restructuring.[89] Other informational RFCs are simply practical jokes (unconventional humour being another archetypal hacker trait).[90]

RFCs that are intended to become Internet standards develop out of documents known as Internet drafts that are normally generated by the relevant Working Group (although an individual outside of a Working Group could also submit one). To progress an Internet draft towards promotion as a standard, the Working Group, through its Area Director, may make a recommendation to IESG that it be accepted as a "Proposed Standard." The IESG will do so if it considers the specification has undergone the requisite community review, and is generally stable, well understood and considered useful.

A six month discussion period on the new Proposed Standard follows, at the conclusion of which it may be reconsidered by the IESG to determine whether it should be promoted to the status of a "Draft Standard." A Draft Standard must be sufficiently stable and unambiguous that applications can be developed by reference to it. At this point, the specification is expected to undergo only minimal revision, and there should also be at least two complete and independent implementations of the standard in software.

In practice, few specifications progress further than this. However the IETF standards process does allow for those that have become very stable and widely used to be promoted by the IESG from a Draft Standard to a full

---

[88]Other document codes are "BCP" which is assigned to policy documents intended to represent "Best Current Practice," and "STD" for specifications which have reached the final stage of standardisation. Experimental and Historical RFCs are also categorised separately.

[89]The references for this section of the book are those RFCsIETF, Defining the IETF ⟨URL: `http://www.ietf.org/rfc/rfc3233.txt`⟩ and Idem, The IETF in the Large: Administration and Execution ⟨URL: `http://www.ietf.org/rfc/rfc3716.txt`⟩, along with Idem, The Internet Activities Board (as in n. 17 on page 6), Idem, The Internet Standards Process—Revision 3 (as in n. 5 on page 31), Idem, The Tao of IETF: A Novice's Guide to the Internet Engineering Task Force (as in n. 5 on page 31) and Idem, The Organizations Involved in the IETF Standards Process ⟨URL: `http://www.ietf.org/rfc/rfc2028.txt`⟩.

[90]Idem, A Standard for the Transmission of IP Datagrams on Avian Carriers ⟨URL: `http://www.ietf.org/rfc/rfc1149.txt`⟩

Internet Standard after four more months of discussion. Internet Standards

> are specifications that are stable and well understood; are technically competent; have multiple, independent and interoperable implementations with substantial operational experience; enjoy significant public support; and are recognisably useful within some or all parts of the Internet.[91]

More parsimoniously, the general criteria for acceptance of an RFC as an Internet Standard have been described as "competence, constituency, coherence and consensus."[92] Consensus is required not only from within the Working Group, nor even the technical area from which the specification originated, but from the IETF as a whole, which includes anyone who subscribes to its public mailing lists.[93]

The IESG can decline to progress an otherwise technically competent and useful specification towards Internet Standard status if it determines that it has not gained the requisite degree of consensus. A recent example is provided by the SPF[94] and the competing Sender ID[95] Internet Drafts, both intended to address the problem of spam emanating from forged addresses. Both specifications, the first a community-developed document and the second based on a Microsoft proposal, provide a facility for recipients to verify that email bearing a certain domain name came from a source that was authorised to send that domain's email.

The IETF formed a Working Group intended to reconcile the two drafts and produce a standards-track specification. However due to each side's intransigence, the compromises required to enable either draft to be reconciled with the other could not be made, and the Working Group was eventually disbanded without reaching consensus. The result is that each specification has been approved only to proceed as an Experimental RFC, and that neither is likely to gain Internet Standard status.

A more successful recent example of the practical operation of the Internet standards development process in the IETF is that of DNSSEC.[96] DNSSEC (DNS Security Extensions) adds the facility for DNS information to be authenticated through the use of digital signatures. The importance of this is that the DNS as originally specified does not certify the authenticity of responses received to DNS queries. In practical terms, this means that

---

[91] ISOC, Annual Report (as in n. 10 on page 33), 18

[92] D Crocker, Making Standards the IETF Way ⟨URL: http://www.isoc.org/internet/standards/papers/crocker-on-standards.shtml⟩

[93] See also section 4.4 on page 308.

[94] IETF, Sender Policy Framework (SPF) for Authorizing Use of Domains in E-MAIL ⟨URL: http://tools.ietf.org/html/draft-schlitt-spf-classic⟩

[95] Idem, Sender ID: Authenticating E-Mail ⟨URL: http://tools.ietf.org/id/draft-lyon-senderid-core-01.txt⟩

[96] See http://www.dnssec.net/.

an Internet user who accesses a certain domain cannot be certain that the Web site that appears in response actually belongs to the registered owner of that domain, rather than an imposter.

The applicable technical area of the IETF dealing with DNS is the Internet Area. A DNS Working Group already existed within that Area when DNSSEC was first proposed in 1995, so in this instance it was not necessary to go through the process of forming one. It took two years until the first Internet Draft developed by the Working Group was published as an RFC, the IESG allotting it the status of a Proposed Standard.[97]

Two years later again in 1999, the specification was refined into what became a new RFC[98] which obsoleted the earlier one, retaining its Proposed Standard status. A new version of the most popular DNS software called BIND (Berkeley Internet Name Daemon)[99] supporting the new DNSSEC specification was released that same year. This implementation of DNSSEC revealed practical problems that required an addition to the specification.

For the publication of this addition, the specification was divided into three Internet drafts. These became RFCs in March 2005,[100] still retaining the Proposed Standard status. By May 2005 there was a second implementation of the latest specification,[101] bringing the RFCs closer to progression to Draft Standards, though this is yet to occur. The first ccTLD to employ DNSSEC for its operations using the latest version of BIND was se (Sweden), in October 2005.

The deployment of DNSSEC within the global DNS root is likely to take somewhat longer, since it raises the political question of whether ICANN, the NTIA, or some more broadly-based body, ought to possess signing authority.[102] If DNSSEC is to be eventually accepted as a full Internet Standard, this will likely occur only once this political issue has been resolved and the DNS-signed root zone has been in successful operation for a number of years.

---

[97] IETF, Domain Name System Security Extensions ⟨URL: http://www.ietf.org/rfc/rfc2065.txt⟩

[98] Idem, Domain Name System Security Extensions ⟨URL: http://www.ietf.org/rfc/rfc2535.txt⟩

[99] See http://www.isc.org/sw/bind/.

[100] Idem, DNS Security Introduction and Requirements ⟨URL: http://www.ietf.org/rfc/rfc4033.txt⟩, Idem, Resource Records for the DNS Security Extensions ⟨URL: http://www.ietf.org/rfc/rfc4034.txt⟩ andIdem, Protocol Modifications for the DNS Security Extensions ⟨URL: http://www.ietf.org/rfc/rfc4035.txt⟩.

[101] See http://www.ninetlabs.nl/nsd/.

[102] Brenden Kuerbis and Milton Mueller, Securing the Root: A Proposal for Distributing Signing Authority ⟨URL: http://www.internetgovernance.org/pdf/SecuringTheRoot.pdf⟩

W3C

The World Wide Web Consortium,[103] or W3C, is an unincorporated body formed in 1994 by the software engineer who designed the protocols that define the Web, Tim Berners-Lee. The W3C develops standards for the World Wide Web that are known as W3C Recommendations. The IETF's relationship with the W3C is a cooperative one, in which the IETF has formally ceded control over standards development in the Web space to the W3C.[104]

The main distinction between the W3C and the IETF is that the W3C was from its inception a paid membership-based organisation, with a sliding membership fee which as at 2008 ranges from USD$953 for small corporate, non-profit or governmental members in developing countries, up to USD$65 000 for full corporate membership in developed countries. This funding is used to support a full-time staff to assist in administration, research, and in the design and development of software conforming to the specifications developed by the organisation.[105]

This difference aside—and it is not a small difference—the organisation operates in a similar manner to the IETF in that members are expected to collaborate, through a variety of Working Groups, on the development of open technical specifications to support and enhance the infrastructure and features of the World Wide Web.[106]

As the IETF's Working Groups work within a number of Areas, so the W3C's Working Groups work within defined Activities, of which there are presently 24. The usual manner in which a new Activity or Working Group is formed is following the successful conclusion of a Workshop on the topic (similar in principle to an IETF BOF), typically arranged by the W3C's staff (its "Team") in response to a member's submission.

Working Group membership is not open to the public as in the IETF, save that invited experts, not affiliated with any W3C member, may be co-opted to the group by its Chair. The first release of a proposed Web standard by a Working Group is known as a "Working Draft" (though like RFCs, there are also some Working Drafts that are not intended to become Recommendations). Comments on the Working Draft are solicited from both within and outside the W3C for a minimum period of three weeks. Once these comments have been addressed in writing, the specification may be progressed to the stage of a Candidate Recommendation.

A Candidate Recommendation is required to be implemented in soft-

---

[103] See `http://www.w3c.org/`.

[104] IETF, The "text/html" Media Type ⟨URL: `http://www.ietf.org/rfc/rfc2854.txt`⟩

[105] See generally Tim Berners-Lee and Mark Fischetti, *Weaving the Web* London, United Kingdom: Orion Business Books, 1999, especially at 100–101.

[106] See generally W3C, Process Document ⟨URL: `http://www.w3.org/2005/10/Process-20051014/`⟩.

ware, preferably in two interoperable forms, before it may progress to a Proposed Recommendation. Comments on a Proposed Recommendation are received for a minimum period of four weeks. The specification finally reaches the status of a W3C Recommendation once it has been endorsed by the W3C Director and the members at large, through an Advisory Committee to which each W3C member appoints a representative and which meets in person biannually.

The W3C's Working Groups are guided by an Advisory Board on issues of strategy, management, legal matters, process, and conflict resolution. The Board's nine ordinary members are elected for two-year terms by the Advisory Committee. The Board's Chair is appointed by the Team.

The Working Groups are also guided in technical issues related to Web architecture by a Technical Advisory Group (TAG). Five of the TAG's eight ordinary members are elected by the Advisory Committee for two year terms, with the balance of its members, and the Chair, being appointed by the W3C Director.

The Director, Tim Berners-Lee, hears appeals from the decisions of Working Group Chairs. He is also responsible for assessing the consensus of the Advisory Committee, for example as to a proposal for the creation of a new Activity. The role of Director is not an elected one, with Berners-Lee essentially holding the position in perpetuity as the W3C's benevolent dictator.

ITU

The International Telecommunications Union[107] was established in 1865 originally as the International Telegraph Union to regulate international telegraph transmissions. It became an agency of the United Nations in 1947. The ITU is now divided into three sectors, the Radiocommunication Sector or ITU-R, the Standardization Sector or ITU-T, and the Development Sector or ITU-D. Unless otherwise noted, references to the ITU in this book are to the ITU-T.

Broadly, the ITU's equivalent to Areas or Activities are Study Groups, of which there are presently thirteen, and its equivalent to ad-hoc Working Groups are Working Parties (who delegate the actual technical work still further, to so-called Rapporteur Groups). Both Study Groups and Working Parties meet face-to-face on a variable schedule, and are not open to the public. A World Telecommunications Standardization Assembly (WTSA), held at least every four years, approves the structure and work programme of Study Groups and the draft Recommendations that they produce.

Until quite recently this meant that a telecommunications standard could not be developed in fewer than four years, but since 2000 a faster

[107] See `http://www.itu.int/`, and specifically ITU, ITU-T Guide for Beginners ⟨URL: `http://www.itu.int/itudoc/gs/promo/tsb/87029.pdf`⟩.

Alternative Approval Process (AAP), and the introduction of self-organised Focus Groups as an alternative to Working Parties established by Study Groups, have been introduced enabling some Recommendations to be finalised more quickly. The use of the AAP is restricted to Recommendations which do not have policy or regulatory implications, and therefore do not require formal consultation with Member States.

A Telecommunication Standardization Advisory Group, constituted by representatives from the ITU membership and convening between WTSA meetings, offers a role akin to that of the W3C's Advisory Board in reviewing and coordinating the activities of the Study Groups. The General Secretariat is the staff of the ITU which manages its administrative and financial affairs, headed by a Secretary-General and his Deputy. Within the General Secretariat is the Telecommunication Standardization Bureau (TSB) which exercises oversight over the ITU-T process at large, and whose Director is elected by the members.

The ITU's membership includes governments who join as Member States, and since 1994 private organisations who join as Sector Members. In 2007–2008, full membership fees ranged from CHF 19 875 for developing Member States or CHF 31 800 for Sector Members, up to CHF 12.72m and CHF 2.54m respectively. Up to 25% of the Member States form the Council of the ITU, which spans all three sectors and guides the policy of the Union in between four-yearly Plenipotentiary Conferences at which all members meet.

Until they are released, ITU Recommendations are not open for public comment (though a Study Group may request permission to open its email mailing lists or FTP area to outsiders). In fact, even when they have been released, copies of ITU Recommendations must be purchased. In response to criticism of this policy, since 2001 three free electronic copies of Recommendations have been offered to registered users per year. The ITU's definition of an "open standard" does not preclude the practice of charging to provide the specification, nor for the use of intellectual property comprised in the specification.[108]

Historically, the ITU has had little involvement in Internet standards development. Its experience lies in the tightly-regulated, hierarchically managed world of circuit switched telecommunications. But being well aware of the advance of packet switched technology as pioneered by the IETF's TCP/IP protocol pair, and of the incipient convergence of IP and traditional telephony, the ITU has lately attempted to enter the Internet standards space, relying on the breadth of the definition of "telecommunications" in its Constitution for its mandate to do so.[109]

---

[108]See ITU, TSB Director's Ad Hoc IPR Group Definition of "Open Standards" ⟨URL: `http://www.itu.int/ITU-T/othergroups/ipr-adhoc/openstandards.html`⟩

[109]"Any transmission, emission or reception of signs, signals, writing, images and sounds or intelligence of any nature by wire, radio, optical or other electromagnetic means": *International Telecommunication Union (ITU) Constitution; Convention; Optional Protocol on the Compulsory*

Its first significant entree to the world of data networking was as early as 1982, when the ITU introduced the OSI (Open Systems Interconnection) suite of network protocols, building on its earlier X.25 suite, which it intended as computer networking standards.[110] OSI had much going for it, not least the backing of the ISO which approved the OSI specifications as official standards. The IETF even established an Area devoted to the integration of OSI with the Internet's protocols.[111] Yet OSI has been a resounding failure.[112]

The poor reception of the ITU's networking standards is often attributed to the fact that they are complex, generally hierarchical in design, and, compared to Internet standards, over-engineered. For example, like their predecessor X.25, the OSI protocols placed Postal Telegraph and Telephone (PTT) authorities firmly at the top of a hierarchy, and assumed that computer owners would interconnect with those networks rather than directly to each other.[113] In comparison, Internet standards are generally much simpler, more likely to be decentralised in design, and more amenable to implementation in multiple interoperable forms.

For example, the ITU's X.400 standard for email is broadly equivalent to the IETF Internet standard SMTP (Simple Mail Transport Protocol),[114] though the specification is very much larger and more complex.[115] It was assumed that X.400 mail servers would be operated by centralised PTTs, for example in that the standard specified automated procedures for X.400 messages to be transferred to facsimile, telex and postal mail services. An individual or business wishing to send X.400 email to a third party had to pay, in Australia's case, Telstra $20 per hour for access to its X.400 network.[116]

Similarly, the X.500 standard for directory services roughly equates to the IETF Internet standard LDAP (Lightweight Directory Access Protocol),[117] which, to be fair, was based on X.500 but greatly simplified. X.500 was built as an application layer protocol on top of six other layers of OSI

Settlement of Disputes relating to the ITU Constitution, to the ITU Convention and the Administrative Regulations, 22 Dec 1992, 1994 ATS No 28 (entry into force for Australia 29 Sep 1994), Annex para 1012.

[110]See generally John Larmouth, Understanding OSI ⟨URL: `http://www.packetizer.com/osi/understandingosi/`⟩.

[111]See `http://www.ietf.org/html.charters/OLD/oim-charter.html`.

[112]Geoff Huston, ICANN, the ITU, WSIS, and Internet Governance, Internet Protocol Journal 8:1 2005, ⟨URL: `http://www.cisco.com/web/about/ac123/ac147/archived_issues/ipj_8-1/internet_governance.html`⟩

[113]Franda (as in n. 43 on page 42), 26

[114]IETF, Simple Mail Transport Protocol ⟨URL: `http://www.ietf.org/rfc/rfc821.txt`⟩

[115]It runs to the size of several large books, whereas the basic SMTP protocol is specified in an RFC of 68 pages.

[116]Known as Keylink: Paula Garrett, What Can the Internet Do for You? Join the Revolution ⟨URL: `http://www.csu.edu.au/special/online97/proceedings/onl203.htm`⟩.

[117]IETF, Lightweight Directory Access Protocol (v3) ⟨URL: `http://www.ietf.org/rfc/rfc2251.txt`⟩

network protocols. As useful as X.500 may have been, it was prohibitively complex to implement the protocols that lay underneath it. It was also unnecessary to do so when LDAP provided most of the same functionality but used TCP/IP as its underlying network protocols.[118]

As the ITU's standards are complex, hierarchical and over-engineered, so too the organisation that produced them is complex, hierarchical and highly bureaucratised. In the same way that the open, transparent architecture of the Internet reflects the culture of its founders, so too elements of the ITU's more closed, opaque culture can be discerned in the standards that the ITU develops. It should therefore come as no surprise that the ITU's Recommendations have failed to gain purchase on the Internet, since they are technically, and the processes by which they are developed are culturally, antithetical to the Internet's architecture.

There are nevertheless a few instances in which ITU Recommendations have been deployed on the Internet; mostly where it borders the telephone network, for example in the technologies by which users connect to their ISPs. Four other examples can be given:

- ENUM is an IETF standard for mapping telephone numbers into the DNS.[119] The telephone numbers themselves, though, are of course defined by an ITU specification, E.164.
- The SNMP (Simple Network Management Protocol) used by some Internet routers and hosts is another IETF Internet standard based in part around ITU protocols (much in the same way that LDAP was based on X.500).[120]
- The ITU's H.323 voice over IP protocol and related specifications enjoyed some early popularity in proprietary software such as Microsoft Netmeeting, but are now being overtaken by simpler community-developed standards such as SIP.[121]
- Finally, ITU-specified X.509 digital cryptography is still widely used in securing otherwise unencrypted Internet protocols such as those used for email (using a specification called S/MIME) and the Web (through a protocol called TLS). The success of the strongly hierarchical X.509 specification[122] over alternative community-developed

[118] See Norbert Klasen, Directory Services for Linux ⟨URL: `http://www.daasi.de/staff/norbert/thesis/html/thesis.html`⟩, chapter 3.

[119] IETF, E.164 Number and DNS ⟨URL: `http://www.ietf.org/rfc/rfc2916.txt`⟩

[120] Idem, A Simple Network Management Protocol (SNMP) ⟨URL: `http://www.ietf.org/rfc/rfc1157.txt`⟩

[121] Idem, SIP: Session Initiation Protocol ⟨URL: `http://www.ietf.org/rfc/rfc3261.txt`⟩

[122] X.509 relies on a hierarchy of Certification Authorities (or CAs) to certify the identity claimed by an applicant for the issue of a cryptographic key signed by that CA. The most successful commercial CA happens to be Verisign, which also operates the com and net gTLD registries.

> cryptography standards[123] is explained by the strong backing the specification received from the private sector; most notably Microsoft Corporation and Netscape Communications.[124] The success of X.509 thus illustrates an instance of the triumph of commercial interests, which favoured an hierarchical trust model that supported e-commerce,[125] over a decentralised model that empowered end users, in the adoption of a *de facto* Internet standard.[126]

Even so, these remain isolated successes, and in general the ITU has been relegated to a subsidiary role in standards development by participating in the IETF process (on an equal footing with all other IETF members).

Having failed to make significant inroads into the standards development sphere of Internet governance, the ITU instead sought a role in technical coordination and public policy governance, through its adoption of Resolution 102 at its Plenipotentiary Conference in 2002, by which it undertook to "contribute to policy development related to the management of Internet domain names and addresses."[127] The resolution also directs the ITU-D:

> to organize international and regional forums, in conjunction with appropriate entities, for the period 2002–2006, to discuss policy, operational and technical issues on the Internet in general and the management of Internet domain names and addresses in particular for the benefit of Member States, especially for least developed countries ...

In pursuit of this directive, the ITU has held several joint workshops with ICANN on ccTLD management and the int gTLD since 2003, hosted fora on various other Internet governance issues such as spam and cybersecurity since 2004, and most significantly established the WSIS.[128]

---

[123]For example, OpenPGP does not rely on a small number of corporate CAs to certify the identities of the parties to a transaction, but allows those parties to choose any other third parties whom they trust to fulfil that role: see IETF, OpenPGP Message Format ⟨URL: `http://www.ietf.org/rfc/rfc2440.txt`⟩.

[124]Microsoft and Netscape were then firmly locked in the "browser wars" in which each company matched the other feature for feature in a frenzied series of new product releases. Both released new email clients to accompany their Web browsers, boasting support for S/MIME, within months of each other in 1997. The combined market share of Microsoft's and Netscape's browsers was then as high as 98%: Maryann Jones Thompson, Behind the Numbers: Browser Market Share ⟨URL: `http://www.cnn.com/TECH/computing/9810/08/browser.idg/`⟩.

[125]See Lessig, *Code and Other Laws of Cyberspace* (as in n. 25 on page 9), 39.

[126]Lessig's explanation for this phenomenon is that the architecture of the Internet is vulnerable to being manipulated by corporations (see Ibid. at 34 and 52) and governments (at 43–44) to their own ends through other mechanisms of governance such as markets and rules.

[127]ITU, Management of Internet Domain Names and Addresses ⟨URL: `http://www.itu.int/osg/spu/resolutions/2002/res102.html`⟩

[128]See section 5.1 on page 322.

ISO

The International Organization for Standardization (ISO),[129] formed in 1947, is a network of generalised national standards institutes, such as Standards Australia,[130] the European Committee for Standardization (CEN), and the American National Standards Institute (ANSI),[131] coordinated by a Central Secretariat in Geneva. Some of its members are governmental organisations, but ISO membership is equally open to private sector national standards groups that are the most representative of standardisation efforts in their country. The ISO's membership fees are calculated based on the GDP of the member's country of origin, but each has a single vote on the General Assembly.

Proposals put to the General Assembly are developed by the ISO Council which meets twice per year and is made up of a rotating board of eighteen member body representatives, headed by a President who is elected for two years. There are also three general policy development committees of the ISO Council whose responsibilities span technical areas, two standing committees on Finance and Strategy, and a number of ad-hoc advisory groups. The ISO's staff is headed by a Secretary-General.

The ISO does not usually initiate the development of specifications, but rather receives those that have already been approved as standards by one or more of its members or by other international standards organisations. From this point, a specification progresses towards recognition as an ISO standard within a Technical Committee, of which there are presently 192 (some of which are inactive). Technical Committees (and in some cases their SubCommittees - often referred to as TCs and SCs respectively) are staffed by experts appointed by the members who have volunteered to work on the Committee.

A Committee with at least five members who wish to work on a proposed work item may adopt that item into its work programme by majority vote. A Working Group (WG) of experts will then normally be convened to produce a specification. The Convener of the Working Group and the Chair of its parent Committee are successively tasked with assisting their respective groups to reach consensus on the form of that specification. During this process, it is the responsibility of delegates to national committees to ensure that they present a position that fairly represents the views of all stakeholders from their country.

Once a Committee has developed a specification that meets with consensus within the group, the specification moves into the so-called enquiry stage, when it is released as a Draft International Standard for consideration by all ISO members within a five-month period. It is during this period that many members also solicit input from the public at large in their home

---

[129] See `http://www.iso.org/`.

[130] See `http://www.standards.org.au/`.

[131] See `http://www.ansi.org/`.

jurisdictions. If any of the comments received require the specification to be amended, this may entail the preparation and circulation of further drafts. At the conclusion of this enquiry phase, the Committee must vote as to whether the specification should proceed further: a two-thirds vote that it should do so, with not more than one-quarter in the negative, is required for it to become a Final Draft International Standard.

A Final Draft International Standard is then resubmitted to the ISO members for them to vote upon within a period of two months. Again approval is required by two-thirds of the ISO members that have participated actively in the standards development process, with approval by 75% of all members that vote. A specification that passes this vote becomes an International Standard. If it does not, it may be returned to its originating Committee for further work.

Like the ITU, the ISO has found the need for an accelerated process to be available for the standardisation of specifications in fast-moving fields such as the Internet. This may be achieved through:

- International Workshop Agreements (IWA), which were introduced in 2001. These bypass the ISO's traditional standards development process altogether, instead utilising an IETF-like process that involves any interested external stakeholders. An IWA is intended to produce a *de facto* standard, with a maximum duration of six years, which may then be converted to an International Standard using an accelerated process.
- Alternatively, Technical Committees may output interim standards (known as Publicly Available Specifications, or Technical Specifications) which can be made available very quickly, but which have a shorter review period than International Standards (three rather than five years) and must be withdrawn or revised to become full International Standards after their second review.
- Similarly, specifications that were developed by other bodies or other standards organisations can be fast tracked through the ISO process, bypassing the Technical Committee stages or even the enquiry stage. It is in a manner similar to this that a number of the ITU's Recommendations, notably those that define OSI such as X.400 and X.500, became ISO standards.

Appointing and overseeing the Technical Committees, in an equivalent role to the ITU's Telecommunication Standardization Advisory Group and the W3C's Advisory Board, is the twelve-member Technical Management Board appointed by the Council. There are also Technical Advisory Groups to assist with cross-sectoral issues and a Committee on Reference Materials.

As far as Internet standards development is concerned, the relevant Technical Committee is the JTC 1, which is unique in that it is the only joint committee, convened with the IEC or International Electrotechnical Commission[132] which in fact predates the ISO. It has 18 SubCommittees grouped into 11 "Technical Directions," each SubCommittee potentially having a number of Working Groups. For example, the Motion Picture Experts Group which is responsible for the MPEG family of video and audio compression standards is Working Group 11 within SubCommittee 29 of JTC 1.

An example of an Internet standard developed by the ISO/IEC is SGML (Standard Generalized Markup Language), which formed the inspiration for the W3C's HTML and later XML. Much like the ITU's X.500 which fell into disuse after being re-implemented in simplified form as LDAP, SGML has now been largely superseded by the simpler XML.

Another example of the ISO/IEC's output that is in wide use on the Internet is the image format commonly known as JPEG,[133] whose namesake the Joint Photographic Experts Group is a joint ISO/IEC and ITU committee. JPEG is the most popular image format found on the Web, more so than the W3C's PNG (Portable Network Graphics) format.

Perhaps even more fundamental than JTC 1's specifications to a number of Internet services are the more basic language code (ISO 639), country code (ISO 3166) and character set (eg ISO 8859-1, aka Latin-1) specifications. ISO 639 is used in standards such as HTML and XML, ISO 3166 provides the names of the ccTLDs used in the domain name system, and ISO 8859-1 was the character set originally used in HTML (but is now becoming obsoleted by the consortium-developed Unicode standard that offers better multilingual support).

The ISO charges for many of its standards, but makes others—mostly those of JTC 1—available for free, and unlike the ITU its draft standards are made freely and publicly available.

Industry consortia

Standards can also be developed by smaller, more responsive groups whose membership is restricted to industry. This has been an increasingly attractive option for industry in the wake of the failure of OSI which exposed the limitations of the ITU and ISO processes. Although many consortia may not accept the input of the public or of other standards groups into their specifications, some of the standards they develop can nevertheless effectively become Internet standards (though not of course in the IETF's sense of that term).

One reason why they may gain this status is because they are referenced by IETF or W3C standards; for example, the Unicode Consortium's Unicode

[132]See `http://www.iec.ch/`.

[133]More formally known as IS 10918-1 | T.81; see `http://www.jpeg.org/`.

standard[134] for encoding multilingual character sets is central to the W3C's XML standard. A second reason is that there may not be an open standard covering the same ground as the industry standard in question, and the standard underpins a popular Internet service or technology. One example is the Open Mobile Alliance's WAP (Wireless Application Protocol)[135] standard, which is something like a wireless version of the W3C's HTTP protocol, and another is ECMAScript, more commonly known as JavaScript, which was submitted for standardisation to Ecma International by its original developer, Netscape Communications.[136]

Some of the standards developed by consortia are then submitted to more open standards groups for registration. For example, the IP/MPLS Forum's[137] ATM (Asynchronous Transfer Mode) standard, which is a high-bandwidth packet switching and transmission system often used to encapsulate TCP/IP data for transmission across Internet-connected networks, has become an ITU recommendation.

Other industry consortia develop higher-level standards "on top" of open standards, often in niche areas of specialisation. An example is OASIS which develops standards for e-business and Web services based on the W3C's XML.[138]

Finally some consortia have attempted to "go it alone" in pushing their specifications as Internet standards, but the track record of such attempts has been poor. A prominent example is the SET (Security Electronic Transactions) specification introduced jointly to much publicity by Visa and Mastercard in 1997. The specification was an advance on the existing protocol for securing Web transactions, SSL (Secure Sockets Layer, which evolved into TLS or Transport Layer Security), in that it allowed a consumer to pay for an online transaction by credit card without revealing the credit card details even to the merchant from whom the purchase was made. However the added complexity of SET for the end user offered them little tangible benefit over and above SSL. As early as 1999 the SET project was floundering from lack of support,[139] and the SET consortium's Web site vanished from the Internet before the end of 2002.

Criticisms

If standards organisations ought to aim, as the IETF does, to achieve technical excellence, prior implementation and testing, clear, concise and

---

[134]See `http://www.unicode.org/`.

[135]Formerly the WAP Forum—see `http://www.openmobilealliance.org/`.

[136]See `http://www.ecma-international.org/`.

[137]Formerly the MFA Forum and before that the ATM Forum—see `http://www.ipmplsforum.org/`.

[138]See `http://www.oasis-open.org/`.

[139]Tim Clark, Visa, Mastercard Try to Revive SET ⟨URL: `http://www.news.com/2100-1017-225723.html`⟩

easily understood documentation, openness and fairness, and timeliness in their specifications,[140] then the grounds upon which such organisations can be, and frequently are criticised follow naturally: technical mediocrity, lack of field implementation or testing, obscure documentation, closed or partial procedures, and delay. There are standards organisations and processes that have been accused of all of these things.[141]

However rather than examining each of these failings, this subsection of the book will focus on three specific areas of criticism common to the IETF and W3C that are of particular relevance to the practice of Internet governance. These are criticisms of whether private standards bodies *can* make decisions by consensus within their membership, if so whether they *do* make decisions by such a process, and if so whether they *should* make decisions by such a process—or in short, criticisms of their effectiveness, their inclusiveness, and their broader legitimacy.

Effectiveness

A weakness of the standards processes of both the IETF and the W3C is the ease with which they can be disrupted by those who, because they have a proprietary specification of their own to push, or for some other reason, are able to stymie the achievement of consensus on the acceptance of a competing standard. This has been observed in the case of S/MIME and OpenPGP, and that of SPF and SenderID, in both of which cases the outcome was to fragment the standards landscape into two competing segments, neither of which might ever reach the status of a full Internet standard.

Although this is a criticism of the IETF and W3C processes, in a sense it reveals no fault in those processes. After all, they produced exactly the outcome they were intended to—that in the absence of consensus, there should be no standard. It is considered better not to specify a standard at all, than to release a so-called standard that a segment of the affected Internet community refuses to implement. To the extent that this policy can be criticised, so too can that of any other organisation that operates by consensus.

As Chapter 4 will discuss in more detail,[142] the answer to this criticism, such as it is, is that when consensus fails, another mechanism of governance will determine the dominant specification: typically, this mechanism will be markets (though it could also be rules). Once this mechanism has run its course, the specification most successful in the marketplace (or that which has been mandated by law) can be returned to the standards body to be formalised as a standard.

---

140 IETF, The Internet Standards Process—Revision 3 (as in n. 5 on page 31)

141 John G Waclawsky, Closed Architectures, Closed Systems And Closed Minds, Business Communications Review October 2004

142 See section 4.4 on page 311.

Inclusiveness

On the other hand not every failure of the Internet standards development processes of the IETF or W3C can be attributed to differences between stakeholders. On other occasions those bodies' failure to produce a standard can be attributed to deficits in the design or implementation of their processes, which have prompted the development of competition from other standards bodies, or in some cases from other mechanisms of governance altogether.[143]

At the root of these procedural deficiencies is a lack of inclusiveness in the standards development process. For example in 2004, a rival to the W3C with no membership fees, the Web Hypertext Application Technology Working Group (WHATWG),[144] was formed in response to concerns about "the W3C's direction with XHTML, lack of interest in HTML and apparent disregard for the needs of real-world authors."[145]

Similarly in 2006 the W3C was publicly accused of failing to acknowledge or respond to comments on a specification, even from one of its own staff, leading another long-time commentator to allege, "Beholden to its corporate paymasters who alone can afford membership, the W3C seems increasingly detached from ordinary designers and developers."[146] In response to such criticisms, in 2007 the W3C relaunched an HTML working group designed to facilitate the active participation of some of its critics.[147]

As for the IETF, whilst its membership may be more open than that of the W3C in theory, in practice it is a meritocracy that can be quite impenetrable to non-technical stakeholders.[148] A self-critical RFC from 2004 frankly acknowledged this problem:

> The IETF is unsure who its stakeholders are. Consequently, certain groups of stakeholder, who could otherwise provide important input to the process, have been more or less sidelined because it has seemed to these stakeholders that the organization does not give due weight to their input.[149]

---

143 This process is also described at section 4.2 on page 211.

144 See `http://www.whatwg.org/`.

145 WHATWG, The WHATWG and HTML 5 FAQ ⟨URL: `http://wiki.whatwg.org/wiki/FAQ`⟩

146 Jeffrey Zeldman, An Angry Fix ⟨URL: `http://www.zeldman.com/2006/07/17/an-angry-fix/`⟩; and another, "The process is stacked in favour of multinationals with expense accounts who can afford to talk on the phone for two hours a week and jet to world capitals for meetings": Joe Clarke, To Hell with WCAG 2 ⟨URL: `http://www.alistapart.com/articles/tohellwithwcag2/`⟩.

147 W3C, W3C Relaunches HTML Activity ⟨URL: `http://www.w3.org/2007/03/html-pressrelease`⟩

148 See section 4.2 on page 203.

149 IETF, IETF Problem Statement ⟨URL: `http://www.ietf.org/rfc/rfc3774.txt`⟩

Legitimacy

This leads to the third main criticism (mirroring a similar criticism made of ICANN) that the IETF and W3C have strayed into areas of public policy without being legitimately entitled to do so by reason of either carrying a democratic mandate to develop policy, or having established a broad community consensus. Whilst they do establish consensus internally in support of the specifications they standardise, as noted above this is in general neither broad nor community-based.

For example, in 1995 the W3C developed a specification called PICS, or Platform for Internet Content Selection,[150] that provided Web publishers with the ability to mark their pages with computer-readable metatags rating the content of the page. It was envisioned that this would enable parents and teachers to proactively restrict childrens' access to certain Internet content, without the need for that content to be censored altogether.

The W3C's press release about PICS[151] proudly announced that it had received input from 23 companies and organisations, most of which were ISPs, media or software companies, and only one of which—the Center for Democracy and Technology (CDT)—claimed to represent users. It should not therefore have come as a surprise to the W3C to find that opposition to the technology began to mount from quarters it had not consulted when developing the technology.[152] These critics maintained that just as easily as parents or teachers could utilise PICS, so too could it be used by a paternalistic ISP or a repressive government to filter out PICS-rated content automatically without any input from the end user.[153]

A lesson that the W3C might have drawn was that altering the architecture of the Internet so as to compromise its inherent values such as interactivity, openness, egalitarianism, and resilience,[154] is to tinker with its fundamental stuff. To do so essentially for public policy reasons, with input from only one representative of users and none of governments, was brash to say the least. Lessig states of PICS, "Given that [the consortium] is a pretty powerful organization, it should be more open. If they want to do policy, they have to accept the constraints on a policy-making body, such as openness in who can participate."[155]

The IETF placed itself in a similar position to the W3C when making a

---

[150] See `http://www.w3.org/PICS/`.

[151] W3C, Industry and Academia Join Forces to Develop Platform for Internet Content Selection (PICS) ⟨URL: `http://www.w3.org/PICS/950911_Announce/pics-pr.html`⟩

[152] ACLU, Fahrenheit 451.2: Is Cyberspace Burning? ⟨URL: `http://www.aclu.org/privacy/speech/15145pub20020317.html`⟩

[153] Irene Graham, Will PICS Torch Free Speech on the Internet?, Commmunications Law Bulletin 17:1 1998

[154] See section 1.3 on page 9.

[155] Attributed to Lessig in Simpson L Garfinkel, The Web's Unelected Government ⟨URL: `http://www.technologyreview.com/InfoTech/wtr_11776,258,p1.html`⟩, 4 (brackets in original).

policy decision not to include support for wire-tapping in the protocols it develops, despite the fact that national legislation or policy might require wire-tapping to be conducted on networks utilising those protocols.[156] This decision was less publicly controversial than the introduction of PICS, perhaps because it was more congruent with the Internet's underlying values (or perhaps because it could be naïvely characterised as an abstention from action on the public policy issues in question).

Even so, the decision was one with considerable public policy implications, made without consultation outside the IETF's membership. This raises questions over the democratic legitimacy of the process; questions that will be revisited in the conclusion to this chapter, and in Chapter 3.[157]

For now, it may at least be concluded that in standards development, as in technical coordination, public policy issues are inherently engaged, and that standards development bodies cannot abnegate responsibility for policy development by denying or ignoring that this is so.

2.3 Public policy governance

The difference between the public policy sphere of governance, and the technical coordination and standards development spheres, is that whereas the latter engage public policy issues in an indirect and subsidiary manner, public policy governance, by definition, does so directly and primarily. Just as the main instruments of technical coordination are norms and markets, and of standards development norms and architecture, the principal mechanism for the exercise of public policy governance is through the use of rules.

Although rules are found in other hierarchical power relationships than that between government and governed, it is in that context that they find their most common and effective expression, and are known as law. Law may of course be further subdivided in any number of ways, for example into that produced by legislative, executive or judicial arms of government, but the more relevant distinction for present purposes is between international law, and national or sub-national law (which together we may call domestic law).

In this section, a brief survey will be made of a range of laws and other rules on a selection of Internet-related public policy issues at both international and domestic levels, taking the particular example of Australia where possible, and omitting discussion of WSIS and the IGF which are the subject of Chapter 5.[158] In doing so, it is hoped that some of the gaps

156 IETF, IETF Policy on Wiretapping ⟨URL: `http://www.ietf.org/rfc/rfc2804.txt`⟩

157 See section 3.4 on page 145.

158 The arrangement below is intended to highlight the relevant issues rather than the relevant actors, however those involved in technical coordination and standards development

Table 2.1: Public policy issues

WGIG para	WGIG description	Agenda paras
15	Administration of the root zone files and system	
16	Interconnection costs	49, 50
17	Internet stability, security and cybercrime	40, 43, 44, 45
18	Spam	41
19	Meaningful participation in global policy development	52
20	Capacity-building	51
21	Allocation of domain names	63, 64
22	IP addressing	38
23	Intellectual property rights (IPR)	
24	Freedom of expression	42
25	Data protection and privacy rights	39, 46
26	Consumer rights	47
27	Multilingualism	49, 53

in the existing governance regimes applied to those public policy issues will be identified, and the scope of the IGF's potential work programme illustrated.

Internet-related public policy issues

The Tunis Agenda itself identifies numerous public policy issues for consideration of the IGF, but nowhere are these itemised in clear terms. The report of WGIG to WSIS had however earlier identified thirteen Internet-related public policy issues in more concrete terms,[159] most of which can be traced forward to one or more paragraphs of the section on Internet governance in the Tunis Agenda. Table 2.1 itemises the thirteen public policy issues identified by WGIG by paragraph and brief description, and their equivalent paragraphs in the relevant section of the Tunis Agenda, if any.

The omissions from the Internet governance section of the Tunis Agenda that are present in the WGIG report call for comment. The subject of paragraph 15 of the WGIG Report, relating to administration of the DNS root servers, is conspicuous in its absence from the Tunis Agenda. As will be explained in greater detail in Chapter 5, this is because the United States

have already been surveyed in the first two sections of this chapter, and some of the most prominent intergovernmental organisations are described in chapter 3. A clear and complete tabular overview of all the organisations active in Internet governance is found in table 1 of Mathiason et al. (as in n. 3 on page 30).

[159] WGIG, Report of the Working Group on Internet Governance (as in n. 2 on page 29), 5

had made it quite clear that it was not willing to divest its control of the DNS root,[160] and during the negotiations that preceded the final meeting of WSIS, this position was conceded. Accordingly, save for the observation that "Countries should not be involved in decisions regarding another country's country-code Top-Level Domain (ccTLD)," and the vague promise of "enhanced cooperation" in future,[161] the Tunis Agenda specified that the IGF "would have no involvement in day-to-day or technical operations of the Internet."[162]

Thus paragraphs 21 and 22 from the WGIG report on domain names and IP addressing were included in the Tunis Agenda only in respect of their public policy rather than their technical dimension (namely the assertion that national oversight of these activities was needed). These items requires no further consideration here as domain name and IP address allocation have already been considered as functions of technical coordination, rather than of public policy governance. The policy issue of governmental oversight of these activities will however be revisited in Chapter 5.[163]

The omission of the topic of paragraph 23 of the WGIG report relating to intellectual property rights from the Tunis Agenda (save for a fleeting reference to software licensing in paragraph 49), and the omission of trade issues from both the WGIG list and the Tunis Agenda, is more obscure—or perhaps not. One commentator states:

> In the preparatory process of the Geneva phase it soon became clear that developed country governments (the United States and European Union in particular) would do everything in their power to avoid broadening out the WSIS agenda to include … the policies promoted by developed countries within such bodies as the WTO and the World Intellectual Property Organisation (WIPO) with respect to international trade or intellectual property rights (IPRs).[164]

In less conspiratorial terms, this is confirmed by a background paper released by WGIG along with its report.[165] Although trade—or in the Internet context, e-commerce—is not included, e-government forms the subject of paragraph 48 of the Tunis Agenda (though it is absent from the WGIG list), and it raises many of the same issues.

---

[160]See NTIA, US Principles on the Internet's Domain Name and Addressing System (as in n. 38 on page 40).

[161]See section 5.1 on page 344.

[162]WSIS, Tunis Agenda for the Information Society (as in n. 5 on page 2), paras 63 and 77.

[163]See section 5.1 on page 344.

[164]Pablo Accuosto, WSIS Wraps Up With Mixed Emotions ⟨URL: http://www.choike.org/nuevo_eng/informes/3730.html⟩

[165]WGIG, Background Report ⟨URL: http://www.wgig.org/docs/BackgroundReport.pdf⟩, 3

Finally, there are a number of issues described separately in the Tunis Agenda that can be usefully combined for present purposes. These are paragraphs 16, 19, 20 and 27 of the WGIG Report; interconnection costs, meaningful participation in global policy development, IT capacity building and multilingualism, which can be combined under the heading of "development," in that they all concern the development of Internet architecture to support uniformity of access to the Internet and participation in Internet public policy governance, particularly by users from disadvantaged economies.

Taking the public policy issues from the WGIG report with the items from paragraphs 16, 19, 20 and 27 combined, removing DNS and IP addressing issues that fall outside the scope of this section, adding e-government from the Tunis Agenda and combining it with e-commerce, and adding back the notably omitted issue of intellectual property, leaves the following list of Internet-related public policy issues for discussion:

- Internet stability, security and cybercrime
- Spam
- Intellectual property rights (IPR)
- Freedom of expression
- Data protection and privacy rights
- Consumer rights
- Development
- e-commerce and e-government

It is not contended that this is an exhaustive list, and some of the categories are rather broad (though as will be seen, less so than the four categories upon which the IGF eventually settled for its first meeting). However the list does provide a useful indication of the topics that might be expected to find a place on the IGF's work programme.

Internet stability, security and cybercrime

The Internet has provided fertile ground for the commission of old crimes in new ways, such as the use of P2P file sharing services to distribute child pornography, and the use of encrypted email to plan terrorist attacks. It has also enabled the commission of new crimes more peculiar to the Internet, that involve the subversion of its architecture. One example of the second class of crimes is the Distributed Denial of Service (DDoS) attack, by which the criminal typically causes a distributed network of home computers to be infected with a virus that covertly places them under the criminal's control, and then uses that control to cause each computer to bombard a victim's Internet server with data until the server's capacity to respond to legitimate requests is overwhelmed.

This second class of new offences is normally termed "cybercrime," and it has been the main focus of bodies involved in Internet public policy governance. There are no fully international instruments addressing this topic, apart from a non-binding *UN General Assembly Resolution on a Global Culture of Security*,[166] which was based on an earlier OECD (Organization for Economic Cooperation and Development) document.[167] However the most notable regional activity, which now has global reach, is the *Convention on Cybercrime* passed by the Council of Europe in 2001[168] dealing with computer fraud, information security, and the content regulatory issues of child pornography and copyright. This convention has also been acceded to by other non-European countries such as South Africa, Canada, the USA and Japan. Although Australia has not ratified the convention, its *Cybercrime Act 2001* (Cth) was based on it in part.

Public policy governance by the executive arms of international, regional and domestic governmental bodies in the area of cybercrime has been at least as significant as that of their legislatures. The G8 Group (the United States, the United Kingdom, France, Germany, Italy, Germany, Japan and Russia), formed a High-tech Crime Subgroup in 1997 which has established a network of cybercrime points of contact in each country.[169] The European Union in 2004 formed an agency of its own, the European Network and Information Security Agency (ENISA), which aims to provide assistance to the European Commission and Member States in addressing security issues in hardware and software, and to promote standards and activities to minimise information security risks.[170]

In Australia's region, APEC (Asia-Pacific Economic Cooperation) has a Telecommunications and Information Working Group (TEL) that has drafted a cybersecurity strategy for its member states,[171] and there is an Australian High Tech Crime Centre to provide a nationally coordinated approach to high tech crime across all Australian jurisdictions.[172]

The war against cybercrime is also waged in non-governmental fora.

---

[166] General Assembly of the United Nations, Creation of a Global Culture of Cybersecurity: Resolution ⟨URL: http://documents-dds-ny.un.org/doc/UNDOC/GEN/N02/555/22/pdf/N0255522.pdf⟩

[167] OECD, OECD Guidelines for the Security of Information Systems and Networks: Towards a Culture of Security ⟨URL: http://www.oecd.org/dataoecd/16/22/15582260.pdf⟩

[168] *Council of Europe Cybercrime Convention*, 23 Nov 2001, 2003 S Treaty Doc No 108-11

[169] See http://www.cybercrime.gov/g82004/g8_background.html.

[170] See http://enisa.europa.eu/.

[171] APEC, Recommendation by the APEC TELWG to SOM for an APEC Cybersecurity Strategy ⟨URL: http://www.apec.org/apec/apec_groups/working_groups/telecommunications_and_information.MedialibDownload.v1.html?url=/etc/medialib/apec_media_library/downloads/som/mtg/2002/word.Par.0204.File.v1.1⟩

[172] See http://www.ahtcc.gov.au/.

National computer emergency response teams such as the eponymous CERT®[173] and Australia's AusCERT,[174] some of which are government-linked and others of which are private sector or civil society organisations, join together in the Forum of Incident Response and Security Teams (FIRST).[175] They provide services and support, some voluntary and some for-fee, to those whose computer systems or networks are attacked by cyber-criminals and those investigating such attacks.

The CA/Browser Forum[176] provides another example of a purely private approach to combatting cybercrime; specifically phishing, a "social engineering" attack in which victims are induced (usually through spam email) to provide confidential details to a bogus Web site masquerading as that of a legitimate online business such as a bank. The CA/Browser Forum contains no governmental members, but is simply a consortium of CAs and vendors of Web browser software. Their approach to the problem is based on architecture: the introduction of a new type of SSL certificate that requires more rigorous verification by the issuing CA, and is flagged as such by the user's Web browser.

As for crimes that are not Internet-specific but which are committed by use of Internet services, there are of course a number of relevant but general international instruments such as conventions on drug trafficking and organised crime,[177] and a number of active executive bodies such as Interpol. These fall outside the scope of this book, though some will be alluded to later at section 3.4 on page 157.

However mention should at least be made of the Optional Protocol to the Convention on the Rights of the Child on the sale of children, child prostitution and child pornography,[178] which was passed in recognition of "the growing availability of child pornography on the Internet," and of the Virtual Global Taskforce (VGT), which is a transnational network of police services combatting online child exploitation.[179]

Spam

Of all the public policy issues examined here, spam provides one of the best illustrations of the necessity of taking an international approach. As the reach of Internet email is international, spam can effectively be sent

---

[173] See `http://www.cert.org/`, though CERT now disavows the origin of its name.

[174] See `http://www.auscert.org.au/`.

[175] See `http://www.first.org/`.

[176] See `http://www.cabforum.org/`.

[177] See Christine Van den Wyngaert, *International Criminal Law: A Collection of International & European Instruments* Boston: Kluwer Law International, 2000.

[178] *Optional Protocol to the Convention on the Rights of the Child*, 25 May 2000, 2007 ATS No 6 (entry into force for Australia 8 Feb 2007)

[179] See `http://www.virtualglobaltaskforce.com/`.

from whichever corner of the globe restricts it the least, rendering domestic prohibitions on the sending of spam next to ineffectual.

There is no international instrument on spam; the closest perhaps being the European Union's *e-Privacy Directive* prohibiting the sending of spam,[180] which all member states were required to implement by 31 October 2003. A Contact Network of Anti-Spam Enforcement Authorities (CNSA) has been formed by 13 of the EU's national anti-spam regulatory authorities.[181]

This has however been eclipsed by a broader international network of 38 anti-spam regulators, and 25 private sector members, in a forum formed in 2004 known as the London Action Plan (LAP).[182] The activities of the LAP are based around an agreement for cooperation in international enforcement of domestic anti-spam laws, and education of users and businesses.

Remaining on the international front, the OECD has formed an *ad hoc* Spam Task Force which has contributed usefully to international coordination of anti-spam enforcement by compiling a variety of reports on spam, and an online anti-spam Toolkit.[183] The ITU has also sought to become involved by releasing a survey of spam legislation and hosting thematic meetings on spam and network security.[184]

Australia's activities in anti-spam networks include the ACMA's and the ACCC's membership of the LAP, a multilateral Seoul–Melbourne Multilateral Anti-Spam Agreement signed by twelve regional agencies, and additional bilateral agreements concluded between the ACMA and agencies from Taiwan, South Korea, Thailand, the United States and the United Kingdom, by which the respective parties agreed to exchange information about anti-spam policies and strategies, and security issues.[185]

Australia can also boast a strong domestic legislative response to the spam problem. The *Spam Act 2003* (Cth) prohibits the sending of spam (or, in the legislation's terms, unsolicited commercial electronic messages) on pain of penalties of up to $220 000 per day, or up to $1.1 million for repeated infringements. There is no specific minimum number of messages that must be sent before they are qualified as spam; a single message can be caught by the legislation. The Act also prohibits the use of address harvesting software or harvested address lists.

---

180 European Commission, Directive on Privacy and Electronic Communications ⟨URL: http://eur-lex.europa.eu/LexUriServ/LexUriServ.do?uri=CELEX:32002L0058:EN:HTML⟩

181 Idem, European Countries Launch Joint Drive to Combat "Spam" ⟨URL: http://europa.eu/rapid/pressReleasesAction.do?reference=IP/05/146⟩

182 Idem, Directive on Privacy and Electronic Communications (as in n. 180), and see http://www.londonactionplan.org/. The membership numbers given are as at 2008.

183 See http://www.oecd-antispam.org/.

184 See http://www.itu.int/osg/spu/spam/.

185 See http://www.acma.gov.au/WEB/STANDARD/pc=PC_310313.

Equivalent legislation from Australia's partners in LAP varies considerably. In contrast to the Australian and EU legislation which requires users to have opted in before receiving commercial email, the United States *CAN-SPAM Act* which came into force in 2004[186] allows spam to be sent in the first instance so long as an "opt-out" facility is provided. It does however require spammers to provide their street address in any communications they send.

Initiatives in the war against spam are also being taken within the private sector and civil society. The Anti-Spam Technical Alliance, whose founding members include America Online, British Telecom, Comcast, EarthLink, Microsoft, and Yahoo!, released a proposal containing a range of technical recommendations for the control of spam.[187] MAAWG (the Messaging Anti-Abuse Working Group) is another similar group.[188] Developments within the IETF of course included SPF and SenderID, and in 2003 the IRTF also chartered an Anti-Spam Research Group (ASRG) which has an active mailing list.[189]

Spam filtering software and services, both open source[190] and proprietary,[191] have proliferated. Amongst these are services known as DNS blocklists. These are lists of IP addresses known to have been used by, or to be open to abuse by spammers. Third parties such as ISPs and knowledgeable individual users can use these lists within their mail server or spam filter software to automatically refuse the receipt of email emanating from those same IP addresses.[192]

Conversely, there are services that will assure receipients of the *bona fides* of email sent from a given domain. The Domain Assurance Council,[193] formed in 2006, is an association of such assurance providers, which is promoting the use of an IETF standards-track specification called DKIM (Domain Keys Identified Mail)[194] as a standard protocol for the provision of domain assurance services.

---

[186] *Controlling the Assault of Non-Solicited Pornography and Marketing Act 2003* 117 Stat 2699 Public Law 108-187

[187] ASTA, Technology and Policy Proposal ⟨URL: `http://postmaster.info.aol.com/asta/proposal_adobe.pdf`⟩

[188] See `http://www.maawg.org/`.

[189] See `http://www.irtf.org/charter?gtype=rg&group=asrg`.

[190] The most popular being Spam Assassin, see `http://spamassassin.apache.org/`.

[191] The most popular being Symantec Brightmail, see `http://www.symantec.com/business/products/overview.jsp?pcid=2242&pvid=835_1`.

[192] For a list, see `http://www.spambouncer.org/reference/blocklists.shtml`.

[193] See `http://www.domain-assurance.org/`.

[194] See `http://www.ietf.org/html.charters/dkim-charter.html`.

Intellectual property rights (IPR)

As noted above, IPR issues on the Internet were excluded from the Tunis Agenda, on the grounds that they fall within the purview of other existing international organisations such as WIPO and the WTO (World Trade Organization). In practice however, it will be seen that this has not altogether excluded them from consideration by the IGF.

WIPO administers the principal intellectual property conventions, which include the *Berne Convention* regarding copyright,[195] the *Paris Convention* regarding patents, trademarks and registered designs,[196] and the *Rome Convention* also regarding copyright.[197] The *WIPO Copyright Treaty* (WCT)[198] and the *WIPO Performances & Phonograms Treaty* (WPPT),[199] both of which came into force in 2002, update these earlier instruments in light of new digital technologies including the Internet. Australia is not a signatory to these WIPO treaties, but its *Copyright Amendment (Digital Agenda) Act 2000* (Cth) amendments to the *Copyright Act 1968* (Cth) are consistent with them.

Amongst the changes introduced by the *Copyright Amendment (Digital Agenda) Act* most relevant to the Internet were to bestow on copyright owners a new exclusive right to communicate works to the public (eg by making electronic copies or uploading them to an online repository), and allowing temporary reproductions of copyright works made automatically in the course of accessing them online (for example, when a user's Web browser caches a copy of a site it accesses to disk).

WIPO was also of course instrumental in drafting the UDRP by which trademark rights could more easily be enforced against domain name registrants (this was backed up in the United States by domestic legislation[200] that enhanced trademark owners' rights against domain name registrants still further). It is less commonly known that in 2001 WIPO proposed new rights to domain names, such as extending protection to the names and acronyms of intergovernmental organisations and to the official long and short names of countries.[201] It is fair to say that these recommendations

[195] *Berne Convention for the Protection of Literary and Artistic Works*, 9 Sep 1886, as revised 13 Nov 1908, completed 20 Mar 1914, revised 2 Jun 1928 and revised 26 Jun 1948, 1969 ATS No 13 (entry into force for Australia 1 Jun 1969)

[196] *Paris Convention for the Protection of Industrial Property*, 20 Mar 1883, as revised 14 Dec 1900, 2 Jun 1911, 6 Nov 1925, 2 Jun 1934, 31 Oct 1958, and 14 Jul 1967, 1972 ATS No 12 (entry into force for Australia of substantive provisions 27 Sep 1975)

[197] *International Convention for the Protection of Performers, Producers of Phonograms and Broadcasting Organisations*, 26 Oct 1961, 1992 ATS No 29 (Rome Convention) (entry into force for Australia 30 Sep 1992)

[198] *WIPO Copyright Treaty*, 20 Dec 1996

[199] *WIPO Performances and Phonograms Treaty*, 20 Dec 1996

[200] *Anticybersquatting Protection Act 1999* (US) 113 Stat 1501, Public Law 106-113

[201] WIPO, Joint Recommendation Concerning the Protection of Marks and Other Industrial Property Rights in Signs on the Internet ⟨URL: `http://www.wipo.int/about-ip/en/`

were in advance of public or political consensus on the issues raised, and no country has adopted them into law.

The other intergovernmental organisation referred to above in respect of its contribution to IPR law is the WTO, whose TRIPS convention[202] covers copyright and industrial property (eg patents, trademarks and registered designs). It largely incorporates the substantive content of the WIPO-administered conventions, but with the important difference that it treats non-compliance as a barrier to trade, and allows the WTO to impose sanctions on member countries in breach. It also provides for the resolution of disputes between nations through the WTO.

Numerous private sector and civil society organisations have played a significant role in public policy governance of IPR on the Internet. Perhaps the most significant has been that of the music industry as often represented by the RIAA (and in Australia by APRA, the Australian Performers Rights Association), and the motion picture industry as often represented by the Motion Picture Association of America (MPAA).

One of the biggest challenges posed to these IPR owners by the Internet has been the prevalence of the exchange of copyright music, software and video, often using P2P technology. The music and motion picture industries have used the force of domestic law against those involved at all levels: the authors of file sharing software,[203] those who publish cracks for DRM (Digital Rights Management) or copy-protection technologies,[204] Internet Service Providers,[205] and end users.[206]

The same industries were also strong campaigners for the passage of the United States *Digital Millennium Copyright Act* (DMCA)[207] which provides a streamlined process for the resolution of disputes between those who are (or claim to be) copyright owners, and ISPs who host allegedly infringing content. They also campaigned for the extension of that regime to Australia through the Australia–United States Fair Trade Agreement (FTA),[208] pursuant to which further reforms to the *Copyright Act 1968* were

---

`development_iplaw/pdf/pub845.pdf`⟩

[202] *Agreement on Trade-Related Aspects of Intellectual Property Rights*, 15 Apr 1994, 1995 ATS No 38 (entry into force for Australia 19 May 1995)

[203] *MGM v Grokster* (2004) 380 F 3d 1154

[204] The most celebrated being the DeCSS crack for the Content Scrambling System (CSS) used on DVD (Digital Versatile Discs): *Universal City Studios Inc v Reimerdes* (2000) 111 F.Supp.2d 294. Taken to an extreme, in 2007 the licensor of the Advanced Access Content System (AACS) began to issue take-down demands to those publishing a hexadecimal number—09 F9 11 02 9D 74 E3 5B D8 41 56 C5 63 56 88 C0—which with the appropriate software could be used to circumvent copy protection on high definition DVDs: see `http://www.chillingeffects.org/notice.cgi?sID=3218`.

[205] *RIAA v Verizon Internet Services* (2003) 351 F 3d 1229, and for an early perspective see Jeremy M Malcolm, Opinion: APRA v Telstra, Intellectual Property Forum 32 1998.

[206] Cassavoy (as in n. 30 on page 11)

[207] *Digital Millennium Copyright Act 1998* (US) 112 Stat 2860, Public Law 105-304

[208] See eg the submission of ARIA (the Australian Recording Industry Association) submission

passed in 2004. In addition to providing a DMCA-like safe harbour scheme for ISPs, these amendments also extended the term of copyright protection from 50 years from the date of the author's death (or from the date of first publication in the case of a corporate author), to at least 70 years.[209]

On the other side of the coin, there are bodies which oppose the extension of IPRs over Internet activities, such as the EFF[210] and its Australian counterpart, the EFA.[211] There are also organisations such as Creative Commons, and the FSF that seek to subvert the dominance of the IPR paradigm, through facilitating the release of copyright works on the Internet under free licences, some of which licences are designed to be "viral" or self-perpetuating in adaptations of the works.[212]

These interests have also sought to build representation within WIPO, through their adoption in September 2007 of a "Development Agenda" for the organisation, which includes amongst its recommendations the preservation of the public domain and the exchange of experiences on open collaborative projects.[213]

Freedom of expression

The United Nations High Commissioner for Human Rights (OHCHR) has addressed the issue of freedom of expression on the Internet by calling on all states to:

> refrain from imposing restrictions which are not consistent with the provisions of article 19, paragraph 3, of the International Covenant on Civil and Political Rights, including on: ... (c) Access to or use of modern telecommunications technologies, including radio, television and the Internet.[214]

This resolution is vague and aspirational, but little more can be expected of an intergovernmental statement in one of the most naturally contentious areas of public policy governance of the Internet.[215]

---

to the Senate enquiry on the FTA at http://www.aph.gov.au/Senate/committee/freetrade_ctte/submissions/sub133.pdf.

[209] See Jeremy M Malcolm, Dark Shadows of the Australia-United States Free Trade Agreement ⟨URL: http://www.ilaw.com.au/public/ftaarticle.html⟩.

[210] See http://www.eff.org/.

[211] See http://www.efa.org.au/.

[212] See section 4.2 on page 211.

[213] WIPO, Member States Adopt a Development Agenda for WIPO ⟨URL: http://www.wipo.int/pressroom/en/articles/2007/article_0071.html⟩

[214] OHCHR, The Right to Freedom of Opinion and Expression ⟨URL: http://www.unhchr.ch/huridocda/huridoca.nsf/(Symbol)/E.CN.4.RES.2002.48.En⟩

[215] See section 3.4 on page 167.

The converse of freedom of expression on the Internet is content regulation, and the approaches taken domestically on this issue range from the almost *laissez faire* approach of countries such as the United States which has established a Global Internet Freedom Task Force (GIFT) to promote online freedom of expression internationally,[216] to the very strict censorship exercised by countries such as Burma, China, Cuba, Laos, Saudi Arabia, Syria, Tunisia, Vietnam and Yemen which route all Internet connections through government-controlled filters.[217]

In between are the approaches of countries such as France, the United Kingdom, Canada and Australia, which prohibit certain types of content online. For example in November 2000 French courts gave US-based Yahoo! Inc three months to prevent French citizens from accessing Nazi memorabilia available using Yahoo!'s auction service, although the sale of such material is legal in the United States. Yahoo! in response sought a declaration that the French court order could not be enforced in the United States.

This eventually failed on appeal in 2006, partly on the basis that Yahoo! had already in large measure complied with the French court order by localising the content presented to French visitors.[218] Even those visitors who did not specifically access Yahoo!'s French portal could be identified as French by tracking the IP addresses from which they accessed the site back to the networks of French ISPs (a technique known as geolocation which is discussed at section 3.4 on page 157).

It should be noted that legal guarantees of the freedom of expression, even in the United States which strongly protects this freedom through the First Amendment to its Constitution, do not extend to the private sector. Thus Google, one of whose corporate principles is "Don't be evil," also used geolocation technology when it bowed to demands of the Chinese government in applying content restrictions to the Chinese version of its search engine,[219] as had Yahoo!, Cisco and Microsoft before it.[220]

Similarly, the UK's largest telecommunications provider and ISP, British Telecom (a former government monopoly), applies a filter called Cleanfeed to its wholesale and retail Internet service. The selection of content to be blocked, currently limited to child pornography, is undertaken by the Internet Watch Foundation (IWF), a non-profit self-regulatory Internet industry body.[221] In 2006 the government put other UK ISPs on notice to

---

[216] See http://www.state.gov/g/drl/rls/78340.htm.

[217] Christopher Cox, *Who Rules the Net? Internet Governance and Jurisdiction* Washington, DC: Cato Institute, 2003, chap. Establishing Global Internet Freedom: Tear Down This Firewall

[218] *Yahoo! Inc v La Ligue Contre le Racisme* (2006) 433 F3d 1199

[219] Eric Auchard, Google Agrees to Censor Service to Enter China ⟨URL: http://www.news.com/8301-10784_3-6030773-7.html⟩

[220] Jack L Goldsmith and Tim Wu, *Who Controls the Internet?: Illusions of a Borderless World* Oxford: Oxford University Press, 2006, 1–10, 93–96

[221] See http://www.iwf.org.uk/.

expect a regulatory response if they did not also filter their Internet services by the following year.[222] Canada's ISPs have recently adopted a similar voluntary filtering scheme, with a network called C-CAICE,[223] that also includes governmental representatives, acting in the place of the IWF.

Australia's content regulation regime is found in the *Broadcasting Services Act 1992* (Cth). Since the passage of amendments to that Act in 1999 which commenced the following year, Australian Internet content is subject to the same rating criteria as motion pictures, save that content is only rated *ex post facto* once a complaint is made. If Internet content were to be rated R if it were a film, it may only be hosted on the Web in Australia subject to an age verification system. If it would be rated X or refused classification, it may not be hosted in Australia at all.

The Federal government has also claimed an election mandate to introduce a compulsory programme of ISP-side filtering of Internet content in 2008, akin to the voluntary programmes of the UK and Canada, and building upon the previous government's programme introduced in 2007 to offer free client-side Internet filtering software to all Australian Internet users.[224]

The PICS content labelling standard developed by the W3C, criticism notwithstanding, is still in use, though it has to a large degree been supplanted by a newer XML-based W3C standard called RDF (Resource Description Framework). The most popular RDF-based schema for rating Internet content, based on its suitability for children, is that of the UK-based Internet Content Rating Association (ICRA).[225] The ICRA is comprised of nine large corporate members, mostly ISPs and software companies such as America Online (AOL) and Microsoft, and a much larger number of associate members ranging from the proprietors of adult Web sites, to regional self-regulatory associations.

Before moving on from the topic of content regulation, brief mention should be made of defamation law, which also falls within that field. Australian defamation law made an international mark on the Internet with the decision in *Dow Jones v Gutnick*.[226] This was a case in which noted Australian businessman Joseph Gutnick sued Dow Jones for publishing an article, which he alleged to be defamatory of him, in the online version of Barron's magazine.

Although Dow Jones and its Web site were based in the United States, the High Court ruled that the case could be heard in Australia, on the

---

[222] Lilian Edwards, From Child Porn to China, in one Cleanfeed ⟨URL: `http://www.law.ed.ac.uk/ahrc/script-ed/vol3-3/editorial.pdf`⟩

[223] Canadian Coalition Against Internet Child Exploitation; see `http://www.cybertip.ca/app/en/projects_overview`.

[224] See Lachlan Heywood, Onus on Providers to Clean Up Web Content ⟨URL: `http://www.news.com.au/story/0,23599,22989028-421,00.html`⟩.

[225] See `http://www.icra.org/vocabulary/`.

[226] *Dow Jones & Company, Inc v Gutnick* (2002) 194 ALR 433

ground that a sufficient link to the jurisdiction was established by Gutnick's residence and established reputation here, and the availability of the magazine in Australia via the Internet, and in a few printed copies. The result was that Dow Jones was required to defend itself in a jurisdiction much friendlier to defamation plaintiffs than the United States.

Data protection and privacy rights

There is no international standard of privacy in the form of an international legal instrument, although the right to privacy is recognised in general terms in Article 12 of the Universal Declaration of Human Rights, and Article 17 of the International Covenant on Civil and Political Rights. The United Nations has also recognised the particular importance of maintaining the privacy of those whose personal information is contained in electronic records, through guidelines on this topic that were the subject of a General Assembly resolution in 1990.[227]

Absent a more formal agreement on privacy, the leading intergovernmental document is a set of guidelines of the OECD adopted in 1980.[228] These informed the drafting of the APEC Privacy Framework released by its Electronic Commerce Steering Group (ECSG) in 2004, that is designed to promote consistency in information privacy protection across APEC member economies. In 2007, Google called for the multi-stakeholder development of a new transnational privacy standard based upon the APEC Framework.[229] The OECD guidelines also provided the basis for the eleven Information Privacy Principles set out in Australia's *Privacy Act 1988* (Cth), which was extended to apply to the private sector in 2001.

The other regional privacy regime that is of significant international importance is the EU *Data Protection Directive*.[230] The most controversial provision of the directive provides that personal data of EU citizens may not be transferred to "third countries" (ie countries outside the EU) unless those countries have adequate levels of privacy protection of their own. The United States, which offers no broad protection for the privacy of personal data, did not meet this criterion, with the result that trade between the US and the EU was in danger of being significantly disrupted when the directive took effect.

---

[227] General Assembly of the United Nations, Guidelines for the Regulation of Computerized Personal Data Files ⟨URL: http://www.un.org/documents/ga/res/45/a45r095.htm⟩

[228] OECD, Guidelines for the Protection of Privacy and Transborder Flows of Personal Data ⟨URL: http://www.oecd.org/document/18/0,2340,en_2649_34255_1815186_1_1_1_1,00.html⟩

[229] Peter Fleischer, Call for Global Privacy Standards ⟨URL: http://googlepublicpolicy.blogspot.com/2007/09/call-for-global-privacy-standards.html⟩

[230] European Commission, Directive on the Protection of Individuals With Regard to the Processing of Personal Data and on the Free Movement of Such Data ⟨URL: http://eur-lex.europa.eu/LexUriServ/LexUriServ.do?uri=CELEX:32002L0058:EN:HTML⟩

The compromise that the two parties reached was to negotiate a special "Safe Harbor" for US businesses whereby they could individually certify their own compliance with EU data protection standards as codified in the Safe Harbor principles, rather than simply adhering to the lesser privacy standards of US law.[231]

Another area of controversy occasioned by the disparity in privacy standards between Europe and the United States is seen in the case of the ICANN WHOIS database. WHOIS is a database containing contact information of domain name registrants maintained by TLD registries. The content of ccTLD WHOIS registries is subject to the policy of the ccTLD in question, and in auDA's case, since 2002 it has omitted the registrant's address, telephone and fax number, providing only an email address.[232]

However the WHOIS policies for certain of the gTLDs are less stringent. They not only include personal address, telephone and fax details of the registrant, but also allow bulk access to WHOIS data to be purchased. Registrants have found themselves in receipt of direct marketing material directed to their WHOIS contact details, and some have fallen victim to cyber-stalking and identity theft. In response, many registrants have taken to supplying false WHOIS data, in breach of their registration agreements. Following much criticism of this situation, ICANN's GNSO Council formed a WHOIS Task Force in 2005 to review the WHOIS policy that should apply to gTLDs in future. Its final report of 2007 recommended an overall restriction of publically available WHOIS data, but the GNSO Council rejected these recommendations in November that year.[233]

Two privacy protection initiatives from the private sector and civil society are worthy of note. The first are private sector privacy certification schemes, the best known of which is that of TRUSTe,[234] a private non-profit organisation founded by the EFF and Commerce.Net, that certifies online business for their adherence to privacy standards. TRUSTe also certifies online businesses for compliance with the EU Safe Harbor scheme. There are over 1500 TRUSTe member Web sites, most of which display a seal as a sign of their compliance with TRUSTe's standards. BBBOnline is a similar programme restricted to North American members, with almost 700 Web sites bearing its Privacy Seal,[235] and WebTrust is a much smaller programme with fewer than 30 members whose adherence to privacy standards has been audited by a Certified Public Accountant (CPA).[236]

The second non-governmental privacy initiative is the P3P (Platform

---

231 See http://www.export.gov/safeharbor/.

232 auDA, WHOIS Policy ⟨URL: http://www.auda.org.au/policies/auda-2003-08/⟩

233 GNSO Council, Recent GNSO Policy Development Activities on WHOIS ⟨URL: http://gnso.icann.org/issues/whois-privacy/gnso-council-report-board-whois-15nov07.pdf⟩

234 See http://www.truste.org/.

235 See http://www.bbbonline.com/.

236 See http://www.cpawebtrust.org/.

for Privacy Preferences) recommendation of the W3C. P3P is an XML-based language in which a Web site's privacy policy can be expressed in computer-readable form. This can be automatically read by an access device that supports P3P (such as a compliant Web browser or mobile phone) in order to regulate a user's Internet usage in accordance with their expressed privacy preferences in an automated way.

P3P was initiated by the Internet Privacy Working Group, established by the CDT in 1996 and counting amongst its members ISPs such as AOL, hardware and software manufacturers such as IBM and Microsoft, and civil society representatives such as the EFF. P3P was subsequently taken up by the W3C the following year and became a Recommendation in 2002.[237]

P3P has not yet come into wide use and seems unlikely to in the future. One factor in this may be that P3P software is not simple and transparent enough that users are attracted to use it, particularly in that only a comparatively small number of Web sites have published P3P-compatible privacy policies. The limitations of the protocol itself should also not be overlooked. In particular, there is nothing in the protocol to verify that a Web site actually complies with the policy it advertises.

Both P3P[238] and the various privacy certification schemes described above[239] have been criticised by privacy advocates for being too solicitous to the interests of business, by allowing businesses to easily derogate from consumers' privacy rights so long as the consumers' consent can be obtained.

Consumer rights

There is no international instrument protecting consumer rights. The European Union passed a *Distance Sales Directive* in 1997[240] to protect EU consumers in transactions made online, for example by providing consumers with a cooling off period and requiring them to be provided with detailed information about the transaction. This was followed by a similar Directive on distance marketing of financial services in 2002.[241]

---

[237] Lorrie Faith Cranor, The Role of Data Protection Authorities in the Design and Deployment of the Platform for Privacy Preferences ⟨URL: `http://lorrie.cranor.org/pubs/paris-talk0901.html`⟩

[238] Agrawal (as in n. 92 on page 24)

[239] Roger Clarke, Meta-Brands ⟨URL: `http://www.anu.edu.au/people/Roger.Clarke/DV/MetaBrands.html`⟩; Erlanger

[240] European Commission, Directive on the Protection of Consumers in Respect of Distance Contracts ⟨URL: `http://eur-lex.europa.eu/LexUriServ/LexUriServ.do?uri=CELEX:31997L0007:EN:HTML`⟩

[241] Idem, Directive Concerning the Distance Marketing of Consumer Financial Services ⟨URL: `http://eur-lex.europa.eu/LexUriServ/LexUriServ.do?uri=CELEX:32002L0065:EN:HTML`⟩

In the absence of an international agreement on consumer rights, the OECD is again at the forefront of international governance on this issue through the *OECD Guidelines for Consumer Protection in the Context of Electronic Commerce*[242] developed by its Consumer Policy Committee and formally adopted by the OECD Council in December 1999.

These formed the basis for the Australian Federal Government's *Building Consumer Sovereignty in Electronic Commerce: A best practice model for business*,[243] a voluntary resource designed to foster a self-regulatory approach to consumer protection in e-commerce by Australian business. The process by which this was drafted incorporated public comment from the private sector, civil society and academia, as well as member government representatives. Whilst the best practice model has no force of law, businesses adhering to it are entitled to display a logo to indicate their compliance.

More recently in 2003 the OECD also released its *OECD Guidelines for Protecting Consumers from Fraudulent and Deceptive Commercial Practices Across Borders*,[244] which focuses on the issue of cross-border fraud, particularly on the Internet, and is intended to provide a framework for international cooperation in tackling this problem through coordination of the activities of national agencies and private sector bodies such as financial institutions and domain name registrars.

This dovetails with the work of the International Consumer Protection and Enforcement Network (ICPEN),[245] an organisation that brings together the consumer protection bodies of 33 countries, including the United States Federal Trade Commission (FTC) and Australia's ACCC.

One example of cooperation between such regional executive agencies is seen in the prosecution of a stock tout operating through the use of unsolicited email, both in Australia at the instigation of the Australian Securities and Investments Commission (ASIC)[246] and in the United States through its Securities Exchange Commission (SEC).[247]

Finally in Australia's region, APEC drafted *Voluntary Consumer Protection Guidelines for the Online Environment* in 2003, though these saw no domestic adoption and now regrettably appear to have disappeared from the Web.[248] There is however an Australasian Consumer Fraud Taskforce

---

[242]OECD, OECD Guidelines for Consumer Protection in the Context of Electronic Commerce ⟨URL: `http://www.oecd.org/dataoecd/18/13/34023235.pdf`⟩

[243]See `http://www.treasury.gov.au/contentitem.asp?NavId=014&ContentID=1083`.

[244]Idem, OECD Guidelines for Protecting Consumers from Fraudulent and Deceptive Commercial Practices Across Borders ⟨URL: `http://www.oecd.org/dataoecd/24/33/2956464.pdf`⟩

[245]See `http://www.icpen.org/`.

[246]*R v Hourmouzis* (unreported Victorian County Court, decided 30 October 2000)

[247]*SEC v Hourmouzis* (unreported, District Court of Colorado, no 00-N-905, decided 1 May 2000)

[248]See `http://web.archive.org/web/20050204094737/http://www.export.gov/apecommerce/consumer_protection.html` for the former content.

formed in 2005, which brings together Australian State, Commonwealth and New Zealand authorities to address consumer fraud both on and offline.[249]

Development

The "digital divide" between the developed and the developing world (or between "North" and "South") is an aspect of a much broader social problem than falls within the scope of Internet governance. The United Nations' Millennium Development Goals (MDG) are an umbrella programme for addressing such issues at the broadest level,[250] including the need for investment in Internet infrastructure and services in regions suffering from the digital divide. Within the broader field of ICTs for development, there are a few discrete issues that more directly raise questions of Internet-related public policy, and hence fall within the ambit of Internet governance.

The first of these isolated by the WGIG Report and Tunis Agenda is that of interconnection costs. By way of background to this issue, in traditional telephony each country's telecommunications provider raises its own connection charges for initiating or receiving a call, and the charges are divided between them when financial settlements between providers are calculated. This does not occur on Internet networks, where typically a smaller network—such as that of a developing nation—will pay the whole cost of its connection to a larger backbone network. The larger network thereby receives access to any Internet content available on the smaller network effectively for free.

This issue formed the subject of Recommendation D.50 from ITU's Study Group 3, which sought to establish a more equitable settlements regime between Internet network operators, but for commercial reasons this has proved highly controversial and is unlikely to be implemented in its current form.[251]

A second development issue is that of capacity building. This is an ill-defined term which in the present context refers to the development of institutional and individual capacity for the governance and application of Internet infrastructure.[252] This is more of an operational than a governance issue, which fits more comfortably within the existing intergovernmental structures for international aid and development work.[253]

---

[249] See `http://www.scamwatch.gov.au/`.

[250] See `http://www.un.org/millenniumgoals/`.

[251] European Commission, Internet Network Issues ⟨URL: `http://ec.europa.eu/information_society/topics/telecoms/international/itu/internet_traffic.pdf`⟩

[252] See section 4.3 on page 285.

[253] See section 6.2 on page 441.

The development agency with particular responsibility for telecommunications networks is the ITU-D, the development arm of the ITU. However infrastructure development for ICT is also supported by such bodies as the World Bank,[254] UNESCO (the United Nations Educational, Scientific and Cultural Organization),[255] the United Nations Conference on Trade and Development (UNCTAD),[256] and UNDP (the United Nations Development Programme).[257] On a regional level, the G8's Digital Opportunities Task Force (DOT Force)[258] and the EU's eEurope programmes[259] are both notable for having taken a multi-stakeholder approach to capacity building, foreshadowing the similar approach of WSIS.[260] In the private sector, the Global Information Infrastructure Comission (GIIC) formed in 1995 is a confederation of executives notable for its work in this area,[261] as in civil society is the Association for Progressive Communications (APC).[262]

A third issue of equity is that of meaningful participation in global policy development. The prominence of this issue was raised in 2002 by a report of the Panos Institute which demonstrated how poorly developing countries are represented in global ICT governance.[263] The conclusions of this *Louder Voices* report were presented to the third meeting of the United Nations ICT Task Force (UNICTTF),[264] a multi-stakeholder body formed in 2001 at the request of UNESCO to play a coordinating role amongst stakeholders working in the area of ICT for development.[265]

The final equity issue raised by the WGIG Report and the Tunis Agenda is multinationalisation (more commonly known as internationalisation, or I18N[266]) of the Internet. The two principal sub-issues involved here are the support of multilingual content by Internet services, and the ability to both access and represent that content using multilingual character sets. This issue was pressed by UNESCO in 2003 when its member States adopted a *Recommendation concerning the Promotion and Use of Multilingualism and Universal Access to Cyberspace*.[267]

---

[254]See http://www.worldbank.org/.

[255]See http://www.unesco.org/.

[256]See http://www.unctad.org/.

[257]See http://www.undp.org/.

[258]DOT Force, Digital Opportunities for All: Meeting the Challenge ⟨URL: http://www.g7.utoronto.ca/summit/2001genoa/dotforce1.html⟩

[259]See http://europa.eu/scadplus/leg/en/lvb/l24221.htm.

[260]See section 5.1 on page 322.

[261]See http://www.giic.org/.

[262]See http://www.apc.org/.

[263]Don MacLean et al., Louder Voices: Strengthening Developing Country Participation in International ICT Decision-Making ⟨URL: http://www.panos.org.uk/download.php?id=59⟩

[264]See http://www.unicttaskforce.org/.

[265]See http://www.unicttaskforce.org/thirdmeeting/openpage.html.

[266]So called because there are 18 letters between the "i" and the "n" in "internationalisation."

[267]UNESCO, Recommendation Concerning the Promotion and Use of Multilingualism and Universal Access to Cyberspace ⟨URL: http://portal.unesco.org/ci/en/ev.php-URL_ID=

Although internationalisation is just as much a development issue as interconnection and capacity building, it can unlike those latter issues be addressed within the technical rather than the economic arena. Most work in this area has been the province of standards organisations such as the IETF and the Unicode consortium[268] (which defines a universal character set capable of displaying typographical symbols from all human languages). Internationalisation is also an Activity of the W3C.[269] Additionally, the W3C has produced a related recommendation on making Web content accessible to those with disabilities.[270]

The current focus of multinationalisation efforts is on the support of multilingual domain names, which allows other character sets such as Arabic and Chinese to be used to access Internet addresses using the DNS. The IETF and ICANN have been principally responsible respectively for the development and implementation of this technology, with support from another civil society organisation, the Multilingual Internet Names Consortium (MINC),[271] in delivering advocacy and education. In recent years slow but steady progress has been made towards resolving some final implementation issues for multilingual domain names, with one of the most recent developments being the testing of eleven multilingual TLDs in October 2007.[272]

For some countries, progress has been too slow; leading China for example to establish its own DNS root in 2005 to serve the Chinese-character equivalents of the com and net gTLDs.[273]

e-commerce and e-government

The final public policy issue under consideration is that of e-commerce, which is simply the conduct of business over electronic networks, relevantly the Internet, and is closely related to e-government, which is the relation of government and its citizens over such networks using the same sorts of technologies. Here the focus is to be on e-commerce, but e-government will be discussed again at section 4.3 on page 268.

13475&URL_DO=DO_TOPIC&URL_SECTION=201.html⟩

[268] See http://www.unicode.org/.

[269] See http://www.w3.org/International/.

[270] W3C, Web Content Accessibility Guidelines 1.0 ⟨URL: http://www.w3.org/TR/WAI-WEBCONTENT/⟩

[271] See http://www.minc.org/.

[272] ICANN, IDN Status Report ⟨URL: http://www.icann.org/announcements/announcement-28oct07.htm⟩

[273] DNS.net, PRC Government Approves Chinese Character Internet Domain Names ⟨URL: http://www.i-dns.net/newsroom/news/OL050427-01.html.en⟩. An Arabic root has also been established by Saudi Arabia, and there have been reports of Russia having similar plans for a Cyrillic root: Catherine Rampell, A Script for Every Surfer ⟨URL: http://www.washingtonpost.com/wp-dyn/content/article/2007/10/10/AR2007101002642.html⟩.

UNCITRAL, the United Nations Commission on International Trade Law,[274] is the intergovernmental body which regulates international trade in conjunction with the WTO. UNCITRAL's particular focus is on the modernisation and harmonisation of laws bearing on international business. To this end, it released in 1996 a *Model Law on Electronic Commerce*,[275] followed in 2001 by a *Model Law on Electronic Signatures*.[276] Both model laws prescribe a technology-neutral model for the treatment of electronic contracts and signatures as legally equivalent to their paper-based equivalents. Australia's *Electronic Transactions Act 2001* (Cth) and its State counterparts were based on the *Model Law on Electronic Commerce*.

UNCITRAL has also developed a convention, not yet adopted by Australia,[277] which aims to clarify for legal purposes such matters as the location of a party to a contract formed electronically, the time and place that that contract will be taken to have been formed, the use of automated message systems in forming contracts, and the criteria to be used in establishing functional equivalence between electronic and paper communications.

This convention, once adopted, will help to resolve the long-obscure question of whether the "postal acceptance rule" applies to electronic contracts; that is to say, whether a contract concluded by email, where the offer is emailed say from Australia to a recipient overseas, is governed by Australian or overseas law, and at what time the contract is formed.

Along similar lines, the Hague Conference on Private International Law, an intergovernmental organisation of sixty member states, finalised in 2005 an international convention on choice of law agreements,[278] to establish rules for the enforcement of contracts that specify that the law of a particular jurisdiction is to apply, and the circumstances in which other countries must recognize the judgments of courts of that jurisdiction. The convention is not yet in force.

Criticisms

It lies outside the scope of this book to investigate the many different substantive criticisms of particular Internet-related public policy initiatives that have been developed by bodies engaged in public policy governance. Even so, it should already be evident that the main problem confronting those

[274] See `http://www.uncitral.org/`.

[275] UNCITRAL, UNCITRAL Model Law on Electronic Commerce ⟨URL: `http://www.uncitral.org/uncitral/en/uncitral_texts/electronic_commerce/1996Model.html`⟩

[276] Idem, UNCITRAL Model Law on Electronic Signatures ⟨URL: `http://www.uncitral.org/uncitral/en/uncitral_texts/electronic_commerce/2001Model_signatures.html`⟩

[277] *UN Convention on the Use of Electronic Communications in International Contracts*, 23 Nov 2005; see `http://www.uncitral.org/uncitral/en/uncitral_texts/electronic_commerce/2005Convention.html`.

[278] *Hague Convention on Choice of Law Agreements*, 30 Jun 2005; see `http://www.hcch.net/index_en.php?act=conventions.pdf&cid=98`.

bodies is the difficulty of making rules that are both globally consistent yet substantive in content.

This difficulty arises from the fact that on the Internet, national regimes can be transcended with a keystroke, potentially both rendering domestic laws ineffective against those physically outside the jurisdiction (as in the case of the hosting of prohibited content, the sending of spam or the commission of cybercrime by a foreign national), whilst conversely subjecting Internet users to laws of foreign jurisdictions to which they owe no allegiance as citizens (as illustrated by the Yahoo! Nazi memorabilia case and the Gutnick defamation case). Such jurisdictional problems, and related problems with enforcing international law in the absence of an effective international court system or police force, are discussed at section 3.4 on page 157.

Regulators recognise these problems. For example, in considering the application of Australia's telecommunications regulation regime to VoIP (Voice over IP) telephony, the Privacy Commissioner stated, "The consequences of not having a globally consistent approach is that information may end up in the country with the lowest privacy protection standards."[279] It recommended the Australian Government initiate discussions through appropriate international fora about how to deal with major international jurisdictional issues arising from global reach of new technologies such as VoIP.[280]

Whilst these inherent difficulties may not themselves provide grounds for criticism of bodies engaged in public policy governance by rules, those bodies can be criticised for a lack of coordination between the rules they develop, and conflicting international or domestic rules. For example, prior to the passage of the *CAN-SPAM Act*, many American States had their own spam laws, which more often than not were inconsistent with each other. For example, when sending unsolicited commercial email with adult content, senders might have been required to prepend "ADV:ADLT" to the subject line in one state and "ADV-ADULT" in another. Bizarrely, in Louisiana, there are two separate provisions, one of which requires the first-mentioned subject prefix[281] and the other the latter.[282]

One of the purposes of the IGF, at least as put forward in this book, is to avoid the sorts of discrepancies that result from an uncoordinated patchwork of regulation and other governance mechanisms as described in this section, by addressing Internet-related public policy at a global

---

[279]Office of the Privacy Commissioner, Getting in on the Act: The Review of the Private Sector Provisions of the Privacy Act 1988 ⟨URL: `http://www.privacy.gov.au/act/review/review2005.htm`⟩, 266. For a more in-depth analysis see Jeremy M Malcolm, Privacy Issues with VoIP Telephony, Privacy Law Bulletin 2:2 2005.

[280]See also ACA, *Regulatory Issues Associated with Provision of Voice Services Using Internet Protocol in Australia* Canberra: Australian Government Information Management Office, 2004.

[281]*Louisiana Revised Statutes*, Title 51, Trade and Commerce, Chapter 19-C

[282]*Louisiana Revised Statutes*, Title 14, Criminal Law, s106

level through a network of all affected stakeholder groups, using an open, consensual process analogous to some of those employed in the standards development sphere of Internet governance.

The closest to such a process that has been encountered in this section is in the cooperative arrangements of domestic executive agencies within government networks such as the London Action Plan and the Virtual Global Taskforce. They are not so well illustrated by the harmonisation activities of domestic lawmakers, which are likely to be more restricted in scope and less inclusive of all stakeholders; for example as in the bilateral (or unilateral) process by which Australia was induced to "harmonise" its IPR laws with those of the United States in the Australia–United States FTA.

As for public policy development within intergovernmental organisations, the position is more complex. Traditionally, these have not been venues very inclusive of external stakeholders, nor have they operated at a speed adequate to respond to the development of public policy issues on the fast-paced Internet. However as Chapter 3 will discuss in detail, certain intergovernmental organisations are beginning to reform their processes to become more responsive and inclusive of non-governmental stakeholders.[283]

To remedy the remaining deficits of participation in intergovernmental policy development fora is another of the purposes put forward in this book for the IGF (and, parenthetically, a good reason why IPR and e-commerce should not be excluded from its mandate).[284]

But more broadly, the establishment of the IGF opens the door to a more coordinated approach to the development of public policy for the Internet than has characterised the *ad hoc* application of various mechanisms of governance to produce the measures described in this section.

2.4 Governance mechanisms revisited

The purpose of this chapter has been to describe three spheres of Internet governance—technical coordination, standards development and public policy governance—and to give examples of how the five mechanisms of governance outlined in the Introduction have been brought to play in each sphere.

It was noted in the Introduction that governance can be exercised through any, or a combination, of these mechanisms of rules, norms, markets, architecture and networks. Biegel, Weber and Vedel, whose models of Internet governance (along with those of Rhodes, Lessig and others)

[283]See section 3.4 on page 147.
[284]See section 6.2 on page 436.

Table 2.2: Governance types and mechanisms

	Technical coordination	Standards development	Public policy
Rules	ICANN/NTIA JPA	ITRs	*Cybercrime Act*
Norms	IAB oversight	RFCs	Spam blocklists
Markets	gTLD registries[a]	S/MIME[b]	Content regulation[c]
Architecture	IPv4 allocation[d]	DNSSEC[e]	CA/Browser forum
Networks	ICANN SOs and ACs	P3P	LAP

[a] gTLD registries are given as an example of technical coordination through markets because their operations are governed by contracts negotiated with ICANN on commercial terms.

[b] S/MIME is an example of standards development through markets because of the influence that RSA, Microsoft and Netscape had on the development and adoption of the S/MIME specification.

[c] This is an example of public policy governance through markets because of the Australian government's reliance on a co-regulatory code of practice drafted by industry as a component of its content regulation regime (and also its spam regime; see section 4.2 on page 207).

[d] Because the architecture of IPv4 constituted IP addresses as a limited resource, RIRs were required to tightly control the allocation of addresses from the pools they administered. Otherwise, IP addresses might have been allocated in a similar manner to domain names, without any limit on the number that an applicant could request.

[e] The design of the DNSSEC protocol was constrained by the requirement that it be interoperable with the architecture of the existing DNS.

contributed to this typology, all agree that since each form has its own advantages and disadvantages, reliance upon any single mechanism of governance is likely to be insufficient, and that their application in concert may often be the most successful approach.[285]

This has been confirmed by this chapter's survey of some of the most notable Internet governance institutions and initiatives in each sphere, and can be concisely illustrated by arraying the five mechanisms and three spheres in a matrix, as in Table 2.2.

Accepting the need for balance between each of the mechanisms of governance, it would still be useful if there were some theoretical or empirical basis upon which to determine which mechanism or mechanisms, either alone or in combination, are most likely to be effective in a given issue area. For this purpose, Biegel proposes a five-step framework in which

> we first identify the category of allegedly problematic conduct … and determine through this identification, certain representative characteristics of the problem. Next, we explore the potential for consensus among the various stakeholders regarding both the nature and extent of the problem and the

[285] Biegel (as in n. 60 on page 19), 358; Weber (as in n. 70 on page 20), 100; Vedel (as in n. 74 on page 21), 67

> prospects for *any* sort of regulatory solution. Then we examine just how uniquely cyber this problem might be, and analyze the extent to which such a determination might help answer the question of *how* we might regulate the problem area. Informed by the analysis in the first three steps, we continue by exploring in detail the potential applicability of each of the three basic regulatory models identified in part 2. After going through all these steps, we seek to identify a synthesis, pointing whenever possible towards a combination of realistic approaches while trying in general to avoid major changes in the current regulatory structure.[286]

Although the three basic regulatory models of which Biegel speaks have been expanded into five mechanisms here, his approach remains capable of application by analogy. However the approach can be refined in two respects.

First, the sphere of governance in which the mechanism is to be applied should also be considered, to determine whether the mechanism in question is likely to be adequately legitimate and effective for application in that sphere.[287] Taking legitimacy first, this is the normative basis upon which the exercise of a mechanism of governance is seen as justified by those it addresses.[288] What is legitimate in one sphere of governance may not be in another. For example, to be perceived as legitimate, the authority that underlies the exercise of public policy governance must normally be accepted by the governed through some form of political process, such as democratic accountability to a broad range of stakeholders.[289] The same is not normally required in the sphere of standards development, where provided that public policy issues are not engaged, technical merit alone is seen as sufficient to justify compliance.

It is therefore no coincidence that the predominant mechanism of governance in the public policy sphere has been rules, since the authority of the rule-maker is normally negotiated through a political process seen as legitimate within the international and/or domestic legal systems of its subjects. In contrast, the legitimacy of the other, more decentralised mechanisms of governance—norms, markets and architecture—is much weaker in the public policy sphere, as they are too often invisible and unamenable to stakeholder input. Such policy-making may for example be driven, in the case of markets, by the "invisible hand of commerce,"[290] or in the case of architecture by unexamined accidents of network design that conflict

[286] Biegel (as in n. 60 on page 19), 224

[287] As to the selection of legitimacy and effectiveness as criteria for evaluating governance, compare Kooiman (as in n. 72 on page 20), 182.

[288] See section 3.4 on page 145.

[289] But not limited to this: Chapter 4 will discuss the options in detail.

[290] Lessig, *Code and Other Laws of Cyberspace* (as in n. 25 on page 9), 30

with more fundamental social values, or in the case of norms by prejudice or vigilantism.

Moving on from legitimacy, the likely effectiveness of a given mechanism within a particular sphere of governance should also be considered. Whilst it makes sense to favour, by default, the continued use of the mechanisms of norms and markets for technical coordination, and norms and architecture for standards development, as these have generally been very successful in those spheres, they have been less effective as mechanisms of public policy governance. One reason is that since the type of regulatory issue involved in public policy governance "usually produces winners and losers and may be heavily contested," its governance is more likely to require some sort of hierarchical force in order to be sufficiently effective.[291]

The mechanism of rules does not suffer from the same limitation. However it does suffer from other limitations that have already been observed, such as its incompatibility with the Internet's cosmopolitanism and culture of decentralisation. Thankfully, the means of addressing these limitations has already been presented: by the use of rules not in an uncoordinated fashion as has largely occurred to date, but instead through the hybrid governance mechanism of networks. By exactly the same token, the limitations on the legitimacy of norms, markets and architecture in public policy governance can also be addressed.

This leads to the second refinement to Biegel's approach that is needed, which lies in his failure to identify the "we" whom he refers to in recommending that "we identify a synthesis ... of realistic approaches." It is contended here that "we" should be a multi-stakeholder governance network, which can combine the merits (and overcome the limitations) of both hierarchical and decentralised modes of governance, by coordinating the application of the most appropriate mechanisms of governance for a given issue area, and rendering their application accountable to the stakeholders of which the network is formed.

The purpose of the next chapter will be to bring this ideal down to earth, by considering how the currently rather abstract concept of a multi-stakeholder governance network might fit within the existing international system consisting largely of discrete geographically-bounded states and intergovernmental bodies formed by agreement between them.

A foretaste of the answer can be found in this chapter's mention of government networks such as the London Action Plan, and the reforms that have begun to permeate more traditional intergovernmental bodies. Although such bodies have historically claimed authority to make rules through the democratic legitimacy they draw from their composition by national governments, this does not preclude them from adopting the alternative governance mechanism of networks, involving other stakeholders

[291] Holitscher (as in n. 4 on page 30), 1. Naturally, this will vary from one issue area to another: see section 4.2 on page 196.

outside the governments' constituencies.[292]

In fact increasingly, even in contexts other than the Internet, international law is being made through networks rather than through rules as in years past. It can even be said that the international order itself, in the post-Westphalian age that is to be defined in the next chapter, has become an archetype of network governance writ large, characterised by multicentric authority and the use of soft power.

And the reverse may also be true: that public policy governance exercised through networks can, regardless of whether the organisation leading the process is traditionally intergovernmental in character, become a form of international (or, more subtly, transnational) law. This is another question that the following chapter will address.

[292]Conversely, the fact that a body was established to act using networks as its dominant mechanism of governance does not prevent it from attempting to act using rules instead. For example, although ICANN was formed (for the sake of argument) through the consensus of a network of stakeholders, and claims to operate in the same manner, it can be seen in many cases to have actually exercised its authority through rules—that is, through unilateral action backed up by hierarchical authority: see Weinberg, ICANN and the Problem of Legitimacy (as in n. 71 on page 49).

Chapter 3

The international system

> Globalization operates on Internet time.
>
> Kofi Annan

In the course of the preceding chapter, an overview was given of a number of international legal instruments bearing on public policy governance of the Internet, and of some of the institutions responsible for their development. This chapter takes a step back from those details to look at the underlying issues of what international law is, where it comes from, and the extent to which civil society in particular—that is, people organised into non-commercial social groups *other* than states—has a role to play in developing it, particularly through governance networks such as the IGF.

The importance of this is that if Internet governance is to be exercised by networks as the previous chapter has suggested, the status of those networks in the international legal system will determine whether their actions are likely on the one hand to be accepted, or on the other to be undermined (or simply ignored) by states. Although the geographical nexus that characterises governance through rules by states may on some accounts be anachronistic and largely irrelevant to life in cyberspace,[1] even citizens of cyberspace still hold dual citizenship with the state in which they are physically located. Those states will be more likely to honour the actions of networks of Internet governance if those actions can somehow claim legitimacy in the international legal system.

[1] See section 4.3 on page 272.

3.1 International law and international relations

In examining this possibility, the theoretical background to this chapter shifts into the fields of international law and international relations. The two are not synonymous. International law is the largely normative study of the legal relations that exist (or should exist) between international legal actors—generally states. International relations, on the other hand, is a branch of political science with a more descriptive programme and a more empirical method, which examines how international legal actors *actually* relate.

International law

The distinction between the "legal relations" of states and their other modes of interaction can be a fine one, but the positivist definition discussed earlier at section 1.4 on page 21 would have it that a legal rule is a binding and enforceable obligation, regarded as law, that has been posited through a political process by a body politic, to whom obedience to the legal rule is owed.

Traditionally, international lawyers would explicitly or implicitly qualify this definition by requiring that the bodies by whom international law is posited be states,[2] consigning the activities of other actors in the international arena to "political" rather than "legal" status. The extent to which this constriction is problematic depends on whether it is intended to be semantic or empirical. That is to say, if international law is *defined* by the fact that it is the result of agreements between states, then that may be a useful way to narrow the field of study, but may at the same time consign the field of international law to irrelevance if as a matter of fact, bodies other than states have an equally important practical role to play in international governance. As Slaughter puts it:

> If, for instance, the primary actors in the system are not States, but individuals and groups represented by State governments, and international law regulates States without regard for such individual and group activity, international legal rules will become increasingly irrelevant to State behaviour.[3]

There are however schools of international lawyers who have adopted a broader treatment of their subject, which incorporates the activities of

[2]For example, Michael Akehurst, *A Modern Introduction to International Law*, 2nd edition London: George Allen & Unwin, 1970, defining international law at page 9 as "the system of law which governs relations between states."

[3]Annie-Marie Slaughter, International Law in a World of Liberal States, Eur J Int' Law 6:4 1995, 2

bodies other than states, recognising international law as a supranational regime of governance—that is, a regime which in certain circumstances can prevail over the sovereignty of states, and in which states are therefore by definition not the ultimate authorities. As a corollary of this, non-state actors are not, or at least not by definition, precluded from participating in such a regime in their own right.

This is already uncontroversial in some contexts, for example in that individuals are the subject of international human rights instruments, even possessing direct rights of audience before the Human Rights Committee of the United Nations in respect of alleged infringements of their rights[4] (and conversely, facing their international obligations at war crime tribunals such as those of Nuremberg and the International Criminal Court). The more controversial question is as to the extent that non-state actors can be involved not only as subjects of international law, but as its authors.

The New Haven school of international law, whilst not in the mainstream, does accommodate this possibility. New Haven scholars contend that international law is characterised by the conjunction of authority and control; that is, the authority of a decision-maker to posit an obligation, as perceived by those to whom it is directed, and the control of their actual behaviour by the posited obligation.[5] Put more simply, international law can be found wherever a lawmaker's claim to exercise authority is accompanied by submission to it in practice. Accordingly for the New Haven scholar, expectations of authority can be drawn not only from states, but from members of the international community at large.[6]

Another school of international legal scholarship more receptive to the inclusion of non-state actors as sources of authority, and which also seeks to unify the study of domestic and international, public and private law, is described as the study of "transnational legal process,"[7] "transnational law"[8] or "global law."[9]

As radical as these schools of international law may be to the mainstream

---

[4]Optional Protocol 1 to the *International Covenant on Civil and Political Rights*, 16 Dec 1966, 1980 ATS No 23 (entry into force for Australia (except Article 41) 13 November 1980); see Ivan Shearer, United Nations: Human Rights Committee: The Toonen Case, ALJ 69 1995.

[5]Eisuke Suzuki, The New Haven School of International Law: An Invitation to a Policy-Oriented Jurisprudence, Yale Stud In World Pub Order 1 1974, 36; Harold D Lasswell and Myres S McDougal, *Jurisprudence for a Free Society: Studies in Law, Science, and Policy* New Haven, CT: New Haven Press, 1992

[6]See Arend (as in n. 75 on page 21), 76–85.

[7]Harold H Koh, Transnational Legal Process, Neb LR 75 1996; Idem, *Transnational Legal Processes: Globalization and Power Disparities* London: Butterworths, 2002, chap. Opening Remarks: Transnational Legal Process Illuminated

[8]Philip Jessup, *Transnational Law* New Haven, CT: Yale University Press, 1956; Peer Zumbansen, Globalization and the Law: Deciphering the Message of Transnational Human Rights Litigation, German LJ 5:12 2004

[9]Gunther Teubner, *Global Law Without a State* Brookfield: Dartmouth, 1997, chap. Global Bukowina: Legal Pluralism in the World Society

scholar, in many ways they are commonplace to the liberal student of international relations.

International relations

The theoretical divergence between the studies of international relations and international law that began early in the 20th century became a schism with the collapse of international order in the second World War, which exposed notions of an international "rule of law" as idealistic. While international lawyers retreated to the United Nations, international relations theorists developed what became the first dominant paradigm of post-war international relations theory to succeed the former "idealism" that they had inherited from their legal colleagues; that of realism.[10]

The realist (or neo-realist, though the distinction is not presently relevant) believes that rules of international law do not have any significant influence on state behaviour. Rather, a state's behaviour is determined by a range of political and sociological factors; predominantly concern for its own internal and external security, and to a lesser extent its economic welfare.[11] There are naturally diverging foci between realist theorists, including a school of behavioural or scientific scholars with a more quantitative systematic approach,[12] rational choice theorists who draw strongly on economics,[13] and cognitive theorists who inherit their approach from psychology.[14] Notwithstanding these divergences, the four assumptions central to the position of the realist, according to one author, may be paraphrased as follows:

- The most important actors in international politics are nation states.
- The international system is a natural anarchy in which nation states compete with each other.
- States seek power, *vis a vis* other states, in order to achieve their interests.

[10]James P Muldoon Jr, *The Architecture of Global Governance: An Introduction to the Study of International Organizations* Oxford: Westview Press, 2004, 66–80.

[11]See Hans J Morgenthau, *Politics Among Nations: The Struggle for Power and Peace*, 5th edition New York: Alfred A Knopf, 1978, 4-15.

[12]See Muldoon Jr (as in n. 10), 83–84.

[13]See Yale H Ferguson and Richard W Mansbach, Between Celebration and Despair: Constructive Suggestions for Future International Theory, International Studies Quarterly 35:4 1991, 373.

[14]Michael D Young and Mark Schafer, Is There Method in Our Madness? Ways of Assessing Cognition in International Relations, Mershon International Studies Review 42 1998

- States, like consumers in the economic free market, tend to act rationally.[15]

Leaving aside critical approaches such as Marxist or neo-Marxist and postmodern or poststructuralist theories,[16] the second main group of post-war theories of international relations are generally described as liberal (or, again, neo-liberal, though the distinction will not be pursued here). In general, liberal theories temper the cynicism of realism in which states are the only relevant actors, with an awareness of the influence of domestic and international civil society on international relations, including its influence on the growing body of new international law that has burgeoned in the post-war period.[17]

Beyond its acknowledgment of the relationship between state and society, liberalism in international relations theory is nothing if not heterogeneous, with insights again being drawn from a range of other fields including economics and game theory. Different strains of liberal theories have different foci: for example, institutionalism stresses the role that international rules and institutions can play in constraining state behaviour,[18] institutions being defined as "persistent and connected sets of rules (formal and informal) that prescribe behavioral roles, constrain activity, and shape expectations."[19]

Taking this further is functionalism (along with neo-functionalism, though again the distinction is not presently relevant), which is sometimes placed outside the liberal canon, and which concentrates on the forces that drive states to integrate rather than to compete, as demonstrated most markedly by Europe's experience.[20] Also tangential to the liberal canon is constructivism, which applies social constructivist analysis to international relations theory.

One of the most pertinent insights of many liberal scholars, that is sometimes referred to as pluralism,[21] is that the arena of international relations

---

[15]Michael Mastanduno, *International Order and the Future of World Politics* Cambridge: Cambridge University Press, 1999, chap. An Institutionalist View: International Institutions and State Strategies, 21–22, and cf Slaughter, International Law in a World of Liberal States (as in n. 3 on page 98), 5.

[16]But see Muldoon Jr (as in n. 10 on the facing page), 84–87 and 92–94, and Ferguson and Mansbach (as in n. 13 on the preceding page).

[17]See Muldoon Jr (as in n. 10 on the facing page), 80–92 for a survey of liberal theories which include functionalism, rational choice theory, and regime theory which is referred to below, and more generally see Slaughter, International Law in a World of Liberal States (as in n. 3 on page 98), 5–6.

[18]See Arend (as in n. 75 on page 21), 4–5.

[19]Robert O Keohane, *International Institutions and State Power* Boulder: Westview Press, 1989, chap. Neoliberal Institutionalism: A Perspective on World Politics, 3

[20]Robert O Keohane and S Hoffmann, *The New European Community: Decision-making and Institutional Change* Boulder: Westview Press, 1991

[21]Robert Dahl, *Pluralist Democracy in the United States* Chicago: Rand McNally, 1967, 24

involves the interrelation of various competing and yet interdependent bodies, of which states are only a subset. In contrast to the approach of realism, and even mainstream liberal institutionalism,[22] this approach admits of actors other than states as the primary subjects of interest. It acknowledges that international law and the bodies that make it do significantly influence the behaviour of states (and *vice versa*), but that so too do trade unions, terrorists and transnational corporations alike. Like states, these other institutions also powerfully represent social interests in the international sphere; in fact, in the new era of globalisation and international terrorism this has become almost a truism.

Regime theory

But further than this, the institutions that shape international relations need not even be formal organisations, so much as practices applied by international actors to a specific activity or group of activities.[23] As defined by regime theory (which falls within the neo-liberal institutionalist camp), regimes are "sets of implicit or explicit principles, norms, rules, and decision-making procedures around which actors' expectations converge in a given area of international relations."[24] Participants in regimes may include either state or non-state actors (in which case they may be respectively described as international or transnational regimes),[25] or a mixture of both. It is common that one international (typically intergovernmental) organisation, for example the IPU in the case of the international postal network, and the International Coffee Organization (ICO) in respect of international trade in coffee,[26] will play a dominant role in governance of a regime.[27] However, in other regimes such as that for international air transport, a roughly equal role is played by both the public and private sectors; in that example represented respectively by the International Civil Aviation Organization (ICAO)[28] and the International Association of Transport Airlines (IATA).[29]

Recall, from the Introduction to Chapter 2, the WGIG's definition of Internet governance (repeated in the Tunis Agenda):

> Internet governance is the development and application by

---

[22]Cutler, *Private Power and Global Authority: Transnational Merchant Law in the Global Political Economy* (as in n. 76 on page 21), 2

[23]See Arend (as in n. 75 on page 21), 120.

[24]Krasner (as in n. 82 on page 22), 1

[25]Oran R Young, *Governance in World Affairs* Ithaca: Cornell University Press, 1999, 10

[26]See `http://www.ico.org/`.

[27]Idem, International Regimes: Problems of Concept Formation, World Politics 32:3 1980; Franda (as in n. 43 on page 42), 3

[28]See `http://www.icao.int/`.

[29]See `http://www.iata.org/`.

> Governments, the private sector and civil society, in their respective roles, of shared *principles, norms, rules, decision-making procedures*, and programmes that shape the evolution and use of the Internet.[30]

WGIG is here, implicitly but unmistakably, identifying Internet governance as a regime. And that is exactly what it is: a regime in which both state and non-state actors (those identified in Chapter 2) participate in governance.[31] But to say this, which is hardly even controversial, does not necessarily mean that the actors in the Internet governance regime, still less the non-state actors, make international law. On that particular question, we must turn back to the study of international law.

3.2 Actors in international law

Traditionally, states are considered the only subjects of (to use the terminology of international law) or actors in (to use the equivalent international relations term) international law.[32] Thus whilst the actions of non-state actors may prompt the development of an international legal rule, it is only through the acts and agreements of states that it becomes law.[33]

The rise of states to preeminence in the international legal system was one of the defining characteristics of the transition from feudalism to the modern age, marked by the Treaties of Westphalia which ended the Thirty Years' War in 1648.[34] Prior to the Treaties of Westphalia[35] the Western world was characterised by the rise and fall of territories to various princes, each variously challenging the authority of the others, and each subject in turn to the claims of the Holy Roman Emperor to secular power.

The Treaties established the principles that each state should be equal and sovereign within its own territorial boundaries, and should in turn show comity or respect for the sovereignty of its neighbours, without

---

[30] WGIG, Report of the Working Group on Internet Governance (as in n. 2 on page 29), 4, emphasis added.

[31] Franda (as in n. 43 on page 42), 5. More narrowly, Mueller has identified the issue area inhabited by ICANN as a regime: Mueller, *Ruling the Root: Internet Governance and the Taming of Cyberspace* (as in n. 21 on page 35), 212.

[32] Cutler, *Private Power and Global Authority: Transnational Merchant Law in the Global Political Economy* (as in n. 76 on page 21), 21. Strictly, an actor is lesser than a subject, the distinction being that a subject bears rights and duties under international law. The word "agent" is also sometimes seen in the international relations literature, confusingly for lawyers, but its use will be avoided here.

[33] Arend (as in n. 75 on page 21), 43.

[34] Aschendorff/Münster, The Westphalian Treaties from October 24th, 1648 ⟨URL: `http://www.pax-westphalica.de/`⟩

[35] Or more correctly the Peace of Westphalia, marked by the Treaties of Münster and Osnabruück.

interfering in their internal affairs. Westphalian states began to settle their disputes through formal diplomatic relations rather than through warfare, which ushered in an era of comparative peace, certainty and territorial stability.[36] An analogy used to describe the interactions of such states was that they were like balls on a billiard table: autonomous, atomic and impermeable.[37]

But the world has changed since 1648. In the post-globalisation era, the world is returning to a pre-Westphalian state in which multiple overlapping spheres of legal authority co-exist. No longer is the authority in question that of kings, knights, guilds, cities, and the Pope, but that of states, multinational corporations, international organisations and transnational civil society groups. Hall and Biersteker write:

> We find it telling that at the beginning of the twenty-first century there are so many examples of sites or locations of authority that are neither states, state-based, nor state-created. The state is no longer the sole, or in some instances even the principal, source of authority, in either the domestic arena or in the international system.[38]

This condition, aptly dubbed "new medievalism," will be discussed further at section 3.2 on page 129. But suffice it for now to say that reflecting the new reality of globalisation and the accordant diffusion of legal authority, there is growing pressure on intergovernmental bodies such as the United Nations to open up their processes to broader public participation;[39] a trend the United Nations has itself acknowledged.[40]

The Tunis Agenda therefore clearly identifies three groups of stakeholders who are to participate in Internet governance: governments, the private sector (which it also refers to as "business entities"), and civil society.[41] In the remainder of this section, the three stakeholder groups identified in the Tunis Agenda will be outlined in relation to their roles in the development of international law.

---

[36] Cutler, *Private Power and Global Authority: Transnational Merchant Law in the Global Political Economy* (as in n. 76 on page 21), 244–245

[37] Slaughter, International Law in a World of Liberal States (as in n. 3 on page 98), 5

[38] Rodney Bruce Hall and Thomas J Biersteker, *The Emergence of Private Authority in Global Governance* Cambridge: Cambridge University Press, 2002, chap. The Emergence of Private Authority in the International System, 5

[39] See generally David Held and Anthony McGrew, editors, *The Global Transformations Reader: An Introduction to the Globalization Debate*, 2nd edition Malden, MS: Polity Press, 2000.

[40] Kofi Annan, In Larger Freedom: Towards Development, Security and Human Rights For All ⟨URL: `http://documents-dds-ny.un.org/doc/UNDOC/GEN/N05/270/78/pdf/N0527078.pdf?OpenElement`⟩, 41

[41] Arguably, it also identifies intergovernmental organisations and international organisations such as ICANN as separate stakeholder groups. These are not accepted as such here, as will be explained at section 5.1 on page 332.

Governments

Governments of states participate in international law by concluding bilateral or multilateral agreements, and through their involvement in intergovernmental organisations that are typically formed by such agreements.[42]

Such intergovernmental organisations may be categorised by their geographical reach, their manifest purposes and their membership base. The geographical reach of an organisation may be global as in the case of the United Nations, or regional as in the case of APEC. Its manifest purposes may be general or specific, as in the case of the OECD in the first instance and the WTO in the second—and if specific, may be political, economic or socio-cultural. Its membership base may be governmental (as in the case of NATO, the North Atlantic Treaty Organization) or hybrid (as in the case of the International Labour Organisation (ILO) which contains both governmental and non-governmental members), and in either instance may be open to all states, or only to a subset, as in the case of the G8.[43]

In this section, four intergovernmental organisations will be described in turn; beginning with the United Nations which is global in reach, general in purpose and governmental in membership, followed by three organisations that differ on one or more of these variables: the WTO which is specific in purpose, the ILO which is of hybrid composition, and the European Union which is regional in reach.

The United Nations

The United Nations (UN) was established following the Second World War in 1945 as an association of 51 states, succeeding the League of Nations which had been established following the First World War in 1919. As at 2008 the United Nations is headquartered in New York City with 191 states as members.

The UN is notable amongst intergovernmental organisations not simply because of its size, but also because of its supranationality; that is, it occupies a realm of international government and international law that prevails over the sovereign authority of the domestic governments and law of their member states.

An example of this is that its member states are required to submit to decisions of its Security Council relating to international peace and security, which (in theory) limits the circumstances in which they may unilaterally

[42] But not always, as in the case of ICANN's GAC. Intergovernmental organisations may also be recognised by treaty following their formation: Ingrid Detter, *The International Legal Order* Aldershot, England: Dartmouth, 1994, 91.

[43] Muldoon Jr (as in n. 10 on page 100), 100–101

employ the use of military force.[44] Even within a member state, its billiard ball shell may be permeated by the United Nations in the case that the state is abusing its citizens' human rights.[45]

The United Nations is composed of five active principal organs; the General Assembly, the Security Council, the International Court of Justice (ICJ), the Secretariat and the Economic and Social Council (ECOSOC).[46] To use the simplest of analogies to the domestic equivalents of each organ, the General Assembly can be understood as the parliamentary body of the United Nations, the Security Council as its militia, the ICJ as its judiciary, the Secretariat as its public service, and the Economic and Social Council as a peak body of executive ministries.

Taking first the General Assembly, this is a body composed of 191 delegates, one from each member state, whose votes are weighted equally. The General Assembly's power does not have a "hard legal" character, as it is empowered only to make non-binding recommendations.[47] One of its few substantive powers is to resolve a deadlock of the Security Council in circumstances where there appears to be a threat to the peace, breach of the peace or act of international aggression.[48] The General Assembly has a number of subsidiary bodies, including the recently-formed United Nations Human Rights Council.

The Security Council is the only organ of the United Nations with the power to make decisions that are binding on UN members pursuant to the UN Charter. It is empowered to institute action ranging from the imposition of economic sanctions to the use of armed force in order to maintain or restore international peace and security.[49] The Security Council also has various standing and ad-hoc subsidiary bodies.

The Security Council's composition is the same today as it was following the second World War, when the United Kingdom, the United States, France, Russia and China were appointed permanent members (Germany and Japan being omitted for obvious reasons). There are ten other seats on the Council, divided into five regional blocs to which members from the applicable region are elected by the General Assembly for two-year terms. However in order for the Council to pass any resolution, the unanimous approval of the permanent members is required, with the result that it is very easy for the Council to become deadlocked.

---

[44] *Charter of the United Nations*, 26 June 1945, 1945 ATS No 1 (entry into force for Australia 1 November 1945), articles 24, 25, 33.

[45] Robert McCorquodale, *The New World Order: Sovereignty, Human Rights, and the Self-Determination of Peoples* Oxford: Berg, 1996, chap. Human Rights and Self-Determination

[46] The Trusteeship Council, which is no longer active, is excluded from this list.

[47] *Charter of the United Nations*, 26 June 1945, 1945 ATS No 1 (entry into force for Australia 1 November 1945), articles 10–13

[48] General Assembly of the United Nations, Uniting for Peace ⟨URL: `http://www.un.org/Depts/dhl/landmark/pdf/ares377e.pdf`⟩

[49] Articles 39–42

The International Court of Justice exists to settle disputes between UN members—that is, states. It is also empowered to render Advisory Opinions, but only on the request of United Nations bodies.[50] Fifteen judges are elected by the General Assembly and the Security Council to the ICJ for nine year terms. The main limitation on the effectiveness of the ICJ is that it requires the consent of each party before it can exercise jurisdiction.[51] Neither does its power to render advisory opinions function as a form of compulsory judicial review of the acts of other organs of the United Nations. Whilst a party is not bound to consent to the ICJ's jurisdiction, once it has done so, the ICJ's ruling may be enforced by the Security Council.[52] (though the Security Council is not obliged to do so, and the ICJ has no recourse if it does not).

The Secretariat of the United Nations comprises the staff of seventeen departments and offices who facilitate the operations of its other organs, headed by a Secretary-General who is appointed to a five year term by the General Assembly on the recommendation of the Security Council.

Finally, the Economic and Social Council oversees and coordinates the numerous United Nations commissions, programmes and agencies that exist to promote international economic and social cooperation and development. The Council's 54 members are elected by the General Assembly from amongst the UN membership to take three-year terms.

Under the Council's oversight are eight active functional commissions (including the United Nations Commission for Social Development[53]), five regional commissions (including the United Nations Economic and Social Commission for Asia and the Pacific or UNESCAP[54]), ten main programmes and funds (such as UNICEF, the United Nations Children's Fund), five research and training institutes, and a small number of other programmes, offices and fora.

There are also seventeen specialised agencies under the Council's oversight, which were either established by treaty, or have formed the subject of subsequent treaties between UN members. These may be categorised into technical agencies, and economic organisations. The technical agencies include the ITU, the UPU,[55] the ILO,[56] the ICAO, the International Maritime Organization (IMO),[57] WIPO and UNESCO.

---

[50] *Charter of the United Nations*, 26 June 1945, 1945 ATS No 1 (entry into force for Australia 1 November 1945), article 65 para 1

[51] *Statute of the International Court of Justice*, 26 Jun 1945, 1975 ATS No 50 (entry into force for Australia 1 Nov 1945), article 36.

[52] *Statute of the International Court of Justice*, 26 Jun 1945, 1975 ATS No 50 (entry into force for Australia 1 Nov 1945), article 94

[53] See `http://www.un.org/esa/socdev/csd/`.

[54] See `http://www.unescap.org/`.

[55] See `http://www.upu.int/`.

[56] See `http://www.ilo.org/`.

[57] See `http://www.imo.org/`.

The economic organisations are the International Bank for Reconstruction and Development (the World Bank)[58] and the International Monetary Fund (IMF),[59] both of which were formed following a conference in 1944 at Bretton Woods, at which it was also intended to form an International Trade Organisation. Whilst the last of these did not then eventuate, the GATT (General Agreement on Tariffs and Trade) that was formed in 1948, both as an agreement and as a loose organisation sharing its name, became the predecessor of the WTO.

World Trade Organization

The WTO succeeded the GATT in January 1995, following the Uruguay Round of negotiations conducted between 1986 and 1994.[60] Its scope was much broader than that of its predecessor (with services and intellectual property coming within its remit for the first time), and its powers of enforcement were considerably strengthened.

As at 2008 the WTO has 151 members and is headquartered in Geneva, where the most powerful countries have permanent delegations. It is not a body of the United Nations, but operates parallel to it, having the principal responsibility of administrating all multilateral trade agreements and arbitrating disputes that arise under them.

Broadly, the six most fundamental WTO agreements are those establishing the WTO, dealing with trade in goods (GATT), trade in services (GATS), intellectual property (TRIPS), dispute settlement (Understanding on Rules and Procedures Governing the Settlement of Disputes), and review of national trade policies (Trade Policies Review Mechanism).

The WTO meets continuously, but the Ministers of member countries also meet at least once every two years at a Ministerial Conference which is the WTO's peak authority. In between Ministerial Conferences the General Council, also sitting as the Dispute Settlement Body and the Trade Policy Review Body amongst others, consists of all members represented by their permanent delegations if available.

The WTO is administered by a Secretariat located in Geneva which in turn is headed by a Director-General, and four deputies handling different divisions.

One of the main functions of the WTO that sets it apart from other intergovernmental organisations is that it provides a mechanism for member states to challenge the laws of other states on the grounds that they function as a barrier to trade. For example, Antigua and Barbuda recently

---

[58] See `http://www.worldbank.org/`.

[59] See `http://www.imf.org/`.

[60] The principal reference for this section is WTO, Understanding the WTO ⟨URL: `http://www.wto.org/english/thewto_e/whatis_e/tif_e/understanding_text_e.pdf`⟩.

successfully challenged the US prohibition on interstate gambling over the Internet.[61] The Dispute Settlement Process by which this is achieved begins with a 60 day period for consultation between the parties. If the dispute remains unresolved, a panel of between three and five experts is convened in consultation with the parties to hear the dispute. If the parties cannot agree on a panel then it is appointed by the Director-General.

Once a dispute has been heard, the panel must within six months of its appointment make a recommendation to the General Council (sitting as the Dispute Settlement Body), which may reject the panel's recommendation, but only by consensus. An appeal may be taken on questions of fact only to a permanent seven-member appeal body, which must hand down its decision within 60 to 90 days; again, the Dispute Settlement Body may reject this decision, but only by consensus. In all, the dispute resolution process takes approximately one year, or 15 months if appealed. A country whose law is found illegal must amend the law, pay compensation to the other country, or face sanctions.

Another characteristic of the WTO that sets it apart from other intergovernmental organisations is that its decisions are made by consensus, rather than by weighted voting as at the IMF and the World Bank, or by means of a steering committee as in the case of the European Union (where the European Commission fulfils that role). In practice, little or no effort is made to achieve a grass roots consensus on significant agreements or decisions within the membership at large. Instead, the most powerful countries, particularly the so-called "Quad"—the United States, the European Union, Japan and Canada—broker their own agreements and "sell" these to the rest of the membership. This occurs through a process of informal meetings at which decisions are concluded before being presented to the WTO at large. These meetings range from "Heads of Delegation" (HOD) meetings which are open to the full membership, through to the smaller "Green Room" negotiations which are called by committee chairpersons or the Director-General, and similar "mini-ministerials" which are called by a host member to be held outside Geneva.

Although the WTO itself states that "informal consultations within the WTO play a vital role in bringing a vastly diverse membership round to an agreement,"[62] the lack of inclusiveness and transparency associated with the closed-door informal meetings has engendered much criticism from less powerful WTO members, some of whom have made their own alliances through which to oppose the quad.[63]

---

[61] Jonathan Lynn, Antigua Wins Modest Sanctions in US Gambling Case ⟨URL: `http://www.reuters.com/article/politicsNews/idUSL2160157420071221`⟩

[62] WTO, Understanding the WTO (as in n. 60 on the preceding page), 104

[63] These alliances include the so-called Like Minded Group (LMG) of developing nations, ASEAN (the Association of South East Asian Nations), and the Cairns group, an organisation of seventeen nations, including Australia, arguing for agricultural trade liberalisation: Aileen Kwa, Cancun Preparatory Process: "Opaque, Exclusive and Rule-less", South Bulletin 59 2003, ⟨URL: `http://www.southcentre.org/info/southbulletin/bulletin59/bulletin59-04.htm`⟩.

In the face of both public[64] and scholarly[65] pressure, the WTO has embarked upon programmes to increase its transparency and accountability, although these have been of limited scope. The WTO's inaugural public symposium held in July 2001 included a session addressing the relationship between the WTO and civil society, and in May 2002 the General Council increased the availability of WTO working documents on its Web site. However it has been implacable in its opposition to the involvement of non-members in the decision-making processes. Article V of the agreement establishing the WTO[66] provides:

> The General Council may make appropriate arrangements for consultation and cooperation with non-governmental organizations concerned with matters related to those of the WTO.

A framework within which such consultation and cooperation could take place was adopted by the General Council in July 1996,[67] but it contained little other than a unilateral commitment to publish derestricted documents on the Internet, an acknowledgment that discussions with NGOs may take place by informal means, and a recitation of the supposedly "broadly held view that it would not be possible for NGOs to be directly involved in the work of the WTO or its meetings."

Commencing in Singapore in 1996, qualifying NGOs could become accredited to attend Ministerial Conferences, but they were not permitted to speak at them, nor even to circulate documents, until 1998 when the WTO began to circulate a monthly list of civil society position papers to its members, and to accept *amicus curiae* briefs from NGOs to its Dispute Settlement Body on broader issues engaged by disputes, such as environmental or human rights concerns. In 2001 the General Council agreed to increase its briefings to civil society, and to hear presentations from selected NGOs. However despite these limited reforms, it may still be said that the WTO's consultations with civil society have been less of a dialogue than a monologue.[68]

Ironically, prior to the establishment of the IGF, the WTO was put forward as a possible model for international public policy governance of the

---

[64] Vandana Shiva, Doha: Saving WTO, Killing Democracy ⟨URL: `http://www.globalpolicy.org/socecon/bwi-wto/wto/2001/1204dem.htm`⟩

[65] Keohane and Nye have argued that what the WTO lacks is political leadership to intermediate between itself and its constituencies: Robert O Keohane and Joseph S Nye, *Governance in a Globalizing World* Washington, DC: Brookings Institution Press, 2000, chap. The Club Model of Multilateral Cooperation and Problems of Democratic Legitimacy.

[66] *Marrakesh Agreement Establishing the World Trade Organization*, 15 Apr 2004, 1995 ATS No 8 (entry into force 1 Jan 1995) (WTO Agreement)

[67] WTO, Guidelines for arrangements on relations with Non-Governmental Organizations ⟨URL: `http://www.wto.org/english/forums_e/ngo_e/guide_e.htm`⟩

[68] Ngaire Woods and Amrita Narlikar, Governance and the Limits of Accountability: The WTO, the IMF, and the World Bank, International Social Science Journal 53:170 2001, 580

Internet.[69] Yet recalling the manner in which IANA presented its private blueprint for ICANN in response to the US Government's White Paper as a *fait accompli* in the guise of consensus, perhaps the suggestion is not so far fetched. Perhaps consensus is simply too unwieldy an instrument for the governance of a large intergovernmental or multi-stakeholder organisation. This is a charge to be investigated further in Chapter 4.[70]

International Labour Organization

The ILO is as exceptional an intergovernmental organisation as the WTO, but in quite different respects. Formed in 1919 as an agency of the League of Nations, and becoming the first specialised agency of the United Nations upon its formation in 1946, the ILO was structured from the outset to include private sector and civil society representatives as full voting members.[71]

Article 2 of the Constitution of the ILO[72] establishes its three constituent bodies: the General Conference, the Governing Body and the International Labour Office.

The General Conference of the ILO, better known as the International Labour Conference, meets annually in Geneva. Each state delegate may (and most do) appoint a representative from the country's peak employers' and workers' bodies to attend with them. In Australia's case, these are representatives from the Australian Chamber of Commerce and Industry (ACCI)[73] and the Australian Council of Trade Unions (ACTU).[74] The employer and worker representatives are permitted to speak and vote independently of each other and of their governments. The Conference elects a President and three Vice Presidents, the latter including representatives of governments, employers and workers.

The fundamental purpose of the Conference is to approve by a two-thirds majority Conventions and Recommendations on labour standards and other employment related issues. ILO Conventions, once signed and ratified, become binding international agreements, whereas its Recommendations are "soft law" for the guidance of member states, often supplementing the subject matter of a Convention. The Conference also adopts the ILO's biennial work programme and budget which are prepared by the Executive Council of the Governing Body.

---

[69] Biegel (as in n. 60 on page 19), 184

[70] See section 4.4 on page 311.

[71] See generally ILO, The ILO: What it is. What it Does. ⟨URL: http://www.ilo.org/public/english/bureau/inf/download/brochure/pdf/broch_0904.pdf⟩.

[72] *Instrument for the Amendment of the Constitution of the International Labour Organization of 28 June 1919, as amended*, 9 Oct 1946, 1948 ATS No 8 (entry into force 20 Apr 1948) (ILO Constitution)

[73] See http://www.acci.asn.au/.

[74] See http://www.actu.asn.au/.

The Governing Body (also known as the Executive Council) manages the ILO's work programme between each Conference. It meets three times per year in Geneva and is composed of 28 government members and 14 members each from the worker and employer groups, all sitting for a three year term.[75] Ten of the government seats are reserved for the major industrial powers, and the remainder are elected by the other government delegates of the Conference. The employers and workers each elect their own representatives.

One of the main purposes of the Governing Body is to prepare the agenda for the Conference, and to ensure that members have been properly consulted before a Convention or Recommendation is put before the Conference for adoption. The Conference itself may also require an item to be added to the agenda, by two-thirds vote.[76] The Governing Body also elects the Director-General who heads the International Labour Office for a five-year term.

The International Labour Office is the ILO's permanent Secretariat in Geneva. Underneath the leadership of the Director-General, it is subdivided into thirteen offices and departments which carry out a variety of administrative and substantive functions. Of these, the four departments that are engaged in supporting the ILO's substantive work programme, each headed by an Executive Director, are:

- Standards and Fundamental Principles and Rights at Work, which deals with such issues as international labour standards and child labour;
- Social Protection, which deals with such issues as social security, conditions of work, HIV/AIDS, occupational health and safety and migration;
- Employment, which deals with economic and labour markets analysis, employment policy, improving skills and employability, and job creation and enterprise development; and
- Social dialogue, which focuses on promoting and facilitating open discussion between representatives of governments, employers and workers, on issues of common interest.

There is also an ILO office for each of the five regions which liaises with and assists the tripartite constituents in those regions to further the ILO's goals.

Apart from its tripartite structure, another distinguishing feature of the ILO is the extent to which it supervises the implementation of its

[75] *ILO Constitution*, Article 7

[76] *ILO Constitution*, Articles 14–16

Conventions and Recommendations by member states. Each member state is required to present a periodic report on this topic, which must also be submitted to its worker and employer representatives who may present their own reports in response. A Committee of Experts on the Application of Conventions and Recommendations, comprised of 28 independent experts in labour law and policy, receives the reports and compiles an annual report of its own to the tripartite Conference Committee on the Application of Conventions and Recommendations.

An additional check on states' compliance with Conventions is the facility for employer and worker organizations to initiate "representations" against a member state alleging that it has failed to comply with a Convention that it has ratified. Representations are examined by a tripartite body that submits its findings to the Governing Body. States too can submit complaints alleging that another state has failed to comply with a convention they both have ratified.

Article 12 of its Constitution authorises the ILO to make whatever arrangements it thinks fit to consult with other intergovernmental organisations and with civil society. Pursuant to this Article, in May 2005 the Governing Body agreed upon a policy permitting qualifying NGOs to attend Conferences provided that their request to do so was received at least one month in advance of the opening session of the Governing Body preceding the opening of the Conference.[77]

The European Union

The complex structure of the European Union (EU) is quite different from that of the United Nations, or that of any other intergovernmental body. Whilst the earliest predecessor of the EU, the Council of Europe established in 1949,[78] was more traditionally intergovernmental in character, the unified face of Europe became increasingly supranational with the establishment of the European Coal and Steel Community (ECSC) in 1951, and the European Economic Community (EEC) in 1958. The ECSC and the European Atomic Energy Community (or Euratom) merged with the EEC in 1965.[79] Following the *Treaty of Maastricht* of 1993,[80] the EEC—or now the EC; the European Community—forms the first pillar of today's European Union.

The EU exhibits supranational features to an even greater extent than the UN, in that EU law is capable of overriding the domestic law of its

[77] ILO, Representation of International Non-Governmental Organizations at the International Labour Conference and Other ILO Meetings ⟨URL: http://www3.ilo.org/public/english/standards/relm/ilc/pdf/note.pdf⟩

[78] It still exists, though now mainly as a human rights watchdog; see http://www.coe.int/.

[79] See Derek W Urwin, *The Community of Europe: A History of European Integration since 1945*, 2nd edition New York: Longman Publishing, 1995.

[80] *Treaty on European Union*, 7 Feb 1992, 1992 O J (C 191), 31 ILM 253

members. For example, the legal sovereignty of the EU is exclusive in areas such as trade, agriculture and customs, as it might be in a federation of states such as the Commonwealth of Australia. The European Court of Justice may also rule against a member state, and to impose sanctions, for its breach of a European Commission Directive. On the other hand sovereignty is shared with its member states in such areas as consumer and environmental protection, and is excluded altogether in favour of its members' sovereignty in areas such as domestic law enforcement and housing policy.

The EU is composed of five main organs: the European Parliament, the Council of the European Union, the European Commission, the European Council and the European Court of Justice.

The European Parliament is analogous to the General Assembly of the United Nations, the main differences being that that it has proportionately more representatives from the more populous countries, and that since 1979 they have been directly elected by their constituents. Since the passage of the most recent governing treaty of the EU, the *Treaty of Nice* in 1999,[81] the total number of MPs has been capped at 732. These Members of the European Parliament (MEPs) hold office for five years, and elect a President who serves for half that term. Much of the Parliament's day to day work is performed within its 20 standing committees organised along functional lines.

The power of the European Parliament has been progressively enlarged from its initial status as a merely consultative body. This began in 1986 with the passage of the *Single European Act*,[82] and continued in the *Treaty of Maastricht* when it was first given "co-decision" powers, which were expanded to additional policy areas in the *Treaties of Amsterdam*[83] and *Nice*. Co-decision is a process by which the European Parliament must reach agreement with the Council of the European Union on the text of any EU law proposed by the European Commission (which in simple terms is known as a directive if it requires domestic implementing legislation, and a regulation if it does not).

The Council of the European Union is constituted by one serving minister from each of the member states, drawn from their national parliaments. Different ministers may however serve on the Council as it deals with different issues. The Council is the main decision-making body of the EU, responsible for passing laws put forward by the European Commission, subject to the oversight of the European Parliament through the co-decision procedure. Councillors are assisted by a Secretariat on administrative matters, and by a Committee of Permanent Representatives—somewhat like

---

[81] *Treaty of Nice amending the TEU, the Treaties establishing the European Communities and certain related acts*, 26 Feb 2001, 2001 OJ (C 80) 1

[82] *Single European Act*, 17 Feb 1986, 1987 O.J (L 169) 1, 25 ILM 506

[83] *Treaty of Amsterdam amending the Treaty on European Union, the Treaties establishing the European Communities and related acts*, 2 Oct 1997, 1997 OJ (C 340) 1, 37 ILM 56

the civil service of a domestic ministry—on policy matters. The Presidency of the Council rotates on a six-monthly basis.

Originally decisions of the Council were required to be made by consensus, but "qualified majority" voting was introduced on certain issues with the *Single Europe Act*, and subsequently extended to additional issues with the *Treaty of Maastricht* and the *Treaty of Nice*. The effect of the latter treaty was also to introduce new weighting of members' votes and to impose a triple-majority requirement: that the majority of weighted votes be in favour, along with a majority of states voting in favour, and that these represent at least 62% of the EU's population. This stipulation has proved difficult to satisfy in practice.

The European Commission is composed of up to 27 members who serve for terms of five years. Pursuant to the *Treaty of Nice*, one Commissioner is appointed by each member state subject to approval by the European Parliament, provided that if there are more than 27 states (which from January 2007 there are), the member state omitted from representation on the Commission rotates. Commissioners do not sit as representatives of their appointing states, but as independent officials of the EU.

The four main roles of the Commission are to propose new policies to form the agenda of the Council of the EU in consultation with member states, to monitor the application of the EU treaties by its members and other EU institutions, to oversee the implementation of EU policies by member states, and to represent the EU in other fora such as the WTO. The Commission is supported in these activities by approximately 35 Directorates General and Services (divided further into directorates and departments) which offer policy, administrative and logistical support.

There is also a European Council (distinct from the Council of the European Union, and from the Council of Europe) which is constituted by the heads of the member states, and the President of the European Commission. The role of the European Council was first formalised in the *Single Europe Act*, which accorded it the role of peak oversight of the EU as a whole. However the character of this role is one of guidance and persuasion rather than formal legal authority.

Finally the European Court of Justice is akin to the International Court of Justice, save that it not only adjudicates upon disputes between states, but also between states and EU institutions and even between citizens of EU states and EU institutions. Domestic courts can also refer questions of EU law to the European Court of Justice for decision. Its power extends to the ability to declare domestic legislation unconstitutional for inconsistency with EU law.

The European Court of Justice is assisted by a Court of First Instance and by a Civil Service Tribunal who now share some of its former workload. Each member state ordinarily appoints one judge to each court, for a term of six years.

Apart from the five main organs of the EU referred to above, there are also a number of supporting organisations under the EU umbrella, including the European Ombudsman,[84] and two advisory bodies; the Economic and Social Committee (EESC) which represents the interests of civil society to the organs of the EU,[85] and the Committee of the Regions (CoR) which does the same for sub-national governments.[86]

Both of these last-mentioned advisory bodies contain 317 members nominated by member states in rough proportion to their population, who hold office for four years, along with a president whom the committee elects for two years. Each committee is divided into functional subcommittees, and its operations are supported by a bureau and a secretariat-general. In certain circumstances, the Commission or the Council of the European Union are obliged to consult with these committees, but in other cases the committees remain at liberty to submit unsolicited advisory documents and opinions to those organs or to the European Parliament.

The private sector

The economic and political influence of the private sector in international relations, particularly that of multinational (or transnational) corporations (MNCs), exceeds that of many states. It is, after all, often noted that the sales revenue of the largest MNCs exceeds the GDP of mid-sized nations.[87] The private sector has accordingly begun slowly to win new rights of direct access to intergovernmental fora,[88] most relevantly including WSIS.[89]

The formal reception of input from private sector representatives into intergovernmental processes mirrors a process that is known in a domestic political context as corporatism (or neo-corporatism), defined as

> a system that gives a variety of functional interest groups—most predominantly business organizations and trade unions–direct representation in the political system, defusing conflict among them and creating instead broad consensus on policies.[90]

---

[84] See `http://ombudsman.europa.eu/`.

[85] See `http://eesc.europa.eu/`.

[86] See `http://cor.europa.eu/`.

[87] John Cavanagh and Sarah Anderson, Top 200. The Rise of Corporate Global Power ⟨URL: `http://www.tni.org/archives/cavanagh/top200.pdf`⟩; though the comparison is imperfect, as GDP and corporate sales are not directly commensurable.

[88] Cutler, *Private Power and Global Authority: Transnational Merchant Law in the Global Political Economy* (as in n. 76 on page 21), 198–199

[89] See section 5.1 on page 322.

[90] M Ottaway, Corporatism Goes Global: International Organizations, Non-Governmental Organization Networks, and Transnational Business, Global Governance 7 2001, 277.

The ILO is perhaps the archetypal example of modern corporatism.[91]

But the private sector also, of course, exercises considerable influence on government policy development outside of its formal representation in governmental or intergovernmental fora. On a domestic level, this may be done either directly, through lobbying and campaign donations[92] (or their illegitimate counterparts, political cronyism and bribery), or through more indirect means such as regulatory capture, whereby the behaviour of a regulatory authority is unduly influenced by the interests of the regulated industry,[93] and perhaps most significantly of all through control of the mass media.[94]

Another indirect means by which MNCs can influence the development of domestic law is simply in their choice of jurisdictions from which to operate, which may be based on where tax and labour conditions are most favourable.[95] The economic repercussions of MNCs' choices in this regard exert an influence on the domestic law of nations vying for foreign investment in what is often described as a "race to the bottom,"[96] and which has been blamed for the dismantling of the domestic social safety nets of welfare states.[97]

On an intergovernmental level, some of the same effects are observed. For example, MNCs were instrumental in the passage of the WTO's TRIPS agreement. The most active MNC in this endeavour was pharmaceutical MNC Pfizer, which engaged in a broad range of strategies to secure the acceptance of TRIPS, including lobbying, donations, sponsorship of think tanks, and the appointment of its CEO to chair a US government Advisory Committee on Trade Negotiation.[98]

Pfizer was joined by eleven like-minded MNCs in a consortium calling themselves the Intellectual Property Committee (IPC).[99] The IPC continued

---

[91] See section 3.2 on page 111, and compare consociationalism at section 4.4 on page 294.

[92] Alan K Ota, Disney in Washington: The Mouse That Roars ⟨URL: `http://www2.cnn.com/ALLPOLITICS/1990/00/10/cq/disney.html`⟩

[93] As allegedly in the case of Australia's Accounting Standards Review Board (ASRB): R G Walker, Australia's ASRB: A Case Study of Political Activity and Regulatory "Capture", Accounting and Business Research 17:67 1987.

[94] Edwards S Herman and Noam Chomsky, *Manufacturing Consent: The Political Economy of the Mass Media* London: Vintage, 1994

[95] Susan Strange, *The New Realisms: Perspectives on Multilateralism and World Order* Tokyo: United Nations University Press, 1997, chap. Territory, State, Authority and Economy: A New Realist Political Ontology of Global Political Economy

[96] Miles Kahler, Modeling Races to the Bottom ⟨URL: `http://irps.ucsd.edu/assets/014/6739.pdf`⟩

[97] Ramesh Mishra, *Globalisation and the Welfare State* Cheltenham, UK: Edward Elgar, 1999

[98] Peter Drahos and John Braithwaite, Who Owns the Knowledge Economy? Political Organising Behind TRIPS ⟨URL: `http://www.thecornerhouse.org.uk/pdf/briefing/32trips.pdf`⟩, 8–9, 11.

[99] Comprising Bristol Myers, DuPont, General Electric, General Motors, Hewlett Packard, IBM, Johnson and Johnson, Merck, Monsanto, Pfizer, Rockwell, and Time-Warner: Susan K Sell,

to lobby governments and expand its sphere of influence internationally,[100] until the passage of the TRIPS agreement was a *fait accompli*.

A more broadly-based organisation representing private sector interests in international public policy development is the International Chamber of Commerce (ICC), headquartered in Paris.[101] The ICC has acted as a representative for the private sector to most United Nations organs, and to other intergovernmental bodies such as WIPO, the WTO (with whom its ongoing relationship is governed by an MOU), the OECD and the ITU (including most notably by chairing the Coordinating Committee of Business Interlocutors at the WSIS).

The peak body of the ICC is its World Council containing delegates from each of its national committees, with ten members from countries without a national committee being directly represented on the Council. The Council elects a Chairman and Vice-Chairman for two year terms, and (on the Chairman's recommendation) an Executive Council of between 15 and 30 members serving for three years, which is responsible for implementing ICC policy. Assisting them is an International Secretariat headed by a Secretary-General who is appointed by the Council on the recommendation of the Executive Board.

The ICC's work programme is divided between a number of specialised Commissions (currently 16) which formulate its policy and draft papers for submission to governments and intergovernmental organisations. Commissions in turn may contain a number of task forces; for example within the E-Business, IT and Telecoms (EBITT) Commission is the Task Force on Internet and IT Services, which specialises in Internet governance issues.

EBITT is also the policy development foundation for the work of BASIS, or Business Action to Support the Information Society; an initative of the ICC that emerged from WSIS as an umbrella for its post-WSIS programmes.[102] It is officially through BASIS that the ICC participates in the UN fora and activities that have emerged from WSIS, such as the IGF.

The new law merchant

The private sector's involvement in international public policy governance as described above is, by its nature, secondary to the primary lawmaking role of governments and intergovernmental organisations, since it is they who control the fora in which negotiations and drafting take place. But the contribution of the private sector to international public policy governance can also be understood as a primary lawmaking role, in which the tables

Private Power, Public Law: The Globalization of Intellectual Property Rights Cambridge: Cambridge University Press, 2003.

[100] Drahos and Braithwaite (as in n. 98 on the preceding page), 25

[101] See `http://www.iccwbo.org/`.

[102] See `http://www.iccwbo.org/basis/`.

are turned and the private sector exercises principal authority, with states receding into the background.

This is not as revolutionary a notion as it might sound. In medieval times, the "law merchant" or *lex mercatoria* was a system of law developed and enforced by merchants themselves, which enjoyed primacy over domestic law in the regions (mostly along trade routes) where it was applied.[103] The medieval law merchant did not derive its force from the consent of sovereign states, but operated independently and alongside the domestic law of the region. As Cutler explains,

> [t]his gave rise to a dualistic system of commercial governance: the regulation of local transaction under the local systems of law and the regulation of wholesale and long-distance transactions under the autonomous law merchant system.[104]

This is not to say that domestic law of a particular region was suspended where the law merchant had effect. Rather, the authority of each legal system overlapped, and it is this characteristic of private lawmaking that is found also in its modern analogues. Jensen writes:

> States and individuals may be members of different communities for different purposes. Just as we might understand the nation-state as an association between people who share a common language and cultural identity for the purposes of their mutual security and well-being, we might understand the various forms of transnational interaction (which include, but are not limited to, commerce and intellectual exchanges between citizens of different nation-states) as providing the germ for the emergence of numerous communities extending across state boundaries. Each of these communities would possess its own norms of conduct, expressed as either formal rules in treaties and commercial contracts or simply unexpressed mutual understandings. Such norms would enjoy legitimacy because their observance facilitates orderly interaction between members of the community and because they represent the opinion of the many rather than the rationally constructed will of the few.[105]

Thus there are today specialised transnational business communities that create and enforce their own transnational norms and rules, much as the

---

[103]Cutler, *Private Power and Global Authority: Transnational Merchant Law in the Global Political Economy* (as in n. 76 on page 21), 108–140

[104]Ibid., 109

[105]Darryn M Jensen, The Transformation of International Law, Policy 20:1 2004, 42

merchants of medieval times did. Indeed these have been described as the "new law merchant."[106]

As will be noted at section 3.3 on page 133, there are degrees of "legalisation" of international law. So too, there are degrees of legalisation within the new law merchant, ranging from the law-like rules of stock markets and financial networks such as Visa, to softer, more innately private orderings such as the rules of self-regulating professional communities.[107]

There are also degrees of institutionalisation within the new law merchant, ranging from informal industry norms and practices that are not institutionalised at all, through to private international regimes which provide "an integrated complex of formal and informal institutions that is a source of governance for an economic issue area as a whole,"[108] as in the case of international commercial arbitration.

This last case provides perhaps the clearest example of the private sector's development of its own quasi-legal rules, as international commercial arbitration is now the dominant method for the resolution of transnational commercial disputes.[109] The market leading arbitration provider is none other than the International Chamber of Commerce, though there are now numerous competing providers including the American Arbitration Association,[110] the London Court of International Arbitration[111] and the Australian Centre for International Commercial Arbitration (ACICA).[112]

Although each arbitration provider applies its own sets of substantive and procedural rules in resolving disputes, they almost universally incorporate the UNCITRAL Model Law on International Commercial Arbitration[113] or a derivative of this, along with substantive law drawn from international and domestic sources, and unwritten commercial norms.[114] For example, article 33 of the UNCITRAL Model Law (and article 34 of the ACICA Arbitration Rules[115]) provide:

---

[106] But also as transnational commercial law, transnational economic law, the law of private international trade, and international business law: Cutler, *Private Power and Global Authority: Transnational Merchant Law in the Global Political Economy* (as in n. 76 on page 21), 1.

[107] Robert D Cooter, Structural Adjudication and the New Law Merchant: A Model of Decentralised Law, Int Rev Law & Econ 14 1994, 216

[108] A Claire Cutler, Virginia Haufler and Tony Porter, *Private Authority and International Affairs* New York: SUNY Press, 1999, chap. Private Authority and International Affairs, 13

[109] Yves Dezalay and Bryant Garth, Merchants of Law as Moral Entreprenuers: Constructing International Justice from the Competition for Transnational Business Disputes, Law & Soc Rev 29:1 1995

[110] See `http://www.adr.org/`.

[111] See `http://www.lcia-arbitration.com/`.

[112] See `http://www.acica.org.au`.

[113] UNCITRAL, Arbitration Rules ⟨URL: `http://www.uncitral.org/pdf/english/texts/arbitration/arb-rules/arb-rules.pdf`⟩

[114] Christopher R Drahozal, Commercial Norms, Commercial Codes, and International Commercial Arbitration, Vand JTL 33 2000

[115] ACICA, Arbitration Rules ⟨URL: `http://www.acica.org.au/arbitration_rules.html`⟩

1. The Arbitral Tribunal shall apply the law designated by the parties as applicable to the substance of the dispute. Failing such designation by the parties, the Arbitral Tribunal shall apply the rules of law which it considers applicable.
2. The Arbitral Tribunal shall decide as *amiable compositeur* or *ex aequo et bono* only if the parties have, in writing, expressly authorized the Arbitral Tribunal to do so and if the law applicable to the arbitral procedure permits such arbitration.
3. In all cases, the Arbitral Tribunal shall decide in accordance with the terms of the contract and shall take into account the usages of the trade applicable to the transaction.

Whilst the use of international commercial arbitration is normally restricted to business-to-business (B2B) transactions, there are analogous private fora for the resolution of consumer disputes, such as the credit card chargeback system that operates as a private dispute resolution mechanism between consumers and merchants,[116] eBay's Dispute Console for disputes relating to its online auction service,[117] and numerous generic third party mediation and arbitration services such as SquareTrade[118] and Cybersettle.[119]

To be sure, there are differences between the new law merchant and the old. One is that the success of the medieval law merchant in prevailing over domestic law owed more to the feudal nature of society in those times than to the power of medieval capital, whereas the position is now reversed. Another important difference is that the effects of the new law merchant now extend in many cases far beyond the boundaries of the communities that developed them and thus take on a character closer to that of public international law. An example is the role of credit rating agencies such as Moody's and Standard & Poor, which assess not only their members' credit, nor only that of private sector entities, but of entire national economies, with consequences often comparable to those of trade sanctions imposed by an intergovernmental authority such as the WTO.[120]

Is the new law merchant, however, accurately described as law? It is easy enough to argue that it *should* be law. One scholar from the school of law and economics argues that if norms represent the consensus of the community that developed them, and if they are aligned with the broader public good (which the author examines in terms of economic efficiency,

---

[116] Henry H Perritt Jr, The Internet is Changing the Public International Legal System, Kentucky LJ 88 2000, 945

[117] See `http://pages.ebay.com/help/tp/using-dispute-console.html`.

[118] See `http://www.squaretrade.com/`.

[119] See `http://www.cybersettle.com/`.

[120] Saskia Sassen, *Losing Control?: Sovereignty in the Age of Globalization* New York: Columbia University Press, 1996, 16; Timothy J Sinclair, Passing Judgment: Credit Rating Processes as Regulatory Mechanisms of Governance in the Emerging World Order, Review of International Political Economy 1:1 1994

but could equally be analysed by reference to alternative paradigms), such norms should be "elevated" to the level of law by "issuing an authoritative statement of the norm and backing it with the state's coercive power."[121]

Whether such norms can be described as *already* amounting to law is more contentious. Some have argued that the new law merchant amounts to customary international law,[122] but empirical evidence to support this is lacking.[123] On a narrow view, that may be enough for the question to be answered in the negative: that the new law merchant is not international law. But the consequences of that conclusion are as profound as the converse would be. It means that entire private international regimes, by which some of the most significant institutions in our economic and social lives are governed, are entirely invisible to international law.[124] This is surely not a conclusion that should be reached lightly or through the application of overly formalistic criteria. The question will therefore be revisited at section 3.3 on page 142.

Civil society

Civil society and the private sector are the two classes of non-state actor recognised by the United Nations as stakeholders in Internet governance. As such, there is much in common between them, and much that has been written in the previous section is applicable to civil society also.

However the sense in which the phrase "civil society" is generally used in relation to the international system differs somewhat from its usage elsewhere. First, it refers to organised civil society, rather than to civil society at large. It is possible that civil society at large may in some circumstances qualify as an international actor in its own right; for example, in 1992 the UN Security Council authorised action on behalf of civilian populations of Somalia.[125] Also, the IGF allows for the participation of individual actors from civil society, who need have no particular institutional affiliation other than with the IGF itself. However these are exceptions to the usual rule that the participation of civil society in the international system occurs only through organised groups.

---

[121] Cooter (as in n. 107 on page 120), 226

[122] Berthold Goldman, *Contemporary Problems in International Arbitration* London: The Eastern Press, 1986, chap. The Applicable Law: General Principles of Law—The Lex Mercatoria

[123] Stephen Zamora, Is There Customary International Economic Law?, German Yearbook of International Law 32 1989

[124] Fleur Johns, The Invisibility of the Transnational Corporation: An Analysis of International Law and Legal Theory, Melb Univ L Rev 19 1994; A Claire Cutler, *The Emergence of Private Authority in Global Governance* Cambridge: Cambridge University Press, 2002, chap. Private International Regimes and Interfirm Cooperation, 33

[125] Security Council of the United Nations, Resolution 794 ⟨URL: `http://documents-dds-ny.un.org/doc/UNDOC/GEN/N92/772/11/pdf/N9277211.pdf?OpenElement`⟩

Second, "civil society" ordinarily refers to global (or transnational[126]) civil society, rather than domestic civil society. Hence it is the more precise meaning of *organised, global* civil society that will be referred to when the term "civil society" is used here (unless the context indicates otherwise), and NGO will be used where appropriate as the singular form.[127]

Once understood as NGOs, the characteristics of civil society participants in the development of international law may be further narrowed by the following factors:

- Being formal organisations intended for indefinite life, not being *ad hoc*.
- Being, or aspiring to being, self-governing with their own constitutions.
- They are private, neither deriving their power from states nor having authority over them.
- They are non-profit.
- They are transnational in their orientation and/or operations.[128]

The absence of any one of these factors may still render the subject a non-state actor in the international system, but it will be an actor outside the scope of this section. For example, the actor might not be a formal organisation, as in the case of peoples like the Palestinians, Quebecois, and Catalonians. It might not be self-governing or constitutionally convened, as in the case of the Al Qaeda movement. It might not be entirely non-governmental, either because it is government-funded (a QUANGO, Quasi-Autonomous NGO), or because like the IGF itself it is government-organised (a GONGO).[129]

Some would add an additional criterion to the list given above: that they act politically. Civil society traditionally represented the group of citizens who upheld the rule of law of a state, and from amongst whom

[126]David Held, Law of States, Law of Peoples, Leg Th 8 2002, 44—"transnational" is often used in contrast to "international" respectively to differentiate the actions of non-state actors across borders from those of states.

[127]See Steve Charnovitz, Two Centuries of Participation, NGOs and International Governance, Mich J Int'l L 18 1997, 188

[128]Leon Gordenker and Thomas G Weiss, *NGOs, the UN & Global Governance* Boulder: Lynne Rienner Publishers, 1996, chap. Pluralizing Global Governance: Analytical Approaches and Dimensions, 20–21.

[129]Such an organisation can be incorporated privately rather than under treaty, as in the case of the hybrid GONGO ICANN. Conversely, an NGO can be converted to a governmental organisation, as in the cases of the ITU and the International Committee of the Red Cross (ICRC): see Detter (as in n. 42 on page 105), 139.

new regulatory authorities and arrangements might emerge.[130] This constriction would exclude for example cultural or sporting organisations. It is difficult to understand why the definition needs to be so restricted, as it has not been suggested that the involvement of the private sector in the international system should be similarly conditioned. Moreover, it could be said that any NGO that seeks a voice in the international system will be acting politically by definition.

It has also been suggested that NGOs with a positively illiberal programme, such as Hizb ut-Tahrir[131] that have been linked to international terrorism, should be excluded by limiting the definition of civil society to those groups that provide a "civilizing process"[132] and excluding "uncivil society."[133] This particular question is a thorny one that raises questions about how cultural differences should be treated in international law, and will be revisited at section 3.4 on page 170.

Civil society's influence on international law

Much like the private sector, civil society has been active in influencing the development of international law since the 18th century, particularly in areas such as the abolition of slavery, the pursuit of peace, worker solidarity and free trade.[134] Civil society was even central to the development of the international law of intellectual property, with the *Berne Convention* having been drafted by governments based upon the proposals of the International Literary and Artistic Association, a civil society organisation headed by Victor Hugo.[135]

Civil society remains active in influencing the shape of international law today. For example, civil society's participation has been central to the success of climate change negotiations,[136] the prohibition of commercial whaling,[137] and the establishment of the International Criminal Court.[138] The 1997 Mine Ban Treaty,[139] now signed by over 150 states, was also

---

[130] Ronnie D Lipschutz and Judith Mayer, *Global Civil Society and Global Environmental Governance* New York: SUNY Press, 1996

[131] See `http://www.hizb-ut-tahrir.org/`.

[132] See eg Norbert Elias, *The Civilizing Process: State Formation and Civilization* Oxford: Blackwell, 1982.

[133] Fernando Henrique Cardoso, Civil Society and Global Governance ⟨URL: `http://www.ngocongo.org/files/cardoso_paper1.doc`⟩, 5

[134] Charnovitz (as in n. 127 on the previous page), 191–194

[135] Ibid., 201

[136] See Jessica T Matthews, Power Shift, Foreign Affairs Jan-Feb 1997.

[137] Charnovitz (as in n. 127 on the preceding page), 263

[138] See eg the Coalition for the International Criminal Court, at `http://www.iccnow.org/`.

[139] *Convention on the Prohibition of the Use, Stockpiling, Production and Transfer of Anti-Personnel Mines and on their Destruction*, 18 Sep 1997, 1999 ATS No 3 (entry into force for Australia 1 Sep 1999) (Mine Ban Treaty)

largely the product of civil society action.[140] In working on such issues across national boundaries, transnational NGOs have participated in international negotiations directly rather than through the intermediation of governments. As Charnovitz puts it, "[i]t is illogical to tell an NGO like the ICC or the International Confederation of Free Trade Unions to channel its concerns through its own government. Such an instruction negates the purpose of the organization."[141]

Thus civil society has won permanent representation at a variety of intergovernmental organisations and conferences, including the World Bank's Panel of Inspection hearings on environmental issues, and to a limited degree, WSIS.[142] At the United Nations Conference on the Human Environment held in Stockholm, Sweden in 1972, there were more NGO representatives present than governments, and by 1987 in Montreal they were not merely observing but addressing plenary sessions in their own right.[143]

Perhaps the high water mark in this evolution was reached in 1992 with the Rio Declaration on Environment and Development, principle 10 of which recited that "[e]nvironmental issues are best handled with participation of all concerned citizens, at the relevant level." Upon this base, the Aarhus Convention was established in 1998 to set minimum standards for the inclusion of the public in international environmental governance.[144]

In 1994, then Secretary-General Boutros Boutros Ghali had addressed NGOs in the following terms:

> I want you to consider this your home. Until recently, these words might have caused astonishment. The United Nations was considered to be a forum for sovereign states alone. Within the space of a few short years, this attitude has changed. Non-governmental organizations are now considered full participants in international life.[145]

As catalogued by Charnovitz, there are no fewer than ten ways in which NGOs can participate, and have historically participated in intergovernmental organisations.[146] These range from the utilisation of the NGO on an

[140]Maxwell A Cameron, Global Civil Society and the Ottawa Process: Lessons From the Movement to Ban Anti-Personnel Mines, Canadian Foreign Policy 7:1 1999

[141]Charnovitz (as in n. 127 on page 123), 276

[142]See section 5.1 on page 322.

[143]Perritt Jr (as in n. 116 on page 121), 899; Charnovitz (as in n. 127 on page 123), 262

[144]*UNECE Convention on Access to Information, Public Participation in Decision-making and Access to Justice in Environmental Matters*, 25 Jun 1998, 1998 SD No 46 (entry into force 30 Oct 2001) (Aarus Convention)

[145]United Nations Non-Government Liaison Service, NGLS Roundup, November 1996 ⟨URL: `http://www.un-ngls.org/documents/text/roundup/10NGOREV.TXT`⟩

[146]Charnovitz (as in n. 127 on page 123), 281

advisory panel or as a delegate to an international conference, through to allowing it full membership of the organisation. The 2004 Cardoso report on UN–Civil Society recommended to the UN that it "should embrace an array of forums, each designed to achieve a specific outcome, with [civil society] participation determined accordingly."[147]

Taken a step further, whilst normally civil society's actions merely contribute to the formation of international law that must in the end be created by agreements between states,[148] there are cases in which NGOs have negotiated agreements with governments in their own right. For example, principles of the Declaration of Panama regarding tuna fishing standards were negotiated between a group of five environmental NGOs and Mexico in 1995, before being signed by eleven other governments.[149] Greenpeace also negotiated an agreement with France over damages to be paid to Greenpeace for the sinking of the Rainbow Warrior.[150]

Taken a step further still, civil society's role in international public policy governance can bypass governments altogether. For example, it was civil society, including AIDS activists and organisations such as Doctors Without Borders/Médecins Sans Frontières, that were largely responsible for pharmaceutical companies agreeing to reduce the price of AIDS drugs to Africa and other third world regions during 2000–2001.[151] This was a case in which the private sector and civil society together achieved a public policy outcome without state intervention at all.

Civil society's effectiveness in influencing the shape of international law has only continued to increase through the use of technologies such as the Internet,[152] which have assisted the growth of social movements and action groups in civil society and given given them a louder voice in policy networks,[153] by making it easier and less expensive for them to mobilise resources and constituents.

---

[147] Fernando Henrique Cardoso, Cardoso Report on Civil Society ⟨URL: `http://www.capacity.undp.org/indexAction.cfm?module=Library&action=GetFile&DocumentAttachmentID=1236`⟩, 33

[148] Detter (as in n. 42 on page 105), 177.

[149] Michael Scott, The Tuna-Dolphin Controversy, Whalewatcher 30 1996

[150] Charnovitz (as in n. 127 on page 123), 265

[151] Stephen J Kobrin, *The Emergence of Private Authority in Global Governance* Cambridge: Cambridge University Press, 2002, chap. Economic Governance in Global Economy, 65

[152] Slaughter, Democratic Governance and International Law (as in n. 93 on page 25), 200; Perritt Jr (as in n. 116 on page 121), 899. The author also (at 895) argues that the Internet promotes acceptance of international law by states and aids in detecting violations and imposing sanctions.

[153] Ronald J Deibert, *Digital Democracy: Politics and Policy in the Wired World* New York: Oxford University Press, 1998, chap. Altered Worlds: Social Forces in the Hypermedia Environment, 6

ECOSOC and CONGO

Although most of the bodies and specialised agencies of the United Nations have regular dealings with NGOs, by far the largest number of NGOs that collaborate with the United Nations do so within the UN Economic and Social Council. Article 71 of the Charter of the United Nations states that ECOSOC

> may make suitable arrangements for consultation with non-governmental organizations which are concerned with matters within its competence. Such arrangements may be made with international organizations and, where appropriate, with national organizations after consultation with the Member of the United Nations concerned.

A framework to give effect to Article 71 was first entered into by resolution of ECOSOC in 1950, which has been amended twice by further resolutions in 1968 and 1996.[154] The 1996 resolution ("the resolution") seeks to achieve "a just, balanced, effective and genuine involvement of non-governmental organizations from all regions and areas of the world."[155]

An NGO may apply for consultative status to the ECOSOC Committee on NGOs if it satisfies the criteria set out in the resolution, including having been registered for at least two years, having an established headquarters, and not having been established or primarily funded by government.[156] The Committee, which is composed of 19 member states and meets twice per year, may then recommend to ECOSOC that it admit a qualifying NGO to consultative status in one of three tiers; general, special and roster.

The general tier is for large, global NGOs with a track record of contribution to the UN's objectives, such as Care International, Greenpeace and Rotary International. The special tier is for NGOs that are regional or otherwise specialised yet still well recognised within their fields, such as the Aboriginal and Torres Strait Islander Commission, Amnesty International and Reporters Without Borders. The roster tier is for organisations including the International Association of Literary Critics, the Islamic Shipowners Association and the World Chlorine Council, that don't qualify for either of the other tiers, perhaps because their focus is still narrower or more

---

[154]See generally Peter Willets, *"The Conscience of the World" The Influence of Non-Governmental Organisations in the UN System* London: Hurst & Company, 1996, chap. Consultative Status for NGOs at the UN.

[155]ECOSOC, Consultative Relationship Between the United Nations and Non-Governmental Organizations ⟨URL: `http://www.un.org/documents/ecosoc/res/1996/eres1996-31.htm`⟩, paragraph 5

[156]Ibid., paras 9–13

technical, but who can still make "occasional and useful contributions to the work of the Council or its subsidiary bodies."[157]

NGOs in the general tier may propose items for the provisional agenda of meetings of ECOSOC, submit written statements of up to 2000 words for circulation (if longer, a summary will be circulated), and request opportunities to make oral presentations. NGOs in the special tier may submit statements of up to 500 words in their fields of speciality for circulation, and the ECOSOC Committee on NGOs may also recommend to the Council that they be permitted to make oral presentations in those fields. All tiers of NGOs may attend public meetings of ECOSOC as observers, but those on the roster tier only when the meeting concerns matters within their field of competence.[158]

Similar provisions apply to meetings of commissions, subsidiary organs and ad-hoc committees of ECOSOC, with the addition that such organs may request an NGO with special competence in a particular field to "undertake specific studies or investigations or prepare specific papers for the commission."[159]

Organisations with or without consultative status may apply for accreditation to attend a United Nations conference, to the secretariat of the conference (but on the understanding that this "does not entail a negotiating role").[160]

All NGOs with consultative status must present a four-yearly (quadrennial) report on their activities focusing on their contributions to the work of the UN. Failure to provide an adequate quadrennial report can result in an NGO being demoted to a lower tier. Failure to make a "positive or effective contribution to the work of the United Nations" for three successive years is amongst the grounds upon which consultative status can be suspended or withdrawn altogether.[161]

ECOSOC was careful to state in its 1996 resolution that "the arrangements for consultation should not be such as to accord to non-governmental organizations the same rights of participation as are accorded to States," and that "arrangements should not be such as to overburden the Council or transform it from a body for coordination of policy and action, as contemplated in the Charter, into a general forum for discussion."[162]

Before concluding this section, brief mention will be made of the Conference of Non-Governmental Organizations in Consultative Relationship

---

[157]These are described in ECOSOC, Consultative Relationship Between the United Nations and Non-Governmental Organizations (as in n. 155 on the preceding page). In 2007 there were 136 NGOs in the general tier, 1955 in the special tier and 960 on the roster tier.

[158]Ibid., paras 28–32

[159]Ibid., paras 33–40

[160]Ibid., paras 42 and 50

[161]Ibid., paragraph 57

[162]Ibid., paras 18 and 19

with the United Nations (CONGO).[163] CONGO was established in 1948 as an association of NGOs involved in the work of the UN. As at 2008 it comprises 354 members holding consultative status with ECOSOC, as well as 50 associate members not yet with consultative status. All members form the General Assembly of CONGO, from which a President and a Board of 20 are elected.

The principal objective of CONGO is to facilitate the participation of NGOs in the UN system. Amongst its strategies to achieve this objective are training its members in the current arrangements for consultation with the UN, lobbying for reform of those arrangements, and practising outreach to organisations, particularly those in developing countries, who do not yet participate in the UN system. CONGO also has a number of thematic committees which bring together member organisations operating in similar fields to share information and cooperate in their work programmes.

New medievalism

The foregoing discussion of the contributions made not only by governments, but also by the private sector and civil society to the development of international law, are illustrative of the fact that the preeminence of the state's authority has receded since the zenith of the Westphalian age, and is continuing to do so.

In fact, as noted at section 1.3 on page 16, there are those who predict that the ongoing processes of cultural and economic globalisation, led by advances in information technology that erode the power of states (and equally indeed other territorially-based constructs such as national markets),[164] will lead to the increasing irrelevance of nation states.[165] The first signs of this can be seen in the development by non-state actors of their own regulatory arrangements, their own law-like standards, their own arbitration systems, and so on.

Rosenau describes the post-Westphalian age as "a multi-centric world composed of diverse 'sovereignty-free' collectivities [which] has evolved apart from and in competition with the state-centric world of 'sovereignty-bound' actors," and observes that the "authority of states is regarded as undergoing relocation to proliferating actors in the multi-centric world—either 'outwards' to supranational and transnational collectivities or 'inwards' to subnational actors."[166]

---

[163]See `http://www.ngocongo.org/`.

[164]Jean-Marie Guehenno, *The End of the Nation-State* Minneapolis: University of Minnesota Press, 1993; Matthews (as in n. 136 on page 124); Abbe Mowshowitz, *Beyond Calculation: The Next Fifty Years of Computing* New York: Springer-Verlag, 1997, chap. Virtual Feudalism

[165]Kobrin (as in n. 151 on page 126), 62; but see section 4.3 on page 272.

[166]James N Rosenau, *Governance Without Government: Order and Change in World Politics* Cambridge: Cambridge University Press, 1992, chap. Citizenship in a Changing Global Order, 282

Some have gone so far as to portend "the end of the nation state."[167] Hedley Bull, as long ago as 1977, in describing what he called a "neomedieval system" of international relations in emergence stated

> that the demise of the states system is taking place as a consequence of the technological unification of the world—of which the multinational corporations and the non-state groups which conduct international violence are only particular expressions, and which is bound to lead to the politics of "spaceship earth" or of the "global village" in which the states system is only a part.[168]

On this account, governance in the post-Westphalian age occurs through a system of networks between authorities with "overlapping and competing competencies"[169]—international bodies, governments, corporations, civil and political organisations and citizens, mediated by technology.

Like the Internet itself, such a system lacks a central point at which its lines of authority converge. The intersecting governance regimes are not naturally compatible, and there is great variation in their degrees of institutionalisation and legalisation. They have been described as "ungainly in the sense that they lack the hierarchical arrangements to which practitioners of politics have long been accustomed."[170]

Ungainly the new medieval system may be, but it is clearly not anarchistic, contrary to the dreams of Internet pioneers such as John Perry Barlow.[171] In fact a citizen of the neo-medieval world is subjected to more law rather than less (depending on how broadly one defines "law"; a question to be revisited at section 3.5 on page 175). It is again truly an age of legal pluralism, as it was before the Treaties of Westphalia reduced the overlapping spheres of medieval authority to the opaque billiard balls of state sovereignty.

The unavoidable ungainliness of the new medieval system is not its only fault. Perhaps more importantly, it is intrinsically less transparent than the Westphalian states system, at least in liberal states, which provide such protections as regular democratic elections, the separation of powers, judicial review and freedom of information legislation. It may also be less

---

[167]Slaughter, Democratic Governance and International Law (as in n. 93 on page 25), 199; Jan van Dijk, *Digital Democracy* London: Sage Publications, 2000, chap. Models of Democracy and Concepts of Communication, 33.

[168]Hedley Bull, *The Anarchical Society*, 2nd edition New York: Columbia University Press, 1977, 273.

[169]Jörg Friedrichs, *Governance and International Legal Theory* Leiden, The Netherlands: Martinus Nijhoff Publishers, 2004, chap. The Neomedieval Renaissance: Global Governance and International Law in the New Middle Ages, 3

[170]James N Rosenau, The Relocation of Authority in a Shrinking World, Comparative Politics 24:3 1992, 256

[171]Jayakar (as in n. 9 on page 4)

representative overall—or at least, less easily shown to be representative. Who is to say that a new regime of Internet governance that takes shape under the authority of a network of state and non-state actors, really represents the will of those whom it governs—or indeed the will of anyone at all?

Whilst these questions will come to be addressed,[172] it should at least be mooted at this point that our preference for governance by networks over the hegemony of state power may have been premature. Perhaps it is to be be hoped after all that rumours of the death of the nation state have been greatly exaggerated.[173] After all, as we have seen it remains possible for governance to be exercised by rules, albeit with certain limitations and difficulties. As Rosenau puts it:

> Because public order still needs to be maintained, because economies still need a modicum of management, because justice still needs to be dispensed, because systemwide laws still need to be framed and administered, because the resources necessary to carry out these tasks still need to be generated—because there is still a need, in other words, for polities that attend to the demands of societies—there is no reason to anticipate a diminution in the competence of states and their international system to the point where they are irrelevant actors on the world stage.[174]

On this more moderate view, it is not so much the death of states that is heralded by the new medieval age, but rather the fact that they will no longer be privileged over other actors in international fora. They are neither capable of being so privileged, as the governance of many transnational issues is literally outside their competence,[175] nor are they entitled to be so privileged, as their legitimate authority does not extend to those who have neither participated in nor consented to their lawmaking.[176] States are now required, not merely as a matter of courtesy or protocol, but as a linchpin of their legitimacy and therefore their authority, to cooperate with other international actors as equal partners.[177]

---

[172]See section 4.3 on page 226.

[173]Timothy S Wu, Cyberspace Sovereignty? The Internet And The International System, Harv J Law & Tech 10:647 1997

[174]Rosenau, The Relocation of Authority in a Shrinking World (as in n. 170 on the preceding page), 256

[175]See section 3.4 on page 157.

[176]See section 3.4 on page 145.

[177]David Held, *Democracy and the Global Order: From the Modern State to Cosmopolitan Governance* Cambridge: Polity Press, 1995, 22–23

3.3 Sources of international law

Less time needs to be spent discussing the sources of international law than was spent on discussing its actors or subjects. In fact international relations theorists do not even employ a concept of the sources of international law, distinct from the actors who constitute it.[178]

International lawyers on the other hand, having traditionally decreed that states were the only subjects of international law, accordingly determined that international treaties and customary law to which state consent could be traced were its only sources.[179]

The conceptual usefulness of such a narrow view has been limited, even leaving aside most of the implications of new medievalism, and accordingly scholars have found it necessary to expand it. They have done this by drawing a distinction between hard law and soft law, as briefly alluded to in the Introduction.[180]

As might be expected, the divide between hard law and soft law is in reality a continuum. One group of authors has defined three variables of obligation, precision, and delegation by which the hardness or "legalisation" of international law can be measured.[181] Obligation is the extent to which the compliance or non-compliance of states (or, as a slight gloss, international actors) with a rule is subject to scrutiny by international and/or domestic legal institutions. Precision is the degree to which the rule in question is capable of expression in a certain and unambiguous form. Delegation exists where a neutral body has been authorised to implement (for example, to interpret or enforce) the rule in question.

An example of international law which is high on every dimension is the TRIPS convention: it is strongly obligatory, being enforceable through the WTO's Dispute Settlement Process, it is drafted with a high degree of precision, and the determination of a state's compliance or otherwise with the convention has been delegated to the Dispute Settlement Body.

An example which is low on every dimension is the obligation that participants in WSIS assumed when they agreed, for example, to "commit ourselves to promote the inclusion of all peoples in the Information Society through the development and use of local and/or indigenous languages in ICTs."[182] The compliance of individual states with this undertaking is not monitored, the content of the obligation is highly imprecise, and although

---

[178]Cutler, *Private Power and Global Authority: Transnational Merchant Law in the Global Political Economy* (as in n. 76 on page 21), 77

[179]Ibid., 21

[180]See section 1.4 on page 21.

[181]Kenneth W Abbot et al., The Concept of Legalization, International Organization 54:3 2000, 404–406

[182]WSIS, Tunis Commitment ⟨URL: `http://www.itu.int/wsis/docs2/tunis/off/7.html`⟩, paragraph 32

there is a WSIS follow-up process,[183] no legal consequences flow from it for participants who fail to implement the commitment.

Hard law

Even leaving soft law aside for now, the breadth of sources of law that traditional hard law encompasses is in itself considerable. Article 38 of the Statute of the International Court of Justice is often used as a codification of the sources of international law. It provides:

1. The Court, whose function is to decide in accordance with international law such disputes as are submitted to it, shall apply:

   a) international conventions, whether general or particular, establishing rules expressly recognised by the contracting States;
   b) international custom, as evidence of a general practice accepted as law;
   c) the general principles of law recognised by civilised nations;
   d) subject to the provisions of Article 59, judicial decisions and the teachings of the most highly qualified publicists of the various nations, as subsidiary means for the determination of rules of law.

2. This provision shall not prejudice the power of the Court to decide a case *ex aequo et bono*,[184] if the parties agree thereto.

3. These sources will be examined in turn, save for judicial decisions and juristic writings as these are merely subsidiary means for the determination of the content of international law.

International conventions

International conventions range from bilateral agreements, such as extradition treaties and the Australia–United States Fair Trade Agreement, through to multilateral agreements such as the Geneva Conventions to which almost all countries of the world are signatories. A treaty or convention only has the status of international law for those states that have signed and ratified it. How this is accomplished, and the effect its ratification may have in local law, is a domestic matter that varies from one jurisdiction to another.

In Australia, treaties and conventions may be ratified by the Federal Cabinet, without the need for the passage of legislation or to be debated in

---

[183] See section 5.1 on page 351.

[184] "In justice and fairness."

Parliament. However since 1996, a policy has been adopted requiring a treaty to be tabled in both houses of Parliament for 15 sitting days, for a Parliamentary Joint Standing Committee on Treaties to engage in public consultation concerning the proposed ratification of the treaty, and a National Interest Analysis in respect of the treaty to be prepared, before it is ratified.[185]

In order to comply with its obligations under the instrument in question, it will then usually be necessary for the government to introduce legislation into Parliament which will be debated in the usual manner. This is also necessary in order for the instrument to have any effect in Australian law, other than as a general guide for the exercise of executive discretion and statutory interpretation.[186] This differs from the position in certain other jurisdictions, such as the United States, although there the President requires the concurrence of two-thirds of the Senate before entering into a treaty.[187]

International custom

Customary international law is found where there is both a "common, consistent and concordant"[188] pattern of behaviour amongst states, without substantial dissent from other states,[189] coupled with the acknowledgment that the practice is observed because it is as a legal obligation; or in law Latin, that *opinio juris sive necessitatis* or simply *opinio juris* is present.[190] *Opinio juris* (and indeed some evidence of state practice) can in appropriate cases be determined from the declarations that a state makes in international fora,[191] from its domestic legislative, executive and judicial institutions, and even from the existence of a treaty on the topic that other states have ratified but that it has not.[192]

Therefore in simple terms, it could be said that customary international law is law because it is regarded as such by international actors.[193] More so than domestic law, it is thus a social construction, since its very existence depends on the subjective beliefs of the actors who comply with it. In

[185] Commonwealth of Australia, Review of the Treaty Making Process ⟨URL: `http://www.austlii.edu.au/au/other/dfat/reports/review_treaty_making.html`⟩

[186] *Minister for Immigration and Ethnic Affairs v Teoh* (1995) 183 CLR 273

[187] *Constitution of the United States of America*, 17 Sep 1787, Article VI and Article II, section 2

[188] *Fisheries Jurisdiction Case (United Kingdom v Iceland) (Merits)* [1974] ICJ Reports 3, 50

[189] *Case Concerning Military and Paramilitary Activities in and against Nicaragua (Nicaragua v United States of America) (Merits)* [1986] ICJ Reports 14, 98

[190] *Polyukhovich v The Commonwealth* (1991) 172 CLR 501, 559–560

[191] Benjamin Langille, It's "Instant Custom": How the Bush Doctrine Became Law After the Terrorist Attacks of September 11, 2001, B C Int'l & Comp L Rev 26:1 2001, 151–152

[192] *North Sea Continental Shelf Cases (Federal Republic of Germany v Denmark; Federal Republic of Germany v Netherlands)* [1969] ICJ Reports 3, 41

[193] Arend (as in n. 75 on page 21), 33.

that respect, the process for formation of customary international law does not seem so very different from the New Haven approach referred to at section 3.1 on page 98, according to which international law is found wherever there is a confluence of authority (that is, where a decision is perceived to be made legitimately by those whom it purports to cover) and control (that is, the decision does in fact influence their behaviour). In New Haven terms, control equates to state practice and authority to something like *opinio juris.*[194]

Much of what begins as customary law ends up being codified by treaty, as for example in the case of the rules of war that are now found in the Geneva Conventions. However, new customary international law is in the process of formation all the time, and there are circumstances in which this can take place extremely quickly. The International Court of Justice itself has noted:

> With regard to the time factor, the formation of law by State practice has in the past frequently been associated with the passage of a long period of time. There is no doubt that in some cases this may be justified.
>
> However, the great acceleration of social and economic change, combined with that of science and technology, have confronted law with a serious challenge: one it must meet, lest it lag even farther behind events than it has been wont to do.
>
> To give a concrete example: the first instruments that man sent into outer space traversed the airspace of States and circled above them in outer space, yet the launching States sought no permission, nor did the other States protest. This is how the freedom of movement into outer space, and in it, came to be established and recognized as law within a remarkably short period of time. Similar developments are affecting, or may affect, other branches of international law.[195]

To give a more recent example of this, following the 11 September 2001 terrorist attacks on New York City and Washington DC, United States President George W Bush declared that in bringing those responsible to justice, "we will make no distinction between the terrorists who committed these acts and those who harbor them." Subsequently dubbed the "Bush Doctrine," this principle has since been affirmed by resolutions of the United Nations General Assembly and Security Council and begun to be acted upon by states. On one account, it thereby became a new principle of "instant" customary international law.[196]

---

[194] Where New Haven scholars diverge from orthodoxy is of course in contending that non-state actors can be involved in this process.

[195] *North Sea Continental Shelf Cases,* 230 per Lachs J

[196] Langille (as in n. 191 on the preceding page)

On this basis, it is certainly possible for norms of Internet governance to become customary international law in the orthodox sense quite quickly. In such cases, sufficient evidence of state practice and *opinio juris* may simply take the form of each affected state communicating their recognition of the practice as customary law, or by means of a resolution of a body such as the General Assembly of the United Nations.[197]

Whilst there is doubt as to whether the new law merchant can be said to have made this transition (it is, after all, largely created and observed by non-state actors),[198] the early and full involvement of states in the IGF (and through the GAC in ICANN) may make many of the norms of Internet governance more promising candidates for promotion to the status of international law.[199] This question will be reconsidered in the conclusion to this chapter.

General principles of law

Little need be said about the general principles of law that form another source of hard international law, save that they are thought to include the principles of equity and estoppel, which are broadly comparable to those concepts as known in common law jurisdictions, and provide a moderating influence on the strict application of the law in cases where it is necessary to avoid unfairness.[200]

Some would also include within this category the *jus cogens*—literally, compelling law—which Article 53 of the Vienna Convention defines as "a peremptory norm of general international law ... accepted and recognised by the international community of states as a whole as a norm from which no derogation is permitted and which can be modified only by a subsequent norm of general international law having the same character."[201] Examples include the prohibitions upon torture, slavery, piracy and genocide.

Soft law

The fora in which treaty law is developed are in general highly bureaucratised and subject to much diplomatic formality. Often it can be slow and expensive at best, and practically impossible at worst, to conclude treaties

---

[197] E R C Van Bogaert, *Aspects of Space Law* The Hague: Kluwer Law International, 1986, 20

[198] Zamora (as in n. 123 on page 122); C M Chinkin, The Challenge of Soft Law: Development and Change in International Law, ICLQ 38:4 1989, 857

[199] Biegel (as in n. 60 on page 19), 172

[200] Margaret White, Equity—A General Principle of Law Recognised by Civilised Nations?, QUTLJJ 4 2004

[201] *Vienna Convention on the Law of Treaties*, 23 May 1969, 1974 ATS No 2 (entry into force 27 Jan 1980)

in such fora.[202] Once made, treaty law is also (by design) difficult to avoid when circumstances change.[203]

On the other hand the degree of "legalisation" of customary international law is often lower than desirable for purposes of certainty, and its content is more difficult to control, only being susceptible to conclusive determination by a judgment of the International Court of Justice.

Soft law can overcome many of the shortcomings of both these types of hard law.[204] The difference between soft law and hard law is akin to the difference between guiding principles and binding rules. Whereas hard law is consummated through diplomacy, soft law is developed through the exercise of "soft power," which is characterised by more horizontal power relationships in which consensus can be built, and by the exchange of information rather than the use of threats and rewards.[205]

Soft law is cheaper and easier to establish than hard law, and offers greater scope for the participation of international actors other than states.[206] The flexible and adaptive nature of soft law is also an attraction, since for the private sector voluntary codes of conduct and private arbitration are a "softer touch" than black-letter regulation and national court systems, and for states soft law leaves them more room for "cheating," and is thus less restrictive of their sovereignty.[207]

Three of the principal forms of soft law are resolutions and declarations of international bodies, codes and model laws, and standards. These will briefly be examined in turn.

Resolutions

Resolutions and declarations of intergovernmental meetings such as the General Assembly of the UN and WSIS are by nature not binding in nature. However they are regarded as a form of soft law, used to guide the behaviour of states both internationally and domestically. For example, General Assembly resolutions can be used to establish state practice and *opinio juris* as a precondition of the recognition of new customary interna-

[202]Negotiations towards a new protocol to the UN Framework Convention on Climate Change, and the stalled Dohor Development Round of WTO talks, provide two contemporary examples.

[203]Cutler, *Private Power and Global Authority: Transnational Merchant Law in the Global Political Economy* (as in n. 76 on page 21), 23

[204]Strictly, this section describes what is tautologically described as "non-legal" soft law. "Legal" soft law can in fact include treaties, albeit treaties that are so vaguely worded that they impose no discernible obligations on their signatories: Ferguson and Mansbach (as in n. 13 on page 100), 851.

[205]Slaughter, The Role of Law in International Politics (as in n. 93 on page 25)

[206]Cutler, *Private Power and Global Authority: Transnational Merchant Law in the Global Political Economy* (as in n. 76 on page 21), 23

[207]Idem, The Emergence of Private Authority in Global Governance (as in n. 124 on page 122), 35

tional law,[208] are authoritative on questions within the General Assembly's competence such as the interpretation of the UN Charter,[209] and can be used as a guide to the interpretation of municipal law.[210]

Pre-eminent in its impact amongst all declarations of the General Assembly, and perhaps amongst all instruments of soft law of any kind, is the Universal Declaration on Human Rights, proclaimed in 1948.[211] Although not binding, the Declaration strongly influenced the first two major treaties on human rights that followed, the International Covenant on Civil and Political Rights,[212] and the International Covenant on Economic, Social and Cultural Rights.[213]

Similar resolutions and declarations are also regularly made by NGOs, such as the International Law Association (ILA) and the Institut de Droit International/Institute of International Law (IIL).[214] The accession of international actors to such documents constitutes them as forms of soft law,[215] which much like resolutions of the General Assembly, can have a similar influence upon the later formation of *opinio juris* and the development of treaty law. Thus the United Nations' International Law Commission has acknowledged that these private bodies have "had a considerable effect on the development of international law."[216]

Codes

A code in soft law may take a number of forms. It may simply be a draft treaty; that is, a document that, if it were eventually signed and ratified, would become an ordinary treaty, but in respect of which "the law has not yet been sufficiently developed in the practice of States" for that to occur.[217] The progressive development of international law in this manner

[208] *Case Concerning Military and Paramilitary Activities in and against Nicaragua (Nicaragua v United States of America) (Merits)* [1986] ICJ Reports 14

[209] *Case Concerning East Timor (Portugal v Australia)* [1995] ICJ Reports 90

[210] They would naturally be less persuasive than a treaty that Australia had actually ratified: *Minister for Immigration and Ethnic Affairs v Teoh* (1995) 183 CLR 273.

[211] General Assembly of the United Nations, Universal Declaration of Human Rights ⟨URL: `http://www.un.org/Overview/rights.html`⟩

[212] *International Covenant on Civil and Political Rights*, 16 Dec 1966, 1980 ATS No 23 (entry into force for Australia (except Article 41) 23 Mar 1976)

[213] *International Covenant on Economic, Social and Cultural Rights*, 16 Dec 1966, 1976 ATS No 5 (entry into force for Australia 10 Mar 1976)

[214] See `http://www.idi-iil.org/`, not to be confused with the International Law Institute, an unrelated American educational institution; see `http://www.ili.org/`.

[215] Anthony D'Amato and Kirsten Engel, *International Environmental Law Anthology* Cincinatti: Andersen Publishing Company, 1996, 55–60

[216] International Law Commission, Introduction—International Law Commission ⟨URL: `http://untreaty.un.org/ilc/ilcintro.htm`⟩

[217] Ibid.

is one of the two objects of the International Law Commission, which was established by the General Assembly of the UN in 1947.

Secondly, a code may be a codification of existing law, which was the second object with which the International Law Commission was formed. Codification is "the more precise formulation and systematization of rules of international law in fields where there already has been extensive State practice, precedent and doctrine."[218] Naturally, the signature and ratification of such a code by states would effect its promotion to hard law and supplant the underlying customary international rules for those states.

Third, a code may be in the form of a recommendation (or a "code of conduct," "guideline," etc), which is conceptually much like a resolution, but in a more legalised form similar to that of a treaty. A body may conclude a recommendation rather than a treaty because a treaty is beyond its competence, as in the case of an NGO or the General Assembly of the UN,[219] or because the subject matter of the recommendation is too far in advance of the actual practice of states, as is commonly the case with recommendations of the ILO and WIPO. A good example of this is WIPO's *Joint Recommendation Concerning Provisions on the Protection of Marks, and Other Industrial Property Rights in Signs, on the Internet.*[220]

The European Commission can issue non-binding recommendations to member states, in place of its hard law regulations or directives.[221] The EU Commission also issues other soft law instruments to its member states and other EU organs that are not explicitly provided for in the EU treaties, including guidelines and communications.[222]

Fourth, a code may be a model law; this is a somewhat stronger form of a recommendation in that it is intended for direct adoption or incorporation by states into domestic law, with a view to harmonising national legislation. One of the most active intergovernmental bodies engaged in drafting codes of this nature today is UNCITRAL, whose 1996 *Model Law on Electronic Commerce*[223] formed the basis of Australia's *Electronic Transactions Act 2001* (Cth). Its *Model Law on International Commercial Arbitration* has also been received into a number of public and private legal systems, including the law of Canada.[224]

---

[218] International Law Commission (as in n. 216 on the preceding page)

[219] Detter (as in n. 42 on page 105), 218–219.

[220] WIPO, Joint Recommendation Concerning the Protection of Marks and Other Industrial Property Rights in Signs on the Internet (as in n. 201 on page 77)

[221] Directives are slightly softer than regulations, in that they prescribe a minimum standard that a member state's laws must adhere to, without dictating their form, and may contain provisions from which a state is permitted to "opt out."

[222] Various examples can be accessed at `http://ec.europa.eu/information_society/topics/telecoms/regulatory/maindocs/comgreen/text_en.htm`.

[223] UNCITRAL, UNCITRAL Model Law on Electronic Commerce (as in n. 275 on page 89)

[224] A Claire Cutler, *Canadian Foreign Policy and International Economic Regimes* Vancouver: University of British Columbia Press, 1992, chap. Canada and the Private International Trade

UNIDROIT, the International Institute for the Unification of Private Law,[225] is another intergovernmental organisation involved in drafting models laws, as well as other forms of hard and soft law including its codification of contract law, the UNIDROIT Principles of International Commercial Contracts.[226]

Of the four types of codes examined, three of them—draft treaties, recommendations and model laws—offer a template for multi-stakeholder Internet governance, in that while non-state actors are not precluded from drafting them, they are readily able to be received into hard law, whether that be by treaty or by custom. This is not simply a hypothetical observation. For example, the International Commercial Terms (or "Incoterms") are a code drafted by the International Chamber of Commerce that is almost universally incorporated into transnational commercial contracts, to such an extent that it has arguably begun to evolve into customary international law.[227]

Standards

Standards are much like codes in the "recommendation" sense, but may be distinguished from these in that they fall within the standards development sphere of governance, rather than the sphere of public policy governance; in other words, standards are usually documents of technical specification, that do not explicitly (but may implicitly) engage issues of public policy.

The development of international standards is consequently seen as a form of "low politics"; that is, a realm of politics that does not strike at the core security concerns of states.[228] States are therefore more ready to delegate the development of standards to bodies that include non-state members, such as the ISO and ITU, than they would be willing to so delegate matters of "high politics" such as trade or defence policy.

Although treated here as a species of soft law, international standards can also be found in hard law, such as the *Metric Convention Treaty*,[229] and

---

Law Regime, which contains a review of the central role of the private sector in the unification of trade law in Canada.

[225]See `http://www.unidroit.org/`.

[226]UNIDROIT, UNIDROIT Principles of International Commercial Contracts ⟨URL: `http://www.unidroit.org/english/principles/contracts/principles2004/blackletter2004.pdf`⟩

[227]Michael C Rowe, *The Transnational Law of International Commercial Transactions* Deventer: Kluwer Law International, 1982, chap. The Contribution of the ICC to the Development of International Trade Law; but compare Hans van Houtte, *The Law of International Trade* London: Sweet & Maxwell, 1995, 151.

[228]Arend (as in n. 75 on page 21), 123.

[229]*Convention Concerning the Creation of an International Office of Weights and Measures*, 20 May 1875, 1947 ATS No 22 (entry into force 20 Dec 1875) (Metric Convention)

in customary international law, such as those standards promulgated by specialised agencies such as the ICAO and IMO.[230]

However the majority of international standards—*de facto* standards as opposed to the *de jure* standards of hard law[231]—are soft law because of their non-binding nature. This is the category into which Internet standards fall, as whilst it is convenient that all countries in the world use the same DNS root servers, it has never been suggested that China would be in breach of international law for establishing its own servers in competition to those of the official root.[232]

There is no uniform mechanism, analogous to ratification, by which a state is required to adopt an international standard that is not contained in a treaty. It may incorporate the standard by reference in domestic legislation or policy, but equally the state may have no involvement in a country's adoption of a standard at all, its adoption being purely left to market forces. Neither is there any legal distinction between the adoption of a standard promulgated by a public standards body such as the Codex Alimentarius[233] or the International Organisation of Legal Metrology,[234] and that of an NGO such as IETF or the W3C.

For example, Standards Australia which serves as the peak standards body for Australia is non-governmental, although it receives government funding. As at 2006 there were 6850 published Australian standards, about 2400 of which were referenced in legislation or delegated legislation by Australian governments.[235] ITU standards are also referenced directly in Commonwealth regulations such as the *Radiocommunictions Regulations 1993* (Cth). Internet standards of the IETF and W3C are not explicitly specified in any Australian legislation, but have been recognised at an executive level.[236]

Private law

Both categories of sources of international law considered above, hard law and soft law, are sources of public international law. Private international

[230] These have the force of customary law because the standards in question, such as the IMO's International Code of Signals, can be considered binding even on states that are not members of the IMO, due to their importance to international air and maritime safety: IMO, International Code of Signals ⟨URL: `http://www.gyc.com/ICOSbook.pdf`⟩.

[231] Crocker (as in n. 92 on page 54)

[232] Michael Geist, China and the Break-Up of the Net ⟨URL: `http://news.bbc.co.uk/1/hi/technology/4779660.stm`⟩

[233] See `http://www.codexalimentarius.net/`.

[234] See `http://www.oiml.org/`.

[235] Productivity Commission, Standard Setting and Laboratory Accreditation ⟨URL: `http://www.pc.gov.au/__data/assets/pdf_file/0012/11325/standards.pdf`⟩, 38

[236] For example in the Australian Government Web Publishing Guide at `http://webpublishing.agimo.gov.au/`.

law is traditionally considered something else entirely. In fact, some scholars take the view that it is a misnomer to call it international law at all, since the conflict of laws rules used to determine which state's law should apply to an international dispute are domestic, and so are the laws that it is eventually decided should apply.[237]

Whilst this observation may be true, it implicitly limits the scope of international law to its traditional narrower sense of relations between states. If states are not the only international actors, and public law is not the only law, then private international law is indeed international law, and the private sector, not states, are its principal players.[238] This is particularly so when considering private international law not simply as a regime of conflict of laws, but as an independent and private source of governance which co-exists with (and may also be adopted into) national legal systems or hard international law, as for example in the case of the international commercial arbitration regime.[239]

Even in the narrower sense in which private international law is restricted to rules of conflict of laws, these rules can be seen as limitations on state sovereignty, in that they define the extent to which a state's authority extends to private arrangements made in the transnational arena. This alone gives them the quintessential character of public international law.

Private international law in this narrower sense will fall for consideration later in the discussion of the jurisdictional limitations of international law,[240] whilst private law in the broader sense of transnational law will be discussed here.

Transnational law

An outline of the content of transnational law—or at least, that subset of it found in the new law merchant—has been given at section 3.2 on page 118, but it has not been precisely defined. For present purposes, transnational law comprises those forms of international governance that exist apart from formal state or intergovernmental institutions, or as Rosenau puts it, "regulatory mechanisms in a sphere of activity which function effectively even though they are not endowed with formal authority."[241]

It was foreshadowed above that we would here revisit the question of whether such law can be considered to be international law proper. In the

---

[237] P E Nygh, *Conflict of Laws in Australia*, 6th edition Sydney: Butterworths, 1995, 4

[238] See Cutler, *Private Power and Global Authority: Transnational Merchant Law in the Global Political Economy* (as in n. 76 on page 21), 32–54; Mark W Janis, Why Do We Continue to Distinguish Between Public and Private International Law?, Am Soc'y Int'l L Proc 79 1985

[239] Cutler, *Private Power and Global Authority: Transnational Merchant Law in the Global Political Economy* (as in n. 76 on page 21), 40

[240] See section 3.4 on page 157.

[241] Rosenau, Governance Without Government: Order and Change in World Politics (as in n. 64 on page 19), 5

absence of sufficient evidence of state practice and *opinio juris* to support its elevation into customary international law, the answer has to be that it cannot, in conventional terms. At most, individual rules or specific regimes may attain that status, but not the full corpus of transnational law.

But the very fact that we must consider the legal status of *private* law in terms of whether sufficient evidence of *state* practice has been amassed reveals the perversity of the exercise and how impoverished the conventional understanding of international law is. Twining writes,

> A *ius humanitatis*, a transnational *lex mercatoria*, Islamic law, transnational humanitarian and human rights law, and, in a different way, some new regional orderings, and even parts of public international law itself are all arguably more or less clear examples of the amorphous category "non-state law." ... [A]n account of the phenomenon of law in the contemporary world would for most purposes be incomplete if it did not treat of [these] legal families and legal cultures.[242]

Whilst one might demur at whether some of these examples do or should have the status of law, the criteria by which their claim to do so can be assessed should surely be capable of empirical assessment, rather than turning upon a formalistic Westphalian doctrine that only admits of laws made by or agreed between governments as law. So, what is law, fundamentally?

H L A Hart's classic examination of this question in *The Concept of Law* concluded that a legal system is a system of primary and secondary rules—primary rules governing conduct that are generally obeyed by the citizens, and secondary rules governing how primary rules are made, amended, repealed, interpreted etc, that are accepted by public officials.[243] But Hart did not claim to offer a definitive definition of law,[244] and indeed he did not do so, as by his own concession his conclusions were problematic for international law which lacked many of the features of a fully developed legal system, yet was widely recognised as law.

A more recent attempt to accommodate diverse legal phenomena within a single framework is Tamanaha's *A General Jurisprudence of Law and Society*, in which he reassesses Hart, abstracts out some of the conceptual underpinnings of his *Concept of Law*, and concludes simply that "Law is whatever people identify and treat through their social practices as law."[245] If this sounds familiar, it may be the echo of the authority and control test of the New Haven School, or even the *opinio juris* test for the existence of custom-

[242] William Twining, *Globalisation and Legal Theory* London: Butterworths, 2000, 52
[243] H L A Hart, *The Concept of Law*, 2nd edition Oxford: Clarendon Press, 1987, 116
[244] Ibid., 213
[245] Brian Z Tamanaha, *A General Jurisprudence of Law and Society* Oxford: Oxford University Press, 2001, 194

ary international law, as all of these are to a large degree restatements of the same recurrent theme, expressed with greater or lesser generality.

On this basis, it can be concluded that whilst transnational law may not be international law as such, the formal defining criteria of international law are too narrow to be complete (or perhaps even useful) in the post-Westphalian age, as they leave a gaping hole between international law and domestic law, for which there is no conceptually consistent reason, and to which orthodox international lawyers are wilfully blind.

The concept of transnational law *as law* fills that hole, allowing non-state actors and their private law the conceptual place in international society that they already, plainly, possess in fact. This is even beginning to be recognised within the United Nations. As Fernando Cardoso, Chair of the High Level Panel on UN–Civil Society, commented in 2003:

> This on-going process of building a cosmopolitan law represented a great leap towards a world order that is not based on the uncontested will of sovereign states, but on universally agreed principles and norms. In a major break with the past, individuals were acknowledged as subjects not only of national law, but also of cosmopolitan rules, enforceable by transnational institutions.[246]

The relevance of this conclusion is that it greatly broadens the potential lawmaking role of the IGF, since it is primarily transnational law, and only incidentally (if at all) international law, that is the product of public policy governance by network.[247]

3.4 Limitations of international law

The international (and similarly the transnational) lawmaker is faced with a number of problems and limitations that do not face the domestic lawmaker to the same extent. Not the least of these is the very legitimacy of the exercise itself. Whereas the domestic lawmaker inherits the legitimacy of the national legal system by which she was appointed or elected, from what source do lawmakers in international arena, particularly non-state actors, gain their legitimacy? If their constituents can be identified, what checks and balances are in place on an international level to ensure that they are accountable to those constituents?

Once this has been settled, the lawmaker then encounters very significant substantive problems in reconciling the transnational character of

[246] Cardoso, Civil Society and Global Governance (as in n. 133 on page 124), 3

[247] Even so, to avoid confusion this will be described in future chapters as a "policy-setting" rather than a "lawmaking" role: see section 6.2 on page 420.

the lawmaking to which she is called with the legacy of the Westphalian system. Both legal questions of jurisdiction, and practical problems of enforcement loom large.

Even the use of soft law does not overcome all of these difficulties. Say that a model law is drafted to be adopted into the legal systems of any states that choose to do so. How would such a law take account of the differences between legal systems of different heritage, such as common law and civil law (or indeed Islamic law)? How could a law of uniform content bridge the ideological differences between East and West, or indeed North and South?

These difficult questions will now be examined, although answers cannot be provided to all of them. Problems and limitations of other forms of large-scale decision-making outside the international public policy arena will not be considered here, but will be discussed in Chapter 4.

The legitimacy of authority

Calls for broader participation in transnational public policy-making generally flow from criticisms either of the effectiveness, or the legitimacy (or both), of those processes when dominated by intergovernmental bodies. The question of the effectiveness of rule-based governance has already been dealt with at some length in previous chapters and will be revisited at section 3.4 on page 157,[248] but the issue of legitimacy will be addressed here.

Authority and legitimacy are closely related concepts. One simple definition of authority is that it is legitimised power.[249] That authority can be multi-layered is not a novel concept, even to the Westphalian international lawyer; since even assuming that the nation state is autonomous within its sphere, authority is also exercised at other levels ranging from the family, the church congregation, the classroom and the workplace, to the market and the intergovernmental arena.[250] Naturally the governance exercised at

---

[248]For a broader taxonomy of variables impacting upon the effectiveness of international institutions, both endogenous and exogenous to the institutional arrangements in question, see Oran R Young, *Governance Without Government: Order and Change in World Politics* Cambridge: Cambridge University Press, 1992, chap. The Effectiveness of International Institutions: Hard Cases and Critical Variables.

[249]Helen Milner, The Assumption of Anarchy in International Relations: A Critique, Review of International Studies 17:1 1991. Another is that it is effective governance: Ferguson and Mansbach (as in n. 13 on page 100), 376. The difference between the two definitions is mostly one of focus—on the legitimacy of the authority in the first case, and its effectiveness in the second. Yet neither definition is entirely satisfactory. As to the first, it is possible, at least for the legal positivist, for law to exist that is illegitimate; but it would be inaccurate to say that such law necessarily lacks authority. As to the second definition, Rosenau at least would regard it as tautologous; see Rosenau, Governance Without Government: Order and Change in World Politics (as in n. 64 on page 19), 5.

[250]Idem, The Relocation of Authority in a Shrinking World (as in n. 170 on page 130), 259

each level is not necessarily of the same type—governance by rules may predominate at one level, by norms at another, and so on—yet they can all be equally legitimate in their respective spheres.

Understanding this, the concepts of legitimacy and effectiveness can be brought back together, in that legitimacy is one of the factors that makes authority effective. The legitimacy of an actor is that which induces those to whom it addresses its authority, to accept it. Thus Franck speaks of legitimacy in an international law context as

> a property of a rule or a rule-making institution which itself exerts a pull towards compliance on those addressed normatively because those addressed believe that the rule has come into being and operates in accordance with generally accepted principles of right process.[251]

In a broader context, this is the "belief in legality" which Max Weber isolated in 1909 as the main ground of legitimacy for a social order, and which forms the basis for legal (sometimes called "legal-rational") authority. The three other sources of legitimacy identified by Weber were tradition (upon which "traditional authority" rests), affectual faith (based on an emotional response to the charismatic authority of a leader), and value-rational faith (in which the validity of the authority has been deduced as an absolute—natural law is given as an example).[252]

Thus for Weber, different forms of legitimacy can ground the exercise of authority in the three spheres of state, economy and society. So it is too, in the present context, that the three stakeholder groups who dominate those spheres—governments, the private sector, and civil society—draw their legitimacy as actors in transnational public policy governance from different sources.

It is for this reason that moves to involve the private sector and civil society in transnational governance are intended to do more than plug the holes in the representativeness of intergovernmental fora. That would imply that a single stakeholder group would suffice if only the group's composition could be made adequately representative. Rather, the effect of such reforms is to balance the legitimacy of the government stakeholders with those of the other groups.

What, then, are the sources of legitimacy from which the three stakeholder groups draw their authority? This question will now be addressed, taking each stakeholder group in turn.

---

[251] T M Franck, *The Power of Legitimacy Among Nations* Oxford: Oxford University Press, 1990, 16.

[252] Max Weber, *Economy and Society: An Outline of Interpretive Sociology*, edited by Guenther Roth and Claus Wittich New York: Bedminster Press, 1968, 36–37, 215

Governments

As the legitimacy of individual states in transnational governance and that of intergovernmental organisations differ conceptually, they will be treated here in turn, beginning with that of states.

Since Westphalia, states drew their legitimacy from their claims of territorial sovereignty, which for Weber is a form of traditional authority.[253] It is on this basis too that states claimed a monopoly on the legitimate use of international violence.[254] One of the characteristics of traditional authority is that citizens' recognition of the state's authority is largely habitual,[255] so that states do not actually need to exercise physical coercion in order to secure widespread compliance.

Increasingly however, in the post-Westphalian age, states must ground their legitimacy in something more than tradition, by showing that their authority has been conferred democratically (which is a legal-rational basis, for Weber). For example, democratic rule is now an important criterion for the recognition of a new state, particularly if it wishes to exercise the unfettered right to participate in international affairs.[256] The primary ground upon which a state authority is now seen as legitimate is therefore that its government represents the interests of its citizens.

This is not to say however that the state fully and transparently represents all of the interests of its citizens, for if it did there might be no need of the other other three stakeholder groups. To so argue would assume that once the people have vested their authority in the state, they have somehow disposed of it altogether. The contrary position is that there remains "the possibility of authority and legitimacy being relocated and the right to engage in coercive action thereby being redefined."[257] For one thing, the Internet has facilitated citizens' creation of and participation in new transnational civil society networks which coincide with no one state's territorial reach.

True it is that a state can still indirectly exercise control over such civil society networks by reason of its authority over those of the networks' members within its borders, but for it to do so is no more a legitimate exercise of its authority than it would be for the European Commission

[253]See also Ferguson and Mansbach (as in n. 13 on page 100), 370.

[254]Though as noted above this monopoly has to a large extent been formally ceded to the United Nations Security Council pursuant to articles 24, 25 and 33 of its charter.

[255]Ibid., 381

[256]See Detter (as in n. 42 on page 105), 73; Gregory H Fox, *Democratic Governance and International Law* Cambridge: Cambridge University Press, 2000, chap. The Right to Political Participation in International Law, 90; Sean D Murphy, *Democratic Governance and International Law* Cambridge: Cambridge University Press, 2000, chap. Democratic Legitimacy and the Recognition of States and Governments, 153, Susan Marks, *Democratic Governance and International Law* Cambridge: Cambridge University Press, 2000, chap. International Law, Democracy and the End of History, 548.

[257]Rosenau, The Relocation of Authority in a Shrinking World (as in n. 170 on page 130), 258

to seek to control the participation of EU member states in the United Nations. Citizens, like states, can divide their loyalties, and the civil society networks that they choose to participate in, also like states, are social entities in themselves, more than just the sums of their members.[258] Such transnational social entities are not legitimate subjects of any territorially-based authority. Post writes:

> The proper presumption for a Liberal theory would seem to be a presumption of a-territoriality; a law's reach is confined and bounded ultimately by the network of those who have participated in its adoption and consented to its application. If that network is itself bounded or defined by physical geography, the presumption of territorial reach and the power of the territorial agent is well-founded, if not, not.[259]

Thus states, whilst legitimate in their sphere, cannot be the only legitimate actors in transnational governance.

As for intergovernmental organisations, the legitimacy of their authority is inherited from that of their member states. What intergovernmental organisations contribute on their own account is not legitimising force, but the expertise of their secretariats, and their instrumental value as a forum for discussion and an enabling infrastructure for state action.

However there is a significant problem with their inheritance of legitimacy from that of their member states, namely that it is weakened in its derivative form. The further removed the processes of intergovernmental organisations are from the ultimate source of their legitimacy—the people—the more liable they are to charges of suffering from democratic deficits.

In a truly representative intergovernmental organisation, policy would bubble up from the norms and practices of states as implemented by the citizens' elected representatives, into intergovernmental fora, to be debated and in due course adopted as international law. But in reality, the reverse is often the case. That is, public policy is often generated in intergovernmental organisations in advance of it being adopted by states.[260]

This is made explicit in the *Convention on the Elimination of All Forms of Discrimination against Women*[261] which requires signatories to take all appropriate steps:

---

[258] Jeremy M Malcolm, Do Corporations Have Rights? ⟨URL: `http://www.malcolm.id.au/honours/`⟩, Chapter 1

[259] David G Post, The "Unsettled Paradox": The Internet, the State, and the Consent of the Governed, Ind J Global Legal Stud 5 1998, 542.

[260] Jensen (as in n. 105 on page 119), 38.

[261] 18 Dec 1979, 1983 ATS No 9 (entry into force for Australia 27 Aug 1983)

> To modify the social and cultural patterns of conduct of men and women, with a view to achieving the elimination of prejudices and customary and all other practices which are based on the idea of the inferiority or the superiority of either of the sexes or on stereotyped roles for men and women.

Thus one of the most commonly voiced criticisms made by the anti-globalisation movement of governance by intergovernmental organisations such as the WTO, the World Bank and the IMF is that they are undemocratic.[262] Whilst there are many ill-informed and isolationist voices within the anti-globalisation movement, on this particular point there is accord with many mainstream commentators, and even within the UN.[263] Paulus writes,

> The reliance on democratic principles and the consent of the governed, which legitimize political decisions in the Western tradition, are of little help in international affairs. The "democratic deficit" of international organizations is a commonplace. Rather, the international lawyer must justify his authority by the acceptance of the results of his activity by his audience and addressees, in particular states, and increasingly non-governmental actors.[264]

But is the perceived democratic deficit within intergovernmental organisations, commonplace as it may be, truly inevitable, or is there in fact scope for intergovernmental organisations to be made more representative? Reformists such as the Campaign for a More Democratic United Nations (CAMDUN)[265] and the World Federalist Movement,[266] along with many international relations scholars, believe that there is (whilst admitting that "in the end, there is no single answer").[267]

The first-mentioned groups above are amongst those which have called for the establishment of a United Nations Parliamentary Assembly (or Global Parliamentary Assembly, or Citizens' Assembly) to exercise popular oversight over the activities of the UN.[268] Such calls are not new,[269] but

---

[262]Shiva (as in n. 64 on page 110)

[263]Cardoso, Cardoso Report on Civil Society (as in n. 147 on page 126), 24

[264]Andreas L Paulus, *Governance and International Legal Theory* Leiden, The Netherlands: Martinus Nijhoff Publishers, 2004, chap. From Territoriality to Functionality? Towards a Legal Methodology of Globalization, 61

[265]See `http://www.camdun-online.gn.apc.org/`.

[266]See `http://www.wfm.org/`.

[267]Joseph S Nye, Globalization's Democratic Deficit: How to Make International Institutions More Accountable, Foreign Affairs 80:4 2001

[268]See generally CAMDUN, Main Options for a UN Peoples' Assembly ⟨URL: `http://www.camdun-online.gn.apc.org/options.html`⟩.

[269]See Grenville Clarke and Louis B Sohn, *World Peace Through World Law* Cambridge, MA: Harvard University Press, 1958.

have been growing louder in recent years, most notably with the European Parliament issuing a resolution in June 2005 in which it called:

> for the establishment of a United Nations Parliamentary Assembly (UNPA) within the UN system, which would increase the democratic profile and internal democratic process of the organisation and allow world civil society to be directly associated in the decision-making process ...[270]

It is said by its proponents that such a body would increase the legitimacy of the United Nations, provide a new mechanism for the enforcement of international law, and perhaps even defuse international conflict.[271] Most likely, such a body might begin with only advisory powers, but could be inclined as the European Parliament has been, to accumulate power through the moral force that it is perceived to inherit from its democratic composition.[272]

Other intergovernmental organisations have been subject to similar calls as the UN to become more democratically accountable to citizens; particularly the EU in which the unelected European Commission's powers are wide-ranging.[273] In March 2002 an intergovernmental conference was convened, along with a forum for the reception of non-state views, to discuss the preparation of a new constitution for the European Union to supersede the existing EU Treaties.

The draft constitution that resulted[274] would have provided a mechanism whereby the Commission could be requested to consider any legislative proposal put forward by a petition of one million citizens.[275] However, whilst the constitution was eventually signed in October 2004, it failed ratification by referendum in France and the Netherlands, leaving it in a state of limbo which continues to the present.

Amongst the other intergovernmental organizations most often the subject of complaints of democratic deficit particularly from within the anti-globalization movement, are the WTO which has already been discussed,[276] the World Bank and the IMF. Like the WTO, the progress of the World Bank

---

[270] European Parliament, Resolution on the Reform of the United Nations ⟨URL: `http://www.europarl.europa.eu/sides/getDoc.do;jsessionid=77601C56E1A79956D73972A5D4FA233C.node1?pubRef=-//EP//TEXT+TA+P6-TA-2005-0237+0+DOC+XML+V0//EN`⟩

[271] Andrew Strauss, Taking Democracy Global: Assessing the Benefits and Challenges of a Global Parliamentary Assembly ⟨URL: `http://www.oneworldtrust.org/documents/taking%20democracy%20global.pdf`⟩, 1–3.

[272] Ibid., 4

[273] But see Andrew Moravcsik, Reassessing Legitimacy in the European Union, JCMS 40:4 2002.

[274] *Treaty Establishing a Constitution for Europe*, 29 Oct 2004

[275] Article I-47

[276] See section 3.2 on page 108.

and the IMF in addressing or even acknowledging the issue of democratic deficit has been slow.

The World Bank established an independent Inspection Panel in 1994 to hear complaints from citizens about World Bank programmes,[277] and since 2001 the IMF has had an Independent Evaluation Office which fulfils a similar function.[278] The two organisations also jointly host a Civil Society Forum in conjunction with each of their Annual Meetings, which NGOs may apply for accreditation to attend.[279] However this does not provide them with rights to speak or to formally table papers at the Annual Meeting, or to participate in any other IMF or World Bank deliberations.

The traditional position of the World Bank and IMF has been that it is sufficient that they are accountable to their "shareholders," the member states, and that "sovereign governments are, and must be, in the first instance accountable to their respective civil societies"[280]—a position which ignores both the phenomenon of transnational civil society, and the further remove of diplomats in intergovernmental organisations from the grass roots constituencies to which their home parliaments are accountable.[281]

Private sector

The private sector draws its legitimacy from the superior efficiency of free markets in the distribution of goods and services; a value-rational justification in Weberian terms. Adam Smith famously used the metaphor of an "invisible hand" to describe how, without the imposition of central planning, the self-interested behaviour of producers and consumers in a market can in fact promote the common good.[282]

Welfare economists have since confirmed this mathematically, demonstrating by their so-called first theorem that in a perfect free market, the distribution of wealth will be Pareto-optimal: that is, the natural state of the market is such that no participant will be able to be made better off without making at least one other participant worse off.[283]

However there may be many Pareto optimal distributions of wealth in an economy, and the theorem makes no normative distinction between

[277]See http://www.worldbank.org/inspectionpanel/.

[278]See http://www.ieo-imf.org/.

[279]See http://www.imf.org/external/am/index.htm.

[280]However, this statement was removed from the IMF's Web site in 2006 (it remains accessible at http://web.archive.org/web/20060721144628/http://www.imf.org/external/np/exr/ccrit/eng/crans.htm), and replaced in 2008 with the claim that the IMF "has sought to become more accountable, not only to the governments that own it, but also to the broader public": see http://www.imf.org/external/np/exr/facts/civ.htm.

[281]See generally section 4.3 on page 260.

[282]Adam Smith, *The Wealth of Nations*, volume IV Chicago: University of Chicago, 1976, 477

[283]Kenneth J Arrow and Gerard Debreu, Existence of an Equilibrium for a Competitive Economy, Econometrica 22:3 1954

them—it is equally efficient for wealth to be distributed evenly between all consumers, as it is for the same wealth to be concentrated in the hands of an elite whose neighbours are left to starve. Although the second theorem of welfare economics does posit that a fair distribution can be attained by means of the government imposing a lump-sum redistribution of wealth, as to what this fair distribution is, it gives no answer.[284] It is thus unfortunate that other important social values besides efficiency, such as distributional equity and human rights, are less easily susceptible to economic analysis.

Unregulated markets also fail to guard against the impact of externalities; the external effects of the decisions of a producer or consumer that are costless to them, but costly (or more costly) to others or to society.[285] This can lead to outcomes such as the "tragedy of the commons," in which it is in each individual's self-interest to deplete a shared resource to nothing, because the benefits of such depletion accrue only to them, while its costs are also borne by others.

And these are only the products of a theoretically perfect market; in practice, no market is perfect, and the less perfect it is (as in the case of a monopolistic or oligopolistic industry), the less benevolent are the movements of the invisible hand. Moreover, MNCs are not parties to the international human rights instruments that are binding on states, with the United Nations' voluntary Global Compact[286] providing a weak substitute at best.

For all these reasons, the private sector's role in the operation of markets, whilst legitimate in its sphere, is insufficient. It is one of the roles of the liberal state to intercede in markets and societies to ensure that markets work efficiently and that other social values are upheld.

Civil society

A widely-held view is that the third stakeholder group, civil society, claims its legitimacy as "a specialist, a scholar, or an expert whose authority derives from specialized knowledge and practices that render such knowledge acceptable, and appropriate, as authoritative."[287] In Weberian terms, the application of such expertise as the most efficient means to an end is instrumental-rational; in other words, it is instrumentally-rational for a decision maker to defer to civil society to gain the benefit of its technical

---

[284] Arrow and Debreu (as in n. 283 on the preceding page)

[285] Coase (as in n. 90 on page 24)

[286] See `http://www.unglobalcompact.org/`.

[287] Cutler, The Emergence of Private Authority in Global Governance (as in n. 124 on page 122), 26; Charnovitz (as in n. 127 on page 123), 274; and compare "consensual knowledge": Rodney Bruce Hall and Thomas J Biersteker, *The Emergence of Private Authority in Global Governance* Cambridge: Cambridge University Press, 2002, chap. Private Authority as Global Governance, 209.

expertise.[288] But this can be true only of a limited subset of civil society, including certain of the more active NGOs.

An alternative and preferable view is that it is not just the expertise that civil society brings, but rather the values it puts forward, that justifies its participation in international governance. It therefore draws its legitimacy from the promotion of substantive values for their own sake,[289] which is a value-rational ground. Put in more familiar terms, to include civil society in governance because of its expertise would be an instrumental justification for doing so (and doubtless private sector consultants could fulfil that role just as well), whereas to include it by reason of its promotion of substantive values is a normative justification.

On the face of it, this seems to overlap with the legitimacy of states, as are not democratic governments intended to provide a mechanism for the transmission of the substantive values of their citizens? Perhaps so, but as noted above, that is not to say that those citizens thereby forfeit their right to form other communities of interest through which to express their values in other fora, that may transcend the state's boundaries. A state cannot therefore be considered the sole and sovereign agent of its citizens while they may choose to delegate their sovereignty outside and across its borders too. Post writes,

> Normative Liberal theory does not merely give "non-governmental organizations" a place at a negotiating table whose shape and agenda is defined by existing state actors; it places non-governmental institutions of all kinds and states on equal footing and asks, as a threshold matter: to which institution(s) has the "sovereign" delegated its power?[290]

The argument can be taken further: that NGOs are potentially *better* representatives of their constituents' interests than are states, because they have "the function of representing people acting of their own volition, rather than by some institutional fiat."[291] There will be no impetus for the formation of an NGO if its members' interests are already adequately represented by their states. But inevitably there are interests that states inadequately represent, and for which NGOs have become the dominant representatives.

Take for example Amnesty International[292] in representing the interests of political prisoners (whose interests are by definition ignored by their

[288] But importantly, Weber did not relate this to a form of authority or consider it a ground of legitimacy for a social order.

[289] Friedrichs (as in n. 169 on page 130), 20

[290] Post, The "Unsettled Paradox": The Internet, the State, and the Consent of the Governed (as in n. 259 on page 148), 536.

[291] Gordenker and Weiss (as in n. 128 on page 123)

[292] See `http://www.amnesty.org/`.

states), the International Campaign to Ban Landmines[293] in campaigning against the use of landmines (against the military interests of states), and Greenpeace[294] in lobbying for environmental protection (against states' economic interests).

These are not isolated cases, but examples of a systemic problem inherent in the concentration of authority in state organs. Just as the free market imperfectly achieves the value of efficiency to which it aspires (let alone other social values), so too the state, although it may be structured along democratic lines and aspire to fairly represent its citizens' interests, is inclined to represent powerful interests more successfully than those of social minorities and the economically powerless.[295]

For Marxists, this is primarily because the capitalist state is a dictatorship of the bourgeoisie which subdues competing interests through cultural hegemony. A more nuanced approach within the Marxist tradition is that of Poulantzas, for whom the state, although enjoying relative autonomy from the capitalist class, is bound to support the long-term interests of capitalists in order to ensure its own continued existence. Thus the state will broker only so many concessions to the interests of the working class as are necessary to subdue a socialist revolution.[296]

This is of course in contrast to the liberal pluralist conception of the state, which constructs it as a neutral vessel to which all classes and their interests have equal access to shape policy. However liberal neo-pluralists such as Robert Dahl and Charles Lindblom have since conceded that:

> common interpretations that depict the American or any other market-oriented system as a competition among interest groups are seriously in error for their failure to account of the distinctive privileged position of businessmen in politics.[297]

Yet a third approach to the study of the state alongside Marxism and pluralism is that of institutionalism,[298] according to which the state, and the interest groups that participate in domestic political processes, are institutions in themselves, with their own interests independent of, and perhaps in conflict with, those of the citizens whom the system is intended to represent. As such,

---

[293]See `http://www.icbl.org/`.

[294]See `http://www.greenpeace.org/`.

[295]See more generally section 4.3 on page 226 regarding the limitations of democratic governance.

[296]Nicos Poulantzas, *Political Power and Social Classes* London: New Left Books, 1968

[297]Robert Dahl and Charles Lindblom, *Politics, Economics and Welfare* New Brunswick, NJ: Transaction Publishers, 1991, xli

[298]Or new institutionalism, of which the scholarship of the so-called "historical" branch is described here.

> the political demands that come to be expressed in politics are not an exact reflection of the preferences of individuals but rather deviate considerably from this potential "raw material" of politics. Various institutional factors influence the political processes that adjudicate among conflicting interests and may hence privilege some interests at the expense of others.[299]

Cutting across these three approaches, Cutler describes the "material, ideological, and institutional" power of capital as the power of the "mercatocracy."[300]

Thus the basis of transnational civil society's legitimate authority in international governance is that it acts as a check on the power of the state to the extent that the state's authority fails to adequately represent the interests of its citizens—particularly including interests that cut across states, and those that are not valued by the mercatocracy. Indeed, the Secretary-General of the United Nations in 1994 acknowledged NGOs as "a basic form of popular representation in the present day world" that is "a guarantee of the political legitimacy of those international organizations" in which they participate.[301]

Does this mean that civil society groups should take the place of states as representatives of substantive values? Not at all, for three main reasons: their inability to independently implement policy at state level, their lack of representativeness, and their lack of accountability.

The first of these reasons is that civil society often depends upon states to actually implement the policies for which NGOs lobby.[302] Naturally, exceptions are easily found, such as the campaigns of the Rainbow Warrior and the direct humanitarian action of NGOs such as Oxfam, but it remains that domestic law reform is often the primary objective of the work of civil society in intergovernmental organisations.

As for the issue of representativeness, it goes without saying that states remain the dominant form of large scale social ordering, and thus for all their faults will always be more representative of their citizens than any NGO could be. NGOs may compensate for the deficiencies of states' representativeness of their citizens, but neither claim to nor do provide the broad representation of society that states do. As Cardoso puts it:

> The legitimacy of civil society organizations derives from what they do and not from whom they represent or from any

[299] Ellen M Immergut, The Theoretical Core of New Institutionalism, Politics and Society 26:1 1988, 17

[300] See Cutler, *Private Power and Global Authority: Transnational Merchant Law in the Global Political Economy* (as in n. 76 on page 21), 186

[301] United Nations Non-Government Liaison Service (as in n. 145 on page 125), and see Charnovitz (as in n. 127 on page 123), 274.

[302] Fred Halliday, Global Governance: Prospects and Problems, Citizenship Studies 4:1 2000

> kind of external mandate. In the final analysis, they are what they do. The power of civil society is a soft one. It is their capacity to argue, to propose, to experiment, to denounce, to be exemplary. It is not the power to decide.[303]

As to civil society's accountability, whilst the extent to which states reflect their citizens' values may be obscure, the extent to which many NGOs do so is even more obscure, as they may not be particularly democratic internally. In fact it is precisely the NGOs that possess the resources to participate actively in international fora that may be most at risk of being unduly influenced by powerful interests. Whilst, as we have seen, states are subject to the same risk, at least liberal democratic states are constrained in this respect by certain institutional checks and balances that NGOs may lack.[304]

Ameliorating this concern to some degree is ECOSOC's requirement that organisations in consultative status with the United Nations

> shall have a democratically adopted constitution, a copy of which shall be deposited with the Secretary-General of the United Nations, and which shall provide for the determination of policy by a conference, congress or other representative body, and for an executive organ responsible to the policy-making body.

It is also required that the organisation possess

> a representative structure and possess appropriate mechanisms of accountability to its members, who shall exercise effective control over its policies and actions through the exercise of voting rights or other appropriate democratic and transparent decision-making processes.[305]

Thus although civil society acts legitimately in international governance, it does so only in collaboration with other legitimate stakeholders. As a corollary, organisations involved in international public policy governance lay their strongest claim to legitimacy when their processes incorporate all three complementary founts of authority: states, markets and society—the very forces that have defined the study of sociology since Weber.

No stakeholder will ever take the place of the others in international governance, because their legitimacy and consequent authority is independently derived. It is this, rather than the fact that any individual stakeholder

[303] Cardoso, Civil Society and Global Governance (as in n. 133 on page 124), 7

[304] See section 4.3 on page 226.

[305] ECOSOC, Consultative Relationship Between the United Nations and Non-Governmental Organizations (as in n. 155 on page 127), paras 10 and 12.

will be ineffective in attempting to exercise governance without the others, that lies at the core of the need for governance by networks in which all stakeholders are involved.

Jurisdiction

The second set of issues that particularly confront international and transnational lawmakers, especially those engaged in public policy governance of the Internet, concerns the intersection of the international and domestic legal systems. These issues include the limited range of mechanisms available for the enforcement of international law, given that the international system lacks a conventional police force or judiciary. There are also difficulties in determining the appropriate domestic law that should govern a particular factual circumstance and in enforcing that law internationally, as well as difficulties in containing the extraterritorial effects of either domestic law or the conduct to which such law is directed. These problems will be dealt with in turn.

Enforcement of international law

There are few formal mechanisms for the enforcement of international law. Whilst there is the International Court of Justice, the main limitation of its jurisdiction is that it requires the consent of each party in order to be enlivened.[306] Furthermore whilst judgments of the ICJ against states may be enforced by the Security Council of the UN, the veto powers of each of the permanent members make it unlikely that such a judgment would ever be enforced against them.

Austin even concluded in 1832 that international law was not law at all because it lacked a judiciary or an executive to enforce it.[307] Yet it has nevertheless been observed that "almost all nations observe almost all principles of international law and almost all of their obligations almost all of the time,"[308] prompting research by international relations scholars (particularly institutionalists) as to why this should be so.[309] It is now more widely accepted that the lack of a conventional mechanism of enforcement for international law is not fatal to its status as law,[310] and that in any case

[306] *Statute of the International Court of Justice*, 26 Jun 1945, 1975 ATS No 50 (entry into force for Australia 1 Nov 1945), article 36.

[307] John Austin, *The Province of Jurisprudence Determined, and the Uses of the Study of Jurisprudence* London: Widenfeld and Nicolson, 1954

[308] Louis Henkin, *How Nations Behave: Law and Foreign Policy* New York: Columbia University Press, 1979, 47

[309] Slaughter observes that it is not all states, but more particularly liberal states who tend to comply with international law: Slaughter, International Law in a World of Liberal States (as in n. 3 on page 98). But see *contra* Koh, Transnational Legal Process (as in n. 7 on page 99) and Idem, Why Do Nations Obey International Law, Yale LJ 106:8 1997.

[310] Arend (as in n. 75 on page 21), 30–31

there are a number of informal institutions by which it is enforced.

First, states can exercise self-help measures against other states believed to be in breach of their international law obligations. An obvious example is found in the United States military offensive against Iraq in the 2003 Gulf War. However as this action was taken in defiance of UN Security Council resolutions, it also illustrates the lack of legitimacy that such unilateral measures may carry as against actions authorised by the United Nations.

Second, particular international organizations have created frameworks within which international law can be enforced through methods other than reference to the ICJ or the Security Council. The best example is the WTO, the Dispute Settlement Body of which can impose a number of innovative penalties on non-compliant states including ordering the payment of compensation to other affected states. Of course, if the payment is not made then the WTO falls back on its ultimate self-enforcing remedy of trade sanctions.

Third and more fundamentally, there are forces which drive states towards voluntary compliance with international law, such as "concerns for reputation, reciprocity, perceptions of legitimacy, trust, and the like, which do not rest on coercion or sanctions."[311] Indeed, regime theory is built on the assumption that states will only establish an international regime (which includes a regime of law) if they consider it is in their long term best interests to do so.[312]

Conflict of laws

Domestic law (including the rules of conflict of laws) tends to be premised on the assumption that events can be located territorially. Thus for example the postal acceptance rule provides that a contract is formed in the "place" where the acceptance is communicated to the offeror.[313] But what if that place is the Internet? One of the earliest preoccupations of academics writing on cyberspace law was in tracing the implications of jurisdictional problems such as these where the location of a legally relevant event is obscure.

The difficulties in assigning online conduct to a jurisdiction have however sometimes been overstated,[314] and most are soluble by the use of

[311]Cutler, *Private Power and Global Authority: Transnational Merchant Law in the Global Political Economy* (as in n. 76 on page 21), 75; Franck, *The Power of Legitimacy Among Nations* (as in n. 251 on page 146).

[312]Robert O Keohane, *After Hegemony: Cooperation and Discord in the World Political Economy* Princeton, NJ: Princeton University Press, 1984

[313]*Adams v Linsell* (1818) 106 ER 250

[314]Jack L Goldsmith, *Who Rules the Net? Internet Governance and Jurisdiction* Washington, DC: Cato Institute, 2003, chap. Against Cyberanarchy; Herbert Kronke, *Internet: Which Court Decides? Which Law Applies?* The Hague: Kluwer Law International, 1998, chap. Applicable Law in Torts and Contracts in Cyberspace

general principles of conflict of laws. Difficulty in finding a state to assume jurisdiction over online activity is unusual; more often there is more than one that might do so. But that is rarely a problem in a contractual context, as it is enough that one jurisdiction can be found to hear the case and generally irrelevant that more than one might.

Similarly in tort and criminal cases, the law to be applied is normally the *lex loci delicti commissi* (broadly that of the place where the act was committed), and even if there is more than one such place, then principles of *forum non conveniens* in civil matters and of double jeopardy in criminal matters will normally prevent the case from being tried twice before different tribunals.

True, the prospect of a multiplicity of states extending their jurisdiction over a single dispute is productive of some uncertainty, but in contractual cases that uncertainty can easily be resolved by the parties selecting their desired jurisdiction for the agreement pursuant to article 3(1) of the *Rome Convention*[315] (and if they so wish having it enforced in some other jurisdiction of their choosing pursuant to the *New York Convention*[316]). These choices can in general be elected online even more easily than they can offline, for example using so-called click-wrap agreements hosted on one party's Web site[317] (subject of course to any compulsory consumer protection provisions applicable in the jurisdiction of either party, such as article 12(2) of the EU *Directive on Distance Contracts*).[318]

Where no such election has been or can be made contractually, there is still some provision through a patchwork of bilateral and multilateral instruments for the enforcement of court judgments between various jurisdictions, including the states of the EU,[319] and between Australia and some 36 states and Canadian provinces pursuant to the *Foreign Judgments*

---

[315]Goldsmith (as in n. 314 on the preceding page), 67–69

[316]*Convention on the Recognition and Enforcement of Foreign Arbitral Awards,* 10 Jun 1958, 1975 ATS No 25 (entry into force for Australia 24 Jun 1975) (New York Convention), an UNCITRAL treaty which provides for the enforcement of both agreements to arbitrate and the resulting arbitral awards in the state of each signatory to the Convention (presently numbering over 130). Compare also the *Hague Convention on Choice of Law Agreements*, concluded on 30 June 2005 (see `http://www.hcch.net/index_en.php?act=conventions.pdf&cid=98`), though this is yet to come into force and will not require signatories to enforce the awards of other states.

[317]J D Kunkel and G Richard, Recent Developments in Shrinkwrap, Clickwrap and Browsewrap Licenses in the United States, E LAW 9:3 2002, ⟨URL: `http://www.murdoch.edu.au/elaw/issues/v9n3/kunkel93_text.html`⟩

[318]Matthew Burnstein, *Internet: Which Court Decides? Which Law Applies?* The Hague: Kluwer Law International, 1998, chap. A Global Network in a Compartmentalised Legal Environment, 33. It provides, "Member States shall take the measures needed to ensure that the consumer does not lose the protection granted by this Directive by virtue of the choice of the law of a non-member country as the law applicable to the contract if the latter has close connection with the territory of one or more Member States."

[319]Pursuant to the Brussels Regime which comprises the *EEX Convention*, the *Convention on Jurisdiction and the Enforcement of Judgments in Civil and Commercial Matters*, 16 Sep 1988 (EVEX Convention) and European Commission, Directive on Privacy and Electronic Communications (as in n. 180 on page 75).

Act 1991 (Cth).

As for criminal matters, the ability of a state to enforce its laws against a defendant in another jurisdiction will depend on the existence of an agreement between the two nations in question for the extradition of criminal defendants. The procedure by which Australia makes and receives extradition requests is set out in the *Extradition Act 1988* (Cth), and the countries from which it receives requests are provided in regulations to that Act. This includes most of the same countries as included in the regulations to the *Foreign Judgments Act*, but with the notable addition of the United States.

Spillover effects

A more serious issue arises in cases where the problem is not so much in locating an event in a particular jurisdiction, but in dealing with its effects that cross multiple jurisdictions. The effects may be those of wrongful conduct, such as tortious, criminal or intellectual property law infringements, or they may be those of the laws themselves, whereby an attempt by one jurisdiction to regulate conduct on the Internet impacts too widely against other sovereign jurisdictions. Such effects are known as "spillover effects."[320]

Spillover effects are seen in one of two forms. First, the least stringent regulations applicable to any Internet-connected jurisdiction may be those that prevail in practice; a "lowest common denominator" effect. This can be seen in the case of spam regulation, where the greatest amount of spam is sent from those countries with the weakest anti-spam laws, often on behalf of advertisers from elsewhere in the world.[321] It is also a hallmark of content regulation that content providers will relocate their hosting operations to less highly-regulated jurisdictions offshore,[322] as in the examples previously given of Australia's *Interactive Gambling Act* and *Broadcasting Services Act*.[323]

Taking full advantage of this phenomenon is Havenco,[324] a Web hosting company located on the (self-declared) sovereign principality of Sealand, previously an abandoned anti-aircraft platform in the North Sea off the coast of Great Britain.[325] Until 2007, Havenco's Web site warned that "Sealand's laws prohibit amongst other things child pornography and spam," but confided that "Sealand currently has no specific regulations regarding patents, libel, restrictions on political speech, cryptography,

---

[320] Goldsmith (as in n. 314 on page 158)

[321] See `http://www.spamhaus.org/statistics/countries.lasso`.

[322] See section 2.3 on page 79.

[323] See section 1.4 on page 21.

[324] See `http://www.havenco.com/`.

[325] See `http://www.sealandgov.org/`.

restrictions on maintaining customer records, DMCA or music sharing services."[326]

The second and converse effect of spillover is that online behaviour may be required to conform to the most stringent regulations in force worldwide, the potential for which is illustrated by the Gutnick defamation case and the Yahoo! Nazi memorabilia case both previously examined above,[327] as well as by the effect of the EU *Data Protection Directive* which has, for example, led Microsoft Corporation to change the way it manages user data for its dot-NET Passport service, not only within Europe, but worldwide.[328]

Without overstating the point, the protection of the First Amendment of the US Constitution, in particular, can result in very different regulatory regimes being applied inside and outside the United States in cases such as these. Taking the example of libel, it is for example necessary for American plaintiffs to demonstrate that a false statement published in the press was written with actual malice.[329] Such differences as these may result in the more tightly regulated country's laws "spilling over" upon those in the more loosely regulated jurisdiction.

In either case, whether it is conduct or law that spills over into less regulated jurisdictions, the outcome is that at least one sovereign nation's law is effectively being trumped by another's.

Goldsmith argues that the effects of spillover have again been overstated, in that it remains possible for indirect regulation to be exercised over much conduct that spills over jurisdictions, for example by criminalising the use of off-shore hosting facilities,[330] or by controlling intermediaries within the local jurisdiction, such as banks, ISPs and domain registrars.[331] A recent example of the latter is found in the withdrawal of credit card processing facilities by the Visa International network to AllofMP3.com, a Russian music download service that allegedly contravened United States (but arguably not Russian) law.[332]

---

[326] See `http://web.archive.org/web/20060324014814/http://www.havenco.com/legal/aup.html`. Since 2007 the site has listed a shorter but more restrictive set of terms of service, including "No infringement of copyright": see `http://www.havenco.com/law.html`.

[327] See section 2.3 on page 79.

[328] Matt Loney, Microsoft Agrees to Passport Changes ⟨URL: `http://www.news.com/2100-1001-982790.html`⟩

[329] *New York Times Company v Sullivan* (1964) 376 US 254

[330] Goldsmith (as in n. 314 on page 158), 49

[331] Goldsmith and Wu (as in n. 220 on page 80), 72; Joel R Reidenberg, States and Internet Enforcement, Uni Ottowa Law & Tech LJ 1 2003-2004

[332] Greg Sandoval, Visa Halts its Service for Allofmp3.com ⟨URL: `http://www.news.com/Visa-halts-service-for-allofmp3.com/2100-1027_3-6127168.html`⟩. The closure of the site was subsequently procured by the United States as a condition of Russia's membership of the WTO, but it reopened shortly afterwards under a new brand at `http://www.mp3sparks.com/`: Tony Halpin, Russia Shuts Down Allofmp3.com ⟨URL: `http://www.timesonline.co.uk/tol/news/world/europe/article2016297.ece`⟩.

The spillover of law on the other hand, for Goldsmith, is unexceptional, as it is well within the competency of states to pass laws with extraterritorial effect in order to regulate effects within their own jurisdictions.

Post on the other hand, whilst not denying this as a general proposition, contends that there are sufficient differences between the way in which such laws impact upon online and off-line conduct that differential treatment of the former is warranted.[333] One difference that he notes is scale, such as the way in which the automatic distribution of millions of Usenet messages through thousands of servers worldwide could lead to unreasonable liability in the event that a message so distributed infringed copyright.[334] This, and the extent to which, in cyberspace, "virtually *all* events and transactions have border-crossing effects," along with the fact that domestic regulation of same will almost always impact upon those who are not subject to that state's sovereignty, point Post to the need for reforms to mitigate these effects.

And, indeed, there have been a number of efforts to do so, both technical and legal. Technical reforms aimed at overcoming the spillover effects of online conduct include filtering and geolocation. These work in approximately opposite ways. Filtering prevents content that is prohibited in a particular jurisdiction (such as unwanted speech or offensive images) from entering that jurisdiction via the Internet. In Australia, for example, both the spam[335] and content regulation[336] legislative regimes make use of co-regulatory codes drafted by industry groups and registered with the ACMA, pursuant to which ISPs are required to make appropriate filtering products or services available to their users.

Geolocation on the other hand, prevents content that is made accessible on the Internet, from being accessed from a particular jurisdiction. For this purpose the IETF has proposed a DNS-based method for determining the geographical location of Internet addresses,[337] though more *ad hoc* geolocation services, both commercial[338] and non-commercial,[339] are currently more widely used.

Neither filtering nor geolocation technologies are foolproof, however, as both measures run counter to the Internet's decentralised and cosmopolitan architecture. A 2002 study of six popular filtering products found that depending on how they were configured they would block between 89%

---

[333] David G Post, *Who Rules the Net? Internet Governance and Jurisdiction* Washington, DC: Cato Institute, 2003, chap. Against "Against Cyberanarchy"

[334] For a description of Usenet, see section 4.1 on page 183.

[335] See `http://www.acma.gov.au/WEB/STANDARD/pc=PC_310325`.

[336] See `http://www.acma.gov.au/WEB/STANDARD/pc=PC_90080`.

[337] IETF, A Means for Expressing Location Information in the Domain Name System ⟨URL: `http://www.ietf.org/rfc/rfc1876.txt`⟩

[338] See eg Quova, Inc at `http://www.quova.com/`, and MaxMind LLC at `http://www.maxmind.com/`.

[339] See `http://www.hostip.info/`.

and 91% of pornographic Web sites, but also between 33% and 91% of safe sex information sites.[340] Similarly, the highest accuracy claimed for geolocation technology admits an approximate 10% error rate at the city level.[341] These figures do not take into account users' ability to deliberately attempt to evade the technologies in question by means such as encrypted tunnels or proxies.

As for the options to mitigate the effects of spillover through law reform, the first example to emerge was the development of a consistent doctrine in United States case law to determine whether a Web site, available internationally, should fall subject to local regulation, in the early case of *Zippo Manufacturing v Zippo Dot Com, Inc.*[342]

The test established by that case described a sliding scale from "passive" Web sites, which were merely information-based, with minimal interaction with the user, through to "active" Web sites, of which the predominant purpose was to conclude business with the user. In between were the intermediate category of "interactive" Web sites. It was adjudged that the jurisdiction of the user in question could assert authority over active sites but not passive ones, whereas for interactive sites the level of interactivity and the commercial nature of the information exchanged would determine whether it would be treated as one or the other of the other categories.

Whether or not this test is an adequate one,[343] it applies on a domestic level only. Since spillover is a transnational issue, it calls out for a uniform transnational solution. There are three ways in which this could be approached. The first and least radical would be to unifiy domestic choice of law rules. Such a project had already taken place in Europe as early as 1968, when the first convention of the so-called Brussels Regime unified the conflict of law rules of EU member states.[344]

This convention formed the starting point for negotiations commenced by the Hague Conference in 1992 over a similar more broadly international convention, the proposed *Hague Convention on Jurisdiction and Foreign Judgments in Civil and Commercial Matters.*[345] However extended negotiations over this draft convention eventually fell through, largely due to objections

[340] Kaiser Family Foundation, See No Evil: How Internet Filters Affect the Search for Online Health Information ⟨URL: `http://www.kff.org/entmedia/3294-index.cfm`⟩

[341] See `http://www.quova.com/page.php?id=106`.

[342] (1997) 952 F Supp 1119

[343] See Michael Geist, *Who Rules the Net? Internet Governance and Jurisdiction* Washington, DC: Cato Institute, 2003, chap. The Shift Towards "Targeting" for Internet Jurisdiction for criticism and an alternative proposal.

[344] *Convention on Jurisdiction and the Enforcement of Judgments in Civil and Commercial Matters*, 27 Sep 1968, OJ L/299/32 (EEX Convention), now largely superseded by European Commission, Directive on Privacy and Electronic Communications (as in n. 180 on page 75).

[345] Hague Conference on Private International Law, Preliminary Draft Convention on Jurisdiction and Foreign Judgments in Civil and Commercial Matters ⟨URL: `http://www.state.gov/www/global/legal_affairs/991030_forjudg.html`⟩

from the United States.[346]

The next most radical approach is the imposition of a *sui generis* Internet law regime, which could still in appropriate cases be applied in domestic tribunals. A *sui generis* regime could take shape through the unification of Internet-related law through formal international agreements as has begun to happen with the UNCITRAL model law on Economic Commerce, or simply through the continued development of private transnational law, in what could become like the process by which the common law developed.[347]

A final and even more radical solution would be the removal of Internet legal issues into a specialised Internet jurisdiction. This was the early approach of scholars like Johnson and Post, who reasoned that due to the inevitable jurisdictional problems associated with the application of domestic laws to the Internet, cyberspace should be left apart from territorial regulation to develop its own self-regulatory structures based on shared norms.[348]

Whilst to date even the least radical of these alternatives has proved to be a dream, elements of all of them can be seen in development. Whilst we do not have the *Hague Convention on Jurisdiction*, we do have the *Hague Convention on Choice of Law Agreements*. We may not have a *sui generis* legal regime covering all Internet-related issues, but we do have the UNCITRAL model law. And whilst the world lacks a legal system exercising specialised Internet jurisdiction, there is such a system for the resolution of domain name disputes, the UDRP. These are the seeds from which bodies such as the IGF may be able to grow a more comprehensive transnational legal regime for the Internet in the future.

Universality

The last category of limitations of international and transnational law to be discussed is the difficulty of applying uniform rules across a diversity of legal systems and cultures. Although the distinction can be a narrow one (particularly in Islamic states), the differences between national legal systems will be examined first, followed by consideration of ideological and cultural differences.

---

[346] *Hague Conference on Private International Law*, Some Reflections on the Present State of Negotiations on the Judgments Project in the Context of the Future Work Programme of the Conference ⟨URL: `http://www.cptech.org/ecom/hague/hague16feb2002-bureaurefects.rtf`⟩

[347] Burnstein (as in n. 318 on page 159), 28

[348] David R Johnson and David G Post, Law and Borders—the Rise of Law in Cyberspace, Stan LR 48 1996, ⟨URL: `http://www.cli.org/X0025_LBFIN.html`⟩, but see Lawrence Lessig, The Zones of Cyberspace, Stan LR 48:5 1996.

Differences between legal systems

Unlike some of the jurisdictional issues that are magnified in an Internet-related context, issues of the universal application of international and transnational law across multiple legal systems are no novelty to international society. Thus, article 9 of the *Statute of the International Court of Justice* requires that common law, civil law and socialist law jurists be represented in the Court's panel. But although these are the most prominent legal systems present within the membership of the United Nations (less so socialist law, of course, since the fall of communism in Eastern Europe and Russia), they are not the only ones. Notably omitted are customary and religious legal systems such as Hindu law, Talmudic (Jewish) law, and Islamic theocratic law, or Sharia.

Of these, Sharia law is applicable within the greatest number of member states; though to varying degrees, since there are states within the Muslim world such as Lebanon, Syria and Egypt that largely follow Western civil law, others such as Saudi Arabia, Oman and Yemen drawing strongly from the Sharia, and still others such as Iraq, Jordan and Libya possessing something of a hybrid.[349]

There is a similar degree of heterogeneity within the other legal systems referred to above. For example the code law systems of East Asia are heavily influenced by Confucian ideas that of course are absent in Europe,[350] and those of the new democracies in Eastern Europe bear the legacy of socialist law.[351] Likewise, within common law systems, there is significant divergence between United States law and Anglo Australian law.

One of the relevant differences between such legal systems is the structure and procedures of their legislative, executive and judicial institutions, which may impact on a state's ability to comply with international instruments presupposing a different set of institutions and procedures. For example, Japan has interpreted references to its police force in international instruments to include the country's fire service.[352] They also may include constitutional differences, which may influence how international law is received into or implemented in domestic law. For example, since Australia's international obligations are required to be implemented in legislation before having domestic effect, it is easier for Australia than for the United States to fall into non-compliance with a treaty that it has signed and ratified.

As noted above, these sorts of differences are nothing new to inter-

[349] H S Shaaban, Commercial Transactions in the Middle East: Which Law Governs?, Law and Pol'y Int'l Bus 31:1 1999

[350] Herbert H P Ma, Law and Morality: Some Reflections on the Chinese Experience Past and Present, Philosophy East and West 21:4 1971

[351] Christopher Lehmann, Bail Reform in Ukraine: Transplanting Western Legal Concepts to Post-Soviet Legal Systems, Harv Hum Rts J 13 2000

[352] See `http://www.unhchr.ch/html/menu3/b/treaty4_asp.htm`.

national law, and they are dealt with largely by leaving them up to the state to resolve. The *Vienna Convention on the Law of Treaties*[353] provides in article 27 that "A party may not invoke the provisions of its internal law as justification for its failure to perform a treaty." The only concession allowed on account of legal and constitutional differences between states is the acknowledgment in articles 19 to 23 that certain treaties may allow for signatories to accede with reservations in respect of specific articles. For example, there are extensive reservations (and interpretative declarations, whereby a party indicates its intention to interpret articles in a particular way) to the *International Covenant on Civil and Political Rights*.[354] To paragraph 6 of Article 14 for instance, regarding compensation payable to a person wrongly convicted of crime, Australia entered the following reservation:

> Australia makes the reservation that the provision of compensation for miscarriage of justice in the circumstances contemplated in paragraph 6 of Article 14 may be by administrative procedures rather than pursuant to specific legal provision.

As for transnational law, differences between legal systems may impact upon a state's ability to participate in programmes of private law harmonisation with other states, although bodies acting in this area such as UNCITRAL have striven at least to include a balance of civil and common law traditions in its working groups.[355] Such differences will also affect a state's willingness to recognise foreign judgments. For example, the award of civil damages by jury in United States courts, which tend to be of much greater quantum than damages assessed by judges in other common law jurisdictions, has precluded Australia from adding the United States to those jurisdictions whose judgments will be recognised and enforced in Australia pursuant to the *Foreign Judgments Act 1991*.

Despite these issues, the difficulties of reconciling differences between legal systems are not widely taken as cause for a wholesale programme of legal unification. On the contrary, the advantage of a multiplicity of legal systems and laws addressing common problems is that this fosters jurisdictional competition,[356] which can lead to the most efficient laws gaining an evolutionary advantage, and only then perhaps influencing law reform efforts elsewhere. On one (controversial)[357] view, an example of this

[353] 23 May 1969, 1974 ATS No 2 (entry into force 27 Jan 1980)

[354] See `http://www.unhchr.ch/html/menu3/b/treaty4_asp.htm`.

[355] John Honnold, The United Nations Commission on International Trade Law: Mission and Methods, Am J Comp Law 27 1979

[356] Simon Deakin, Two Types of Regulatory Competition: Competitive Federalism Versus Reflexive Harmonisation. A Law and Economics Perspective on Centros, CYELS 1 1999

[357] Nicholas L Georgakopoulos, Statistics of Legal Infrastructures: A Review of the Law and Finance Literature, Amer Law Econ Rev 8:1 2006

is found in the relative financial strength[358] and quality of government[359] of countries that have adopted legal systems based on the common law.

More importantly than supporting jurisdictional competition, taking a non-prescriptive approach as to the form of domestic law on the part of international and transnational lawmakers, and perhaps also allowing reservations to be made in respect of provisions that are manifestly unsuitable for adoption by a particular state, allows the difficult task of adapting the law for a variety of legal systems to be delegated to authorities at the domestic level. This is much the same approach—known as subsidiarity—that the EU takes in passing directives that prescribe an objective to be achieved, but not the form and means by which it is put into effect by member states.[360]

Since the IGF's contribution to transnational law can only be in the form of non-binding soft law,[361] it follows that the use of codes (whether so described or described as guidelines, best practice recommendations or the like), or even draft treaties, is to be preferred to the use of model laws in order to ensure that they are applicable across the greatest number of states.

Ideological differences

More intractable than the differences between legal systems are the cultural and ideological differences between states. Ideologies are normally to be taken to be sets of political and economic values and beliefs, such as liberalism, socialism and fascism, whereas cultures are both broader—incorporating language, history, art, etiquette and so on—and at the same time narrower, in that states that share political ideologies may have vastly different cultures.

The history of most of the 20th century was characterised by a clash of ideologies, particularly the three major ideologies mentioned above. But the end of the Cold War to a large extent brought this era to an end, with liberal democracy apparently emerging victorious. This outcome has been characterised as the "end of ideology,"[362] or by Fukuyama even as the "end of history."[363] What is it about liberalism that could account for its dominance, and why should this be expected to be more than transitory?

The liberal's own answer is that liberal states aim to construct a society in which individuals are free to pursue their own conception of the good,

[358] R La Porta et al., Law and Finance, Journal of Political Economy 106 1998

[359] Idem, The Quality of Government, Journal of Law, Economics, and Organization 15:1 1999

[360] See section 6.2 on page 432.

[361] WSIS, Tunis Agenda for the Information Society (as in n. 5 on page 2), paragraph 77

[362] James Kurth, War, Peace and the Ideologies of the Twentieth Century, Current History 98:924 1999

[363] Francis Fukuyama, The End of History?, The National Interest 1989

consistent with the same freedom being afforded to others. The fundamental unit of value to the liberal is the individual human being, rather than the state, the community or the family. Kant treated this as follows:

> Now I say that man, and in general every rational being, exists as an end in himself, *not merely as a means* for arbitrary use by this or that will: he must in all his actions, whether they are directed to himself or to other rational beings, always be viewed *at the same time as an end*.[364]

The role to be assumed by the classical liberal state is therefore straightforward: to administer institutions that facilitate individual autonomy and inhibit interference with the same.[365] Such institutions include the free market, private property, and human rights, which are assumed to be morally neutral, insofar as human autonomy (or as variously expressed the right to freedom,[366] or equal concern or respect,[367] or to be treated with equal dignity[368]), is a transcendent, universal value.

However since even before the publication of the *Communist Manifesto* in 1888, the assumption of the moral neutrality of the free market and private property has been disputed. In that tract, Marx and Engels wrote vividly:

> The bourgeoisie, wherever it has got the upper hand, has put an end to all feudal, patriarchal, idyllic relations. It has pitilessly torn asunder the motley feudal ties that bound man to his "natural superiors," and has left remaining no other nexus between man and man than naked self-interest, than callous "cash payment." It has drowned the most heavenly ecstasies of religious fervour, of chivalrous enthusiasm, of philistine sentimentalism, in the icy water of egotistical calculation. It has resolved personal worth into exchange value, and in place of the numberless and feasible chartered freedoms, has set up that single, unconscionable freedom—Free Trade. In one word, for exploitation, veiled by religious and political illusions, naked, shameless, direct, brutal exploitation.[369]

Even within the liberal tradition itself, Rawls' *A Theory of Justice* attempted to accommodate some of the intuitive unease of liberals at the disinterest

---

[364] I Kant, *Groundwork to the Metaphysics of Morals*, volume Paton, H (trans) New York: Harper & Row, 1965, 95. Emphasis in original.

[365] Robert Nozick, *Anarchy, State and Utopia* New York: Basic Books, 1974

[366] H L A Hart, Are There Any Natural Rights?, Philosophical Review 64 1955

[367] R Dworkin, *Taking Rights Seriously* London: Duckworth, 1977, 275

[368] Kant (as in n. 364)

[369] K Marx and F Engels, *The Communist Manifesto* New York: Signet Classic, 1998, 53

of their ideology in distributive justice, by demonstrating that from a given (though contrived) original position in which they were ignorant of their own capacities and preferences, rational beings would forge a social contract that would not only uphold basic human rights for all, but would also limit social and economic inequality to cases where there is equality of opportunity for all, and the inequality improves the lot of the least fortunate member of society.[370] This was a more egalitarian conception of distributive justice than the more libertarian normative liberal conceptions of the good such as Mill's utilitarianism,[371] or Posner's wealth maximisation.[372]

Although Rawls' social liberalism addresses the objections of Marx to some degree in theory (as in practice do the social programmes of modern welfare liberal states), criticisms have also been made of another more fundamental assumption of classical liberalism: that human autonomy is a fundamental value, common to all human beings by virtue of their having been born into a free state of nature.[373] This individualist assumption is challenged by communitarians on the ground that humans are not born as atomistic individuals but as members of families and communities,[374] which contrary to the assumptions at least of Rawls' original position, are partly constitutive of our identities.[375] The true value of such communal orderings is therefore not counted either in the ("deontological") liberalism of Kant and Rawls that recognises pre-legal rights and duties of individuals, nor in the calculus of utilitarian ("teleological") liberalism.[376]

However, unlike Marxism, communitarianism has no normative political program for the dismantling or radical reform of the liberal state. Indeed, without an underlying system of liberal rights and the rule of law, a communitarian society would have no safeguard against the community visiting tyranny upon minorities.[377] Rather, the implications of the communitarian critique for the modern social liberal state, insofar as they are directed to the state at all, are largely limited to the greater inclusion of civil society in public policy development,[378] and as discussed at length above

[370] John Rawls, *A Theory of Justice* Cambridge, MA: Harvard University Press, 1971, but see in response Nozick (as in n. 365 on the facing page)

[371] John Stuart Mill, *Utilitarianism*, 12th edition London: Routledge, 1895

[372] R Posner, Utilitarianism, Economics and Legal Theory, JLS 8 1979. It was also more strongly put, being accorded the ontological priority of a right, or "primary good," which no individual conception of the good could displace: Rawls, *A Theory of Justice* (as in n. 370), 93.

[373] J Locke, *Two Treatises of Government*, Revised edition New York: Cambridge University Press, 1963, 301–311

[374] Amy Gutmann, Communitarian Critics of Liberalism, Philosophy & Public Affairs 14:3 1985

[375] Michael Sandel, *Liberalism and the Limits of Justice* Cambridge: Cambridge University Press, 1998, 150

[376] Malcolm, Do Corporations Have Rights? (as in n. 258 on page 148), chapter 3

[377] Gutmann (as in n. 374), 318–320

[378] Robert D Putnam, Bowling Alone: America's Declining Social Capital, Journal of Democracy 6:1 1995, 76–77; Michael Sandel, Morality and the Liberal Ideal, The New Republic 190:May 7 1984, 17

this is precisely one of the programmes of reform that the liberal state and international society have already begun to undertake.

What liberalism can claim, that communism cannot and communitarianism does not attempt, is evolutionary success. The neo-Marxist criticisms of the 1960s and the communitarian critiques of the 1980s have been heard and the liberal state has sought to adapt accordingly, even if it has in a narrow sense lost theoretical coherence in doing so. Empirically, liberal states have come to dominate the globe,[379] they generally have strong and stable economies, and have also maintained a remarkable record of peace with each other.[380] By definition, liberal democracies are simply better at what they do—representing their people—than authoritarian and totalitarian states, as their authority is grounded in the legal-rational force of the liberal democratic order rather than purely on their territorial sovereignty.[381]

Cultural differences

Cultural differences can pose as much of an impediment as ideological differences to international and transnational lawmakers seeking to apply public policy uniformly across a multitude of states. Indeed, the difficulties are greater, in that cultural differences exist not only between liberal and illiberal states, but also amongst liberal states, as demonstrated by the Yahoo! dispute. And whereas there are perhaps a handful of major political ideologies, one of which has achieved dominance, there are hundreds if not thousands of distinct world cultures.[382]

Of these, the impact of Islamic culture and its clash with Western culture, as epitomised most infamously by the events of 11 September 2001, have become one of the defining phenomena of the first part of the 21st century. It is of significance in this context that the Sharia broaches no clear distinction between law, politics and religion. Thus, to the Muslim the clash of cultures is just as much a clash of political ideologies. Moreover, at least in Islamic states that strictly apply Sharia law, Westphalia never happened; there is no division of religious and secular authority in the Muslim world.[383]

An examination of the points of variance between Islamic culture and Western culture would exceed the scope of this book. But in general

[379] Fukuyama, The End of History? (as in n. 363 on page 167)

[380] Michael Doyle, Kant, Liberal Legacies, and Foreign Affairs, Philosophy and Public Affairs 12 1983

[381] Perritt Jr (as in n. 116 on page 121)

[382] Certainly, these can be categorised into major groupings ("civilisations"), but this still leaves at least seven or eight.; on one account Western, Confucian, Japanese, Islamic, Hindu, Slavic-Orthodox, Latin American and possibly African: S P Huntington, The Clash of Civilizations?, Foreign Affairs 72 1993, 25.

[383] L Ali Khan, *A Theory of Universal Democracy: Beyond the End of History* The Hague: Kluwer Law International, 2003, 106

Western culture, reflecting liberalism itself, is far more individualistic than Islamic culture, which places greater emphasis on submission to the will of Allah than it does on individual autonomy and rights.[384]

Consequently, international human rights instruments such as the *International Covenant on Civil and Political Rights*, which were drafted without the participation of most Islamic states,[385] are incompatible with various provisions of the Sharia.[386]

But by the same token, just as Islamic states may breach international human rights instruments which offend their cultural norms, those instruments fail to address grave breaches of Sharia law that are considered equally or more fundamental by Muslims as the freedoms enshrined in the *International Covenant*. Most notable amongst these grave breaches are defamation of Islam or of the prophet Muhammad, as allegedly perpetrated by the publication of cartoons depicting Muhammad in the Danish newspaper *Jyllands-Posten* on 30 September 2005, which resulted in protests and riots worldwide.[387]

In 1993 Samuel Huntington wrote in *The Clash of Civilisations?*:

> The end of ideologically defined states in Eastern Europe and the former Soviet Union permits traditional ethnic identities and animosities to come to the fore. Differences in culture and religion create differences over policy issues, ranging from human rights to immigration to trade and commerce to the environment. Geographical propinquity gives rise to conflicting territorial claims from Bosnia to Mindanao. Most important, the efforts of the West to promote its values of democracy and liberalism as universal values, to maintain its military predominance and to advance its economic interests engender countering responses from other civilizations.[388]

Given such dramatic gulfs between the cultural norms of the West and those of the Muslim world, how can it ever be possible for international

---

[384] Kimberley Younce Schooley, Cultural Sovereignty, Islam, and Human Rights—Towards a Communitarian Revision, Cumb LR 25 1995, 694–695

[385] Makau wa Mutua, Why Redrew the Map of Africa: A Moral and Legal Enquiry, Mich J Int'l L 16 1995, 1122

[386] Pavani Thagirisa, A Historial Perspective of the Sharia Project and a Cross-Cultural and Self-Determination Approach to Resolving the Sharia Project in Nigeria, Brook J Int'l Law 29:1 2003, 493–498. This is particularly evident in respect of the equal rights of women, as enshrined in Article 3 of the International Covenant. Schooley writes, "Regulating the life and home of a woman within a particular non-western culture by a universal measure that is in truth western offends the deeply religious culture of Islam. Islamic culture has no concept of the western standards embodied in international documents": Schooley (as in n. 384), 659.

[387] Flemming Rose, Why I Published Those Cartoons ⟨URL: `http://www.washingtonpost.com/wp-dyn/content/article/2006/02/17/AR2006021702499.html`⟩

[388] Huntington (as in n. 382 on the preceding page), 29

and transnational lawmakers to settle upon a set of universal moral rules that are culturally neutral? Some commentators have indeed expressed the view that it will be difficult or impossible to do so.[389]

If that is so, then Islamic states are faced with the prospect that they must simply find a way to accommodate Western liberal values if they wish to participate in international society; since for better or worse,

> [v]irtually all of the norms that are now identified as essential ingredients of international law and global society have their roots in the jurisprudence of European scholars of international law and in the notions and patterns of acceptable behavior established by the more powerful Western European states.[390]

Whilst the bias of international legal norms towards Western liberal values may be hegemonic from a Muslim perspective, and although "[o]ne cannot gain traction or start a normative dialogue with devout Muslims by quoting Locke or Kant,"[391] even Muslims must agree that it is now too late to seek to call into question the cultural underpinnings of norms that have been accepted by the majority of United Nations member states, including states of other ideologies such as North Korea and Cuba.

Consequently, the most fundamental differences between cultures that impact upon international norms will continue to tend to be settled in favour of liberal states. For example in the context of Internet-related public policy, Internet access will be framed as a human rights issue. Specifically, article 19 of the *International Covenant on Civil and Political Rights* which protects the freedom to "seek, receive and impart information and ideas of all kinds" will prevail over religious considerations to mandate that reasonable Internet access be allowed to each state's citizens.[392]

On the other hand, even if this approach is defensible on liberal democratic grounds, the ultimate outcome of such trampling of Islamic cultural

---

[389] Isha Khan, Islamic Human Rights: Islamic Law and International Human Rights Standards, Appeal 5 1999, 79–81; Arend (as in n. 75 on page 21), 18

[390] Ethan A Nadelmann, Global Prohibition Regimes: The Evolution of Norms in International Society, International Organization 44 1990, 484

[391] Amitai Etzioni, Leveraging Islam, The National Interest 83 2006, 104

[392] Save that the article does allow for restrictions to be prescribed by law for purposes such as "the protection of national security or of public order (ordre public), or of public health or morals." This approach is evident in the statement of Abid Hussain, Special Rapporteur to the United Nations Commission on Human Rights, that "The instinct or tendency of Governments to consider regulation rather than enhancing and increasing access to the Internet is ... to be strongly checked:" ECOSOC, Report of the Special Rapporteur on the Protection and Promotion of the Right to Freedom of Opinion and Expression ⟨URL: `http://www.unhchr.ch/huridocda/huridoca.nsf/(Symbol)/E.CN.4.1999.64.En?OpenDocument`⟩, and compare also Council of Europe, Recommendation of the Committee of Ministers to Member States on Measures to Promote the Public Service Value of the Internet ⟨URL: `https://wcd.coe.int/ViewDoc.jsp?id=1207291`⟩.

values is not difficult to fortell, as the fruits of the *Jyllands-Posten* caricature dispute demonstrate. Thus, the UN has endeavoured to reach a pragmatic medium with Islamic interests.

In December 2005, the Organization of the Islamic Conference (OIC),[393] an intergovernmental organisation of Islamic states, sponsored a resolution of the General Assembly of the UN to the following effect:

> The General Assembly ...
> *Alarmed* at the continuing negative impact of the events of 11 September 2001 on Muslim minorities and communities in some non-Muslim countries, the negative projection of Islam in the media and the introduction and enforcement of laws that specifically discriminate against and target Muslims, ...
> Noting with deep concern the increasing trend in recent years of statements attacking religions, Islam and Muslims in particular, especially in human rights forums, ...
> *urges* States to provide, within their respective legal and constitutional systems, adequate protection against acts of hatred, discrimination, intimidation and coercion resulting from defamation of religions, to take all possible measures to promote tolerance and respect for all religions and their value systems and to complement legal systems with intellectual and moral strategies to combat religious hatred and intolerance ...[394]

There have also been efforts to develop, if not a "thick consensus" that provides a complete system of culturally-neutral values for the development of international and transnational law, then at least a "thin" consensus on values which might be sufficient to establish a minimal set of determinate answers.[395]

The way forward for international and transnational lawmakers in seeking a culturally sensitive medium for public policy development prob-

[393] See `http://www.oic-oci.org/`.

[394] General Assembly of the United Nations, Combatting Defamation of Religions ⟨URL: `http://documents-dds-ny.un.org/doc/UNDOC/GEN/N05/496/60/pdf/N0549660.pdf?OpenElement`⟩

[395] T M Franck, *Fairness in International Law* New York: Clarendon Press, 1995. The "golden rule," or the ethic of reciprocity (that is, that one should treat others as one wishes to be treated by them), has been suggested as a plausible value that is common to almost all religious traditions, and for that matter almost all secular ethical traditions dating back at least to Hobbes (see respectively Brian D Lepard, *Rethinking Humanitarian Intervention: A Fresh Legal Approach Based on Fundamental Ethical Principles in International Law and World Religions* University Park, PA: Pennsylvania State University Press, 2002, 50–52, and Thomas Hobbes, *The Leviathan*, edited by Edwin Curley Indianapolis: Hackett Publishing Company, 1994, 99). In fact, the *Declaration of Independence of Cyberspace* nominates it as a shared value for the online community as well. However such a general principle does not scale to a sufficient level of granularity to account for all principles of international law; for example, it may not prevent the amputation of limbs as a punishment for theft as the Sharia allows: Schooley (as in n. 384 on page 171), 688–689.

ably lies in between the extremes of strict cultural relativism, in which no culturally inappropriate international norms can be considered, and universalism in which the Western liberal paradigm is treated as universal and immutable. This middle ground of moderate cultural relativism requires some "minimum standard of protection [of human rights] that must be evaluated and legitimated through culture."[396] The programme of evaluating and legitimating international norms within the framework of Sharia would fall to liberal Muslims, in collaboration with others in international society.[397]

So in summation, although there is no simple solution to the complex problem of how to accommodate cultural differences in international and transnational lawmaking, the beginnings of an answer are found in a fourfold approach:

- Firstly, to engage affected cultural groups at all stages of policy development to see whether norms originating in the Western liberal tradition can be explicated in culturally appropriate forms—or, importantly, *vice versa* in the case of norms important to other cultures that they may seek to have recognised in international fora. Whilst this exercise is open to criticism on the ground that it seeks to retro-fit norms that presuppose underlying values of Western liberal individualism into a culture that does not hold those underlying values[398] (or *vice versa*), it may still be the only workable compromise in a fundamentally multicultural world.

- Second, the inability of an international forum to conclude an instrument that is universally culturally acceptable does not mean that the instrument cannot still be widely adopted. Even hard international law is not automatically binding on nation states, as they remain free either not to accede to it at all, or in some cases to do so with reservations. Thus if international or transnational law is developed with an intrinsic liberal character, it will only be appropriated by liberal actors: so be it. In the case of Internet-related public policy, this may be inevitable, as Internet culture largely reflects liberal values such as freedom of expression, and indeed embeds them deeply in its technical and social architecture. The Internet itself is not a culturally neutral artifact, any more than other communications technologies

---

[396]Schooley (as in n. 384 on page 171), 679

[397]Etzioni (as in n. 391 on page 172). This approach is reflected in the new constitutions of Afghanistan and Iraq, the former of which provides in Article 3 that "In Afghanistan, no law can be contrary to the beliefs and provisions of the sacred religion of Islam," yet in Article 7(1) that "The state shall abide by the UN charter, international treaties, international conventions that Afghanistan has signed, and the Universal Declaration of Human Rights": *Constitution of the Islamic Republic of Afghanistan*, 4 Jan 2004.

[398]Schooley (as in n. 384 on page 171), 713–714

are.[399] Internet-related public policy therefore cannot be expected to be either.

- Third, it is common for certain issues, such as matters of security, to be left out of the sphere of the governance of an international regime, in which case national regulation is left to "fill in the gaps."[400] It is likely that the most contentious matters of Internet-related public policy can be dealt with in this way. For example, a policy on content regulation can be drafted in broad principles, leaving details to be implemented on a national level with regard to domestic cultural norms. Whilst this will not result in a uniform and comprehensive international content regulation regime, it will still be more than exists now. In fact for liberals, this is not merely a pragmatic compromise, but rather the just outcome in cases where cultural differences between peoples preclude a uniform approach.[401]
- Finally, and as a proviso to the other points, there may be some cases in which customary international law or even *jus cogens* has developed from which states are unable to opt out, even if it does conflict with their cultures. This is most likely to be the case in respect of human rights. In these cases, where the issues involved are ideological rather than merely cultural, there is likely to remain some trampling of cultural values that are plainly at variance with international norms. Little more can be said than that this is an instance in which the hegemony of the liberal majority is (justly, by its own standards) exercised over the illiberal minority. In most instances, this will not apply to the work of the IGF which is only involved in the development of soft law.

3.5 Internet governance as law

The purpose of this chapter was to survey the field of international law, as the dominant international order for the governance of public policy

[399] Harold A Innis, *The Bias of Communication* Toronto: University of Toronto Press, 1991

[400] Franda (as in n. 43 on page 42), 206

[401] Goldsmith and Wu (as in n. 220 on page 80), 152–153. It is also consistent with the principle of subsidiarity: see section 6.2 on page 432.

A practical example of this is found in the approach advocated by the Keep the Core Neutral campaign that opposes ICANN's application of cultural as well as technical standards for the approval of new gTLDs (see `http://www.keep-the-core-neutral.org/`), on the basis that "[i]f Saudi Arabia objects to the .allah domain or the Vatican city dislikes .jesus then they will be free to block them, but we should not limit the capabilities of the network just because of these sectional interests": Bill Thompson, Time To Led a Thousand Domains Bloom? ⟨URL: `http://news.bbc.co.uk/1/hi/technology/6262386.stm`⟩. The Council of Europe's Cybercrime Convention also illustrates this approach, in that its provisions to curb the promulgation of xenophobic content online are contained in an Additional Protocol against Racism, in order to allow countries such as the USA for whom these provisions conflict with free expression principles to ratify only the balance of the Convention.

issues, in order to describe the context in which any institution seeking involvement in Internet public policy governance must operate. In the course of this survey, it has been revealed that apart from international law there are also other international orders for the governance of public policy issues, of which the new law merchant is a specific case, and which in their generalised context have been described as transnational law.

The obvious question that remains, and which has been touched on obliquely but not resolved, is whether Internet public policy governance takes place, or will in the future take place, in the environment of international law, or transnational law—or perhaps both, or neither.

As outlined in Chapter 2, the most mature institutions for governance of the Internet are those involved in standards development, rather than those involved in public policy governance. Since international standards are as we have seen a form of soft law,[402] it is therefore arguable, for what it is worth, that Internet standards already constitute international law.

Similarly, the regime that has been described in this book as technical coordination also constitutes international law in the same "soft law" sense. ICANN, the preeminent body of technical coordination of the Internet, is an active subject of international society, directly entering into agreements with states over ccTLD administration,[403] and convening its own intergovernmental advisory panel, the GAC.

Although it may have been accurate in earlier days to say that bodies such as ICANN "have no authority and no ability to implement anything, other than what they care to make available and hope that people use,"[404] ICANN's perceived legitimacy and thereby its authority have grown as its actions in the administration of the DNS system have been accepted (or at least not directly challenged) by states.[405] At the very least, this illustrates that ICANN operates as a subject of international society under *de facto* delegation from the international community.[406]

Is it possible to go further and contend that the international legal order, by accepting the ICANN regime, has elevated it to the status of customary international law? There is certainly widespread state practice to support such a contention; universal in fact if the use of ccTLDs under the ICANN

[402] See section 3.3 on page 136.

[403] See `http://www.icann.org/cctlds/agreements.html`.

[404] A Rutkowski, Regulate the Internet? Try If You Can., Communications Week International April 26 1999

[405] Ian Hurd, Legitimacy and Authority in International Politics, International Organization 53:2 1999; Strange (as in n. 95 on page 117). On one view though, the contribution to this phenomenon of the underlying authority of the United States government should not be underestimated: A Michael Froomkin, Form and Substance in Cyberspace, 94. On the other hand see section 5.1 on page 344.

[406] Council of Europe, Building a Free and Safe Internet ⟨URL: `http://www.intgovforum.org/Substantive_2nd_IGF/CoE_Building%20a%20free%20and%20safe%20Internet.pdf`⟩, 7

root is used as a measure.[407]

Opinio juris is more difficult to demonstrate without empirical evidence, of which none has been collected, but there is no reason in principle why this could not be found and why customary international law could not therefore form from the norms of the Internet community,[408] either directly or by the intermediate soft law stages of an international code (such as the Incoterms), or standard (such as the International Code of Signals). According to one commentator, such norms have already impacted upon the development of Internet-related domestic law, including

> the generally accepted activity of linking without permission, the aggressive commitment to a libertarian view of free-speech rights, and the ongoing consensus regarding the perceived right to remain anonymous.[409]

However it must be acknowledged that even if the ICANN system for management of the DNS root has attained (or is on the way to attaining) the status of customary international law, Internet governance at large as outlined in Chapter 2 involves far more than just ICANN. Whilst its various other constituent institutions from all stakeholder groups (the IETF, the W3C, the EFF, the LAP, the ITU, WIPO, CERT, TRUSTe, the OECD, UNCITRAL and many others) may be accepted by state and non-state actors alike as legitimate authorities in their fields, the corpus of their work is not accepted as international law.

But if the governance of these institutions is acknowledged by the existing international order as legitimate and authoritative, yet is not accepted as law, then what is it accepted as? A regime is the most obvious answer. And what is a regime, but part of an autonomous transnational legal order distinct from and coexistent with that of orthodox international law. The acceptance of the regime of Internet governance as an autonomous legal order is shown both in the words of international actors—the very words of the Tunis Agenda acknowledge it[410]—and also through their actions, such as their conclusion of agreements with ICANN and their passage of domestic and international instruments that complement rather than seeking to trump the existing regime.[411] A like case is the way in which

[407] The final ccTLDs—those for North Korea (kp), Serbia (rs) and Montenegro (me)—were delegated in 2007, leaving only four minor territories whose ccTLD remains unassigned: see `http://www.iana.org/domains/root/db/`.

[408] Weber (as in n. 70 on page 20)

[409] Biegel (as in n. 60 on page 19), and see *1267623 Ontario Inc v Nexx Online Inc* (unreported Ontario Superior Court of Justice, OJ No 2246, decided 14 June 1999) in which it was ruled that "sending unsolicited bulk e-mail is in breach of the emerging principles of Netiquette, unless it is specifically permitted in the governing contract." Compare also Mueller, Net Neutrality as Global Principal for Internet Governance (as in n. 20 on page 8).

[410] See section 3.1 on page 102.

[411] For example, the *Spam Act 2003* (Cth) and the *UNCITRAL Model Law on Electronic Commerce*.

states recognise and support the new law merchant through accession to the *New York Convention* and the *UNCITRAL Model Law on International Commercial Arbitration* which reinforce the transnational commercial arbitration regime.

Recognition of Internet governance as a regime is not limited to the United Nations. It is also accepted by scholars such as Spar who considers it as a private international regime,[412] and Franda who considers it an international regime in formation, in which the parameters of its governance are shaped by "a wide variety of private business firms, governments, universities and scientific, professional and epistemic communities spread across the globe."[413]

However the terminology of regime theory, being rooted in international relations theory, obscures something very important about Internet governance that has been lost since we have ceased to speak of its reception into customary international law, and that is the scope for the institutions of Internet governance to be seen *as law* (for a regime is nothing other than transnational law, restricted to a single issue-area).[414]

It is important to make that point, because if it is not made, it is implicitly being accepted that governance of the Internet fundamentally depends for its force upon the old Westphalian system of international and domestic law. While it is true that some of the institutions acting in Internet governance remain loosely tied to that system (ICANN to the United States government, the IGF to the United Nations), it is vital to comprehend that the transnational law that they create need not be so tied, loosely or otherwise.

This is not to say that the two systems of law cannot interact. They can, and inevitably will. But the fundamental point is that the transnational law of Internet governance need not collapse if states ceased to take any part of it. It need not even do so even if states ceased to recognise it, as they do at present, for a state's failure to recognise an independent and coexistent system of law does not extinguish it.[415]

Having said that, in practice the fate of the nascent regime of Internet governance as it matures under the leadership of the IGF remains a matter of speculation. Whilst it does have the potential to flourish into a fully formed transnational legal institution that would survive cut free of its roots, there is also the risk that it will become dominated by state hegemony

---

[412]Though she allows that the private sector will control "not the Internet of course, but their own growing corners of commerce and communication ... through a combination of formal and informal rules, administrative and technical means": Debora L Spar, *Private Authority and International Affairs* New York: SUNY Press, 1999, chap. Lost in (Cyber)space: The Private Rules of Online Commerce, 48.

[413]Franda (as in n. 43 on page 42), 5

[414]Rosenau, Governance Without Government: Order and Change in World Politics (as in n. 64 on page 19), 8

[415]*Mabo v Queensland* (#2) (1992) 175 CLR 1

and be absorbed into the old international legal system.

It is important that the IGF does not allow this to happen, becoming just another intergovernmental organisation beholden to its Westphalian masters, but rather that it should live up to its mandate to initiate "a transparent, democratic, and multilateral process, with the participation of governments, private sector, civil society and international organizations." How the IGF is to do this is question to be examined in the next chapter.

Chapter 4

Designing a governance network

> Who rules the Net? You and I and 600 million others, in some measure.
>
> Vinton Cerf

To resolve that public policy governance of the Internet should be the province of a network of governments, private sector and civil society organisations does not presuppose that its form should be that which has in fact taken shape in the IGF. The structure and processes of the IGF, which are to be examined in Chapter 5, were not organised spontaneously, nor inevitably. A network can in fact take any of a number of different forms. The main purpose of this chapter is to examine and compare four such forms that might be used to structure a governance network such as the IGF.

As background to this exercise, an instructive analogy is found in the topology of computer networks such as the Internet. During the NSFNET period, the Internet was arranged in an hierarchical (or tree) structure whereby networks connecting to the Internet were required to establish direct links to the NSFNET backbone network (or if they were too small to justify a direct link, to link to larger networks that were in turn connected to the NSFNET backbone). So for example, in order for one university network to reach another, rather than sending its data across a link that directly connected the two universities, the data would be sent by the first university to the NSFNET backbone which would route it through to the second university by reference to an authoritative table of routing information that was maintained by the NSF.[1] This is a "top–down" structure.

[1] P S Ford, Y Rekhter and H W Braun, Improving the Routing and Addressing of IP, IEEE

The topology of the modern day Internet on the other hand is a distributed mesh network, in which the routing function is decentralised. Any node on the network can communicate with any other node across a multiplicity of possible paths, none of which need include any given central point. The redundancy of any given link in such a network makes the network as a whole more resilient against failure. Although it contrasts starkly with the top–down model, this is not so much a bottom–up structure—since that still implies the existence of a hierarchy, though inverted—as middle–out; or in computer network terminology, peer-to-peer.

Top–down and peer-to-peer computer networks have their equivalents in what we will respectively term hierarchical and consensual organisations. Whilst on the Internet the consensual paradigm is dominant, in organisations, the hierarchical paradigm prevails. This is in part the legacy of Weber, who theorised that a bureaucracy structured along hierarchical lines, with a strict division of labour and standardised procedures, was the most efficient (or rational) form an organisation could take.[2]

However examples of post-bureaucratic organisations, in which decisions are made by dialogue and consensus between peers,[3] have also more recently begun to emerge, and in fact are exemplified by a number of the institutions of Internet governance.[4] For such organisations, electronic communications are an enabling force,[5] not merely making old structures more efficient, but offering new ways of organising of which Weber could not have conceived, characterised by the fluidity of authority and the use of soft power.

These organisational forms, hierarchical and consensual, will be discussed below as two of the possible structures for a governance network such as the IGF. However, two other structures for which no ready analogue is found in computer networking are also possible: the bottom–up form, which will be described as democratic, and the absence of ordering altogether which will be described as anarchistic.[6]

Network 7:3 1993

[2]Max Weber, *The Theory of Social and Economic Organization* New York: Free Press, 1964

[3]C Heckscher, *The Post-Bureaucratic Organization: New Perspectives on Organizational Change* Thousand Oaks, CA: Sage Publications, 1994, chap. Defining the Post-Bureaucratic Type

[4]See section 4.4 on page 302.

[5]Fulk and DeSanctis (as in n. 95 on page 25)

[6]It might seem a retrograde step to be considering top–down and bottom–up structures for a governance network, when governance by network has already been distinguished from governance by rules in its lack of hierarchy. However this can be explained by distinguishing between governance *by* network, which is a mechanism of governance through which public policy issues are addressed in concert by a coalition of affected stakeholders, and governance *of* the network, which is the coordination of the application of that mechanism through whatever internal structures and processes the stakeholders may devise. There is no reason why governance *of* the network might not involve a hierarchy of organisational roles.

To put this more concretely, an organisation consisting of governmental, civil society, private sector and intergovernmental stakeholders could equally conduct its affairs through the leadership of an elite subcommittee, or by democratic vote, or through consensus, or without relying

This chapter describes each of these four forms of organisational structure in turn, with consideration of their inherent merits, as well as where relevant their compatibility with the international system described in Chapter 3, and with the culture of the Internet as described in Chapter 2. The aim is that by the end of the chapter we will have settled (if at a fairly abstract level) upon an appropriate organisational structure for international public policy governance of the Internet, which satisfies the criteria developed in previous chapters.

4.1 Anarchistic

It is often mistakenly thought that anarchists favour disorder and chaos. In fact the essence of anarchy as a political philosophy is the promotion of private, voluntary ordering as an alternative to the hierarchical ordering of, principally, the state. Malatesta writes

> of the destruction of all political order based on authority, and the creation of a society of free and equal members based on a harmony of interests and the voluntary participation of everybody in carrying out social responsibilities.[7]

Anarchism thus does not imply so much lack of ordering, or even a lack of authority *per se*, as lack of hierarchy. Authority that stems from the natural influence of an expert amongst her peers is welcomed by the anarchist. As Bakunin wrote:

> In general, we ask nothing better than to see men endowed with great knowledge, great experience, great minds, and, above all, great hearts, exercise over us a natural and legitimate influence, freely accepted, and never imposed in the name of any official authority whatsoever, celestial or terrestrial.[8]

Anarchism is therefore quite a natural structure for a governance network between peers. Social movements structured in such manner have been

---

on any predefined mechanism at all.

This is not to say that a governance network may adopt *any* internal management structure and still correctly be described as exercising governance by network. If it possesses an hierarchical or democratic internal structure which is such as to negate the participation of the stakeholders who are nominally involved, the organisation may in effect be exercising governance by rules led by the dominant participant or participants.

[7] E Malatesta, *Anarchy* London: Freedom Press, 1974, 13

[8] Mikhail Aleksandrovich Bakunin, *God and the State* New York: Courier Dover Publications, 1970, 35

termed SPINs: "segmentary, polycentric, integrated networks," and have been the subject of study for well over 30 years.[9]

Anarchy and the Internet

The compatibility of the architecture and culture of the Internet with these ideals was recognised early in its development. Bruce Sterling famously described the Internet in 1993 as "a rare example of a true, modern, functional anarchy."[10] A few years later, John Perry Barlow issued the *Declaration of Independence of Cyberspace*;[11] an anarchist tract *par exemplar*.

With the inroads that governments have since begun to make into the Internet's inherent architectural anarchism, those who would practise anarchy on the Internet have not so much retreated as regrouped. Today, self-styled crypto-anarchists utilise technologies such as strong encryption, virtual private networks (VPNs), and electronic cash,[12] in an endeavour to forge a stateless anarchist society online.[13]

These technologies further this aim by enabling users to craft online spaces, known as cypherspace (or cipherspace), in which they may act anonymously or pseudonymously, thereby rendering domestic laws on such matters as copyright, content regulation, and taxation unenforceable and thus, it could be said, inapplicable.[14]

Predictably, resources hosted in cypherspace include unlicensed copies of copyrighted media, child pornography, and even supposed confessions to murder, but also anonymous support fora for victims of sexual assault, communiques from dissidents and whistle-blowers, and lively pseudonomous chat and discussion fora.

Usenet

Anarchy is also a familiar governing principle for some more conventional and widely-used Internet services. An early example is found in the

---

[9]Luther Gerlach, *Waves of Protest: Social Movements Since the Sixties* Lanham, MD: Rowman & Littlefield Publishers, 1999, chap. The Structure of Social Movements: Environmental Activism and Its Opponents

[10]Bruce Stirling, A Short History of the Internet ⟨URL: `http://www.library.yale.edu/div/instruct/internet/history.htm`⟩

[11]Barlow (as in n. 3 on page 1)

[12]For example e-gold; see `http://www.e-gold.com/`, and compare Ripple at `http://ripple.sourceforge.net/`, which is an open source implementation of electronic cash, the value of which depends upon the trust between debtor and creditor, rather than being backed by a valuable commodity.

[13]Timothy C May, *Crypto Anarchy, Cyberstates, and Pirate Utopias* Cambridge, MA: MIT Press, 2001, chap. Crypto Anarchy and Virtual Communities

[14]One of the tools used in this way is Tor, which was discussed at section 1.3 on page 9.

governance of Usenet. Usenet was one of the early applications deployed on the Internet, preceding the World Wide Web by six years, but even before that it existed as an independent online network of computers running the Unix operating system (the name Usenet being derived from Unix User Network).

Unix users were no strangers to anarchistic governance regimes. Richard M Stallman, founder of the GNU project to create a free Unix-like operating system,[15] discussed the philosophy that lay behind a previous operating system developed by hackers, the Incompatible Time-sharing System (ITS) of the Artificial Intelligence Lab at MIT. ITS was designed to solve problems of users hacking into each other's accounts and bringing down the computer, precisely by not putting any controls in to begin with: the system had no passwords, and could be brought to its knees by any user typing the command "KILL SYSTEM." Stallman boasted,

> If I told people it's possible to have no security on a computer without people deleting your files all the time, and no bosses stopping you from doing things ... nobody will [*sic*] would] believe me. For a while, we were setting an example for the rest of the world.[16]

Usenet provides a discussion board system, that unlike most similar systems before or since, is distributed. That is to say that, in keeping with the principle of decentralisation that underlies Internet architecture generally, there is no central archive of Usenet messages (or posts); rather, each site that participates in the Usenet network maintains its own copies of posts, and periodically synchronises them with its peers. New posts can therefore enter the Usenet network from any such site. Haubern writes that

> Usenet should be seen as a promising successor to other people's presses, such as broadsides at the time of the American Revolution and the Penny Presses in England at the turn of the 19th Century. Most of the material written to Usenet is by the same people who actively read Usenet. Thus, the audience of Usenet decides the content and subject matter to be thought about, presented and debated. The ideas that exist on Usenet come from the mass of people who participate in it. In this way, Usenet is an uncensored forum for debate - where many sides of an issue come into view. Instead of being force-fed by an uncontrollable source of information, the participants set the tone and emphasis on Usenet.[17]

---

[15] See `http://www.gnu.org/`, GNU standing for "GNU's Not Unix."

[16] Levy (as in n. 16 on page 5), 427.

[17] Michael Hauben and Ronda Hauben, Netizens: On the History and Impact of Usenet and the Internet ⟨URL: `http://www.columbia.edu/~hauben/netbook/`⟩, chapter 3

Usenet posts are categorised by topic in fora known as newsgroups. From the inception of the network in 1979 until 1985, anyone could create a newsgroup and anyone could delete one.[18] As the network grew larger, it became evident that this procedure did not scale well, as there was no way to enforce the addition and deletion decisions made at one site by others. Additionally, some newsgroups were straining under the weight of off-topic or offensive posts, or vituperative and insulting exchanges—"flame wars."[19]

But as anarchy does not imply disorder, rather collaborative and voluntary order, the solution to these problems came from within. To address the issue of coordination, one Usenet administrator, Gene Spafford, from 1985 to 1993 published a monthly list of "officially recognised" newsgroups which other Usenet-connected sites could (but were not obliged to) follow in deciding what groups to carry for users on their own servers.[20]

To address the issue of inappropriate posts, rather than censoring ("cancelling") such posts, the facility for the establishment of new moderated groups was introduced—but even in this case, the architecture behind the moderation technology was advisory rather than hierarchical. A message would automatically pass through into a moderated group if an "Approved" header—which could easily be forged—was inserted. [21]

In 1985, a group of system administrators of those servers that had come to function as something of a backbone of the Usenet network, and who styled themselves with some irony as the "Backbone Cabal," reordered the newsgroups into an hierarchical structure. At the root of the hierarchy at this time were the prefixes comp, misc, news, rec, sci, soc and talk, respectively for discussion on computing, miscellany, Usenet, recreation, science, society and controversial topics that were likely to produce flame wars. The decision of the Backbone Cabal to sideline controversial topics in the "talk" (originally "flame") branch of the hierarchy, which could be easily omitted from a site's Usenet feed, was productive of much dissent from ordinary Usenet users.[22]

Still further controversy resulted from the refusal of Backbone Cabal members to carry the newly-formed groups rec.sex and rec.drugs. The process by which new newsgroup could be formed had by around this time been formalised, such that proposals should first be discussed on the news.groups newsgroup, and a vote taken: if 100 more votes favoured the

---

[18] Bryan Pfaffenberger, "If I Want It, It's OK": Usenet and the Outer Limits of Free Speech, The Information Society 12:4 1996, 371

[19] Ibid., 373

[20] Ibid., 371

[21] Later, the facility for the moderator to be authenticated using digital cryptography was added to prevent such forgeries, though this was only adopted in a minority of moderated groups: Greg G Rose, The PGP Moose: Implementation and Experience ⟨URL: `http://db.usenix.org/publications/library/proceedings/lisa96/full_papers/ggr/ggr.ps`⟩.

[22] Pfaffenberger (as in n. 18), 375–376

creation of the newsgroup than opposed it, being at least two-thirds of the total number of votes, it would be added to the list of officially recognised groups.[23] Yet although rec.sec and rec.drugs had passed this test (or a less formal precursor of it), Spafford declined to add them to his "official" list.[24]

Whilst this may have suggested that Usenet was no longer organised along anarchistic lines after all, but had become subject to the dominance of the Backbone Cabal, this did not account for the fact that Usenet's anarchistic origins had been embedded in its technical architecture. Accordingly in 1987 a small group of Usenet administrators, dissatisfied with the policies of the Cabal, simply bypassed it by establishing a new hierarchy of alt ("alternative") newsgroups, amongst the first of which were alt.sex, alt.drugs, and for good measure, alt.rock-n-roll.[25]

In the alt hierarchy, new newsgroups could once again be created or deleted by anyone, though normally a site would only choose to carry a group upon request, or following the emergence of sufficient consensus as to the utility of the group on the alt.config newsgroup. The alt hierarchy soon became, and remains, the biggest on Usenet.

A regular posting to the newsgroup news.announce.newusers, intended for new Usenet users and originally authored by Chip Salzenberg, states under the heading "Usenet is not a democracy," that "[s]ince there is no person or group in charge of Usenet as a whole—ie there is no Usenet 'government'—it follows that Usenet cannot be a democracy, autocracy, or any other kind of '-acy.'"[26] Whilst much else has changed in Internet governance in the intervening years, Salzenberg's statement remains accurate.

This is not to say that Usenet is a utopia. Far from it. The anarchistic system by which it is governed has resulted in a measure of chaos and antisocial conduct online, ranging from the omnipresent newsgroup spam that originated with lawyers Canter and Siegel,[27] to the creation of groups such as alt.binaries.pictures.erotica.rape and alt.kill.jews. However, the anarchistic project is not to create a utopia. Rocker writes,

> Anarchism is no patent solution for all human problems, no Utopia of a perfect social order, as it has so often been called, since on principle it rejects all absolute schemes and concepts. It does not believe in any absolute truth, or in definite final goals for human development, but in an unlimited perfectibility of

[23]David C Lawrence, How to Create a New Usenet Newsgroup ⟨URL: http://www.faqs.org/faqs/usenet/creating-newsgroups/part1/⟩

[24]Henry Edward Hardy, The History of the Net ⟨URL: http://www.eff.org/Net_culture/net.history.txt⟩

[25]Pfaffenberger (as in n. 18 on the preceding page), 377

[26]Chip Salzenberg, Gene Spafford and Mark Moraes, What is Usenet? ⟨URL: http://www.faqs.org/faqs/usenet/what-is/part1/⟩

[27]Campbell (as in n. 85 on page 23)

> social arrangements and human living conditions, which are always straining after higher forms of expression, and to which for this reason one can assign no definite terminus nor set any fixed goal.[28]

Wikipedia

The popular online encyclopædia Wikipedia[29] provides an example of how an organisation both more formal and more recent than Usenet might be successfully governed along anarchistic lines.

Wikipedia is the world's largest encyclopædia. Its one millionth article in its English language edition was published in March 2006, at which time there were also 228 other language editions, eleven containing 100 000 articles or more. In February 2007 Wikipedia reached its highest ranking of eighth amongst the most popular Web sites worldwide.[30]

Wikipedia is only the most prominent example amongst thousands of "wikis"; Web sites constructed and hosted using software which allows visitors to the site to collaboratively edit its content using a convenient Web-based interface.[31] Other typical characteristics of wikis are the heavy use of cross-hyperlinking between pages, and that contributors are required to license their contributions under an open source style licence, so as to allow other users to freely make their own adaptations of the content.[32]

The problems that might have been expected to result from such a liberal regime have indeed arisen in Wikipedia's case: regular vandalism of pages, "edit wars" between users who compete to have the last word by undoing ("reverting") each other's changes, and the publication of inaccurate or erroneous information. Given that the mission of the site is to act as an encyclopædia, it is this last problem that has drawn the most comment from critics. A correspondent to the *Washington Post* is representative of these, writing:

> It combines the global reach and authoritative bearing of an Internet encyclopedia with the worst elements of radicalized bloggers. You step into a blog, you know what you're getting. But if you search an encyclopedia, it's fair to expect something

---

[28] Rudolf Rocker, *Anarcho-Syndicalism: Theory and Practice*, 6th edition Edinburgh: AK Press, 2004, 15

[29] See `http://www.wikipedia.org/`.

[30] See `http://meta.wikimedia.org/wiki/Wikipedia.org_is_more_popular_than...`.

[31] See generally Bo Leuf and Ward Cunningham, *The Wiki Way: Quick Collaboration on the Web* Boston: Addison-Wesley Professional, 2001. The original Wiki software, WikiWikiWeb (see `http://c2.com/cgi/wiki/`), was released in 1994, but numerous reimplementations and improvements upon the idea have since been written, including MediaWiki (see `http://www.mediawiki.org/`) upon which Wikipedia is built.

[32] See section 4.2 on page 211.

else. Actual facts, say. At its worst, Wikipedia is an active deception, a powerful piece of agitprop, not information.[33]

However, other commentators have been impressed with Wikipedia's accuracy. A 2005 report in *Nature* found Wikipedia's accuracy to be roughly comparable to that of *Encyclopædia Britannica* (whilst this was strongly repudiated by *Britannica*,[34] *Nature* has defended its original report[35]).

The level of overall accuracy that Wikipedia has attained, and its resilience against attacks from vandals and disruption from disputes between editors, are not accidental. They are matters directly addressed by the norms of the Wikipedia community, and formalised in its structure, and its official policies and guidelines. As at September 2006, there were 42 policies[36] and hundreds of guidelines in place (guidelines being less imperative and more advisory in nature than policies).[37] These policies are grouped into five categories, which are described on Wikipedia as follows:

- Behavioral: standards for behavior on Wikipedia to make it a pleasant experience for everyone.
- Content: which topics are welcome on Wikipedia and give quality and naming standards.
- Deletion: the body of policies dealing with the issue of article deletion.
- Enforcement: what action authorised users can take to enforce other policies.
- Legal and copyright: law-based rules about what material may be used here, and remedies for misuse.

Tellingly however, there is one policy that explicitly overrides all others: "If the rules prevent you from improving or maintaining Wikipedia's quality, ignore them." It is this policy that reinforces the distinction between the rules of an hierarchical community and the norms of an anarchistic one such as Wikipedia.

[33]Frank Ahrens, Death by Wikipedia: The Kenneth Lay Chronicles ⟨URL: http://www.washingtonpost.com/wp-dyn/content/article/2006/07/08/AR2006070800135.html⟩

[34]Encyclopædia Britannica, Fatally Flawed: Refuting the Recent Study on Encyclopedic Accuracy by the Journal Nature ⟨URL: http://corporate.britannica.com/britannica_nature_response.pdf⟩; and Brittanica staff have attacked Wikipedia's accuracy elsewhere also: Robert McHenry, The Faith-Based Encyclopedia ⟨URL: http://www.tcsdaily.com/article.aspx?id=111504A⟩.

[35]See http://www.nature.com/nature/britannica/.

[36]See http://en.wikipedia.org/wiki/Wikipedia:List_of_policies.

[37]See http://en.wikipedia.org/wiki/Wikipedia:List_of_guidelines.

A further illustration of the difference between policies as rules and policies as norms is in respect of the consequences of their breach. A Wikipedia editor who goes by the username "the Cuncator" explains that breaches of policy "should not be used as reasons to violently delete other people's work. Rather, if you believe in the rules, you should attempt to convert those people to your view. Use words, not force."[38]

Notwithstanding these sentiments, there has been a continuing tension between those Wikipedia administrators and editors such as the Cuncator who favour the retention of an anarchistic approach to the editing of the encyclopædia, and pragmatists such as Wikipedia's original co-founder Larry Sanger[39] who have proposed to create a hierarchy of more trusted users with elevated privileges,[40] such as exists on other community-developed Web sites such as the venerable news discussion site, Slashdot.[41]

Although Sanger's views have not found favour within the broader Wikipedia community, this is not to say that the project is completely egalitarian. Outside of its substantive work, the administration of the project combines anarchistic with consensual, democratic, and even hierarchical models of ordering.[42]

As an example of consensual ordering, ordinary users cannot delete articles: this ability is reserved to Wikipedia administrators, and then only after the issue has been put up for discussion by all Wikipedia users for about a week, and a rough consensus has been reached in favour of deletion. Anyone may nominate themselves (or another user) for the status of administrator, and requests are assessed in much the same way as proposals to delete an article; once a consensus is reached following a discussion period amongst Wikipedia editors.[43]

As for democratic ordering, Wikipedia has a Mediation Committee and an Arbitration Committee which take a more substantive role in the

---

[38] J Thurgood, How to Build Wikipedia ⟨URL: `http://en.wikipedia.org/wiki/User:The_Cunctator/How_to_build_Wikipedia`⟩

[39] Sanger, whilst agreeing with the Cuncator that the Wikipedia project is organised anarchistically, criticises it for being "anti-elitist (which, in this context, means that expertise is not accorded any special respect, and snubs and disrespect of expertise is tolerated)": Larry Sanger, Why Wikipedia Must Jettison Its Anti-Elitism ⟨URL: `http://www.kuro5hin.org/story/2004/12/30/142458/25`⟩.

[40] Marshall Poe, The Hive ⟨URL: `http://www.theatlantic.com/doc/200609/wikipedia`⟩

[41] See `http://slashdot.org/`.

[42] These are to be discussed at sections 4.3 on page 240, 4.3 on page 226 and 4.2 on page 196.

[43] See `http://en.wikipedia.org/wiki/Wikipedia:Administrators`. As well as the power to delete articles, administrators exclusively possess the power to temporarily lock articles and ban users in order to combat the most serious instances of vandalism and edit wars. There are also a few other classes of special users on Wikipedia, to which various criteria for appointment or election are attached. These include bureaucrats (who can grant administrator status, but not remove it), stewards (who can grant and remove administrator and bureaucrat status), and developers (who have control of the MediaWiki software and the databases that underlie Wikipedia). These are largely technical functions that must be exercised in accordance with the wishes of the community.

editing process, by assisting to resolve disputes between editors. Whilst membership of the Mediation Committee is open to any who volunteer and who are approved by consensus discussion, the twelve members of the Arbitration Committees are elected for three year terms by a vote of Wikipedia editors.[44]

The MediaWiki software and databases themselves of course require computer hardware and network connectivity in order to operate, and these in turn require funding, as well as administrative oversight. These issues are the responsibility of the five-member Board of Trustees of the Wikimedia Foundation, a non-profit organisation that has owned the infrastructure of the Wikipedia project since 2003.[45]

All active Wikipedia editors are eligible to vote in the biannual elections of the Board of Trustees, and to nominate for one of two Board positions. However the remaining Board positions are held by Wikipedia's founder Jimmy Wales, and two members appointed by him. The authority that Wales exercises in perpetuity is an example of hierarchical ordering within the Wikipedia project.[46]

Thus the Wikipedia project does not embody anarchistic governance in its purest form, but can perhaps be fairly described, in the words of the Cuncator, as "a noble attempt at a limited anarchistic society."[47] It illustrates well for present purposes is how an Internet-based social entity of significant size can, successfully and consistently with the principles of anarchism, be internally governed largely through the non-hierarchical mechanisms of architecture (the MediaWiki software) and norms (Wikipedia's policies and guidelines).

Anarchistic Internet governance

It is appealing on an intuitive level to consider that the same anarchistic principles could be applied in structuring a governance network to deal with Internet-related public policy issues. The fact that anarchistic ordering is consistent with the Internet's core architectural principles on a technical level, and also philosophically consonant with many of them on a cultural level (decentralisation, openness, egalitarianism, anonymity and cosmopolitanism in particular), a network forged on anarchistic principles is likely to be more successful than one modelled on, say, the hierarchical authority of traditional intergovernmental organisations, by reason of being more culturally appropriate.

---

[44]See `http://en.wikipedia.org/wiki/Wikipedia:Elections`.

[45]See `http://www.wikimedia.org/`. In January 2006 the Board of Trustees also established a series of twelve subcommittees to deal with largely financial and administrative matters.

[46]Wales himself, an objectivist, could be described as a "minarchist" if not an anarchist: Poe (as in n. 40 on the preceding page).

[47]Thurgood (as in n. 38 on the facing page)

How would this work in practice? In essence, it would simply mean involving all stakeholders in Internet governance, but disallowing any of them to coerce the others (even by democratic or meritocratic claims). The applicable structures of governance in an anarchistic order could thus not be posited in advance, but would be those that emerge from spontaneous networks between stakeholders that form and reform as required. Reagle, an anarchist who has examined these characteristics in the Internet's technical governance, writes,

> With the cacophony of ideas, proposals, and debates, and a lack of a central authority to cleave the good from the bad, how does one sort it all out? It sorts itself out. We need not delegate our values to a central authority—subject to tyrannical or partisan tendencies. The success of any policy is based simply on its adoption by the community.[48]

Johnson and Post ground their preference for anarchistic ordering in Internet governance in the fact that the geography of online activities does not coincide with the sovereignty of any existing legal authority. They posit the emergence of responsible self-regulatory structures on the net, based upon common consensus, much in the same manner as the law merchant emerged from amongst those engaged in transnational commerce.[49]

This should be carefully distinguished from self-regulation, at least in the conventional sense. Such self-regulation is a form of governance in which stakeholders develop standards or codes to which they prospectively agree to bind themselves, typically as a trade-off against the threat of external coercion (such as governmental regulation). This is both inconsistent with anarchism and a misreading of Johnson and Post, for whom no structured regulation should be presupposed at all; rather, spontaneous regulation should be left to emerge through consensus. To distinguish this notion from self-regulation in the first sense given above, the phrase "decentralised collective action"[50] may be used.

The "rules" that emerge from decentralised collective action do not derive their force from hierarchical authority, which leaves markets, norms and architecture as the three possible mechanisms of internal governance for an anarchistic governance network.[51]

---

[48]Joseph Reagle, Why the Internet is Good: Community Governance That Works Well ⟨URL: `http://cyber.law.harvard.edu/people/reagle/regulation-19990326.html`⟩

[49]Johnson and Post (as in n. 348 on page 164)

[50]David R Johnson and Susan P Crawford, The Idea of ICANN ⟨URL: `http://www.icannwatch.org/archive/the_idea_of_icann.htm`⟩

[51]Though anarchists of the collectivist and communist schools, contrary to anarcho-capitalists, would omit the first of these, since market forces are supported by governmental enforcement of private property rights: Ruth Kinna, *Anarchism: A Beginner's Guide* Oxford: Oneworld Publications, 2005, 25.

An example of the use of markets in anarchistic Internet governance is found in some of early experiments in gTLD administration. At around the time of the IAHC, other DNS systems such as eDNS[52] were set up on a free market model, that in the case of eDNS would have allowed an unlimited number of registrars to administer up to ten new domains each, whilst still interoperating with the legacy IANA and NSI-administered domains.[53] There was even a similar project in Australia, the AURSC, which ended up with 28 new TLDs.[54] Both, having been superseded by ICANN (whose registry contracts prohibit dealings with alternate roots),[55] are now defunct, though there do remain a number of other active alternate roots with limited use.

The result would have been either a market of competitors offering similar services, or the market's convergence on a single winner through the force of network externalities,[56] producing a succession of serial monopolies. Either of these outcomes could have been alternatives to the ICANN model in which a single body is institutionalised in the role through the hierarchical force of its contract with the United States Department of Commerce.[57] Higgs has even applied game theory to the issue of multiple DNS roots, and concluded that it would be rational for multiple DNS roots to voluntarily cooperate,[58] as in practice many of them have.[59]

As for the use of norms within an anarchistic transnational network, the London Action Plan provides a good example. Whilst its members do agree to cooperate in the battle against spam through the use of tools such as domestic anti-spam legislation and education of users and businesses, they are not legally compelled to do so as they would be under a traditional intergovernmental agreement (not to mention that a traditional intergovernmental agreement would not include the private sector stakeholders that the LAP does). Rather, the LAP relies solely upon its members' shared norms as its internal mechanism of governance.

As well as being culturally appropriate for the governance of networks

---

[52] Previously at `http://www.edns.net/`; see `http://web.archive.org/web/19981201040715/http://www.edns.net/`.

[53] Rony and Rony (as in n. 18 on page 35), 544

[54] Australian Root Server Consortium; see `http://www.aursc.ah.net/`. Two other similar projects, uDNS and AlterNIC, are not only defunct but also no longer live on the Web.

[55] Mueller, *Ruling the Root: Internet Governance and the Taming of Cyberspace* (as in n. 21 on page 35), 220–221

[56] That is, the service becomes more valuable when more people use it: see M L Katz and C Shapiro, Technology Adoption in the Presence of Network Externalities, Journal of Political Economy 94 1986.

[57] Mueller, *Ruling the Root: Internet Governance and the Taming of Cyberspace* (as in n. 21 on page 35), 56

[58] S Higgs, Applying Game Theory To The Domain Name Root System ⟨URL: `http://www.higgs.com/archive/internet/drafts/draft-higgs-dns-game-theory-00.txt`⟩

[59] See `http://www.publicroot.org/`, a project to unify all known operational TLDs under a single independently-maintained root.

engaged in Internet public policy development, decentralised collective action also offers a number of practical benefits over hierarchical methods for the internal governance of networks. These include the ability to be more responsive to changes in the environment, to transcend the archaic territorial focus that is implicit in the Westphalian state system, and to develop and implement policies less expensively and more quickly.[60] In short, decentralised collective action is not only more culturally acceptable on the Internet, but can also be more efficient than hierarchical alternatives.

Criticisms

On the other hand, there are also other factors to be considered in assessing the appropriateness of anarchistic organisation for a governance network. At root, these factors are the network's legitimacy and its effectiveness.[61] It has already been determined that a network involving all stakeholders is the most legitimate mechanism of public policy governance for the Internet, and there is no reason to reopen that question here.[62] However, where that network is organised along anarchistic lines, its involvement of all stakeholders to the requisite degree is likely to be more difficult to demonstrate.

The two main indicia of an organisation's legitimacy are its accountability and transparency. These are important to whichever organisational structure is adopted by a governance network, and hence although they will be considered here to illustrate the main shortcomings of anarchistic ordering for a governance network, they are to be discussed in more depth at section 4.3 on page 260.

Briefly then, considering accountability in respect of the anarchistic structure in particular, the fluidity with which the arrangements between stakeholders in such a structure may form and reform make it difficult to ensure that at any given point, those arrangements are adequately inclusive of all stakeholders. Governments may, for example (and do), enter into arrangements between themselves without consultation with the private sector and civil society, or vice versa. Even where all stakeholder groups are represented, their power within the network may be unequal, replicating similar inequalities in the larger international system.[63]

This is not important in other contexts—Wikipedia, for example, publishes an encyclopædia; it does not deliberate upon issues of public policy that might affect stakeholders other than its own users, and therefore is not required to be accountable to them. But for a public policy governance network, stakeholders' uncertainty of the state of power relations in a gov-

[60] Weber (as in n. 70 on page 20), 80, 83–84

[61] See section 3.4 on page 145.

[62] See section 2.4 on page 91.

[63] See section 4.3 on page 289.

ernance network at any given time, and (by definition) their lack of control over the same, is a serious shortcoming of the anarchistic structure.

As for transparency, the London Action Plan, for example, has a "Members Only" section of its Web site that conceals a number of the details of its activities. Less formal governance networks of anarchistic structure are likely to be even less transparent.

As far as effectiveness is concerned, certainly, the efficiency of anarchistic ordering, and its cultural appropriateness (which increases the likely effectiveness of its internal governance by norms), both of which have already been noted, are positive indicators. On the other hand, detracting from the effectiveness of an anarchistically ordered governance network is its very voluntariness. Without denying that norms and architecture can effectively channel cooperative behaviour, there are also cases in which if stakeholders are given the choice to cooperate or to act strategically on their own, they will take the latter course.

In fact, rational choice theorists claim that strategic behaviour will be the rule rather than the exception in such cases. The prisoner's dilemma famously and simply illustrates the problem. If two accused prisoners in adjoining cells could cooperate and minimise each other's sentence by remaining silent, or could betray the other in order to go free themselves, it would always be in their rational self-interest to betray each other (or to "defect" in the language of game theory). This is so even though cooperation would have resulted in the least collective deprivation of liberty for them both.[64]

Whilst the anarchist's response is that cooperation does begin to become a rational strategy over the long term (which it does), even in such cases it is rarely the only rational strategy.[65] Thus for liberals, the institution of the state is necessary to protect individual rights that might be infringed by the strategic behaviour of others that game theory predicts.[66] In other contexts, it may be necessary for some other hierarchical authority to take the state's place in performing this function.

It may also be properly objected by anarchists that rational choice theory tends to leave aside the forces of norms and institutions which can result in cooperative behaviour emerging sooner than rational choice theory might predict;[67] however in the present context the point remains that there is little empirical evidence of stable governance networks that are

---

[64] William Poundstone, *Prisoner's Dilemma* New York: Doubleday, 1992, 120

[65] Andrew Rutten, Can Anarchy Save Us From Leviathan?, The Independent Review 3:4 1999, 587–591; Russell Hardin, *The Good Polity: Normative Analysis of the State* New York: Basil Blackwell, 1989, chap. Political Obligation, 115

[66] Robert Sugden, *The Good Polity: Normative Analysis of the State* New York: Basil Blackwell, 1989, chap. Maximizing Social Welfare: Is it the Government's Business?, 83

[67] Donald Green and Ian Shapiro, *Pathologies of Rational Choice Theory: A Critique of Applications in Political Science* New Haven, CT: Yale University Press, 1994, 121–123

truly inclusive of governments, the private sector and civil society forming spontaneously.[68]

But for the supranational authoritative force of the United Nations, for example (admittedly exercised through a soft law process), it is doubtful that the IGF would have come into being. There are many more examples (and the IGF may become one of them) in which governments have strategically gained the dominant position in what should have been a multi-stakeholder network—in the ITU, for example—and other cases in which non-governmental stakeholders have done so, as in the case of the ill-fated IAHC and its gTLD-MoU.

What is perhaps needed to overcome the problem of short-term strategic behaviour, and the other problems of anarchistic ordering that have been noted, is a hybrid which preserves the efficiency and cultural fit of decentralised collective action, with the greater (or at least more certain) accountability, transparency and effectiveness made possible by more structured organisational forms that utilise governance by rules. One such hybrid is called co-regulation. But it is hardly anarchistic; which takes us to the second of the four organisational structures to be considered in this chapter.

4.2 Hierarchical

To suggest that a governance network should be structured along hierarchical lines might hardly seem worth considering, in light of the conclusion already reached that its structure should concord with the architectural values of the Internet. But there are three reasons why this option should be in fact be considered.

First and most fundamentally, it should be recalled that the appropriate internal organisational structure for a governance network is a conceptually separate issue from the given fact that it must be inclusive of three separate stakeholder groups in its operation as a network. No structure that fails to adequately accommodate multi-stakeholderism can be considered for a governance network such as the IGF, whether it is hierarchical or otherwise—but the extent to which it does so should not be prejudged.

Second, but similarly, the adoption of an hierarchical structure for a governance network leaves open the question of how, and by whom, the structure would be established, as it cannot hoist itself into being by its own bootstraps (unless it could do so by force). There would have to be an existing organisation superior to, or at least preceding, the governance network, by which it was formed. That organisation need not itself necessarily be organised along hierarchical lines, but could emerge by a consensual

---

[68] Vedel (as in n. 74 on page 21), 65

process involving all stakeholders (as, supposedly, ICANN emerged from the IFWP).

The third reason why the hierarchical option for the form of a governance network should not be discounted is that in the present context, it is not to be taken as implying authoritarianism, but simply top–down ordering, which includes forms such as bureaucracy, oligarchy and meritocracy. These will be examined in turn, before discussion turns to some examples of these forms of structure in domestic politics (including the case of co-regulation mentioned above), and in Internet governance.

Bureaucracy

An hierarchically-structured bureaucracy was considered by Weber as the most efficient form an organisation could take. Thus the bureaucratic form is often found in governance networks, especially those in which governments take the lead role.[69]

There are a number of features central to the ideal type of a bureaucracy for Weber. which include:

- The use of impersonal rules as an internal mechanism of governance, covering such issues as the division of labour into a hierarchy of offices, criteria for selection to hold those offices and to advance within the organisation, and procedures for the conduct of the organisation's work programme.
- Offices within the organisation are separated from the persons holding them, so that for example office holders do not own the tools with which they perform their service, and interactions between office holders are conducted on an impersonal level, thereby limiting the scope for interpersonal conflict within the organisation.
- Permanent written records of the organisation's activities are to be maintained, which not only supports the separation of person from position, in that if an office holder is replaced, a record of their actions remains, but also provides a body of evidence from which the efficiency of the organisation's rules can be assessed and refined.[70]

It may appear from this that a Weberian bureaucracy is not necessarily incompatible with the multi-stakeholderism required of a governance network, in that it does not preclude those in authority from allowing their subordinates to contribute to the governance process through formal channels. On the contrary, it is structured as it is precisely because the

[69]Skelcher et al. (as in n. 97 on page 26), 578, 591

[70]Weber, *The Theory of Social and Economic Organization* (as in n. 2 on page 182)

division of labour that it specifies provides each member of an organisation with a unique and formally-defined role that contributes to the working of the larger whole.

The separation of organisational roles from the identities of those who occupy them, and the reliance upon merit as the sole criterion for appointment to such roles, might also be said to also support the participation of all stakeholders, by ensuring that positions of authority are held by those best qualified for them, and that they conduct their duties in accordance with impartial rules rather than in their own personal interests.

However on closer examination, herein also lies a fatal limitation with the use of a bureaucratic structure, even in its ideal form, as a model for the internal structure of a governance network. Requiring that stakeholders participating in a bureaucratically-structured governance network act in roles precisely defined by formal rules, completely obviates the reason for involving those stakeholders in the first place.

The reason for requiring that a governance network include all stakeholders is *precisely because* they represent their own values. Governments represent the interests of their citizens, the private sector represents the value of the free market, and civil society represents the values of the public outside of their national affiliations. Requiring these stakeholders instead to anonymously act out predefined roles in support of an amorphous collective interest dictated from above would defeat this purpose altogether.

However saying this does raise an interesting question: what if the interest from above was not that dictated by a single stakeholder representative (whomever was judged as most meritorious to exercise authority over the others), but rather by a panel on which all three stakeholder groups were represented?

Such a panel would be an oligarchy.

Oligarchy

The principal advantage of oligarchical rule, in which power is restricted to a small defined group, is that by reducing the number of participants, decisions can be made more quickly and with less contention amongst the decision-makers than in a system, such as democracy, with a broader power base. These benefits of oligarchy accrue at the cost of it being less representative and accountable to the governed than democracy, and therefore offering them less protection against tyranny.

However, the force of this objection is lessened by two observations. First, there *is* no transnational *demos* to which the interests of all three stakeholder groups can be traced. Therefore, at least until such a polity is brought into being, democratic representation is not an option, leaving oligarchy as perhaps the only practical alternative.[71]

Second, there is empirical evidence that oligarchy may be the natural state of any organisation, no matter how it is initially structured; whether as a bureaucracy, democracy or anarchy. This is Michels' "iron law of oligarchy": that in any small group there is a tendency for power to be concentrated in the hands of an elite who have both the will and the means to organise others.[72]

ICANN as an oligarchy

This latter point is evident in the context of Internet governance. Because ICANN for example, whilst claiming to operate upon consensual principles, has in practice been driven largely by its professional staff and select corporate and government stakeholders, it has been described as an "authoritarian–pluralist" institution.[73] Former ICANN board member Karl Auerbach explains, "ICANN is an oligarchy. ICANN claims it's a private organization yet it claims immunity from things like antitrust because it derives its powers via contracts with the government."[74] Weinberg agrees that "ICANN demonstrates Aristotle's fear of the degeneration of aristocracy into oligarchy."[75]

One of the factors to which the ICANN board's unilateralism in policy formation is attributed is that there has been widespread disengagement from and apparent apathy towards many of the issues in question by the Internet community. However this may be explained in part by the fact that the constituencies for community participation in ICANN's policy processes were established in a top–down fashion,[76] that the avenues for the receipt of input have been unduly limited,[77] and indeed that the community's input, when provided, has been largely disregarded.[78]

In any case, if Michels' Law holds, then attempting to reform ICANN to redress its perceived lack of public accountability is a misguided endeavour. An alternative, putting idealism aside, is to recognise ICANN for the oligarchy that it perhaps inevitably is, and allow it to make policy according

[71] Though this question will be revisited at section 4.3 on page 226.

[72] Robert Michels, *Political Parties: A Sociological Study of the Oligarchical Tendencies of Modern Democracy* New York: Free Press, 1962

[73] John G Palfrey Jr, The End of the Experiment: How ICANN's Foray into Global Internet Democracy Failed ⟨URL: `http://cyber.law.harvard.edu/publications/2004/The_End_of_the_Experiment`⟩, 40, 45

[74] Richard Koman, Karl Auerbach: ICANN "Out of Control" ⟨URL: `http://www.oreillynet.com/pub/a/policy/2002/12/05/karl.html`⟩

[75] Jonathan Weinberg, Geeks and Greeks, Info 3:4 2001, 327

[76] See section 2.1 on page 33.

[77] For example, a 2007 request for public comments on ICANN's performance was held open for less than one month: see `http://www.icann.org/announcements/announcement-08may07.htm`.

[78] Palfrey Jr (as in n. 73), 34, 50–52

to its own best judgment, without being distracted by the need for token efforts at public engagement. After all, nobody (not even ICANN) ever claimed that the organisation was a democracy. To the extent that its board exercises a representative function at all, it is more in the nature of guardianship than agency. Franda writes:

> For business people generally, the idea of a board member's representation is not the public representational function of someone duly authorized by an election or other legitimizing process to speak for a large constituency. Rather, it is the idea that someone will know and understand a specific business interest and be able to speak for that interest in forums where such interests are being challenged.[79]

Thus the EFF, for example, was often described as a representative body long before it actually had an open membership, by dint of its demonstrated ability to advocate for the rights and interests of online communities.[80]

On this view, an "autocratic approach might well be most efficient way to structure ICANN in order to carry out its mission."[81]

The IGF as an oligarchy

The same argument applies in principle to the IGF. If power within a governance network such as the IGF would inevitably evolve (or devolve) into an oligarchical form anyway, concentrated in the hands of those who have the initiative to put the most into the process, then perhaps it is quixotic to insist that the IGF should ever pretend to anything other than an oligarchical structure. If those whose power was most critical to the IGF's establishment were those who would lead it, the IGF would perhaps be an oligarchy of the United States and European Union, the ICC and ISOC for each of the respective stakeholder groups. No doubt they would do at least as good a job of policy development between themselves as ICANN has in its domain.[82]

But there are two problems, one procedural and the other normative. The procedural problem is that we still have no answer as to how the

[79]Franda (as in n. 43 on page 42), 67. To similar effect is the proposition discussed within the IGF's Advisory Group that its "members should be chosen on the basis of how large and diverse a community they connect to (which is different than 'represent')": IGF Secretariat, Advisory Group Discussion 6 December 2007 to 15 January 2008 ⟨URL: http://intgovforum.org/AGD/AG_Discussion_Thread.pdf⟩, 3.

[80]M Godwin, The Electronic Frontier Foundation and Virtual Communities ⟨URL: http://w2.eff.org/Misc/EFF/?f=virtual_communities.eff.txt⟩

[81]Palfrey Jr (as in n. 73 on the previous page), 57

[82]The IGF's stakeholders have indeed divided into a small number of factions, but not quite along the lines suggested here: see section 5.2 on page 356.

governance network is to operate, save that its composition is to be limited to a small number of powerful members. How are those participants to resolve disagreements between themselves? The specification of the oligarchical form alone provides no answer. Perhaps the power of certain large stakeholders will exceed that of others. For example the ICC had much less to do with the final form of the Tunis Agenda than did the other stakeholder representatives nominated in the previous paragraph. What would prevent those other representatives from vetoing the power of the ICC within the IGF oligarchy, and thus effectively excluding the private sector as a stakeholder altogether?

The second and more fundamental problem is that there are no normative criteria implicit in the oligarchical form by which to determine who is to be privileged with the status of membership. Indeed, this question is entirely exogenous to the oligarchical structure, which simply entrenches existing power relations. Whilst it may be true that organisations will tend towards oligarchy in any case, it is fatalistic simply to allow that "those who will rule, will rule" without questioning how it came about that they should do so. Would those who might form an oligarchical governance network be the most public spirited amongst the stakeholder representatives, or simply the most politically and economically powerful?

Even the bureaucratic organisation, whilst already rejected as unsuitable for a governance network, provides normative guidelines for the progression of suitable candidates up the hierarchy of authority, by requiring that promotion should be on the grounds of merit, rather than on other grounds such as nepotism or political influence. But can the concept of merit be applied to a governance network, and if so, how would it fall to be assessed? These are questions central to another form of hierarchical governance: meritocracy.

Meritocracy

The idea that rule should be exercised by those who are the best was originally conveyed by the term aristocracy, for which it is the literal meaning of the Greek. Though it is not named for him, aristocracy is often associated with Aristotle, who championed it in his *Politics* in the third century BC.[83] However the modern understanding of aristocracy, especially since the French revolution in 1789, is no longer associated with individual merit but with the hereditary power of an idle bourgeoisie, whose rule could often more suitably be described as plutocracy (rule by the rich).

The more modern term meritocracy is used to denote a system of rule by which those best qualified to do so, by reason of their personal attributes

[83] Aristotle, *Politics* Oxford: Clarendon Press, 1943

or their technical expertise.[84] Of all the hierarchical forms of organisation considered so far, meritocracy could be said to hold the most promise, in that it provides a normative basis upon which the most competent representatives of each of the stakeholder groups, rather than necessarily the most powerful, could be afforded the right to lead the governance network.

This conception of a peak body of moral leaders or technical experts is not even so far from the way in which representative democracy functions, whereby the people delegate their power to those representatives who they believe not only share their political preferences, but are also the most capable and well informed in political matters.

Unlike representative democracy of course, there is no democratic process by which the most meritorious candidates are selected. Therefore in order for the principle of merit to prevail over the "law of the jungle" of oligarchy it will be necessary for the rules by which merit is assessed to be either agreed by consensus, or be settled by some other objective means.[85]

The requirement of objectivity rules out the basis upon which Aristotle, a virtue ethicist, assessed merit. For Aristotle, merit was earned by doing virtuous deeds, where the virtuous choice in most cases would be found by pursuing the "Golden Mean" between two extreme ethical alternatives.[86] But there are a variety of alternative and incompatible ethical systems, including deontological, teleological and consequentialist variants, and at least one secular teleological ethical system, Objectivism, which explicitly claims to be objectively valid.[87] No such claim is compatible with the liberal neutrality that allows all to pursue their own conception of the good life, subject only to the observance of the equal rights of others to do the same.[88]

Assuming that some consensual or objective basis for the assessment of merit exists, it will also be necessary for the continuing merit of the incumbent authorities to be periodically measured against the same standard, lest they begin to act with unmeritorious self-regard and the meritocracy thus degenerate into oligarchy, a fate of which Aristotle warned.[89]

---

[84] The latter is more specifically termed technocracy.

[85] As an aside, why *objective*? Simply because a meritocracy subjectively so declared by hierarchical means, and an oligarchy with no normative basis for its composition, are indistinguishable to the governed; each is equally arbitrary and hegemonic. If an authority is to establish a meritocracy that can be properly so called regardless of the lack of consent of the governed, then it must be able to demonstrate that merit by objective means.

[86] Aristotle, *Nicomachean Ethics* Raleigh, N C: Alex Catalogue, 2000

[87] Ayn Rand, *The Virtue of Selfishness: A New Concept of Egoism* New York: New American Library, 1964

[88] See section 3.4 on page 167.

[89] Aristotle, *Politics* (as in n. 83 on the preceding page), 138–139

The IETF as a meritocracy

In the context of Internet governance, the IETF provides an example of an organisation in which merit is assessed using a consensually-agreed standard. Despite its open membership and bottom–up character, the IETF been described as a technical meritocracy (or technocracy) because of the priority that is afforded by the community to the views and preferences of those who have demonstrated their superior technical expertise.[90] In this, the standard of merit that prevails within the IETF mirrors the principle of the Hacker Ethic that "hackers should be judged by their hacking."[91]

Although the assessment of merit within the IETF is principled, it is inherently imprecise. In other online contexts, less *ad hoc* metrics for the assessment of merit have been used. For example, on Wikipedia, users are more likely to be promoted to the status of administrator if they can demonstrate the range, extent and quality of their contributions to the project to the Wikipedia community. Although no formal criteria apply, a number of members of the community have established their own metrics for the assessment of applicants' merit, including the length of time they have been participating and the number of articles of particular types that they have edited.[92]

Even more quantitative measurements of merit (or reputation) are used elsewhere online, as for example on eBay, where each registered user has a feedback score comprised of the total of positive, neutral or negative ratings by other users with whom they have transacted business, and which has been found to have a direct correlation with the selling price of items they sell at auction.[93] Similarly on discussion sites such as Slashdot, a user can earn "karma" by means such as posting comments that other users rate as "insightful" or "interesting." A higher karma score elevates the user's privileges on the site.[94]

Whilst most reputation-tracking mechanisms are specific to a particular Internet site or service, there are also those designed to be used across various sites or services that a user might inhabit. For example Playerep is a Web-based reputation-tracking service which allows players of online games to rate each other on factors such as competency, knowledge, fairness and sociability.[95]

More relevant to the IGF, there are also products designed for online

[90]Mueller, *Ruling the Root: Internet Governance and the Taming of Cyberspace* (as in n. 21 on page 35), 91

[91]Levy (as in n. 16 on page 5), 43

[92]See `http://en.wikipedia.org/wiki/Wikipedia:Requests_for_adminship`.

[93]Paul Resnick et al., The Value of Reputation on eBay: A Controlled Experiment, Experimental Economics 9:2 2006

[94]Froomkin, Habermas@discourse.net: Toward a Critical Theory of Cyberspace (as in n. 40 on page 13), 863–867

[95]See `http://www.playerep.com/`.

deliberation and collaboration, such as the Dialog Dashboard, which incorporate the facility for participants to attribute reputation points to one another based on their contributions to the discussion process. Unchat is a similar product which allows contributors to choose which of them should be granted moderation privileges (or have them revoked) based on their contribution to the discussion as it occurs. Both of these products will be revisited at section 4.3 on page 276.

All of the forms of meritocracy described here are notable in that the process by which the recognition of merit is bestowed is not a unique event, but a conditional and ongoing one, thus fulfilling Aristotle's admonition that a meritocracy must be guarded against its tendency to degrade into a mere oligarchy. However, therein lies the problem with each of the meritocracies described (although it is not so much a problem, as an ontological issue): at what point does a meritocracy in which positions of authority are assigned through a democratic or consensual process, cease to be hierarchical at all, and simply become a democratic or consensual organisation?

For consistency, that dividing line must be reached when the power of the meritocracy is conditioned upon the ongoing consent of the governed. Thus if criteria for the assessment of merit are at first decided by consensual means and the composition of the meritocracy is thereafter only to be determined by reference to those agreed criteria, the organisation may be described as an hierarchical meritocracy. If the criteria are subject to ongoing review by either consensual or democratic means, then the organisation is more accurately described as democratic or consensual.

By this definition, it may be concluded that the IETF, even if it is a meritocracy, is not in fact an hierarchical one, as the criteria by which technical merit is assessed are informal and subject to continual re-evaluation by the community.

The IGF as a meritocracy

This is not however to say that there is no organisation in the context of Internet governance which is both meritocratic and hierarchical (that is, the structure of which is not subject to displacement by consensual or democratic means). Take the example of the IGF's Advisory Group, a steering committee tasked with the preparation of the substantive agenda and programme for the IGF's annual meetings. Rather than through a democratic or consensual process, this group was appointed through the hierarchical power of the United Nations.[96]

Unfortunately the question of how the Advisory Group's merit was assessed is somewhat obscure, as the process by which its members were selected was not public. Nonetheless as the selection process did not

[96]See section 5.2 on page 355.

avail itself of (what is, let us accept for now)[97] the inherent normative force of a democratic or consensual process, and as the United Nations has no legitimate authority to unilaterally prescribe the composition of a multi-stakeholder group,[98] some other objective normative basis must be presented for the attribution of merit to those selected, if the Advisory Group is to be considered as anything other than an oligarchy.

There are two possible such criteria by which the merit of the members of a multi-stakeholder governance network formed by hierarchical means might be assessed. First (and most fundamental) is the extent to which they embody the values that that stakeholder group brings to the governance network. Second is the extent to which they contribute to the substantive work of the governance network. Taking these in turn:

- It is not too difficult to objectively determine which stakeholder group a member represents. However, beyond this there is no objective basis upon which to compare their relative merit within each stakeholder group. For example, there could have been no objective basis for the United Nations to determine that the values of civil society were better represented within the Advisory Committee by ICANN than the IETF, or of the private sector by Microsoft rather than Red Hat.

  This is not to say that there are no objective metrics that could be used to distinguish these stakeholders from each other: for example, GDP in the case of governments, net profits in the case of the private sector, and membership numbers in the case of civil society. Neither is it even to say that these metrics are irrelevant to the values that the stakeholders in question bring to a governance network.[99] Rather, the lack of objectivity is in the assumption that *size matters* (or that any other applicable quantifier for the metric chosen does).

  The argument is easier to understand when the respective merits of stakeholders *inter se* are considered in other contexts. For example, does the United States have more merit as a stakeholder within the United Nations than China? Does McDonalds better embody the values of the market than The Body Shop? Is Greenpeace more important than World Vision within civil society? In each case, perhaps so. But equally, perhaps not; and the point is not to decide the question either way, but simply to acknowledge that it is a subjective one.

- It may be possible to objectively analyse the participants' capacities to contribute to the workload of a governance network, based on much the same criteria as would have been used in assessing their

[97]See section 4.3 on page 226.

[98]See the introduction to this section and section 6.3 on page 452.

[99]That is, the merit of citizen representation for government, of market efficiency for the private sector, and of transnational substantive values for civil society.

> suitability for employment. There are, certainly, a wealth of more-or-less objective criteria by which work-related competencies can be judged.[100] And there is in fact nothing wrong with the use of this criterion to judge the productive merit of members of a governance network, in so far as it goes. The problem is simply that without having been able to objectively determine which stakeholders were most meritorious by the preceding criterion, this criterion alone is a poor substitute. To rely upon it solely is to assess the merit of members of a governance network, by reference to their instrumental worth rather than their intrinsic worth as stakeholders, is to treat them as cogs in a decision-making machine, rather than as the very source of the values from which their decision-making draws its legitimacy.

A fundamental difficulty with the selection by hierarchical means of a meritocracy to lead a governance network is thus exposed. Democratic and consensual processes aside, there is no objective basis for adequately assessing the merit of candidates to lead a governance network engaged in the development of public policy. Thus in the end, although hierarchical meritocracy has come much closer than bureaucracy and oligarchy, it is still not quite an appropriate organisational form for a governance network.

Hybrid models

This does, however, suggest the way forward: a hybrid between hierarchical ordering in the form of meritocracy, and a more participatory form of anarchistic, democratic or consensual ordering, to fill the normative holes in the hierarchical option, while retaining many of its benefits (such as the greater efficiency of a smaller governance body). Such a mixed system of governance is in fact precisely what Aristotle recommended.[101] It is also widely seen in Internet governance. ICANN, most notably has been described as a "semi-democracy,"[102] combining hierarchical and democratic elements, through the composition of its board which is drawn partly from the meritocratic Supporting Organisations and partly from the At Large community.[103] The same idea is found in other organisations in which a standing committee is appointed alongside elected members, for example in the Wikimedia Foundation and the W3C.

[100] For example, David Dubois and William Rothwell, *The Competency Toolkit* Amherst, MA: HRD Press, 2000.

[101] Aristotle, *Politics* (as in n. 83 on page 201), 195

[102] Palfrey Jr (as in n. 73 on page 199)

[103] Weinberg, Geeks and Greeks (as in n. 75 on page 199), 329

Co-regulation

Another example of an effective hybrid of hierarchical and participatory forms, as foreshadowed at the close of the discussion of anarchism, is the case of co-regulation.

Co-regulation illustrates a possible compromise between anarchistic forms of ordering (by norms, markets and architecture) and governance by rules, in which decentralised collective action is guided or directed by government (or to generalise this case, by some other hierarchical authority). To be more specific, co-regulation is the process by which an industry or industry segment is permitted to draft its own code of conduct on a particular issue, which if acceptable to the executive agency responsible for regulating that issue area, will be "registered" by it to serve in lieu of government regulation. Once registered the code applies to the entire industry sector in question, so that even those who are not signatories to it can be directed by the agency to comply with it.

There are numerous possible variations of this model along a continuum between pure hierarchical ordering and pure decentralised collective action (or between "command and control" and self-regulation, in simpler if less precise terms),[104] and these are sometimes known by other names such as "enforced self-regulation"[105] and "policy co-ordination,"[106] but the name and description given reflect the dominant practice in Australia.

Examples of co-regulatory regimes already in place in Australia include the various codes on topics such as billing and customer complaints developed by Communications Alliance Ltd for the telecommunications industry under the *Telecommunications Act 1997* (Cth), the Internet content regulation regime established under the *Broadcasting Services Act 1992* (Cth) and drafted by the Internet Industry Association (IIA) for the Internet industry, and two codes under the *Spam Act 2003* (Cth), one of which was drafted by a committee of the IIA for the Internet industry and the other by the Australian Direct Marketing Association (ADMA) for the direct marketing industry.[107] In all of these cases, the government agency responsible for the registration of the codes is ACMA.[108]

The benefits of co-regulation can be described by comparison to either of the pure forms of which it is a hybrid. Over pure hierarchical organi-

---

[104] Darren Sinclair, Self-Regulation Versus Command and Control? Beyond False Dichotomies, Law & Policy 19:4 1997, 544

[105] John Braithwaite, Enforced Self-Regulation: A New Strategy for Corporate Crime Control, Mich LR 80 1982

[106] Wolfgang Kleinwächter, Global Governance in the Information Age: GBDe and ICANN as "Pilot Projects" for Co-regulation and a New Trilateral Policy? ⟨URL: `http://www.cfi.au.dk/publikationer/cfi/003_kleinwachter`⟩, 20

[107] Jeremy M Malcolm, Australia's Stand on Spam ⟨URL: `http://www.ilaw.com.au/public/spampaper.html`⟩

[108] See `http://www.acma.gov.au/WEB/STANDARD/pc=PC_2525`.

sational forms, it offers many of the same benefits as self-regulation, such as its greater speed and reduced expense over traditional governmental regulation, the ability of industry to develop or modify codes swiftly in response to environmental stimuli, as well as the pull towards voluntary compliance that is associated with governance by norms.[109]

As for the benefits of co-regulation over anarchistic forms of ordering, the ability for compliance with a co-regulatory code to be independently enforced addresses the limited effectiveness of anarchistic ordering that results from its voluntary nature.[110] Although a registered co-regulatory code does not have the full force of law, pursuant to section 121 of the *Telecommunications Act 1997* (Cth), a member of an industry covered by a code can be directed to comply with its provisions by ACMA. It is an offence to fail to comply with such a direction.

The substantive content of the code is also more likely to reflect public policy concerns, rather than serving only the interests of its drafters as is often found in cases of pure self-regulation.[111] This is achieved in much the same way as in the case of directives of the European Union, whereby the government regulator specifies certain minimum outcomes that code is required to achieve, but not how those outcomes are to be achieved, which is left to the discretion of the industry.[112]

The problems of accountability and transparency associated with anarchistic ordering can also be addressed in co-regulatory structures, by establishing systems for the regulator to monitor compliance and for complaints to be independently heard. For example, clause 12 of the Internet Industry Spam Code of Practice drafted by the IIA provides that consumers may make complaints about an ISP's breach of the code to ACMA, which may refer them to the Telecommunications Industry Ombudsman (TIO) for determination.[113]

Since these are all benefits to government more so than to industry, it is a misapprehension to consider that phenomena such as co-regulation represent a loss of power by states to the private sector. Rather, the sharing of state authority with private actors is a process for which states are largely responsible, and which serves their own ends first and foremost.[114]

However whilst addressing some of the shortcomings of each of the pure regulatory forms, the co-regulatory form does introduce or exacerbate

[109]Weber (as in n. 70 on page 20), 80, 83–84

[110]Braithwaite (as in n. 105 on the preceding page), 1470

[111]A C Page, Self Regulation and Codes of Practice, Jnl of Bus L 1980

[112]Neil Gunningham and Joseph Rees, Industry Self-Regulation: An Institutional Perspective, Law & Policy 19:4 1997, 401

[113]IIA, Internet Industry Spam Code of Practice ⟨URL: `http://www.iia.net.au/files/IIA/Codes%20of%20Practice/Spam/iia%20spam%20code.pdf`⟩

[114]Saskia Sassen, *The Emergence of Private Authority in Global Governance* Cambridge: Cambridge University Press, 2002, chap. The State and Globalization

certain other problems. These include the risk of regulatory capture,[115] and the inherent incentive for industry to "cheat," for example by writing loopholes into its codes.[116]

These dangers underline the need for broadly-based oversight of co-regulatory arrangements, from civil society as well as government.[117] For example section 117 of the *Telecommunications Act* requires codes registered under that Act to be subjected to an open process of public consultation. All codes registered to date have also been subject to regular review, with the first review of the Spam Code for example taking place one year after its registration.

Hybrid models in Internet governance

The model of domestic co-regulation could in principle be extended to the international arena, as self-regulatory arrangements are naturally extensible transnationally, as for example in the case of the International Bar Association's[118] International Code of Ethics.[119] However in practice this is complicated by the limited choice of international authorities to assume the regulator's role. Although there may already be an appropriate regulator in some issue areas, such as the WTO (which with the assistance of its members could transform international commercial arbitration into a co-regulatory regime), in other issue areas such as Internet governance new intergovernmental agreements may be required to establish a regulatory framework.

For this reason there are few existing international or transnational examples analogous to domestic co-regulation, but the European Union's CE mark found on consumer and industrial goods offers one. The requirement for goods sold within the European Union to conform to EU standards and to carry the CE mark is mandated by EU resolution, but a product's conformity to those EU standards is self-assessed by or on behalf of the product's manufacturers, who must create a test report and declaration of conformity to support their assessment.[120]

Hybrid regulatory models are found in the context of Internet governance also. Most significantly, ICANN remains contracted until at least 2009 to the NTIA, which allows ICANN to manage the DNS essentially

[115] Braithwaite (as in n. 105 on page 207), 1492

[116] Ibid., 1495–1496

[117] Gunningham and Rees (as in n. 112 on the facing page), 402–405

[118] See http://www.ibanet.org/.

[119] International Bar Association, International Code of Ethics ⟨URL: http://www.ibanet.org/images/downloads/international_ethics.pdf⟩

[120] European Commission, Guide to the Implementation of Directives Based on the New Approach and the Global Approach ⟨URL: http://ec.europa.eu/enterprise/newapproach/legislation/guide/document/1999_1282_en.pdf⟩

independently, while the NTIA retains ultimate authority over the DNS root.

auDA provides another good example. The process by which control of the au ccTLD passed from a pure self-regulatory regime under Robert Elz and later ADNA, to auDA has already been described.[121] In particular it was noted that this was facilitated by NOIE, a Commonwealth government agency, and that the Commonwealth reserved authority to itself under the *Telecommunications Act 1997* to take over from auDA in the event that it ceased to act effectively.

In the context of the IGF, the scope for a co-regulatory approach can be found in the fact that one of the concessions made by governments in the Tunis Agenda was that the issues of DNS management and IP address allocation would be left outside the IGF's mandate, and remain under the private management of the ICANN regime. There is no reason why the governmental stakeholders in the IGF could not similarly agree to leave other issues to be regulated through the decentralised collective action of the stakeholders at large, whilst retaining ultimate authority to intervene on a domestic or intergovernmental level should decentralised collective action fail to adequately address the issues in question.[122]

Governments as a proxy for the meritocracy

Would an IGF structured in such a manner, as a hybrid between the hierarchical power of governments and the anarchistic ordering of all other stakeholders, still amount to a governance network as it has been described in this book? It is not exactly the hybrid between meritocracy and decentralised collective action that was previously considered, as it substitutes governments for a meritocratic elite drawn from amongst all stakeholders. This is in one way indefensible, in that it privileges one stakeholder group over the others; a stakeholder group that we have already found lacks the legitimacy to exercise authority over transnational public policy issues.

Yet in another way, it could be argued that if it is necessary to concede to hierarchical ordering in order to address some of the identified limitations of anarchistic ordering, governments are in a better practical position to hold this elevated position than any of the other stakeholder groups. After all, it is they who can most effectively wield the coercive power of rules.

---

[121] See section 2.1 on page 44.

[122] That may be the practical effect of the prevailing hegemony of states in any case; that is, provided that a public policy issue is technically amenable to being addressed by rules, there would be nothing to stop governments or intergovernmental authorities from trumping the IGF's recommendations even if the IGF were not structured in such a manner as to facilitate their doing so. The distinction though, formal as it may be, is between a multi-stakeholder governance forum structured to include a role for formal intergovernmental oversight, and one in which policy development is undertaken in the shadow of the exogenous power of states to intervene in and override the process.

And to allow governments to wield hierarchical power would neatly sidestep the dilemma of how to select a meritocratic elite to do so. Whilst it was vaguely suggested above that such an elite could be selected through democratic or consensual means, most governments can be presumed already to have been selected by such means (though admittedly not in respect of transnational issues). Why then should it be necessary to reinvent the wheel? Reflecting this view, former ICANN President and CEO M Stuart Lynn has argued,

> Although governments vary around the world, for better or worse they are the most evolved and best legitimated representatives of their populations—that is, of the public interest. As such, their greater participation in general, and in particular their collective selection of outstanding non-governmental individuals to fill a certain portion of ICANN Trustee seats, could better fill the need for public accountability without the serious practical and resource problems of global elections in which only a relatively few self-selected voters are likely to participate.[123]

If this view were to prevail, it would be that all stakeholders are equal within the IGF, but that some are more equal than others. Perhaps, however, this is the only practical outcome. The following discussion of hierarchy within open source software development may provide an insight into that suggestion.

Hierarchy and open source software

Although the burgeoning success of open source software and the philosophy underpinning it has been often described as the "open source revolution,"[124] open source software is actually nothing new; in fact it is older than proprietary software. Levy describes how even in the late 1950s and early 1960s, software for the first generation of minicomputers was made available "for anyone to access, look at, and rewrite as they saw fit."[125]

Another common observation is that it is no coincidence that the rise of open source software has coincided with that of the Internet.[126] As never before, the Internet facilitated the development of open source software *en*

[123] M Stuart Lynn, President's Report: ICANN—The Case for Reform ⟨URL: `http://www.icann.org/general/lynn-reform-proposal-24feb02.htm`⟩

[124] Chris DiBona, Sam Ockman and Mark Stone, editors, *Open Sources: Voices from the Open Source Revolution* Sebastopol, CA: O'Reilly & Associates, 1999

[125] Levy (as in n. 16 on page 5), 65

[126] Eric S Raymond, *The Cathedral and the Bazaar: Musings on Linux and Open Source by an Accidental Revolutionary*, Revised edition Sebastopol, CA: O'Reilly & Associates, 2001, 51

masse by geographically distributed groups of hackers. But the relationship goes back still further, as the technical infrastructure of the Internet was itself largely built on open source software—even before it was known by that name. Prior to the term "open source" being coined in 1998,[127] it was more commonly known simply as "free software."[128]

However, the software is free in more than one sense. Free or open source software[129] is in the FSF's words not only free in the sense of "free beer," but also in the sense of "freedom," encompassing:

- The freedom to run the program, for any purpose (freedom 0).
- The freedom to study how the program works, and adapt it to your needs (freedom 1). Access to the source code is a precondition for this.
- The freedom to redistribute copies so you can help your neighbor (freedom 2).
- The freedom to improve the program, and release your improvements to the public, so that the whole community benefits (freedom 3). Access to the source code is a precondition for this.[130]

Although it is not required in order to satisfy this definition, certain open source software licences, most notably the GNU General Public License (GPL) which is used by a majority of all open source software,[131] require any work copied or derived from software covered by the GPL to be distributed under the same licence terms. This characteristic is referred to by the FSF as "copyleft," as a play on "copyright," in that it requires those who base their own works on copyleft-licensed software to forgo the exclusive rights that copyright law gives them to copy and modify their works, and to share those rights freely with the community.

More significant than the freedoms associated with open source software are the larger cultural and organisational consequences to which their exercise gives rise. These include the widespread voluntary service that

---

[127] Eric S Raymond, Goodbye, "Free Software"; Hello, "Open Source" ⟨URL: `http://www.catb.org/~esr/open-source.html`⟩

[128] It is still so known by many, notably including the Free Software Foundation; see `http://www.fsf.org/`.

[129] Both appellations being encompassed by the acronym FOSS or F/OSS; FLOSS is also sometimes seen, adding the French *libre*.

[130] Richard M Stallman, The Free Software Definition ⟨URL: `http://www.fsf.org/licensing/essays/free-sw.html`⟩. A similar but more comprehensive list of ten requirements of open source software was first published by the Open Source Institute in 1998 in its Open Source Definition (see `http://www.opensource.org/docs/osd`).

[131] FSF, GNU General Public License ⟨URL: `http://www.gnu.org/licenses/gpl.html`⟩

members of the open source community provide in coding and documenting the software projects to which they contribute,[132] and the typical high quality, timeliness and innovation of their output.[133]

Eric Raymond, a hacker himself, has famously described the difference between the development methodology for proprietary software and that for open source software as that between "the cathedral and the bazaar," in his essay of that name. To be built like a cathedral, in that context, is to be "carefully crafted by individual wizards or small bands of mages working in splendid isolation, with no beta to be released before its time," whereas the bazaar style of development was epitomised by the Linux kernel development process, which

> seemed to resemble a great babbling bazaar of differing agendas and approaches (aptly symbolized by the Linux archive sites, who'd take submissions from *anyone*) out of which a coherent and stable system could seemingly emerge only by a succession of miracles.[134]

The same phenomenon of "peer production" has begun to propagate beyond software development into other fields. It has already been observed in the hours that hundreds of contributors devote each week to the Wikipedia project, producing the most comprehensive encyclopædia ever written. The licensing model employed by Wikipedia is equivalent to that of open source software, although the material licensed may be more accurately described as "open content," and the license employed is the GNU Free Documentation License (GFDL).[135]

There are, of course, other open content licences. Creative Commons is a project to draft and promote licences suitable for the release of all manner of literary, musical, artistic and dramatic works as open content.[136] The Creative Commons Web site makes some of this content available, though Creative Commons licensed content is also found on many other sites including the Internet Archive[137] and the OpenCourseWare project,[138]

[132]Guido Hertel, Sven Niedner and Stefanie Herrmann, Motivation of Software Developers in Open Source Projects: An Internet-based Survey of Contributors to the Linux Kernel ⟨URL: http://opensource.mit.edu/papers/rp-hertelniednerherrmann.pdf⟩

[133]Joseph Feller and Brian Fitzgerald, *Understanding Open Source Software Development* Harlow, England: Pearson Education, 2002, 131

[134]Raymond, *The Cathedral and the Bazaar: Musings on Linux and Open Source by an Accidental Revolutionary* (as in n. 126 on page 211), 21–22

[135]FSF, GNU Free Documentation License ⟨URL: http://www.gnu.org/licenses/fdl.html⟩

[136]See http://creativecommons.org/, though for criticism of the openness of the Creative Commons licences see Benjamin Mako Hill, Towards a Standard of Freedom: Creative Commons and the Free Software Movement ⟨URL: http://www.advogato.org/article/851.html⟩.

[137]See http://www.archive.org/.

[138]See http://ocw.mit.edu/.

inaugurated by MIT and since extended to other institutions[139] for the publication of course materials.

The success of the open source development methodology is often explained by economic sociologists in terms of the low transaction costs associated with communication between developers,[140] and the network effects which increase the value of the open source "commons" to all as more people become involved.[141] Although puzzled as to what individual incentives developers have to voluntarily build up this open source commons,[142] they posit that it is a barter or gift exchange system in which developers exchange their labour for such goods as feedback from users and an enhanced reputation amongst their peers,[143] or that it is a means of improving their future employment prospects.[144]

To developers such as Raymond the question is less of a mystery: they do it because it is fun.[145]

Linus Torvalds, original author of the Linux operating system kernel, concurs with this view in his autobiography (which is suitably enough titled *Just For Fun*),[146] as does Levy in his history of the hacker community.[147] Software development is only one application of the open source ethic, but the fun extends to publishers of other forms of open content too: Jimmy Wales of Wikipedia for example unpretentiously states, "The goal of Wikipedia is fun for the contributors."[148]

The same motivation also extends to projects small enough to be pursued by a single developer. Whilst these might not be thought of as organisations, lacking a community of developers, they are still aimed at a community of users or readers[149] and thus fulfil similar social needs as more structured virtual communities.[150] Take the example of blogs ("Web logs"); self-published online journals numbering over 100 million as at

---

[139]See `http://www.ocwconsortium.org/`.

[140]Yochai Benkler, Coase's Penguin, or, Linux and The Nature of the Firm, Yale LJ 112 2002

[141]Eric von Hippel, *Democratizing Innovation* Cambridge, MA: MIT Press, 2005

[142]Josh Lerner and Jean Tirole, The Economics of Technology Sharing: Open Source and Beyond ⟨URL: `http://opensource.mit.edu/papers/lernertirole3.pdf`⟩, 7

[143]Rishab A Ghosh, Cooking Pot Markets: An Economic Model for the Trade in Free Goods and Services on the Internet ⟨URL: `http://www.firstmonday.dk/issues/issue3_3/ghosh/index.html`⟩

[144]Lerner and Tirole (as in n. 142), 8

[145]Raymond, *The Cathedral and the Bazaar: Musings on Linux and Open Source by an Accidental Revolutionary* (as in n. 126 on page 211), 60; Luthiger

[146]Linus Torvalds and David Diamond, *Just For Fun: the Story of an Accidental Revolutionary* New York: HarperCollins, 2001, 248

[147]Levy (as in n. 16 on page 5), 46

[148]Poe (as in n. 40 on page 190).

[149]William Davies, You Don't Know Me, But... Social Capital and Social Software ⟨URL: `http://www.theworkfoundation.com/Assets/PDFs/you_dontknowme.pdf`⟩, 32

[150]H Rheingold, *The Virtual Community* Reading, MA: Addison-Wesley Publishing, 1993

2008.[151] Tim Wu observes that "in general, bloggers writing for fun—or out of single-minded obsession—can thump reporters trying to get home by 6pm."[152]

But what underlies the fun? It might be argued that it is inherent in the creative process, but that begs the question, what underlies *that*?

At least to some extent, the answer is empowerment: the power to independently create or achieve something one perceives to be of value.[153] The desire for such power is known by psychologists as a mastery, competence or achievement motive,[154] and Maslow placed it at the pinnacle of his hierarchy of human needs, naming it the need for self-actualisation.[155] Sociologists as far back as Weber came to the same realisation that increasing the bureaucratic rationalisation of work could be dehumanising; Weber describing this trend as an "iron cage" in which humanity was destined to be trapped.[156] Scholars of organisational behaviour have inherited this insight, and proposed strategies by which employees can be empowered (and thus made happier and more productive) by increasing their autonomy at work.[157]

Although the emergence of the open source methodology has been quite orthogonal to this scholarship, it is an exemplar of its programme in the extent to which it empowers the members of the open source community to pursue their own objectives, in their own way, in a manner that is not possible within an hierarchical bureaucracy.[158]

It follows that the licence under which open source software is released, as important as it may be to the success of the software and to the movement as a whole, is not the most critical factor in its success as a software

---

[151] According to blog analysis firm Technorati; see `http://www.technorati.com/about/`.

[152] Tim Wu, The Power of Fun ⟨URL: `http://www.slate.com/id/2138537/entry/2138647/`⟩

[153] Karim R Lakhani and Robert G Wolf, *Perspectives on Free and Open Source Software* Cambridge, MA: MIT Press, 2005, chap. Why Hackers Do What They Do: Understanding Motivation and Effort in Free/Open Source Software Projects

[154] Gerald Matthews, Ian J Deary and Martha C Whiteman, *Personality Traits* Cambridge: Cambridge University Press, 2003, 128

[155] Abraham Maslow, *Motivation and Personality*, 3rd edition New York: Harper & Row, 1987

[156] Max Weber, *The Protestant Ethic and the Spirit of Capitalism* Mineola, NY: Dover Publications, 2003, 181

[157] Heloisa Fragoso, An Overview of Employee Empowerment: Do's And Don'ts ⟨URL: `http://www.angelfire.com/nb/ba1199/lesson028/emp4.htm`⟩

[158] This does not necessarily mean that the open source software development methodology is the only one to so empower its users; the so-called "agile" development methodologies for proprietary software also do so to some extent, and in fact share some of the characteristics of the open source model such as promoting short release cycles and involving the end user in the development process; see J Highsmith and A Cockburn, Agile Software Development: The Business of Innovation, Computer 34:9 2001. However, there are many other advantages of open source software over proprietary software besides the extent to which its developers are empowered; for example, its contribution to bridging the digital divide; see Jeffrey James, *Bridging the Global Digital Divide* Cheltenham, UK: Edward Elgar, 2003, 60.

development methodology; rather, it is the empowerment of its contributors that is central. The licence is simply the means by which hackers have institutionalised in law (or rules) the ethic that "all information should be free"[159] in respect of open source software and open content, as they embedded it in the architecture of the Internet in respect of data communications.

On this basis, the egalitarianism of the open source software development model can be seen as reflecting that of the Internet itself. Both are models of anarchistic ordering largely of hackers' own creation.[160] Thus as already observed it is no coincidence that the Internet is an enabling force for the open source paradigm, levelling the playing field between media juggernauts and software powerhouses, and teenagers writing or coding in their attic.[161] Freed of the hegemony of hierarchy, hackers and others pursing their need for self-actualisation become more empowered, fulfilled and happy.

However, to characterise the open source software development model as purely anarchistic is simplistic. In most projects, anarchy is balanced with hierarchical control.[162]

It is in fact common for open source software development projects to be governed by a "benevolent dictator for life" (or BDFL).[163] These are found in projects ranging from the Linux operating system kernel itself, of which Linus Torvalds is the BDFL,[164] Linux-based operating system distributions such as Ubuntu led by Mark Shuttleworth,[165] application software such

[159] Levy (as in n. 16 on page 5), 40

[160] Christian Imhorst, Anarchy and Source Code—What Does the Free Software Movement Have to Do With Anarchism? ⟨URL: `http://opensource.mit.edu/papers/imhorst.pdf`⟩

[161] Glenn Reynolds, *An Army of Davids: How Markets and Technology Empower Ordinary People to Beat Big Media, Big Government, and Other Goliaths* Nashville, TN: Nelson Current, 2006

[162] Jesper Holck and Niels Jørgensen, *Free/Open Source Software Development* Hershey, PA: Idea Group Publishing, 2005, chap. Do Not Check In On Red: Control Meets Anarchy in Two Open Source Projects

[163] Reagle (as in n. 48 on page 192)

[164] See `http://www.kernel.org/`.

[165] Ubuntu, founded in 2004 (see `http://www.ubuntu.com/`), is based on an earlier Linux distribution called Debian GNU/Linux, founded in 1993. The Debian project is the most egalitarian of the two; for example its elected Project Leader is directed by clause 5.3 of its constitution to "attempt to make decisions which are consistent with the consensus of the opinions of the Developers" and to "avoid overemphasizing their own point of view when making decisions in their capacity as Leader": Debian Project, Debian Constitution ⟨URL: `http://www.debian.org/devel/constitution`⟩. In contrast, Mark Shuttleworth, who founded the Ubuntu distribution in 2004 and termed himself its SABDFL (self-appointed benevolent dictator for life), appoints the members of both of its main decision-making bodies (the Technical Board and the Ubuntu Community Council) and exercises a casting vote in those bodies.

A prominent former Debian Developer who resigned in 2006 compared the Debian and Ubuntu distributions by saying, "There's a balance to be struck between organisational freedom and organisational effectiveness. I'm not convinced that Debian has that balance right as far as forming a working community goes. In that respect, Ubuntu's an experiment—does a more rigid structure and a greater willingness to enforce certain social standards result in a more

as the Samba networking suite coordinated by Andrew Tridgell,[166] and programming languages such as Perl,[167] PHP[168] and Python[169] in which Larry Wall, Rasmus Lerdorf and Guido van Rossum respectively act as project leaders in perpetuity.[170]

In the case of the Linux kernel, Torvalds who is perhaps the archetype of a BDFL, possesses ultimate authority to decide which contributions ("patches") to the Linux operating system kernel should be accepted and which should be refused. Torvalds no longer personally manages the whole of the kernel and has delegated authority to a number of trusted associates to manage particular subsystems and hardware architectures, but it remains his authority to appoint these so-called "lieutenants" and to supervise their work. A document distributed with the Linux kernel source code that is subtitled "Care And Operation Of Your Linus Torvalds" describes him as "the final arbiter of all changes accepted into the Linux kernel."[171]

Thus contrary to what might be assumed from Raymond's claim about "the Linux archive sites, who'd take submissions from *anyone*," the Linux kernel development process is neither anarchistic nor consensual: if Torvalds does not like a patch, it does not go in to the kernel.[172] This has often antagonised other kernel developers, one of them commencing a long-running thread on the kernel development mailing list by saying:

> Linus doesn't scale, and his current way of coping is to silently drop the vast majority of patches submitted to him onto the floor. Most of the time there is no judgement involved when this code gets dropped. Patches that fix compile errors get dropped. Code from subsystem maintainers that Linus himself designated gets dropped. A build of the tree now spits out numerous easily fixable warnings, when at one time it was warning-free. Finished code regularly goes unintegrated for months at a time, being repeatedly resynced and re-diffed against new trees until the code's maintainer gets sick of it.

---

workable community?" (quoted in Bruce Byfield, Maintainer's Resignation Highlights Problems in Debian Project ⟨URL: `http://www.linux.com/articles/56883`⟩, which links to the original source).

166 See `http://www.samba.org/`.

167 See `http://www.perl.org/`.

168 See `http://www.php.net/`.

169 See `http://www.python.org/`.

170 The position of BDFL normally falls to the developer who initiated a project, though in the case of multiple original core developers, the phenomenon of a benevolent oligarchy for life is not unknown (for example Matt Mullenweg and Ryan Boren for the WordPress blog engine at `http://wordpress.com/`).

171 See Documentation/SubmittingPatches within the kernel source tree which can be downloaded from `http://www.kernel.org/`.

172 For a more detailed case study of Linux kernel development see S Schach et al., Maintainability of the Linux Kernel, IEEE Proceedings—Software 149:1 2002.

> This is extremely frustrating to developers, users, and vendors, and is burning out the maintainers. It is a huge source of unnecessary work. The situation needs to be resolved. Fast.[173]

Torvalds' initially unapologetic response[174] recalls another classic example of his sardonic view of his position as BDFL, when announcing the selection of a penguin logo for Linux. Acknowledging the comments of those who had expressed reservations about it, Torvalds concluded with the quip, "If you still don't like it, that's ok: that's why I'm boss. I simply know better than you do."[175]

The Mozilla[176] and OpenOffice.org[177] projects provide a slightly different example of hierarchical ordering in open source software development.[178] In these cases, the authority is not that of an individual, but a corporation: originally Netscape Communications in the case of Mozilla,[179] and Sun Microsystems in the case of OpenOffice.org.[180]

This kind of collective hierarchical control over an open source software project can also be exercised by a civil society organisation. The non-profit Mozilla Foundation, for example, succeeded to the rights of Netscape, such as the trademark and rights under the Netscape Public License.[181] Membership of its governing body (or "staff") is by invitation only. Another example of such an organisation, also taken from one of the most prominent and successful open source projects, is the Apache Software Foundation (ASF),[182] which is best known for the Apache HTTP Server which powers

---

173 Rob Landley, A Modest Proposal—We Need a Patch Penguin ⟨URL: http://www.cs.helsinki.fi/linux/linux-kernel/2002-04/0320.html⟩

174 See http://www.cs.helsinki.fi/linux/linux-kernel/2002-04/0389.html.

175 Originally published on Usenet at news:4sv02t$j8g@linux.cs.Helsinki.FI, now archived at http://groups.google.com/group/comp.os.linux.advocacy/msg/ee350cc97f7d0e69.

176 See http://www.mozilla.com/.

177 See http://www.openoffice.org/.

178 For more detailed case studies of these projects see Holck and Jørgensen (as in n. 162 on page 216) and A Mockus, R T Fielding and J D Herbsleb, Two Case Studies of Open Source Software Development: Apache and Mozilla, ACM Transactions on Software Engineering and Methodology 11:3 2002 for Mozilla, and Fridrich Strba, From TrainedMonkey to Google SoC Mentor ⟨URL: http://marketing.openoffice.org/ooocon2006/presentations/wednesday_c11.pdf⟩ for OpenOffice.org.

179 As well as leading development, Netscape originally held the "Mozilla" trademark (as Linus Torvalds does for "Linux" in various jurisdictions: see http://www.linuxmark.org/), and until 2001 required modifications to its source code to be licensed under terms that exclusively exempted it from the copyleft provisions applicable to other users: see http://www.mozilla.org/MPL/FAQ.html in its description of the Netscape Public License.

180 Sun requires contributors to the OpenOffice.org project to assign joint copyright in their work to it: see http://www.openoffice.org/licenses/jca.pdf.

181 See http://www.mozilla.org/foundation/.

182 See http://www.apache.org/. The Apache Software Foundation is a non-profit corporation governed by a board of nine directors who are elected by the Foundation's members for one-year terms, and who in turn appoint a number of officers (66, in 2008) to oversee its day-to-day operations. As of 2008 there are 249 members of the ASF, each of whom was invited

the majority of Web sites on the Internet.[183]

The case of the ASF also illustrates well that there are also various strata of developers underneath the BDFL. One study has categorised these into core members (or maintainers), active developers, peripheral developers, bug reporters, readers and passive users,[184] and confirmed previous findings that the core developers are generally the smallest group but write the majority of the project's code.[185] Whilst developers in lower strata are mostly self-selected,[186] in many projects, including those of the ASF, the core developers are selected by the BDFL, applying stringent meritocratic standards.[187]

In fact of the examples given of open source projects in which a significant hierarchical structure exists or has existed—the Linux kernel, Mozilla, OpenOffice.org and Apache, as well as Samba and Ubuntu mentioned earlier—all are the most widely-used open source projects in their class, and have large and active communities of developers. How can this be reconciled with the earlier hypothesis that it was the very lack of hierarchy that empowered developers and attracted them to volunteer their services to open source projects?

Despite the fact that its significance to developers had earlier been downplayed, the answer is found in the open source licence. It is the open source license that enforces benevolence upon the dictator. It does this by ensuring that for any open source project, there is always relatively costless freedom of exit, in that any developers who feel they are being oppressed by a project leader can simply cease participating in the project, take its source code, and use it as the base for a new project of their own (known as a "fork" of the original project). This "exit-based empowerment"[188] enjoyed by developers mitigates the power of the project leaders.

As Torvalds has put it,

> I am a dictator, but it's the right kind of dictatorship. I can't really do anything that screws people over. The benevolence is built in. I can't be nasty. If my baser instincts took hold, they

to join on the basis of their previous contributions to ASF projects, and whose invitation was extended by a majority vote of the existing members.

[183]See http://news.netcraft.com/archives/web_server_survey.html.

[184]Yunwen Ye et al., *Free/Open Source Software Development* Hershey, PA: Idea Group Publishing, 2005, chap. The Co-Evolution of Systems and Communities in Free and Open Source Software Development

[185]Mockus et al. (as in n. 178 on the preceding page)

[186]Ye et al. (as in n. 184), 64

[187]For a more detailed case study of Apache see Mockus et al. (as in n. 178 on the preceding page).

[188]Mark E Warren, Controlling Corruption Through Democratic Empowerment: Market-Style Accountability Revisited ⟨URL: http://www.politics.ubc.ca/fileadmin/template/main/images/departments/poli_sci/Faculty/warren/Market-Style_Accountability_Reconsidered_APSA_2006.pdf⟩, 2

wouldn't trust me, and they wouldn't work with me anymore. I'm not so much a leader, I'm more of a shepherd.[189]

The Linux kernel has, indeed, been forked numerous times. One prominent fork was that maintained by Red Hat Linux developer Alan Cox, who released a series of kernel source trees that contained patches not yet accepted by Torvalds.[190] However since 2002, a technical solution to Torvalds' backlog was found in the use of specialised revision control software,[191] which has placated many of Torvalds' critics, and resulted in the obsolescence of many former forks of the kernel.

Both Mozilla's Firefox browser and the OpenOffice.org office suite have also been forked. The Debian project, for example, has replaced Firefox in its distribution with a forked version called Iceweasel, to escape the onerous trademark licence conditions imposed by the Mozilla Foundation for the use of the Firefox name and logo.[192] As for OpenOffice.org, a prominent fork called NeoOffice[193] has been customised to integrate more smoothly with the Mac OS X operating system. Debian itself has also spawned a number of derivative distributions, Ubuntu being one.[194]

Admittedly, forking an open source project is not completely costless. Although the cost of the infrastructure required to host a new project is minimal (often even free),[195] a new name and logo will be required (either because the originals are protected by trademarks as in the case of Firefox and OpenOffice.org, or simply because of the practical necessity to distinguish the two projects).

Usually the most significant cost however is that it will be necessary for the new project leader to establish a community of users and developers to support the project in the long term. For economic sociologists, this is the cost of developing social capital.[196] Thus, the more successful the parent project is (and the more cohesive its communities of developer and users),

---

[189] Steve Hamm, Linus Torvalds' Benevolent Dictatorship ⟨URL: `http://www.businessweek.com/print/technology/content/aug2004/tc20040818_1593.htm?tc`⟩

[190] Jonathan Corbet, Where Does Kernel Development Stand? ⟨URL: `http://lwn.net/2001/1011/kernel.php3`⟩

[191] Originally, ironically, a proprietary product called BitKeeper, and subsequently an open source equivalent called Git written by Torvalds himself: see `http://git.or.cz/`.

[192] Idem, Debian and Mozilla—A Study in Trademarks ⟨URL: `http://lwn.net/Articles/118268/`⟩

[193] See `http://www.neooffice.org/`.

[194] The same phenomenon is found in other open content development communities. For example in 2002, Spanish Wikipedians who were dissatisfied with the Wikipedia project created their own fork, Enciclopedia Libre ("free encyclopædia"), as permitted by the GNU Free Documentation License under which Wikipedia's content is licensed: see `http://enciclopedia.us.es/`. More recently Larry Sanger has attempted to do the same, creating "a responsible, expert-managed fork of Wikipedia" titled Citizendium: see `http://www.citizendium.org/`.

[195] For example from Sourceforge at `http://sourceforge.net/`.

[196] N Uphoff, *Social Capital, A Multifaceted Perspective* Washington, DC: The World Bank, 1999, chap. Understanding Social Capital: Learning from the Analysis and Experience of Participation.

the higher its social capital will be, the higher the transaction costs of a fork, and the more effectively that fork will have to differentiate itself from its parent in order to overcome those costs.

This is illustrated by the case of Samba-TNG which forked from the highly successful Samba project in 1999,[197] seeking to differentiate itself by first offering the facility to replace a Microsoft Windows server as the Primary Domain Controller for an office network. However it struggled to build a development community comparable in size and expertise to that of its parent project, which in the meantime implemented its own version of Samba-TNG's differentiating feature. In comparison, forks of less dominant and stable projects have been forked more often and more successfully.[198]

This characteristic of the transaction costs associated with migration from one open source project to another provides a cohesive force against the unnecessary fragmentation of open source projects, that will only be overcome if enough developers become sufficiently dissatisfied to form a viable competing project (which the project leaders have an incentive not to allow to happen, lest they lose their base of developers). In comparison, developers within Microsoft Corporation face much higher transaction costs in replicating their work and their communities elsewhere if they are dissatisfied, if indeed it is possible for them to do so at all.

Thus it is from the unexpected source of the open source licence that a solution is found to the problem of maintaining an organisation under an hierarchical structure to address the limitations of anarchistic ordering, in that it provides an implicit ongoing consensual check on the power of the authority which side-steps the difficult task of objectively assessing the authority's merit antecedently.

Anarchistic–hierarchical Internet governance

What has been described is essentially a hybrid of anarchistic and hierarchical governance; but the distribution of power in this hybrid is much more even than in the case of co-regulation described previously. It is closer to the kind of voluntary association that anarchist Colin Ward describes in stating

Social capital can be formally defined as "the value of those aspects of the social structure to actors, as resources that can be used by the actors to realize their interests": J Coleman, *Foundations of Social Theory* Cambridge, MA: Harvard University Press, 1990, 305.

[197]See http://www.samba-tng.org/.

[198]For example, the oft-criticised PHP-Nuke content management system: see http://phpnuke.org/ and Jonathan Corbet, PHP Nuke Remains Vulnerable ⟨URL: http://lwn.net/2001/1011/security.php3⟩. These forks include Post-Nuke at http://www.postnuke.com/, Envolution at http://sourceforge.net/projects/envolution, MyPHPNuke at http://sourceforge.net/projects/myphpnuke and Xoops at http://www.xoops.org/.

> that there are at least two kinds of organisation. There is the kind which is forced on you, the kind which is run from above, and there is the kind which is run from below, which can't force you to do anything, and which you are free to join or free to leave alone. We could say that the anarchists are people who want to transform all kinds of human organisation into the kind of purely voluntary association where people can pull out and start one of their own if they don't like it.[199]

How, if at all, is this insight applicable to Internet governance?

To answer this will require the implications of the "open source-style" hybrid structure to be isolated; specifically, the assumptions that must be satisfied to ensure that the stakeholders in a governance network that is structured in hierarchical form are not at risk of being oppressed.[200] These assumptions can be reduced to three:

- the existence of perfect substitutes for the product of the governance network;
- freedom of exit from the network; and
- that stakeholders are not coerced to accept the product of the governance network by exogenous forces.[201]

If these assumptions sound familiar, it is because the first two are amongst those that underlie the ideal of the perfect free market (along with additional assumptions not needed here, as we do not require that the governance network be effective, only that it not be oppressive),[202] and the third is one of those underlying deliberative democracy, to be discussed in the next section.[203] With these three criteria satisfied,

> [i]t does not matter whether online discussion groups or even entire networks of such groups are internally autocratic, since individuals can always choose "their own more congenial online homes." Cyberanarchists, then, see cyberspace as a market of alternative rule regimes. It is the ease of exit and the abundance of alternatives—in essence consumer choice

[199] Colin Ward, Anarchism as a Theory of Organization, Anarchy 52 1965, 171

[200] That is, being subjected to hierarchical power that has not passed the normative tests of either objective merit or consent.

[201] Or in anarchistic terms, other than by the "natural and legitimate influence" of other stakeholders: Bakunin (as in n. 8 on page 183), 35.

[202] See section 1.4 on page 23.

[203] See section 4.3 on page 245.

in conditions approaching perfect competition—that bring to fruition the liberal ideals of liberty and consent.[204]

The next question then is the extent to which these assumptions can be fulfilled in the case of a governance network as they are in the case of open source software development. Examining each of them in turn:

- In the case of a governance network, the substitutes for governance through that network are governance either through another network, or through another mechanism: that is, by rules, norms, markets and/or architecture. In few cases is the substitution likely to be perfect, and the closest available substitute will vary from one case to another. However, it may be good enough in many cases to persuade stakeholders who feel oppressed to opt out of the governance network in favour of pursuing the same end by that substitute means.
- Freedom of exit from a governance network is impeded by the transaction costs of switching to an acceptable substitute mechanism of governance, or developing a new governance network afresh. As suggested in the preceding point, the quantum of the transaction costs incurred may vary considerably from case to case. However in general, as seen from the example of open source software, these costs will be higher the more social capital the original project (or in this context, the original network) has developed, and the less the defecting project has to offer to differentiate itself
- Whether the requirement of lack of coercion is satisfied in the case of a governance network depends on who it is that has authority over the network. At section 4.2 on page 210, it was suggested that on pragmatic grounds, governments might be the best parties to act as the authorities of a governance network structured in hybrid anarchistic/hierarchical form, following the example of co-regulation.

  However if it is required that no coercion be exercised from outside the governance network, governments are the very worst stakeholders who could lead it, as they are the only stakeholders who can exercise significant coercive power over all other stakeholders through their domestic legal regimes, even if those stakeholders have opted out of the governance network in favour of other mechanisms of governance.

An example will put these observations in more concrete terms. Let us assume that the IGF has an hierarchical leadership, which drafts a code governing the issue of Internet interconnection costs. This code is entirely

[204] Neil Weinstock Netanel, Cyberspace Self-Governance: A Skeptical View from Liberal Democratic Theory, Calif L Rev 88 2000, 404–405

satisfactory to all of the other stakeholders, except for the private sector who claim that interconnection costs should continue to be left to the free market (an alternative mechanism of governance, which it is costless for them to substitute for that of the IGF).

Are the three criteria satisfied? Yes, there is a perfect (or at least a costless) substitute for the code of the IGF. Yes, there is freedom of exit from the IGF so that even if its hierarchical leadership required all IGF members to subscribe to the code, the private sector would be at liberty simply to withdraw from the network. And as to whether the private sector could be coerced to accept the code, regardless of its departure from the IGF—well, this depends on whether the authority behind the IGF is governmental or not. If it is, then it can ignore the private sector's concerns and pass the code into international or domestic law regardless, which defeats the very purpose of developing it through a governance network.

Let us change the scenario a little. In this case, the hierarchical leadership of the IGF has managed to address the concerns of the private sector in a new code on interconnection costs that is now acceptable to all. A few private sector stakeholders however decide to opt out of the IGF regime and revert to reliance on the market to set interconnection prices. They immediately find that the success of the IGF's code has permanently lowered market prices for interconnection, and that the costs of differentiating their service so that it can be sold at higher prices are insurmountable. The hierarchical leadership of the IGF (unless composed of governments) not only cannot coerce these private sector stakeholders into accepting the code, but *it does not need to*. The IGF's very success has made it self-governing.

Granted, less extreme examples could be given in which the applicable transaction costs would vary markedly from these. But the lesson from open source software remains that if conditions are right, the question of how to impose hierarchical ordering on a governance network (for example by attempting to select a meritocracy through objective or consensual means), becomes redundant. If the hierarchical leadership, however selected, does not act in the best interests of the IGF, then its output will be ignored (the more so, the greater the segment whose interests are disregarded) and it will become powerless. If it does act in the best interests of the IGF, then its power will grow.

It can best do this by engaging all stakeholders in the process of public policy development using a participatory process, much as open source developers collaboratively work on open source software projects. In doing this, the stakeholders will become empowered, the social capital of the governance network will increase, and its effectiveness will grow.

Criticisms

At the commencement of this section on hierarchical organisation it may have seemed unlikely that such a structure could be suited for a governance network; and indeed, like anarchism, it was found to be unsuitable in its pure form. To recap briefly, the bureaucratic form of hierarchical organisation was found unacceptable because it devalued the identities of participants by limiting them to the performance of defined roles; oligarchy was unacceptable because it provided no normative basis to justify the authority of the oligarchs; and meritocracy was found unacceptable in cases where the merit of its incumbents was assessed by hierarchical means.

However when combined with a participatory form of governance such as anarchism, it has been found that an hierarchical structure does have merit. In particular, the following two hybrid cases have shown promise:

- A meritocracy established by a democratic or consensual process, such as either a vote of all stakeholders, or a consensually-appointed nominating committee (a Nomcom in IETF and ICANN parlance); or
- An hierarchical structure whose leaders' merit is ensured by the force of certain idealising assumptions drawn from the example of open source software.

Both of these options remain vulnerable to criticism. As for the first, it was found necessary that the meritocracy not only be established by, but remain subject to the supervision of some democratic or consensual process, which begs the question, what such process? Whilst there may be an answer to this, it has not yet been discussed.

As for the second option, the idealism of the assumptions required for this form of hierarchical ordering to become tenable is its main downfall. For example, all that holds it together are the transaction costs that make other mechanisms of governance relatively more expensive. What is to ensure that these transaction costs are set at the right level, particularly in the short term?[205] While they are too low, the governance network may lack cohesion, reducing its effectiveness. If they are too high, then its stakeholders may still be oppressed, reducing its legitimacy.

Even where the assumptions of this model do hold, some of the same shortcomings of the free market may be replicated in a forum whose authority is drawn from its success in what Netanel describes as the market for "alternative rule regimes." For example, he states,

[205]In the longer term, if the market for governance regimes works well, network effects should reduce the number of competing governance networks to a sustainable number, whilst the oppression of stakeholders should be minimised by the prospective entry of new entrants into that market. However such an equilibrium might take decades to achieve.

> In cyberspace, no less than in real space, consumer decisions may represent an impoverished account of individuals' true preferences for many types of social goods. By the same token, market failure is no less endemic to online decision making than to its offline counterpart. In particular, the cyberanarchist vision would countenance some of the very externalities that liberal democracy seeks to minimize, including status discrimination and the suppression of minority viewpoints.[206]

That is, just as the free market is regulated in order to more closely conform with society's norms of distributive justice, it may be necessary to mediate disparities between the power of participants in a governance network (such as civil society and governments) if the network is not to exhibit the same imbalances as exist in the broader international system. The anarchistic/hierarchical hybrid does not do this (and neither for that matter does pure anarchistic ordering).

Even apart from this, all that has really been shown is that the success of a governance network such as the IGF depends upon it not upsetting its stakeholders enough that they are forced to seek alternative mechanisms of governance. Like the first option above, it still begs the question of how it is to make decisions that are most acceptable to the IGF at large, save that it be through some participatory mechanism.

Thus, although we have come close to an acceptable form of organisation for a multi-stakeholder governance network, there remain significant unresolved issues. If these issues can be resolved, then it may be through one of the democratic or consensual forms of organisation that have yet to be considered, but to which we now turn.

When previously considering a democratic method for the selection of an hierarchical leadership for a multi-stakeholder governance network, it was a considered problematic that there was no existing democratic polity to represent all stakeholders transnationally. But does this necessarily defeat the ideal of democratic ordering? This is one of the principal questions next to be addressed.

4.3 Democratic

Democracy is most often associated with the political system of liberal democratic states. However for the liberal, democracy is not an end in itself but rather a means of securing the greatest possible measure of justice for the individual. There may in fact be other forms of government that would secure this end just as well: for example, libertarians posit that a minar-

[206]Netanel (as in n. 204 on page 223), 405–406

chic (minimal, near-anarchistic) government could do so.[207] Conversely, a democracy would not serve this end as well if it were permitted to degenerate into a tyranny of the majority,[208] which may require an hierarchical hand to restrain their excesses.

Even so, mainstream liberal democratic theory turns on the assumption that it is through some form of democratic government coupled with the recognition of individual civil and political rights, that its citizens' freedom to exercise their autonomy may be maximised. At the root of this assumption is that democratic government best provides citizens with freedom of self-determination; that "citizens should always be able to understand themselves also as authors of the law to which they are subject as addressees."[209] Put even more simply, following Locke, it is to ensure that at some level government operates with the consent of the governed.[210] This will be described here simply as "the democratic principle."

As democracy is thus an instrumental rather than a primary good for liberals, it is necessary for them to construct a theory by which the democratic principle can be shown to support their fundamental moral intuition of the primacy of the value of human autonomy. One of the most popular such theoretical models, common to Rousseau, Kant and Rawls amongst others, is that of the social contract. This is a thought-experiment by which one considers what constitutional principles a society would consensually adopt if it it found itself in an anarchistic original position (in Rawls' case, without its members even knowing their own capacities and preferences).

An alternate model by which the democratic principle can be supported is that of discourse theory, of which Habermas is the most prominent scholar, and which will be discussed in more detail below. But at root, this and all other liberal models of democracy serve the same purpose: to demonstrate that a democratic system of government fulfils the liberal moral intuition that any interference with a person's liberty requires their consent.[211]

---

[207] Nozick (as in n. 365 on page 168)

[208] F A Hayek, *The Road to Serfdom* London: Routledge & Kegan Paul, 1976, 53

[209] Jürgen Habermas, *Between Facts and Norms: Contributions to a Discourse Theory of Law and Democracy* Cambridge, MA: MIT Press, 1996, 449

[210] Locke (as in n. 373 on page 169)

[211] A contrast is provided by the main competing broad theoretical conception of democracy, which is the civic republican model (see generally Held, *Democracy and the Global Order: From the Modern State to Cosmopolitan Governance* (as in n. 177 on page 131), 6–7). Civic republicanism emphasises the duties of citizens over their rights, as on this account it is through active citizenship (that is, participation in public affairs) that the democratic republic is constituted and sustained. Today communitarians are the intellectual successors of this political philosophy.

Unlike the so-called "protective democracy" of the classical liberal state, the civic republic is not limited to the maintenance of institutions to protect the liberty of the citizen, such as a market economy and the rule of law, because civic republicanism does not avoid the pursuit of a particular conception of the good. Rather, it assumes that such a conception can be discerned from the unified popular will of a relatively homogeneous political society. It does not merely

However, what democracy means for a liberal democratic nation state is not necessarily the same as what it means for a multi-stakeholder governance network. Notions such as "one vote, one value" and an institutionalised rule of law may well be quite foreign to a context in which collectivities join individuals as stakeholders, and in which the only decisions made are non-binding.

In particular it was already observed at section 3.2 on page 129 that governance networks are likely to lack the institutional guarantees that liberal states provide of representativeness (such as universal suffrage and regular elections) and of accountability and transparency (such as the separation of powers, judicial review and freedom of information legislation). What, then, are the criteria for a governance network that would satisfy the democratic principle, outside of the nation state? To answer this question by examining the essential nature of liberal democratic governance is the purpose of this chapter. This endeavour will be conducted under the four headings of representation, consent, transparency and accountability, and inclusion.

Under the first heading we will consider what it means for a governance network to be representative (or "democratic" in the narrowest sense). A point that will be made in that discussion is that one of the usual characteristics of the representative democratic model, that is a deficiency from a liberal perspective, is that it is possible for the rule of a majority to override minority interests.

Under the heading of consent, we will consider ways in which this deficiency can be addressed. Whilst consent is an overriding principle, in this context it is used to illustrate how participatory forms of democracy, such as deliberative democracy, can help to include all affected viewpoints, including those of minorities, in the democratic decision-making process.

Next, the related issues of transparency and accountability will be considered. The importance of accountability lies in the fact that as Aristotle observed, in its absence pure democracy is liable to regress into oligarchy. The essence of transparency on the other hand is that democratic justice must not only be done, it must also be seen to be done (*nemo judez in sua causa*, in law Latin). When both transparency and accountability are assured along with representation and consent (in the sense given above), one is left with a system of governance which operates in accordance with

---

presuppose such relative homogeneity, but aims to foster it by encouraging the citizen's pursuit of civic virtue. For the civic republican, it is by following a lifestyle that is conducive to the benefit of the community as a whole, that the community is enabled in turn to guarantee the freedom of the citizen. As a corollary, governance of a democratic republic is not left purely to popular will. Rather, a mixed form of government is likely to be preferred (which as has already been noted, was also Aristotle's preference): Sandel, *Liberalism and the Limits of Justice* (as in n. 375 on page 169).

Whilst the civic republican model of democracy is mentioned for completeness, it is the dominant liberal conception of democracy that will mainly be discussed here, as it is this model that prevails within the international legal system (as illustrated for example in the prominence of the discourse on human rights, and the absence of a balancing discourse on civic responsibility).

the consent of the governed, through a process by which their interests are considered rather than just aggregated, and the adherence of which to these standards is demonstrable.

This leaves the remaining issue of inclusion, which concerns the fact that even if procedures exist to institutionalise the other principles of liberal democracy, these will be to no avail if the governed do not take recourse to those institutions. Here, the Internet is both an example of how participation in democratic governance may be extended, and of its limitations on account of the so-called "digital divide."

If, at the conclusion of the chapter, it is resolved that a governance network can be structured that is democratic in every important sense of the word, then the result will be a holy grail of transnational governance—the flexibility and balanced legitimacy of a network, with the procedural justice and accountability of a liberal democracy.

Representation

In its original ancient Athenian form, democracy was of course literally what its name suggests—the rule (or power, *kratos*) of the people (the *demos*). Today known as direct democracy, it was a form of self-government in which citizens participated in making decisions in a political forum without the intermediation of elected representatives. Much subsequent democratic rhetoric has appealed to the same notions of popular rule; for example, Abraham Lincoln's mantra from the Gettysburg Address describing a "government of the people, by the people, for the people."

Yet neither in Athens, nor in any subsequent democratic society of large scale, have all the people really participated in government. For example only adult male citizens of Athens and surrounding Attica were permitted to participate in its assembly, which comprised less than a fifth of its resident population.[212] Such a society could hardly be called a democracy today, though by the same token Dahl refuses to grant that appellation to modern liberal states either, preferring to describe them as "polyarchies."[213]

Dahl's conception of the appropriate constitution of the *demos* is more inclusive than that of the Athenians, though he would still exclude transients and those shown to be mentally defective.[214] Alternative formulations focus more on the principle of consent; for example that the people entitled to make a law ought to be those who are subject to it,[215] or those who

[212]Josiah Ober, *Mass and Elite in Democratic Athens: Rhetoric, Ideology, and the Power of the People* Princeton, NJ: Princeton University Press, 1991, 128

[213]Robert Dahl, *Who Governs?: Democracy and Power in the American City* New Haven, CT: Yale University Press, 1961

[214]Idem, *Democracy and its Critics* New Haven, CT: Yale University Press, 1989, 129

[215]See Graham (as in n. 56 on page 18), 72

are significantly affected by it,[216] or all but those who have no legitimate material interest in it.[217]

Direct versus representative

There are a few isolated cases in which the *demos* so constituted does still act directly to some extent today. Examples include the initiative (by which the Parliament can be required by citizens to consider a bill), the referendum (by which the people can pass a bill into law or repeal an existing law), the recall (by which they can remove an official from office) and the plebiscite (by which they can make constitutional changes).[218]

The most significant present-day example of direct (or plebescitary) democracy at the national level is in Switzerland, where a petition signed by 1% of the electorate may call for a referendum on an issue currently before the Parliament, or signed by 2% of voters if the issue is not yet before the Parliament.[219] The referendum itself in most cases passes with a simple majority of those voting, though at the national level there must also be a majority of states in which a majority of votes were in favour of the proposal.

California has had since 1911 a system of a "ballot propositions" similar to the Swiss system, save that the required percentages of registered voters to put forward a proposed statute or constitutional amendment are 5% and 8% respectively, and that only a simple majority is required at referendum in either case. Many other states of the United States have adopted similar procedures.[220] Although there is no equivalent at the national level, at the local government level, by-laws proposed in New England are commonly enacted by a Town Meeting open to all registered voters.[221]

Direct democracy is of course also seen in the private sector and in civil society, although more often in smaller, grass roots organisations. The clearest example of direct democracy in action in the private sector is at general meetings of public companies, which in countries including Australia are required to be open to all shareholders of the company.[222]

In civil society, it is seen at levels ranging from the local bridge club, up to the scale of political parties and trade unions. Sweden is particularly

[216]Held and McGrew (as in n. 39 on page 104)

[217]John Gastil, *Democracy in Small Groups* Philadelphia: New Society Publishers, 1993, 19

[218]Roger Clarke, The Internet and Democracy ⟨URL: `http://www.agimo.gov.au/publications/2004/05/egovt_challenges/community/democracy`⟩

[219]Kris W Kobach, *The Referendum: Direct Democracy In Switzerland* Dartmouth: Dartmouth, 1993

[220]Joseph F Zimmerman, *The Initiative: Citizen Law-Making* Westport, CT: Praeger, 1999

[221]For example, this is required for any town of Massachusetts with a population of up to 6000, and is optional in larger towns. See *Constitution of the Commonwealth of Massachusetts*, 25 Oct 1780, article LXXXIX.

[222]*Corporations Act 2001* (Cth), part 2G.2

notable here, with political parties at both the local[223] and national levels,[224] as well as a large trade union,[225] organised along direct democratic lines.

However by far the dominant form of democratic rule is representative democracy, which rather than allowing the *demos* the right to rule directly, grants it the power and responsibility to delegate skilled specialist representatives to rule on its behalf. Seminal liberal scholar John Stuart Mill was amongst those who saw representative democracy as necessary to overcome not only the cost and logistical difficulty of implementing direct democracy on a large scale, but also the disinterest and indeed the incapacity of many citizens to act directly.[226] In more recent times, Dahl has agreed, contending "that representative government by elites is appropriate and that direct (as opposed to indirect through voting) participation is unworkable in the modern bureaucratic state."[227]

Filter versus mirror

There is however a division between the populist conception of representative democracy represented to some extent by Dahl, and the elitist conception of Mill. On the former account, representative democracy is favoured over direct democracy mainly as a concession to practicality. The peoples' representatives are expected to act as a mirror of the community's views, reflecting the views they would express in person if given the opportunity.

The alternative conception is of a representative assembly as a form of protection against ill-informed populism, including the tyranny of the majority.[228] Its function is to compensate for the deficiencies of direct democracy, such as the phenomenon whereby broad but shallow interests will always be trumped by narrow and deep interests pushed by organised groups.[229]

This division of opinion has a long heritage; it created a schism during the Constitutional Convention that drafted the United States Constitution,[230] Representing the populist position, John Adams for example urged

[223] Demoex; see http://demoex.net/en/.

[224] Aktiv Demokrati; see http://aktivdemokrati.se/.

[225] Sveriges Arbetares Centralorganisation (Central Organization of the Workers of Sweden); see http://www.sac.se/en/.

[226] John Stuart Mill, *Considerations on Representative Government: Remarks on Bentham's Philosophy* Cedar City, UT: Classic Books, 2000

[227] Dahl, *Democracy and its Critics* (as in n. 214 on page 229)

[228] D Walton, *Appeal to Popular Opinion* University Park, PA: Pennsylvania State University Press, 1999

[229] M Olsen, *The Logic of Collective Action: Public Goods and the Theory of Groups* Cambridge: Cambridge University Press, 1965

[230] J S Fishkin, Virtual Democratic Possibilities: Prospects for Internet Democracy ⟨URL: http://cdd.stanford.edu/research/papers/2000/brazil_paper.pdf⟩, 2–10

that a representative assembly "should be in miniature, an exact portrait of the people at large. It should think, feel, reason, and act like them."[231] The alternate view that the representative assembly should be a filter through which the public views would be refined was expressed by Madison, who held that the purpose of representation was

> to refine and enlarge the public views by passing them through the medium of a chosen body of citizens, whose wisdom may best discern the true interest of their country, and whose patriotism and love of justice will be least likely to sacrifice it to temporary or partial considerations. Under such a regulation, it may well happen that the public voice, pronounced by the representatives of the people, will be more consonant to the public good than if pronounced by the people themselves.[232]

These perspectives illustrate a real, and not easily resolved, tension which continues today between the conception of government as the agent of the people, and that of government as separate from the people and potentially acting against its collective wishes.[233]

Whilst it might be assumed that the liberal approach is the former, brief mention of insights from from two quite different theoretical perspectives will suffice to demonstrate that this is not the case, and that the pure direct democratic, and populist representative democratic models are deficient from a liberal standpoint. The root problem from which both theoretical insights stem lies in the difficulty of selecting a voting system which precludes the majority, as determined by the aggregation of individual votes, from tyrannising minorities and thereby compromising the democratic principle.

The first theoretical perspective is Dworkin's observation that the preferences of voters expressed in a democratic forum will tend to include preferences as to distributions of benefits that *other* voters should receive. These so-called "external" preferences are not entitled to be given any weight in a democratic calculus which attempts to aggregate individual preferences in order to maximize overall welfare.[234] An example of this problem is that the community may express its preferences through the ballot box as to the rights that should be accorded to (or withheld from)

---

[231] John Adams, *The Political Writings of John Adams* Washington, DC: Regnery Publishing, Inc, 2000, 484

[232] Charles Rossiter, editor, *The Federalist Papers* New York: Signet Classic, 2003, 76–77

[233] B Holden, *Understanding Liberal Democracy* Oxford: Philip Allen, 1998, 20

[234] Dworkin (as in n. 367 on page 168), 277

homosexual couples, whereas it is only the preferences of the couples themselves that should be counted on that issue.[235]

The second perspective comes from economist Kenneth Arrow, who has demonstrated that it is impossible even in theory to construct a democratic voting system that simultaneously satisfies all the criteria that might be considered necessary to produce an outcome fairly representing the voters' collective best interests.[236]

Amartya Sen extended Arrow's impossibility theorem to demonstrate a further and even more fundamental shortcoming of democracy for the liberal, which has come to be known as the liberal paradox: that it is impossible to devise a voting system that both upholds individual rights, and results in a Pareto optimal outcome. Put another way, if individual liberty is to be upheld, then the outcome of any voting system will always be inferior to some alternative that all voters would have been happier with.[237]

These observations of Dworkin, Arrow and Sen illustrate just some of the significant shortcomings with all democratic voting systems in expressing the true preferences of the *demos* (and there are further practical shortcomings not even mentioned, such as those of strategic voting and institutional effects).[238] Whilst they do not detract from the democratic principle, they do demonstrate that its implications extend well beyond a system of voting.

They also give licence to elected representatives to pursue the democratic ideal beyond the expressed preferences of their constituents. Even to state this fact immediately heralds its risks. Whilst further thoughts will be offered in the succeeding section on transparency and accountability, for now it can be foreshadowed that any representative democratic au-

---

[235]As will be seen, Dworkin's answer to this paradox is that it is the purpose of human rights to prevent most such external preferences from being given expression in a democratic political system.

[236]Kenneth J Arrow, *Social Choice and Individual Values*, 2nd edition New Haven, CT: Yale University Press, 1963. These criteria are:

- non-dictatorship (that a single voter's preferences cannot be permitted to hold sway);
- unrestricted domain (that the voting system selected must be capable of ordering preferences in a consistent way that does not operate randomly across iterations);
- independence of irrelevant alternatives (that if only a subset of alternatives are considered, changes in voters' ordering of preferences outside this subset should have no impact on the result);
- monotonicity (that if an individual voter changes a preference to rank it higher, it should not be possible for this to cause the voting system to rank it *lower* overall); and
- non-imposition (that it should be possible to achieve any given overall ordering of preferences from an appropriate set of individual preferences).

[237]Amartya Sen, Liberty and Social Choice, Journal of Philosophy 80:1 1983

[238]Gary W Cox, *Making Votes Count: Strategic Coordination in the World's Electoral Systems* Cambridge: Cambridge University Press, 1997

thority must "be held in check by institutional constraints that guarantee turnover in government and provide dissenters with many opportunities for political veto."[239]

Procedural versus substantive

Another perspective on the observed procedural shortcomings of representative democratic government (or governance) comes from the proponents of what can be called substantive democracy. What distinguishes procedural democracy from substantive democracy is a difference in focus: an institutional focus in the former case, and a social focus in the latter. Where the procedural democrat may be satisfied that democratic institutions and procedures are in place, the substantive democrat looks behind them to examine outcomes: does a particular system of governance *actually* reflect the aggregated preferences of the electorate, and if not, why not?

In practice, what this means is that procedural democracy is concerned mainly with the establishment and maintenance of a free and fair electoral system, whereas the concern of substantive democracy is broader and encompasses the maintenance of a society in which electors are, and remain, free to form and change their preferences.[240] The liberal, therefore, is a substantive democrat, who requires of the state not only a fair electoral system, but also to maintain the bedrock upon which that system stands. Such a liberal scholar is Dahl, who posits five criteria that a democratic polity should satisfy (most of which will fall, or have fallen, for separate discussion within the four slightly broader headings of this section on democracy):

- effective participation (that all citizens are equally empowered to participate in the political process);
- enlightened understanding (that these citizens are provided with adequate information to allow them to contribute meaningfully);
- control over the agenda (that citizens should be empowered to decide which issues should be placed on the public agenda);
- voting equality at decisive stages (that all citizens should have a vote of equal weight at every point when a decision is made); and
- inclusiveness (that the rights of citizenship should be available to all besides transients and the mentally deficient).[241]

[239] Immergut (as in n. 299 on page 155), 14

[240] Gregory H Fox and Georg Nolte, *Democratic Governance and International Law* Cambridge: Cambridge University Press, 2000, chap. Intolerant Democracies, 400–401, and see section 3.4 on page 167

[241] Dahl, *Democracy and its Critics* (as in n. 214 on page 229)

The satisfaction of these criteria in turn requires the state to ensure that their preconditions are safeguarded even against infringement by the state itself (as in a protective democracy). The first of two related ways in which this can be done is by recognising these preconditions as rights, and there are in turn two main categories into which such rights could be classed.

The first category of rights required to meet the criteria of a democratic society are the basic civil and political rights of individual autonomy common to liberal scholars from Kant to Nozick, that Habermas describes as the "*right to the greatest possible measure of equal individual liberties*,"[242] and with which he includes the right to freedom of political association and due process. These are the rights necessary for even procedural democracy to function as designed, and which international law recognises through the *International Covenant on Civil and Political Rights.*

In the second category, and more peculiar to substantive democrats, are what Dahl refers to as rights to support the agency of individuals,[243] and that Habermas describes as rights to the basic living conditions that are necessary in order for the citizens to exercise their other rights.[244] These rights, which include the right to a basic standard of living and to an elementary education,[245] are amongst those found in the *International Covenant on Economic, Social and Cultural Rights.*[246]

Deontological liberalism has long recognised such fundamental pre-legal rights (at least of the first category) as being sacrosanct against the state, though such priority is more difficult to invoke in terms of teleological liberalism (and does raise difficult questions about how conflicting rights claims are to be resolved).[247]

A second and complementary way in which to safeguard the preconditions of democratic governance against infringement by the state is to

---

[242]Habermas, *Between Facts and Norms: Contributions to a Discourse Theory of Law and Democracy* (as in n. 209 on page 227), 122 (emphasis in original)

[243]Robert Dahl, *Democracy's Edges* Cambridge: Cambridge University Press, 1999, chap. Can International Organizations be Democratic? A Skeptic's View; Idem, *Democracy and its Critics* (as in n. 214 on page 229), 170

[244]Habermas, *Between Facts and Norms: Contributions to a Discourse Theory of Law and Democracy* (as in n. 209 on page 227), 123

[245]See General Assembly of the United Nations, Universal Declaration of Human Rights (as in n. 211 on page 138), Articles 25 and 26.

[246]This second category of rights, which are in the nature of entitlements rather than freedoms, are more controversial than the first because their fulfilment is likely to require the redistribution of property (normally through taxation) in violation of the property rights of others: Nozick (as in n. 365 on page 168). But by the same token, the status of the right to private property, and the free market system which arises from it, is itself controversial. Some liberals point out that the right to private property may be distinguished from other fundamental rights in that its exercise is rival: Albert Weale, *The Good Polity: Normative Analysis of the State* New York: Basil Blackwell, 1989, chap. The Limits of Democracy, 42. It is unnecessary for present purposes to enter this debate.

[247]Held, *Democracy and the Global Order: From the Modern State to Cosmopolitan Governance* (as in n. 177 on page 131), 217

elevate them to constitutional level. This is the manner in which the political institutions of representative democracy are generally enshrined in law, including the separation of powers and the rule of law, both of which will be discussed in more detail in the section on transparency and accountability below.

However a constitution can also be used to enshrine rights, as Kant for example observed,[248] (which avoids the difficulty of the recognition of pre-legal rights and duties in teleological liberal theory, since a constitution is still law, though its most fundamental example). Rawls identifies the purpose of constitutional rights as preserving or mirroring the justice of the original position, a position of equality and fair representation from which common principles are identified that are to the mutual benefit of all.[249] For Dworkin on the other hand, the purpose of rights is to compensate for the deficiencies of procedural democracy described above.[250]

Habermas, too, sees the place of rights as being constitutional principles, generated through a public discourse that constitutes its citizens as legal subjects, whereafter they are constrained from determining discursively the form that their discursive creation of other law will take. Thus for Habermas, "the requirement of legally institutionalizing self-legislation can be fulfilled only with the help of a code that *simultaneously* implies the guarantee of actionable individual liberties."[251]

In summary of the last three subsections, then, it has been found that liberal democratic governance requires the establishment of accountable and transparent institutions that allow for the public to effectively participate as authors of the laws to which they are subject, subject to various superadded guarantees such as the protection of civil and political, and probably some degree of economic and social rights of individuals, through constitutional and international law.

Transnational democracy

Unfortunately however, even this is not enough in the transnationally interconnected world of the new medieval era, since democracy might well be protected by such measures within the state, and yet still be impeded by forces from outside the state such as other states or transnational institutions (including government networks, civil society and the private sector),[252] which take roles in governance without the concomitant consti-

[248]Immanuel Kant, *Kant: Political Writings*, edited by Hans Reiss, 2nd edition Cambridge: Cambridge University Press, 1991, 191

[249]Rawls, *A Theory of Justice* (as in n. 370 on page 169), 221–222

[250]Dworkin (as in n. 367 on page 168), 277

[251]Habermas, *Between Facts and Norms: Contributions to a Discourse Theory of Law and Democracy* (as in n. 209 on page 227), 455 (emphasis in original).

[252]Held, *Democracy and the Global Order: From the Modern State to Cosmopolitan Governance* (as in n. 177 on page 131), 226; Idem, *Cosmopolitan Democracy: An Agenda for a New World Order*

tutional and international legal responsibilities of states.[253] Since decisions made in such fora may affect individuals across diverse territorial boundaries, it becomes difficult to determine whose consent to them should be required, and how that consent could be measured.[254]

The study of transnational democracy addresses this dilemma, and puts the normative position that it is necessary to extend democratic guarantees of autonomy on a transnational basis at all applicable levels of governance. There are however three broad approaches to achieving this end.

The first of these is liberal institutionalism (of which regime theory is a special case).[255] For the liberal institutionalist, transnational democracy is furthered through pluralism of transnational governance and by increasing the transparency of the operations of each of the actors, which approximates to the position put forward at section 3.5 on page 175. Fukuyama has describes it as a vision of "a world populated by a large number of overlapping and sometimes competitive international institutions, what can be labelled multi-multilateralism."[256] Civil society has a central role to play here both instrumentally (in facilitating this process) and normatively (as a participant in it).[257]

A limitation of the liberal institutional approach is that its normative programme does not include any mechanism to ensure that there is an overall balance of views represented amongst the various actors participating in transnational public policy governance. For example, an issue area such as IPR may be dominated by private sector rights holders, governments beholden to them, civil society organisations representing them, and WIPO, leaving alternate perspectives under-represented.

This is one of the insights that may be drawn from the second approach to transnational democracy, which can be termed radical democratic pluralism[258] or radical plural democracy.[259] The radical democratic pluralist is critical of the ability of powerful interests to capture pluralistic governance processes, and in response urges direct action by grass roots social move-

---

Cambridge: Polity Press, 1995, chap. Democracy and the New International Order, 99–100

[253]Sol Picciotto, *The Market or the Public Domain?: Global Governance and the Asymmetry of Power* London: Routledge, 2001, chap. Democratizing Globalism, 342

[254]Held, Cosmopolitan Democracy: An Agenda for a New World Order (as in n. 252 on the preceding page), 102

[255]Anthony McGrew, *Democratic Theory Today: Challenges for the 21st Century* Cambridge: Polity Press, 2002, chap. Transnational Democracy

[256]Francis Fukuyama, *America at the Crossroads: Democracy, Power, and the Neoconservative Legacy* New Haven, CT: Yale University Press, 2006, 158

[257]Myres S McDougal, Harold D Lasswell and W Michael Reisman, *International Law Essays: A Supplement to International Law in Contemporary Practice* New York: Foundation Press, 1981, chap. The World Constitutive Process of Authoritative Decision, cited in Charnovitz (as in n. 127 on page 123), 271–273

[258]McGrew (as in n. 255)

[259]Susan Hekman, Radical Plural Democracy: A New Theory For the Left? ⟨URL: `http://www.datawranglers.com/negations/issues/96w/96w_hekman.html`⟩

ments to achieve transnational governance outcomes through a variety of fora at different levels.[260]

This position is antagonistic to the dominance of the existing liberal world order even in its pluralistic form, so for example the radical democratic pluralist would likely not seek to work within the IGF, but to subvert it. From a liberal perspective this is the main shortcoming of the approach, along with the fact that although it aims to develop a structure of checks and balances to hold the hegemony of powerful interests to account, the legitimacy, transparency and accountability of these grass roots endeavours themselves remain, if anything, even more obscure than those of a governance network structured within the liberal paradigm.

The third transnational democratic approach is cosmopolitan democracy, which builds on liberal institutionalism in its vision of multi-layered governance, but has a more ambitious normative program. It proposes, in the words of its foremost scholar David Held, "the establishment of an international community of democratic states and societies committed to upholding a democratic public law both within and across their own boundaries: a cosmopolitan democratic community."[261] This requires all transnational governance institutions, including private regimes such as the new law merchant, to be held to an overarching cosmopolitan legal framework that upholds accountability to liberal democratic norms such as the rule of law.[262]

In the long term, this will mean nothing less than the creation of a global parliament and an internationalised global legal system.[263] The short-term objectives of the cosmopolitan programme are not much less ambitious; including the creation of a second chamber of the UN, the reform of the UN Security Council, enhanced political regionalisation on the model of the EC, the creation of a new international Human Rights Court with compulsory jurisdiction, and the establishment of an international military force.[264]

It is to criticism of these high-flown ideals that cosmopolitan democracy is most vulnerable, with Keohane and Nye dramatically pointing out that "a cosmopolitan view that treats the globe as one constituency, implies the existence of a political community in which citizens of 198 states would be willing to be continually outvoted by a billion Chinese and a billion Indians."[265]

---

[260]McGrew (as in n. 255 on the previous page), 274

[261]Held, *Democracy and the Global Order: From the Modern State to Cosmopolitan Governance* (as in n. 177 on page 131), 229

[262]Ibid., 234; Idem, Law of States, Law of Peoples (as in n. 126 on page 123)

[263]Idem, Cosmopolitan Democracy: An Agenda for a New World Order (as in n. 252 on page 236), 113

[264]Ibid., 111; Idem, *Democracy and the Global Order: From the Modern State to Cosmopolitan Governance* (as in n. 177 on page 131), 279–280

[265]Keohane and Nye (as in n. 65 on page 110), 33.

On this account, cosmopolitanism falls victim to its own ambition. It encounters the same problems discussed at section 3.4 on page 167 as to the extent to which diverse communities can form a single normative regime that also has adequate content to be of any value.[266] Keane, for example, doubts that even the principles of procedural democracy, that the cosmopolitan programme seeks to instil in all transnational governance institutions, are culturally neutral:

> Daoist celebrations of natural, virtually anarchistic spontaneity and Legalist defences of centralised political order through carefully controlled punishments and rewards—to mention two randomly chosen but important Chinese intellectual traditions—do not see eye to eye with such "cosmopolitan" regulative principles. Why should they? Why should they or the rest of the world even engage in a reasoned public debate with cosmopolitans, whom they might (understandably) dismiss out of hand or indeed suppose, wielding their own plausible reasons, to be wrong-headed, or utterly mistaken?[267]

These criticisms lose some of their cogency when the principles of cosmopolitan democracy are applied to a governance network such as the IGF rather than to the international system as a whole. In this narrower context, the preparedness of affected stakeholders to accept the democratic principle should be widespread enough that few will be excluded (and for those who are, the IGF exercises only soft power anyway, and is unable to enforce its output upon them).

On the other hand it is true that the range of substantive issues upon which it would then be possible for stakeholders to go on to decide by democratic means may be limited: cultural or ideological differences may either prevent decisions from being made at all, or if the decision-making method employed (such as a voting system) allows the forum to push through a majority decision, it may yet be defeated by the minority's ability to boycott it. Granted that this provides an incentive for the forum to aim towards consensus, but if the only decisions that can thus be made are amorphous platitudes, it would still be as well if no decisions were made at all.

Whilst this criticism is relevant and will be addressed in detail later,[268] it does not foil the cosmopolitan democratic programme. Such cases are simply examples of those in which it is not appropriate for the decision in question to be dealt with at such a high level, and where it should fall back to be dealt with at a lower layer of governance in accordance with the principle of subsidiarity.

[266] McGrew (as in n. 255 on page 237), 276

[267] John Keane, *Global Civil Society?* Cambridge: Cambridge University Press, 2003, 124–125

[268] To some extent in the following subsection, and again at section 4.4 on page 311.

Held has developed tests of extensity, intensity, and comparative efficiency to determine whether it is most appropriate for governance to be exercised at a grass roots level (the corporation or city, for instance), the national level, or a higher, supranational or transnational level.[269] These three tests respectively examine how extensive is the range of people affected within and across borders, how intensely each particular group of people is affected, and whether a lower governance level would likely be ineffective, requiring it to be dealt with at a higher level.

The appropriate constituency in any given case is to be "defined according to the nature and scope of controversial transnational issues."[270] In some cases it may be unavoidable that the closest fit is not a perfect one, and in others the best outcome may be for an issue to be dealt with in overlapping and competing ways at multiple layers of governance. This equates to Fukuyama's "multi-multilateral" model, and illustrates the commonality of the core of the cosmopolitan democratic approach with that of liberal institutionalism.

In fact, leaving aside the most overreaching ambitions of cosmopolitan democracy and the postmodern excesses of the radical democratic pluralist programme, all three approaches affirm the importance of the democratic principle not just at the level of the state, but at all levels of transnational ordering, public and private,[271] extending beyond the state-centric *demos*, to the *cosmos*; that is, to all humankind.[272]

Consent

One problem that transnational democratic theory does not resolve is how to extend the limited range of decisions upon which agreement can be reached, given that freedom of exit from a governance network provides an in-built check on its power to oppress its stakeholders. That is, because its authority is non-binding, stakeholders can simply ignore or avoid the dictates of a governance network that do not accord with the democratic principle of consent. As Rosenau puts it,

> governance is a system of rule that only works if it is accepted by the majority (or, at least, by the most powerful of

[269] Held, *Democracy and the Global Order: From the Modern State to Cosmopolitan Governance* (as in n. 177 on page 131), 234

[270] Idem, *Models of Democracy*, 2nd edition Cambridge: Polity Press, 1996, 355

[271] Idem, *Democracy and the Global Order: From the Modern State to Cosmopolitan Governance* (as in n. 177 on page 131), 252

[272] Idem, *The Political Philosophy of Cosmopolitanism* Cambridge: Cambridge University Press, 2005, chap. Principles of Cosmopolitan Order

> those it affects), whereas governments can function even in the face of widespread opposition to their policies.[273]

Whilst this characteristic of governance networks is well aligned with the most basic principle of democratic governance—that of the consent of the governed—it may also be inclined to splinter an ideologically and culturally diverse network into smaller, more agreeable but also more homogeneous groups,[274] unless there were some other mechanism to hold the larger network together.

In the discussion of open source software, it was suggested that transaction costs could serve this purpose, and that those transaction costs would be the higher, the greater the social capital that the governance network had developed, making it relatively more attractive to its stakeholders than alternative mechanisms or fora of governance.[275]

It is possible to go further and say that social capital is the defining attribute of a successful network, as such success is measured by its ability to coordinate mutually beneficial collective action (or MBCA) among its stakeholders, which is effectively the "income" that social capital returns.[276] In order to maximise the range of decisions that a democratic governance network such as the IGF might make, the long-term value of its social capital to its stakeholders, and thus the transaction costs of defecting from it to alternative fora, should be high enough to persuade them to voluntarily abide by and implement the network's decisions even when they go against their own short-term interests.

How, then, may social capital be cultivated within a governance network, in order to achieve this end? One of the most important factors is the inculcation of norms that reinforce voluntary participation in the activities of the network, with the expectation that this will be reciprocated by other stakeholders to the common benefit.[277] These norms of cooperation in turn depend upon the stakeholders being institutionally empowered to participate in governance through the network. As suggested in the discussion of open source software, but as research also confirms,[278] there is a strong positive link between empowerment and participation, which is simply to state the perhaps obvious point that in order to encourage the participation of stakeholders in democratic or consensual governance, they must be able to see that their participation can influence the outcome.

---

[273]Rosenau, Governance Without Government: Order and Change in World Politics (as in n. 64 on page 19), 4

[274]For example, consider the factions into which the WTO is effectively divided: see section 3.2 on page 108.

[275]See section 4.2 on page 211.

[276]Uphoff (as in n. 196 on page 220), 218–219

[277]Ibid., 228–229

[278]Michal Lyons, Carin Smuts and Anthea Stephens, Participation, Empowerment and Sustainability: (How) Do the Links Work?, Urban Studies 38:8 2001, 1236

Institutionalising the empowerment of stakeholders can also foster the development of an environment in which stakeholders trust each other to reciprocate the participation they each contribute to the governance network, resulting in a "virtuous circle" (or conversely, avoiding a vicious circle) that encourages their continued and enhanced participation in turn. Ironically, experience from open source software development suggests that it is counter-productive to pay stakeholders for their participation in the network, because this will only demotivate those who participate voluntarily in the knowledge that others are doing the same.[279]

Although these instrumental benefits may seem reason enough to empower stakeholders to participate in democratic governance, to do so is defensible on the broader theoretical basis that it better fulfils the democratic principle of consent (hence the title of this subsection of the book). Recall that democracy is a means rather than an end for the liberal, the end being a form of governance that permits the smallest possible encroachment upon individual liberty. Thus for the liberal, a democracy in which everyone's views are heard and taken into consideration in more than just a token way, is simply a better democracy than one in which only the majority participates.

However the gulf between this ideal and the way democracy most often works in practice is quite wide. Conventionally, decisions made by the simple aggregation of preferences through representative democratic procedures can be quite arbitrary. Even without infringing upon any citizen's human rights, the majority's decision could still be entirely capricious and unreasoned. Although generally some deliberation takes place in representative fora (such as parliaments), at the level of broadest democratic participation (such as the ballot box), no reasons need be presented at all. Many voters may lack the time or inclination to assimilate all the information they need to even form a reasoned position, and it may be entirely rational for them, individually, not to do so.[280]

This illustrates a practical tension between developing a democratic polity in which a large number of stakeholders are directly involved, and one in which the decisions they make are the product of reasoned deliberation—something of a trade-off between "quantity and quality." Yet in fact these are not the end-points of a continuum, but rather variables. Although the forms of democratic governance cannot be neatly plotted against these variables in a tabular or matrix form,[281] the chart below is a limited attempt to visualise their relationship, showing various forms and conceptions of democratic governance, the number of participants generally involved, the degree to which they involve greater or lesser

---

[279] Steven J Vaughan-Nichols, Disgruntled Debian Developers Delay Etch ⟨URL: `http://www.linux-watch.com/news/NS3128387759.html`⟩

[280] Anthony Downs, *An Economic Theory of Democracy* New York: Harper & Row, 1957

[281] Though for one attempt see Fishkin, Virtual Democratic Possibilities: Prospects for Internet Democracy (as in n. 230 on page 231), 12

Figure 4.1: Conceptions of democracy

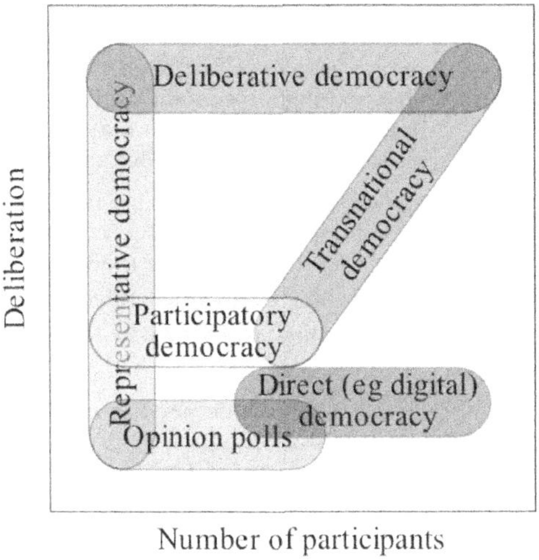

deliberation, and the other forms or conceptions with which they intersect.

Although this chart by no means includes all major forms or conceptions of democratic governance, it does demonstrate for example that representative democracy can result in well reasoned decisions, but that these are the result of the deliberations of very few, and that at the other extreme direct democracy can involve the entire *demos*, but typically with a low level of deliberation.

Potentially rating highly on both variables is deliberative democracy, which is to be discussed below, and which intersects at its apex with transnational democracy (illustrating the theoretical case in which deliberative democratic principles are institutionalised at all levels of transnational democratic governance). Preceding that discussion and by way of drawing a contrast to it, a more conventional conception of democratic governance will be described: that of participatory democracy.

Participatory democracy

Participatory or collaborative democracy is that in which the process of policy development by a representative democratic decision-making body, but not the final decision-making process itself, is open to the reception of direct input from all stakeholders, in a process known as consultation or dialogue. This is already a matter of practice for most domestic governments, and a matter of legal obligation for some others,[282] and traditionally takes place through the reception of written submissions and the holding of open public hearings.

As the participants in such processes are usually self-selected,[283] opportunities for public participation in policy making are generally advertised through the media, though briefings to known interest groups may also be initiated by government (a feature of so-called pluralist democracy).

A number of civil society and private sector organisations are involved in advancing the cause of participatory democracy, putting forward principles or providing services by which consultation can be made more effective.[284] Such organisations from civil society include the United States-based Centre for Collaborative Policy,[285] and those from the private sector include Dialogue by Design[286] and Citizen Space.[287]

At an intergovernmental level, participatory democracy has most notably been promoted by the OECD in a publication which distinguishes three levels of citizen engagement in government: information, consultation and active participation.[288] Of these, the first level, information provision, does not qualify as participatory democracy as it is described here, as it does not involve any element of participation on the citizens' part.[289]

The second and third levels, consultation and active participation, describe a continuum which extends from participatory democracy of a purely formal kind, through to the use of the deliberative democratic techniques described at section 4.3 on page 253 (subject to the proviso that "responsibility for the final decision or policy formulation rests with government"[290]—which may or may not be consistent with the deliberative democratic programme, depending on how accountable the government is for the consideration of the citizens' input through institutionalised political pro-

---

[282] Judith E Innes and David E Booher, Reframing Public Participation: Strategies for the 21st Century, Planning Theory & Practice 5:4 2004, 5

[283] Though not always: for example for the Australia 2020 Summit held in April 2008, one thousand "leading Australians" were nominated as delegates by a ten-member non-governmental steering committee: see `http://www.australia2020.gov.au/`.

[284] Lyn Carson, Innovative Consultation Processes and the Changing Role of Activism, Third Sector Review 7:1 2001; Government of Western Australia, e-Engagement: Guidelines For Community Engagement Using Information And Communications Technology (ICT) ⟨URL: `http://www.citizenscape.wa.gov.au/documents/e_engagement.pdf`⟩, 11

[285] See `http://www.csus.edu/ccp/`.

[286] See `http://www.dialoguebydesign.net/`.

[287] See `http://www.citizenspace.co.uk/`.

[288] OECD, Engaging Citizens in Policy-Making: Information, Consultation and Public Participation ⟨URL: `http://www.oecd.org/dataoecd/24/34/2384040.pdf`⟩

[289] Though is still a vital component of democratic transparency, to be discussed at section 4.3 on page 260.

[290] Ibid., 2

cesses.)[291]

Drawing on these principles, both the OECD,[292] and Australia's AGIMO, have drafted sets of guidelines for effectively conducting public consultations online.[293] AGIMO has applied these principles in proposing the introduction of an Australian Government Consultation Blog, which unlike the Commonwealth government's current public consultations Web site,[294] could enable respondents not only to present their own views, but also to deliberate upon and debate the views of others (though without necessarily being empowered to actively shape government policy).[295]

Consistent with this at a State level is a Victorian report on Electronic Democracy that recommended that "online consultation should allow citizen-to-citizen communication, moderated only to prevent incidence of defamation or legal risk,"[296] though this recommendation has not been implemented to date.

Deliberative democracy

Deliberative democracy takes this notion of citizen-to-citizen communication further. It is concerned with citizens exercising their votes (or otherwise engaging in democratic decision-making processes) in a considered manner that reflects their reasoned deliberations formed during engagement with other citizens on the issue at hand.[297] Thus where direct democracy fails because its ability to produce reasoned decisions is predicated upon the existence of a more well-informed citizenry than exists in practice, and representative democracy cannot, even in theory, fairly represent the interests of all citizens (and in practice best represents those of powerful elites),[298] deliberative democracy aims to remedy both those deficiencies,[299] resulting in closer adherence to the democratic principle of consent.

---

[291] Habermas, *Between Facts and Norms: Contributions to a Discourse Theory of Law and Democracy* (as in n. 209 on page 227), 380

[292] OECD, Guidelines for Online Public Consultation ⟨URL: http://www.oecd.org/document/40/0,2340,en_2649_34495_37539752_1_1_1_1,00.html⟩

[293] AGIMO, Principles for ICT-enabled Citizen Engagement ⟨URL: http://www.agimo.gov.au/__data/assets/pdf_file/0008/55745/Principles.pdf⟩

[294] See http://www.regulations.gov/.

[295] Idem, Australian Government Consultation Blog Discussion Paper ⟨URL: http://www.agimo.gov.au/__data/assets/pdf_file/0014/61601/Consultation_Blog_Discussion_Paper.pdf⟩

[296] Scrutiny of Acts & Regulations Committee, Inquiry into Electronic Democracy: Final Report ⟨URL: http://www.parliament.vic.gov.au/SARC/E-Democracy/Final_Report/Final_Report.pdf⟩, 147

[297] See Philip Pettit, *Debating Deliberative Democracy* London: Routledge, 2003, chap. Deliberative Democracy, the Discursive Dilemma, and Republican Theory 138–139.

[298] See section 3.4 on page 152.

[299] John S Dryzek and Christian List, Social Choice Theory and Deliberative Democracy: A Reconciliation, British Journal of Political Science 33 2003

Cohen writes,

> The notion of a deliberative democracy is rooted in the intuitive ideal of a democratic association in which the justification of the terms and conditions of association proceeds through public argument and reasoning among equal citizens. Citizens in such an order share a commitment to the resolution of problems of collective choice through public reasoning, and regard their basic institutions as legitimate in so far as they establish the framework for free public deliberation.[300]

He suggests a set of four criteria by which a system of democratic governance can be compared against the deliberative democratic ideal:

- It should be free; that is, participants should not be constrained either in considering proposals, or in implementing them once agreed, by external claims of authority.
- It should be reasoned, in that arguments should not be based upon force or unexamined preferences.
- It should be equal, such that parties to the deliberation are identically placed both in procedural terms, and also in that their status outside the forum does not impinge upon consideration of their substantive contributions.
- It should aim to achieve a rational consensus.[301]

Some more insight into what deliberative democracy is may be obtained from distinguishing it from some of those things that it is not:

---

[300] Joshua Cohen, *The Good Polity: Normative Analysis of the State* New York: Basil Blackwell, 1989, chap. Deliberation and Democratic Legitimacy, 21. Cohen also here formally defines deliberative democracy by identifying five essential features that may be summarised as follows:

- Deliberative democracy takes place within an organisation with an ongoing and independent existence.
- Its members share a common conception that their affairs should be governed by the principle of deliberation among equals.
- The organisation is pluralistic, containing members of diverse opinions and preferences.
- The organisation's adherence to the principle of deliberation among equals is manifest and public.
- All members recognise the capacity of all other members to participate in this public deliberative process.

[301] Ibid., 22–23; Idem, *Deliberative Democracy* Cambridge: Cambridge University Press, 1998, chap. Democracy and Liberty, 194, and compare the eight criteria of Coleman at Stephen Coleman and John Gøtze, Bowling Together: Online Public Engagement in Policy Deliberation ⟨URL: `http://www.bowlingtogether.net/bowlingtogether.pdf`⟩, 5.

- Unlike participatory democracy it is concerned not simply with understanding but with decision-making;[302] however the dialogue that participatory democracy fosters can be a preliminary stage to deliberation.[303]

- On the other hand unlike direct democracy, deliberative democracy is concerned not only with decision-making, but also with opinion formation.[304]

- At the other extreme, a democracy concerned only with opinion formation, as a means of developing a community of civically virtuous citizens, would be an example of "developmental democracy";[305] a species of civic republicanism from which deliberative democracy should also be distinguished.

- It may again be distinguished from "grass roots democracy" which holds that democracy is to be exercised at the lowest possible level.[306] Whilst deliberative democratic procedures may be applied at the grass roots level, they are equally applicable within other layers of governance that may be further removed from the grass roots.

- Similarly deliberative democracy is broader than empowered participatory governance,[307] because to empower stakeholders with the authority to make decisions affecting them only fulfils one of "two key elements: giving community members the authority to make decisions and choices and facilitating the development of the knowledge and resources necessary to exercise these choices."[308] A distinguishing feature of deliberative democracy is its focus on the latter.

- Finally in its focus on the refinement of preferences through reasoned deliberation, deliberative democracy also departs from rational choice theory, which tends to regard democratically-expressed preferences as relatively "stable and exogenous to the decision process, [whereas] deliberative democracy [regards them] as transformable and endogenous."[309]

---

[302]Or at least, decision-shaping; see section 6.2 on page 423.

[303]David Schoem and Sylvia Hurtado, editors, *Intergroup Dialogue: Deliberative Democracy in School, College, Community and Workplace* Ann Arbor: University of Michigan Press, 2001

[304]Van Dijk (as in n. 167 on page 130), 38–39.

[305]C B Macpherson, *The Life and Times of Liberal Democracy* London: Oxford University Press, 1977, 43

[306]Michael Kaufman and Haroldo Dilla Alfonso, editors, *Community Power and Grassroots Democracy: The Transformation of Social Life* London: Zed Books, 1997

[307]Archon Fung, Erik Olin Wright and Rebecca Abers, editors, *Deepening Democracy: Institutional Innovations in Empowered Participatory Governance* London: Verso, 2003

[308]Allison Zippay, The Politics of Empowerment, Social Work 40:2 1995, 264

[309]Claudia Landwehr, Rational Choice, Deliberative Democracy and Preference Transformation, Studies in Social and Political Thought 11 2005, 41

Perhaps the most important corollary to the above criteria follows from the proposition that opinions cannot be shaped by force. This being so, any position contended for must be supported by reasons that appeal not just to the proposer but to all, or at least to a majority. This results in a tendency for democratic deliberation to be framed in terms of the common good, simply because a participant's appeal solely to his own self-interest is unlikely to be successful in convincing others.[310]

This bias away from arguments based on pure self-interest makes it important that the preferences of participants in the deliberative democratic process are open to reasoned adaptation in response to other viewpoints, and that such adaptation is not constrained by underlying power relations. This does not mean that participants may not privately hold preferences for selfish reasons, but simply that for these preferences to prevail will require others to be convinced of them (perhaps on quite different grounds), through no other force than that of reason.

To put this same proposition more starkly, it is the position of the deliberative democrat that a decision that "cannot arise from free reasoning among equals . . . . is for that reason undemocratic."[311] Note that this does not imply that the participants in a deliberative democratic process will always be *able* to reach a consensual collective ordering of preferences. It merely sets out an impartial procedure by which such preferences *could* be justified.

Habermas phrases the same concept slightly differently and terms it the "discourse principle": that "just those norms deserve to be valid that could meet with the approval of those potentially affected, insofar as the latter participate in rational discourses."[312]

To give a concrete example of the effect of this principle, it might be that, if a majority of the citizens in a democratic polity were of Caucasian extraction, they would all privately prefer to receive preferential treatment in taxation or social services than citizens of other racial backgrounds. Yet as it would be difficult for them to justify such discriminatory treatment as policy through the use of public reason, the measure would would be less likely to pass into law in a deliberative democracy than in (for example) a direct democracy in which public deliberation was not required.

Effectively, deliberative democracy thus resolves the tension between the filter and the mirror conceptions of representative democracy. It is no

[310]Cohen, The Good Polity: Normative Analysis of the State (as in n. 300 on page 246), 25; John S Dryzek, *Deliberative Democracy and Beyond* Oxford: Oxford University Press, 2002, 171

[311]Cohen, Deliberative Democracy (as in n. 301 on page 246), 221

[312]Habermas, *Between Facts and Norms: Contributions to a Discourse Theory of Law and Democracy* (as in n. 209 on page 227), 127. In fact, for Habermas it is specifically in the discourse principle, rather than the democratic principle, that the legitimacy of a democratic society that upholds popular sovereignty and fundamental human rights is founded: Idem, *The Inclusion of the Other: Studies in Political Theory* Cambridge, MA: MIT Press, 1998, chap. Three Normative Models of Democracy.

longer necessary in order to overcome ill-informed populism for the people to cede authority to a sagacious elite whose task it is to filter their raw, uninformed preferences to reveal a kernel of truth. Rather, deliberative democracy provides the people themselves with the opportunity to form more informed and public-spirited judgments before their preferences are counted.[313]

It is this phenomenon, in which the act of public deliberation transforms the democratic process from something potentially quite arbitrary into an approximation to the liberal ideal, that makes the impossible (according to Arrow's theorem) possible.[314] Not only does the deliberative democratic process thus produce better (more reasoned) outcomes, but because it takes place through a process of open and equal public deliberation, its transparency and accountability are also of a high standard, which in turn contributes to the perceived legitimacy of its output and the breadth of that output's acceptance.[315]

Another feature of deliberative democracy is that it is not conceptually limited to the state, as prevalent models of electoral democracy are.[316] First, there is no theoretical upper limit to the scale at which deliberative democratic principles can be applied; it can for example complement the existing international system, working across states within intergovernmental fora, as easily as it is applied at the domestic level.[317]

Second, its focus on deliberation renders the quixotic endeavour to achieve numerically proportional representation in transnational fora less central. More important is to ensure that all relevant perspectives are considered, and in fact for this purpose it may in some cases be necessary to

[313]This does raise the deeper question of whether a system of governance can truly be called democratic if it refuses to accept people's raw preferences, requiring them instead to submit to a process of public deliberation by which those preferences are refined before they may be counted as valid: see Gastil (as in n. 217 on page 230), 13 note 8.

Picciotto sees this dilemma as an expression of the tension between universalism—the notion that there is absolute truth in the realm of values, which is generally thought untenable in postmodern times—and pure ethical relativism, in which there are no universal values at all. He writes of the deliberative democratic compromise between these positions, that "truth is seen as an emergent property of the deliberative interaction between perspectives, rather than based on a single objective standard. In other words, there is an objective truth, although we can only know it through subjective interactions": Picciotto (as in n. 253 on page 237), 344.

The mirror proponent might still object that this is an idealised truth, as it does not equate to what the population actually think, but what they would think if they were better informed: Fishkin, Virtual Democratic Possibilities: Prospects for Internet Democracy (as in n. 230 on page 231), 3. This is, perhaps, a gloss on the democratic principle, but it is one which accords with the plausible intuition that it is better to think about a collective outcome, than not to think about it and to accept whatever arbitrary outcome the simple accumulation of unexamined private preferences might suggest.

[314]Dryzek and List (as in n. 299 on page 245)

[315]Innes and Booher (as in n. 282 on page 244), 429

[316]Habermas, The Inclusion of the Other: Studies in Political Theory (as in n. 312 on the preceding page), 248

[317]Dryzek, *Deliberative Democracy and Beyond* (as in n. 310 on the facing page), 120, 175

specifically engineer disproportional representation of particularly affected or otherwise marginalised groups (thus, deliberative democracy sits firmly within the substantive democratic paradigm). An example is provided in the case of Australia's deliberative poll on reconciliation which is to be described below, in which Aboriginal stakeholders were provided greater than proportional representation.[318]

Deliberation in the public sphere

Although deliberation can (and occasionally does) take place within the existing institutions of representative democracy, a more ambitious deliberative democratic program that coincides with the program of transnational democracy is that the ideals of decision-making through the public use of reason should be extended from the "organs of governments to every active, state-related organization."[319] This would require that appropriate conditions exist within (or perhaps alongside) each of those organisations to enable such deliberation to take place.

In an idealised historical European context, such conditions were according to Habermas exemplified by the coffee-houses of eighteenth-century London, which provided fora within which a broad range of participants could engage with one another, exchanging and comparing their various perspectives on social and political issues of the day. Habermas describes such fora collectively as "the public sphere"; "a communication structure rooted in the lifeworld through the associational network of civil society."[320]

It perhaps goes without saying that today's Starbucks does not provide quite the same facility for public deliberation that the eighteenth century coffee houses may have done.[321] Yet the existence of an effective public sphere within which social issues can be debated, springing from civil society and permeating each of the layers of democratic governance, could provide the basis for the extension of deliberative democratic principles on a transnational basis.

Whilst there is no such public sphere in the international system as it exists,[322] the conditions of developing one sufficient to support transnational deliberative democracy can be stated in five points:

[318]Innes and Booher (as in n. 282 on page 244), 429

[319]Jürgen Habermas, *The Theory of Communicative Action: Lifeworld and System: A Critique of Functionalist Reason*, volume vol 2 Boston: Beacon Press, 1987, 256

[320]Idem, *Between Facts and Norms: Contributions to a Discourse Theory of Law and Democracy* (as in n. 209 on page 227), 359

[321]Though the extent to which even they ever did so has been questioned, since they excluded many potential participants on the grounds of class and gender: Nancy Fraser, Rethinking the Public Sphere: A Contribution to the Critique of Actually Existing Democracy, Social Text 25/26 1990.

[322]Habermas, The Inclusion of the Other: Studies in Political Theory (as in n. 312 on page 248)

- As Dryzek notes consistently with the views of Habermas,[323] "a flourishing civil society provides both a resource for future democratization of the state and a check against reversal of the state's democratic commitments."[324] In this context, suggestions that activity in civil society is not in fact flourishing but withering are of potential concern.[325]

- It has already been noted that both civil and political rights, as well as economic and social rights, are required to be observed within organs of governance in order to satisfy the conditions of substantive democracy. At least according to Habermas, the superadded requirements of deliberative democracy call for the separate protection of "rights to equal opportunities to participate in processes of opinion- and will-formation in which citizens exercise their *political autonomy* and through which they generate legitimate law."[326] These rights must

  > guarantee participation in all deliberative and decisional processes relevant to legislation and must do so in a way that provides each person with equal chances to exercise the communicative freedom to take a position on criticizable validity claims. Equal opportunities for the political use of communicative freedoms require a legally structured deliberative praxis in which the discourse principle is applied.[327]

- Representing the "legally structured deliberative praxis" referred to above, institutional constructs are needed in order to give effect to these rights to the public use of communicative freedom. This is done within a democratic state by enshrining them in law, or more particularly as noted above from Kant, in constitutional law. Thus institutionalising the procedures of deliberative democracy dispenses with the need for individual actors within the system to deliberately uphold others' public communicative rights, because they have been "hard-coded" into the political system.[328]

What should the content of these institutional constructs be? More than one option exists, but the least ambitious within the context of

[323] Habermas, *Between Facts and Norms: Contributions to a Discourse Theory of Law and Democracy* (as in n. 209 on page 227), 371. Rawls however would disagree, as he excludes deliberation within civil society from his conception of public reason: John Rawls, *Political Liberalism* New York: Columbia University Press, 1993, 213, 220.

[324] Dryzek, *Deliberative Democracy and Beyond* (as in n. 310 on page 248), 171

[325] Putnam (as in n. 378 on page 169)

[326] Habermas, *Between Facts and Norms: Contributions to a Discourse Theory of Law and Democracy* (as in n. 209 on page 227), 123 (emphasis in original).

[327] Ibid., 127

[328] Ibid., 341

the liberal democratic state amounts to "a public sphere based in civil society with the opinion- and will-formation institutionalized in parliamentary bodies and courts."[329] In such a system, citizens have influence over public policy development through the public sphere, but direct political power is reserved to accountable and transparent parliamentary and judicial institutions. This separation between deliberation and the ultimate decision-making power of the state encourages participants in deliberation to do so freely and with open minds.[330]

- A responsible mass media is one important means[331] by which to manage the availability of information to participants in public deliberations.[332] For the deliberative model to be effective, participants should be presented with "a wide range of alternative views supported by sincere arguments and reasonably accurate information."[333] In many cases, the participants themselves will generate these arguments by contributing from their own knowledge and experience. However, depending on the composition of the group (including its professional, cultural and gender composition), it may be that the viewpoints of all affected participants are not being voiced, and that not all relevant factual material is being heard. The media is one mechanism through which these deficiencies can be addressed.

- Finally there must be a mechanism by which public opinion generated within civil society can be put on the public agenda to be formally considered and implemented within the political arena.[334] Tools of direct democracy such as the initiative, and of participatory democracy such as open public hearings and the solicitation of public submissions by parliamentary committees and agencies, can be drawn upon here. However, in order to avoid the biases inherent in the usual self-selection of contributors to such processes, a pro-active programme of outreach should be undertaken to draw in viewpoints from the public sphere that would otherwise go unheard.[335]

---

[329] Habermas, *Between Facts and Norms: Contributions to a Discourse Theory of Law and Democracy* (as in n. 209 on page 227), 371

[330] John S Dryzek, Deliberative Democracy in Divided Societies: Alternatives to Agonism and Analgesia, Political Theory 33:2 2005

[331] Habermas, *Between Facts and Norms: Contributions to a Discourse Theory of Law and Democracy* (as in n. 209 on page 227), 378

[332] K S Hanna, The Paradox of Participation and the Hidden Role of Information: a Case Study, Journal of the American Planning Association 66:4 2000

[333] Fishkin, Virtual Democratic Possibilities: Prospects for Internet Democracy (as in n. 230 on page 231), 12

[334] Habermas, *Between Facts and Norms: Contributions to a Discourse Theory of Law and Democracy* (as in n. 209 on page 227), 380

[335] Particular examples of how this ideal can be applied in practice will be discussed at section 4.3 on the facing page.

These five conditions for the realisation of deliberative democracy within existing organs of governance through an empowered public sphere, make somewhat stronger normative claims upon the democratic process than arise from classical liberal democratic theory (though weaker than those arising from civic republicanism).[336] Indeed, some scholars have proposed additional conditions that have not been included here, such as the requirement of Rawls that those engaged in the use of public reason act with civility to one another.[337]

Similarly Picciotto, one of the few scholars who has combined the studies of transnational and deliberative democracy, adds a condition of responsibility, which he defines as the means by which participants in deliberation and debate fulfil the democratic norms attaching to those processes, for example by adhering to relevant ethical, professional and scientific standards of discourse; a "deontology of deliberation."[338]

Deliberation in domestic politics

In any case, it has already been noted that even the above five conditions do not yet exist in the international system. However this does not render the foregoing discussion a purely abstract and aspirational exercise, as it may still be possible to realise those same or similar conditions at a lower layer of governance. Most research in this area has been directed to the case of the domestic political system.

The dominant paradigm of participatory governance at the domestic level is the public consultation model of participatory democracy. Hence these new frameworks for deliberative democracy, in which all stakeholders subject their perspectives to the light of public reason in working towards a joint decision, are designed to supplant older processes by which self-selected activists seek to influence governance processes taking place at higher levels. The change of paradigm is significant enough that most of these deliberative democratic frameworks are still only used experimentally, and with a few exceptions to be discussed below, not widely institutionalised in government.

Since there is no single template by which deliberative democratic norms can be institutionalised domestically, four major institutional frameworks

[336] Habermas, *Between Facts and Norms: Contributions to a Discourse Theory of Law and Democracy* (as in n. 209 on page 227), 298

[337] Rawls, *Political Liberalism* (as in n. 323 on page 251), 217–218; to which Dryzek has responded, "deliberative democracy is not an exclusive gentlemen's club": Dryzek, *Deliberative Democracy and Beyond* (as in n. 310 on page 248), 169.

[338] Picciotto (as in n. 253 on page 237), 349. Picciotto also (at 344) recognises conditions of transparency, accountability, and empowerment, which will be left aside here since transparency and accountability, although important in deliberative democratic structures, are equally important in other democratic structures, and hence will be dealt with separately in the following section, whereas empowerment essentially subsumes the second, third and particularly the fifth conditions already outlined above.

for deliberative democracy will be dealt with here. These are the 21st Century Town Meeting, Deliberative Polling, the citizens' jury and its close variants, and speed exchanges. Although there are a number of others in use,[339] most of these are variations or hybrids of one or more of these four popular methods, which themselves share a number of common elements.

The 21st Century Town Meeting®, developed by America*Speaks*,[340] was inspired by the traditional New England town meeting. It is a large scale forum of hundreds or thousands of citizens who meet face to face in small table groups. All groups are provided with background material to read covering the issues under consideration in a balanced manner, and the meeting at large also hears presentations on these issues from experts. Each group is assisted by a trained facilitator to discuss the issues, and once it has formed a view on them, relays this to the meeting at large through networked laptop computers and voting keypads. The views expressed most strongly by table groups form the basis for a set of recommendations upon which the group as a whole votes, with the results being declared before the participants leave.

Although to date 21st Century Town Meetings have taken place only within the United States, they have been perhaps more enthusiastically adopted by government than any other method of democratic deliberation, with hundreds of meetings having been held across 31 states since 1997. The "Listening to the City" event at which the future for the site of the former World Trade Center in New York was discussed is one high profile example of a successful 21st Century Town Meeting.[341]

Deliberative Polling®, the product of the Centre for Deliberative Democracy at Stanford University,[342] is another large-scale exercise in which a random sample of citizens is selected to take part in a preliminary opinion poll and to receive background briefing materials on an issue. They then come together and are divided into smaller groups to discuss the issue in depth, assisted by a facilitator. Questions from individual groups are put to experts in plenary sessions. The groups then deliberate again and at the conclusion, are polled once more. The strength of this method is that by polling before and after the event, the effect of the deliberative process can be gauged.

As at 2008 Deliberative Polling has been successfully conducted in ten countries including Australia, and across the European Union. Australia's

[339] America*Speaks*, a non-profit organisation active in this area (see `http://www.americaspeaks.org/`), has listed eight presently used in the United States: Joe Goldman and Lars H Torres, Approaches to Face-to-Face Deliberation in the US ⟨URL: `http://www.deliberative-democracy.net/resources/library/f2f_matrix_030304.pdf`⟩.

[340] See Carolyn J Lukensmeyer and Steve Brigham, Taking Democracy to Scale: Creating a Town Hall Meeting for the Twenty-First Century, National Civic Review 91:4 2002.

[341] Civic Alliance to Rebuild Downtown New York, Listening to the City: Report of Proceedings ⟨URL: `http://www.listeningtothecity.org/background/final_report_9_20.pdf`⟩

[342] See `http://cdd.stanford.edu/`.

first Deliberative Poll was held by Issues Deliberation Australia[343] preceding the 1999 referendum on whether Australia should become a republic. Following deliberation the preconceptions of participants were altered dramatically.[344] A second poll held in 2001 on Aboriginal reconciliation, and a third in 2007 on Muslims and non-Muslims in Australia, resulted in similar dramatic shifts.[345] A distinction of the 2001 poll was that Aboriginal representatives were provided with greater than proportional representation amongst the otherwise randomly-selected participants, in order to ensure that all of the smaller groups had direct access to Aboriginal perspectives.

The third method to be noted here is the citizens' jury (or planning cell). This is a random group of citizens chosen much like a jury and of similar size, who are presented with a range of expert opinions on the issue in question, and given time to deliberate on them privately. This usually takes place over a period of a few days. Citizens' juries or planning cells have been used in the United States, Germany, the United Kingdom and Australia.[346] The method's main weakness against most of its alternatives is its small size, and thus weaker claim to represent a diverse cross-section of views.

A citizens' assembly is much the same as a citizens' jury, but typically of a larger size. These have been successfully used in Canada, with an Citizens Assembly on Electoral Reform of 161 members from British Columbia reporting in 2004, followed by a similar assembly of 103 members from Ontario in 2007.[347] A standing citizens assembly, also on electoral reform, concluded in the Netherlands in 2006.[348]

A consensus conference is very similar again, except that it takes place on a still larger scale, potentially also over a longer period, and that those who attend are given greater control over the agenda and the choice of experts who are called.[349] These are widely used in Denmark,[350] and has

[343] See `http://www.ida.org.au/`.

[344] Support for the republic increased from 53 to 73 percent, support for a directly elected President dropped from 50 to 19 percent, and those who believed the President should be non-political rose from 53 to 88 percent: J S Fishkin, Consulting the Public Through Deliberative Polling, Journal of Policy Analysis and Management 22:1 2003.

[345] Issues Deliberation Australia, Australia Deliberates: Muslims and Non-Muslims in Australia ⟨URL: `http://ida.org.au/content.php?p=dpprelease`⟩, 7

[346] Carson (as in n. 284 on page 244), 11

[347] See `http://www.citizensassembly.gov.on.ca/`.

[348] J H Snider, Citizens Assemblies: A Mechanism for Enhancing Legislative Transparency and Accountability ⟨URL: `http://www.w3.org/2007/06/eGov-dc/papers/NAS-eGovernmentPositionPaper.pdf`⟩. Its Web site at `http://www.burgerforumkiesstelsel.nl/` was not accessible as at April 2008, but an archived version can be found at `http://web.archive.org/web/20070716172416/http://www.burgerforumkiesstelsel.nl/`.

[349] Carson (as in n. 284 on page 244), 12

[350] S Joss, Danish Consensus Conferences as a Model of Participatory Technology Assessment: An Impact Study of Consensus Conferences on Danish Parliament and Danish Public Debate, Science and Public Policy 25:1 1998

also been trialled in the United States, Australia and New Zealand.

Australia's first large scale consensus conference, convened by the Australian Museum, was held on the topic of Gene Technology in the Food Chain in 1999.[351] As in the case of the two Deliberative Polls, the consensus conference was nationally televised. Although the lay panel's report was not formally received by the Commonwealth government, shortly after it was released the government established Biotechnology Australia largely in conformity with some of the panel's recommendations.[352]

The final method of democratic deliberation to be briefly outlined here is the speed exchange or speed dialogue, a technique developed by the American Bar Association.[353] It differs from the other methods discussed above in two respects: that it is not usually used as a decision-making tool, and that so far it has been used in an intergovermental rather than a governmental context; namely by the ITU. However it is worthy of discussion here because of the brief period for which it was included on the agenda for the second meeting of the IGF in Rio.

Speed dialogues have much in common with the 21st Century Town Meeting, in that they are conducted in table groups, each of which is equipped with a flip chart and staffed by an expert moderator. The main distinction is that each table group generally discusses a different issue (or a different facet of a given issue), and has a limited time period in which to do so; 20 minutes, in the ITU's implementation of the process.

After the expiration of this time period, table groups rotate, so that by the close of the session, all participants have deliberated upon all of the issues that were set for the group's deliberation. The moderators of each table group then summarise the discussion and any areas of agreement that were reached, for the consideration of the meeting at large.

Apart from the strong support of the Danish government for consensus conferences, state support for the practice of deliberative democracy has been less forthcoming. Most of the research into and promotion of deliberative democratic techniques has come from civil society.[354]

In Australia, neither of the three Deliberative Polls nor the consensus conference was government organised. At a state level, the Western Australian government has shown the greatest resolve to make use of deliberative forms of citizen participation,[355] having experimented at an

---

[351] See `http://www.abc.net.au/science/slab/consconf/`.

[352] See `http://www.biotechnology.gov.au/`.

[353] ITU, Introduction to Action Line C5 Speed Exchanges ⟨URL: `http://www.itu.int/osg/spu/cybersecurity/pgc/2007/events/docs/c5-speed-exchange-information-document-14-may-2007.pdf`⟩

[354] Most organisations active in this area are members of the Deliberative Democracy Consortium (see `http://www.deliberative-democracy.net/`). Lyn Carson is an Australian researcher who has also instigated a number of projects in this field: see `http://www.activedemocracy.net/`.

[355] Government of Western Australia, A Voice For All: Strengthening Democracy ⟨URL:

executive level with the use of 21st Century Town Meetings, Deliberative Polling and Citizens' Juries.[356] The Dialogue with the City for example, held by the Department of Planning and Infrastructure in 2003 and reportedly "the biggest interactive consultation ever held in the southern hemisphere," incorporated a 21st Century Town Meeting attended by 1100 participants.[357]

Deliberation in non-state entities

To conclude the present review of deliberative democracy, it remains to consider how deliberative processes may be institutionalised at layers of governance other than those of the state and the civil society public sphere. These include layers constituted by the governance of private sector or civil society organisations such as Microsoft and the IETF respectively, and that of networks such as the IGF.

Taking the case of private sector organisations first, a starting point is found in the literature on "participative-democratic" forms of organisation design. This illustrates the potential for companies to adopt structures such as that of Rensis Likert's System 4 organisation, in which the communicative freedom of their staff is institutionally upheld, in broad concordance with deliberative democratic principles.[358]

However it is a limited conception of the democratic principle that considers a corporation to have obtained "the consent of the governed" merely by extending the power of governance from its owners to its staff. A broader conception of the democratic principle that looks to all those significantly affected by a decision[359] requires yet other stakeholders to be considered, including the corporation's customers, and the public at large.

Although at variance with early established principles of corporate law,[360] this is no longer a revolutionary concept. Now known as "corporate social responsibility" or CSR,[361] it was as long ago as 1943 that it was embodied in the corporate credo of Johnson & Johnson, which explicitly put customers first, employees second, the community third, and shareholders fourth and last.[362]

---

http://www.citizenscape.wa.gov.au/documents/citizenship_strategy.pdf⟩, 6

[356] See http://www.dpi.wa.gov.au/communityengagement/727.asp.

[357] Department for Planning & Infrastructure, Dialogue With the City—Final Report of Proceedings ⟨URL: http://www.dpi.wa.gov.au/mediaFiles/dialogue_finalproc.pdf⟩, 4

[358] Rensis Likert and Jane Gibson Likert, *New Ways of Managing Conflict* New York: McGraw-Hill, 1976

[359] Held and McGrew (as in n. 39 on page 104)

[360] See *Parke v Daily News Ltd* [1962] Ch 927

[361] Archie B Carroll, Corporate Social Responsibility: Evolution of a Definitional Construct, Business & Society 38:3 1999

[362] See http://www.jnj.com/our_company/our_credo/index.htm.

There are a number of strategies by which companies seeking to fulfil their corporate social responsibility can empower stakeholders to participate in decisions of the company that affect their interests, not all of which could be described as deliberatively democratic. Even those that could, do not much resemble the models by which deliberative democracy is pursued in the public sector. As Parker puts it,

> Making corporations democratically accountable is not simply about copying public institutions of representative democracy within the corporate microcosm .... Rather, the challenge is to understand the norms of democracy and then to create new institutions for applying them to the unique world of corporate enterprise.[363]

She goes on to suggest three best practice guidelines by which deliberative democracy can be institutionalised within the corporation:

- to draw on the cultures, values and self-identities of employees to build organisational integrity;
- to consult with legitimate external stakeholders to introduce their perspectives into the decision-making process, then to report back to them and allow them to challenge those decisions once made; and
- to integrate into the company's management systems the means to inform itself of, learn from, and respond to its social and legal responsibilities.[364]

Similarly in civil society organisations, the prevalent governance structures, in this instance often based around the strictures of *Robert's Rules of Order*,[365] are being challenged by newer, less divisive and more collaborative models that are more consistent with deliberative democratic principles.[366] One example of these is Gastil's model of small group democracy, which defines it by reference to five characteristics, most of which can be traced back to other conceptions of deliberative democracy discussed above:

- Group power (which essentially incorporates the same conditions as Picciotto's "empowerment");

[363] Christine Parker, *The Open Corporation: Effective Self-Regulation and Democracy* Cambridge: Cambridge University Press, 2002, 37

[364] Ibid., 197–198

[365] Henry M Robert and Sarah Corbin Robert, *Robert's Rules of Order Newly Revised* Cambridge, MA: Perseus Books Group, 2000

[366] L Susskind, *The Consensus Building Handbook: A Comprehensive Guide to Reaching Agreement* Thousand Oaks, CA: Sage Publications, 1999, chap. A Short Guide to Consensus Building. An Alternative to Robert's Rules of Order for Groups, Organizations, and Ad Hoc Assemblies that Want to Operate by Consensus

- Inclusiveness (that all those significantly affected by the group's decisions are invited to participate; this condition is derived from Dahl's conception of the appropriate constitution of the *demos* discussed at section 4.3 on page 229);
- Commitment to the democratic process (a condition also found in Cohen's conception of deliberative democracy);[367]
- Relationships between group members (whereby members acknowledge each other's individuality and competence, recognise the mutuality of the group, and act in a congenial manner to each other—which as noted above Rawls specified as a requirement of the exercise of public reason);[368] and
- Deliberation (which describes the rights and responsibilities of both speakers and listeners in the deliberative process).[369]

As for governance networks such as the IGF, the most appropriate structure may be based on that of this small group model, or on the private sector, the domestic political, or the public sphere models, or a hybrid of one or more of these, depending on the network's size, extent and composition. It is unnecessary to be too prescriptive about the appropriate structure of a deliberative democratic IGF at this point, at least until Chapter 6 when the IGF's present structure and composition are outlined.

It is more important however to have settled upon some essential principles of deliberative democracy that can be applied in various circumstances through a variety of implementations, than to find the blueprint for an implementation that is equally applicable across all organs of governance. Lacking such a blueprint, the closest approximation to the transnational democratic programme that can reasonably be pursued in the short term, and the most effective in furthering the democratic principle, is to simultaneously implement separate strategies for the deliberative democratisation of all appropriate domestic, international and transnational governance fora, by various techniques all drawing from the common underlying principles discussed in this section.

A corollary of this pragmatically heterogeneous approach is that the adoption of a deliberative democratic organisation structure for a governance network such as the IGF need not await the development of an international public sphere (essentially the "transnational *demos*" whose absence was earlier assumed to preclude the adoption of a democratic organisation structure for a transnational governance network). Rather, deliberative democratic theory equips such governance networks to pursue the democratic principle here and now, by pursuing a variety of strategies

[367] Cohen, The Good Polity: Normative Analysis of the State (as in n. 300 on page 246), 21
[368] Rawls, *Political Liberalism* (as in n. 323 on page 251), 217–218
[369] Gastil (as in n. 217 on page 230), 16

to draw in all affected viewpoints and perspectives and subject them to the transformative power of dialogue.[370]

Transparency and accountability

Although fundamental, the criteria of transparency and accountability are not constitutive of the democratic organisational form in the same way as the principles of representation and consent. Thus, the lack of transparency or accountability alone does not entail that a democratic polity lacks formal legitimacy (though it may cause it to lack the appearance of legitimacy, which is much the same thing in practice).

Rather, transparency and accountability are auxiliary precautions against the potential for the regression of democracy into hierarchical forms such as bureaucracy or oligarchy, which in turn may offer a mask for inefficiency and corruption.[371] The allegation of democratic deficit is most often levelled against organisations that although democratic in form, in practice lack transparency and accountability because their operations are closed to their constituents.

Transparency

Transparency has been described as the "distinguishing feature" of democracy by one author, who explains:

> Only when a record becomes public are citizens in a position to judge it, and hence to exercise one of the fundamental prerogatives of any citizen in a democracy: the control of his rulers.[372]

In the context of the liberal state, transparency is often known as open government. Amongst the principal guarantees of transparency in government are freedom of information legislation, and regulations or policy providing for the open and accessible publication of public documents and ensuring public access to parliamentary, executive and judicial fora of deliberation.

The extent to which these institutions have in fact effectively exposed the liberal democratic process to public observation has been mixed. Clarke's assessment of the state of access to information in Australia in 1999 was that access to "personal data has been becoming increasingly open, information

[370] N C Roberts, editor, *The Transformative Power of Dialogue* Amsterdam: JAI, an imprint of Elsevier Science, 2002

[371] Warren (as in n. 188 on page 219); Aristotle, *Politics* (as in n. 83 on page 201)

[372] Norberto Bobbio, *Cosmopolitan Democracy: An Agenda for a New World Order* Cambridge: Polity Press, 1995, chap. Democracy and the International System, 36

held by corporations remains largely protected, and information held by governments is largely protected, but subject to some limited access provisions."[373]

Thus as in the case of deliberative democracy in the liberal state, in which civil society plays a central role in the maintenance of a public sphere for deliberation, it is necessary to look outside government in order to find institutions to further its transparency. As again in the case of deliberative democracy, foremost amongst these is the mass media, supported by associated institutional guarantees of its independence such as freedom of the press.

The Internet also has an important role to play in increasing democratic transparency, by broadening the potential accessibility of information and reducing the cost of its provision. It has also played a secondary role in heightening public expectations of the transparency of their governments' actions; for example, expectations of the free public dissemination of the law.[374] This may be traced to the principle of the hacker ethic, reflected in the culture of the Internet, that "information wants to be free."[375]

The importance of transparency to democratic governance of course extends beyond the context of the liberal state to international and transnational governance fora also. Thus transparency is the first of seven critical variables identified by Young as contributing to the effectiveness of international institutions of governance,[376] and is also nominated by Picciotto as the first of four constitutive principles for democratizing globalism.[377]

Certain of the criteria by which the democratic transparency of the liberal state may be judged, the basic strategies by which it may be pursued, and the institutions by which it may be safeguarded, are equally applicable outside it. Examples include the maintenance of records of governance processes and outcomes, the provision of access to those records and to other documents developed in the pursuit of governance functions, and the facilitation of public access to deliberative processes by means such as the publication of agenda for open meetings.

However as the following section will illustrate, there are fewer established metrics for the assessment of the transparency of international or transnational fora of democratic governance, which renders problematic any endeavour to rate or compare the transparency of such institutions.

---

[373] Roger Clarke, Freedom of Information? The Internet as Harbinger of the New Dark Ages ⟨URL: http://firstmonday.org/issues/issue4_11/clarke/⟩

[374] Graham Greenleaf et al., AustLII—Changing the Nature of Public Access to Law ⟨URL: http://austlii.edu.au/~graham/NZLLG/AustLII_NZLLG-AustLII.html⟩

[375] Roger Clarke, "Information Wants to be Free ..." ⟨URL: http://www.anu.edu.au/people/Roger.Clarke/II/IWtbF.html⟩; Levy (as in n. 16 on page 5), 40

[376] Young, Governance Without Government: Order and Change in World Politics (as in n. 248 on page 145), 176

[377] Picciotto (as in n. 253 on page 237), 344

Accountability

Accountability is so called because it describes the process by which one exercising authority is required to account either to those by whom that authority was delegated for its use[378] (which can be called bottom–up accountability), or to another institution or another branch of the same institution exercising hierarchical oversight over it (that is, top–down accountability).[379]

For the liberal democratic state, the most basic guarantees of accountability are fair and regular elections, the separation of powers, and the rule of law. Of these, elections are a classic example of bottom–up accountability, in that not only do they fulfil the democratic principle, by ensuring that the government holds office with the consent of the governed, but they also publicly and regularly demonstrate the state's fulfilment of that democratic principle.

The separation of powers on the other hand is more of a mechanism of top–down accountability, designed to maintain mutual oversight between the legislative, executive and judicial arms of government.[380] A stricter separation of powers exists in the United States than in countries with a Westminster system of government inherited from the United Kingdom. In Australia for example, the legislative and executive powers are effectively conflated within Parliament,[381] though the Parliament is prohibited from intruding upon judicial functions.[382]

Finally the content of the rule of law (which intersects both bottom–up and top–down spheres of accountability) was classically defined by Fuller: that the laws should be cast in general terms, that they should be public, they should not be retrospective, they should be intelligible, they should not be contradictory, that they should not be impossible to comply with, they should be sufficiently stable to provide a guide for the citizen's conduct, and that they should be administered as announced.[383]

The main limitation of the use of these three measures of democratic accountability is that they have limited application outside the context of the liberal state. For example, in a deliberative democratic forum, elections may not occur; the democratic principle may instead be satisfied by the

---

[378]Stewart Ranson and John Stewart, *Management for the Public Domain: Enabling the Learning Society* Basingstoke: Macmillan, 1994, 4

[379]Mary Rundle, Beyond Internet Governance: The Emerging International Framework for Governing the Networked World ⟨URL: `http://cyber.law.harvard.edu/publications/2005/Beyond_Internet_Governance`⟩, 17

[380]Charles de Montesquieu, *Montesquieu: The Spirit of the Laws*, edited by Anne M. Cohler, Basia Carolyn Miller and Harold Samuel Stone Cambridge: Cambridge University Press, 1989, 157

[381]*Victorian Stevedoring & General Contracting Co Pty Ltd & Meakes v Dignan* (1931) 46 CLR 73

[382]*Waterside Workers' Federation of Australia v JW Alexander Ltd* (1918) 25 CLR 434

[383]Lon L Fuller, *The Morality of Law* New Haven, CT: Yale University Press, 1969, 39

representation of all affected viewpoints during an open and inclusive deliberative process. Similarly, within a democratic governance network there may be no need for separate legislative, executive and judicial functions, and neither would the rule of law assume much prominence within a network that lacks coercive power.

There are alternative models for accountability besides that of the democratic state, such as that of the domestic administrative agency, which may have closer application to governance networks in some respects. For example, this is the model which ICANN has employed, though somewhat haphazardly, by adopting the participatory democratic approach of open public comment before policy making and in institutionalising mechanisms of review.[384]

Other applicable mechanisms to ensure the accountability of government agencies that could be applied to democratic governance networks also include rules to combat corruption (for example by prohibiting bribery), and nepotism (by documenting objective selection criteria for appointments and contracts), the requirement to declare conflicts of interest, and submission to independent audits of dealings with assets or compliance with standards.

A strong civil society that lies outside the power of the state (or the network in this case) is another important influence upon a network's public accountability,[385] and so too, once again, is an independent mass media (as ICANN, for example, has found).[386] Similarly, other networks or institutions that may be its competitors in the market for governance solutions, rather than its constituents or overseers, can provide what may be termed "peer-to-peer" accountability (in distinction to bottom–up and top–down).[387]

Even so, as previously noted when considering the most appropriate structure by which to implement deliberative democratic principles, it is difficult to lay down any universal prescriptions as to how accountability may be assured within a forum of democratic governance, since there is so much potential for variation amongst these in terms of their size, structure, culture and hybridisation with other forms of governance.

Lacking such a uniform set of expected institutional protections, or in most cases any direct vertical accountability to national parliaments, it is perhaps no wonder that, as noted above at section 3.2 on page 129, transnational governance networks are left with "at best, weak or obscure mechanisms of accountability."[388]

---

[384]Weinberg, ICANN and the Problem of Legitimacy (as in n. 71 on page 49), 225–226

[385]John Keane, *Democracy and Civil Society* London: Verso, 1988, 237

[386]See `http://www.icannwatch.org/`.

[387]Milton Mueller and Hans Klein, What to Do About ICANN: A Proposal for Structural Reform ⟨URL: `http://internetgovernance.org/pdf/igp-icannreform.pdf`⟩, 3

[388]Held, *Democracy and the Global Order: From the Modern State to Cosmopolitan Governance* (as

For example, Slaughter refers to the Basel Committee on Banking Supervision, an organisation of the world's central banks, which in 1988 adopted new capital adequacy requirements for the banks under their supervision. This decision was made under the radar of any domestic or international representative political process, yet had significant economic impact worldwide.[389] Barr and Miller illustrate this vividly:

> Imagine a club of central bankers meeting secretly in one of Switzerland's wealthiest cities, known for its discretion, its iconic graphic design school, and boring bars. The members of the Basel Committee develop regulations governing the very lifeblood of domestic economies in ways that expand the reach of distant, unaccountable bureaucrats. Legislators may find themselves out of the loop and international banks can find no escape from burdensome rules. No wonder sober commentators such as former U.S. House Financial Services Committee ranking member John LaFalce has called the Basel process "fundamentally flawed" and "dangerous" and former Federal Deposit Insurance Corporation (FDIC) Chairman William Isaac described it as a "runaway train."[390]

In criticising Slaughter's enthusiasm for government networks, Alston complains that:

> It implies the marginalisation of governments as such and their replacement by special interest groups, which might sometimes include the relevant government bureaucrats. It suggests a move away from arenas of relative transparency into the back rooms, the emergence of what she [Slaughter] terms a "real new world order" in which those with power consolidate it and make the decisions which will continue to determine the fate of the excluded, and the bypassing of the national political arenas to which the United States and other proponents of the importance of healthy democratic institutions attach so much importance.[391]

Slaughter's response is that the use of soft power (characterised by persuasion rather than coercion) as is typical in government networks differentiates them normatively from the hierarchical arrangement of democratic

---

in n. 177 on page 131), 139

[389] Slaughter, Democratic Governance and International Law (as in n. 93 on page 25), 215–216.

[390] Michael S Barr and Geoffrey P Miller, Global Administrative Law: The View from Basel, EJIL 17:1 2006, 17. To be fair, they go on at 24–28 to record the reforms that the Committee has put in place to improve its transparency and accountability, while also recommending that reforms continue: 45–46.

[391] Philip Alston, The Myopia of the Handmaidens: International Lawyers and Globalization, Eur J Int'l Law 8:3 1997, 440.

institutions, and that therefore "[w]e may need to develop new metrics or even new conceptions of accountability geared towards the distinctive features of power in the Information Age."[392]

Kingsbury, Krisch, and Stewart have taken up this challenge and begun to sketch the outlines of a new global administrative law designed to provide

> structures, procedures and normative standards for regulatory decisionmaking … that are applicable to formal intergovernmental regulatory bodies; to informal intergovernmental regulatory networks, to regulatory decisions of national governments where these are part of or constrained by an international intergovernmental regime; and to hybrid public–private or private transnational bodies.[393]

Similarly, Mathur and Skelcher have begun to develop metrics of accountability and transparency of governance networks in order for the extent of their democratic deficit to be assessed, and thereby more methodically addressed. They describe two approaches to this exercise. First, they present a universalist approach whereby such metrics are devised by *a priori* reasoning from theory.[394] A limitation of this approach is that it may not produce very specific and measurable criteria. In contrast, the second approach is to undertake an empirical exercise to identify specific best practices within similar existing organisations,[395] though this may fail to identify any shortfall between current best practice and theory.

Primarily utilising the second approach, Skelcher, Mathur and Smith have developed 27 criteria to assess the democratic deficit of certain types of governance networks (specifically, domestic public–private partnerships), grouped into four categories of public access (which is largely synonymous with transparency), internal governance (which concerns matters of structure such as the quorum of the executive committee), member conduct (such as the declaration of conflicts of interest by executive committee members) and accountability (which focuses on financial and top–down accountability).[396]

These criteria are incomplete, and not necessarily all directly applicable to transnational governance networks, any more than the criteria applicable to liberal democratic states or to domestic administrative agencies.

---

[392] Slaughter, The Role of Law in International Politics (as in n. 93 on page 25), 195

[393] Benedict Kingsbury, Nico Krisch and Richard Stewart, The Emergence of Global Administrative Law, L & CP 68 2005, 5

[394] This is an equivalent approach to that of Habermas in devising the conditions of deliberation within the public sphere.

[395] Navdeep Mathur and Chris Skelcher, The Democratic Performance of Network Governance: Conceptual and Methodological Issues ⟨URL: `http://www.inlogov.bham.ac.uk/research/pdfs/Democratic_performance.pdf`⟩, 8

[396] Skelcher et al. (as in n. 97 on page 26), 584

However a similar approach can be taken when eventually assessing the accountability of the IGF in Chapter 6, by surveying best practices of the most closely analogous other institutions and networks, and then determining by reference to more general principles of democratic transparency and accountability whether these leave any gaps that remain to be filled by top–down, bottom–up or peer-to-peer mechanisms.

Inclusion

The final heading under which the content of the liberal conception of democracy is discussed is inclusion, as although a transparent and accountable deliberative democracy frees the liberal democrat from the quixotic imperative of fairly and accurately aggregating dissonant preferences, it remains true that the wider the participation of the *demos* in deliberation, the more likely that all its perspectives will be adequately represented.

There is no reason in theory why all members of the *demos* who wish to do so should not participate in an appropriate form of democratic deliberation (as the public sphere theory of Habermas comprehends). The logistical difficulties of direct democracy on the other hand remain, but these have not dissuaded its advocates from seeking to address and overcome them.

In particular, advocacy of direct democracy has gained momentum as the facilitating potential of ICT has become apparent. Before the Internet even existed, futurist Alvin Toffler foresaw a hybrid of representative and direct democracy in which

> the elected representative would cast only 50 percent of the votes, while the current random sample—who are not in the capital but in their own homes or offices—would electronically cast the remaining 50 per cent. Such a system would not merely provide a more representative process than "representative" government ever did, but would strike a devastating blow at the special interest groups and lobbies who infest the corridors of most parliaments.[397]

More recently, direct democratic theory has been revitalised by a number of variations on the idea of direct democracy by delegable proxy,[398] such as representative direct democracy[399] and liquid democracy,[400] each of which

---

[397] Alvin Toffler, *The Third Wave* New York: Bantam Books, 1981, 426

[398] James Green-Armytage, Direct Democracy by Delegable Proxy ⟨URL: http://fc.antioch.edu/~james_green-armytage/vm/proxy.htm⟩

[399] See Aktiv Demokrati, Partyprogram for Aktiv Demokrati ⟨URL: http://wse75376.web16.talkactive.net/ads%20websida/Party%20program.html⟩

[400] sayke, Liquid Democracy In Context or, An Infrastructuralist Manifesto ⟨URL: http://seed.sourceforge.net/ld_k5_article_004.html⟩

would allow citizens the option of representing themselves directly in fora of deliberation, or temporarily delegating their right to be so represented to one or more proxies in respect of particular issues. Whilst such voting systems would once have been impracticable, Internet-based communications have for the first time made them viable.

Large-scale experiments in online direct democracy have also gradually begun to emerge in the real world. ICANN's At-Large elections of 2000, which are to be discussed below,[401] provide a pertinent example, though this particular experiment was soon terminated on the grounds that it was thought open to abuse and capture, and to be an imprudent use of ICANN's limited funds.[402]

Even so, the potential for the use of ICT to increase popular participation in democratic governance deserves particular consideration in the transnational context of the Internet. As the Internet itself transcends geographical limitations, it would be ironic if such boundaries were to constrain the ability of those who wished to participate in its governance from doing so.

Having said that, none of the specific implementations of so-called "digital democracy" mentioned above are intrinsically consistent with deliberative democratic principles, any more so than the process for nomination of evictees from the Big Brother house. However, the issues of greater participation and deeper deliberation are largely distinct, and there is no reason why compatible approaches to the pursuit of both objectives could not be combined.

In this subsection, a distinction will be drawn between two conceptions of digital democracy: what will be termed e-democracy on the one hand, and Internet democracy on the other. The former has been defined as "a collection of attempts to practise democracy without the limits of time, space and other physical conditions, using ICT or CMC [computer-mediated communication] instead, as an addition, not a replacement for traditional 'analogue' political practices."[403]

Internet democracy on the other hand is a broader and more ambitious conception of the revolutionising potential of ICTs for democracy, that foretells the "use of information and communication technologies to realise the utopian goal of self-governance."[404]

---

401 See section 5.4 on page 404.

402 At-Large Study Committee, Final Report on ICANN At-Large Membership ⟨URL: `http://www.icann.org/at-large/final-report-05nov01.htm`⟩

403 Kenneth L Hacker and Jan van Dijk, *Digital Democracy* London: Sage Publications, 2000, chap. What is Digital Democracy?, 1

404 Charles Leadbeater, *Living on Thin Air: The New Economy* London: Viking, 1999, 224

e-democracy

Under the first conception, the Internet is simply considered as a communications medium with greater range and better efficiency than traditional media for facilitating communication with the *demos*.[405] In the context of the nation state, this makes e-democracy simply a subset of e-government, which as noted at section 2.3 on page 88 involves the use of ICT in the relation of governments and their citizens online (but in a broader context, including for example the delivery of government services over the Internet).

Support for e-democratic reform at the state level has emerged from within all stakeholder groups, including governments such as that of Australia (at a Federal[406] and State level),[407] intergovernmental organisations such as the Council of Europe, which issued a 2004 recommendation supporting the use of ICTs in democratic processes,[408] private sector bodies servicing this new industry such as the CyberVote consortium, and[409] civil society organisations such as the United States-based Information Renaissance.[410]

The breadth of this support illustrates that rather than challenging existing democratic institutions, e-democracy simply streamlines their operation in much the same way that e-commerce streamlines the operation of online markets such as eBay, bringing them closer to the economic model of the free market than their offline equivalents.[411] Thus e-democracy "can be defined as a political system in which the use of ICT ensures democratic values"[412] by supporting (but generally not transforming) existing democratic processes, such as:

- campaigning and lobbying;
- consultation and deliberation;
- voting; and

---

[405] See Graham (as in n. 56 on page 18), 66.

[406] See `http://agimo.gov.au/practice/delivery/cop/e-democracy`.

[407] Queensland established the Community Engagement and Development Unit of the Department of Communities in 2001 to spearhead e-democracy initiatives. It has so far arranged online public consultations, Internet streaming of Parliamentary debates, and electronic lodgment of petitions to Parliament: see `http://www.getinvolved.qld.gov.au/`. See also Scrutiny of Acts & Regulations Committee (as in n. 296 on page 245), 3, 20.

[408] Council of Europe, Electronic Governance ("E-Governance") ⟨URL: `http://www.coe.int/t/e/integrated_projects/democracy/02_activities/01_e%2Dgovernance/00_recommendation_and_explanatory_memorandum/`⟩, 8–9

[409] See `http://www.eucybervote.org/`.

[410] See `http://www.info-ren.org/`.

[411] Hasenpusch (as in n. 89 on page 24)

[412] Michel Catinat and Thierry Vedel, *Digital Democracy* London: Sage Publications, 2000, chap. Public Policies for Digital Democracy, 185

• mechanisms of democratic transparency and accountability.[413]

Taking these processes in turn, the advantages of e-democratic campaigning and lobbying over traditional methods are characteristic of those of the other e-democratic processes, and consist firstly of improvements in the efficiency of communications—the ability of the Internet to provide a highly available, near-instantaneous and inexpensive channel of communication[414]—and secondly of the new modes of interaction between citizens and government that the Internet facilitates.[415]

For example, political party Web sites, and more recently also party political blogs[416] and online campaign videos[417] are now commonplace in e-democratic campaigning. In many cases these take advantage of the interactive capacity of Internet communications by allowing citizens to post comments on campaign documents. An even better example of this capacity is provided by wiki sites in which political candidates and their would-be constituents actually collaborate on content.[418]

As for lobbying, in addition to numerous blogging and commentary sites and wikis, political organisations such as MoveOn.org Political Action in the United States,[419] and GetUp in Australia,[420] have leveraged interactive Internet technologies to coordinate lobbying of politicians on issues of collective concern.

Internet communications have also facilitated the mobilisation of large groups of activists in the offline world, such as the 45 000 protesters who disrupted the 1999 World Trade Organization meeting in Seattle.[421] These protests were accompanied by the launch of a mock WTO Web site hosted at what appeared to be (but was not) an official WTO domain name.[422] Taken further, so-called "hacktivism" is the use (or the subversion) of Internet architecture as a weapon of protest or civil disobedience, by means such as the launch of DDoS attacks against or the cracking and defacement of

---

[413] See Clarke, The Internet and Democracy (as in n. 218 on page 230).

[414] Government of Western Australia, e-Engagement. Guidelines For Community Engagement Using Information And Communications Technology (ICT) (as in n. 284 on page 244), 7

[415] Lawrence Grossman, *The Electronic Republic: Reshaping American Democracy for the Information Age* New York: Penguin Books, 1996, 31

[416] Peter Chen, e-lection 2004? New Media and the Campaign ⟨URL: http://eprints.infodiv.unimelb.edu.au/archive/00000772/01/e-lection_2004.pdf⟩

[417] A dedicated YouTube channel supplemented by content from other Google properties was supported by all parties in the 2007 Australian federal elections: see http://www.google.com.au/election2007/.

[418] See http://campaigns.wikia.com/ and http://congresspedia.org/.

[419] See http://www.moveon.org/.

[420] See http://www.getup.org.au/.

[421] Stefano Baldi, The Internet for International Political and Social Protest: the Case of Seattle ⟨URL: http://baldi.diplomacy.edu/articles/protest.htm⟩

[422] See http://www.gatt.org/.

political or corporate Web sites.[423]

Consultation and deliberation as e-democratic processes also benefit from the same efficiencies enabled by the use of Internet communications in other contexts, such as greater accessibility to those who are geographically remote or otherwise unable to participate (for example by reason of low mobility). Online engagement is also more attractive to certain demographic groups such as youth, who although able to participate, would otherwise be less inclined to do so.[424]

An additional advantage more specific to deliberation is that more information can be provided, to be digested over a longer time period, than the small sound-bites normally disseminated through the mass media. Neither is the media any longer the only source for political information for the public, as citizens themselves take on the mantle of journalists to inform and provoke their peers.[425] Thus on the Internet the consumption and production of political information and other public speech tend to merge.[426] It is this which distinguishes Internet fora such as threaded discussion groups from the broadcast and print media, and allows (certain) online communities more closely to approximate the idealised democratic public sphere that Habermas found in 19th century coffee houses.[427] As one commentator puts it,

> [n]ew media, and particularly computer-mediated communication, it is hoped, will undo the damage done to politics by the old media. Far from the television dystropias, new media technology hails a rebirth of democratic life. It is envisaged that new public spheres will open up and that technologies will permit social actors to find or forge common political interests. People will actively access information from an infinite, free virtual library rather than receiving half-digested "programing," and interactive media will institutionalise a right to reply.[428]

Some examples of e-democratic consultation have already been given in the discussion of participatory democracy at section 4.3 on page 243, and

[423] The Pull, Confessions of a Hacktivist ⟨URL: `http://www.hacktivismo.com/public/tfiles/confessionhacktivist.txt`⟩

[424] A Macintosh et al., Electronic Democracy and Young People, Social Science Computer Review 21:1 2003

[425] See `http://www.youdecide2007.org/`, a forum for citizen journalism established for the 2007 Australian federal election.

[426] Mark Poster, *Virtual Politics: Identity and Community in Cyberspace* Thousand Oaks, CA: Sage Publications, 1997, chap. Cyberdemocracy: The Internet and the Public Sphere, 222

[427] S M Schneider, Creating a Democratic Public Sphere Through Political Discussion: A Case Study of Abortion Conversation on the Internet, Soc Sci Computer Rev 14 1996; Froomkin, Habermas@discourse.net: Toward a Critical Theory of Cyberspace (as in n. 40 on page 13)

[428] Cathy Bryan, Roza Tsagorousianou and Damian Tambini, *Cyberdemocracy* London: Routledge, 1998, chap. Electronic Democracy and the Civic Networking Movement in Context, 5

more will be said of a variety of online mechanisms for deliberation at section 4.3 on page 276. Their limitations will be considered at section 4.3 on page 285.

Voting, in both elections and referenda, is another democratic process that can be conducted in e-democratic form in order to realise similar benefits of efficiency and accessibility. Ross Perot's 1992 campaign for the Presidency of the United States incorporated a prominent proposal to put electronic direct democracy into place through interactive televised discussions that he called "electronic town halls."[429] Two years later, then United States Vice President Al Gore grandiosely heralded "a new Athenian age of democracy forged in the fora that the Government's information infrastructure will create."[430]

However, early enthusiasm for the possibilities of Internet voting has since been widely tempered with caution over the risks of abuse.[431] The Internet has also raised new challenges for offline electoral processes, for example by enabling votes cast offline to be traded in online markets.[432]

Actual voting over the Internet was first seen overseas in the Estonian national elections of 2007.[433] On a smaller scale, Internet voting was used for the Arizona presidential primary elections in 2000,[434] though plans to expand earlier trials to allow overseas personnel to vote over the Internet in the 2004 general presidential elections were abandoned due to security concerns.[435] Canadian municipal elections have also been held over the Internet.[436]

The same has not yet taken place in any Australian jurisdiction. The closest approach has been in the Australian Capital Territory where the Parliamentary elections held since 2001 have allowed for votes to be cast from specially-equipped public computer terminals utilising open source software, although these are not linked to the Internet.[437] Victoria since emulated this model in 2006 in a trial for vision impaired users, though with a proprietary software product.[438]

---

[429] Mark Balnaves, Lucas Walsh and Brian Shoesmith, Participatory Technologies: The Use of the Internet in Civic Participation and Democratic Processes ⟨URL: http://www.public-policy.unimelb.edu.au/egovernance/papers/03_Balnaves.pdf⟩, 10

[430] Al Gore, Forging a New Athenian Age of Democracy, Intermedia 22:2 1995, 4

[431] A Bacard, Electronic Democracy: Can We Retake Our Government?, Humanist 53:4 1993

[432] Joanna Glasner, Vote Swaps Revamped for 2004 ⟨URL: http://www.wired.com/techbiz/media/news/2004/09/64777⟩

[433] See http://www.vvk.ee/engindex.html.

[434] Rachel Gibson, Elections Online: Assessing Internet Voting in Light of the Arizona Democratic Primary, Political Science Quarterly 116:4 2001

[435] David McGlinchey, Pentagon Scraps Plan for Online Voting in 2004 Elections ⟨URL: http://www.govexec.com/dailyfed/0204/020504d2.htm⟩

[436] Richard Brennan, E-vote a Virtual Cinch to Take Off, The Toronto Star Nov 16 2006

[437] See http://www.elections.act.gov.au/elections/evacsprocess.html.

[438] Sandra Rossi, Victoria the First to Cast E-Vote in a State Election ⟨URL: http://www.

The final democratic process in which there has been significant e-democratic reform has been in furthering transparency and accountability. Transparency has been increased mainly through the capacity for policy, legislation and parliamentary debates to be inexpensively and accessibly published online.[439] Accountability has been improved firstly by streamlining the process by which citizens can communicate with their representatives, and secondly by allowing them to report government misfeasance to the world.

On the first count, Web-based services such as e.thePeople for the United States,[440] WriteToThem.com in the United Kingdom,[441] and Australia's National Forum,[442] are designed to simplify the process of contacting politicians not only by email, but also by postal mail and fax. The UK government has gone further in establishing an official Web site for the presentation of petitions to the Prime Minister online.[443]

On the second count, anonymous and pseudonomous Internet services can assist citizens wishing to "blow the whistle" on their governments. Governments not wishing to be made so accountable have however sought to overcome the Internet's inherent architectural anonymity by bringing the mechanism of rules to bear against Internet hosts within their borders. For example, China has compelled Yahoo to give up the account details of dissident bloggers who were later arrested and imprisoned,[444] prompting an Amnesty International campaign and the presentation of a petition to the first meeting of the IGF.[445]

Internet democracy

Digital democracy in the second sense, referred to here as Internet democracy, aims not merely to support the existing institutions of representative democracy, but to displace them in favour of a form of direct democracy that challenges the roles of parliaments, political parties, the media and all other intermediate institutions head on,[446] much in the same way as the

---

computerworld.com.au/index.php/id;1353237299;fp;16;fpid;1⟩

[439]The Australian Federal Parliament's Hansard for example is published at http://www.aph.gov.au/hansard/, and an enhanced interface to the UK Hansard developed by a civil society organisation, mySociety, is found at http://www.theyworkforyou.com/.

[440]See http://www.e-thepeople.org/.

[441]See http://www.writetothem.com/, and for a converse service from the same developers, that facilitates communication from politicians to the public, see http://www.hearfromyourmp.com/.

[442]See http://portal.nationalforum.com.au/.

[443]See http://petitions.pm.gov.uk/. Estonia has a similar site to receive suggestions from the public for new legislation: see http://www.eesti.ee/tom/.

[444]Jane Macartney, Dissident Jailed "After Yahoo Handed Evidence to Police" ⟨URL: http://www.timesonline.co.uk/tol/news/world/asia/article729210.ece⟩

[445]See http://irrepressible.info/.

[446]Catinat and Vedel (as in n. 412 on page 268), 185

open source movement has upturned the conventional proprietary models of software and content development.[447] As van Dijk puts it,

> [t]he basic problem to be solved, according to this model, is the centralism, bureaucracy and obsoleteness of institutional politics which fail to live up to the expectations (the primacy of politics) and are not able to solve the most important problems of modern society.[448]

What makes the Internet the solution to this basic problem, for Internet democrats, is in part the same as the source of its appeal to e-democrats; its capacity to efficiently support interactive communication. However, Internet democrats focus more on the unique attributes of the virtual communities enabled by the Internet, which are typified by uncoerced, horizontal communications.

The classic early text on virtual communities is Howard Rheingold's, defining them as "social aggregations that emerge from the Net when enough people carry on public discussions long enough, with sufficient human feeling, to form webs of personal relationships."[449] A more recent account isolates four key structural features of community that may be present in online or virtual communities just as they are present in the real world: limited membership, shared norms, affective ties, and a sense of mutual obligation.[450]

Virtual communities have the potential to be very well suited to the deliberative democratic model, in that they tend to cut across divisions of class, race and gender to a greater extent than real life communities, allowing participants to organise themselves along lines of underlying shared interests.[451] Since an early study found electronic communications to mediate differences in status and expertise,[452] further research has suggested that hierarchies are devalued within virtual communities in part because of the failure of the medium to transmit social context cues of dominance associated with status, race and gender.[453] Research has also shown that online fora thereby allow participants in small group

---

[447] Douglas Rushkoff, Open Source Democracy: How Online Communication is Changing Offline Politics ⟨URL: `http://www.demos.co.uk/files/OpenSourceDemocracy.pdf`⟩, 56

[448] Van Dijk (as in n. 167 on page 130), 45

[449] Rheingold, *The Virtual Community* (as in n. 150 on page 214), 5

[450] William A Galston, *The Internet in Public Life* Lanham, MD: Rowman & Littlefield Publishers, 2004, chap. The Impact of the Internet on Civic Life: An Early Assessment, 65

[451] Barry Wellman and Milena Gulia, *Communities in Cyberspace* London: Routledge, 1999, chap. Virtual Communities as Communities: Net Surfers Don't Ride Alone, 186

[452] Vitaly J Dubrovsky, Sara Kiesler and Beheruz N Sethna, The Equalization Phenomenon: Status Effects in Computer-Mediated and Face-to-Face Decision-Making Groups, Human-Computer Interaction 6:2 1991

[453] Jordan (as in n. 49 on page 16), 80; Froomkin, Habermas@discourse.net: Toward a Critical Theory of Cyberspace (as in n. 40 on page 13), 803

discussions to talk with increased frankness, and to experience greater participation and more equality than in face-to-face discussions.[454] Or in the words of the classic New Yorker cartoon, "On the Internet, nobody knows you're a dog."[455]

There is, however, some variance in the political implications that are extrapolated from these features of virtual communities. Taken to an extreme, the so-called Californian ideology, seen as the convergence of "the 'hippie' dream for a direct, self-empowered citizen government, and the 'yuppie' dream for material wealth,"[456] and typified by numerous hyperbolic articles from *Wired* magazine during the 1990s,[457] theorised that "existing social, political and legal power structures will wither away to be replaced by unfettered interactions between autonomous individuals."[458]

Such a conception of Internet democracy is hardly recognisable as democratic at all, and indeed other commentators simply identify it as anarchism:

> The Net itself is a metaphor and/or precursor of a new anarchic political community in which traditional political identities linked to territorial and sectional interests are undermined, and new forms of politics emerge free of state coercion. The new communications revolution can lead to more "horizontal" and less "vertical" communication.[459]

Another school of thought attributes almost transcendent potential to the interactions that the Internet enables. Joichi Ito states:

> It is possible that there is a method for citizens to self-organize to deliberate on and address complex issues as necessary and enhance our democracy without any one citizen being required to know and understand the whole. This is the essence of an emergence, and it is the way that ant colonies are able to "think" and our DNA is able to build the complex bodies that we have. If information technology could provide a mechanism for citizens in a democracy to participate in a way that allowed self-organization and emergent understanding, it is possible that a form of emergent democracy could

---

[454] L Sproull and S Kiesler, *Global Networks: Computers and International Communication* Cambridge, MA: MIT Press, 1993, chap. Computers, Networks and Work; Froomkin, Habermas@discourse.net: Toward a Critical Theory of Cyberspace (as in n. 40 on page 13), 800

[455] Peter Steiner, On the Internet, Nobody Knows You're a Dog, The New Yorker 69:20 1993

[456] Martin Hagen, *Digital Democracy* London: Sage Publications, 2000, chap. Digital Democracy and Political Systems, 59

[457] J Katz, Birth of a Digital Nation, Wired US 5.04 1997; Wired, The Wired Manifesto for the Digital Society, Wired UK 2.10 1996

[458] R Barbrook and A Cameron, The Californian Ideology, Science as Culture 26 1996, 53

[459] Bryan et al. (as in n. 428 on page 270), 7

address many of the complexity and scalability issues facing representative governments today.[460]

Even Tim Berners-Lee, inventor of the World Wide Web, posits:

> If we lay the groundwork right and try novel ways of interacting on the new Web, we may find a whole new set of financial, ethical, cultural and governing structures to which we can choose to belong, rather than having to pick the ones we happen to physically live in. Bit by bit those structures that work best would become most important in the world, and democratic systems might take on different shapes.[461]

If such predictions were to prove accurate, their consequences would begin to resonate not only in global institutions, but amongst individuals in families, workplaces and social life. As Knight contends,

> the technological revolution has the potential of creating in the minds of people around the world a sense of global citizenship which could result eventually in the transfer of individuals' loyalties from "sovereignty-bound" to "sovereignty-free" multilateral bodies.[462]

However, this potential has not yet been realised sufficiently to be verified by empirical studies,[463] and at the moment can best be characterised as a somewhat speculative ideal. Likewise, returning to the macroscopic level, this idea of Internet democracy offering an alternative to institutional politics (wherein those existing institutions are relegated to the role of the executive government),[464] may be regarded for now simply as cyberlibertarian idealism.

In the current institutional political climate, the impact of the deliberations of Internet-based virtual communities on governance is indirect at best. Whilst the blogosphere and Facebook may make news headlines, this is often as far as their influence extends: to the media, rather than to the sphere of institutional politics in which real power ultimately remains.[465]

---

[460] Joichi Ito, Emergent Democracy ⟨URL: `http://joi.ito.com/joiwiki/EmergentDemocracyPaper`⟩

[461] Berners-Lee and Fischetti (as in n. 105 on page 56), 224

[462] W Andy Knight, *Future Multilateralism: The Political and Social Framework* Tokyo: United Nations University Press, 1999, chap. Engineering Space in Global Governance: the Emergence of Civil Society in Evolving "New" Multilateralism, 277

[463] Pippa Norris, *Governance in a Globalizing World* Washington, DC: Brookings Institution Press, 2000, chap. Global Governance and Cosmopolitan Citizens

[464] Van Dijk (as in n. 167 on page 130), 49

[465] Rheingold, *The Virtual Community* (as in n. 150 on page 214), 289

Perhaps a more moderate and yet still substantive assessment of the implications of Internet democracy is that it does not pose as significant a threat to existing institutions of power such as the state, as it does to intermediaries. Grossman writes:

> The big losers in the present-day reshuffling and resurgence of public influence are the traditional institutions that have served as the main intermediaries between government and its citizens—the political parties, labor unions, civic associations, even the commentators and correspondents in the mainstream press.[466]

On this account, Internet democracy is less about displacing existing institutions, and more about providing new venues for public deliberation that take advantage of the high degree of congruence between the inherent features of virtual communities (such as egalitarianism and cosmopolitanism), and the requirements of the Habermasian discourse principle for the conduct of rational political discourses.[467] This creates the potential for the development of a true public sphere such as has not existed since the demise of the English coffee houses of Habermas, and has in fact never existed on such a transnational scale before now.[468]

Whilst the Internet democratic programme is an ambitious one, there are existing virtual communities, such as that of the IETF, that arguably already exemplify what is required of such political fora.[469] Thus, virtual communities do have an important role in the formation of opinions within civil society. In turn, civil society has a vital role within transnational governance networks; however, it is not a role that supplants that of the other stakeholder groups.

Online deliberation

Common to both conceptions of digital democracy is the potential for the use of online tools for democratic deliberation. This potential has recently begun to attract academic attention,[470] although governments have not been widely seized of the same vision, any more so than they have for the

[466] Grossman (as in n. 415 on page 269), 161

[467] C Ess, *Philosophical Perspective on Computer-Mediated Communication* Albany, NY: SUNY Press, 1996, 216

[468] Ibid., 216

[469] Froomkin, Habermas@discourse.net: Toward a Critical Theory of Cyberspace (as in n. 40 on page 13)

[470] See `http://www.online-deliberation.net/`.

potential of deliberative democracy in general[471] (save to some extent at a local level).[472]

This is unfortunate in that online deliberation has the potential to achieve many of the same benefits as offline deliberative democracy, whilst also leveraging the efficiencies of digital democracy that could allow deliberation to be facilitated at a far lower cost than many of those offline techniques such as the 21st Century Town Meeting.

In fact to date, two of the institutional frameworks for deliberative democracy that were examined at section 4.3 on page 253 have already been successfully transplanted to an equivalent form online. The inventor of Deliberative Polling, James Fishkin, presided over the first online Deliberative Polls in September and October 2005 using audio conferencing software,[473] and has proposed this technique as a possible method for the governance of ICANN.[474]

Similarly, an online citizens' jury was implemented by the South Kesteven District Council, retaining a typical size of twelve members for the jury, but allowing for it to call any number of witnesses during its deliberations.[475] There is no reason why the larger variations of the citizens' jury, such as the consensus conference, could not also be implemented online.

However by the same token, it would be short-sighted to limit the forms of online deliberation to implementations of offline forms; and indeed, they have not been so limited in practice. The forms of online deliberation that are not based on the mainstream frameworks for offline deliberation may be most usefully divided into the following categories:

- Group discussion
  - Synchronous
  - Asynchronous
- Collaborative authoring
  - Pre-deliberation
  - Post-deliberation

[471] Coleman and Gøtze (as in n. 301 on page 246), 36

[472] A Gronlund, Emerging Infrastructures for E-Democracy: In Search of Strong Inscriptions, e-Service Journal 2:1 2003

[473] See http://www.pbs.org/newshour/btp/articles/events_dop.html.

[474] J S Fishkin, Deliberative Polling As a Model for ICANN Membership ⟨URL: http://cyber.law.harvard.edu/rcs/fish.html⟩. eDecide is the name of another software product implementing the functionality of the Deliberative Poll, but which does not require the user's computer to be equipped with audio facilities: see http://www.communitypeople.net/.

[475] See http://skdc.citizensjury.org.uk/.

• Decision-making

The main place of synchronous (or instantaneous) group discussion is where deliberation takes place concurrently in face-to-face meetings as well as online. It can also be used where it is necessary or desirable for a group to deliberate and reach a decision quickly, and where broad participation is not compromised by the need for all to be present online at the same time.

Software to facilitate synchronous group discussion online has a long history, dating back to 1988 in the form of the IRC (Internet Relay Chat) protocol,[476] which is still widely used today. IRC is a text-only protocol, in that although it allows participants to exchange messages and files between themselves, they cannot ordinarily hear or observe each other as they speak.

Although audio and video conferencing software also exists, both proprietary such as Skype[477] and open source such as Ekiga,[478] technology has not yet advanced to the point where these are practical for the simultaneous use of large groups of users, and they also place significantly greater demands than text-only chat upon the computing power and speed of Internet access available to the user. The same is true of virtual reality software such as Second Life,[479] although the Second Life world has been used by the ICANN community to host virtual conferences in conjunction with official ICANN meetings, commencing with the 2006 meeting in Sa o Paulo, Brazil.[480]

Asynchronous group discussion also has a long history; Usenet is one of the earliest implementations, but others include email mailing list management software (one of the earliest of which is Majordomo),[481] and more recently Web-based discussion fora such as SMF (Simple Machines Forum)[482] which is notable for its use by the IGF Secretariat.[483] Morrisett explains why asynchronous discussion fora such as these have certain advantages over synchronous alternatives in their suitability for online deliberation:

> In [such] a computer conference, people have access to questions, facts, and opinions and can take their time about when they are ready to give their own opinion. Input can be made at any time, and the ongoing output of the system can

[476] IETF, Internet Relay Chat Protocol ⟨URL: `http://www.ietf.org/rfc/rfc1459.txt`⟩

[477] See `http://www.skype.com/`.

[478] See `http://www.ekiga.org/`.

[479] See `http://secondlife.com/`.

[480] See `http://www.icannwiki.org/Ninca_Island_in_Second_Life`.

[481] See `http://www.greatcircle.com/majordomo/`.

[482] See `http://www.simplemachines.org/`.

[483] See `http://intgovforum.org/forum/`.

> be studied until someone believes he or she has something to say.[484]

Similar observations have been made of blogs, which provide the same facilities in a more decentralised form.[485]

There are also certain asynchronous discussion products, both proprietary such as eConsult,[486] and open source such as DotConsult,[487] that have been specifically developed for use in democratic deliberation, for example because they provide enhanced capabilities for managing citizen panels.

Moving on to the second main class of tools for online deliberation, collaborative authoring can also be subdivided into two categories. First are tools that facilitate the production of the balanced briefing material that is required to inform deliberation. One of the few tools specifically designed for this purpose is GRASS, for Group Report Authoring Support System.[488]

In the second (though overlapping) sub-category of collaborative authoring tools are those used as a more efficient mechanism than discussion alone for drafting an agreed text such as a standard or code. The modern archetype of such collaborative authoring software is the wiki. Along similar lines, a new generation of editors allows multiple users to edit documents synchronously, actually seeing each other's changes as they are typed. SynchroEdit[489] is one of these, which to a large extent also incidentally fulfils the role of synchronous discussion software. Another innovative tool is stet, recently used in the drafting of version 3 of the GNU GPL, which allowed the public to attach comments to any parts of the text, with more-commented sections being highlighted in darker colours.[490]

The third class of tools are those for decision-making, which includes conventional voting software such as the open source GNU.FREE,[491] and also more relevantly for present purposes software that is designed to foster and support deliberation in the decision-making process, such as the proprietary hosted product eDecide, which implements an online Deliberative Poll. Each question in an eDecide poll is linked to further information putting alternative perspectives. A similar effect can be achieved through the use of the polling capabilities that are built in to certain asynchronous

[484] Lloyd Morrisett, *Democracy and New Media (Media in Transition)* Cambridge, MA: MIT Press, 2004, chap. Technologies of Freedom?, 29

[485] Lawrence Lessig, *Free Culture* New York: Penguin Books, 2004, 42

[486] See `http://www.communitypeople.net/econsult.htm`.

[487] See `http://www.dotconsult.org/`.

[488] See `http://www.wagenvoort.net/grass/`.

[489] See `http://www.synchroedit.com/`.

[490] See `http://gplv3.fsf.org/comments`.

[491] See `http://www.free-project.org/dev/`.

Figure 4.2: Tools for online democracy

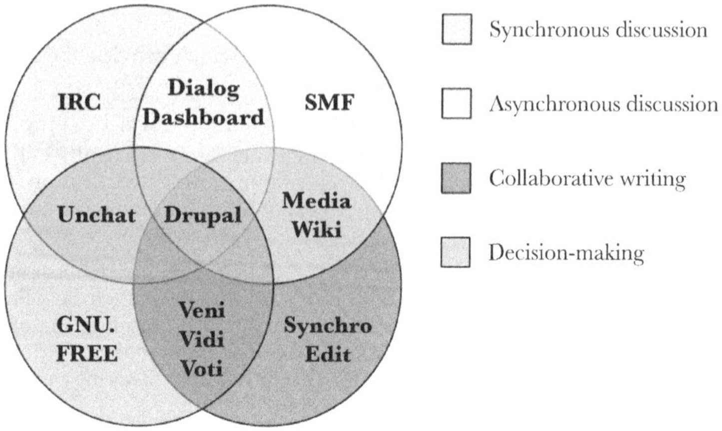

discussion tools such as SMF, provided that the facilitator only opens a poll once satisfied that the issues bearing on it have been sufficiently discussed to bring out all relevant facts and perspectives.

Other examples of some tools for online deliberation which cross over between two categories are given in the figure above. Although it is by no means intended to be comprehensive, some of the products there described are worthy of separate mention. Unchat is a a proprietary synchronous discussion product which incorporates a voting facility, along with other features designed for democratic deliberation such as a document repository linked to the discussions, and the ability for discussions to be moderated, unmoderated, or self-moderated.[492]

The Dialog Dashboard is another proprietary product specifically designed for online deliberation which combines synchronous and asynchronous modes of discussion. MediaWiki, the wiki software used by Wikipedia, is shown in the diagram as a hybrid of collaborative authoring and asynchronous discussion, simply because every page of substantive content is accompanied by a discussion page on which all editors are encouraged to discuss their ideas for the page and to resolve disagreements.

Intersecting the collaborative authoring and decision-making categories, VeniVidiVoti is a somewhat complex though powerful open source software

[492] As at April 2008, its Web site at `http://www.unchat.com/` is inaccessible. An archived version may be found at `http://web.archive.org/web/20070806084821/http://www.unchat.com/`.

library designed for the drafting of agreed texts.[493] Its most interesting feature is that the decision-making system that it incorporates is based upon the principles of direct democracy by delegable proxy that were briefly alluded to at section 4.3 on page 266.

The final segment of the diagram is the centre, in which all four categories of tool for online democracy intersect. There is yet no such tool that is specifically designed to meet all of the technical requirements of an online deliberative democracy.[494] However the example given, Drupal,[495] is a general-purpose Web content management system which can be extended by means of a variety of modules to meet these requirements at a basic level.[496] As will be explained in the next chapter, Drupal was used to develop a community Web site for the first meeting of the IGF.

Thus although development is continuing apace on a number of fronts, there is already a rich variety of software suitable for the facilitation of online deliberation. Even so, software is not enough. Unmoderated and un-

---

[493]See `http://vvv.sourceforge.net/English/vvv/element/specifications.html`.

[494]However towards this end, Wilson, Ramsey and Nyerges' research into "analytic-deliberative" online participation (that is, deliberation informed by expert information, a condition implicit to many of the offline deliberative democratic techniques), proposes the development of systems for the implementation of eleven "participatory games": Matthew W Wilson, Kevin S Ramsey and Timothy L Nyerges, Design Considerations for Supporting Online, Analytic-Deliberative, Public Participation ⟨URL: `http://www.online-deliberation.net/conf2005/viewpaper.php?id=37`⟩. These games—which include goal statement, brainstorming, negotiation, synthesis, refinement, voting or survey, and review—could all be facilitated using the more generic categories of software described above coupled with effective moderation and facilitation.

Another project worthy of mention, though currently quite immature in its development cycle, is an open source platform for online deliberation called Deme, developed at Stanford University (see `http://groupspace.org/`). The goal of the developers of Deme is to create a system for online deliberation that will fulfil four criteria in its application to an existing offline group or network:

- Supportiveness (the system should support the group's activities, so that these are rendered more effective as a whole, or at least no less effective than before);
- Comprehensiveness (there should be nothing significant that the group can do in face-to-face meetings that it cannot do using the online platform—and thus no reason for an insistence upon face-to-face meetings to justify a practice of "inner-circle, closed-door decision making");
- Participation (the system should maximise the ability for affected parties to participate in democratic deliberation); and
- Quality (the quality of participation enabled by the platform should subjectively meet or exceed that of face-to-face discussion).

(See Todd Davies et al., An Online Environment for Democratic Deliberation: Motivations, Principles, and Design ⟨URL: `http://www.stanford.edu/~davies/deme-principles.pdf`⟩, 5.)

These objectives are highly pertinent to the IGF, as a network composed of widely geographically dispersed stakeholders seeking to come together in a forum convened by the authority of an intergovernmental organisation; a stakeholder group within which the prevalence of "inner-circle, closed-door decision making" has been widely noted.

[495]See `http://drupal.org/`.

[496]It also exists in a forked version called CivicSpace that has been refined for the use of communities: see `http://www.civicspacelabs.org/`.

structured discussion is very far from deliberation, as Coleman and Go"tze note, stating that "[i]n free-for-all discussions anyone can say anything, but no-one can have much expectation of being heard or of influencing policy outcomes."[497] Their research emphasises the role of expert moderation or facilitation of online deliberation, which accords with the requirements of most of the deliberative democratic techniques designed for offline settings.

The skills that such moderators or facilitators require, whether online or offline, include the facilitation of relevant discussion, conflict resolution, project management, and summarising and providing feedback to the group. It may also be necessary to split the group into sub-groups of managable size, in order to allow them to function as communities rather than simply as audiences for the views of their most outspoken members.[498] In all, the moderation and facilitation of online discussion is a very similar role to that of the BDFL of an open source software project, and provides an example of the place of a hybrid of hierarchical and democratic ordering, where the hierarchical role is limited to the support of the institutions of the online deliberative process.

Criticisms

By this point, it has become fairly clear that a democratic organisation structure for a governance network possesses advantages that the anarchistic and hierarchical structures do not, and that it overcomes many of their shortcomings, at least in the case where deliberative democratic principles are followed, and ideally where online participation is also facilitated.

However some significant criticisms of such an organisation structure could also be made. These may be divided into conceptual criticisms of deliberative democracy generally, some problems specific to online deliberation, and some broader political issues with implementing an online or offline deliberative democratic structure within a transnational governance network such as the IGF.

Conceptual criticisms

One perceived issue with deliberative democracy, which is really a more particular criticism of procedural democracy in general, is as to the supposed neutrality of the process. Although deliberative democracy claims to require nothing more of its participants than that they commit to resolve their differences as equals through a process of public reasoning, it has been contended that the "norms of deliberation are culturally specific and

[497] Coleman and Gøtze (as in n. 301 on page 246), 17
[498] Davies (as in n. 149 on page 214), 28

often operate as forms of power that silence or devalue the speech of some people."[499]

Thus whereas Habermas only accepts rational argument as a means of communication in deliberative fora, Dryzek plausibly suggests that alternative modes of communication such as rhetoric, testimony or storytelling, and greeting, should also be admitted provided that they are exercised noncoercively and are "capable of connecting the particular to the general"[500]—that is, essentially, that rational reasoning underlies them, even if they are not expressed in an argumentative form. In an online deliberative context, the mode of storytelling could well be extended to include the use of blogging as an input into the deliberative process.[501]

The question of whether the additional modes of communication noted by Dryzek, or others, should be allowed within deliberative fora, is not one that goes to the root of the deliberative democratic programme, but rather one that the moderator or facilitator of a deliberative process can be called upon to manage with due regard to the composition of the group in question. Having said that, neither Dryzek, nor any liberal, would or could go further to admit inherently irrational or coercive forms of discourse into deliberative fora, as any strong form of postmodern skepticism about the neutrality of rational discourse is fundamentally at odds with the liberal paradigm upon which democratic theory rests.[502]

A second criticism is that deliberative democracy does not work well in large groups. This is both a practical observation and a conceptual one. Dealing with the practical issue first, it is true that in any large group, discussion tends to be dominated by a few active participants, with the majority remaining silent (the latter group being known in the context of virtual communities as "lurkers").[503] This phenomenon can be addressed by a combination of measures, including:

- designing the framework for deliberation so as to institutionalise the process by which the views of all participants are solicited;
- active engagement by the moderator or facilitator in encouraging silent stakeholders to participate and discouraging dominant stakeholders from becoming too overbearing;
- limiting the size of groups, as in of the citizens' jury; or

[499] Iris Marion Young, *Democracy and Difference* Princeton, NJ: Princeton University Press, 1996, chap. Communication and the Other: Beyond Deliberative Democracy, 123

[500] Dryzek, *Deliberative Democracy and Beyond* (as in n. 310 on page 248),

[501] Coleman and Gøtze (as in n. 301 on page 246), 34

[502] See further section 4.4 on page 311.

[503] Blair Nonnecke and Jenny Preece, *Proceedings of the SIGCHI Conference on Human Factors in Computing Systems* The Hague: ACM Press, 2000, chap. Lurker Demographics: Counting the Silent

- if a large group is involved, splitting it up into smaller units, as in the case of the 21st Century Town Meeting.

The conceptual problem with large groups is that by definition they limit the effective ability of any one member's participation to make a difference to the outcome, which in turn makes it more difficult to ensure that the organisation is acting accountably; a difficulty that is magnified in the case of international organisations.[504]

However, this is more of a problem in a representative democracy, where the participation of a large number makes it easier to produce an accurate (but not necessarily meaningful) picture of their preferences in aggregate, without necessarily doing anything to produce better (more reasoned) democratic outcomes. The deliberative approach is designed to mitigate this problem, by allowing a small number of participants who may have cogent views to express, to exert a greater than proportionate influence over the outcome to which the organisation as a whole eventually agrees.

This in turn gives rise to the further conceptual criticism that whilst deliberative democratic processes may facilitate grass roots participation in governance, it is simplistic to assume that rule from the grass roots is always good.[505] As Netanel argues, the diffusion of sovereignty over Internet-related public policy issue areas from states to a broader base of stakeholders opens the door to "invidious status discrimination, narrowcasting and mainstreaming content selection, systematic invasions of privacy and gross inequalities in the distribution of basic requisites for netizenship and citizenship."[506]

The deliberative democrat agrees entirely with this, but takes it as a valid criticism only of orthodox direct democracy, not of deliberative democracy which builds in procedures requiring the preferences of the grass roots to be passed through the filter of public reason before being accepted, thereby ensuring that minority viewpoints and the opinions of relevant experts are heard and taken into account. To continue to object to the broadening of authority to the grass roots following this process of filtering and refinement might indicate that such elitism carries an underlying hierarchical programme.

The final, and roughly converse, criticism of the deliberative democratic ideal is that it is very much only an ideal in its insistence that that underlying power relations must play no part in the deliberative process.[507] Much like the assumptions of the economist that underlie models based upon the free market, to the extent that those assumptions fail to hold in practice, the soundness of the model itself is compromised. In a deliberative

[504] Dahl, Democracy's Edges (as in n. 243 on page 235)

[505] Held, *Democracy and the Global Order: From the Modern State to Cosmopolitan Governance* (as in n. 177 on page 131), 286

[506] Netanel (as in n. 204 on page 223), 498

[507] Cohen, The Good Polity: Normative Analysis of the State (as in n. 300 on page 246), 22–23

democratic context, and specifically giving the example of a governance network such as the IGF, this means that to the extent that representatives of governments (for example) are able to use the threat of the exercise of their authority to govern by rules to sabotage the freedom and equality of the process, they will retain a hegemonic influence over the network that belies its apparently democratic form.

This criticism is the most cogent of those examined here, and to the extent that it can be managed at all, this can only be through the development of internal norms within the governance network which value cooperation over coercion, and whereby the equal importance of each stakeholder group to the success of the process is acknowledged by all. This problem will be revisited, and an alternative approach to resolving it discussed, at section 4.4 on page 294.

Digital deficits

In addition to the criticisms of deliberative democracy discussed above, there are a number of further limitations of online deliberation in particular that warrant separate treatment.

The first is that online communities tend to be insular and prone to balkanisation,[508] which in turn results in the development of polarised preferences and perspectives. An explanation for this is that it is more difficult for people to be "accidentally" exposed to political information on the Internet (or at least on the World Wide Web), than in the case of traditional media, as audiences can choose what information they wish to receive and when they wish to receive it.[509] Whilst this might be seen as an advantage over traditional media by the users in question, it allows them to crowd into virtual ghettos and reinforce each others' preconceptions, trending towards ever more extreme views.[510]

A number of other dysfunctional behaviours common within virtual communities also work against deliberative democratic principles. These include the prevalence of "flaming" (sending intentionally insulting or abusive messages),[511] and an odd dichotomy between the tendencies of virtual communities either to adopt rash decisions with insufficient research,[512] or conversely to bog themselves down in a much drawn-out

[508]M Van Alstyne and E Brynjolfsson, Electronic Communities: Global Villages or Cyberbalkanization?, Proceedings of the International Conference on Information Systems 17 1996

[509]Robert J Klotz, *The Politics of Internet Communication* Lanham, MD: Rowman & Littlefield Publishers, 2004, 64

[510]Cass R Sunstein, *Debating Deliberative Democracy* London: Routledge, 2003, chap. The Law of Group Polarization, 89; Idem, *Republic.com* Princeton, NJ: Princeton University Press, 2001

[511]Sproull and Kiesler (as in n. 454 on page 274), 108–110

[512]Laura J Gurak, *Communities in Cyberspace* London: Routledge, 1999, chap. The Promise and the Peril of Social Action in Cyberspace, 259

decision-making process.[513]

Each of these dysfunctional tendencies gives the lie to the assumption that citizens will spontaneously and effectively engage in reasoned deliberation if they are only provided the opportunity and the technical means to do so. Rather, they reinforce the importance of effective moderation and facilitation of online deliberation if it is to adhere to deliberative democratic principles.

It is less easy for a facilitator or moderator to overcome the next limitation of online deliberation, however; the fact that participants lack the context of verbal, facial and body language cues that accompany face-to-face deliberation, and thereby often fall into misunderstanding.[514] Whilst, as already noted, the lack of such cues is in some cases an advantage in that they might otherwise perpetuate differences in offline status and power,[515] they can also exacerbate differences in written language skills,[516] which can be significant in a multicultural and multilingual forum.[517]

These limitations can be partially addressed by educating participants in online discussions to make their mood, tone of voice or actions known, where relevant, by textual means. These include the use of emoticons such as the ubiquitous smiley :-), the use of capital letters to indicate shouting, and by describing one's actions as one performs them.[518]

Deliberation in a virtual reality environment such as Second Life also allows the possibility of directing one's avatar (virtual persona) to adopt the facial expressions, body language or actions that the user would present in face-to-face deliberation—or at least, those that she would consciously present, and therefore desire to be transmitted. As previously noted however, the accessibility of virtual reality environments for deliberation is presently limited by the demands they place on a user's computer hardware and Internet connection.

This leads to the final and most significant criticism of online deliberation to be dealt with here, which is a criticism of digital democracy generally: that whilst the Internet may provide an efficient and relatively cost-effective means of communication for deliberation (particularly in a transnational context, where the alternative is international air travel), there is still a digital divide between those with adequate access to the Internet and those without. As a result, the composition of any online deliberative democratic polity will not be widely representative, but rather

---

[513]Sproull and Kiesler (as in n. 454 on page 274)

[514]H Rheingold, *High Noon on the Electronic Frontier* Cambridge, MA: MIT Press, 1996, chap. A Slice of My Life in My Virtual Community, 427

[515]Jordan (as in n. 49 on page 16), 80

[516]Fishkin, Virtual Democratic Possibilities: Prospects for Internet Democracy (as in n. 230 on page 231), 14–15

[517]See also section 4.4 on page 311.

[518] For example in IRC this may be done by typing "/me shakes his head," which renders the code "/me" as the user's pseudonymous screen name.

will tend to be biased towards privileged users and against economically disadvantaged minorities.[519]

The digital divide is primarily an economic divide. Thus internationally, there is a considerable disparity between the incidence of Internet use in developed countries and in less developed countries, although the gap has been closing over time. At the extremes, in 2006, over 88% of the Netherlands' population were Internet users, whereas this only applied to approximately 0.01% of residents of Burkina Faso, Dijibouti, Côte d'Ivoire or Sudan. (In Australia the figure was over 50%.)[520]

Domestically—exemplified by United States research—amongst those excluded by the digital divide are low income earners, those with lower levels of education, the elderly, and disabled people, all of whom tend to have lower levels of general computer literacy.[521] In Australia, infrastructure deficiencies have also created something of a digital divide between those resident in metropolitan areas and those in rural, regional and remote areas of Australia.[522]

Although there is no quick fix for the problems of the digital divide, they have begun to be addressed by all stakeholder groups, particularly in the wake of WSIS,[523] which established a number of new follow-up mechanisms to monitor and maintain stakeholders' ongoing commitments to address this issue.[524]

As with other issues of social equity such as those covered by the *International Covenant on Economic, Social and Cultural Rights*, the primary responsibility for addressing them falls upon governments. One of the most basic strategies that they can employ to narrow the digital divide within their own borders is to provide Internet access to schools, and to public places such as public libraries and telecentres, as research has shown that these facilities are most commonly used by those disadvantaged by income or education,[525] and by the citizens of many developing countries with limited telecommunications infrastructure.[526]

As noted above however, access to Internet infrastructure is only one component of the digital divide. To go further and facilitate their citizens' use of the Internet, governments can lead the way by pursuing e-democratic

---

519 Fishkin, Deliberative Polling As a Model for ICANN Membership (as in n. 474 on page 277), 23–24

520 ITU, ICT Statistics Database ⟨URL: http://www.itu.int/ITU-D/icteye/Indicators/Indicators.aspx⟩

521 Klotz (as in n. 509 on page 285), 21, 24

522 Jennifer Curtin, A Digital Divide in Rural and Regional Australia? ⟨URL: http://www.aph.gov.au/library/pubs/cib/2001-02/02cib01.htm⟩

523 WSIS, Geneva Declaration of Principles (as in n. 104 on page 27), para 10

524 See section 5.1 on page 351.

525 Klotz (as in n. 509 on page 285), 23

526 ITU, World Information Society Report 2007 ⟨URL: http://www.itu.int/osg/spu/publications/worldinformationsociety/2006/wisr-web.pdf⟩, 35

strategies such as publishing government information and consulting with their citizens online, as well as by promoting (or mandating within government) adherence to standards of accessibility for local Web sites.

In cases where there is a significant domestic digital divide, it may also be necessary for government programmes to recruit members of marginalised, disadvantaged or otherwise "hard to reach" groups within the community for participation in e-democratic processes. This can be done by specifically inviting members of these groups to participate in online deliberation or consultation, as occurred for example in Australia's Deliberative Poll on reconciliation, rather than relying on random selection or self-selection respectively. It may be necessary to go offline to target members of these groups where they live, work or socialise.[527]

The private sector also has a role to play, particularly in building the telecommunications infrastructure necessary to bring affordable Internet access to the disadvantaged. Although the particular measures required to bring this about will vary from one community to another, a relatively inexpensive package to provide local connectivity to a disadvantaged and isolated community may comprise the provision of low cost or recycled computers,[528] open source software, and low-cost satellite connections coupled with Wireless Local Loop (WLL) technology.[529]

Civil society is also involved in the provision of inexpensive computer hardware through organisations such as the One Laptop Per Child project which aims to produce a $100 laptop for distribution in developing countries,[530] and of course in developing and supporting open source software, sometimes in conjunction with the private sector (as for example in the case of the OpenOffice.org project established by Sun Microsystems).[531]

The digital divide is thus acknowledged by all stakeholders as a significant and ongoing challenge. Even so, returning to the present context, it hardly provides a fatal objection to the process of online deliberation within a multi-stakeholder governance network such as the IGF, for two main reasons.

---

[527] Nicola Brackertz et al., Community Consultation and the Hard to Reach: Concepts and Practice in Victorian Local Government ⟨URL: http://www.sisr.net/cag/docs/HardtoReach_main.pdf⟩, 14–15

[528] James (as in n. 158 on page 215), 49–53

[529] Ibid., 47

[530] See http://www.laptop.org/.

[531] ParTecs is another particularly interesting example of an open source software product upon which the private sector and civil society have collaborated, that directly addresses the impact of the digital divide on online deliberation: see http://partecs.com/products.html. Built on an open source foundation, ParTecs is a tool for asynchronous discussion that allows users to participate using either the online methods of email or the Web, or the offline methods of mail or fax. The software facilitates the bridging of online and offline methods, and even the translation of content where required. Thus for example, one participant may post a message in English to a Web site running the ParTecs software, and another may receive that message in French, by mail, as part of a printed newsletter, whilst a third receives it in Spanish by email.

First, as already noted, the digital divide largely mirrors an underlying economic divide. Therefore although online deliberation does exclude certain stakeholder representatives from participation in a governance network, so too does face-to-face deliberation. As long as the former would exclude fewer participants than the latter, online deliberation will be the preferable option. Furthermore, there is certainly nothing to prevent the network from making use of both forms of deliberation.

Second, as also already noted, deliberative democracy does not depend as representative democracy does upon the achievement of numerically proportional representation. Whereas in a representative democracy the preferences of a minority can be overruled by the majority without the need for justification, in a deliberative democracy this can only occur through the exercise of public reason. Therefore provided that the moderator or facilitator of an online deliberative process can ensure that there is at least one stakeholder representative to put the perspectives of a minority group, it is matters little that other members of that minority group were excluded from participation by the digital divide.

Political issues

The final criticism to be examined here has been raised and answered previously: that the absence of a stable transnational, multi-stakeholder *demos* for the regime of Internet governance by definition precludes the formation of a democratic governance network for that regime.[532] This criticism is encapsulated in the bald statement of Nitin Desai, Chairman of the IGF's Advisory Group, at a conference preceding the first meeting of the IGF, "The forum has no membership, it's an open door, a town hall, all views are welcome. But it's not a decision-making body. We have no members so we have no power to make decision."[533]

This criticism calls for closer examination again now, because its superficial plausibility, particularly within the intergovernmental circles of the existing IGF, may in the end be that organisation's undoing.

At the commencement of this section, the democratic principle was defined as the fundamental liberal tenet that a system of legitimate democratic rule must operate with the consent of the governed (that is, of all those potentially affected by such rule). When deliberative democratic theory was introduced it was posited that this principle is only fully realised where each of the governed is given the opportunity to speak on any question of governance in a forum of public deliberation.

This is all very well in theory. But a governance network actually organised along these lines, at least in the Internet governance regime, would

[532]See section 4.3 on page 257.

[533]Darren Waters, Warning Over "Broken Up" Internet (URL: http://news.bbc.co.uk/1/hi/technology/6037345.stm)

be required to traverse a wide range of issue areas, and the stakeholders potentially affected by decisions made by the network could well vary from one such issue area to another. For example, those potentially affected by decisions made on the regulation of spam might be quite different from those affected by decisions relating to IPR.

This means that there can be no stable *demos* in the Internet governance regime. In other words, the IGF not only does not, but cannot have a defined membership. This is also sound in theory; it allows the organisation to be flexible and adaptive, growing or contracting to accommodate anyone who can, and to exclude anyone who cannot, frame their interest in a particular issue in the discourse of public reason.

However in practice, the notion that a democratic polity can exist in the absence of a defined transnational and multi-stakeholder *demos* is a profoundly counter-intuitive one for politicians, diplomats and even academics alike.[534] Governments in particular are loath to share "their" policy authority in a governance network of uncertain size and composition, and indeed one in which governmental representatives may be outnumbered by those from civil society. As unobjectionable as this may be in theory, it is highly objectionable to diplomats and politicians.

Unless they can be convinced otherwise, the likely outcome for the governance network is that if governments participate in it at all, they will seek to circumscribe its role to being strictly advisory in nature, and will firmly underscore their reservation of authority to disregard its output.

This is quite a familiar tale, in which although a network between governments and citizens may be described as a "partnership," with the implication of equality between the parties, governments perceive their own role in such networks as being superior to those of the other stakeholders.[535] This reflects the US government's relationship with ICANN[536] and the Australian government's with auDA,[537] and as will be shown in Chapter 6, has also been the IGF's experience.

Yet there remains a glimmer of hope. Although a deliberative democratic form for the organisation of a governance network is by far the most suitable yet considered, it could be that its downfall lies in its claim to be a form of democratic rule. As already noted, it is a feature of deliberative

---

[534]For example, Johnson and Crawford write (in Johnson and Crawford, The Idea of ICANN (as in n. 50 on page 192)) that "[t]he principle of one-person-one vote provides a basis for delegating a people's sovereignty to a government. It does not provide legitimacy for a system that seeks voluntary compliance with policies that have the support or acquiescence of all groups particularly impacted by those policies."

Strictly speaking this is correct, however it suggests that "one person, one vote" and democracy are synonymous, whereas in fact deliberative democracy does provide legitimacy for just such a system.

[535]Skelcher et al. (as in n. 97 on page 26), 578; Cardoso, Cardoso Report on Civil Society (as in n. 147 on page 126), 37

[536]McCullagh, Bush Administration Objects to .xxx Domains (as in n. 7 on page 3)

[537]*Telecommunications Act 1997* (Cth), Part 22, Division 3

democracy that it "aims to arrive at a rationally motivated *consensus*."[538] Perhaps, then, recasting the organisation in a formally consensual rather than democratic form, and modifying its procedures as required to accord with this new nomenclature (whilst still holding to the democratic principle), might resolve some of the objections of governments. This prospect is to be considered next.

4.4 Consensual

Much like anarchism, consensus is a widely misunderstood concept. The word itself can be blamed in part for this, because it refers to the desired outcome rather than the process by which it is pursued.[539] A second reason for misunderstanding may be that there are so many consensus-based decision-making processes in use, with little consistent theory underpinning their design. As Butler and Rothstein lament, too "[o]ften, the consensus process is informal, vague, and very inconsistent."[540]

Having said that, the fundamentals of the process of seeking consensus are conceptually very similar to those of deliberative democracy. Whilst there is much variation in the degree of agreement required to qualify as consensus, it need not amount to unanimity. Johnson and Crawford, for example, define consensus as having been reached when "opposition to a particular policy is limited in scope and intensity (or is unreasoned), and opposition does not stem from those specially impacted by the policy."[541]

It can be seen that the elements of this particular test closely resemble those of deliberative democracy, specifically in the requirement that opposition to a proposal be reasoned, and that such opposition stem from those specifically impacted by the proposal. As for opposition being "limited in scope or intensity," this simply substitutes a subjective standard (though a high one) for the objective test of a democratic vote.

Similarly, most of the advantages claimed for consensus are advantages of deliberative democracy also. For example, it is argued that by seeking to reach consensus—even if it is not achieved—the group's members are encouraged to articulate their viewpoints persuasively and to actively seek acceptable compromise.[542] Public deliberation encourages them to do the

---

[538]Cohen, The Good Polity: Normative Analysis of the State (as in n. 300 on page 246), 22–23.

[539]However its use will be retained here because alternative terms such as "collective decision making" (as in Steven Saint and James R Lawson, *Rules for Reaching Consensus* San Francisco, CA: Jossey-Bass/Pfeiffer, 1994) are confusingly generic.

[540]C T Butler and Amy Rothstein, *On Conflict and Consensus: A Handbook on Formal Consensus Decisionmaking* Tahoma Park, MD: Food Not Bombs Publishing, 2004, 9

[541]David R Johnson and Susan P Crawford, Why Consensus Matters: The Theory Underlying ICANN's Mandate to Set Policy Standards for the Domain Name System ⟨URL: `http://www.icannwatch.org/archive/why_consensus_matters.htm`⟩

[542]Gastil (as in n. 217 on page 230), 50–53

same. Also like democratic deliberation, decision-making by consensus is an inherently egalitarian process, because all participants carry equal power to block agreement on a decision from being reached—and once agreement is reached, all can share a sense of ownership of the decision.

In fact perhaps counter-intuitively, the key difference between most consensual decision-making processes and the deliberative democratic process is not that the former require a higher level of agreement, but rather that they are in other respects procedurally less stringent than the latter. So for example, decision-making by consensus need not require that deliberation take place at all. Although it will normally be necessary for it to do so in order to bring all those involved to agreement,[543] it is also possible to gain consensus through purely strategic bargaining techniques.[544]

Some processes for decision-making by consensus do not even require all those amongst whom a consensus is declared, to have expressed their views on the issue in question. It is therefore possible for an organisation governed by consensus to declare that consensus exists on an issue to which not all of its members have even addressed their minds. As Johnson and Crawford point out, there would be no accountability behind such a declaration unless the organisation at least gathered and documented some evidence that consensus existed, by engaging in dialogue with its members.[545]

From the above it might be assumed that a consensual decision-making process would most likely be less useful than one based upon the more theoretically rigorous deliberative democracy for structuring an organisation's decision-making procedures in accordance with the democratic principle. However, well-designed consensual processes can in fact be more useful in at two relevant circumstances.

The first is where it is impossible or impractical to satisfy the preconditions of deliberative democracy. ICANN, for example, purports to act upon the consensus of the entire Internet community,[546] which, until a universal online public sphere develops,[547] is not a body capable of public deliberation in the sense required by deliberative democracy. Another example is where the only criteria for decision-making are technical and objective, since in such a case the views of the organisation's members would not

---

[543] Jürg Steiner, *Amicable Agreement Versus Majority Rule. Conflict Resolution in Switzerland* Chapel Hill, NC: University of North Carolina Press, 1974, 5

[544] Kenneth L Avio, Constitutional Contract and Discourse Ethics: The Agreement Theories of James Buchanan and Jürgen Habermas, Journal of Theoretical Politics 9:4 1997, 544–51

[545] Johnson and Crawford, Why Consensus Matters: The Theory Underlying ICANN's Mandate to Set Policy Standards for the Domain Name System (as in n. 541 on the previous page)

[546] David G Post, ICANN and the Consensus of the Internet Community ⟨URL: `http://www.icannwatch.org/archive/icann_and_the_consensus_of_the_community.htm`⟩

[547] Or an IGF-style open forum representing one in miniature is adopted by ICANN to replace its present rigid hierarchy of ACs and SOs: see sections 4.4 on page 302 and 6.3 on page 444.

be pluralistic as deliberative democracy requires.[548] Thus consensus is the standard of agreement within many technical standards organisations, including the IETF.[549]

The second case in which consensus-based processes can be employed where deliberative democratic processes cannot is where consensus is to be reached between groups rather than individuals (either in their own or in representative capacities). In common with its parent liberalism, deliberative democracy, even more so than representative democracy, has a very atomistic focus, based on the equal rights of individuals to participate in political deliberation. Lacking this theoretical baggage (or in some cases being grounded instead in communitarianism), the pursuit of consensus is a conceptually more suitable mechanism for reaching agreement at higher levels, whilst also adhering more closely to the democratic principle than representative democracy at those levels, due to the democratic deficits to which representative democracy becomes subject the further removed it is from the grass roots.

The relevance of this to the design of a network for the governance of Internet-related public policy issues lies in the fact that one of the most distinctive attributes of such a network is its multi-stakeholder composition. The individualistic focus of the discussion on deliberative democracy may have obscured the significance of the independence of each of the stakeholder groups. The conclusion of the preceding section has however brought this issue back into focus, by illustrating the disruptive tendency of governments to act unilaterally in democratic governance networks; a problem to which deliberative democracy offers no clear solution.

Consensus between stakeholder groups

We will therefore now consider the possibility of requiring that consensus be reached between the stakeholder groups on any proposal that has been democratically agreed within and across those groups, thereby essentially giving each stakeholder group the power to veto it. Since multi-stakeholder governance networks are inherently consensual structures anyway, and possess only soft power with which to enforce their decisions, the recognition of a formal requirement of consensus amongst stakeholder groups is also a more natural fit for this mechanism of governance than democratic voting.

This could address the problem of government unilateralism in two ways. First, it would provide an alternative to the use of the effective power of veto that governments already possess in many issue areas. Instead of denying the competance of the governance network to make even non-

[548] Cohen, The Good Polity: Normative Analysis of the State (as in n. 300 on page 246), 21

[549] Though perhaps in denial of the fact that subjective public policy issues are also often engaged in the development of standards: see section 2.2 on page 65.

binding decisions, and overriding its authority through the use of the coercive force of law, it will be possible for governments to formally veto any proposal the network makes without thereby undermining its authority as a forum for ongoing collaborative policy development.

Secondly, and alternatively, even if governments do continue to deny the independent authority of the governance network to develop soft law and purport to relegate it to an advisory role (which seems more likely, in the IGF's case),[550] the formal requirement that consensus be reached between all stakeholder groups would institutionalise a power of veto for the other stakeholders, that would go some way towards equalising their power with that of governments. The analogy of the "KILL SYSTEM" command of the ITS operating system, referred to at section 4.1 on page 184 is an apt one, in that giving all equal power to undermine the governance process stimulates the development of norms to regulate the use of that power.

Consociationalism

Consociationalism is the theory of a form of organisation designed to institutionalise the reservation of power to distinct stakeholder groups within a consensual decision-making forum. First and most famously described by Arend Lijphart,[551] it describes an ideal form of what may more broadly be called consensus democracy, which includes various other forms of democratic governance characterised by the sharing of power between stakeholder groups at the executive level.[552]

In its ideal type as identified by Lijphart, a consociation exhibits four characteristics:

- power is shared within a "grand coalition" comprised of representatives of all major stakeholder groups;
- the stakeholder groups are elected to the grand coalition by a system of proportional representation;
- they each enjoy a right of veto over any proposal of mutual concern, regardless of whether any of them is in the majority; and
- their "segmental autonomy" is preserved, which is to say that each group is delegated the authority to autonomously govern its own

[550] See section 6.2 on page 420.

[551] Arend Lijphart, Consociational Democracy, World Politics 21 1969

[552] Idem, *Patterns of Democracy: Government Forms and Performance in Thirty-Six Countries* New Haven, CT: Yale University Press, 1999

segment of exclusive concern (such as the governance of a particular territory, or of a particular ethnic, linguistic or religious group).[553]

As the above characteristics may suggest, consociation has been most commonly studied as a form of government, in which the various stakeholder groups of a pluralistic community are divided along territorial, ethnic, linguistic, religious or cultural lines. It is designed to reduce conflict by preserving the independence of groups entitled to be represented in government but which may not be willing to cede control to a majoritarian democracy.

Consociationalism can also be applied to other fora of governance, including multi-stakeholder governance networks.[554] However, some adaptation of Lijphart's ideal type would be required for it to provide an appropriate model of a consociational network for the Internet governance regime. In particular, since the relevant stakeholders would be governments, the private sector and civil society, it would be difficult to provide for proportional representation within the grand coalition, because the size of each stakeholder group's membership is not easily commensurable.[555]

There is however an alternative method of ensuring proportional representation, and thus also fairly institutionalising the power of mutual veto, without restricting the composition of the grand coalition. This is for an executive council of the governance network to be formed, to which each stakeholder group would elect an equal number of representatives. This executive council would be required to ratify all decisions of the grand coalition by consensus. If consensus could not be achieved, the objecting stakeholder group or groups would effectively thus exercise their power of veto.

Although this could be seen as elitist for removing direct power from the grand coalition to a meritocracy, the advantage of doing so is that it would enable the grand coalition to deliberate more freely and less strategically, knowing that ultimate political power lay at a higher level,[556] whilst at that higher level, formal decisions could be made more quickly.[557] By analogy, the grand coalition would become the public sphere of the Habermasian model, and the executive council its parliament.

Another possible objection to the above model of a consociational Internet governance network is that it is not deliberatively democratic, at any of three levels: within the grand coalition where decisions are made, within

[553]Arend Lijphart, *Democracy in Plural Societies: A Comparative Exploration* New Haven, CT: Yale University Press, 1977

[554]Chris Skelcher, Jurisdictional Integrity, Polycentrism, and the Design of Democratic Governance, Governance 18:1 2005

[555]See section 4.2 on page 204.

[556]Dryzek, Deliberative Democracy in Divided Societies: Alternatives to Agonism and Analgesia (as in n. 330 on page 252)

[557]See section 4.2 on page 198.

the executive council where they are ratified, or in the process by which the executive council is elected.

This objection is however quite easily answered, as there is no reason why Lijphart's ideal type could not be adapted to incorporate deliberative democratic principles in the process by which decisions are made by the grand coalition. It has even been said that deliberative democratic principles are already "embedded in the very structure of consociational democracies," since the process of forging consensus between stakeholder groups is naturally much closer to that of democratic deliberation than the process of majoritarian rule in a representative democratic parliament.[558]

The consensus of the executive council on whether to ratify a proposal could also be facilitated by democratic deliberation, though it is less important that it should be, since the executive councillors would already have participated in the process of deliberation within the grand coalition, and the role of the executive council is a more limited one simply designed to institutionalise the stakeholder groups' right of mutual veto. As for the process by which the councillors are elected, it would be cumbersome to attempt to do so by any other method than voting, however it would be possible for a multi-stakeholder nominating committee to deliberate upon a shortlist of candidates to be presented to the grand coalition for election.

This model of a consociational governance network has much in common with the variant of consociationalism found in the European Union. The European Parliament, containing multiple directly-elected MEPs for each country in rough proportion to their size, is the equivalent of the grand coalition. The Council of the European Union, containing only one minister from each country, equates to the executive council. To pass an EU law using the co-decision procedure, the Council is required to reach agreement on the proposed text with the Parliament, much like the process of ratification proposed here. Depending on the issue area in question, it is required to do so either by unanimous consensus, or by the "rough consensus" of qualified majority voting.[559]

Thus the option of consociation for a multi-stakeholder governance network, although relatively novel, is certainly not untested; the ILO with its sharing of power between governments, employers and workers provides another example,[560] and yet another is found in the Forest Stewardship Council (FSC); a non-governmental forum responsible for the development of standards for sustainable forestry.[561] It also accords with the conclu-

[558]Jürg Steiner, André Bächtiger and Markus Spörndli, *The Challenge of Cultural Pluralism* Westport, CT: Praeger, 2002, chap. The Consociational Theory and Deliberative Politics. A Conceptual Framework for a Cross-National Analysis, 77

[559]See section 3.2 on page 113.

[560]See section 3.2 on page 111.

[561]Although the FSC (see `http://www.fsc.org/`) does not conform to Lijphart's ideal type of consociationalism, it follows similar principles that reinforce the equality of all stakeholder groups and the mutuality of their endeavour (see generally Ronnie D Lipschutz and Cathleen

sion of the discussion of hierarchical organisational forms at section 4.2 on page 225, that a meritocracy established by a democratic or consensual process could be the most effective and legitimate structure for the organisation of a governance network, if only an appropriate such process by which for the meritocracy to be established and supervised could be found.

Such a process having been found in deliberative democracy, the resulting meritocratic/democratic/consensual hybrid—the consociational governance network—may be the fulfilment of that earlier prediction. Better yet, it also offers a solution to the problem of government unilateralism that deliberative democracy alone cannot provide.

Deliberative consensus

It next falls to consider various consensual decision-making procedures that preserve the deliberative quality demanded by deliberative democracy. These procedures are not to be considered at a macroscopic level as in the preceding subsection of this book—that is, focusing on the design of political institutions required to support consensus decision-making—but rather at the level of process: how the pursuit of consensus can best be measured, facilitated and managed within any facilitative institutional framework.

Although these questions overlap with those already dealt with in the discussion of deliberative democracy, by stepping outside that paradigm we may find new and more specific insights developed in the practice

---

Fogel, *The Emergence of Private Authority in Global Governance* Cambridge: Cambridge University Press, 2002, chap. "Regulation for the Rest of Us?" Global Civil Society and the Privatization of Transnational Regulation, 136 and Eleonore Schmidt, The Forest Stewardship Council: Using the Market to Promote Responsible Forestry, Yearbook of International Co-Operation on Environment and Development 1998/99).

Its stakeholders are categorised into three chambers according to their predominant interest: Social, Environmental, or Economic. Each chamber is then further sub-divided into North and South for members from the developed and developing worlds respectively. These meet together once every three years as the General Assembly, where any motions for new or amended statutes, by-laws, principles or policies of the FSC are debated and voted upon.

Votes are weighted to give each chamber an equal third of the vote regardless of the number of members it has, and similarly within each chamber's voting bloc, half is allocated to each of North and South. In order to pass, a motion must achieve consensus, which "is defined as the absence of sustained opposition but does not require unanimity": FSC, By-laws ⟨URL: `http://www.fsc.org/keepout/en/content_areas/77/84/files/1_1_FSC_By_Laws_2006.pdf`⟩, Article 15. Specifically, it requires a simple majority of each sub-chamber (that is, of both the North and South constituencies of each chamber), together with a two-thirds majority of the weighted votes overall. To ensure the broadest possible participation, members who are unable to afford to attend General Assembly meetings may apply to the Board for financial support, with priority being afforded to Southern members.

The Board of Directors of the FSC contains three members from each chamber, including at least one from each sub-chamber, who are elected by the General Assembly by postal ballot for three year terms. These are chosen from a slate of candidates put forward by a nominating committee headed and appointed by the Chair of the Board, which is in turn made up of one member from each chamber, including at least one each from the North and the South.

of other consensual decision-making processes, that are also compatible with the pursuit of consensus within a deliberative democratic framework. Conversely, some other pitfalls to avoid may also be revealed.

Offline consensus

Just as there are a variety of implementations of deliberative democracy such as the 21st Century Town Meeting, Deliberative Poll and citizen's jury, so too there are various implementations of consensus-based processes; indeed, there is much overlap between the two. Three examples applicable in an offline setting, that are compatible with democratic deliberation yet not explicitly derived from liberal democratic theory, will be briefly outlined here: Formal Consensus, Saint and Lawson's private sector model of consensus, and the Consensus Workshop.

Formal Consensus is a consensus-based process developed by Butler and Rothstein for decision-making within a civil society organisation, which is compatible with the ideals of deliberative democracy as applied in such a setting, but without sharing the same roots in liberal theory.[562] It was formerly known as "Secular Consensus," to differentiate it from the process used by the Quakers at their meetings, with which it shares a number of similarities.[563]

The process begins with an introductory phase in which the facilitator clarifies the process to be used, presents the proposal or issue, and facilitates the resolution of any questions put by the group for the limited purpose of clarifying the proposal or issue presented. Discussion of the proposal then takes place, and if it appears that it has the general approval of the group, a call for consensus is made immediately.

If it does not, then the process enters the next phase in which all concerns the group has with the proposal are listed, and related concerns are grouped together. This sets the stage for the following phase in which the concerns (or groups of concerns) are discussed in turn by the group with the objective of resolving them. Once all concerns have been resolved, a call for consensus is made.

If consensus still cannot be reached, then the group has three choices: to declare the proposal blocked, or for the objectors to stand aside and allow the decision to be adopted with their concerns noted, or to send the proposal to a committee which can endeavour to generate additional options to be brought back to the larger group at a later time.

Saint and Lawson have also developed a formal method for consensus-based decision-making, very similar to that of Formal Consensus, but from

[562] Butler and Rothstein (as in n. 540 on page 291), 11–15

[563] Monteze Snyder et al., *Building Consensus: Conflict And Unity* Richmond, IN: Earlham Press, 2001

a private sector perspective. The four stages of the process they put forward are as follows:

- Preconsensus (determining the group's membership and agreeing on its purpose, values and authority, settling on a definition of consensus, and setting standards for interpersonal behaviour);
- Understanding the proposal (stating and clarifying the proposal, stating any objections or concerns, and making an initial call for consensus);
- Resolving concerns (an iterative process based around discussion of the each of the expressed concerns with reference back to the group's purpose and values, followed by further calls for consensus); and
- Closing options (which include extending the time for discussion and perhaps engaging a mediator to assist the group, withdrawing the proposal or the outstanding objections, allowing the proposal to be agreed by a supermajority, or even excluding the minority from the group).[564]

Similar again but with a slightly different focus is the Consensus Workshop, one of a package of complementary techniques for participatory decision-making called the Technology of Participation or ToP®, developed by the Institute of Cultural Affairs (ICA).[565] A Consensus Workshop breaks the process of seeking consensus into five stages:

- Contexting (preparing for discussion by ensuring that all are aware of the purpose of the workshop and the process to be followed);
- Brainstorming (generating new ideas to address the issue or dispute under discussion, without yet passing judgment on any of them);
- Ordering (identifying relationships amongst the ideas and grouping them into related clusters—this is normally done by rearranging cards on which the ideas are written, but a flip-chart can also be used);
- Naming (giving each cluster a name, and then discussing them in turn beginning with the largest cluster); and
- Evaluating (once agreement is reached, the resolution is confirmed, and the significance and implications of the consensus and the next steps to be taken are discussed).[566]

[564]Saint and Lawson (as in n. 539 on page 291)

[565]See `http://www.ica-international.org/`.

[566]Laura Spencer, *Winning Through Participation* Dubuque, IA: Kendall/Hunt Publishing, 1989, 57–76

None of these three processes are prescriptive of the exact manner in which discussion of the proposal or objections must proceed, leaving the facilitator with some discretion in this regard. However there are a variety of common techniques upon which the facilitator can draw for various purposes.

For example, to determine who is entitled to speak, the facilitator's choices range from the formal such as the use of *Robert's Rules of Order*[567] (although taking care that its strict application does not provoke division rather than fostering cooperation and open discussion),[568] through to the informal such as allowing participants to engage in uninterrupted storytelling,[569] depending on the size and composition of the group.

To provide a quick, non-binding overview of the group's overall position on an issue, straw polling can be conducted,[570] using methods ranging from the conventional such as a show of hands or the use of coloured cards (holding up green to indicate agreement, red to object, and yellow to abstain or stand aside), through to the unconventional such as the use of humming to indicate agreement. This latter option, which has been used within the IETF, carries the benefit that the group can discern whether there is broad or narrow agreement upon a proposal, without the need for a vote or the identification of specific objectors.[571]

Finally to creatively overcome objections and generate solutions, techniques ranging from the relatively unstructured such as brainstorming or mind mapping,[572] through to more highly structured tools such as Dialogue Mapping,[573] policy Delphi and the Nominal Group Technique can be employed.[574] As noted above, the Consensus Workshop also incorporates a structured brainstorming session, which draws from the Delphi technique.

Online consensus

There is again much overlap between the tools available to facilitate online deliberation and those for online consensus, especially since the tools most often used for either purpose, such as discussion boards and mailing lists, are generic in design.

---

[567] Robert and Robert (as in n. 365 on page 258)

[568] Susskind (as in n. 366 on page 258)

[569] Allan J Stitt, *Mediation: A Practical Guide* London: Routledge Cavendish, 2004, 69

[570] Butler and Rothstein (as in n. 540 on page 291), 44; Saint and Lawson (as in n. 539 on page 291), 45

[571] IETF, IETF Working Group Guidelines and Procedures ⟨URL: `http://www.ietf.org/rfc/rfc1603.txt`⟩

[572] Stitt (as in n. 569), 87

[573] Jeff Conklin, *Dialogue Mapping: Building Shared Understanding of Wicked Problems* Chichester: John Wiley and Sons Ltd, 2005

[574] Andre L Delbecq, Andrew H Van de Ven and David H Gustafson, *Group Techniques for Program Planning: A Guide to Nominal Group and Delphi Processes* Glenview, IL: Scott Foresman, 1975

For example, the coloured cards technique for straw polling has been implemented by an open source software project called Monit simply by means of its developers' mailing list, to which votes of +1, 0 or -1 may be posted as the equivalents of green, yellow and red cards respectively. The circumstances in which the last of these is to be used is described on the Monit Web site as follows:

> On issues where consensus is required, this vote counts as a veto. All vetos must contain an explanation of why the veto is appropriate. Vetos with no explanation are void. No veto can be overruled. If you disagree with the veto, you should lobby the person who cast the veto. Voters intending to veto an action item should make their opinions known to the group immediately so that the problem can be remedied as early as possible.[575]

There are however also a few tools that have been developed specifically for the purposes of facilitating online consensus. These can be divided in turn into those that implement the equivalents of offline techniques, and those unique and perhaps specific to the online environment.

In the former category, there are online implementations of each of the three structured techniques for consensus decision-making noted at the end of the discussion of offline consensus above. Dialogue Mapping, which is a method of visually representing deliberative processes, can be implemented using a free product called Compendium[576] or a proprietary one called Decision Explorer.[577] Policy Delphi, which is a moderated, consensus-oriented decision-making method based upon the use of questionnaires, is implemented by the DEMOS (Delphi Mediation Online System) Project.[578] Finally the Nominal Group Technique is a method of discussion and brainstorming in which participants individually rank the group's ideas, and those rankings are aggregated with the aim of isolating an alternative that meets with the group's consensus. This has also successfully been implemented online, in a form that incorporates both synchronous and asynchronous participation.[579]

An example of a technique for facilitating online consensus that is unique to the online environment is Consensus Polling.[580] As presently implemented, Consensus Polling takes place in three main stages:

---

575 See `http://www.tildeslash.com/monit/who.php`, and compare ASF, How the ASF Works ⟨URL: `http://www.apache.org/foundation/how-it-works.html`⟩.

576 See `http://compendium.open.ac.uk/institute/index.htm`.

577 See `http://www.banxia.com/dexplore/`.

578 See `http://demos-project.org/`.

579 Kuo-Hung Tseng, Using Online Nominal Group Technique to Implement Knowledge Transfer, Journal of Engineering Education 95:4 2006

580 See `http://www.aboutus.org/Portal:ConsensusPolls`.

- Framing the issue (settling upon an agreed form of the question or problem to be addressed);
- Concurrently developing:
  - Concerns and interests (in a forum where participants discuss the interests they wish to be met by whatever solution is adopted, and the concerns they wish it to address); and
  - Background information (the compilation of a comprehensive and accurate archive of relevant background information, which can inform the listing of concerns and interests);
- Concurrently developing:
  - Solution pieces (various possible approaches for addressing the issue in question that are evaluated against all of the concerns and interests that were isolated in the preceding stage); and
  - Solution (assembling these into a composite solution upon which consensus can be reached).

At each stage, a "Yes meter" is used which records each participant's state of agreement with the current articulation of the solution being considered in that stage: either "yes, or "not yet." Consensus can be deemed to be reached when all reach "yes," or when some other high standard of agreement, such as 90%, is reached. Since participants can change between "yes" and "not yet" at any time, there must also be a defined period for which a consensus must be maintained, and a defined minimum number of participants. These variables are all settled upon before the poll begins.

The ICANN community has established an experimental Consensus Poll on the question, "What should ICANN policy with respect to new TLDs be?",[581] utilising a customised version of MediaWiki.

Consensus in Internet governance

As will be recalled from Chapter 2, consensus is the dominant method for the internal governance of the existing institutions of Internet governance that preceded the IGF, including ICANN, the IETF and the W3C. A significant factor in this is that the decentralised norms of consensus decision-making are more compatible than those of hierarchical decision-making structures with the Internet's cultural norms of decentralisation, interactivity, openness, egalitarianism and cosmopolitanism.[582]

However, as foreshadowed by the introduction to this section, there is considerable variation in each organisation's conception of consensus,

---

[581] See `http://www.icannwiki.org/Consensus:New_TLDs`.

[582] See section 2.2 on page 57.

including the degree of agreement required, the processes by which it should be fostered, and how and by whom it is declared.

Here, the different conceptions of consensus held by four of the major institutions of Internet governance—ICANN, APNIC, the IETF and the W3C—will be briefly compared, without retreading ground already covered when analysing their organisational structures.[583]

ICANN

In July 1999, then ICANN Chair Esther Dyson testified before the United States House of Representatives that

> ICANN is nothing more or less than the embodiment of the Internet community as a whole. It reflects the participation of a large and growing number of technical, business, public-interest, academic, and other segments of the Internet community. It is this collection of diverse interests and experiences that produces ICANN policies and decisions, as a statement of the consensus of the participants.[584]

Taking this statement at face value, it implies the existence of something like an online public sphere within which consensus on ICANN policies and decisions is developed, along with mechanisms by which for that consensus to be transmitted to its Board of Directors and implemented.[585] As such, it provides a simple but conceptually sound model of a governance network that draws upon the consensus of all stakeholders both to ground its legitimacy and to structure its decision-making processes.

Unfortunately however, it is quite fictitious.[586] None of its assumptions were fulfilled by ICANN in 1999, and they are still yet to be fully realised today, with the result that ICANN remains closer to an oligarchy than any other organisational form.[587] Even so, it is possible to isolate four basic assumptions behind Dyson's aspirational claim for ICANN, and to sketch ICANN's progress towards fulfilling them:

- If the consensus of the Internet community is to be reflective at all, there must exist a public sphere within which for it to be formed and articulated through public discourse. Although this is the promise of

[583]See sections 2.1 on page 40 and 2.2 on page 51.

[584]Esther Dyson, Prepared Testimony ⟨URL: `http://www.icann.org/correspondence/dyson-testimony-22jul99.htm`⟩

[585]Compare Habermas, *Between Facts and Norms: Contributions to a Discourse Theory of Law and Democracy* (as in n. 209 on page 227), 380

[586]See section 2.1 on page 46.

[587]See section 4.2 on page 199.

Internet democracy and is found in microcosm within certain virtual communities, there is no persuasive evidence that it exists on a large scale.

In an endeavour to provide a forum for outreach and informal consensus-building within the Internet community at large, ICANN holds regular open meetings in various cities around the world,[588] and hosts asynchronous online fora.[589] Open meetings are webcast, and beginning with the Sa o Paulo meeting in December 2006, a Web site designed to facilitate remote participation, based on that developed for the first meeting of the IGF, was also made available.[590] The limitation of these fora is that any consensus developed within them does not feed directly into ICANN's governance processes.

A more direct link exists between ICANN's Board and the narrower, more manageable segments of the Internet community represented by its three Supporting Organisations, which still encompass a fairly broad cross-section of the Internet community through their constituency groups.[591]

However in general, ICANN does not require the SOs or their constituencies to reach consensus (indeed, on one view these top–down structures have been "gerrymandered to prevent emergence of true consensus".)[592] In fact, the only mention of consensus at all in ICANN's current Bylaws applies to the process by which the CCNSO is to build consensus within the community of ccTLD managers over ccTLD-related issues.[593] Consensus is said to exist where at least 14 of the 18 voting members of its Council are in agreement.[594]

None of the other SOs are charged to operate by consensus at all, and neither is there is any mechanism to broker consensus between them. The GNSO Council uses a system of voting based on *Robert's Rules of Order*, save that the gTLD registries and registrars exercise half of the vote, and the other constituencies share the other half.[595] The Address Council of the ASO follows a similar but simpler pro-

---

[588] See `http://www.icann.org/meetings/`.

[589] See `http://forum.icann.org/`.

[590] See `http://sp.icann.org/`, and subsequently `http://public.icann.org`.

[591] In the ASO's case these are the RIRs, in the CCNSO's case are organisations for each of the five geographic regions recognised by ICANN, and in the GNSO's case are commercial and business users, gTLD registries, ISPs, non-commercial users, registrars and intellectual property owners: see `http://gnso.icann.org/` for links to their respective Web sites.

[592] David R Johnson and Susan P Crawford, What's Wrong With ICANN—And How to Fix It ⟨URL: `http://www.icannwatch.org/archive/how2fixicann.htm`⟩

[593] Though Article VI, Section 3(a) of the Bylaw revisions from 31 March 1999 to 12 February 2002 also formerly provided that the SOs are to "be formed through community consensus"; see `http://www.icann.org/general/archive-bylaws/`.

[594] ICANN, Bylaws (as in n. 39 on page 41), Article IX, Sections 1 and 4(11)

[595] GNSO Council, New Rules of Procedure ⟨URL: `http://gnso.icann.org/council/new-procedures.shtml`⟩, Articles 3.6, 5.4

cedure.[596] As for the constituency groups—too many to go into individually[597]—they are left to devise their own means of making decisions.

- Assuming that there were effective fora in the public sphere within which for consensus on ICANN's policies to be formed, ICANN would also require the means to discern this consensus. This is straightforward in the case of the SOs which are represented on ICANN's board, but less so for those other stakeholder groups which are not. This is where ICANN's five Advisory Committees could come in. Unlike the SOs, the ACs are not stakeholders in themselves (and thus do not have voting power within ICANN), but rather act as conduits for the transmission of the views of specified classes of external stakeholders to ICANN's board.

  Thus the Operating Principles of the GAC state that it is "not a decision making body," and simply provide for the Chair to summarise the views expressed by its participants when reporting to the ICANN Board.[598] Similarly, the ALAC's main role is to coordinate the activities of the RALOs, which in turn serve the purpose of drawing in input from their constituent At-Large Structures, and to transmit this to ICANN's Board.[599] However, in the absence of an effective online public sphere, there is no particular reason why such input would or even should amount to consensus.

- Third, but following from the second point, if there exist both effective fora within which for consensus to be formed, and the means of discerning that consensus, there should also be a process for ICANN to document it. Thus earlier in ICANN's history, both Post,[600] and Johnson and Crawford,[601] suggested that ICANN be required when purporting to take actions by consensus, to table a report demonstrating that this was so.

  According to Johnson and Crawford, the report should include amongst other matters an analysis of all substantial impacts of the proposal in question, a description of outreach conducted to those potentially affected, a summary of the arguments made for and against the proposal by impacted parties, and an analysis of why opposition

[596] ASO, Memorandum of Understanding ⟨URL: http://aso.icann.org/docs/aso-mou.html⟩

[597] But see section 4.4 on page 307.

[598] GAC, Operating Principles ⟨URL: http://gac.icann.org/web/home/GAC_Operating_Principles.doc⟩, Principles 2 and 40

[599] See generally ALAC, Charter ⟨URL: http://icannwiki.org/ALAC_Charter⟩

[600] Post, ICANN and the Consensus of the Internet Community (as in n. 546 on page 292)

[601] David R Johnson and Susan P Crawford, What an ICANN Consensus Report Should Look Like ⟨URL: http://www.icannwatch.org/archive/what_icann_consensus_should_look_like.htm⟩

to the proposal is believed to be limited, unreasoned, or arising only from those not impacted by its implementation.

A process broadly similar to this is now enshrined in Annexes A and B to ICANN's Bylaws, which set out a detailed Policy Development Process (PDP) for the development of new policies by the GNSO and CCNSO respectively.[602]

- Finally, ICANN must have both the will and ability to act upon any consensus that has developed amongst its stakeholders and that it has discerned and documented. Its will is limited only by the fact that its Board always retains the discretion not to act upon the consensus of the community, whether expressed informally at public meetings or online fora, or formally through a PDP.

  ICANN's ability to give effect to the consensus of the Internet community is also restricted by institutional limitations on the scope of its activities that are required to be conducted consensually. In fact, a CCNSO PDP, requiring the approval of a two-thirds majority of CCNSO members, is the only means by which ICANN's activities are formally subjected to a consensual test, and a loose one at that.

  It may be that there are certain matters—such as the Board's dealings with registries—that ought not to be governed by consensus, because reliance upon other forms of governance, such as markets, is more legitimate or effective in those circumstances.[603] However, ICANN

[602] A PDP may be initiated either by the ICANN Board, by the Council of the SO in question, or at the request of an Advisory Committee, in all cases subject to the approval of ICANN's General Counsel, and (except in the case of a GNSO PDP initiated by ICANN's Board) also subject to a supermajority resolution of the Council of the applicable SO.

Evidence of the views of stakeholders on the proposed new policy may be gathered by a task force convened for that purpose constituted primarily by representatives from the SO's constituencies. Alternatively their views may be sought by a simple report from the self-organised groups representing each constituency. In either case, comments on the proposal, which will be posted on ICANN's Web site, are also accepted from the public at large.

An initial report on the proposal, either prepared by the task force or produced by compiling the individual reports of constituents and the public, is then posted for comment of all ICANN bodies and the public, and the comments received upon this are in turn incorporated into a final report that is submitted to the Council of the applicable SO.

The process then diverges somewhat between the GNSO and CCNSO. The simpler procedure applies to the former, whose recommendation on the proposal is simply transmitted to ICANN's Board. If the Council's recommendation is reached by a two-thirds majority, then the Board may in turn only veto it by a two-thirds majority of its own, in which case the Board and Council must discuss the impasse before the Council makes a further recommendation to the Board which is treated in the same manner as the first. A final 10 day public comment period precedes the Board's final decision.

As for the CCNSO, its Council is charged to endeavour to reach consensus on the proposal (which is defined as at least 14 of the Council's 18 members), but in any case its recommendation is transmitted in a report to all CCNSO members, who may ratify the proposed policy by a two-thirds majority. If they do, it will then be transmitted to ICANN's Board, which may only veto it by a two-thirds majority, in which case the Board and Council must discuss the matter before the process iterates back again to the Council, the CCNSO members and the Board in like manner as before.

[603] See section 4.1 on page 191.

cannot truly live up to the claims made of it by Esther Dyson in 1999 while the scope of application of consensus decision-making within ICANN is as limited as it presently is. An organisation cannot accurately be said to be governed by consensus unless it is so governed at all levels of policy development, from agenda-setting through to decision-making.[604]

APNIC

Less time needs to be spent on discussing APNIC, the RIR for the Asia Pacific region and a constituent of ICANN's ASO, as its procedures for decision-making by consensus are much simpler and more open than those of ICANN.

APNIC's policy development process is self-described as one in which policies are "developed by the membership and the broader Internet community through a bottom–up process of consultation and consensus."[605]

The main forum in which this process takes place are the twice-yearly APNIC Open Policy Meetings (OPMs), held in various locations within the region, and which are open to APNIC members and non-members alike. For those from developing countries who could not otherwise attend an OPM in person, APNIC grants a number of fellowships. Remote participation is also facilitated using video streaming, audio streaming, live transcripts, Jabber chat software and podcasts.[606]

The other fora for the policy development process are the mailing lists of APNIC's Special Interest Groups (SIGs), of which there are currently seven on topics ranging from National Internet Registries (NIR) to DNS operation, routing and IPv6. These are also open to non-members, and are publicly archived.

A proposal for the adoption or amendment of an APNIC policy begins by tabling notice of the proposal to the relevant SIG mailing list and the SIG Chair at least four weeks prior to an OPM at which it is intended to be agreed. At the OPM, the proposal must meet with consensus both at the relevant SIG session, and also at the plenary Member Meeting. For this purpose, "consensus" is simply defined as "general agreement" as observed by the Chair of the meeting. If consensus is not reached at either stage, the SIG may resolve that the proposal should be amended for submission at a following OPM, or be withdrawn.

Following an OPM at which a proposal meets with consensus, an eight-week comment period begins, during which the proposal remains open for discussion on the relevant SIG mailing list. At the expiry of this period, the

---

[604] Biegel (as in n. 60 on page 19), 223

[605] Tseng (as in n. 579 on page 301)

[606] See http://www.apnic.net/meetings/remote/.

SIG Chair and co-chairs will determine whether any substantial objections to the proposal have been made. If so, then the proposal fails, and again the SIG may determine to amend it before it is proposed again, or to withdraw it.

A proposal that survives the comment period then goes to the Executive Council of APNIC, which will normally simply endorse the proposal as formal APNIC policy, but may refer it back to the SIG for further discussion if the Executive Council itself is unable to agree upon the proposal by majority vote, or may require a majority vote of endorsement by APNIC members. This introduces the possibility that the APNIC policy development process may not remain purely consensual throughout, as the last stage of decision-making may employ a hybrid of consensus and democracy.

IETF

The process for decision-making by consensus within the IETF has more in common with that of APNIC than that of ICANN. The movement of a specification through the IETF standards track from an Internet draft agreed within a Working Group, to a Proposed Standard (and thence a Draft Standard and eventually an Internet Standard) accepted by the community as a whole, has already been described in some detail at section 2.2 on page 52.

The IETF process requires consensus to a proposal to be formed at three levels within each stage of this standards track process. It must first achieve consensus within its originating Working Group. Once a rough consensus appears to have been reached, the Chair makes a "last call" for comments from the Working Group that normally lasts for two weeks, before forwarding the specification to the IESG.

The IESG then publishes the specification to an IETF-wide mailing list where a further "last call" for comments is made, lasting another two weeks for specifications that originate within an IETF Working Group, or four weeks for those submitted from outside the IETF.

The third and final level within which consensus must be obtained to the specification before it passes that stage of the standards track process is the IESG itself. The IESG may approve the document and request the RFC Editor to publish it, send it back to the Working Group for revision, or even reject it outright.[607]

The IETF's definition of consensus, such as it is, is found in RFC 1603 which states:

> IETF consensus does not require that all participants agree

[607] IETF, The Internet Standards Process—Revision 3 (as in n. 5 on page 31), para 6.1

> although this is, of course, preferred. In general the dominant view of the working group shall prevail. (However, it must be noted that "dominance" is not to be determined on the basis of volume or persistence, but rather a more general sense of agreement.) Consensus can be determined by balloting, humming, or any other means on which the Working Group agrees (by rough consensus, of course).[608]

Allowing Working Groups the flexibility of devising their own means of establishing rough consensus is naturally empowering, and limits the scope for the process to be subverted through strategic games. On the other hand, it places a lot of responsibility on the shoulders of Working Group Chairs, leaving them open to challenge if they should declare a rough consensus of the Working Group as a whole over the objections of a small minority.[609]

In the case of disputes such as this that cannot be resolved within the Working Group, nor by the relevant Area Director, the IESG steps in to adjudicate. The IESG will also conduct an internal review when a decision of its own is challenged. These appeals and reviews may be further appealed to the IAB whose decision is final. Only in cases where the above procedures are insufficient to fairly and openly address the concerns of all parties, ISOC's Board of Trustees may also hear an appeal, resolving it by whatever means it sees fit to adopt.[610]

It can be seen from this that the IETF standards process also displays hybrid qualities; being consensual at the grass roots level, but remaining subject to the judicious use of hierarchical power at higher levels of governance when the pursuit of rough consensus has failed. But then, this is only a reflection of the fact that as open and inclusive as the IETF may be, it is fundamentally a meritocracy in practice.[611]

W3C

The implementation of consensus-based decision-making in the standards development process of the W3C falls somewhere in between the formal stakeholder consultation of ICANN's PDP and the self-selected, community-driven processes of the IETF and APNIC. The standards development process itself has already been described at section 2.2 on page 56, so here our focus will be restricted to the means by which consensus is assessed at each stage through which a specification progresses from its genesis as a Working Draft towards its ultimate acceptance as a W3C Recommendation.

---

[608] IETF, IETF Working Group Guidelines and Procedures (as in n. 571 on page 300)

[609] The same observation applies to chairs of APNIC SIGs, who are placed in the same position.

[610] Idem, The Internet Standards Process—Revision 3 (as in n. 5 on page 31), para 6.5

[611] See section 4.2 on page 203.

In contrast to the IETF and APNIC processes, it is not a precondition of the submission of a Working Draft to public review that it has already gained consensus within a Working Group. Rather, a First Public Working Draft is released while the Working Group is still deliberating, in order that early public review of the developing specification from within and outside the W3C may be obtained. This is particularly important for the W3C since its membership is much more exclusive than that of the IETF.

By the time it is finalised however the Chair of the Working Group is encouraged to ensure that a Working Draft represents the group's consensus, defined as where:

> [a] substantial number of individuals in the set support the decision and nobody in the set registers a Formal Objection. Individuals in the set may abstain. Abstention is either an explicit expression of no opinion or silence by an individual in the set. Unanimity is the particular case of consensus where all individuals in the set support the decision (i.e., no individual in the set abstains).[612]

The Chair is also directed to ensure that there is a sufficient level of active participation that a specification does not achieve consensus simply through apathy.[613]

In seeking to reach consensus the Working Group utilises a combination of electronic mailing lists (public for technical work, and private for internal administration), teleconferences, and face-to-face meetings in conjunction with IRC to facilitate remote participation.

Where consensus fails, the Working Group may resort to voting or may proceed despite one or more participants' formal objections, provided that these objections are forwarded to the Advisory Committee when seeking to advance the specification to the stage of Candidate Recommendation.

Before progression to a Candidate Recommendation, the specification undergoes a "Last Call" period of at least three weeks during which public comment is sought and, once received, must be formally addressed in writing. This does not extend so far as to require public consensus on the specification in the sense defined above; one respect in which the W3C process more closely resembles the PDPs of ICANN which emphasise consultation over consensus.

An analogous period of public comment applies to the progression from Candidate Recommendation to Proposed Recommendation, once the specification has been implemented in software, and to the four week period

---

612 W3C, Process Document (as in n. 106 on page 56), para 3.3

613 The same consideration is also reflected in the design of the Consensus Poll, though it contrasts with, say, the Apache Software Foundation's "lazy consensus approach: a few positive votes with no negative vote": ASF (as in n. 575 on page 301).

before a Proposed Recommendation may be considered for acceptance as a W3C Recommendation.

The final level at which consensus is sought before a Proposed Recommendation progresses to a W3C Recommendation is that of the W3C's Advisory Committee, representing the W3C as a whole. The achievement of consensus in this instance is judged by the Director, the W3C Chair and its Chief Operating Officer (COO), by the same standards as those by which it is assessed within a Working Group.

A formal objection to the decision of a Working Group Chair that consensus has been reached may be made to the Director, Tim Berners-Lee. The Director also exercises the final decision on the acceptance of a specification at the stage of W3C Recommendation. These and other powers that may be unilaterally exercised by Berners-Lee, essentially as the W3C's Benevolent Dictator For Life, illustrate that it too is best characterised as possessing a hybrid form displaying both consensual and hierarchical characteristics.

Criticisms

It has been seen that even within the sometimes idealistic Internet technical community, it is rare to find a form of organisation that is governed solely by consensus. This is not so much because the cultural norms of the Internet are any less compatible in principle with consensual than with anarchistic ordering, as because consensus is an ideal case of anarchism, the conditions for which are difficult to realise in a pluralistic world.

This is particularly so in certain issue areas, and for certain types of dispute. These most notably include deep seated culture clashes that Dryzek refers to as "mutually contradictory assertions of identity,"[614] and clashes between competing claims of right, in which it is in neither party's interests to agree to a consensual resolution. These two areas of difficulty will be dealt with in turn, before concluding with a brief look at some of the other deficiencies of consensual ordering.

Consensus and culture

It is a commonly expressed view that the "rough consensus" approach of the IETF is only suited to a largely technical organisation, that is capable of resolving disputes that arise between its members by applying principles that are, if not entirely objective, then at least widely shared. Whilst it may

[614] Dryzek, Deliberative Democracy in Divided Societies: Alternatives to Agonism and Analgesia (as in n. 330 on page 252), 218–219

have been so in the past, the stakeholders of today's Internet are no longer such a group.[615] As Lemley observes:

> Even a brief look at the Net should dispel any notion that netizens are a homogenous group with a strong community of interest. White supremacists, libertarians, communitarians, and communists all coexist on the Net; so do rich and poor, black and white, nerds and literati. If we brought them all together in a room, virtual or real, it is doubtful they would reach even a rough consensus on virtually any subject.[616]

This is not a view confined to Internet cynics. Rather, it can be seen as an application of the broader and more venerable political theory of agonism, which holds that in any pluralistic community, conflict is inevitable and unending. The agonist spurns attempts to broker consensus within such communities, in favour of the accommodation of "a vibrant clash of democratic political positions."[617] Mouffe contends:

> We have to accept that every consensus exists as a temporary result of a provisional hegemony, as a stabilization of power, and that it always entails some form of exclusion. The idea that power could be dissolved through a rational debate and that legitimacy could be based on pure rationality are illusions, which can endanger democratic institutions.[618]

Bearing out the view that the scope for a pluralistic organisation to make decisions by consensus is very limited, Kofi Annan has described the case of the General Assembly of the United Nations:

> In recent years, the number of General Assembly resolutions approved by consensus has increased steadily. That would be good if it reflected a genuine unity of purpose among Member States in responding to global challenges. But unfortunately, consensus (often interpreted as requiring unanimity) has become an end in itself. It is sought first within each regional group and then at the level of the whole. This has not proved an effective way of reconciling the interests of Member States. Rather, it prompts the Assembly to retreat into generalities, abandoning any serious effort to take action. Such real debates

[615]Mueller, *Ruling the Root: Internet Governance and the Taming of Cyberspace* (as in n. 21 on page 35), 163–164

[616]Lemley (as in n. 87 on page 23), 1270

[617]Chantal Mouffe, Deliberative Democracy or Agonistic Pluralism ⟨URL: `http://users.unimi.it/dikeius/pw_72.pdf`⟩, 15–16

[618]Ibid., 17

> as there are tend to focus on process rather than substance and many so-called decisions simply reflect the lowest common denominator of widely different opinions.[619]

This does not imply that a more substantive consensus could not be achieved by a more effective process, involving prior deliberation about principles, norms, and rules rather than just bargaining.[620] However the root difficulty that remains is that to even begin to resolve a dispute communicatively requires what Habermas calls a "shared lifeworld"; a background consensus which provides the participants with resources for managing the conflict and reduces the scope of issues in dispute.[621] In a transnational and cross-cultural context, it may be that even this is lacking,[622] and that the only commonality between the parties will be their agreement to a minimal set of fair procedures.[623]

Dryzek, while frankly acknowledging that "[i]n a pluralistic world, consensus is unattainable, unnecessary, and undesirable,"[624] still maintains that democratic deliberation offers the best prospect of facilitating the development of substantive consensus from such a minimal shared base of agreement on procedural norms. In comparison to agonism which offers no solutions to the difficulties of reaching agreement in the face of clashes of culture and identity, Dryzek maintains that such contentious issues can be engaged deliberatively within a public sphere at some distance from the state, using appropriate communicative forms.[625]

Even granting this, it does not completely address the potential for cultural differences to impair deliberation. A specific case that illustrates just how intractable these differences can be is that of cross-cultural communication.[626] Cognitive linguists have determined that those who speak different languages actually think differently as well. In his pioneering work on linguistic relativity, Whorf wrote that

> each language is not merely a reproducing instrument for voicing ideas but rather is itself the shaper of ideas, the pro-

[619]Annan (as in n. 40 on page 104), 40

[620]Thomas Risse, Let's Argue!: Communicative Action in World Politics, International Organization 54 2000, 20-1

[621]Habermas, *Between Facts and Norms: Contributions to a Discourse Theory of Law and Democracy* (as in n. 209 on page 227), xvi

[622]See section 3.4 on page 170.

[623]Cohen, Deliberative Democracy (as in n. 301 on page 246), 193

[624]Dryzek, *Deliberative Democracy and Beyond* (as in n. 310 on page 248), 170

[625]Idem, Deliberative Democracy in Divided Societies: Alternatives to Agonism and Analgesia (as in n. 330 on page 252)

[626]W Kymlicka, *Democracy's Edges* Cambridge: Cambridge University Press, 1999, chap. Citizenship in an Era of Globalization

gram and the guide for the individual's mental activity, for his analysis of impressions.[627]

Empirical research has supported this observation, for example demonstrating that all languages have lexical gaps in which it is literally impossible to express a thought that can be expressed in in other languages, and that attempting to fill these gaps by paraphrasing generates extraneous implications not present in the original.[628] Further, there is evidence that speakers of a language do not even think of things that they have no way of expressing in language; for example speakers of a language in which a group of items is described by their composition but not their number, will notice the former and not the latter.[629]

Such deep problems of cross-cultural communication are troublesome for Habermas, who makes three idealising assumptions in his model of conflict resolution on the basis of reasoned agreement: that participants can assume that they each mean the same thing by the same words and expressions, that they each consider themselves rationally accountable, and that once agreement is reached the assumptions underlying their consensus (for example as to its truth or justice) will not subsequently prove mistaken. As he acknowledges, to the extent that these assumptions are not realised, agreements reached are open to challenge.[630]

There is no simple solution to such problems, though in general they point to the need for mechanisms by which participants in deliberation are encouraged (or forced) to become more linguistically and epistemologically cosmopolitan.[631] Needless to say, this is potentially an ambitious programme, which although capable of being pursued by deliberative means, may be time-consuming and require expert facilitation.

Having said that, the same sorts of problems are endemic to our multicultural world in many other contexts beyond that of deliberative democratic and consensual decision-making. In particular, there is no reason to think that an hierarchical or anarchistic form for a transnational governance network could overcome them to any greater extent than the deliberative democratic or consensual forms.

---

[627] Benjamin Lee Whorf, *Language, Thought and Reality* Cambridge, MA: MIT Press, 1956, 212

[628] Stephen C Levinson, *Language and Conceptualization* Cambridge: Cambridge University Press, 1997, chap. From Outer to Inner Space, 16–18

[629] Ibid., 34

[630] Habermas, *Between Facts and Norms: Contributions to a Discourse Theory of Law and Democracy* (as in n. 209 on page 227), xv

[631] Thomas C Hilde, *The Internet in Public Life* Lanham, MD: Rowman & Littlefield Publishers, 2004, chap. The Cosmopolitan Project: Does the Internet Have a Global Public Face?, 120–122

Consensus and rational choice

An additional limitation of which consensual forms of organisation are accused is that there are some issues that it would not be rational for participants to agree on by consensus. As this is essentially the same criticism as made of anarchistic ordering,[632] it will not be reiterated in full here.[633]

Instead, particular attention will be given here to one specific instance in which it is said that submission to consensual ordering would be irrational and indeed inappropriate: where there are (in Weinberg's words) competing claims of right, for example between multiple applicants to ICANN for the right to manage new gTLDs.[634]

This criticism has both a narrow application and a broader one. In its narrow application, it holds that the determination of particular competing claims of right, or the distribution of wealth among particular parties, cannot be conducted by consensus. This much is doubtless correct. Certainly, Network Solutions did not consent to the admission of new entrants into its formerly monopolistic market for domain name registration—why should it have?

However, this charge can be accepted without derogating from the use of consensus as an organising principle for ICANN as a governance network. This is because the place of consensus within ICANN is at a policy development, not an operational level. Unlike under an anarchistic regime in which ordering always remains voluntary, it is possible for a consensual governance network to institutionalise the bureaucratic application of consensually agreed policies. Thus for ICANN, whereas policies covering gTLD issues in general are formed by consensus, the grant of custodianship of individual gTLDs by reference to these policies is an operational matter to be decided bureaucratically (or by some other consensually agreed or otherwise legitimate mechanism of governance, such as through markets—or better yet, a hybrid which corrects for market deficiencies).

Although the bureaucratic determination of competing claims of right will necessarily result in wealth being distributed between stakeholders unevenly (an outcome which the affected stakeholders probably could not reach consensus upon antecedently), this does not delegitimize the outcome. After all, for the liberal, consensus is not an end in itself but a means of pursuing the democratic principle. Thus a majority cannot deny a minority benefits that they have gained through a consensual process. Johnson and Crawford put this by saying that although "[t]he creation of

---

[632]See section 4.1 on page 194.

[633]Though one response to that charge, the capacity for norms to support consensual processes, will be dealt with under the next heading.

[634]Weinberg, ICANN and the Problem of Legitimacy (as in n. 71 on page 49), 252; and see Mueller, *Ruling the Root: Internet Governance and the Taming of Cyberspace* (as in n. 21 on page 35), 216.

new TLDs will have an effect on existing registries, registrars, registrants and various other parties like trademark owners . . . [it] will not require any of these actors to implement or abide by a new set of rules."[635]

The second and broader sense of the above criticism of Weinberg implies that consensus could never develop even around the domain name policies that underlie the determination of competing claims of right, due to the intervention of strategic interests. However, this is far from a foregone conclusion. If the procedures by which ICANN developed policy by consensus were more deliberative and its structures were more open, there is no reason why a consensual balance between the interests of all stakeholders could not be reached.

As it stands, ICANN's stakeholders do not for the most part engage with each other in the policy development process, and therefore have no occasion to even attempt to reach such a compromise discursively. The process of seeking consensus by consulting stakeholders separately, aggregating their views, and attempting to balance them by executive fiat, is indeed open to criticism, but such criticism does not extend to decision-making by consensus in general.

Consensual deficits

The final group of criticisms of consensus-based decision-making to be discussed here relate to its potential to become dysfunctional even where complicating factors such as cultural difference and competing claims of right are absent.

One such dysfunction, the phenomenon of "groupthink," is ironically most prevalent in more cohesive groups, because their members are reluctant to break the group's consensus, giving them a propensity to make decisions rashly.[636] Conversely, consensus-based decision-making can lead to polarisation and deadlock,[637] whereby the views with which participants enter the discussion become entrenched in more extreme forms, so that consensus becomes more difficult and takes much longer to achieve. This phenomenon is most evident where the views in question run along stakeholder lines and the stakeholder groups are separated,[638] as occurs in a segmentally autonomous consociation, in ICANN's SOs, and amongst members of self-selecting virtual communities.

---

[635] Johnson and Crawford, Why Consensus Matters: The Theory Underlying ICANN's Mandate to Set Policy Standards for the Domain Name System (as in n. 541 on page 291)

[636] Clark McCauley, The Nature of Social Influence in Groupthink: Compliance and Internalization, Journal of Personality and Social Psychology 57 1987

[637] D J Isenberg, Group Polarization: A Critical Review and Meta-Analysis, Journal of Personality and Social Psychology 50:6 1986

[638] Dryzek, Deliberative Democracy in Divided Societies: Alternatives to Agonism and Analgesia (as in n. 330 on page 252)

These problems may be countered by the use of deliberative democratic techniques designed to introduce participants to a range of viewpoints other than their own (by requiring them to actively engage with other participants, and through the provision of factual background materials), and by requiring them to justify their views against these other perspectives through public reason. As these techniques have been described at length, no more time need be spent on them here.

A much more problematic dysfunction that is inherent to consensual decision-making is that minorities are granted disproportional power over the process. This enables them to abuse their effective right of veto by engaging in blocking tactics and other strategic games rather than seeking mutually satisfactory outcomes in good faith. A common solution to this is to allow for "rough consensus" in place of unanimity, though this can exacerbate the problems of limited deliberation and lack of accountability inherent in some forms of decision-making by consensus, as Mueller notes, stating:

> As soon as one concedes that one can move forward on the basis of "rough consensus" rather than unanimity, one has eliminated what is supposed to be the prime virtue of consensus-based processes: the need to persuade, rather than overrule or ignore, minorities. Unanimity is a stringent check on the abuse of power. "Rough consensus," on the other hand, is informal and cannot be precisely defined and measured. It must be "recognised" or "declared."[639]

Another common solution, which as we have seen is often used in conjunction with the first, is to structure the organisation as a hybrid between consensual and democratic or hierarchical decision-making, wherein either a majority, or a meritocratic elite (who should be consensually or democratically selected), have the institutional power to resolve internal disputes and deadlocks.

A third means to dissuade participants from the abuse of their right of veto is through the development of supportive norms that constrain the use of that power except where it is essential to protect deeply-held interests of the blocking party that the interests of the group ought not to be able to override.[640]

According to Butler and Rothstein, the applicable norms are trust, respect, unity of purpose, nonviolence, self empowerment, cooperation, conflict resolution, commitment to the group, active participation, equal

[639]Mueller, *Ruling the Root: Internet Governance and the Taming of Cyberspace* (as in n. 21 on page 35), 216

[640]Skelcher (as in n. 554 on page 295), 105

access to power, and patience.[641] For Skelcher, the norms of cooperation and recognition of the equality of all parties are most central.[642]

There is no template by which such norms can be inculcated, but they tend to develop spontaneously when members of the network cooperate towards mutually beneficial outcomes, and also tend to be self-reinforcing.[643] This process of building social capital can be "kick-started" by the use of designs for deliberation that encourage participants to find mutually acceptable outcomes rather than to adopt adversarial positions.

But at the end of the day, perhaps the best defence of decision-making by consensus in the context of a transnational governance network is that the failure of consensus is a strong indication that it was not appropriate for the issue in question to be dealt with through the soft power of a governance network anyway, and that it should instead fall through to be dealt with by some other mechanism. Johnson and Crawford write:

> Failure to reach a global consensus may be a success rather than a failure, however, because it leaves undisturbed the power of many diverse and decentralized actors to make their own decisions. These actors may find even better ways to proceed than might have emerged from a compromising committee.[644]

It can thus be considered that a consensual governance network is merely one supplier in a competitive market of governance solutions, and as in the case of the open source software development model, it is freedom of exit—the ability for participants to vote with their feet—that makes these suppliers accountable. The W3C has also conceptualised the process of seeking consensus as being market-driven, stating:

> Groups strive to reach consensus in order to provide a single solution acceptable to the market at-large. If a group makes a decision that causes the market to fragment—despite agreement by those participating in the decision—the decision does not reflect a single market and therefore the group has failed to reach true consensus.[645]

In practice, the achievement of consensus between stakeholders will be central to the success of a transnational governance network no matter

[641] Butler and Rothstein (as in n. 540 on page 291), 20–23
[642] Skelcher (as in n. 554 on page 295), 103
[643] Uphoff (as in n. 196 on page 220)
[644] Johnson and Crawford, The Idea of ICANN (as in n. 50 on page 192)
[645] W3C, Process Document (as in n. 106 on page 56), and compare also the stand-off between the competing SPF and Sender ID specifications referred to at section 2.2 on page 52.

which of the four forms of organisation examined in this chapter it adopts. The main benefit of adopting the consensual form is that it also reflects this reality institutionally in the organisation's design, thereby both providing an early gauge of the likely ultimate adoption of the network's soft law output by its participants, and also ensuring in accordance with the democratic principle that those who are to be governed by that law are those responsible for writing it.

4.5 Multi-stakeholder public policy development

Previous chapters introduced governance by network as the only mechanism capable of bringing together multiple stakeholder groups to address public policy issues in concert. Since governments are amongst these stakeholders, the network may determine that they should address a policy issue through domestic legislation or intergovernmental agreement. If a market-based solution is more appropriate, private sector stakeholders will be in a position to fill it. If an issue is better addressed through norms, civil society can explicate these norms publicly. Or all three groups may act together, by collaboratively developing an independent body of transnational law for the guidance of their respective constituents.

What had not been discussed until this chapter was exactly how they ought to make those sorts of collective decisions. In a sense, consensus is the archetypal decision-making structure for governance networks, since the organisation's internal structure in that case mirrors the relationship of the organisation to its stakeholders. However this chapter has revealed elements from each of the four broad types of organisation structure for decision-making which are instructive for the design of a transnational governance network developing Internet related public policy.

From anarchism, it was found that the most empowering structure for participants in any organisation may in fact be the lack of structure—or rather, the lack of constraint as to the structures they may voluntarily organise themselves, through the non-coercive mechanisms of markets, norms and architecture. Whilst the resulting network is often more efficient, and more consonant with Internet culture than hierarchical alternatives, this very lack of control also makes it difficult to ensure the network's adherence to liberal democratic values such as accountability and transparency. The hybridisation of anarchistic with hierarchical ordering was suggested as a possible method of addressing this deficiency.

From hierarchical ordering, it was found that meritocracy could provide an effective structure for a governance network, being designed to ensure that those most qualified to rule did so, rather than the most powerful or privileged. Perhaps unexpectedly, it was also found to exist prominently on the Internet, within the IETF (in a hybrid consensual form) and many open source software projects. However, in order for it to accord with the democratic principle, it was necessary either that the criteria for selection of the meritocracy be agreed by consensual or democratic means (as in the IETF's case), or that freedom of exit and a number of other conditions found in the case of open source software be fulfilled.

From democracy, liberal theory was identified as the source of the democratic principle, that any interference with an individual's liberty requires their consent. However, it was found that pure direct democracy, or representative democracy that simply mirrored the majority's preferences, could lead to illiberal outcomes including the tyrannical trampling of minority interests. Rather than compelling the majority to respect those interests by hierarchical means, a mechanism was found in deliberative democracy to enable the *demos* to develop its own capacity to produce fairer and more reasoned outcomes. Similarly digital democracy was found to offer the potential to extend the accessibility and improve the efficiency of these deliberative democratic fora.

Thus we return to consensus, which also has a long track record of use in within institutions of Internet governance, usually in hybrid form. Otherwise largely intersecting with deliberative democracy, the unique insight gained from consideration of consensual decision-making was its application at larger scales, through consociationalism. This can allow groups insistent upon retaining their independent power yet wishing to collaborate in governance, to do so in the knowledge that they and the other participating groups share the power of mutual veto over any decision of collective concern.

Drawing together these insights, it can be concluded that an appropriate structure for a transnational network for Internet governance could consist of an open and transparent forum within which members of all stakeholder groups deliberate with the aim of reaching consensus, led by a meritocratic executive council to which each group appoints its representatives using consensual or democratic means, and which would be required to ratify all decisions of the forum by consensus. Such a body would bear much resemblance to the IETF or APNIC, overlaid with a consociational structure closer to that of the EU or the FSC.

This is all very well, except that of course the question of an appropriate design for such a multi-stakeholder governance network is not an abstract one; it has been already asked and answered in the process that led to the establishment of the IGF. As will be seen, the IGF in fact happens to bear very little resemblance to the network outlined above. To outline the structure of the IGF as it now exists and the process from which it emerged is the principal purpose of the next chapter.

Chapter 5

Reform of Internet governance

> The IGF, obviously, is the beginning of something. Yesterday I actually said it wasn't the beginning of something. I said we were mid-process. But clearly if we are in mid-process, we are in the start of that middle process.
>
> Kenneth Cukier

At this point, the theoretical background required to assess the legitimacy and likely effectiveness of present and future arrangements for Internet governance is in place. In Chapter 2 the institutions and main issue areas of Internet governance up to the date of establishment of the IGF were described, in Chapter 3 the international context in which Internet-related public policy-making takes place was laid out, and from Chapter 4 an understanding was given of the organisational forms suitable to this endeavour.

What has not yet been touched upon is how the institutions of Internet governance as outlined in Chapter 2 have been and are being reformed—most importantly, but not exclusively, through the establishment of the IGF—and the context in which this process sits with alternative proposals. The purpose of this chapter is therefore to describe these matters, while the purpose of the next will be to assess the prevailing Internet governance regime as thus outlined against the theoretical background developed over previous chapters.

5.1 WSIS

Although the process of Internet governance reform has been a continual one, marked by occasional milestones such as the foundation of ICANN, a natural point at which to begin discussion of the present regime is with the World Summit on the Information Society, as it was at this summit that the requirement that Internet governance be conducted on a multi-stakeholder basis was first clearly expressed, arguably setting a new norm of customary International law.[1] This marked a departure from the earlier prevailing norm—expressed even by some governments (most notably the United States)—that Internet governance was predominantly a private sector responsibility.[2]

As a summit, rather than a permanent intergovernmental organisation, the only power that WSIS had to make decisions was to make them by consensus. Some of the implications of consensual decision-making that have already been observed, such as the tendency for negotiations to be protracted, and the empowerment of minority groups,[3] were very much in evidence at WSIS, with negotiation sessions being extended time and again, and with the focus of its substantive agenda on development issues having been largely shaped by developing country governments.

Even in comparison to other United Nations summits conducted on the same basis, WSIS took place on a very large scale and over a lengthy period. Its genesis was at the ITU's 1998 Plenipotentiary Conference in Minneapolis, at which it was originally resolved that such a summit should be convened by the ITU. Interest from other UN agencies in the proposed subject matters of the summit soon led to it being broadened into a larger scale event under the umbrella of the UN.

Thus it was that in 2001, the Council of the ITU endorsed a proposal of its Secretary-General to hold the summit in two phases in Geneva in 2003 and Tunisia in 2005, which proposal was endorsed later that year by a United Nations Resolution calling for the full involvement of other agencies and stakeholders.[4] The task of organising the summit was shared by all major UN agencies within a High-Level Summit Organizing Committee (HLSOC), chaired by the Secretary-General of the ITU.

---

[1]WSIS, Geneva Declaration of Principles (as in n. 104 on page 27), para 48. Mueller, Mathiason and Klein posit an extension of this multi-stakeholder principle as one of six norms for a proposed Internet governance regime, without adverting to its status as a foundational principle of the extant Internet governance regime: Milton Mueller, John Mathiason and Hans Klein, The Internet and Global Governance: Principles and Norms for a New Regime, Global Governance 13:2 2007.

[2]Kleinwächter, Global Governance in the Information Age: GBDe and ICANN as "Pilot Projects" for Co-regulation and a New Trilateral Policy? (as in n. 106 on page 207), 18

[3]See section 4.4 on page 316.

[4]General Assembly of the United Nations, World Summit on the Information Society ⟨URL: `http://www.itu.int/wsis/docs/background/resolutions/56_183_unga_2002.pdf`⟩

The Geneva phase of WSIS was to focus on principles, and the Tunis phase on implementation of those principles and follow-up mechanisms.[5] In more concrete terms, the output of each phase was contained in two documents. For the first phase, these were a Declaration of Principles and a Plan of Action, that were adopted by 175 countries after being agreed in a succession of preparatory conferences. As the first phase of WSIS could not resolve differences on (most notably) Internet governance, WGIG was set up by United Nations Secretary-General Kofi Annan to report to the second phase of WSIS on that issue.

The Tunis Commitment and the Tunis Agenda were the output documents produced at the conclusion of the second phase, which presented the summit's conclusions on the issues such as Internet governance that were outstanding from the first phase, as well as reinforcing the content of the two earlier output documents and outlining follow-up steps to be taken.

Preceding each formal phase of WSIS, meetings of the intergovernmental Preparatory Committee ("PrepCom") were held at which the process of intergovernmental negotiation took place,[6] as were a series of regional conferences.[7]

Finally, in the lead-up to each phase and alongside it, there were a range of private sector and civil society events. The WSIS Secretariat rather poetically described the relationship between these events and the high level sessions of the first phase in the following terms:

> To reflect its tripartite nature, the Summit could be pictured as a flower, where the central part represents the meeting of Heads of States and the petals represent civil society and private sector events.
>
> The section of the petals that is rooted onto the core of the flower represents the participation of civil society and private sector representatives in the meeting of Heads of States. This is the space where they would present the positions of their constituencies on the outcomes of the Summit and take an active part in adopting the Plan of Action and final Declaration.

[5] See generally David G Souter, Whose Information Society? Developing Country and Civil Society Voices in the World Summit on the Information Society ⟨URL: `http://rights.apc.org/documents/wsis_EN.pdf`⟩.

[6] Five were held in Geneva prior to the first phase between July 2002 and December 2003 (including the originally unscheduled PrepCom 3A and 3B, also known as 3bis and 3bis+, or 3 resumed and 3 resumed II), along with an intersessional meeting in Paris. For the second phase, the PrepCom 1 was held in Tunis in June 2004, PrepCom 2 and 3 in Geneva, and a reconvened PrepCom 3 in Tunis in November 2005, immediately preceding the formal Tunis summit.

[7] Five were held ahead of the Geneva Phase between May 2002 and February 2003, being for the WSIS regions of Africa, Europe, the Asia-Pacific, Latin America and the Caribbean, and Western Asia. For the Tunis Phase, the regional conferences took place between November 2004 and June 2005 (with the European regional conference being dropped in favour of subregional conferences in Kyrgyzstan and Egypt).

The remaining part of the petals represents the various events organized at the initiative of civil society and private sector during the Summit. ... they could take the form of debates, agora, colloquia, showcasing of projects, training sessions, etc. [8]

Processes

The most direct relevance of WSIS to the IGF is of course that the Tunis Agenda is essentially the IGF's constitutional document, and for that reason this and the other three output documents will be outlined in the next subsection. However the structure and processes of WSIS are also highly relevant to the IGF's endeavour, in that they provide the closest previous example of an attempt to apply multi-stakeholder governance principles to the Internet governance regime.

This is evident from the output documents of the first phase, which establish the so-called "process criteria" for international Internet governance arrangements, specifying that they should be "multilateral, transparent, democratic, and with the full involvement of governments, the private sector, civil society, and international organizations."[9]

It is also reflected in the resolution of the UN General Assembly by which WSIS was endorsed, which "encourages effective contributions from and the active participation of all relevant United Nations bodies, ... international and regional institutions, non-governmental organizations, civil society and the private sector [and invites them] to contribute to, and participate in, the intergovernmental preparatory process of the Summit and at the Summit itself." To this end the resolution recommended the establishment of the PrepCom to "decide on the modalities of the participation of other stakeholders in the Summit."[10]

In this context, civil society's confoundment at being refused the full access, speaking and voting rights that many of its members (together with some private sector representatives) expected to be afforded, is understandable.[11] Instead, civil society and the private sector found themselves at the periphery of the WSIS process, consigned to offering suggestions to the governmental negotiators who maintained authority over the process of drafting the output documents.

---

[8] WSIS Secretariat, Civil Society & NGO Open Ended Bureau Proposal ⟨URL: http://www.worldsummit2003.de/download_en/CS_Bureau_30Jan_ENG.doc⟩

[9] WSIS, Geneva Declaration of Principles (as in n. 104 on page 27), para 48

[10] General Assembly of the United Nations, World Summit on the Information Society (as in n. 4 on page 322)

[11] Wolfgang Kleinwächter and Daniel Stauffacher, *The World Summit on the Information Society: Moving from the Past into the Future* New York: UNICTTF, 2005, chap. Introduction, 3

The WSIS Rules of Procedure that governments developed at the first PrepCom meeting stated:

1. Non-governmental organizations, civil society and business sector entities accredited to participate in the Committee may designate representatives to sit as observers at public meetings of the Preparatory Committee and its subcommittees.

2. Upon the invitation of the presiding officer of the body concerned and subject to the approval of that body, such observers may make oral statements on questions in which they have special competence. If the number of requests to speak is too large, the non-governmental organizations, civil society and business sector entities shall be requested to form themselves into constituencies, such constituencies to speak through spokespersons.[12]

The effect of this was that civil society's participation in intergovernmental negotiations, for example on the text of the output documents, was allowed only on an *ad hoc* basis at the discretion of government delegates. It took little time for civil society representatives to discover how that discretion would be applied, when they were excluded from discussions during the PrepCom 1 meeting on arrangements for their own accreditation to participate further in WSIS.[13] As one civil society observer described it:

> While the WSIS was mandated to be a multistakeholder process, its actual conduct called into question the precise nature of this commitment. The modalities of participation gave Governments and session Chairpersons a good deal of discretion in their treatment of observers, and the private sector and civil society frequently found themselves to be on a yo-yo string—in one moment allowed into the room with sharply limited speaking opportunities, in the next told to sit silently, and in the next thrown out entirely.[14]

[12] WSIS Secretariat, Final Report of PrepCom1 ⟨URL: `http://www.itu.int/dms_pub/itu-s/md/02/wsispc1/doc/S02-WSISPC1-DOC-0011!R1!PDF-E.pdf`⟩, 20. Similarly, the rules provided that written statements from civil society would be distributed to all delegations "provided that a statement submitted on behalf of a non-governmental organization or a business sector entity is related to the work of the Preparatory Committee and is on a subject in which the non-governmental organization or the business sector entity has a special competence": ibid., 21.

[13] Renate Bloem, *The World Summit on the Information Society: Moving from the Past into the Future* New York: UNICTTF, 2005, chap. Multi-Stakeholderism and Civil Society, 99

[14] William J Drake, *Reforming Internet Governance: Perspectives from the Working Group on Internet Governance (WGIG)* New York: UNICTTF, 2005, chap. Why the WGIG Process Mattered, 249

This phenomenon continued throughout the preparatory processes, becoming even more pronounced as the summit dates approached.[15] For example, during PrepCom 3 in September, some governments ejected civil society members who were blogging live from the group sessions. At PrepCom 3b in December, even ICANN President Paul Twomey was excluded from the negotiation room.[16]

Even when civil society was not formally excluded from negotiations, its input was often afforded little weight. One estimate put it that only 25% of civil society contributions were included in the text of the Plan of Action in some form, with 15% otherwise taken into account and the balance disregarded.[17] In the words of Markus Kummer, now of the IGF Secretariat, "[i]t was not surprising therefore that the summit failed to produce what might be termed 'a solution.'"[18]

Stakeholder institutions

Making the most of the limited and variable input they had into the summit, the non-governmental stakeholders took the initiative of organising themselves into more effective groupings, including what were effectively the "constituencies" referred to in the WSIS Rules of Procedure. The private sector's constituency was the Coordinating Committee of Business Interlocutors (CCBI), chaired by the ICC.

The structures into which civil society organised itself were rather more complex, largely because of its relative heterogeneity and also its much greater numbers than the private sector. Its peak body at WSIS was the Civil Society Plenary group, constituted by all members of civil society present whenever WSIS was convened for a PrepCom or summit meeting. There was also a "virtual plenary" based on an electronic mailing list, which existed to facilitate the conduct of intersessional work, rather than for decision-making.[19]

The Civil Society Plenary was sub-divided into self-organised regional, multi-stakeholder and thematic caucuses and working groups. There was a regional caucus for each of the seven WSIS regions, two multi-stakeholder

---

[15] Bloem (as in n. 13 on the previous page), 99; Daniel Stauffacher, *The World Summit on the Information Society: Moving from the Past into the Future* New York: UNICTTF, 2005, chap. A Tribute to Those Who Made it Happen, 85

[16] Wolfgang Kleinwächter, *The World Summit on the Information Society: Moving from the Past into the Future* New York: UNICTTF, 2005, chap. A New Diplomacy for the 21st Century? MultiStakeholder Approach and Bottom-Up Policy Development in the Information Society, 112

[17] Civil Society Working Group on Content & Themes, Does Input lead to Impact? How Governments treated Civil Society Proposals in Drafting the 19 September 2003 Draft Plan of Action ⟨URL: `http://www.worldsummit2003.de/download_en/does_input_lead_to_impact-action-plan.rtf`⟩

[18] Markus Kummer, *Reforming Internet Governance: Perspectives from the Working Group on Internet Governance (WGIG)* New York: UNICTTF, 2005, chap. Introduction, 2

[19] See `http://mailman.greennet.org.uk/mailman/listinfo/plenary`.

caucuses for gender and youth issues, and twenty-three thematic caucuses and working groups organised along thematic lines, such as education and academia, health, human rights, media and IPRs. The civil society caucuses and working groups made much use of online tools in their activities, including open electronic mailing lists which were all accessible from a community-run Web site,[20] and the use of another community Web platform, set up at the initiative of the Swiss hosts, to highlight their activities.[21]

The caucus of most relevance to the IGF is the Civil Society Internet Governance Caucus (CS-IGC),[22] which was formed during PrepCom 2 of the first phase of WSIS in February 2003, as the civil society caucus for Internet governance issues within WSIS.[23] Its significance lies not only in its role as a forum for the development of civil society contributions to the discussion of Internet governance during WSIS (for example by successfully nominating WGIG's civil society representatives), but in that it remains active in representing civil society on these issues at the IGF today. In fact as at 2008, its electronic mailing list contains more members than it did during WSIS.

From PrepCom 2 of the first phase, the Civil Society Plenary and the caucuses and working groups were supplemented by two other bodies formed by a resolution of the Civil Society Plenary and reporting to it: the Civil Society Content and Themes group[24] and the Civil Society Bureau (CSB).[25] Both of these were based in some measure on the equivalent intergovernmental subcommittees of the PrepCom.

The Content and Themes Group was a coordinating body for the caucuses and working groups, which endeavoured to generate and present a unified position on behalf of civil society on substantive issues, for the purpose of drafting papers and statements for presentation to the summit.[26] Its membership was open and its coordinators were consensually appointed. In between PrepCom meetings at which it convened in person, its activities took place on a public and open mailing list.[27]

The CSB was its procedural counterpart, charged with managing organisational aspects of civil society's participation in the WSIS and preparatory

---

[20] See http://www.wsis-cs.org/caucuses.html.

[21] The site at http://www.wsis-online.net/ is no longer functional, but a previous version of the site can be found at http://web.archive.org/web/20050323233954/http://wsis-online.net/.

[22] See http://www.igcaucus.org/

[23] CS-IGC, Initial Reactions to the WGIG Report ⟨URL: http://www.itu.int/wsis/docs2/pc3/contributions/co23.doc⟩

[24] Also known as the Subcommittee on Content and Themes, or WSIS-SCT.

[25] See http://www.csbureau.info/.

[26] WSIS-SCT, Final Report on Prepcom-2 Activities of the Civil Society on Content and Themes ⟨URL: http://www.itu.int/wsis/docs/pcip/misc/cs_sct.pdf⟩

[27] See http://www.wsis-cs.org/content.htm.

processes, including the distribution of funding from the donor-supported Civil Society Facility Fund. The executive positions on the Bureau were filled by one organisational member from each of various "families" of civil society groups. There were 22 such families at the time of the Bureau's creation, divided along broadly similar thematic, demographic and regional lines as the caucuses and working groups, with the addition of some catch-all categories such as "social movements" and "multi-stakeholders partnerships."

Decisions of the CSB were often required to be implemented by the Civil Society Division (CSD) of the WSIS Executive Secretariat (which had in turn been formed under the authority of HLSOC). The CSD, which was essentially also the Secretariat of the Content and Themes group and the Plenary, was generally responsible for facilitating civil society involvement in the WSIS, including processing requests for accreditation and providing civil society with information and working materials.

The Civil Society Internet Governance Caucus

The single caucus of most relevance to the IGF is the Civil Society Internet Governance Caucus (CS-IGC),[28] which was formed during PrepCom 2 of the first phase of WSIS in February 2003, as the civil society caucus for Internet governance issues within WSIS.[29] Its significance lies not only in its role as a forum for the development of civil society contributions to the discussion of Internet governance during WSIS (for example by successfully nominating the WGIG's civil society representatives), but in that it remains active in representing civil society on these issues at the IGF today. In fact as at 2008, its electronic mailing list contains over 300 members; a greater number than during WSIS.

The CS-IGC began to reform ahead of the first meeting of the IGF, adopting a new Charter in October 2006.[30] Although this post-dates WSIS, the continuing activity of the CS-IGC into the era of the IGF makes it worthwhile to briefly review its Charter here, as one possible model for structured civil society participation in multi-stakeholder Internet governance.

The Charter makes provision for two Coordinators to be elected by caucus members in alternate years, each for two year terms. The ability to vote in elections for the Coordinators or on amendments to the Charter may be acquired by anyone who has participated on the CS-IGC mailing list for two months, and indicated their agreement to abide by the Charter. By default, all votes are openly cast, though the Coordinators may determine to make a vote secret.

---

[28]See `http://www.igcaucus.org/`

[29]CS-IGC, Initial Reactions to the WGIG Report (as in n. 23 on the preceding page)

[30]Idem, Charter ⟨URL: `http://www.igcaucus.org/IGC-charter_final-061014.html`⟩

The Coordinators' principal duties are to facilitate the formation of consensus within the CS-IGC. In the case where unanimity is not attained, they are empowered to jointly adjudge the attainment of "rough consensus" upon giving 48 hours notice of their proposed decision, to allow time for any final discussion. The Charter provides:

> Rough consensus, for the purposes of the IGC, is defined as the point at which an overwhelming majority of the IGC appears to agree with a position with any dissenting minority view having been well discussed and respected. Rough consensus can only be called after a serious attempt has been made to accommodate minority points of view.

The Charter also establishes a five-member Appeals Team, the purpose of which is to allow any decision of a Coordinator to be overturned by majority vote, upon the institution of an appeal by at least four members and following a period for comment from the CS-IGC as a whole. The Appeals Team is appointed annually by a randomly-selected Nominations Committee drawn from a pool of volunteers.[31] A successful appeal also lays the ground for a Coordinator to be recalled, which requires the Appeals Team to reach consensus that a recall vote is required, and for that vote to succeed by a two-thirds majority of members.

First phase

The Geneva phase of WSIS took place from 10 to 12 December 2003, attended by almost 50 heads of state, 175 national delegations and approximately 12 000 participants. In addition to the formal plenary sessions, almost 300 other events took place during the Geneva phase from 5 December, including three multi-stakeholder round table discussions.

None of these events will receive further consideration here. Rather, our attention will be limited to the Declaration of Principles and Plan of Action, drafting of which was complete before the Geneva phase of the summit officially even opened. Although the IGF was not conceived until the Tunis phase of the summit, a brief analysis of the Geneva output documents is important not only to set the scene, but because the principles agreed in Geneva remain one of the few fixed points of reference by which any reforms that may be proposed for the IGF will be judged by the international community of states.

[31] An analogous procedure governs the appointment of representatives of the CS-IGC to external bodies, such as the IGF's Advisory Group.

Declaration of Principles

The core of the Declaration of Principles is contained in eleven "key principles for building an inclusive Information Society." Only two of these call for examination here, but the subjects of the others may be gleaned from the headings they are given in the Declaration which are as follows:

- The role of governments and all stakeholders in the promotion of ICTs for development (which first establishes the multi-stakeholder principle and is set out in full below);
- Information and communication infrastructure: An essential foundation for the Information Society (stressing the need for access to ICT infrastructure and services, investment in communications infrastructure, and an enabling policy environment);
- Access to information and knowledge (including the importance of a rich public domain, and the availability of open source and free software alongside proprietary software);
- Capacity building (including the need for the use of ICTs in education and the development of national capability in ICT research and development);
- Building confidence and security in the use of ICTs (which underlines the importance of enhancing information and network security, authentication, privacy and consumer protection, and makes specific mention of the spam problem);
- Enabling environment (which refers to the need for an international and national legal and economic environment to support the development of the Information Society);
- ICT applications: benefits in all aspects of life (which refers to the importance of ICTs in government operations and services, health care and health information, education and training, employment, job creation, business, agriculture, transport, protection of the environment and management of natural resources, disaster prevention, and culture, and to promote the eradication of poverty and other agreed development goals);
- Cultural diversity and identity, linguistic diversity and local content (stressing the need for the creation, dissemination and preservation of content in diverse languages and formats);
- Media (affirming the importance of freedom of the press and freedom of information, along with the concomitant public duties of the media);
- Ethical dimensions of the Information Society (referring to the need to uphold human rights in the use of ICTs); and

- International and regional cooperation (which reiterates the multi-stakeholder principle as well as the importance of regional initiatives).

The need for multi-stakeholder involvement in Internet governance is enshrined in the very first of these principles, which provides in full:

> Governments, as well as private sector, civil society and the United Nations and other international organizations have an important role and responsibility in the development of the Information Society and, as appropriate, in decision-making processes. Building a people-centred Information Society is a joint effort which requires cooperation and partnership among all stakeholders.[32]

This theme recurs in the paragraphs on Internet governance within the explication of the "Enabling environment" principle, which deals with the need for an international and national legal and economic environment to support the development of the Information Society. It defines the agreed roles of the stakeholder groups as they were briefly referred to in the Introduction and will be repeated in the Tunis Agenda:

> We reaffirm that the management of the Internet encompasses both technical and public policy issues and should involve all stakeholders and relevant intergovernmental and international organizations. In this respect it is recognised that:
>
> a) Policy authority for Internet-related public policy issues is the sovereign right of States. They have rights and responsibilities for international Internet-related public policy issues;
> b) The private sector has had and should continue to have an important role in the development of the Internet, both in the technical and economic fields;
> c) Civil society has also played an important role on Internet matters, especially at community level, and should continue to play such a role;
> d) Intergovernmental organizations have had and should continue to have a facilitating role in the coordination of Internet-related public policy issues;
> e) International organizations have also had and should continue to have an important role in the development of Internet-related technical standards and relevant policies.[33]

[32] WSIS, Geneva Declaration of Principles (as in n. 104 on page 27), para 20

[33] Ibid., para 35

The Declaration of Principles continues by calling for the establishment of WGIG, and states:

> The Internet has evolved into a global facility available to the public and its governance should constitute a core issue of the Information Society agenda. The international management of the Internet should be multilateral, transparent and democratic, with the full involvement of governments, the private sector, civil society and international organizations. It should ensure an equitable distribution of resources, facilitate access for all and ensure a stable and secure functioning of the Internet, taking into account multilingualism.[34]

The stakeholder groups revisited

Already, some lack of clarity in the definitions of the stakeholder groups has appeared, which is something of a hallmark of the WSIS output documents. In some paragraphs, either intergovernmental organisations[35] or international organisations[36] appear to be treated as separate stakeholder groups. Even more problematically, the two occasionally seem to be conflated.[37]

Except in such cases where intergovernmental and non-governmental international organisations are treated together, the phrase "international organisations" is generally used in the WSIS output documents to refer to the institutions of the Internet technical community. This much is clear from the definition of their role as a stakeholder group: "the development of Internet-related technical standards and relevant policies."[38]

Although there is no entirely satisfactory basis upon which to reconcile these conflicts, it will be taken that the authoritative statement of stakeholder groups in post-WSIS Internet governance is limited to governments, the private sector and civil society. This is largely consistent with the terms of the WSIS output documents; for example, in that the definition of the roles of stakeholders refers to "all stakeholders *and* relevant intergovernmental and international organizations"[39] which suggests that intergovernmental and international organisations are not to be considered as stakeholders in their own right.

It can also be justified on the conceptual basis that, as already observed, the legitimacy of intergovernmental organisations as a stakeholder group

[34] WSIS, Geneva Declaration of Principles (as in n. 104 on page 27), para 48

[35] Idem, Tunis Agenda for the Information Society (as in n. 5 on page 2), para 73

[36] Idem, Geneva Declaration of Principles (as in n. 104 on page 27), para 48

[37] Ibid., para 20; Idem, Tunis Agenda for the Information Society (as in n. 5 on page 2), para 52

[38] Idem, Geneva Declaration of Principles (as in n. 104 on page 27), para 35

[39] Ibid., para 35

is purely derivative in nature,[40] and by the same token the legitimacy of non-governmental international organisations is, or is drawn from, that of civil society and/or the private sector. It is also consistent with the view of WGIG, which took it that there were only three distinct stakeholder groups[41] (after having specifically considered adding the technical community as a fourth).[42]

This certainly does not mean that intergovernmental and other international organisations should be excluded from multi-stakeholder governance processes. On the contrary; their participation is important on instrumentalist grounds, respectively because of their centrality to the existing international system and to the present architecture of the Internet. For example, even if all stakeholders, including all affected governments, reached agreement on a reform to intellectual property law, it would not be possible to effectuate that reform without also securing the involvement of WIPO; and neither would it be possible to effectuate reforms to the technical architecture of the Internet without the involvement of the IETF.

However, this does not require those institutions to be treated as separate stakeholders rather than as observers,[43] advisers, or as members of one or more of the other stakeholder groups as appropriate. For example, ICANN's GAC could participate as an intergovernmental organisation, the ALAC as civil society, and the GNSO's commercial and business users constituency as a member of the private sector.

Plan of Action

Much less time needs to be spent discussing the Geneva Plan of Action, which builds upon the Declaration of Principles by setting out a range of general objectives to be achieved by the application of those principles. These are categorised into eleven action lines, one for each of the principles, that have been referred to in follow-up documents and activities by their identifiers "C1" to "C11." There are also eight subsidiary lines under C7, "ICT applications: benefits in all aspects of life," namely e-government, e-business, e-learning, e-health, e-employment, e-environment, e-agriculture and e-science.

Most of the objectives are very general, leaving specific targets to be determined on a national level, and making no prescription of the means by which they are to be accomplished. By way of example, action line C5 ("Building confidence and security in the use of ICTs") simply states in

---

40 See section 3.4 on page 147.

41 WGIG, Report of the Working Group on Internet Governance (as in n. 2 on page 29), 8–10

42 Avri Doria, *Reforming Internet Governance: Perspectives from the Working Group on Internet Governance (WGIG)* New York: UNICTTF, 2005, chap. WSIS, WGIG, Technology and Technologists

43 This is the present status of intergovernmental organisations within the IGF's Advisory Group: see section 5.2 on page 364.

respect of spam that parties are to "[t]ake appropriate action on spam at national and international levels."[44] These do not require further consideration here.

One of the more specific action lines is C6 ("Enabling environment"), which requests the UN Secretary-General to establish the WGIG "to investigate and make proposals for action, as appropriate, on the governance of Internet" [*sic*].[45] It was originally expected that governance of the Internet would be dealt with in the Geneva output documents themselves, but when agreement could not be reached, even when PrepCom 3 was twice extended to PrepCom 3A and 3B, the deferral of this issue pending the report of a smaller task force was a compromise reached around 24 hours before the official opening of the summit.[46]

Internet governance was not the only issue so deferred. Another section of the Plan of Action, following the eleven action lines, established a Digital Solidarity Agenda, with the aim of "putting in place the conditions for mobilizing human, financial and technological resources for inclusion of all men and women in the emerging Information Society."[47] As part of this Agenda, calls were made by developing country governments for the establishment of a Digital Solidarity Fund (DSF) for financing ICT infrastructure development.

As agreement on this issue could not be reached within the Geneva phase either, the Plan of Action called for it too to be reviewed by a dedicated task force, which became the Task Force on Financing Mechanisms (TFFM). As it transpired, the DSF was established outside the WSIS process altogether in March 2005, as an independent multi-stakeholder network.[48] This largely disposed of the issue prior to PrepCom 3 of the Tunis phase, and no further discussion of it will be necessary here either.

WGIG

The contention over Internet governance within the Geneva phase that led to the establishment of WGIG can be considered fortuitous, in that as will be seen, WGIG much more faithfully embodied the multi-stakeholder principle than its parent had (or would again, in the Tunis phase). WGIG also considered the issues of Internet governance in a much broader context than would likely have occurred if those issues had remained within the mainstream of WSIS.

---

[44] WSIS, Geneva Plan of Action ⟨URL: `http://www.itu.int/wsis/docs/geneva/official/poa.html`⟩, para 12(d)

[45] Ibid., para 13(b)

[46] Kleinwächter and Stauffacher (as in n. 11 on page 324), 4

[47] WSIS, Geneva Plan of Action (as in n. 44), para 27

[48] See `http://www.dsf-fsn.org/`.

Within WSIS, discussion of Internet governance was focused upon a single issue: the control that the United States was seen to unilaterally possess over what WGIG came to call "infrastructure and the management of critical Internet resources,"[49] such as the DNS system, the root servers, and IP address allocation, through its oversight of the administration of those functions by a Californian corporation, ICANN.

Whilst the United States naturally supported the status quo, and many of its close allies including Australia and New Zealand were content to make evolutionary changes to it, developing countries in particular were implacable in their opposition to the prevailing regime. China and Brazil, for example, pushed for more direct international involvement in ICANN's processes, whilst others such as Pakistan went further and sought that these functions be transferred outright away from ICANN to the ITU.[50] The United States characterised this as a power-play "by those governments who are not very happy with the rapid and innovative changes on the internet, both economically and also with regard to speech, [to prevent those changes] by threatening a veto."[51]

It was in this context that the Secretary-General of the ITU and WSIS, Yoshio Utsumi, urged WGIG to focus on that specific issue, concluding his welcoming address "with a plea; that we do not reopen all of the issues that were already extensively discussed in the first phase. But instead, let us focus on those few issues of substance that were not resolved during the negotiations; namely on the future reform of ICANN."[52]

He soon found that WGIG had other ideas.

Processes

The first task of Markus Kummer, appointed as Executive Coordinator of WGIG's Secretariat in July 2004, was to recommend a multi-stakeholder panel of candidates for the working group to the UN Secretary-General. He set about this task over the succeeding months through a programme of informal discussions with stakeholders, together with an open two-day consultation that was held on 20–21 September and chaired by Nitin Desai, Special Advisor to the Secretary-General for the WSIS. He also received a slate of nominations from the CS-IGC, selected through an open process it had devised.[53]

[49] WGIG, Report of the Working Group on Internet Governance (as in n. 2 on page 29), 8

[50] Ulrika Hedquist, WYSIWYG Guide to WSIS ⟨URL: `http://computerworld.co.nz/news.nsf/news/467909CAE61A19A2CC2570C100678772`⟩

[51] Tim Wu et al., On the Future of Internet Governance ⟨URL: `http://ssrn.com/abstract=992805`⟩, 2

[52] Yoshio Utsumi, First Meeting of the Working Group on Internet Governance (WGIG) ⟨URL: `http://www.wgig.org/docs/Utsumi.pdf`⟩, 2

[53] Bertrand de la Chapelle, *The World Summit on the Information Society: Moving from the Past into the Future* New York: UNICTTF, 2005, chap. WSIS: The First Summit of the Internet Age?,

The WGIG eventually formed on 11 November comprised forty members, with a balance of all stakeholder groups and geographical regions, and a reasonably broad demographic and gender distribution. Amongst those selected were all but one of those that had been nominated by the CS-IGC, and Nitin Desai as Chair.[54] Interestingly no representative of the United States government was selected, though in any case, governmental members were selected in a personal rather than a representative capacity, so that there would be no need for them to refer questions back to their ministries before committing to a position.

WGIG met four times in Geneva between November 2004 and June 2005, for a duration of three or four days. Every meeting of the group included an open consultation session at which both written and oral submissions were received from the public. From the second meeting in February 2005, the proceedings of these consultations were transcribed in real-time into the six official UN languages[55] and streamed over the Internet.[56] In addition to the open consultation sessions, one of WGIG's private meetings was open to observers, and at the others intergovernmental observers were permitted to attend and speak. Documentary submissions received from the public were also posted to the WGIG Web site, and all of these contributions fed into the WGIG's Background Report.[57]

Between meetings, WGIG members communicated using an email mailing list.[58] Limited use was also made of a Web site site which provided members with an asynchronous online discussion forum and a wiki.[59] At its first meeting, WGIG divided into smaller working groups to deal with specific issues, which had their own mailing lists, and which published working papers to the WGIG's Web site for public comment.[60] At its final meeting WGIG divided again into smaller working groups to write sections of its final report, reassembling in plenary to review and consolidate these sections, with final editing of the text being conducted in real-time on a computer-projection screen.[61]

281

[54] See `http://www.wsis-si.org/wgig.html`.

[55] Though only for the final meeting in June was this transcript archived on the WGIG Web site: see `http://www.wgig.org/Meeting-June.html`.

[56] That is "webcast": see the links to each meeting from `http://www.wgig.org/`.

[57] WGIG, Background Report (as in n. 165 on page 71)

[58] Don MacLean, *Reforming Internet Governance: Perspectives from the Working Group on Internet Governance (WGIG)* New York: UNICTTF, 2005, chap. A Brief History of WGIG, 12–13 and see `http://wgig.org/mailman/listinfo/wgig-discuss_wgig.org`.

[59] Ibid., 17 and see `http://www.wgig.org/Plone-instructions.html`. Plone (see `http://plone.org/`) is the same software upon which ParTecs is based: see section 4.3 on page 285.

[60] See `http://www.wgig.org/working-papers.html`.

[61] Ibid., 20–21

Mandate

WGIG's mandate was set out in the Plan of Action which suggested that it should:

i) develop a working definition of Internet governance;

ii) identify the public policy issues that are relevant to Internet governance;

iii) develop a common understanding of the respective roles and responsibilities of governments, existing intergovernmental and

iv) international organizations and other forums as well as the private sector and civil society from both developing and developed countries; [and]

v) prepare a report on the results of this activity to be presented for consideration and appropriate action for the second phase of WSIS in Tunis in 2005.[62]

To take the WGIG's response to each of the four requests in turn, the first was its proposal of the definition of Internet governance that was first cited in the introduction to Chapter 2.[63] One of the most significant achievements of WGIG was that its definition was incorporated into the Tunis Agenda *verbatim* at para 34. The definition is broad enough to cover the full gamut of Internet governance issues—technical coordination, standards development and public policy governance. Extending far beyond the limited issues of Internet naming and numbering to which the ITU had urged the WGIG to restrict its attention, the adoption of this definition alone was enough to frustrate those who would have put forward the ITU, or for that matter ICANN, as the peak body of Internet governance, as clearly neither were competent to adopt such a mantle.

WGIG then proceeded to identify thirteen broad public policy issues that its definition of Internet governance encompassed, which have already been referred to in some detail at section 2.3 on page 70. For each of the thirteen broad issues, WGIG's Background Report analysed the main sub-issues involved, described the existing institutions and mechanisms of governance already engaged in respect of those issues, and assessed the extent to which those institutions and mechanisms conformed with the WSIS process criteria of being multilateral, transparent, democratic and inclusive.

With this background in place, WGIG proceeded to make ten basic policy recommendations in its main report. Much along the lines of the

[62]WSIS, Geneva Plan of Action (as in n. 44 on page 334), para 13(b)

[63]WGIG, Report of the Working Group on Internet Governance (as in n. 2 on page 29), para 10

recommendations in the Geneva Plan of Action, these were rather broad in scope and vague in content; for example, "Ensure that all measures taken in relation to the Internet, in particular those on grounds of security or to fight crime, do not lead to violations of human rights principles."[64] These recommendations do not call for further discussion here.

The third request made of WGIG in the Plan of Action was that it attempt to develop a common understanding of the respective roles of stakeholders in relation to Internet governance. As already noted, WGIG recognised three distinct groups: governments, the private sector and civil society. As to the roles of these stakeholder groups, WGIG was less limiting than the Geneva Declaration of Principles had been in its definitions of stakeholder roles, which would be repeated in the Tunis Agenda.

For example, the WGIG report acknowledged that all stakeholder groups have a role to play in policy development. For governments, their role is in "[p]ublic policymaking and coordination and implementation." The private sector's role is in the "[d]evelopment of policy proposals, guidelines and tools" as well as "participation in national and international policy development" (rather than merely an "important role ... in the technical and economic fields" as allowed by the Declaration of Principles). Civil society has a role in "[e]ngaging in policy processes" and "[c]ontributing to policy processes and policies that are more bottom–up, people-centred and inclusive" (rather than just "an important role ... at community level").[65]

Although not a consensus document, WGIG's Background Report, in particular, takes a more progressive view of the new post-Westphalian international order than the Geneva output documents:

> This emerging new "tri-stakeholderism" involving governments, the private sector and civil society, would suggest the need for a new conceptual framework which is on the one hand embedded in the existing system of international law, but on the other hand goes beyond this, bringing other type [*sic*] of norms (for example, "soft law," self-regulation) to global governance concepts.[66]

The fourth and final part of WGIG's mandate was the open suggestion that it produce proposals for action. In addition to the ten issues in respect of which substantive policy recommendations were made as referred to above, and of more relevance than these for present purposes, WGIG made recommendations for future Internet governance mechanisms. These recommendations were in turn subdivided into four clusters:

- the establishment of an Internet governance forum;

[64] WGIG, Report of the Working Group on Internet Governance (as in n. 2 on page 29), 18
[65] Ibid., 8–9
[66] Idem, Background Report (as in n. 165 on page 71), 66

- mechanisms for global public policy and oversight;
- the need for improved institutional coordination; and
- the need for regional, subregional and national coordination.

The last two recommendations above were dealt with scantly in a paragraph each, simply recommending in the first instance that the secretariats of existing intergovernmental organisations and other organisations of Internet governance improve the coordination of their activities and their exchange of information. In the second, WGIG recommended that the multi-stakeholder approach be replicated at regional and subregional levels of Internet governance, and that governments establish a multi-stakeholder national Internet governance steering committee or similar body.[67]

Much more attention was given to the first two recommendations above, which will be discussed next in turn.

An Internet governance forum

Correctly noting that there was "no global multi-stakeholder forum to address Internet-related public policy issues,"[68] the WGIG report proposed the establishment of a multi-stakeholder Internet governance forum linked to the United Nations,[69] which would:

- Interface with intergovernmental bodies and other institutions on matters under their purview which are relevant to Internet governance, such as IPR, ecommerce, trade in services and Internet/telecommunications convergence.
- Identify emerging issues and bring them to the attention of the appropriate bodies and make recommendations.
- Address issues that are not being dealt with elsewhere and make proposals for action, as appropriate.
- Connect different bodies involved in Internet management where necessary.
- Contribute to capacity-building for Internet governance for developing countries, drawing fully on local sources of knowledge and expertise.
- Promote and assess on an ongoing basis the embodiment of WSIS principles in Internet governance processes.[70]

[67] WGIG, Report of the Working Group on Internet Governance (as in n. 2 on page 29), 16
[68] Ibid., 10
[69] Ibid., 11
[70] Ibid., 11–12

As will be seen, these six suggested functions made their way into the Tunis Agenda in subtly altered form.

Global public policy and oversight

An Internet governance forum alone, however, could not easily provide all that was required to bridge the gap between the existing Internet governance regime as it had evolved, and a future regime that would fulfil a more expansive range of possible Internet governance functions. These more expansive functions are referred to as as "global public policy and oversight" in the WGIG report, which more specifically suggests that they may include the roles of audit, arbitration, coordination, policy-setting and regulation.[71]

The WGIG report correctly observes that a consensual network such as the proposed Internet governance forum may not be sufficiently well adapted to fulfil all of these potential functions. However, there was no consensus within WGIG about the need for all of these roles to be fulfilled, nor as to how they should be; one point of view within WGIG being that "[t]here is no need for a specific oversight organization."[72]

The abstract manner in which this question is considered in the WGIG report seems obscure until it is understood that its implicit context is the issue area of Internet naming and numbering. The real question, therefore—although never stated so baldly in the WGIG report—was whether by making the management of infrastructure and critical Internet resources subject to greater public oversight than exists under the ICANN regime, concerns over US unilateralism would be addressed.

In the end, the only consensus that could be reached on this question was that any new mechanism proposed to fulfil the global public policy and oversight functions should adhere to the following principles:

- No single Government should have a pre-eminent role in relation to international Internet governance.
- The organizational form for the governance function will be multilateral, transparent and democratic, with the full involvement of Governments, the private sector, civil society and international organizations.

---

[71] WGIG, Report of the Working Group on Internet Governance (as in n. 2 on page 29), 12. Compare the five potential roles for multi-stakeholder governance networks put forward in Martens (as in n. 103 on page 27), 21: advocacy, standard setting, financing, implementation and coordination.

[72] WGIG, Report of the Working Group on Internet Governance (as in n. 2 on page 29), 14 and see Wolfgang Kleinwächter, *Reforming Internet Governance: Perspectives from the Working Group on Internet Governance (WGIG)* New York: UNICTTF, 2005, chap. De-Mystification of the Internet Root: Do We Need Governmental Oversight?, 221

- The organizational form for the governance function will involve all stakeholders and relevant intergovernmental and international organizations within their respective roles.[73]

Since no agreement could be reached on a single model for institutional reform of existing Internet governance mechanisms that would accord with the above three principles, WGIG instead presented in the alternative four possible organisational models that its members had considered, without recommending any of them:

- The formation of a new intergovernmental Global Internet Council (GIC) anchored in the United Nations. The GIC would directly set international Internet public policy, and non-governmental stakeholders would participate in this process only in an advisory capacity. Under this model, ICANN would become accountable to the GIC, which would supersede the roles of both the ICANN GAC and the NTIA.
- The enhancement of ICANN's GAC to address concerns of US unilateralism in the control of infrastructure and critical Internet resources. The Internet governance forum separately proposed by WGIG would additionally coordinate between existing Internet governance organisations such as ICANN and their stakeholders, but would not exercise oversight of any of their activities.
- The establishment of an International Internet Council (IIC), distinguishable from the proposed GIC mainly in that it would not be UN-linked. It would intercede in policy areas where national interests were impacted, but which fell outside the scope of existing intergovernmental arrangements. It would thus be likely to play a less dominant role than the GIC outside the issue area of Internet naming and numbering, and to supersede existing organisations of Internet governance to a lesser extent.
- The final option proposed to divide up the "three interrelated areas of Internet policy governance, oversight and global coordination" between three separate organisations:
  - A Global Internet Policy Council (GIPC) which would be a government-led decision-making body in which the other stakeholders merely acted as observers, and which would set policy on issues addressed by existing intergovernmental organizations as well as other public policy issues currently lacking a natural home or cutting across several international or intergovernmental bodies;

[73] WGIG, Report of the Working Group on Internet Governance (as in n. 2 on page 29), 12, drawing in the case of the second and third points from para 48 and 49 of the Declaration of Principles.

- A World Internet Corporation for Assigned Names and Numbers (WICANN) which would be a reformed, internationalised ICANN linked to the United Nations, in which governments would take over the oversight function of the NTIA, and the advisory function of the GAC; and
- A Global Internet Governance Forum (GIGF); which would be a multi-stakeholder advisory body to "facilitate coordination (and discussion) of Internet-related public policy issues," much as outlined above.[74]

WGIG's report was presented to PrepCom 3 of the second phase in July 2005, following a preliminary report to PrepCom 2 in February. Notwithstanding the equivocation on global public policy and oversight, the report had been adopted by its members by consensus, a feat attributed by one member of the secretariat to its clear sense of direction, the consensus based approach fostered by the appointment of members in their individual capacities rather than as representing factional interests, and its efficient working method that combined face to face meetings with ongoing online discussion.[75]

Second phase

The high level segment of the second phase of WSIS was held from 16 to 18 November 2005 in Tunis.[76] Again, there were numerous associated private sector and civil society events held in the lead-up to and alongside the high level segment that do not call for discussion here.

Again also, the actual process of negotiation was over by the time the summit officially reopened—although not long over, with more last-minute compromises being thrashed out during the final hours of an extended PrepCom 3. In the process, there had been a regression from the open and inclusive working methods of WGIG, with attempts by many governments to exclude civil society and private sector representatives from PrepCom 3 drafting sessions.[77]

Of the two outcome documents from the Tunis phase, the Tunis Agenda is the only one that calls for treatment here, as the Tunis Commitment, the shortest of the four outcome documents, was largely confined to confirming the parties' agreement to the Declaration of Principles and reaffirming their commitment to pursuing the initiatives set out in the Plan of Action.

---

[74] WGIG, Report of the Working Group on Internet Governance (as in n. 2 on page 29), 13–16

[75] Tarek Cheniti, *Reforming Internet Governance: Perspectives from the Working Group on Internet Governance (WGIG)* New York: UNICTTF, 2005, chap. The WGIG Process: Lessons Learned and Thoughts for the Future, 31

[76] See `http://www.smsitunis2005.tn/`.

[77] Drake, Reforming Internet Governance: Perspectives from the Working Group on Internet Governance (WGIG) (as in n. 14 on page 325), 250

The Tunis Agenda is divided into an introduction and three substantive parts. The first two substantive parts deals with the two issues omitted during the Geneva phase—financing and Internet governance. The third deals with implementation and follow-up, building on the eleven action lines and the eight subsidiary lines of the Geneva Action Plan.

The first substantive part can be dealt with shortly, since as indicated above, the most contentious aspect of the TFFM report was to a large degree overcome by the establishment of the DSF outside the WSIS process, allowing it to be simply acknowledged in the Tunis Agenda.[78] The balance of this part of the document is in similar general terms to the Plan of Action, for example, "Multilateral development banks and institutions should consider adapting their existing mechanisms, and where appropriate designing new ones, to provide for national and regional demands on ICT development."[79]

The following part of the Agenda, on Internet Governance, begins by adopting without further comment the working definition of that term developed by WGIG, yet repeats unaltered the more restrictive description of the respective roles of the stakeholder groups from the Declaration of Principles.[80] It recognises the academic and technical communities as cutting across the other stakeholder groups—an insight inherited from WGIG[81]—and affirms the importance of adopting a multi-stakeholder approach "as far as possible, at all levels."[82]

The Tunis Agenda then proceeds to record the resolve of the parties to address many of the Internet governance issues isolated by WGIG, as set out in tabular form at section 2.3 on page 70, in very general terms similar to those of the Plan of Action; for example, on spam:

> We resolve to deal effectively with the significant and growing problem posed by spam. We take note of current multilateral, multi-stakeholder frameworks for regional and international cooperation on spam, for example, the APEC Anti-Spam Strategy, the London Action Plan, the Seoul–Melbourne Anti Spam Memorandum of Understanding and the relevant activities of OECD and ITU. We call upon all stakeholders, to adopt a multi-pronged approach to counter spam that includes, *inter alia*, consumer and business education; appropriate legislation, law-enforcement authorities and tools; the continued

[78] WSIS, Tunis Agenda for the Information Society (as in n. 5 on page 2), para 28

[79] Ibid., para 25

[80] Ibid., paras 34 and 35

[81] WGIG, Report of the Working Group on Internet Governance (as in n. 2 on page 29), 8, 10; Doria, Reforming Internet Governance: Perspectives from the Working Group on Internet Governance (WGIG) (as in n. 42 on page 333)

[82] WSIS, Tunis Agenda for the Information Society (as in n. 5 on page 2), paras 36 and 37

development of technical and self-regulatory measures; best practices; and international cooperation.[83]

The more significant paragraphs of this part of the Agenda however are those relating to the reform of Internet governance institutions. This topic is addressed in two ways: through setting in place a process of "enhanced cooperation," and by establishing the Internet Governance Forum that WGIG had recommended. As these were by far the most divisive issues discussed during negotiations at the Tunis PrepCom meetings, some more background of these negotiations is required before discussing the eventual agreement which found form in the Tunis Agenda.

Enhanced cooperation

The WGIG report had not been received with such consensus within WSIS at large as within WGIG itself. Perhaps predictably, the most dissent in respect of its recommendations for a new regime for global public policy and oversight came from the United States, which, along with private sector representatives such as the CCBI, responded to the report by arguing that no significant changes to the status quo were necessary.[84] They also expressed concern that in outlining the respective roles of stakeholders, the role of governments had been overstated and that of the private sector and civil society diminished.[85]

On the other hand, it could be taken that the ITU was not particularly pleased with the WGIG report either (though it did not publish an official response). Although its Secretary-General had painted the ITU as "a multilateral organization with greater international legitimacy and democratic processes" than ICANN, WGIG had found that in fact the ITU was far from this. Relatively few Internet businesses were members, and the ITU's exclusion of civil society from its processes prevented it from fulfilling the multi-stakeholder principle demanded by the Geneva principles.[86]

Thus although three of the oversight options proposed by WGIG proposed new intergovernmental oversight mechanisms for the ICANN function, none of them considered the ITU a serious candidate. Only at its 2006 Plenipotentiary Conference in Antalya did the ITU begin to investigate whether there was scope "to draft any possible amendments to the ITU

[83]WSIS, Tunis Agenda for the Information Society (as in n. 5 on page 2), paras 41

[84]WSIS Secretariat, Compilation of Comments Received on the Report of the Working Group on Internet Governance ⟨URL: `http://www.itu.int/wsis/docs2/pc3/working/dt7rev2.pdf`⟩, 3, 36–43

[85]Ibid., 29–30

[86]Utsumi (as in n. 52 on page 335), 257

basic texts that might be needed in order to facilitate the participation of all relevant stakeholders in the activities of ITU related to WSIS."[87]

If neither the United States nor the ITU were particularly happy with WGIG's recommendations, most of the rest of the world was, with a coalition of developing countries specifically supporting the GIC model for oversight of naming and numbering functions.[88] Although conducted the following year, a 2006 review of ICANN conducted by the NTIA supported WGIG's view that that no single government should have a pre-eminent role in international Internet governance, with over 87 percent of respondents in favour of the transition of naming and numbering functions to an international model.[89]

Thus in the lead-up to its third meeting of the Tunis phase, the PrepCom faced essentially two choices on the global public policy and oversight issue: the *status quo*, which was the only option acceptable to the United States, or some measure of internationalisation of the NTIA's oversight function as most of the rest of the international community demanded.

In the end, the United States forced the issue. Following the completion of the WGIG report, but pre-empting its publication, the NTIA issued a statement in June 2005 affirming its resolve to "maintain its historic role in authorizing changes or modifications to the authoritative root zone file."[90] This effectively ruled out each of the four models WGIG had put forward, save for the status quo, with possible "enhancement" of the GAC.

The reaction both from civil society[91] and many governments[92] was immediate and negative. But it was not until PrepCom 3 had commenced in September that the EU made what the United States described as "a very shocking and profound change,"[93] proposing the following text to a drafting session:

> In reviewing the adequacy of existing institutional arrangements for Internet Governance and policy debate we agree that adjustments need to be made and we propose accordingly: ...

[87] ITU, Study on the Participation of All Relevant Stakeholders in the Activities of the Union Related to the World Summit on the Information Society ⟨URL: http://www.itu.int/council/groups/pp06-plen7.html⟩ and see http://www.itu.int/council/groups/stakeholders/.

[88] Drake, Reforming Internet Governance: Perspectives from the Working Group on Internet Governance (WGIG) (as in n. 14 on page 325), 261

[89] Kieren McCarthy, US Government Told to Take Its Hands Off Internet ⟨URL: http://www.theregister.co.uk/2006/07/15/ntia_inquiry_results/⟩

[90] NTIA, US Principles on the Internet's Domain Name and Addressing System (as in n. 38 on page 40)

[91] CS-IGC, Initial Reactions to the WGIG Report (as in n. 23 on page 327), 12

[92] Most vocally those of Russia, Brazil, Iran and China: Declan McCullagh, Power Grab could Split the Net ⟨URL: http://www.news.com/Power-grab-could-split-the-Net/2010-1071_3-5886556.html?tag=nefd.ac⟩; Tom Wright, EU Tries to Unblock Internet Impasse ⟨URL: http://www.nytimes.com/iht/2005/09/30/business/IHT-30net.html⟩.

[93] Ibid.

> The new model for international cooperation ... should include the development and application of globally applicable public policy principles and provide an international government involvement at the level of principles over ... naming, numbering and addressing-related matters ... .[94]

Now finding itself isolated, the United States through its Secretary of State and Secretary of Commerce immediately requested the EU to reconsider its position, in a strongly worded letter to the UK Foreign Minister that stated, "We regret the recent positions on Internet governance (ie, the 'new cooperation model') offered by the European Union, the Presidency of which is currently held by the United Kingdom, seems to propose ... a new structure of intergovernmental control over the Internet."[95]

The US was in a strong position to maintain its stand. First, the only alternative to the cooperation of the United States in reform of Internet naming and numbering was the establishment of a new internationally-administered alternative DNS root, which although technically feasible, was still a radical step that had not yet been seriously considered at an intergovernmental level.[96]

Second, given the United States' record of exceptionalism in other contexts,[97] the prospect that the US could stymie the achievement of a WSIS resolution on Internet governance was seen as very real. As aptly noted in another context (that of reform to the UN Security Council), "the idea that the remaining superpower will continue to participate—politically or financially—in an institution whose purpose has become to limit its power

[94] EU, Proposal for Addition to Chair's Paper Sub-Com A Internet Governance on Paragraph 5 "Follow-up and Possible Arrangements" ⟨URL: http://www.itu.int/wsis/docs2/pc3/working/dt21.pdf⟩

[95] Kieren McCarthy, Read the Letter That Won the Internet Governance Battle ⟨URL: http://www.theregister.co.uk/2005/12/02/rice_eu_letter/⟩. The EU's stance was not in fact such a profound change as the US suggested, since as long before as 1998, the EU had written in a response to the Department of Commerce Green Paper that "the importance of an international framework for the long-term organization of the Internet underlines the need to associate a wide range of international interests with future policy in this area": Council of the European Union, Reply of the European Community and its Member States to the US Green Paper ⟨URL: http://jgate.ncsi.iisc.ernet.in/cyberspace/law/governance/eu/ReplytoUSGreenPaper.html⟩. The US also overlooked the fact that the EU had specified that its new cooperation model "should adhere, besides the Geneva principles, to ... the architectural principles of the Internet, including the interoperability, openness and the end-to-end principle," which implied that it envisioned far from a traditional intergovernmental policy-making role: Viktor Mayer-Schoenberger and Malte Ziewitz, Jefferson Rebuffed: The United States and the Future of Internet Governance ⟨URL: http://ksgnotes1.harvard.edu/Research/wpaper.nsf/rwp/RWP06-018⟩.

[96] Although certain countries had begun to supplement the ICANN root with their own independent TLDs; see section 2.3 on page 86.

[97] Such as its withdrawal from the Anti-Ballistic Missile Treaty, and its failure to accede to the Kyoto Protocol on climate change or to endorse the International Criminal Court: Ibid., 35.

has no precedent."[98]

Thus PrepCom 3 ended its scheduled term in September in deadlock, with only the days preceding the Tunis Summit available for further negotiation. The outcome of those last-minute negotiations was that the *status quo* would indeed be preserved for the time being, on the strength of an undertaking from the US that it would not interfere with other countries' ccTLDs, and with the inclusion in the Tunis Agenda of a tip of the hat towards the EU's "new cooperation model," in the form of the promise of "enhanced cooperation in the future."

The Tunis Agenda introduces this topic by acknowledging the success of the existing Internet governance regime in adapting to a dynamically changing Internet, largely led by the private sector and civil society, but also facilitated by the enabling environment fostered by governments. The Agenda acknowledges the importance of preserving the "security and stability" of these arrangements, which was also the language used in the NTIA's June 2005 statement on Internet naming and addressing when referring to the desirability of maintaining a single authoritative DNS root.[99]

The Tunis Agenda then however notes that Internet governance extends beyond naming and numbering issues, to include a wide variety of social, economic and technical issues many of which are not addressed by current mechanisms.[100] This points to the need for a new transparent and democratic multilateral process involving all stakeholders, that balances the importance of maintaining an enabling environment for an adaptive and evolving Internet, with the legitimate interests of states in controlling their own ccTLD space and the desire to strengthen cooperation among stakeholders in public policy making for the gTLDs.[101]

This sets the stage for the request that the UN Secretary-General convene a new forum for multi-stakeholder policy dialogue in which governments can take an equal role and responsibility for Internet governance and policy making in consultation with all other stakeholders. Although in doing this they are not to intervene in "the day-to-day technical and operational matters" of existing bodies such as ICANN and the RIRs, those bodies must in turn provide a role for governments to lead the development of globally applicable public policy principles and to also safeguard national and regional interests in management of their own Internet resources.[102]

At first glance, it might be assumed that the IGF is being spoken of here; and, indeed, it clearly is in part. After all, there is no other existing forum

[98] Thomas G Weiss, The Illusion of UN Security Council Reform, The Washington Quarterly 26:4 2003, 153

[99] WSIS, Tunis Agenda for the Information Society (as in n. 5 on page 2), paras 54–57

[100] Ibid., paras 58–60

[101] Ibid., paras 61–64.

[102] Ibid., paras 67–70 and 38

within which for governments to consult with all stakeholders on Internet policy issues. Neither is there any reason to assume that the enhanced cooperation process is to be limited to the issue of Internet naming and numbering to the exclusion of other public policy issues.[103] Moreover, there is no textual division between the discussion of enhanced cooperation and discussion of the IGF.

However on a closer reading, the Agenda speaks more broadly of a "process towards enhanced cooperation" between all "relevant organisations," to be commenced by the end of the first quarter of 2006 (whereas the IGF was to be established by the second quarter), and requests that each such organisation publish an annual performance report on its progress towards this end.[104]

Thus the preferable view is that the enhanced cooperation process is a broader initiative that includes, but is not limited to, the establishment of the IGF. Whilst the IGF has an initial five-year mandate, enhanced cooperation is a model of multi-stakeholder governance for the future, based upon bottom–up coordination subject to a framework of general principles. Even so, whilst there is conceptually a degree of separation between the two processes, there is no reason why they might not interweave, should the IGF become a permanent forum following the completion of its mandated term.

Whilst the intent of the Agenda on enhanced cooperation is thus tolerably clear, it still leaves many details of the process unspecified. What are the "relevant organisations" being referred to? To whom are their annual performance reports to be submitted? By what mechanism, or in what fora other than the IGF, if any, is the process of enhanced cooperation between stakeholders to take place?

These unanswered questions may be part of the reason for a delay in implementation of the enhanced cooperation directive. In March 2006, the UN Secretary-General requested Nitin Desai to begin informal consultations on how to start the process of enhanced cooperation,[105] pursuant to his mandate in the Tunis Agenda. In response to this, Desai commenced informal bilateral consultations with governments and select other stakeholders in May 2006 in a closed process, of which no documentary record was published. No such discussions are known to have taken place with civil society outside of the technical community, though Nominet[106] and the ICC[107] at least were consulted.

[103]See paras 58, 59, 60 and 61, though contra para 70.

[104]WSIS, Tunis Agenda for the Information Society (as in n. 5 on page 2), para 71

[105]United Nations Office of the Secretary-General, Preparations Begin for Internet Governance Forum ⟨URL: `http://www.un.org/News/Press/docs/2006/sgsm10366.doc.htm`⟩

[106]Nominet, Process Towards Enhanced Cooperation

[107]ICC, Global Business' Preliminary Input on WSIS Tunis Agenda Paragraphs 69-71 Regarding "Enhanced Cooperation" and Key Priorities Regarding Internet Governance Forum (IGF)

At a consultation meeting organised by the Secretariat of the IGF in February 2007, Desai indicated that he had, at some time following his consultations, submitted a report on them to the then Secretary-General, describing the respondents' expectations of a process leading to enhanced cooperation. Desai thus considered that his own mandate had been fulfilled, and that the matter was now in the Secretary-General's hands. No further progress had been made at the following open consultation meeting in May, at which Desai said:

> For six months, I personally met with people to find out whether there could be some basis, some common ground which could be found for a process, leaving it very flexible and elastic as to what this process could be. And, essentially, I have sent the report of that to the Secretary-General, the then-Secretary-General. And the fact is that there isn't that common ground as yet. So I think we'll have to try something different, a different approach. So let us see.

In the meantime, the ITU commenced its own process towards enhanced cooperation, resolving at its 2006 Plenipotentiary Conference in Antalya "to take the necessary steps in ITU's own internal process towards enhanced cooperation on international public policy issues pertaining to the Internet," and "as a concrete step, to organize consultations on these issues among the ITU membership and other relevant stakeholders, in order to prepare and submit proposals ... to the 2007 session of the Council."[108]

According to this approach, the process towards enhanced cooperation is limited to a bottom-up initiative of the existing Internet governance institutions, rather than the development of a new overarching framework to which those institutions are made subject. The same approach seems lately to have been taken by the UN Secretary-General also. In March 2008, Under-Secretary-General Sha Zukang, assuming Desai's role in taking the enhanced cooperation process forward, wrote privately to "relevant organisations" such as ISOC to request that they submit an annual performance report on their progress towards the realisation of enhanced cooperation as called for by the Tunis Agenda, to enable those reports to be summarised in the Secretary-General's progress report on WSIS.[109]

The Internet Governance Forum

In comparison to the wrangling over enhanced cooperation, agreement upon the establishment of the IGF could almost have been described as

[108] ITU, ITU's Role With Regard to International Public Policy Issues Pertaining to the Internet and the Management of Internet Resources, Including Domain Names and Addresses ⟨URL: http://www.itu.int/osg/spu/resolutions/2006/final-acts-internet-extracts.pdf⟩

[109] See http://wiki.tools.isoc.org/Policy_Activities/UN_report_request.

smooth. Following the report of WGIG, most governments had expressed their favour for the formation of the forum by the time of the September session of PrepCom 3. The United States was again a notable exception. In the same statement in which it reasserted its authority over the root DNS, and pointedly addressing the WGIG report, it stated:

> Dialogue related to Internet governance should continue in relevant multiple fora. Given the breadth of topics potentially encompassed under the rubric of Internet governance there is no one venue to appropriately address the subject in its entirety. While the United States recognizes that the current Internet system is working, we encourage an ongoing dialogue with all stakeholders around the world in the various fora as a way to facilitate discussion and to advance our shared interest in the ongoing robustness and dynamism of the Internet.[110]

A possible compromise suggested by the United States during the resumed PrepCom 3 in November was that the IGF should become an activity of ISOC; a proposal that was supported by Australia, but rejected by developing country governments. Eventually, the US and the other OECD governments came around to the idea of an IGF independent of ISOC by the inclusion of language to make it clear that it would be a multi-stakeholder body (rather than just a "multilateral" one), that it would not be bound by UN procedures, and that it would not be empowered to create binding obligations.[111]

The private sector was also initially dubious about the merit of an IGF, as was ISOC.[112] ISOC's position had long been that "Significant benefit will come from increased access to the Internet, not centralised government control. The centralised approach is not compatible with the dynamics of the Internet and is antithetical to what has made the Internet such a success to date."[113] In fact by the conclusion of the first round of PrepCom 3, ISOC was one of only two WSIS participants on record as opposing the creation of the IGF.[114]

Most of the balance of civil society had long supported the proposal, although the CS-IGC for one would have preferred that it be established

---

[110]NTIA, US Principles on the Internet's Domain Name and Addressing System (as in n. 38 on page 40)

[111]Heinrich-Böll Foundation, Negotiations Closer to Agreement: Consensus on Internet Governance Forum and—Almost—ICANN Oversight ⟨URL: `http://www.worldsummit2005.de/en/web/825.htm`⟩

[112]WSIS Secretariat, Compilation of Comments Received on the Report of the Working Group on Internet Governance (as in n. 84 on page 344), 31–35

[113]ISOC, Annual Report (as in n. 10 on page 33), 4

[114]The other was WITSA; the World Information Technology and Services Alliance, which had been a co-founder of the CCBI. The ICC had already dropped its opposition by this time.

as a legally free-standing entity rather than being anchored in the United Nations.[115] Its view of the role of the IGF was that:

> The forum should not by default have a mandate to negotiate hard instruments like treaties or contracts. However, in very exceptional circumstances when the parties all agree that such instruments are needed, there could be a mechanism that allows for their establishment. Normally, the forum should focus on the development of soft law instruments such as recommendations, guidelines, declarations, etc.[116]

This was largely consistent with how the proposal eventually found form in the Tunis Agenda. It requested the UN Secretary-General to form an Internet Governance Forum for multi-stakeholder policy dialogue, with the full involvement of all stakeholders, and with a mandate that is to be set out in full below.[117]

The Secretary-General was directed to invite all stakeholders to participate at the IGF's inaugural meeting, giving consideration to the need for balanced geographical representation, and drawing on resources from all interested stakeholders. An effective and cost-efficient bureau was to be established to support the forum, ensuring multi-stakeholder participation. The Secretary-General was also directed to review whether the forum should continue in operation within five years of its creation, and to report on its operation to UN members periodically.[118]

The Tunis Agenda states that the IGF should be multilateral, multi-stakeholder, democratic and transparent in its working and function, with a lightweight and decentralized structure that is subject to periodic review. It is not to replace other relevant fora in which Internet governance issues are discussed or to exercise oversight over them or have any binding decision-making power. In particular, it would have no involvement in day-to-day or technical operations of the Internet, but would work in parallel with those organisations that do, taking advantage of their expertise.[119]

Development action lines

The final part of the Tunis Agenda deals with implementation and follow-up. It specifies that this must take place at an international, regional and

[115] CS-IGC, Initial Reactions to the WGIG Report (as in n. 23 on page 327), 3

[116] Ibid., 3

[117] WSIS, Tunis Agenda for the Information Society (as in n. 5 on page 2), paras 72 and 74 and see section 5.2 on page 353.

[118] Ibid., paras 75, 76 and 78

[119] Ibid., paras 73, 77 and 79.

national level, and at each level involve governments in a leading role, in partnership with other stakeholders.[120]

The follow-up and review mechanisms that apply to all three of these processes in parallel are described as "system-wide."[121] The agency given the lead role in overseeing this system-wide follow-up is ECOSOC, with the Agenda suggesting that it strengthen its Commission on Science and Technology for Development (CSTD) to enable it to manage the role using a multi-stakeholder approach.[122]

Also at a system-wide level, the General Assembly is to make an overall review of the implementation of WSIS outcomes by 2015, which is the same date as set by the Plan of Action for the achievement of its objectives, goals and targets, and also the target date for achievement of the Millennium Development Goals.[123] Periodic evaluation of the WSIS outcomes, including implementation mechanisms, is also to be conducted using an agreed methodology, which includes the use of the Digital Opportunity Index described at section 4.3 on page 285. [124]

In addition to these system-wide mechanisms, implementation and follow-up at the international level is subject to two additional processes: coordination of the activities of UN agencies,[125] and multi-stakeholder implementation.[126] In practice, these two mechanisms have largely merged and may be treated for present purposes as one.

The body responsible for oversight and coordination of this process at the international level is the United Nations Group on the Information Society (UNGIS), which was established in April 2006 in compliance with a mandate given in the Tunis Agenda to the Secretary-General to establish the group within the UN's Chief Executives Board (CEB), with the suggestion that it be led by the ITU, UNESCO and UNDP.[127]

An annex to the Agenda links the eleven action lines and eight subsidiary lines from the Plan of Action with relevant UN agencies that it is suggested might take the leading role as facilitators or moderators in following up on their implementation. Thus for example line C8, "Cultural diversity and identity, linguistic diversity and local content," is provisionally assigned to UNESCO, and the "e-government" subsidiary line of C7 on "ICT applications" is assigned jointly to the UNDP and ITU. The appointment of these suggested facilitators was confirmed, or in some cases

[120] WSIS, Tunis Agenda for the Information Society (as in n. 5 on page 2), paras 100–102
[121] Ibid., paras 104, 105 and 111
[122] Ibid., para 105
[123] Ibid., para 111
[124] Ibid., paras 113–120
[125] Ibid., para 103
[126] Ibid., paras 108–110
[127] Ibid., para 109

modified, during open consultations held in February 2006,[128] and UNGIS has since organised further meetings for the facilitators of each action line in Geneva.[129]

Finally, and outside of the already-complex structures for follow-up and implementation specified in the Tunis Agenda, the Global Alliance for ICT and Development (GAID)[130] was formed in April 2006 as the successor to the UNICTTF whose mandate had expired at the end of 2005. GAID's cross-cutting mission is to provide "a platform for an open, inclusive, multi-stakeholder cross-sectoral policy dialogue on the role of information and communication technology in development."[131] Like its predecessor, GAID is open to all stakeholders and held its first meeting in Kuala Lumpur in June 2006.

5.2 IGF

The Internet Governance Forum's mandate is as set out in paragraph 72 of the Tunis Agenda, which provides:

> We ask the UN Secretary-General, in an open and inclusive process, to convene, by the second quarter of 2006, a meeting of the new forum for multi-stakeholder policy dialogue—called the Internet Governance Forum (IGF). The mandate of the Forum is to:
>
> a) Discuss public policy issues related to key elements of Internet governance in order to foster the sustainability, robustness, security, stability and development of the Internet;
>
> b) Facilitate discourse between bodies dealing with different cross-cutting international public policies regarding the Internet and discuss issues that do not fall within the scope of any existing body;
>
> c) Interface with appropriate inter-governmental organizations and other institutions on matters under their purview;

[128] ITU, Summary Report: Consultation Meeting of WSIS Action Line Facilitators/Moderators ⟨URL: http://www.itu.int/wsis/implementation/docs/consultations/feb2006/summary-report.pdf⟩

[129] See http://www.itu.int/wsis/implementation/.

[130] See http://www.un-gaid.org/.

[131] United Nations Office of the Secretary-General, Global Alliance for Information Technologies and Development to be Launched ⟨URL: http://www.un.org/News/Press/docs/2006/dev2572.doc.htm⟩

d) Facilitate the exchange of information and best practices, and in this regard make full use of the expertise of the academic, scientific and technical communities;
e) Advise all stakeholders in proposing ways and means to accelerate the availability and affordability of the Internet in the developing world;
f) Strengthen and enhance the engagement of stakeholders in existing and/or future Internet governance mechanisms, particularly those from developing countries;
g) Identify emerging issues, bring them to the attention of the relevant bodies and the general public, and, where appropriate, make recommendations;
h) Contribute to capacity building for Internet governance in developing countries, drawing fully on local sources of knowledge and expertise;
i) Promote and assess, on an ongoing basis, the embodiment of WSIS principles in Internet governance processes;
j) Discuss, *inter alia*, issues relating to critical Internet resources;
k) Help to find solutions to the issues arising from the use and misuse of the Internet, of particular concern to everyday users;
l) Publish its proceedings.

This is an expansion of WGIG's suggestions as to the content of the IGF's mandate, which contained six points.[132]

Subparagraph (c) above was derived from the first point in the WGIG list, but omitted the qualifying words, "which are relevant to Internet governance, such as IPR, ecommerce, trade in services and Internet/telecommunications convergence." Although this may not seem a substantive change on its face, the amendment reflected the exclusion of IPR and trade issues altogether from the Tunis Agenda by governments wishing for those issues to be reserved to WIPO and the WTO.[133]

The second point in the WGIG list became subparagraph (g), but in this case with two additions: the words "and the general public" after "appropriate bodies" (which adds a measure of transparency to its mandate), but also the proviso that it would only make recommendations "where appropriate" (which arguably narrows the scope of the IGF's mandate to make recommendations).

The substance of the third and fourth points in the WGIG list can be found in subparagraph (b) above, but in weakened form: the forum is only

[132] See section 5.1 on page 339.
[133] Accuosto (as in n. 164 on page 71)

to "discuss" rather than to "address" issues not being dealt with elsewhere, and there is no longer any reference to it making proposals for action. It is therefore arguable that the IGF has no mandate to make recommendations for action in respect of issues that are not being dealt with elsewhere, unless they also fall within another head of its mandate (for example, because the issues are "emerging").[134]

The fifth and sixth points of the WGIG list are the only ones to be reproduced verbatim in the Tunis Agenda, at subparagraphs (h) and (i). This leaves subparagraphs (a), (d), (e), (f), (j), (k) and (l) as new additions to the IGF's mandate in the Agenda.

The IGF's mandate is to be reviewed by the UN Secretary-General pursuant to the Tunis Agenda in 2011. Thus, there may be only five meetings of the IGF. The choice of Athens as a venue for the first meeting was made in accepting an offer of the Greek government made at WSIS. The offers of the Brazilian, Indian and Egyptian governments made respectively at public consultations in February and May and at the Athens meeting to host the second, third and fourth meetings were accepted by the IGF Secretariat without public consultation. The possibly final meeting, to be held in 2010, was the subject of competing bids from both Lithuania and Azerbaijan in Athens.

Preparations

The first action taken by the UN Secretary-General towards the establishment of the IGF was the appointment of Markus Kummer, formerly of the WGIG Secretariat, to head its interim Secretariat. In January 2006, Kummer established an IGF Web site and wrote an open letter to stakeholder representatives from WSIS, inviting them to attend an open consultation session in Geneva in February and requesting them to submit written contributions as inputs into the consultations.[135]

In response to this request, nineteen contributors from civil society and the private sector provided written submissions.[136] In the interim, Kummer also posted a questionnaire to the IGF Web site which provided the opportunity for comments to be provided in a more structured form.[137] The questionnaire received a limited response, being completed by seven governments (including Australia, but neither the United States nor the EU), three individuals, twelve civil society and private sector organisations, and the ITU.[138]

---

[134] See section 6.2 on page 424.

[135] See http://www.intgovforum.org/inv_letter.htm.

[136] See http://www.intgovforum.org/contributionsg.htm.

[137] See http://www.intgovforum.org/questionnaire.htm.

[138] See http://www.intgovforum.org/contributions_questionnaire_responses.htm.

Submissions

Since respondents prepared their submissions to these first two requests for contributions in isolation, without the opportunity to engage with each other's views, the submissions showed little development from the positions that the stakeholders had taken at WSIS, and indeed some largely repeated their responses to the proposal for the formation of a forum in the WGIG report.

It is not necessary to go into each of them here, but a brief overview will be given, focusing on three key procedural issues: the role of the IGF, its structure, and its processes. The substantive public policy issues that some submissions also addressed will not be outlined here.

Taking first the role of the IGF, what would prove to be a recurrent division can already be seen between those preferring a restrictive interpretation of its mandate, which downplayed or refuted its capacity to make policy recommendations, and those who took an expansive view of its mandate, who saw that capacity as the forum's *raison d'etre*.

The former group largely consisted of those who had opposed the establishment of the IGF at first; the technical community (such as Nominet which stated, "[i]t should not be a decision-making body"),[139] the private sector (such as the CCBI and ICC which stressed "the IGF will not have decision-making powers"),[140] and OECD governments (such as Canada which wrote that "the IGF is to provide a platform for policy discussion, not for the development of policy").[141]

The latter camp was dominated by civil society (such as the APC which saw the IGF producing "[s]pecific recommendations where there is sufficient consensus"),[142] and developing country governments (such as Azerbaijan, which wrote that the Forum should produce "recommendations that ... are not legally binding but could be a very good source for policy-making and decision-making").[143]

Moving to the IGF's structure, there was widespread agreement that the "effective and cost-efficient bureau" referred to in the Tunis Agenda should have a narrow mandate limited to setting the agenda for plenary

---

[139]Nominet, Questionnaire on the Convening the Internet Governance Forum ⟨URL: `http://www.intgovforum.org/contributions/Nominet%20Questionnaire.pdf`⟩, 1

[140]CCBI and ICC, CCBI/ICC Questions and Further Input on the Internet Governance Forum ⟨URL: `http://www.intgovforum.org/contributions/CCBI%20further%20input%20on%20IGF%206%20February%20FINAL.pdf`⟩, 2

[141]Government of Canada, Questionnaire on the Convening the Internet Governance Forum ⟨URL: `http://www.intgovforum.org/contributions/GOC_IGF%20Questionnaire%20Response%20.pdf`⟩, 1

[142]APC, Questionnaire on the Convening the Internet Governance Forum ⟨URL: `http://www.intgovforum.org/contributions/apc-questionnaire.pdf`⟩, 1

[143]Government of Azerbaijan, Proposed Answers to the Questionnaire on the Convening the Internet Governance Forum ⟨URL: `http://www.intgovforum.org/contributions/Azerbaijan_Q.pdf`⟩, 1

meetings, subject to bottom–up consultation[144] (though some civil society stakeholders would have assigned it a more substantial role).[145] The need for a separate lightweight Secretariat was also accepted by many.

Beyond that however, the first camp referred to above (for convenience, "Forum doves")[146] were more likely to de-emphasise structure, as illustrated by the statement that "Australia does not support the IGF establishing a range of sub-groups or subcommittees,"[147] and ISOC's claim that it was important to "[l]imit Forum-related organizational structures."[148]

A more substantial structure tended to be supported by those in the second group referred to above ("Forum hawks," let us call them). For example, Saudi Arabia recommended the formation of "virtual working groups" which would coordinate online,[149] and the Internet Governance Project fleshed this idea out with a comprehensive proposal to structure the IGF rather along the lines of the IETF. [150]

Turning finally to the IGF's processes, the divide already observed continued along much the same lines, between Forum doves who viewed the IGF as principally a meeting (as for example Canada which did "not envisage the establishment of ongoing work programs for the IGF"),[151] and Forum hawks who viewed it as "a process, punctuated by an annual meeting",[152] and who were concerned with how it might arrive at the recommendations that it was to make pursuant to its mandate.

---

144 For example, Government of Canada, Questionnaire on the Convening the Internet Governance Forum (as in n. 141 on the preceding page), 3; Government of Azerbaijan (as in n. 143 on the facing page), 2; CCBI and ICC (as in n. 140 on the preceding page), 5–6; IGP, Building an Internet Governance Forum ⟨URL: `http://dcc.syr.edu/miscarticles/IGP-Forum.pdf`⟩, 5

145 Ibid.; MMWG, Internet Governance Forum Input Statement ⟨URL: `http://www.intgovforum.org/contributions/Internet%20Governance%20Forum%20Input%20Statement1.pdf`⟩

146 From the Internet Governance Project's summary of a forum held by the Oxford Internet Institute on 1 September, found at `http://www.internetgovernance.org/events.html`.

147 Government of Australia, Response to Questionnaire on Internet Governance Forum ⟨URL: `http://www.intgovforum.org/contributions/Au%20Govt%20response%20to%20IGF%20questionnaire%20060213.pdf`⟩, 1

148 ISOC, The Internet Society's contribution on the formation of the Internet Governance Forum ⟨URL: `http://www.intgovforum.org/contributions/ISOC%20IGF%20CONTRIBUTION.pdf`⟩, 2

149 Government of Saudi Arabia, Response to Questionnaire on Convening the Internet Governance Forum ⟨URL: `http://www.intgovforum.org/contributions/questionnaire%20Saudi.pdf`⟩, 2

150 It recommended a twelve-person bureau containing five representatives of governments, and two each from the private sector, civil society and the academic and technical communities, plus a chair. This proposed IGF Bureau would elect a chair for the Forum at large and set the agenda for its plenary sessions, driven by proposals of IGF working groups. It would also approve the formation of such working groups, and exercise oversight of the Secretariat: IGP, Building an Internet Governance Forum (as in n. 144), 5. Compare also MMWG (as in n. 145), 3.

151 Government of Canada, Questionnaire on the Convening the Internet Governance Forum (as in n. 141 on the facing page), 5

152 APC, Questionnaire on the Convening the Internet Governance Forum (as in n. 142 on the preceding page), 2

Perhaps the extreme position from the Forum doves came from the ITU, which suggested in its response to the questionnaire that "the WSIS rules of procedures themselves could be considered as the starting point for the IGF processes and procedures"[153]—referring to the same rules that had notoriously consigned civil society to the sidelines during WSIS.

As for the hawks, Vittorio Bertola, a member of the CS-IGC (though not writing in that capacity), drew upon the model of the IETF in suggesting that working groups of the IGF should develop their recommendations on a rough consensus basis, before presenting these to the plenary body as policy proposals for adoption.[154] The APC largely agreed, and suggested that it should then fall to the Chair to rule on the existence of rough consensus within the plenary meeting.[155]

Consultations

The first open consultations on the establishment of the IGF were held in Geneva on 16 and 17 February 2006, and were chaired by Nitin Desai.[156] Around 300 attended, including approximately 40 governments, along with those who observed the proceedings remotely via webcast. The proceedings were simultaneously translated into the official UN languages, with the webcast being available in English and French.

The consultations were not structured as an interactive discussion, but rather a moderated round table event at which most interventions were read from prepared statements, many of which were also tabled as documents and later made available from the IGF Web site.[157] In consequence, there was little opportunity for consensus-building, and in many cases the participants' views expressed in response to the questionnaire or the WGIG report were simply reiterated.

Even so, there was enough common ground between participants that Desai was able to declare the existence of a broad consensus that the IGF should be an annual event of about four days, open to representatives of all stakeholder groups, with a focus on about three themes.

---

[153]ITU, Preliminary Response to the Questionnaire on the Convening of the Internet Governance Forum ⟨URL: `http://www.intgovforum.org/contributions/IGF%20Questionnaire%20Response%20ITU.pdf`⟩

[154]Vittorio Bertola, An Implementation Proposal for the Internet Governance Forum ⟨URL: `http://www.intgovforum.org/contributions/An%20implementation%20proposal%20for%20the%20IGF.pdf`⟩, 2; and see also, from another CS-IGC member, Avri Doria, The IETF as a Model for the IGF ⟨URL: `http://www.intgovforum.org/contributions/IETF-as-model.pdf`⟩.

[155]APC, Questionnaire on the Convening the Internet Governance Forum (as in n. 142 on page 356), 1–2, 8

[156]See `http://intgovforum.org/meeting.htm`.

[157]See `http://www.intgovforum.org/contributions_interventions_1CIGF.htm`. Except where one of these papers is cited, the source for this section of the book is the transcript of the meeting found at `http://www.intgovforum.org/meeting.htm`.

Beyond this, the areas of difference largely reflected those that had been seen in the earlier written submissions as outlined above—that is, in respect of the three key procedural issues of the role of the IGF, its structure, and its processes—with further disagreement about the substantive issues that should form the agenda for the IGF's first meeting. These will be briefly dealt with in turn.

On the role of the IGF, there had been no progression from the views expressed in response to the initial call for contributions and the questionnaire. From the Forum doves, the CCBI reiterated that "[t]he Tunis Agenda is clear that the IGF does not have decision-making or policy-making authority," and the NRO emphasised that the "IGF must be a multi-stakeholder forum without decision-making attributions."[158] Again, the hawks insisted otherwise, with El Salvador expressing hope "that the Internet Governance Forum will come up with recommendations built on consensus on specific issues," and Brazil even characterising its first meeting as "an excellent opportunity to initiate negotiations on a framework treaty to deal with international Internet public policy issues."[159]

On the structure of the IGF, although a broad consensus was declared on need for a lightweight multi-stakeholder bureau, which respondents also variously described as a "Programmatic Committee,"[160] "Programme Committee"[161] or "steering group,"[162] there was no consensus on what its size, composition or mandate should be. Desai therefore held this issue over for further written input by 28 February. Twelve responses were received, including five from governments.[163]

Most of these respondents, from across both camps and all stakeholder groups, recommended a body of between ten and twenty-five members. The proposal that deviated most sharply from this was that of the Group of 77 and China (the G77).[164] Their proposal was for not one but three bureaus, much as there had been at WSIS,[165] which would have a combined total of forty members—half of those to be governmental.[166]

Moving on the third and final procedural issue, the IGF's processes, the February consultations more clearly illustrated a difference of approach

---

158 NRO, Input on the Internet Governance Forum ⟨URL: http://www.intgovforum.org/contributions/nro-inputs-on-igf.pdf⟩

159 Government of Brazil, Discurso IGF Meeting Fev 2006 ⟨URL: http://www.intgovforum.org/contributions/Discurso%20IGF%20meeting%20fev-2006.doc⟩, 2

160 NRO (as in n. 158)

161 MMWG (as in n. 145 on page 357)

162 Bertola, An Implementation Proposal for the Internet Governance Forum (as in n. 154 on the preceding page), 3

163 See http://www.intgovforum.org/contributions_MSG.htm.

164 Despite the name, the G77 at the time represented 133 developing country governments.

165 That is, a Governmental Bureau, Civil Society Bureau and the CCBI for the private sector.

166 G77, G77 & China Paper on the Proposed Internet Governance Forum ⟨URL: http://www.intgovforum.org/contributions/G77_9_March.pdf⟩, 2–3

between the Forum doves and hawks on an issue that has not already been traversed in discussion of the written submissions: that of online participation.

Almost all stakeholders from both camps expressed general support for the use of online working methods; for example, the CCBI arguing that the IGF should "[u]tilize online tools to make it more inclusive with no stakeholder group excluded from the discussions," and Canada noting that "[b]y building a significant online presence, the IGF can also facilitate ongoing discussion between its physical meetings."[167]

However some Forum doves were less enthused of the idea of using online tools for intersessional work. ISOC said, "It is unrealistic to expect all stakeholders to be able to participate in multiple-layered list-based exchanges on a realtime basis. Many stakeholders do not have the resources or time to spend managing or participating in ongoing discussions."[168] Australia echoed this concern, saying:

> A key concern is the actual human resources such processes would require on an ongoing basis if all stakeholders are to participate in them in a meaningful way. ... We tend to see, in contrast, a focused annual meeting as a more resource efficient and effective means of proceeding. As such, we do not see online processes being mandated from above as an integral part of the IGF, but rather being encouraged as bottom–up initiatives.[169]

The final area of difference between stakeholder representatives attending the February consultations was as to the substantive issues that ought to be included on the agenda of the IGF's first meeting. This question too was

[167]Government of Canada, Canadian Statement, IGF Consultations Feb 16 2006 ⟨URL: `http://www.intgovforum.org/contributions/Canadian%20Statement%20IGF%20consults%20Feb%2016.pdf`⟩, 2

[168]ISOC, ISOC Statement, Internet Governance Forum Meeting 17 February 2006 ⟨URL: `http://www.intgovforum.org/contributions/ISOC%20statement%20Feb%2017.pdf`⟩, 2

[169]Government of Australia, Second Intervention by the Government of Australia ⟨URL: `http://www.intgovforum.org/contributions/Au%202nd%20intervention%20060217.pdf`⟩, 2–3. Addressing this and the concerns more broadly expressed by Forum doves about the establishment of IGF working groups, William Drake, a member of the CS-IGC, responded:

> it need not involve a great deal of resources. It would be an opportunity under the umbrella of the IGF for those people who have a shared interest in a topic to discuss it in a nonbinding way. It's come as you are. If you want to be there, you are. And if you're not ... you're not. So, to us, that is very much a bottom–up process, and the product would be one that is potentially something that could enrich the larger dialogue. The larger plenary then could decide whether, "Hmm, this is an interesting matter that's been brought up by this working group. Perhaps this merits further conversation in a larger, more structured setting," et cetera.

held over by Desai, pending the receipt of written submissions which he invited stakeholders to provide by 31 March.[170]

In the meantime, a short synthesis by the Secretariat of the written contributions and discussions to date produced a list of the ten most frequently mentioned public policy issues, and claimed to identify an emerging consensus that the activities of the IGF should have an overall development orientation, with an overarching priority of capacity building to enable meaningful participation in global Internet policy development.[171]

A somewhat different picture was painted by the submissions on substantive issues that were eventually received and posted on the IGF Web site. Contrary to the report of the Secretariat that capacity building was the issue addressed most frequently, if equal weight was given to each issue nominated, then as the chart below illustrates, the issues nominated most often were:

- e-security and cybercrime;
- spam;
- privacy and digital identity; and
- freedom of expression and access to knowledge.[172]

Together these amounted to almost half of the total, as against the development issues of capacity building, the digital divide, multilingualism and interconnection costs and connectivity, which constituted around a third.

A second round of consultations was held, also in Geneva, on 19 May 2006, immediately preceding the first meeting of the Advisory Group.[173] The IGF's Web site described the purpose of these consultations as to "focus on the substantive preperation [*sic*] of the inaugural meeting of the IGF." As before, further written contributions were also solicited in advance of the meeting, though as only two respondents (David Allen and John

[170]See `http://www.intgovforum.org/contributions_sa.htm`.

[171]IGF Secretariat, The Substantive Agenda of the First Meeting of the Internet Governance Forum ⟨URL: `http://www.intgovforum.org/Summary%20of%20discussions.htm`⟩

[172]Submissions were excluded from analysis if they nominated more than three issues (even if these were grouped into clusters), unless three primary issues could be discerned. Also excluded were submissions listed on the IGF Web site together with those on substantive issues, but which were actually on other topics. This excluded six respondents: the Group of 77 and China, African Civil Society, the Association for Progressive Communications, the German Foundation for Law and Informatics, David Allen and John Mathiason (these latter two actually being submissions for the May consultations), along with additional submissions of the ICC/CCBI and North American Consumer Project on Electronic Commerce (NACPEC). Further details of the method used to produce the chart are on file with the author.

[173]See `http://www.intgovforum.org/contributions_18May.htm` for copies of interventions from three stakeholders and `http://www.intgovforum.org/meeting.htm` for the full transcript.

Figure 5.1: Substantive issues for the IGF

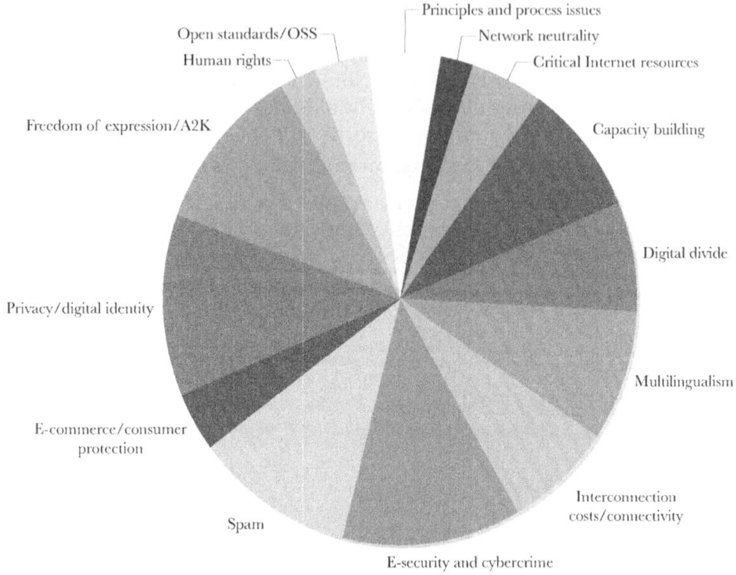

Mathiason, both academics) saw fit to provide them, these do not call for separate treatment here. The consultations were also once again translated and webcast.

The interventions at the May consultations were broadly congruent with those that had been made in February, so detailed analysis of them is unnecessary. However if anything, a strengthening of the views expressed then could be discerned three months later. One notable respect in which this was so is that the broad agreement that development should be made an overarching priority for the IGF's substantive agenda was now more clearly in evidence.

To take one further example of the consolidation of stakeholders' positions, in this case on the role and structure of the IGF, Brazil had become even more forthright in its insistence that the IGF's outputs should include substantive recommendations, stating:

> even though we are not going to take decisions in the forum—that's why we are calling it a forum—we can have recommendations. And to have recommendations, we need to divide ourselves in topics, in groups, for each group to recommend something on specific topics, and then [it] goes back to

> the second plenary and the last one where we are going to approve recommendations. Non-binding recommendations, but it would be recommendations … we are going to send back, I suppose, to the Secretary-General of the United Nations, and then these recommendations can be delivered to specific bodies that takes [*sic*] decisions on matters. Then my suggestion, Mr Chairman, [is] then we have an opening plenary, a closing plenary [and] panels, groups, study groups in between; as many as we want, as we decide, as the group decides. Each one producing recommendations on a consensus basis. Of course there will be no votes. Recommendations goes [*sic*] back to the last plenary, and then we approve, and we are ready to go to [those other bodies].

Saudi Arabia agreed and went further, pointing to the need for the IGF to develop the capacity to engage in intersessional work in order to fulfil its mandate:

> with regards to … coming [up] with concrete proposals out of the IGF, it would be practically not possible to both discuss topics and come to reasonable conclusions in the same meeting. We therefore recommend that the topics be put forward for discussion prior to the meeting itself, and a mechanism be established to allow initial discussions to prepare for the meeting. The results of these discussions should be published electronically for everybody's preparation. The IGF meeting will be used to present the various views, further discussions and conclusions on these issues.

Whilst civil society (well represented in May by Wolfgang Kleinwächter amongst others) was in accord with this strategy, the more circumspect approach of the Forum doves was put most forcefully on this occasion by Nitin Desai himself, who stated, "I would stress that there is a forum for dialogue. This is a forum for discussion. It is not a decision-making forum."

Noting the hawks' position that in order to fulfil its mandate, some decisions would have to be taken by consensus on recommendations to be made by the Forum, Desai responded doubtfully, "consensus between 500 participants from multiple sectors groups… I will put it to the Advisory Group. It's an interesting thought—I will put it to them and see how they feel about it." Whilst the Advisory Group's reaction to the proposal, if Desai did put it to them, is unknown, it will soon be seen that no such consensual decision-making structures were in place for the first meeting in Athens.

Secretariat

The Secretariat of the IGF was formally established by the UN Secretary-General in March 2006.[174] In contrast to the Secretariat of WGIG in which Markus Kummer managed a staff of up to ten, he was initially assisted in the IGF Secretariat by a sole consultant, and an intern from the host nation.[175] As Chair of the Advisory Group, Nitin Desai also worked very closely with the Secretariat and often referred to himself as a member of it.[176]

The Secretariat was not funded by the United Nations, but relied upon voluntary donations to a trust fund. Its early donors included the Swiss Agency for Development and Cooperation which contributed CHF 500 000 (on the proviso that the Secretariat was to be based in Geneva), ICANN which gave US$200 000, and Nominet which donated €15 000.[177] Each host nation was also a major donor, covering all the costs it incurred in hosting an IGF meeting.

As might perhaps be expected from a Secretariat with such limited resources, its services to stakeholders were much more limited than those of the WSIS Secretariat. For example, the IGF's official Web site was very rudimentary, and it was difficult to obtain a response to enquiries and requests directed to the Secretariat. The transparency of the Secretariat's activities was also very limited, as first and most clearly exemplified by the process by which the Advisory Group was appointed.

Advisory Group

The bureau referred to in the Tunis Agenda, and the multi-stakeholder group referred to following the February consultations, eventually became the Advisory Group, also known as the Multi-stakeholder Advisory Group (MAG). It was announced on the IGF's Web site in March that it was to be established as a group of "about forty" members, and—although not openly stated—half of those forty were to be government representatives, with the balance to be divided, not necessarily equally, between civil society and private sector positions.[178]

The written submission of the G77 and China on the multi-stakeholder group, which had proposed almost exactly this structure, had been sent under cover of a letter expressing the groups' hope that Desai would "give

[174] United Nations Office of the Secretary-General, Preparations Begin for Internet Governance Forum (as in n. 105 on page 348)

[175] As at 2008 they have been joined by another intern, a fellow, and two more part-time consultants.

[176] See for example the first passage cited at section 6.3 on page 452.

[177] See `http://www.intgovforum.org/funding.htm`.

[178] Milton Mueller, The Forum MAG: Who Are These People? ⟨URL: `http://www.icannwatch.org/article.pl?sid=06/05/18/226205&mode=thread`⟩

the requisite weight to this input."[179] Evidently that is what he did, since a group of forty members was far larger than any other stakeholder had suggested would be appropriate.

A call for nominations for membership of the Advisory Group was made on 16 March 2006 with a deadline of 18 April. Nominations were not acknowledged by the IGF Secretariat, and the first that unsuccessful nominees heard of the outcomes of their nominations was the Secretariat's announcement of the successful candidates on 17 May.[180] The forty-six originally listed as successful included the Chair, Nitin Desai, and forty representatives of stakeholder groups, with fairly even geographical distribution. In addition a regional coordinator was appointed from each of the five WSIS regions, and initially five special advisors personally appointed by the Chair, who have been referred to in their own right as the Special Advisory Group (SAG).[181]

Intergovernmental organisations, not being otherwise represented in the Advisory Group, were invited to participate as observers; however in practice they exercised much the same speaking rights as other delegates.[182]

The non-governmental positions on the Advisory Group were dominated by those with a connection to the Internet naming and numbering regime, including five current or former board members and one staff member of ICANN, one of the IGF's major sponsors.[183] Even so, the technical community was not recognised as a distinct stakeholder group, as ICANN had requested most recently at the February consultations. Rather, in referring to "civil society, including the academic and technical communities," the Secretariat treated these communities as part of civil society.[184]

The greatest discontent at this decision came from broader civil society, as it left room for only a relatively small number of stakeholders from civil society outside the technical community to be appointed to the Advisory Group. In particular, the CS-IGC had put forward fifteen nominees for appointment, of which only three were selected by the Secretary-General.[185]

The Advisory Group met twice in Geneva before the inaugural IGF meeting in Athens, first following the May open consultations, and again

[179] G77 (as in n. 166 on page 359), 1

[180] United Nations Office of the Secretary-General, Secretary-General Establishes Advisory Group to Assist Him in Convening Internet Governance Forum ⟨URL: `http://www.un.org/News/Press/docs/2006/sga1006.doc.htm`⟩

[181] In May 2006 the number rose to forty-seven when an additional regional coordinator was appointed for an unspecified African sub-region. By the date of the Rio de Janeiro meeting the number of special advisors had risen to twelve: six appointed by each of the then two co-chairs.

[182] IGF Secretariat, Advisory Group Discussion 30 January to 3 February 2008 ⟨URL: `http://intgovforum.org/AGD/AGdiscussion.30.01.-03.02.2008.pdf`⟩, 2

[183] Mueller, The Forum MAG: Who Are These People? (as in n. 178 on the preceding page)

[184] United Nations Office of the Secretary-General, Secretary-General Establishes Advisory Group to Assist Him in Convening Internet Governance Forum (as in n. 180)

[185] See the CS-IGC's contribution to the post-Athens consultation session at section 5.2 on page 381.

following another open consultation meeting in September. Advisory Group members attended these meetings at their own expense, save that the Swiss government offered in February to reimburse the travel expenses of members from developing countries.

Meetings of the Advisory Group were closed, and no reports or minutes of them were released during the preparations for Athens. The Advisory Group also operated an electronic mailing list, but this too was closed, and not publicly archived.[186] Consequently, the detail of the operations of the Advisory Group ahead of the first IGF meeting were known only to its members.

What is known is that the Advisory Group possessed little formal authority; for the most part operating as a forum for discussion akin to the open consultations, at which those in attendance expressed and debated their views, but without the object of taking formal decisions. Instead, the views expressed on the issues discussed were summarised by the Chair in a report to the UN Secretary-General, on the basis of which the Secretary-General made a formal decision in due course.[187] What few decisions the Advisory Group did make on its own behalf on matters such as as the selection of panelists for the plenary sessions were made by rough consensus as declared by the Chair.[188]

The First Meeting

The inaugural meeting of the Internet Governance Forum was held in Athens from 30 October to 2 November 2006. According to the Greek hosts,[189] it was attended by 1350 participants (including 152 media), from 97 countries. Approximately 40% of these were from civil society, about 35% governmental or intergovernmental, and another 25% divided fairly equally between the private sector and the media.[190] There was no cost to register for the event, with all venue expenses being covered by the hosts.

At the Advisory Group's meeting on 22 and 23 May, and as foreshadowed following the February consultations, an overall theme "Internet Governance for Development" was selected for the Athens meeting, with capacity building as a "cross-cutting priority." Within this framework, four

[186]This remains the case, although in February 2008, following considerable criticism of the Advisory Group's transparency, consideration was given to opening the mailing list archives. As this was resisted by certain stakeholders, no changes were made: IGF Secretariat, Advisory Group Discussion 30 January to 3 February 2008 (as in n. 182 on the preceding page), 9.

[187]See section 6.3 on page 452.

[188]Idem, Advisory Group Discussion 6 December 2007 to 15 January 2008 (as in n. 79 on page 200), 2

[189]At the February 2007 follow-up consultations; see section 5.2 on page 381.

[190]See http://www.intgovforum.org/Athens_stats_stakeholder.php. It is assumed that the "technical and academic communities" shown here may be treated as from civil society.

themes for discussion were chosen, being described on the IGF Web site as follows:

- Openness (freedom of expression, free flow of information, ideas and knowledge);
- Security (creating trust and confidence through collaboration, particularly by protecting users from spam, phishing and viruses while protecting privacy);
- Diversity (promoting multilingualism, including IDN, and local content); and
- Access (Internet connectivity: policy and cost, dealing with the availability and affordability of the Internet including issues such as interconnection costs, interoperability and open standards).

The breadth of these themes was such that almost all of the public policy issues previously raised by stakeholders in their interventions and written contributions could be shoehorned into one or more of them, although the omission of explicit reference to Internet naming and numbering issues was notable.[191]

Submissions

Following publication of the agenda, submissions were again solicited, with those received by 2 August being included in another synthesis paper that was prepared by the Secretariat as an input into the inaugural meeting. 79 submissions were received from 45 contributors by this deadline,[192] and were reflected in the Background Paper that was released in all official UN languages one week before the commencement of the Athens meeting.[193] It dealt first with submissions on general aspects of Internet governance, then those that could be grouped under one of the four themes, followed by those that looked at the IGF as an institution.

[191]And was indeed noted by the Russian Federation (see Russian Federation, Proposals of the Russian Federation to the Agenda of the Internet Governance Forum ⟨URL: http://intgovforum.org/Substantive_1st_IGF/Proposals_RF_Agenda_of_Internet_Governance%20Forum.pdf⟩), the Brazilian government (see Government of Brazil, Comments to the "Programme Outline" Document ⟨URL: http://www.intgovforum.org/Substantive_1st_IGF/Brazilian%20Position.doc⟩) and the Internet Governance Project (see IGP, Contribution to the Internet Governance Forum Athens Meeting ⟨URL: http://www.intgovforum.org/Substantive_1st_IGF/IGF-writtencontrib.doc⟩) in their substantive submissions to the meeting.

[192]See http://www.intgovforum.org/contributions_for_1st_IGF.htm, where fourteen submissions from eight other contributors who missed the deadline can also be found.

[193]IGF Secretariat, Inaugural Meeting Background Report ⟨URL: http://www.intgovforum.org/synth/E.doc⟩

Rather than summarising their content here (as the Background Paper has already been that), it will be more productive to review the submissions as products of a process initiated by the Secretariat to fulfil the IGF's role as a forum for multi-stakeholder policy dialogue. On this basis, the process was characterised by three deficiencies: in the substantive moderation or facilitation of the discussion, in the level of deliberation by the participants, and in the orientation of submissions towards the fulfilment of the IGF's mandate. Taking these in turn:

- The Secretariat provided no guidance to stakeholders as to how their submissions should be structured or what they should address. This had both a positive and a negative impact. On the positive side, the submissions displayed much more diversity than those that had been made to the open consultation meetings; ranging from a Swiss civil society proposal for the development of "Internet Quality Labels"[194] through to a primer on Trusted Computing.[195]

  The other side of this coin was that, without guidance on what was expected, many submissions lacked any connection to the IGF's mandate. Some for example, such as those of the OECD and ICC/BASIS, simply provided background material summarising their own activities, without addressing whether those activities fulfilled the WSIS process criteria or what part the IGF might have to play in them in the future.[196]

- As respondents developed their submissions in isolation, without any mechanism by which to address each others' contributions or to review or provide feedback on them ahead of the meeting, it was inevitable that they would speak at cross purposes to each other, rather than seriously engaging with each others' views as a step in the process of democratic deliberation or consensus-building. The Background Paper masks this by declaring superficial areas of consensus, such as, on the theme of openness, the

  > wide spread recognition of the fact that the distributed nature of the Internet whereby control is placed at the ends, or in the hands of users, rather than at a centralized point, is a key architectural feature of the Internet that has ensured that freedom of expression and the free flow of information.[197]

[194] Swiss Internet User Group, Internet Quality Labels ⟨URL: http://www.intgovforum.org/Substantive_1st_IGF/SwissInternetUserGroup.txt⟩

[195] Vittorio Bertola, An Introduction to Trusted Computing ⟨URL: http://www.intgovforum.org/Substantive_1st_IGF/An%20Introduction%20To%20Trusted%20Computing.doc⟩

[196] This was particularly true of the ITU, which submitted fourteen generic reports on its activities, many of which it had also earlier submitted by way of response to the WGIG report: see WSIS Secretariat, Compilation of Comments Received on the Report of the Working Group on Internet Governance (as in n. 84 on page 344), 5.

[197] IGF Secretariat, Inaugural Meeting Background Report (as in n. 193 on page 367), 6

However it also notes that there was little consensus amongst stakeholders on specific public policy issues impacted by this architectural openness, such as the extent to which it calls for reform to the existing legal regime of IPRs, and if so whether an expansion, contraction, or fundamental reconsideration of that regime is called for. As an example of this, concerns expressed by some respondents (including EFF and IP Justice) about the potential for technologies such as DRM to undermine the free flow of information were contrasted with the contentions of others (such as WIPO) that DRM is of central importance in preserving incentives to create and innovate.[198]

- In other areas, there happened to be a greater convergence of views on policy objectives amongst the contributions received, but a lack of consensus on the strategies by which those agreed objectives should be pursued. For example, on the theme of security, the Background Paper notes a broad awareness of the problems of spam, phishing, malware and Internet security,[199] and on the theme of diversity there was yet greater consensus on the substantive issues of multilingual content, internationalised domain names and keyword systems.[200] Yet there was next to no awareness of the possible role of the IGF in addressing these issues as a governance network. Instead, suggestions on how they should be addressed focused on a single layer of governance such as memoranda of understanding between governments[201] or a self-regulatory approach led by the private sector.[202]

  One notable exception came from the Council of Europe, which argued that there was an important role for the Forum in developing substantive answers to unanswered questions regarding the interpretation of human rights as applied in online settings.[203]

The limitations of these submissions and the process by which they were solicited should be understood in the light that they were intended only

[198]Ibid., 6. For the contribution of WIPO, not specifically cited in the Background Paper, see WIPO, Statement of the World Intellectual Property Organization ⟨URL: http://intgovforum.org/contributions/FINALSTAT%5B1%5D.doc⟩.

[199]IGF Secretariat, Inaugural Meeting Background Report (as in n. 193 on page 367), 8; though still with some divergences on issues of spam, privacy and "trusted computing": ibid., 10.

[200]It was also a notably multi-stakeholder consensus, with the Background Paper finding commonality in the submissions of EUROLINC (the European Languages Internet Conference), the Native Language Internet Consortium, the WSIS Civil Society Working Group on Scientific Information, the ITU, ISOC and ICC.

[201]ITU, Report of Meeting of ITU Membership on Mechanisms for Cooperation on Cybersecurity and Combating Spam ⟨URL: http://intgovforum.org/Substantive_1st_IGF/13-IGF-ITU-D_Report_on_WTDC06_Resolution_45.doc⟩, 2

[202]ICC, ICC Policy Statement on "Spam" and Unsolicited Commercial Electronic Messages ⟨URL: http://intgovforum.org/Substantive_1st_IGF/spam.pdf⟩, 2

[203]Council of Europe, Council of Europe Submission to the Internet Governance Forum ⟨URL: http://intgovforum.org/Substantive_1st_IGF/CoE%20submission%20to%20the%20IGF.pdf⟩, 2

as an input into the discussions that would take place in person in Athens, which had the potential to be far more deliberative and, through expert facilitation, to be directed more closely towards the fulfilment of the IGF's mandate. Whether this potential would in fact be realised will shortly be seen.

The Plaza

The agenda for the Athens meeting also indicated that an "open space for showcasing institutions and projects" to be known as the Plaza would be provided at the meeting venue, for the purposes of "bringing participants together, facilitating the exchange of experience and the sharing of best practices."[204]

When space in the Plaza was first released on 14 September 2006, those who had registered their interest in exhibiting found that they could only do so at a cost ranging from CHF5800 to CHF8400.[205] This immediately created a significant impediment to the participation of stakeholders from civil society, developing countries, and the small business sector, who may have wished to exhibit there.

One week following the release of these prices, those who had expressed interest in exhibiting were privately given notice of the Plaza's cancellation. No explanation for the cancellation was given, and none was given on the IGF's Web site, which in fact made no mention of the cancellation. Then on 5 October, prospective exhibitors were notified that the Plaza would be held after all, this time as a free exhibition space.

The space set aside for the Plaza was on a lower level of the meeting venue, away from the plenary sessions, and featured eighteen exhibitors, mostly from civil society.[206]

Plenary sessions

The programme of the inaugural meeting of the IGF included nine plenary sessions:

- the opening ceremony;
- Multistakeholder Policy Dialogue—Setting the Scene;

[204] This description was, but is no longer, given at `http://www.intgovforum.org/athens_outline.htm`.

[205] See `http://www.ottofrei.ch/news_yourexhibit.htm`. As at that date, this amounted to approximately AUD$6200 and AUD$9000 respectively.

[206] Namely Amnesty International, the CDT, Diplo Foundation, the Global Internet Policy Initiative, the Global Knowledge Partnership, Gov2U, GLOCOM, ICANN, ICC/BASIS, the Internet Governance Project, ISOC, the Information Technology Association of America (ITAA), Nominet, the OECD, SIDN (the .nl gTLD registry), Verisign, the W3C and the author.

- a session devoted to each of the themes of Openness, Security, Diversity and Access;
- Conclusions and The Way Forward;
- Emerging Issues; and
- the closing ceremony.

Each session bar the last was three hours in duration, and benefited from simultaneous translation into all official UN languages, using eight translation booths staffed by twenty translators. In addition, the text of each session appeared in English on a large projection screen within moments of its translation or transcription, and was subsequently posted to the IGF's Web site.[207]

The four thematic sessions, along with the Multistakeholder Policy Dialogue and Emerging Issues sessions, were structured as panel presentations with between eleven and fifteen panelists, and were professionally moderated.[208] No formal process of consultation was conducted by the Advisory Group in selecting the panelists or moderators, although the Group did endeavour to ensure that there was a balance of stakeholder groups and geographical diversity amongst the speakers.[209]

Although notionally all plenary sessions were to focus on the developmental dimension of their themes, and to promote capacity building as a cross-cutting priority, this was adhered to by few speakers from outside civil society, and few workshops other than those devoted to development issues. Thus Rikke Frank Jorgensen acknowledged during the security panel in Athens, "we are still rather weak when we talk about this link and what it actually means and how security play [*sic*] into the development agenda."

As the plenary sessions comprised about 25 hours of discussion in all, it lies beyond the scope of this section to attempt even a cursory summary of them. For this reason, the substantive issues under discussion in the plenary sessions will not be dealt with at all here. Instead, our attention will be confined to three specific issues discussed during the plenary sessions that highlight the IGF's own view of its role, structure, and processes, as had previously been the focus of the two open consultation meetings in Geneva.

[207]See `http://www.intgovforum.org/IIGF.htm`.

[208]As for the other sessions, the opening and closing ceremonies were taken up by prepared speeches, whereas the session on "The Way Forward" was conducted in a more open format, whereby rather than interrogating a panel and taking occasional questions from the floor, the moderator gave the entire session over to the floor.

[209]It was somewhat limited in its ability to do this by reason that no budget was available to fund the attendance of speakers who were not already intending to attend the meeting.

These issues are firstly whether the IGF's role should include the making of recommendations, secondly whether some structural evolution of the IGF would be required for the development of such recommendations, and thirdly what procedures could be employed to bring the IGF closer to a consensus of stakeholders on the issues before it. The discussion of each of these issues will be outlined in turn.

First, as to whether the IGF's role extended to the making of recommendations, this was accepted most readily by the Forum hawks of civil society[210] and developing country governments,[211] and resisted most strenuously by the Forum doves of the OECD governments[212] and the private sector and technical community.[213] A representative exchange between the two camps on this issue occurred on the first day during the session on "Multistakeholder Policy Dialogue—Setting the Scene."

ISOC's President Lynn St Amour affirmed ISOC's reluctance to cede a role in governance to the IGF, even if its multi-stakeholder model were fully realised, on the grounds that "that's actually embedding today's political models and trying to put it on top of a development that just doesn't naturally fit." She stated frankly:

> I don't think the Internet Governance Forum is a place for decisions or for recommendations. I don't think the process is nearly inclusive enough. I don't think it's got the right level of participation. ... I think it needs to go back to national level, local level, participation in the forums that are available to you, that are important to you as an individual.

Karen Banks from the Association for Progressive Communications took issue with this, saying that

> to make the connection between the national and the global is a really, really tough task, and it requires a lot of work. And I

[210] For example, civil society's representative during the opening ceremony, Natasha Primo, gave the striking image of the Athens meeting as "the beginning of a process that grows teeth at the same time it finds its feet," and saw the IGF as an institution that would come to "provide leadership and guidance."

[211] For example Tariq Badsha of Pakistan, speaking during the final day's session on "The Way Forward," underlined the need for the IGF to develop the capacity to produce tangible outputs and concrete recommendations in order to fulfil those paragraphs of its mandate that had yet to be addressed.

[212] For example Viviane Reding from the European Commission maintained, "The IGF does not replace negotiation between governments or the enhanced cooperation model"; a contentious statement given that the enhanced cooperation model as outlined in the Tunis Agenda specifies a multi-stakeholder process: see section 5.1 on page 344.

[213] For example, Yoshio Utsumi from the ITU, for which the IGF's very formation was a result of the WSIS negotiations on Internet governance taking an unfavourable turn, stressed during the opening ceremony that "the future of Internet governance is inevitably local rather than global. This is because the best approach is different for each society and economy."

think if the IGF is going to add value, that this is one of the ways that it can. I think there are definitely issues that need to be addressed here that aren't addressed in other spaces adequately, in line with the mandate. ... [W]e can look at the IGF ... as something where we not only have a good discussion, but we think about leaving ... with some sense of working forward around concrete activities and possibly ... recommendations.

As for the second issue of note from the plenary sessions, regarding the compatibility of the IGF's structure with a recommendation-making role, there were three basic views expressed; in this instance, not running cleanly along the lines of the hawk and dove camps. The first view was that since the IGF did not have the structural capacity to pursue a work programme, this should instead be taken up by other institutions in the regime who did possess that capacity.

Thus for example Jean-Jacques Massima Landji from Gambon cautiously agreed with Karen Banks that "We can start perhaps drawing up recommendations on the various points commonly approved," but saw considerable difficulty in bringing the stakeholders to that point, since merely by "discussing this in a forum, you can't actually come to a ... common position." He suggested instead that

UNESCO, as a specialized body, certainly can deal with this, would find the time to come to some sort of compromise and arrangement which would suit all parties. But a forum like this, which cannot take any sort of binding decisions, well, we can't have a recommendation here.

The same suggestion was made independently during the session on diversity by Divina Frau-Meigs of the University of Paris, who called for the formation of a multi-stakeholder working group on issues of cultural diversity and IDNs, not within the IGF, but instead within an intergovernmental body such as UNESCO.

Those who took the second view agreed that the IGF lacked the capacity to take forward a substantive work programme, but for them the solution was different: it should forthwith develop that capacity, through the formation of dedicated working groups. Thus, for example, Rikke Frank Jorgensen of the Danish Human Rights Institute suggested during the panel on security that the IGF should form a multi-stakeholder task force on security and privacy; and in the final day's session on "The Way Forward," former French diplomat Jean-Jacques Subrenat was amongst those who suggested that a structure based on the IETF model could be employed by the IGF, implying the creation of formal working groups within which decision-making would take place by rough consensus.

The third view on this issue was first voiced during the session on access, at which Georg Greve announced the formation of the IGF's first multi-stakeholder "dynamic coalition," on open standards.[214] Such dynamic coalitions could work towards producing some of the concrete outcomes sought by Forum hawks, yet being voluntary and self-organised, would require neither the assent nor the participation of other IGF stakeholders.[215] This view soon came to draw broad support, with a number of participants in "The Way Forward" session speaking for the use of dynamic coalitions (possessing, as Thomas Schneider of the Swiss government underlined, "not formal links but very narrow links with the IGF"), in the place of formal working groups.[216]

The third and final issue which has been isolated for mention from the discussions in the plenary sessions of the Athens meeting is the question of what procedures might be required to bring the IGF's diverse stakeholders closer to consensus on the substantive issues before it. As Carlos Alfonso of the Information Network for the Third Sector, a Brazilian civil society organisation, put the problem during the plenary session on openness, "We know that child pornography is a consensus, but what are other aspects of freedom of information ... which can be accepted universally?"

Andrew Puddephatt, also of civil society, gave a specific example of the kinds of difficulties likely to be encountered:

> there are countries where the state and symbols of the state and nation are protected. And ... if you attack or criticize that country or nation, you're accused and tried for defamation. That would be unacceptable in many other jurisdictions where defamation only applies to individuals' personal reputation. The idea that you could develop a standard on defamation as an agreement among states at the moment I think would be extremely fraught.

Regrettably this was one issue in respect the plenary body could divine no answers. Vittorio Bertola, former WGIG member, simply offered his experience of that multi-stakeholder body which had managed to produce its report by consensus on issues so contentious that they had confounded the governmental delegates at WSIS. He said:

> The only thing we can do in a true Internet spirit is to bring everyone at the same table and have an agreement, in the end,

[214]Curiously, open standards were dealt with as a topic under the access theme in the Athens meeting (and dominated the treatment of that theme in the Secretariat's Background Paper, in comparison to issues such as the digital divide and the cost of access: IGF Secretariat, Inaugural Meeting Background Report (as in n. 193 on page 367), 12). Perhaps for this reason the same topic was shifted to the openness theme for the Rio meeting.

[215]See section 5.2 on page 379.

[216]See section 6.3 on page 457

for [that's] the way that the Internet works. The agreement is beneficial to all the people who participate in it. And that's the way the Internet has been growing since the beginning. The technical standards of the Internet were never decided, were never formally adopted or binding either. They are just there and everyone abides by them because it's beneficial for everyone to be able to talk to everyone. And that's what we can get in this forum.

At the closing ceremony, the final statements of representatives of the stakeholder groups evidenced few signs of development in their views since the Athens meeting had opened. David Appasamy from ICC/BASIS observed:

> Some have asked where the action is, and what tangibles have been achieved. Well, the wisdom and experience gained are of great value in and of themselves. If we go to plant these seeds at the national level and cultivate them by working with all stakeholders at this level, they are certain to bear fruit.

Jeanette Hoffman on the other hand, as the closing speaker from civil society, said it was "vital that all stakeholders recognise and adopt this new venue as an innovative place of policy making" and suggested that the forum should "encourage the development of practical solutions, both in workshops but also in dynamic coalitions that are about to form. Such practical solutions should be put on public record of the forum."

Workshops

Despite Hoffman's entreaty, in Athens the output of the 36 self-organised workshops that were held there could not be received into the official report of the meeting, though individual workshop reports were published *verbatim* on the IGF Web site.[217]

A call for proposals for these workshops had accompanied the publication of the agenda, with a deadline of 24 August 2006.[218] The call specified the following selection criteria:

- Relevance to the overriding themes and topics. Priority will be given to proposals for workshops related to the main themes.
- Demonstratively proposed and organized through multistakeholder collaboration.

[217] See http://www.intgovforum.org/Workshop_reports.php.

[218] See http://www.intgovforum.org/workshops.html.

- Capacity to improve understanding of the IGF themes and topics.
- Proven expertise and experience to manage the staging of the workshop, including raising the funds necessary to do so.

The process by which workshops were selected pursuant to these criteria was a closed one. As workshop proposals were not listed on the IGF Web site as they were made, many workshops on the same topics were proposed independently. The Advisory Group did not seek to amalgamate these, but in the end simply approved all of them, releasing its final schedule of workshops in October.[219] No opportunity was provided for public comment on the workshops selected, nor on their scheduling, which saw them being held concurrently with each other and with the plenary sessions.

Thus for example the topic of multi-stakeholder participation in Internet governance was the subject of no fewer than four workshops, each led by a different stakeholder group or sub-group. On the second day in Athens, both the Internet technical community and non-technical civil society held separate workshops on the topic, respectively organised by ICANN, ISOC and representatives of the RIRs and ccTLDs, and by CONGO. Also on that day, a similar workshop "Enhancing Multi-Stakeholder Participation in ICT Policy Making" was held by private sector stakeholders, and on the following day, a workshop titled "Building Meaningful Participation" took place that had been co-organised by the government of Canada.

The sheer number of workshops precludes any attempt being made here to summarise the discussion that took place within them, even on procedural issues. However, some of the content of "Exploring a Framework Convention" organised by IT for Change and others, which was perhaps the workshop that examined institutional and process issues in the most depth, will be reviewed later in this chapter.[220]

Remote participation

As noted above, a recurring theme of the submissions to the consultation sessions that preceded the Athens meeting was that effective use should be made of online mechanisms for participation in the activities of the IGF. In practice, less effective use was made of such mechanisms than many stakeholders may have hoped.

In September 2006 an SMF-based Web forum was created on the IGF Web site by its Secretariat, however it was configured so that new discussion topics could only be created by administrators. At first there was only one such topic, "Remote Participation," with subsequently the four themes of

[219] See `http://www.intgovforum.org/wksshop_program.htm`.

[220] See section 5.4 on page 407.

the Athens meeting being added two weeks later, and another for "Taking stock and the way forward" after the Athens meeting had concluded.

By October, it became apparent that the suggestions being made on this board on mechanisms that should be put in place for remote participation were not going to be implemented by the Secretariat, or at least not in sufficient time for the Athens meeting. No response was received to direct offers of assistance, such as an offer by the developers of the Dialog Dashboard[221] to host a free public synchronous and asynchronous discussion forum for the IGF's use, just as no response had been made to an offer made by Geneva Net Dialogue during the February consultations to build an interactive Web site for the IGF.[222]

Once it had become became clear that the suggestions being made on remote participation would not be taken forward by the Secretariat, the two most active participants in the discussions on this topic, then-journalist Kieren McCarthy and the author, decided to implement them independently. Launched on 11 October, the Drupal-based IGF Community Site featured synchronous and asynchronous discussion fora, a wiki, and the facility to conduct informal polls, amongst other features. It gained the tacit endorsement of the Secretariat, but no funding or publicity.[223]

The IGF Community Site was announced on various civil society mailing lists and Web sites and by the distribution of printed flyers at the Athens meeting itself. It soon proved to be far more popular than the IGF's official Web forum, with over 200 users registering on the site during or within one week of the conference, and more than a dozen of those posting to their own blogs on the site.

Although having had little to no involvement in this initiative, the Secretariat and host country did provide certain other facilities to link remote participants in with the plenary sessions and workshops, namely:

- Free wireless Internet access was provided at the venue, allowing those present to discuss the proceedings with those outside using tools such as instant messaging and blogs. The quality of the wireless access was variable, ranging from almost entirely absent in the workshop rooms, to weak and intermittent in the plenary sessions.
- The plenary sessions were webcast, though in a proprietary Microsoft format that was no longer supported even on the Microsoft Windows

[221] See section 4.3 on page 276.

[222] The only such suggestion eventually taken on board, on 19 October, was the establishment of an electronic mailing list for those attending the Athens meeting, equivalent to that which had been established for the Advisory Group. However those who had registered to attend the meeting were not informed of the existence of the requested "plenary" mailing list and no mention of it was made on the IGF Web site, so it was not utilised: see http://intgovforum.org/mailman/listinfo/plenary_intgovforum.org.

[223] The Web site was located at http://igf2006.info/, but is no longer operational at that address.

operating system at the date of the meeting. Recordings of the plenary sessions were subsequently archived on the IGF Web site in the open standard MPEG4 format.[224]

- During plenary sessions, the administrators of the IGF Community Site monitored email mailboxes and chat fora hosted on that site and forwarded the comments received to the session moderators. In later sessions, mobile phones were also monitored for text messages by Advisory Group members.

  This fulfilled the Secretariat's earlier promise that "[p]rovisions will be made for remote participants to use instant messaging to send comments into the meetings. It is hoped that volunteers will monitor IM channels and will serve as proxies for the remote participants in making interventions."[225]

On the other hand there were some initiatives that the Secretariat had indicated would be in place for the Athens meeting, that never eventuated. For example, the IGF's Web site had also stated:

> Participants can submit a recorded five minute statement that will be made available on the IGF Web site and also broadcast at the venue on in a loop on three plasma screens for participants to hear. Those who are interested are encouraged to provide these statements both in video (specification: DVD format .vob files (region 2) or .wmv format (384x288 resolution for streaming)) and in written document form.

In fact video statements provided to the Secretariat were neither broadcast at the venue, nor made available on the IGF Web site. Also unfulfilled was the statement, "The blogs being written about the IGF will be monitored and will be reported on during the recap and review sessions in a daily blog report."

Outcomes

The outcomes of the first IGF meeting had been predetermined by the Secretariat and Advisory Group before the meeting opened, and were stated on the IGF's Web site:

> The outcome of the meeting will be the reports of the individual sessions as well as of the meeting as a whole. There will be no negotiated texts such as decisions or resolutions.

[224] See http://www.intgovforum.org/IIGF_webcasts.htm.

[225] See http://www.intgovforum.org/athens_outline.htm.

> The Chairman may also wish to make a summing-up of the meeting. The report of the meeting will be submitted to the Secretary-General and made available on the website.
>
> In addition, all the material that was used as input into the meeting will remain on record on the IGF Web site.
>
> As a third possible outcome, there may be "dynamic coalitions" emerging from Athens, ie a group of institutions or people who agree to pursue an initiative started at the inaugural IGF meeting.[226]

The report of the meeting referred to here was published as an "informal summing up,"[227] and was a brief precis of the six panel sessions only. Although it identified a "broad convergence of views" or "a widely held view" on several substantive issues, such as the need for multi-stakeholder cooperation in addressing issues of Internet security, the report did not attempt to draw any overall conclusions from the discussions that had taken place.

Dynamic coalitions

The emergence of dynamic coalitions as another possible outcome of the Athens meeting became a self-fulfilling prophecy, with the announcement of several such coalitions at the meeting itself, and a number of others shortly afterwards. As at 2008 eleven dynamic coalitions claim to be active.[228]

Save that the mission and contact details of each of these dynamic coalitions is listed on the IGF Web site, as matters stand they have no formal institutional affiliation with the IGF, nor any access to the resources of the IGF Secretariat. As such, there are no strictures upon the objects, structure or processes of dynamic coalitions claiming association with the IGF. Probably the most obvious consequence of this[229] is the diversity that the dynamic coalitions display in these respects, to the extent that the groups currently sharing the appellation of dynamic coalition can be divided into three quite distinct types. These may be described for convenience as networks, working groups, and BOFs.[230]

---

[226] See `http://www.intgovforum.org/athens_outline.htm`.

[227] IGF Secretariat, The Inaugural Session of the Internet Governance Forum ⟨URL: `http://www.intgovforum.org/Summary.Final.07.11.2006.htm`⟩

[228] They are those on Spam (the StopSpamAlliance), Privacy, Open Standards (IGF DCOS), Access and Connectivity for Remote, Rural and Dispersed Communities, The Internet Bill of Rights, Diversite' Linguistique (Linguistic Diversity), Access to Knowledge (A2K@IGF), Freedom of Expression and Freedom of the Media on the Internet (FOEonline), Online Collaboration, Gender and Internet Governance (GIG), and Framework of Principles for the Internet.

[229] Others will be noted at section 6.3 on page 457.

[230] During the September 2007 open consultations, France distinguished "between groups that

The StopSpamAlliance is currently the only dynamic coalition in the first category. It is essentially a coordinating body for the existing programmes of its members, including the London Action Plan (which as already noted, is a multi-stakeholder governance network in its own right), as well as APEC, the ITU, the OECD, the Seoul–Melbourne MOU group and the EU's CNSA (Contact Network of Spam Authorities). As self-described at its meeting in Rio, it allows its members to reduce duplication of work between themselves, and allows them to speak with a single voice to the international community when they are in accord. However the StopSpamAlliance does not currently have an independent programme of its own.

A second type of dynamic coalition is exemplified by the Internet Bill of Rights Dynamic Coalition. It provides a structure within which for its members to collaborate on a joint programme of work; in this case, the definition of an Internet Bill of Rights that could be promulgated either through the informal moral authority of the IGF, or through intergovernmental and/or other mechanisms, to improve the recognition and enforcement of human rights online. Already that dynamic coalition has made progress to this end, having secured the agreement of Brazilian and Italian officials "to facilitate together the process of defining an Internet Bill of Rights with a view to frame and enforce fundamental rights in the Internet environment."[231]

The third type of dynamic coalition are the BOFs, which are open fora for those sharing an interest in a particular issue area, but which have not yet adopted a joint programme of work. As in the case of their namesakes within the IETF and APNIC, groups that begin as BOFs may later develop into working groups, and indeed there is some overlap between the two categories. The FOEonline dynamic coalition, which brings together those with an interest in freedom of expression and freedom of the media on the Internet, is a good example of a BOF.[232]

Follow-up

In the week following the conclusion of the Athens meeting, the Secretariat called for written comments on what had worked well, and what should be done in preparation for the Rio meeting to address what had worked less well. Thirteen documentary submissions, and ten others submitted using an online questionnaire form, were summarised by the Secretariat in another synthesis paper that was released a few days ahead of an open

are advocacy group or facilitation groups," which approximately equate to BOFs and networks respectively.

[231]Gilberto Passos Gil Moreira and Luigi Vimercati, Joint Declaration on Internet Rights by the Minister of Culture of Brazil and the Undersecretary for Communications of Italy ⟨URL: http://internet-bill-of-rights.org/file/pdf/Joint%20Declaration%20Brazil-Italy.pdf⟩. Also in this category are the dynamic coalitions on Access to Knowledge, Framework of Principles for the Internet, Online Collaboration, Open Standards and Privacy.

[232]Those on Access and Connectivity for Remote, Rural and Dispersed Communities, Diversite' Linguistique, and Gender Equality also currently best fit into this category.

consultation meeting on the same topic that was held in Geneva on 13 February 2007.[233] The open consultation itself was again translated and webcast, and a transcript later posted to the IGF's Web site.[234]

In both the written submissions and the interventions at the open consultation, there were certain aspects of the IGF's first meeting that met with a broad positive or negative consensus. There was, for example, general agreement that the meeting had succeeded in creating a valuable space for discussion across stakeholder groups, and that the real-time transcription service and unrestricted seating arrangements had been amongst the factors contributing to this success; but on the other hand that the plenary sessions had been too long, that there had been too many panelists, and that there had been excessive overlap between the plenary sessions and the workshops (many of which themselves overlapped in content).

But beyond these broad areas of agreement, many fundamental gulfs remained. These can again be usefully grouped into the three procedural issues of the role of the IGF, its structure, and its processes. In addition, one substantive issue—that of Internet naming and numbering—drew strong comment, with the Third World Network amongst those who were particularly critical of the exclusion of this issue from the agenda of the first meeting.[235]

As to the procedural issues, there was no perceptible relaxation of the restrictive stance of the Forum doves as to the role of the IGF. For example, ICC/BASIS maintained its position that "[t]he emphasis on discussions without negotiated conclusions is an essential principle for the Forum. It avoids the pressure to reach consensus, establish strict criteria for representation, or spend time on what could be protracted political negotiations and wordsmithing."[236]

However the Forum hawks (civil society and developing country governments) had a different perspective. For example, the government of Brazil said:

> we also believe that it is important for us to envisage some kind of written conclusions, be it a reporting, recommendations, or concluding statement, that would be a reference of

[233] IGF Secretariat, Stock-taking Session Synthesis Paper ⟨URL: http://www.intgovforum.org/Feb_igf_meeting/Synthesis.Paper.Feb.2007.rtf⟩

[234] See http://www.intgovforum.org/Feb_igf_meeting/13_February_Consult_2007.txt.

[235] Third World Network, Statement for the Preparatory Session for the Internet Governance Forum ⟨URL: http://www.intgovforum.org/Feb_igf_meeting/TWN.doc⟩, 1

[236] ICC, ICC/BASIS Feedback on First Internet Governance Forum (IGF) in Athens, Greece ⟨URL: http://www.iccwbo.org/uploadedFiles/BASIS/Documents/ICCBASIS_input_on_IGF_Athens_Final_12_01_07.pdf⟩. ETNO (the European Telecommunications Network Operators), the ITAA and ISOC spoke to similar effect: see ISOC, From Athens to Rio de Janeiro: Building on the Success of the First Internet Governance Forum ⟨URL: http://www.intgovforum.org/Feb_igf_meeting/ISOC%20IGF%20FEB%2007.pdf⟩, 1.

> the meeting. In fact, the mandate that was given to the IGF on [paragraph] 72, item g of the Tunis Agenda refers to the possibility of making recommendations where appropriate. And we should have that in mind. We are aware that the format that has been used on the first meeting, while it allows for the wider discussion, it may not be the best format in order to negotiate texts. And I don't think that we are aiming at a binding negotiated text, but we should consider having some kind of reporting for the fact that the IGF is not an isolated path.[237]

Even Nitin Desai acknowledged for the first time that "there is language in paragraph 72 which talks of recommendations as appropriate, and we still do not have a process for figuring out how to get to those recommendations. But these are things which will evolve." The CS-IGC recommended that a "meta-governance" theme be included in the Rio agenda to deal with such issues as these in a more overt and open fashion.

One simple and practical way in which the IGF could fulfil its mandate in sub-paragraph 72 (c) to "[i]nterface with ... other institutions on matters under their purview" was suggested by IT for Change: that those other organisations be invited to present their own sessions at the next IGF meeting. The ITU, at least, indicated at the open consultation that it would in principle be likely to accept such an invitation.

Leading into discussion of the second main procedural issue, the structure of the IGF, the dynamic coalitions were now becoming widely accepted as a first step for the IGF towards developing the capacity to produce recommendations. Thus the EU (through Germany) stated, "we feel that Athens has provided an opportunity for a concrete outcome, not least in the form of dynamic coalitions. We welcome this development, and we hope to see it continued in the meeting in Rio de Janeiro, providing the different dynamic coalitions with an opportunity to present their work." Switzerland and Australia spoke to similar effect.

The other main issue that was discussed in relation to the structure of the IGF is what should become of the Advisory Group. The two main opposing views were that it should be retained in its present form with new members only brought in to replace those who have departed, or that it should be reconvened in a more inclusive and democratic manner, to address charges of lack of transparency in its appointment and operations that were acknowledged in the synthesis report.

The first view was most strongly represented by the Forum doves (including the United States, Canada, ITAA and SIDN), and the second by the Forum hawks (such as the CS-IGC and the governments of Egypt

[237] Similar remarks were made by IT for Change, an India-based civil society group: see IT For Change, Taking Stock and the Way Forward ⟨URL: `http://www.intgovforum.org/ITfC%27s%20contribution%20to%20IGF%27s%20Stock%20Taking%20Meeting.doc`⟩, 1–2.

and the Russian Federation). The CS-IGC for example decried the under-representation of civil society, and said:

> We think that clear terms and rules should be established for the Advisory Group between now and Rio, through an open process involving all the participants in the IGF, as a shared foundation for our common work. We further consider that if these rules and the quotas for representation from each stake-holder group were openly established, it would be possible for the Secretary General to delegate the actual process of selection of Advisory Group members to the stakeholder groups themselves.

The final procedural issue dealt with in the post-Athens submissions and consultation session was as to the IGF's processes. It was argued by many, for example France,[238] that more use should have been made of online tools. Indeed, this deficiency had already been noted within the Advisory Group, with Desai acknowledging, "[i]f we are talking of Internet governance, if you do not use the capacities of the Internet to allow people to connect and interact with one another, then, in a sense, we are failing in our duty." The Online Collaboration Dynamic Coalition was one of four coalitions that presented a report to that open consultation meeting, and it announced its resolve to help redress this deficit.

Other suggestions made for the improvement of the IGF's processes were based around developing more creative formats to increase the interactivity of the discussion, as ICC/BASIS put it at the consultation. For example, the CS-IGC suggested that workshops could be broken into table groups, or could use online tools to engage with those outside, and ISOC was amongst those who suggested that the opportunity should be provided for sharing of national best practices, and that more prominent use should have been made of the Plaza.[239]

Another issue directly raised by the Secretariat for discussion was as to the effectiveness of the use of input papers for the Athens meeting, and more specifically the synthesis paper which attempted to summarise them. There was no disagreement that a synthesis paper, translated into the UN languages, was potentially invaluable in providing participants, especially those who did not speak English, with background briefing material covering a variety of perspectives, which could in turn allow the discussions at the plenary sessions to be more focused, in-depth and practical.

---

[238] Government of France, Lessons From the Inaugural Meeting of the IGF in Athens and Recommendations for the Second Annual Meeting ⟨URL: `http://www.intgovforum.org/Feb_igf_meeting/IGF%20Stoktaking.doc`⟩

[239] ISOC, From Athens to Rio de Janeiro: Building on the Success of the First Internet Governance Forum (as in n. 236 on the facing page), 3

However, several respondents, including the ITAA, noted that this had not happened in Athens.[240] Not only did moderators fail to draw upon the synthesis paper as a base for questioning panelists, but in fact no reference was made to it during the plenary sessions in Athens at all, which left several potentially valuable proposals hanging. Part of the reason for this may well have been because the paper was distributed so late, as a number of respondents also noted.[241]

Nothing more was heard from the Secretariat or Advisory Group on any of these suggestions until May, when their consultations shifted from a focus on taking stock of Athens, to preparing in earnest for Rio.

The Second Meeting

The second meeting of the IGF was held in Rio de Janeiro between 11 and 14 November 2007. It was attended by 1363 participants; similar to the number in Athens and similarly broken down by stakeholder group.[242]

A draft programme for the IGF's second meeting in Rio de Janeiro was released by the Secretariat on 1 May 2007.[243] It addressed certain of the most widespread criticisms made of the format of the Athens meeting during the follow-up process, notably by reducing the size of the panels in main sessions by about half to a maximum of six, and reducing the length of those sessions from three to two hours.

However there were other criticisms, both procedural and substantive, that the programme overlooked. Foremost amongst the former were criticisms of excessive overlap between parallel sessions,[244] since rather than reducing the number of parallel events, they were increased from four in Athens to as many as seven for Rio. The most glaring substantive omission from this initial agenda was the continued absence of Internet naming and numbering.

The main changes to the agenda for Rio in this draft programme were:

---

[240] ITAA, ITAA IGF Comments ⟨URL: `http://www.intgovforum.org/ITAA%20IGF%20-%20Feb%202%202007.pdf`⟩, 3

[241] More generally it was suggested that a more formalised procedure for the distribution of working documents in advance of sessions should have been devised; perhaps, as ENSTA (École Nationale Supérieure de Techniques Avancées) and EUROLINC recommended, drawing from the example of the IETF's RFC document series: ENSTA and EUROLINC, Taking Stock and the Way Forward ⟨URL: `http://www.intgovforum.org/ensta-eurolinc_form_igf.rtf`⟩, 2.

[242] IGF Secretariat, Second Meeting of the Internet Governance Forum: Chairman's Summary ⟨URL: `http://www.intgovforum.org/Rio_Meeting/Chairman%20Summary.FINAL.16.11.2007.pdf`⟩, 1

[243] The original is no longer available, but is on file with the author. The version as most recently revised before the Rio meeting is at `http://www.intgovforum.org/Rio_Schedule_final.html`.

[244] IGF Secretariat, Stock-taking Session Synthesis Paper (as in n. 233 on page 381), 5

- Each plenary session would be preceded by a two-hour speed dialogue session which would feature a succession of three round-table discussions to be held in groups of ten to twenty on issues relating to the theme of the plenary session;
- There would again be three concurrent streams of workshops, but these would now be divided into thematic workshops on the main themes of openness, security, access and diversity, and open workshops that would be available for any Internet governance topic proposed by the workshop's organisers, as in Athens;
- The second of two additional concurrent streams would alternate between an "open forum" and a "best practices forum." The former would provide an opportunity for other Internet governance organisations to present and discuss their activities, essentially as IT for Change had suggested in February. The latter would be moderated sessions designed to allow stakeholders to present their own experiences of best practices in Internet governance at a regional and local level.
- The final new stream was to be set aside for meetings of dynamic coalitions, and other meetings that stakeholders might wish to arrange.

Not all of these changes were to be reflected in the meeting that eventually took place.[245]

Written comments on the draft programme were received during a period of consultation that commenced on 3 April, ahead of the following open consultation meeting in May.

Consultations

Two open consultation meetings were held to seek input from stakeholders on the agenda and programme for the Rio meeting. The first was held on 23 May 2007 in Geneva, and like previous meetings was webcast.[246] A document synthesising nineteen written contributions to the meeting was prepared and released one day in advance.[247]

---

[245]Similarly, the promise that prepared video statements would be shown in a loop at the venue and made available on the IGF's Web site again failed to eventuate: Idem, Draft Programme Outline for the Second Meeting of the Internet Governance Forum ⟨URL: http://www.intgovforum.org/Rio_Meeting/DraftProgramme.24.09.2007.rtf⟩, 2.

[246]A transcript of the proceedings is available at http://www.intgovforum.org/May_contributions/IGF-23May07Consultation.txt.

[247]IGF Secretariat, Open Consultations Geneva, 23 May 2007: Summary of Contributions Prepared by the IGF Secretariat ⟨URL: http://www.intgovforum.org/May_contributions/SynthesisPaper.23.May.rtf⟩

The contribution most notable in its influence on the discussion over the substantive programme for Rio was that of China, whose voice now joined those of others[248] in recommending that "the Second IGF meeting should discuss the critical Internet resources issues such as the DNS root servers and IP Address, as these issues are the core of Internet governance and just because of which that the IGF was founded" [*sic*].[249] Even Forum doves such as Canada and Australia conceded for the first time at the May consultation that the discussion of critical Internet resources was now inevitable.

Besides agreeing that a session on "core Internet resources and their current governance institutions" was required, the CS-IGC recommended the inclusion of three other new plenary sessions for the Rio meeting, including one on the role and mandate of the IGF, and another on issues and institutions of global Internet public policy more generally.[250] However the position of the Forum doves on the IGF's role in global public policy development had not changed, with ICC/BASIS and Canada both referring with approval at the May consultation to the contribution of ISOC that claimed:

> IGF Athens worked because ... it was an open environment free of the intergovernmental pressures of negotiated texts and political maneuvering. Suggestions that might change the structure and nature of the IGF for Rio or future meetings need to be approached with great caution.[251]

On the structure of the IGF, ENSTA and EUROLINC amplified their argument made at the February 2007 consultation that the limitations of the Advisory Group were significant enough to warrant its replacement by a multi-stakeholder bureau, which should include segments for government, civil society, the private sector and the Internet technical community.[252] Although others from civil society (such as the APC) received this proposal coolly, as did the Forum doves (such as ICC/BASIS, Canada and Australia),

---

[248] Including El Salvador, Brazil, Argentina, Iran and the Russian Federation at the consultation meeting.

[249] People's Republic of China, Comments on the Draft Programme Outline for the Second Meeting of the Internet Governance Forum (IGF) ⟨URL: http://www.intgovforum.org/May_contributions/China%20Input.doc⟩, 1

[250] CS-IGC, Input into the Open Round of Consultations on 23 May 2007 to Discuss Program and Agenda for the Second Meeting of the IGF in Rio de Janeiro ⟨URL: http://www.intgovforum.org/May_contributions/IGC%27s%20contribution%20to%20Rio%20agenda%200507.pdf⟩

[251] ISOC, Contribution to the Internet Governance Forum Consultations May 2007 ⟨URL: http://www.intgovforum.org/May_contributions/ISOC%20IGF%20May%2007.pdf⟩, 1

[252] EUROLINC, Thoughts for Rio: a Bureau for the IGF ⟨URL: http://www.intgovforum.org/May_contributions/Propositions-Rio-V10.3.F1.pdf⟩; Francis Muguet, A Legal Analysis of the Internet Governance Forum Process ⟨URL: http://www.intgovforum.org/May_contributions/legal-igf.pdf⟩, 21

support for the establishment of a "multi-stakeholder bureau office" was also voiced by Brazil, which linked it to the need for the IGF to develop non-binding recommendations:

> As in many other international fora, there is always the possibility of, for instance, a chairman's report. But the chairman alone would not have the required legitimacy to prepare such a report without the help of a representative, multi-stakeholder, and regionally balanced group. So how do we call such group? Friends of the chair? Bureau? Supporting committee? I think that there are many options. What we believe is that we need to have this kind of support. Otherwise, the chairman alone will not be able to deliver to the expectations that are already created by the international community.

Little new was said during the May consultation meeting on the IGF's working procedures, save that Nitin Desai ironically expressed doubt as to the wisdom of the Secretariat's own proposal to conduct speed dialogue sessions at the Rio meeting.

Although the mandate of the existing Advisory Group had been fulfilled with the conclusion of the Athens meeting, the decision as to whether to renew that mandate or to restructure the group was officially one for the UN Secretary-General, who had not yet made a decision by the date of the May consultations. Consequently the private Advisory Group meetings planned for 24 and 25 May were belatedly declared open to all parties (although this was not announced ahead of their commencement, and the meetings were not webcast or transcribed).

During the first of these meeting days, there was general acceptance that it would be necessary, after all, for the IGF to develop the capacity to develop a set of agreed recommendations in order to fully comply with its mandate. The desperation of the Forum doves to avoid this reform was made clear when Chris Disspain of auDA wrote to Markus Kummer and Nitin Desai, copying the private Advisory Group mailing list,[253] stating:

> [W]e are concerned that there appear to be fundamental changes being mooted which are unacceptable to and may lead to the withdrawl [*sic*] of some non government and perhaps even government participants. ...
>
> Chief amongst our concerns is the concept, that seems to have been "agreed" in today's session, of final recommendations arising from the igf. In effect, a negotiated document. This is way outside of the mandate of the igf and is, simply,

[253] And subsequently leaked: copies of the message and Kummer's reply are on file with the author.

unacceptable to the majority of non government people here.

...

There is a grave danger that financial support and general involvement of non government participants will be withdrawn.

When a revised programme was released in June 2007, "Critical Internet resources" had been added as a new plenary session to be held on the first day, and the speed dialogue sessions had been quietly removed. By August, the Advisory Group had also been re-appointed by the new UN Secretary-General Ban Ki-moon, largely with the same composition as the previous group, but now with two co-chairs; Nitin Desai being joined by Hadil da Rocha Vianna of Brazil's Ministry of External Relations. In September, the Advisory Group met again following a second open consultation meeting that does not call for specific discussion here.

For the first time, the Advisory Group released an agenda and a brief report of its private meeting shortly after it had concluded, pursuant to a communique from the Secretary-General which "asked [it] to enhance the transparency of the preparatory process by ensuring a continuous flow of information between its members and the various interested groups."[254] However, at the same meeting, it was determined not to open the meeting to observers.

The report of the Advisory Group meeting referred to two papers that had been tabled by Everton Lucero, a special advisor to the Brazilian co-chair.[255] The first, dealing with the role and procedures of the Advisory Group itself, was presented "as a starting point for preparing the session entitled 'Stock taking and the way forward' at the 2nd IGF in Rio de Janeiro," and asked for comments of Advisory Group members to be incorporated into a synthesis paper that would be used in that session. Amongst the paper's recommendations were that "[e]ach stakeholder group shall appoint their representatives to the AG according to its own procedure, which should be transparent, democratic and inclusive."[256]

Lucero's second paper dealt with the substance, structure and outcomes of the Rio meeting. It recommended that as well as considering the role of the Advisory Group, the stock-taking session should "be devoted to a discussion on the structure for future meetings," and that the meeting's outcomes should include a "Rio message on Internet Governance" prepared by the Chairman as a summary of the meeting, along with reports of all the

---

[254] United Nations Office of the Secretary-General, Advisory Group to Prepare for Internet Governance Forum Meeting in Rio de Janeiro ⟨URL: http://www.un.org/News/Press/docs/ /2007/pi1791.doc.htm⟩

[255] IGF Secretariat, Advisory Group Meeting Summary Report ⟨URL: http://www.intgovforum.org/Summary.AG.05.09.07.rtf⟩

[256] Everton Lucero, Elements to be Considered for Structuring the IGF ⟨URL: http://www.intgovforum.org/EL_paper1_3Sept2007.doc⟩

workshops, dynamic coalition meetings and other events as attachments to that summary.[257]

No discussion of Lucero's papers was recorded in the report of the Advisory Group's meeting, and their recommendations were not carried forward.

Submissions

A background paper synthesising the substantive contributions made for the Rio meeting was released in English towards the end of September 2007, about a month sooner than that for the Athens meeting had been, but at the cost that just over a third as many submissions, by fewer than a third as many contributors, were received in time to be included.[258] Of the twenty-eight submissions that were summarised, nine of them, from BASIS, were identical to those it had submitted for Athens. In view of the paucity of source material, the Secretariat also drew upon a handful of posts to its Web forum and some contributions to the intervening open consultation meetings in the background paper.

The paper was divided into sections on each of the themes of the substantive agenda, followed by consideration of the role and functioning of the IGF. Only the latter need be considered here.

Firstly as to the role of the IGF, the Forum doves such as the ITAA and ETNO continued to oppose a recommendation-developing capacity for the IGF; ENTO specifically commending the Secretariat for dropping speed dialogues from the agenda, and even asserting that it was important "that IGF itself does not sponsor nor recommend any best practice" highlighted during Best Practice Forums.[259] Amongst the Forum hawks of civil society, IT For Change found this attitude confounding, and noted:

> The sudden position of antipathy among many actors—many of whom were represented in the WGIG—to any recommendation-making role for the IGF is difficult to understand, or logically defend. WGIG also had the exact same role of giving policy recommendations to a legitimate policy-making body, the Summit, in that instance. In this light, it seems illogical

[257] Everton Lucero, A "Package" Deal for Rio ⟨URL: http://www.intgovforum.org/EL_paper2_3Sept2007.doc⟩

[258] IGF Secretariat, IGF Second Meeting Synthesis Paper ⟨URL: http://www.intgovforum.org/Rio_Meeting/IGF.SynthesisPaper.24.09.2007.rtf⟩

[259] ETNO, ETNO Reflection Document in Reply to the Consultation "Preparing for the Second Meeting of the IGF" ⟨URL: http://www.intgovforum.org/Substantive_2nd_IGF/ETNO_Reply_to_the_preparing_consultation_for_Rio.pdf⟩, 2–3

to hold that WGIG was worthwhile but a recommendation providing-IGF is not.[260]

In respect of IGF's structure, the hawks were largely content with the status quo; ETNO simply recommending some fine-tuning to the composition of the Advisory Group, and the NRO suggesting that the non-governmental stakeholder groups should be given greater representation.[261] IT For Change on the other hand was amongst the doves who continued to push for more major reform; in its case, that the Advisory Group should be supplemented by a WGIG-like standing committee.[262]

However in one respect, a consensus on the need for reform to the IGF's structures had now developed: namely on the need to develop some criteria for the recognition of dynamic coalitions. This proposition, that originated with civil society,[263] had been repeated by Marcus Kummer at the September 2007 consultations where it also met with the agreement of the ICC and WITSA, and was finally recorded in the background paper as possessing general support.[264]

Plenary sessions

As demanded in the open consultations that followed the Athens meeting, the panels of the plenary sessions of the Rio meeting were smaller, comprising between four and seven members, who were selected by the Secretariat on the advice of the Advisory Group from a slate of nominees. No formal call for speakers had been made to produce this slate; rather it was the outcome of the private solicitations of the Secretariat and Advisory Group and of nominations made by recognised stakeholder representative groups such as the CS-IGC and the ICC.

The reduction in the number of panelists seemed to make little difference to the extent of interaction between the panel and the audience. This was for a number of reasons. First, the sessions had also been shortened by one hour, and other than during the final session on "Emerging Issues," in which the professional moderator strictly limited both the panelists and the floor to brief statements, panelists often overran their allotted time. For

---

[260] IT For Change, Four Critical Issues for the IGF, Rio, from a Southern Perspective ⟨URL: `http://www.intgovforum.org/Substantive_2nd_IGF/IT%20for%20change_Four%20Critical%20Issues%20for%20the%20IGF%20Rio.pdf`⟩, 10

[261] IGF Secretariat, IGF Second Meeting Synthesis Paper (as in n. 258 on page 389), 14 (recorded as being a submission of AfriNIC).

[262] IT For Change, Four Critical Issues for the IGF, Rio, from a Southern Perspective (as in n. 260), 11

[263] It was originally made of working groups for the IGF (for example MMWG (as in n. 145 on page 357), 3), and later of dynamic coalitions (for example during the session on Taking Stock and The Way Forward by the writer, and at the February 2007 open consultations by the CS-IGC).

[264] IGF Secretariat, IGF Second Meeting Synthesis Paper (as in n. 258 on the previous page), 15

example, the plenary session on security was one in which the panelists' presentations took up more than half of the allotted time of the session.

The other main reason why there remained only limited scope for interaction with the floor during the panel sessions was that despite the reduction in the number of panelists, the Secretariat had also selected for each panel a similar number of "discussants" from amongst those who had been nominated for but missed out on a seat on the panel, to be given preference in making statements or questions. The position of discussant was not one that had been raised during open consultations.

Most of the plenary sessions were attended by fewer participants than in Athens. On the second and third days in particular, the plenary sessions attracted smaller audiences not only than the workshops overall, but even than some individual workshops. Some attributed this to the fact that the content of the plenary sessions had developed little from Athens.[265] However the limited impact of the plenary sessions even extended to the new and potentially divisive subject of critical Internet resources.

During the opening ceremony, Roberto Mangabeira Unger, Brazilian Extraordinary Minister for Strategic Affairs, had explicitly called for ICANN "to pass on its power to a more inclusive organisation," which he called upon global civil society to form in a participatory democratic process. But none of those selected to form the panel on critical Internet resources made a similar call. The most radical views on the panel were those of Milton Mueller, who simply questioned the primacy of the GAC amongst ICANN's Advisory Committees but without proposing that a successor body was required, and Carlos Alfonso, who outlined his modest programme for ICANN to attain independence from the US government.

Workshops, open fora and best practices fora

As in Athens, many of the workshops proposed for the Rio meeting covered quite similar themes, since the Secretariat had provided no institutionalised mechanism for stakeholders to coordinate their proposals. However on this occasion, an even greater number of workshops were put forward than the venue could accommodate. By 4 July 2007 when sixty proposals had been made, the Secretariat issued a request to proponents "to contact potential organizers of similar workshops and initiate discussions on how to merge them. ... In parallel, the Secretariat will contact workshop proponents to seek clarifications and/or to make suggestions."[266]

In the end, there were 36 workshops in the Rio meeting, along with 23 best practice fora (most of which were effectively indistinguishable from

[265] APC, APC Statement on the Second Internet Governance Forum ⟨URL: http://pakistanictpolicy.bytesforall.net/?q=node/104⟩

[266] See http://info.intgovforum.org/wsl2.php.

workshops), eight open fora and sundry other meetings (including those of the dynamic coalitions to be separately treated below).

The most significant new events amongst these were the open fora, which opened the Rio meeting to other participants in the Internet governance regime, potentially thereby addressing the disconnect between the IGF and the other institutions with which its mandate required it to interface.[267]

However few signs of this potential being realised were evident in Rio. For example, in ICANN's open forum, its Chairman Peter Dengate Thrush merely outlined the history of the organisation, took reports from some of its constituent bodies, and invited discussion of a few of the current issues on its agenda, but without considering questions such as the organisation's performance against the WSIS process criteria, or the IGF's role in the development of public policy principles on matters under ICANN's purview.

Dynamic coalitions

Each of the dynamic coalitions held a meeting in Rio. However no mechanism had been developed since the Athens meeting by which their findings and recommendations could be considered by the plenary body, other than that they could present a summary of their meetings during a subsequent reporting back session.

Ironically rather than addressing this omission, the Advisory Group intended on further limiting dynamic coalitions' access to the plenary forum, having resolved at its meeting of September 2007 that "in future no Dynamic Coalition should have an automatic right to report to the main session."[268] However neither had the Advisory Group begun to consider the development of any criteria pursuant to which the dynamic coalitions could earn such a right.

The Advisory Group's position contrasted with the view, expressed by William Drake and Bertrand de la Chapelle amongst others during the last day's session on "The Way Forward," that the plenary sessions could be more productively used to receive and consider the dynamic coalitions' output. In Drake's words:

> After two years of the configuration of openness, access, security, diversity, one could argue that doing the same thing again the next year might be of relatively limited value, whereas … what we could do is try to have essentially the dynamic coalitions and the workshops … [bring] some of the ideas,

[267] WSIS, Tunis Agenda for the Information Society (as in n. 5 on page 2), para 72(c)
[268] IGF Secretariat, Advisory Group Meeting Summary Report (as in n. 255 on page 388)

> some of the key points that have come out of their work ... to the larger community for discussion in a plenary setting. ... In this manner, also, those ideas might feed back, then, into other institutions and back to the national level.

Even Nitin Desai, when summarising the session, acknowledged the view that the connection between the main sessions and the workshops and dynamic coalitions would need to be addressed for future meetings.

Remote participation

Despite the criticisms that had attended the limitations of the facilities provided by the Secretariat for remote participation in the Athens meeting of the IGF, these were developed very little for the Rio meeting. In some respects they actually regressed, for example in that questions for the floor of plenary sessions were only received from remote participants in two languages rather than the four promised, and the email addresses at which they were to be received were not published until after the first day's sessions had commenced, with the result that they were even less used than in Athens.

One of the most significant improvements that was planned was developed by a team from the Brazilian Ministry of Culture led by Jose Murilo Junior, a member of the Online Collaboration Dynamic Coalition. This combined chat and webcast facility would have allowed remote and in-person participation to be integrated much more closely by displaying online discussion on the plenary session in near real-time on a large projection screen at the venue, subject to light moderation for inappropriate content.[269] Although completed, the use of this facility for projection into the venue was not taken up by the Secretariat.

The OCDC itself also had limited success in improving upon the facilities that its founders had provided for the Athens meeting through the IGF Community Web site. It was originally intended to expand the facilities of this site using a dedicated server that a member had pledged to donate in February 2007, but one month ahead of the date of the Rio meeting this donation had yet to eventuate. Even so, shortly before the Rio meeting opened a successor to the Athens IGF Community site was rapidly assembled and launched.[270] Although it carried several improvements to the original, including a ribbon menu at the top of each page that linked between all of the official and community sites, the Secretariat once again

[269] This would have implemented suggestions of the author that were recorded in the synthesis paper for the May 2007 open consultation meeting: IGF Secretariat, Open Consultations Geneva, 23 May 2007: Summary of Contributions Prepared by the IGF Secretariat (as in n. 247 on page 386), 8.

[270] See `http://igf-online.net/`.

declined to publicise the availability of the site to IGF participants, with the result that it was also less used than in Athens.

Follow-up

The process of taking stock of and following up from the Rio meeting that began in the plenary session on "The Way Forward" continued with a call in December for stakeholders to provide written feedback both on the success of the second IGF meeting, and on possible reforms to the Advisory Group, such as the rotation of its members. These were collected in a synthesis paper published in the week preceding an open consultation meeting on these topics on 26 February 2008.[271]

Whilst the deeper divides between hawks and doves on the IGF's role and structure remained, a number of areas of broad agreement on procedural reforms to the IGF's annual meeting could be found amongst both the eleven contributors to the synthesis paper and those who contributed in person to the open consultation meeting.[272] Most notably, the paper records a widespread view that in view of the lukewarm reception of the plenary sessions in Rio, for the following meeting in Hyderabad, India "the main sessions should be focused on a more in-depth discussion of a limited number of specific issues drawing on the outcomes (including recommendations) of the relevant workshops."[273]

The synthesis paper also recognised

> that in order to strengthen the dynamic coalitions, they should be given more visibility during and also between the IGF meetings, and their work should be better reflected into the meetings during reporting back sessions. There should also be some way for the IGF to promote the outcomes from the dynamic coalitions.[274]

As to the reform of the Advisory Group, some demonstrable progress to this end had been made even before the open consultation meeting opened, with the publication in February 2008 of a commitment on the front page of the IGF's Web site to make "[d]igests of the discussion held within the Advisory Group ... available on the Forum Section on a regular basis." The first two of these digests, published in anonymised form, were a selection of postings considering the topics of the Advisory Group's rotation,[275] and

[271] IGF Secretariat, Synthesis Paper—Open Consultations, Geneva, 26 February 2008

[272] Archived at `http://www.intgovforum.org/feb26/Geneva-IGF-2-26-08%20Full%20Day%20ver1.txt`.

[273] Ibid., 3

[274] Ibid., 4

[275] IGF Secretariat, Advisory Group Discussion 6 December 2007 to 15 January 2008 (as in n. 79 on page 200)

how its transparency could be further improved.[276] By the end of March 2008 five more digests had been posted.[277]

The synthesis paper's treatment of reform to the Advisory Group comprised little more than a summary of the views expressed in the first two digests. Whilst proposals for more sweeping reform were voiced at the open consultation meeting,[278] the Secretariat's view of such proposals was made clear in the report of the subsequent closed meeting of the Advisory Group that was held over the following two days. The report notes that there was a range of views on the need for rebalancing the representation of the various stakeholder groups, but ominously states that "the group was informed"—presumably by its Chair—that no proposal to reduce the 50% representation of governments would be entertained.[279]

5.3 Regional initiatives

Having surveyed the reforms wrought by WSIS and the IGF to the regime of Internet governance, it still remains in this chapter to touch on a couple of the most significant regional and sub-regional multi-stakeholder initiatives that have accompanied those larger reforms.

Since the main concern of this book is international and transnational governance, only a cursory survey of regional developments will be given here. However they cannot be overlooked altogether, since regional consultation and coordination were key to the WSIS process from its commencement. For example, apart from the regional conferences that were held ahead of each phase of WSIS, in the Asia-Pacific region an Open Regional Dialogue on Internet Governance (ORDIG) took place during 2004 and 2005 as a project of UNDP's Asia-Pacific Development Information Programme (UNDP-APDIP) to feed into the WGIG and the broader WSIS processes.[280]

Accordingly, international and regional cooperation was specified as a key principle for building an inclusive Information Society in the WSIS Declaration of Principles, and was also the subject of a key recommendation in the WGIG report.[281]

[276] Idem, Advisory Group Discussion 30 January to 3 February 2008 (as in n. 182 on page 365)

[277] See http://intgovforum.org/forum/index.php?topic=426.0.

[278] For example, the Russian Federation spoke "in favor of changing the format of the group in conformity with the procedures within the UN system"—that is, adopting the procedures of an intergovernmental bureau—whereas Brazil suggested the recognition of the academic community as a fourth class of stakeholder within the Advisory Group, and the CS-IGC continued to push for the greater representation of civil society within the group.

[279] Idem, Multistakeholder Advisory Group Meeting Summary Report ⟨URL: http://www.intgovforum.org/Feb_igf_meeting/MAG.Summary.28.02.2008.v2.pdf⟩, 1

[280] See http://www.apdip.net/projects/igov/ and Danny Butt, *Internet Governance: Asia-Pacific Perspectives* New Delhi: Elsevier, 2005, chap. The Open Regional Dialogue on Internet Governance.

[281] WGIG, Report of the Working Group on Internet Governance (as in n. 2 on page 29), 16

Although not specifically contained in the IGF's mandate, IGF participants have also long called for the development of supportive regional processes. At the first open consultation in February 2006, Morocco and the Dominican Republic were amongst those recommending the initiation of regional IGF events. Nitin Desai summed up these calls in saying:

> I think one aspect of it which may require a little advanced work is a message I have heard very strongly from many people here, and that is the need for some type of regional process to contribute to this. And that's not something which can be done at the last minute. You can't just say suddenly, you know, three months or four months before, "Oh, please get off the ground." So ... I would suggest, to the UN that they may wish to get in touch with the regional commissions to see how, within the resources that the regional commissions have, they could start thinking about what sort of regional contribution they could make to this process.

However aside from the appointment of designated "regional coordinators" to the Advisory Group, any further regional programmes were left to emerge through bottom–up coordination.

This occurred only to a very limited degree ahead of the Athens meeting; mainly through limited public consultation processes conducted by delegations attending the WSIS summit[282] and the IGF.[283]

A few new regional programmes were announced between the Athens and Rio meetings. First came the launch of Nominet's Best Practice Challenge, which invited UK civil society and the private sector to nominate themselves as demonstrating best practice in the categories of openness, security, access or diversity, with selected nominees to be showcased in Rio.[284] There were also two preparatory seminars held in Brazil during July and September 2007 by CGI.br,[285] and one in Tokyo organised by Nippon Keidanren in May.[286] Finally a one-day Dialogue Forum on Internet Rights was hosted by the Italian government in Rome in September.[287]

---

[282] Such as that of Australia's DCITA in August 2005: DCITA, World Summit on the Information Society and Internet Governance Public Forums ⟨URL: http://www.dbcde.gov.au/__data/assets/pdf_file/0003/29775/World_Summit_on_the_Information_Society-WSIS_and_Internet_Governance_Forums_3_4_Aug_05.pdf⟩.

[283] Such as that of the United Kingdom's Department of Trade and Industry in January 2006: Department of Trade & Industry, Points Raised at the Internet Governance Forum Consultation Meeting ⟨URL: http://www.intgovforum.org/contributions/igf.pdf⟩.

[284] See http://www.nominet.org.uk/about/bestpracticechallenge/.

[285] See http://www.nupef.org.br/atividade_IGF_seminarios_pre1.htm and http://www.nupef.org.br/atividade_IGF_reuniao_2.htm.

[286] See http://www.iccwbo.org/policy/law/iccbdeda/index.html.

[287] See http://www.dfiritaly2007.it/.

Following the Rio meeting, a so-called United Kingdom Internet Governance Forum was launched in March 2008, taking the rather unassuming form of a two-hour seminar.[288] Finally in January 2008 the European Parliament passed a resolution to encourage "the organisation of a 'European IGF' before mid-2009 to reinforce the European dimension of the whole IGF/WSIS process."[289]

CGI.br

A more advanced model of sub-regional reform in multi-stakeholder Internet governance is exemplified by the Brazilian Internet Steering Committee (CGI.br).[290] Established in May 1995 by Interministerial Ordinance, this national multi-stakeholder body is unusual in that its responsibilities span the realms of both technical coordination and public policy governance. That is, CGI.br coordinates and exercises oversight over the activities of the national IP address and ccTLD registries (NIC.br and registro.br respectively), as well as operating the local computer emergency response team CERT.br,[291] but also has a role in the development of policies and procedures for the regulation of the Internet in Brazil.

Since last reconstituted as a legal entity by Presidential Decree in 2003,[292] CGI.br has been composed of twenty-one members, including:

- nine federal government representatives, with one representative from each of nine relevant ministries and agencies;
- four private sector representatives, with one representative each of ISPs, telecommunications infrastructure providers, the hardware and software industries, and general private sector Internet users;
- four representatives of civil society;[293]
- three representatives of the scientific and technical community; and
- one non-voting Internet expert nominated by the Ministry of Science and Technology.

---

[288] See `http://www.nominet.org.uk/about/events/UKIGF/`.

[289] European Parliament, European Parliament Resolution on the Second Internet Governance Forum, held in Rio de Janeiro from 12 to 15 November 2007 ⟨URL: `http://www.europarl.europa.eu/sides/getDoc.do?type=MOTION&reference=B6-2008-0041&language=EN`⟩

[290] Comitê Gestor da Internet no Brasil; see `http://cgi.br/`.

[291] Centro de Estudos, Resposta e Tratamento de Incidentes de Segurança no Brasil; see `http://www.cert.br/`.

[292] *Decree No 4,829 of 3 Sep 2003* (Brazil), DOU of 4 Sep 2003, Section I, p 24

[293] Or "the third sector" as it is known within CGI.br.

Each of these constituencies democratically elects its own representatives for three year terms, save for the governmental constituency whose representatives are appointed. For this purpose, the constituency is represented by an electoral college (or in the case of the private sector, one electoral college for each segment) on which any relevant representative bodies that have existed for at least two years prior to the election are eligible to be enrolled. Each qualifying representative body is entitled to nominate one candidate for election, and to vote for as many candidates as there are places in its constituency or segment. The elections are conducted using a secure Web portal.

There are also three working groups of CGI.br, respectively dedicated to network engineering, computer security and capacity building, which meet in person as well as operating electronic mailing lists. Aiming to act by consensus, they provide recommendations to the full group on issues within their areas of expertise. CGI.br also endeavours to act by consensus, but falls back to voting where this cannot be achieved. Minutes of the meetings of CGI.br are published on its Web site.[294]

5.4 Other proposals

The process that led to the establishment of the IGF at WSIS did not take place in a vacuum. It was rather the outcome of the convergence of pre-existing forces driven by diverse actors seeking to reform existing Internet governance arrangements, and produced a compromise that adequately accommodated the heterogeneous interests of the most powerful of those actors. Some of those interests may have been addressed by the IGF's establishment, but others were not; as seen in the continued pressure for movement on "enhanced cooperation," from the Forum hawks in particular.

Many of the actors involved in the WSIS process had, and some still have, their own agenda for Internet governance reform, and some of these will be briefly discussed here. The purpose of doing so is not to provide a catalogue of other proposals for Internet governance reform, but simply to take the opportunity, before drawing the book's final conclusions, to consider whether any other proposals contain pearls of wisdom missing from all other alternatives considered before now.

Although there is insufficient space to mention all such proposals, the selection of those that are of most interest is made easier by the fact that previous chapters have established firstly that Internet public policy governance must, particularly in some issue areas, be conducted on a global basis, and secondly that governance by network should exist at the core of

[294] See http://www.cgi.br/acoes/realizadas.htm.

any Internet governance regime, although other mechanisms of governance such as rules, norms, markets and architecture will also come into play.

That being so, the typology that will be adopted here, drawing from Chapter 4, considers proposals not according to which mechanism of governance they favour, since most will require the use of several mechanisms of governance (and should therefore be broadly consistent with a core of governance by network), but rather according to the form that the institutions utilising or embodying those mechanisms are most likely to take: anarchistic, hierarchical, democratic or consensual.

Anarchistic

A plausible model of anarchistic self-governance of the Internet is one of governance through networks of consensual arrangements between Internet stakeholders at various levels, potentially incorporating the use of any other mechanisms of governance besides rules. To relate this to the relevant layers of the Internet's network stack, these may include the use of interconnection agreements between ISPs at the network layer (an example of governance through markets), the application of IETF standards at the transport layer (utilising governance by architecture), and the promulgation of AUPs (Acceptable Use Policies) and netiquette at the application layer (demonstrating governance by norms).

But because these existing mechanisms leave gaps in the sphere of public policy governance of the Internet, comprehensive anarchistic proposals for reform cannot simply be arguments for the status quo, but should call for or at least accommodate a superadded Internet public policy governance network (if a very loose and decentralised one).

Even in John Perry Barlow's utopian vision of an anarchistic Internet, he understood its self-governance as a regime under development, rather than one fully-formed; thus writing, "We *are forming* our own Social Contract. This governance *will arise* according to the conditions of our world, not yours."[295]

Writing in the same year, Johnson and Post sought to explain how such a regime of independent self-governance for the Internet might come into being, in an international system already populated with governmental and intergovernmental authorities. They argued that the role of states in such a regime is simply to grant comity to the decentralised, emergent governance of Internet stakeholders,[296] just as medieval governments recognised and accorded independent status to the law merchant. Essentially, governments are called upon to regard cyberspace as a distinct jurisdiction of its own.[297]

[295] Barlow (as in n. 3 on page 1), emphasis added.
[296] Johnson and Post (as in n. 348 on page 164), 1391–94
[297] This is a concept that Zittrain derides as "Internet separatism," describing Johnson and

Reidenberg provides more detail of how such a regime might function in practice, noting that since ISPs and computer network administrators wield significant control over cyberspace, they provide a convenient locus of control for an Internet governance regime, with each network essentially taking the place of a state in the international public policy governance regime.[298] This is already seen in some issue areas, such as the extent to which AUP terms imposed by ISPs and content providers are used to regulate spam, cybercrime and even IPRs.

However, to the extent that the public policy choices embodied in these terms are made by the private sector unilaterally, they may not reflect broader public values.[299] It is on this basis that the Council of Europe has argued at the IGF that in delegating governance authority to a non-state body such as ICANN, states are not excused from their duty of oversight to ensure that human rights are protected, and should ensure that they maintain some way to make such bodies ultimately answerable to the international community.[300]

The same problem applies to the reliance upon architecture as the foundation of an anarchistic governance network. Although certain core values embedded in the architecture of the Internet cannot be modified without fundamentally reconstituting the network, the code that shapes the end user's Internet experience is distributed throughout all layers of the network stack, and there are various points at which it can more easily be reshaped to accord with alternative sets of values.[301]

Biegel examines how architectural or "code-based changes" in this broader sense can be actively used as a mechanism of Internet governance, rather than merely acting as such by default in disseminating the core values of the hacker ethic. He distinguishes between changes made:

- at the root server level of the domain name system;[302]

Post's article as "now thoroughly dated": Jonathan Zittrain, *Who Rules the Net? Internet Governance and Jurisdiction* Washington, DC: Cato Institute, 2003, chap. Be Careful What You Ask For: Reconciling a Global Internet and Local Law, 22. See also Joel R Reidenberg, Technology and Internet Jurisdiction, Uni Penn LR 153 2005.

[298] Idem, Governing Networks and Rule-Making in Cyberspace, Em LJ 45 1996; Idem, States and Internet Enforcement (as in n. 331 on page 161)

[299] Biegel (as in n. 60 on page 19), 219. Since these may also vary from one computer network to another, there is also the potential for a "race to the bottom," whereby users are attracted to the network enforcing the least stringent standards, though this outcome is difficult to avoid in any anarchist model: see section 3.4 on page 160.

[300] Council of Europe, Council of Europe Submission to the Internet Governance Forum (as in n. 203 on page 370), 10. On the other hand to the extent that, being developed in the shadow of the law, AUPs simply reflect underlying governmental regulation, they are also deficient.

[301] Lessig, *Code and Other Laws of Cyberspace* (as in n. 25 on page 9), 43–44

[302] Though he does not specifically acknowledge the quite limited scope for governance of public policy issues at this level: Biegel (as in n. 60 on page 19), 197; and see section 3.4 on page 170.

- at the application layer of TCP/IP (by which he appears to mean "over TCP/IP," and in which category he places architectures of identification, content filtering and copyright management);
- on individual users' hard drives (which refers to end-user application software such as filtering tools and surveillance software, excluding software deployed by ISPs and content providers which would fall into the preceding category); and
- in the design of digital products that may be sold or distributed either online or offline (which is much the same as the preceding category, save that the software is embedded in hardware or firmware, such as the DRM software in media players).[303]

What is required in order for the anarchist programme to become consistent with democratic principles is that the public policy choices underlying the contractual regulation of Internet usage by ISPs and content providers, and those embedded in the Internet's architecture and other code by any of the means identified by Biegel, be consensually developed within a multi-stakeholder forum, rather than unilaterally by the private sector or the technical community. Even for the anarchist, there is no reason why the IGF could not be that forum. However, it would be an IGF which substantially differs from that which exists now.[304]

Hierarchical

Other proposals for reform to Internet governance arrangements take issue with anarchistic models on the basis that they are, by nature, voluntary, which is a significant limitation in certain issue areas such as cybercrime, in which antisocial behaviour cannot be sufficiently curtailed through norms, markets or architecture. Thus Rony and Rony list authority amongst the criteria to be considered in selecting a new Internet governance regime.[305]

There are three main hierarchical models of Internet governance that are consistent with governance by network in some measure. The most radical of these is for an extensive autonomous body of Internet-specific international law to be developed by an intergovernmental authority (in consultation with other stakeholders), which would in one stroke solve many of the most acute jurisdictional issues to which the Internet gives rise. As Goldsmith and Wu write, it would mean "no conflicting laws, no

[303] Ibid., 193–207

[304] See section 6.2 on page 431.

[305] Together with stability, accountability, security, priority (that is, accommodating the first-come, first-served principle), structure, and harmonisation (that is, integration with domestic law on issues of international property and privacy: Rony and Rony (as in n. 18 on page 35), 10–11.

worries about complying with 175 different legal systems, no race to the bottom."[306]

Neither would it be without precedent: international maritime law in fact provides a close analogy for what is proposed.[307] In an online context, though on a less comprehensive scale, the UDRP also offers an example of this model in action, in that case with WIPO acting as the relevant intergovernmental authority, being the progenitor of the scheme and the dominant provider of UDRP arbitration services.

On a larger scale, this model would require a legal framework for the Internet to be developed under the auspices of either a new intergovernmental entity established to do so,[308] or an existing intergovernmental authority. The WTO has been proposed by some for this purpose,[309] given that it offers a ready-made mechanism of enforcement lacking in current Internet governance institutions. However at least some commentators, in anticipation of the WSIS principles, have acknowledged the need for multi-stakeholder participation, which would count quite strongly against the selection of the WTO as a forum for the development of a legal regime for the Internet. Schuler for example stated in 1998:

> Although government needs to assume a stronger role in this area, its objectives must not be accomplished through edicts or heavy-handed bureaucracies, but through innovative, flexible experiments conducted in partnerships with citizen groups, NGOs, and, perhaps, business.[310]

Kobayashi and Ribstein concur,[311], proffering instead a second model of hierarchical Internet governance based not around a single regulatory regime but a multiplicity of networked regimes. This would limit "the extent to which powerful interest groups can control regulation and secure inefficient rules that transfer wealth from weaker interest groups," whilst offering a variety of regulatory approaches to "suit different sets of preferences, including a preference for no regulation," and thereby promoting "an evolutionary process as individuals and firms choose the laws under which they prefer to operate."[312] This roughly equates to the model of competi-

---

[306] Goldsmith and Wu (as in n. 220 on page 80), 26

[307] See Johnson and Post (as in n. 348 on page 164), although the authors do not concur with the view that the body of law should be developed by an intergovernmental authority.

[308] Franda (as in n. 43 on page 42), 74; Jonathan Zittrain, ICANN: Between the Public and the Private—Comments Before Congress, Berkeley Tech LJ 14 1999

[309] Weber (as in n. 70 on page 20), 78; Biegel (as in n. 60 on page 19), 182

[310] Doug Schuler, How Do We Institutionalize Democracy in the Electronic Age? ⟨URL: `http://www.scn.org/ip/commnet/its98.html`⟩

[311] Bruce H Kobayashi and Larry E Ribstein, *Who Rules the Net? Internet Governance and Jurisdiction* Washington, DC: Cato Institute, 2003, chap. Multijurisdictional Regulation of the Internet, 214

[312] Kobayashi and Ribstein (as in n. 311), 176

tion between hierarchically-organised networks described at section 4.2 on page 221.

However in order for this to work, freedom of exit from each jurisdiction would be required. Although exit from a jurisdiction's reach can, at least for purposes of trade and commerce, be as simple as the exercise of a contractual choice of law clause, it is a more formidable obstacle in other issue areas, particularly for those whose geographical roots are firmly planted, as are most individual Internet users. This model therefore works better where the competing regulatory regimes include a range of governance mechanisms other than the rule of states, between which Internet users, no matter where situated, actually have a meaningful choice. However, so modified, the model loses its hierarchical quality.

The third model of hierarchical Internet governance is something of a compromise between the first two, in that it calls for an intergovernmental authority to assume responsibility for public policy issues that are specifically impacted by existing Internet governance processes and institutions, but without seeking to establish a broader regime of governance for all Internet-related issue areas, which are left to be dealt with by diverse other mechanisms. This model is exemplified by the early support of commentators for direct involvement of the ITU and WIPO in addressing the disconnect between the DNS and trademark law.[313]

In more recent times it is the ITU that has most vocally advocated the position that an intergovernmental authority would be more legitimate and effective than a hotchpotch of civil society and private sector organisations in dealing with public policy issues arising in the administrative and technical governance of the Internet, and that the ITU in particular, representing all national telecommunications regulatory authorities, would be the most appropriate intergovernmental authority to assume this role.[314]

The ITU's position is that it is difficult for governments to participate in processes that are not formally intergovernmental, such as those of ICANN which is formally a US company and therefore subject to the control of its domestic authorities. Whilst governments can (and do) still participate informally in bodies such as ICANN and the IETF, the Director of the ITU's TSG contended ahead of the Tunis summit of WSIS that "there is a big difference between the legitimacy that comes from formal participation, as compared to informal participation," and stated:

> The usual solution to this difficult problem is to charge an intergovernmental organization with the task of developing internationally agreed public policies (that is, advice to private companies), which policies are then transposed as appropriate

[313]W A Foster, *Coordinating the Internet* Cambridge: MIT Press, 1997, chap. Registering the Domain Name System: An Exercise in Global Decision-Making

[314]Huston (as in n. 112 on page 59)

into national laws and apply to private companies as appropriate. ...

Concretely, it might be helpful to build on ITU's unique position as an intergovernmental organization that has private sector members—especially since those active ITU members are also major players in providing Internet infrastructure—and to consider relying on ITU (and other IGOs as appropriate) to provide appropriate public policy frameworks at the international level for what concerns Internet matters.

... it is preferable to have existing inter-governmental organizations under the UN system to take care of issues that require inter-governmental coordination, while recognizing the role of existing international and private sector organizations with respect to technical and operating matters. It would be cost-effective to charge existing UN family organizations with this task.[315]

Since the Tunis phase of WSIS, the ITU's ambitions in this regard have of course been dealt a serious, and probably fatal setback. However the ideal of "enhanced cooperation" to which they have given way can be regarded as the successor of this hierarchical model for Internet governance. Exactly what it is to entail in practice however, and the extent to which the IGF will have a role to play in it, remain very open questions.

Democratic

Although the division between democratic and consensual models of Internet governance reform is somewhat arbitrary, for present purposes democratic models of Internet governance may be defined as those in which representation is applied as a key criterion. Most notable of these is the NTIA's Green Paper on the future ICANN, that specified the four criteria of stability, competition, private sector coordination and representation.[316]

The high water mark in ICANN's pursuit of the principle of representation was in the method by which five At-Large representatives on the ICANN board were selected in 2000,[317] prior to the development of the RALO model in 2002.[318] This experiment in large-scale online democracy

[315]Zhao (as in n. 2 on page 1), 12–13

[316]NTIA, Request for Comments on the Registration and Administration of Internet Domain Names ⟨URL: `http://www.ntia.doc.gov/ntiahome/domainname/DN5NOTIC.htm`⟩. These distilled six "appropriate principles" earlier specified in the NTIA's Notice of Inquiry.

[317]See ICANN, Membership Implementation Task Force: Call for Expressions of Interest ⟨URL: `http://www.icann.org/committees/at-large/call-1dec99.htm`⟩.

[318]ICANN, Evolution and Reform Committee's Final Implementation Report and Recommendations ⟨URL: `http://www.icann.org/committees/evol-reform/final-implementation-report-02oct02.htm`⟩

followed the recommendations of the Berkman Center for Internet & Society at Harvard Law School, in a report to ICANN's Membership Advisory Committee (MAC) that stated:

> At-large membership should primarily represent those individuals and organizations that are not represented by the Supporting Organizations (SOs). The goals of the at-large membership are as follows:
>
> 1. to include any Internet user with access and verifiable identity in order to reflect the global diversity of users (membership should not be limited to IP address or domain name holders),
> 2. to elect Directors to the ICANN Board by procedures that are valid and authentic,
> 3. to ensure that ICANN's corporate structure operates for the benefit of the Internet community as a whole, is not captured, and continues to provide fair and proportional representation of the entire user community,
> 4. to provide input from the user community to the ICANN Directors and
> 5. to do so in a cost-efficient manner.

In response to that report, ICANN formed a Membership Implementation Task Force to build a broadly constituted base of at least 5000 individual members to participate in the inaugural elections. Registration of members required a name, email address and verification by postal mail (the cost of which was defrayed by a public grant). In the end, 143 806 members registered, 76 183 of whom were authenticated by postal mail, and 34 035 of whom actually voted.

Following a review by yet another ICANN-formed committee, the At-Large Study Committee, in 2001, this direct election model was abandoned, on grounds that "such an approach is administratively and financially unworkable on a global scale for a sizeable electorate, and fraught with potential dangers ranging from capture to outright fraud."[319] In the place of direct election, the committee recommended a model that would have seen only the holders of domain names as at-large members of ICANN.

This recommendation was however trumped by the still more damning comments of ICANN's then President M Stuart Lynn,

> that the concept of At Large membership elections from a self-selected pool of unknown voters is not just flawed, but fatally flawed, and that continued devotion of ICANN's very

[319] At-Large Study Committee (as in n. 402 on page 267)

finite energy and resources down this path will very likely prevent the creation of an effective and viable institution.

However Karl Auerbach, the director chosen to represent North America in those 2000 elections, considers that democratic election remains a model worthy of serious consideration by Internet governance bodies. He states:

> We could easily model elections for representatives on internet governance bodies on the elections that are held among shareholders of publicly held corporations. These are usually done over the internet or via paper mail. These are inexpensive and technically easy to administer.[320]

The problem is that the shareholders of a corporation are a fixed and ascertainable class of electors, but the stakeholders of a governance network are not. This opens the door to mischiefs such as the manipulation of a large bloc of voters who, although formally qualified, would not otherwise have voted, to support a particular candidate. This, and more rudimentary methods of election fraud such as multiple voting under false identities, were suspected of having occurred in the ICANN elections.[321]

The way in which CGI.br has tackled such problems in the elections for its constituencies is through the use of an electoral college constituted by relevant representative organisations. Although a better solution than individual direct election, this does have a distorting effect in that the votes of organisations with large memberships are not weighted differently to those of small organisations. Unless accountablity is strictly maintained, it also introduces the danger of democratic deficits emerging through the interpolation of layers of representation that distance the polity from the grass roots. Finally there is also still some potential for electoral fraud, illustrated by the fact that the use of GONGOs and other front NGOs within intergovernmental fora, including WSIS, is notorious.[322]

Despite these problems, at worst ICANN and CGI.br "can be seen as 'pilot projects' to explore the feasibility of new policy mechanisms which go beyond the traditional governmental top-down system," utilising "new principles in global policy-making like bottom–up coordination, rough consensus, openness and transparency."[323] Beyond adherence to these principles, all else that is really needed to constitute them as democratic

[320] Karl Auerbach, Stakeholderism—The Wrong Road For Internet Governance ⟨URL: http://www.cavebear.com/archive/rw/igf-democracy-in-internet-governance.pdf⟩, 4

[321] At-Large Study Committee (as in n. 402 on page 267)

[322] Kenneth Neil Cukier, *The World Summit on the Information Society: Moving from the Past into the Future* New York: UNICTTF, 2005, chap. The WSIS Wars: An Analysis of the Politicization of the Internet, 161

[323] Kleinwächter, Global Governance in the Information Age: GBDe and ICANN as "Pilot Projects" for Co-regulation and a New Trilateral Policy? (as in n. 106 on page 207), 3

governance networks is a structure that adequately fulfils the democratic principle of consent. In the absence of a sound method of representing stakeholders proportionally in their policy development structures, this means the development of adequate mechanisms for democratic deliberation within those structures.

Consensual

For present purposes, consensual models of Internet governance are those that are more likely to emphasise consensus than authority or representation as a key design criterion for the reform of Internet governance institutions. This is, for example, the view of Biegel who writes that "consensus among the various stakeholders will be an essential component" of any programme of Internet governance reform.[324]

Although there is some overlap with both anarchistic and democratic proposals, the consensual model may be differentiated from them in that it more closely reflects the underlying dynamics of governance by network. Unlike in the democratic model, such a network can only operate with the consent of all its participants; yet unlike in the anarchistic model, it also requires the processes by which consensus is reached to be institutionalised by some, perhaps hierarchical, mechanism. Thus Vedel claims that governance by network (or "associative regulation" in his terms) rarely exists or is maintained in the absence of state intervention.[325]

Specific proposals for Internet governance reform that fall into the consensual class may be further subdivided into two categories. First are those that are situated within the existing international law paradigm, thus anchoring the institutions and processes of Internet governance in the international system. Second are consensual governance networks placed outside or parallel to the international system, and which require it to accommodate their autonomous operation, much in the same way as ICANN's regime of Internet naming and numbering has been accommodated within the international system.

Anchored in the international system

The first proposal in the former category is one that emerged from within civil society at WSIS for the establishment of a new specialised agency of the United Nations to be called UNMSP (United Nations Multi-Stakeholder Partnerships).[326] It would essentially act as a bridge between new multi-

[324] Biegel (as in n. 60 on page 19), 360

[325] Vedel (as in n. 74 on page 21), 65

[326] See `http://www.unmsp.org/` and Civil Society Scientific Information Working Group, Substantive Contributions as Material to Synthesis Papers in View of the First Meeting of the Internet Governance Forum ⟨URL: `http://intgovforum.org/Substantive_1st_IGF/`

stakeholder governance networks and the existing international system, by streamlining the process by which such networks are formed and by facilitating states' participation in them.[327]

The proposed new agency would contain a separate assembly for each stakeholder group, including a General Assembly for governments and Conferences for the private sector and civil society. Conferences would be subdivided by topic, each with a President whom it would elect or appoint, and could convene virtually rather than meeting in person. Conference members would submit proposals for resolutions or recommendations for approval by the General Assembly.

A proposed new multi-stakeholder network formed between participants in the UNMSP would be entitled to receive the UNMSP's formal imprimatur of endorsement once it had a charter and the sponsorship of at least two states. There would be no need for a treaty to formalise the involvement of these or other states in the network, because this would be covered by the umbrella UNMSP treaty.

Along somewhat similar lines is the proposal for a Framework Convention on Internet Governance,[328] following the model of the Framework Convention on Climate Change.[329]

Such a Framework Convention could be thought of as a constitutional document that would establish the facts, principles and norms of the Internet governance regime,[330] and delineate the respective roles of both intergovernmental and non-governmental institutions of Internet governance.[331] As a practical example of the application of such a Framework Convention, it could supplant the JPA between the NTIA and ICANN in providing a mechanism of international oversight of the management of Internet naming and numbering.

The Tunis Agenda seems to anticipate the development of such an instrument as an element of the programme of enhanced cooperation, stating that the "process could envisage creation of a suitable framework or mechanisms, where justified, thus spurring the ongoing and active evolution of the current arrangements in order to synergize the efforts in this regard."[332] This need not necessarily be a hard law instrument; for example Anriette Esterhausen of APC suggested at a Best Practice Forum on public participation in Internet governance held in Rio that the Aarhus

---

si-synthesis-oa.pdf⟩, 18.

[327]Compare the Partnership Development Unit recommended by the Cardoso Report: Cardoso, Cardoso Report on Civil Society (as in n. 147 on page 126), 38.

[328]John Mathiason, A Framework Convention: An Institutional Option for Internet Goverance ⟨URL: http://www.internetgovernance.org/pdf/igp-fc.pdf⟩, 1–2

[329]*UN Framework Convention on Climate Change*, 9 May 1992, 1994 ATS No 2 (entry into force 21 Mar 2004)

[330]Mueller et al. (as in n. 1 on page 322)

[331]Holitscher (as in n. 4 on page 30), 6

[332]WSIS, Tunis Agenda for the Information Society (as in n. 5 on page 2), para 61

Convention could be used as the basis for a soft law agreement on Internet governance to which different institutions, both public and private, could become signatories.

The third proposal that seeks to situate multi-stakeholder Internet governance in the international system is really a group of related proposals for the establishment of an Internet Bill of Rights. These proposals include:

- the APC's Internet Rights Charter;[333]
- the "Tunis Mon Amour" initiative from the Tunis phase of WSIS that evolved into the Internet Bill of Rights dynamic coalition of the IGF; and
- the Declaration of Lima 2003 drafted by Latin American civil society at the Geneva phase of WSIS, which endeavoured to develop a set of principles for cyberspace akin to those enshrined in international law for the high seas and outer space.[334]

Although an Internet Bill of Rights would not, in the same manner as the previous two proposals, provide a meta-structure for a multi-stakeholder Internet governance network, it could, if all stakeholders were involved in its development, provide a baseline of protection for consensually agreed individual rights and interests against incursion from future state (and, indeed, private) action.

A shortcoming of the Bill of Rights proposal is its limited responsiveness to change, since it crystallises the interests of those involved in its development, assuming that the general principles they develop in a specific set of circumstances will remain applicable (or even comprehensible) across heterogeneous issue areas as the Internet continues to evolve.

More fundamentally, for this or indeed the other two proposals noted above to seek to place Internet governance within the existing international system, can be seen as an unprincipled concession to state hegemony that undervalues the legitimacy of the independent role of the other stakeholders in governance. In other words, it reduces transnational law to international law.

Autonomous transnational law

In contrast are those proposals for Internet governance reform that are situated apart from the international system. Being divorced from intergovernmental authority does not necessarily mean that these lack an

[333] APC, Internet Rights Charter ⟨URL: http://rights.apc.org/documents/APC_charter_EN.pdf⟩

[334] GIC, Declaration of Lima ⟨URL: http://www.alfa-redi.org/ar-dnt-documento.shtml?x=3499⟩

institutionalised structure or process. However it does beg the question, if a governance structure is not anchored in the superstructure of the international system, does it (and, indeed, does it need to) draw upon some other hierarchical source?

Generally, if the Internet governance regimes put forward in these proposals are anchored anywhere else at all, it is in other institutions of Internet governance. Thus Gould suggests that an unwritten constitutional framework could emerge from existing Internet governance institutions, with the addition of an "Internet regulator" which could be ultimately responsible to the Internet Society.[335] Similarly, Stuckey talks of the passage of a constitution for cyberspace, explicating the roles of its existing governance institutions, and providing a base for the development of its own corpus of law and self-regulation.[336] More recently, the self-described Working Group on Constitutional Internet Governance (WGCIG) has inaugurated an online Constitutional Convention alongside the IGF.[337]

An apparent problem with such proposals is that they seek to pull the Internet governance regime up by its own bootstraps, by establishing a transnational legal framework for consensual governance through institutions such as ISOC whose authority only exists as part of that same regime, in a chain of paradoxical self-reference. However, this is not so much of a problem as it may seem: it is possible for a transnational legal regime to establish a self-supporting superstructure, in the same way that the adjudication of international trade disputes occurs pursuant to a system of international commercial arbitration that is itself the product of contract.[338]

However by the same token, it is also possible for a consensual Internet governance network to exist entirely autonomously, supported by nothing other than the inherent force of its own "running code."[339] This alludes to the famous maxim of David Clark from MIT, which became the credo of the IETF: "We reject kings, presidents and voting. We believe in rough consensus and running code."[340] In other words, on this account, the institutions and processes of a consensual Internet governance network gain nothing from being anchored in any external authority, so long as their output has been tested in practice and proven effective.

And indeed, it is from the IETF that a number of such initiatives have drawn inspiration. These include the Internet Law and Policy Forum

[335] Mark Gould, *Coordinating the Internet* Cambridge, MA: MIT Press, 1997, chap. Governance of the Internet: a UK Perspective, 58

[336] Kent D Stuckey, *Internet and Online Law* New York: Law Journal Press, 1996, xxiii

[337] See `http://www.wgcig.net/`.

[338] Teubner (as in n. 9 on page 99)

[339] Einar Stefferud, Image Online Design, Inc comments on the Registration and Administration of Internet Domain Names ⟨URL: `http://www.ntia.doc.gov/ntiahome/domainname/not-emailed/imageonline.htm`⟩, 515

[340] See Reagle (as in n. 48 on page 192) for an extended analysis of the maxim.

(ILPF)[341] and the Internet Societal Task Force (ISTF).[342]

Originally known as the Internet Law Task Force, the ILPF was established in 1993. It was a private sector organisation divided into six working groups on substantive issue areas, ranging from content regulation to privacy and spam. New working groups could be formed by consensus of the membership, and were responsible for carrying out the ILPF's work programme, including the production of reports and the development of Consensus Principles. The ILPF also held workshops on specific topics along with an annual conference. The ILPF appears to have become inactive since 2003, having been largely superseded by the CCBI and subsequently BASIS at WSIS.

The ISTF was a project of ISOC formed in 1997 as a complement to the IETF and IRTF. The ISTF was based around a series of working groups and open mailing lists that endeavoured to produce white papers, analogous to the IETF's RFCs, on public policy issues such as accessibility, privacy and content regulation. Prophetically, Vint Cerf acknowledged in 1999 that this was "taking up a challenge which governments ought to take up."[343] By the time the ISTF was eventually disbanded in 2002, this is exactly what governments had begun to do, leaving the ISTF's efforts sidelined.

The weakness of the ISTF, as with the ILPF before it, was that despite the acknowledgement from Vint Cerf that they were seeking to usurp a traditionally public function, and given that Internet governance cannot legitimately be regarded as the domain of the private sector and technical communities alone,[344] there was still no clear understanding of the process by which the participation of states could be attracted without formal intergovernmental sponsorship.

In this respect, ICANN provides a better possible model. ICANN has long been recognised by commentators as a "private corporation that is sculpting itself to perform public-interest functions."[345] More recently, it has also begun to acknowledge this itself. The last of eleven core values listed in its bylaws, added to that document in the wake of WSIS, states, "While remaining rooted in the private sector, recognizing that governments and public authorities are responsible for public policy and duly taking into account governments' or public authorities' recommendations."[346]

Having said that, ICANN itself (apart from its other problems) has too narrow a mandate to have ever been seriously proposed as a body for generalised Internet public policy governance, as People for Internet

---

[341] See `http://www.ilpf.org/`.

[342] See `http://istf-docs.norrnod.se/`.

[343] Alan McCluskey, The Future of the Internet ⟨URL: `http://www.connected.org/is/vint.html`⟩

[344] At least, it cannot in the post-WSIS era; the proposition was more arguable in 1997.

[345] Franda (as in n. 43 on page 42), 76

[346] ICANN, Bylaws (as in n. 39 on page 41), Article 1, section 2

Responsibility (PFIR) noted in their prescient proposal of 2000 for the formation of a multi-stakeholder Representative Global Internet Policy Organization. Although this proposal was not taken up, its themes would recur strongly in the WGIG report some five years later. PFIR argued at the time:

> Attempts to keep the Internet policymaking process free of government input have often resulted in governments swooping in later, frequently with what might be characterized as "knee-jerk" reactions, often to the detriment of the Internet and its global community. It would be far better to define the participatory role of governments in the first place, and have them as part of the team, rather than as an after-the-fact "spoiler" kept on the sidelines for most of the deliberations process. They deserve to be involved, and they should be involved.[347]

But there is a thin line to tread here. On the one hand, it is necessary to secure the participation of states in any consensual governance network, which will require that they are comfortable with its structure and processes. But on the other, there is no warrant for such a network to submit to the authority of states either as an entre'e into the international system (which may compromise the network's consensual form), or to confer legitimacy upon its output (which state hegemony would only weaken rather than enhance). It is unclear that ICANN, or any other institution of Internet governance, has yet struck the most appropriate balance.

5.5 The need for further reform

The purpose of this chapter has been to return focus to the implementation of Internet governance in practice, following the abstraction of the preceding two chapters. The chapter began by surveying the recent processes of reform to the existing regime of Internet governance outlined in Chapter 2. It was seen that the reforms that began in earnest at WSIS, partially implementing the recommendations of the WGIG report, led both to the establishment of the IGF for a term of at least five years, and to the promise of a longer term model of enhanced multi-stakeholder cooperation in policy development.

But it was also clear that the Tunis Agenda's mandate for each of these initiatives has yet to be fulfilled. In fact, agreement has been lacking even as to whether and how it should be fulfilled, with the role of the IGF, its structure, and its processes remaining the subject of contention throughout the entire process. Interestingly, the division between stakeholder groups

[347]Lauren Weinstein, PFIR Statement on Internet Policies, Regulations, and Control ⟨URL: http://www.pfir.org/statements/policies⟩

was less significant in this regard than that between the cross-cutting camps of Forum "hawks" and "doves." Susan Crawford of ICANN was not understating the point when she described the IGF as "highly political."[348]

The purpose of the next chapter is to make a more detailed assessment of the success of the IGF and to propose whatever reforms are required to enable it to fulfil not only its express mandate in the Tunis Agenda, but also—if the political will were to exist for it to do so—a broader mandate more consistent with the recommendations of the WGIG report, that acknowledges the legitimate role of non-state actors in the development of public policy as transnational law.

This assessment of how closely the IGF approximates a legitimate and effective multi-stakeholder Internet governance network will be conducted by two parallel methods: firstly by reference to best practices of other organisations that have been observed throughout this book, and secondly by applying the theoretical principles that were developed principally in chapters 3 and 4.

Foreshadowing this approach, the preceding section of this chapter outlined a number of other proposals for reform, mostly from outside the WSIS process, to determine what they could add to the background of theory developed over the preceding chapters that will be used in assessing the IGF.

Consolidating the findings of Chapter 4, it was found that proposals that would require states to accommodate the decentralised governance of an anarchistic network of Internet stakeholders carry no assurance of multi-stakeholder participation or democratic accountability unless conducted within a more formal structure. On the hierarchical account, this is where the need for oversight and coordination comes in, which is the essence of the "process towards enhanced cooperation"; however, the need to ensure freedom of exit from the network limits the legitimate use of governmental or intergovernmental power in any such structure.[349]

Also in accord with previous findings, little promise was found in democratic models of governance that sought to implement a system of representative elections, unless they also incorporated a deliberative process, which would make them a special case of the consensual model. But even such consensual networks presented a difficult question: whether they should be anchored to the international system through a treaty of some kind, or exist as autonomous transnational legal institutions.

In the former option lay the danger that the network would become beholden to government, but the latter carried the perhaps even more acute risk that states would refuse to participate in the network, significantly curtailing its legitimacy and effectiveness. On balance, it would be perverse

[348] Andrew Noyes, Biggest Threat to Internet Could Be a Massive Virtual Blackout ⟨URL: http://www.govexec.com/dailyfed/0407/040507tdpm2.htm⟩

[349] Though it may well not limit its application in practice: see section 4.3 on page 289.

to refuse to countenance a thin link between any consensual network of Internet governance and the existing international system, at least until the network builds up sufficient social capital across all stakeholder groups to break free and become fully autonomous.

Such a network does not exist in any of the alternative models of Internet governance reform that were examined in this chapter, but it does describe the IGF of the Tunis Agenda quite well. It describes the IGF as it actually exists somewhat less well; however the required theoretical and factual background is now in place to enable us to identify the deficiencies of the IGF as it stands, and to make the necessary recommendations for its reform.

Chapter 6

The IGF's report card

> In managing, promoting and protecting [the Internet's] presence in our lives, we need to be no less creative than those who invented it. Clearly, there is a need for governance, but that does not necessarily mean that it has to be done in the traditional way, for something that is so very different.
>
> Kofi Annan

The purpose of this final chapter is to recommend how the Internet Governance Forum may be reformed to improve its legitimacy and effectiveness as a governance network. Before commencing to do so, it will be useful to review how the chapters preceding this have helped to set the ground for that exercise.

The book began by developing a taxonomy of five available mechanisms of governance, and describing the object of their application, the Internet, in terms of seven persistent features of its technical and social architecture: decentralisation, interactivity, openness, egalitarianism, anonymity, cosmopolitanism and resilience. It was posited that the mechanism of governance by network, which brings together each of the other mechanisms and the stakeholders by whom they are used, may be the most legitimate and effective mechanism for the governance of that domain.

Chapter 2 illustrated that most existing institutions of Internet governance in the spheres of technical coordination and standards development were based upon the non-hierarchical forces of norms, markets, and architecture, whereas the bodies seeking to exercise public policy governance tended to be governmental or intergovernmental and thus to rely upon the hierarchical power of rules; a mechanism much more at odds with many of the architectural features of the Internet that had earlier been identified.

As Chapter 3 described, this clash of cultures was indicative of a deeper deficiency of the international system, that was beginning to be recognised and addressed systemically through the increasing incorporation of civil society and private sector participation in the development of hard and soft international law, but also extra-systemically through the development of parallel transnational legal orders for public policy governance, such as international commercial arbitration and the ICANN regime.

However whilst this "new medieval" system addressed the exclusion of transnational non-state interests from the dominant international order by admitting of a more pluralistic conception of law, it offered in itself no greater assurance of the legitimacy and effectiveness of governance by such non-state actors and networks.

The challenge of Chapter 4 was therefore to examine possible structures and processes for a governance network that would be as legitimate and effective as possible across the contexts of both the international system and cyberspace. In particular, it should be more legitimate than alternative models of reform based around international law or private sector leadership, and more effective than the prevailing models of domestic law and decentralised collective action.

On both counts, the key was to be found in the facilitation of multi-stakeholder participation. This would enable the governance network to draw from the legitimacy of all stakeholder groups, and also improve its effectiveness over the two alternatives of an hierarchical international legal regime shoehorned into the decentralised and egalitarian architecture of cyberspace, or a private transnational legal regime seeking an autonomous role within an international system still shackled to its Westphalian past.

Although this still left many details unspecified, Chapter 4 drew elements from anarchistic, hierarchical, democratic and consensual organisational models in attempting to strike an appropriate balance between the pursuit of the democratic principle of consent (already well illustrated within "native" Internet governance institutions such as the IETF) and the stability and accountability of the liberal democratic model (better exemplified by institutions of the existing international system).

It was suggested that an appropriate balance could be found in an open and transparent multi-stakeholder forum whose members would deliberate upon public policy issues with the objective of reaching consensus, subject to the oversight of an executive council to which each group would appoint representatives using consensual and/or democratic means, and which would have the responsibility of ratifying any decisions of the larger group by consensus.

However as Chapter 5 revealed, this is by no means a description of the

Internet Governance Forum as it exists today. In tracing the progress of recent reforms to the Internet governance regime, that chapter accentuated the very real influence of political forces on the role, structure and working processes of the IGF, to the extent that it is yet unclear whether it will even be in a position to fulfil its mandate in the Tunis Agenda. Does this mean that the theoretical model of a legitimate and effective multi-stakeholder Internet governance network, that was settled upon in Chapter 4, may after all prove too idealistic to consummate in practice?

This chapter aims to address that question, drawing together the insights gained in the preceding chapters to examine the extent to which the Internet Governance Forum presently falls short of its ideal, and to propose how the gap between theory and practice might be bridged. This undertaking is to begin at the macroscopic and end at the microscopic level. That is, maintaining the method of Chapter 5, we will begin by looking at the roles in which the IGF legitimately acts, before moving on to discuss the effectiveness of its structure and its processes in the conduct of those roles.

6.1 Other organisations as models

It will be helpful to make reference back to the models and experiences of some of the other organisations discussed throughout this book, which will provide anecdotal evidence of prevailing best practices in Internet governance to corroborate the conclusions drawn from theory. The difficulty with this is that over two hundred organisations have been referenced in this book, making it impractical to refer to all or even a significant fraction of them in this concluding chapter.

To narrow the scope of the endeavour, but in a principled rather than an entirely arbitrary way, the following method will be used to highlight a small number of organisations most likely to provide useful lessons for the IGF:

- An initial shortlist of forty organisations will be nominated based upon the author's subjective perception of their likely relevance. This produces the following list: APNIC, the ASF, auDA, the CA/Browser Forum, CGI.br, CONGO, the CS-IGC, the CSB, the Debian project, ECOSOC, the EFF, the EU, the FSC, GAID, the GKP, the gTLD-MoU, the IAB, ICANN, the ICC, ICPEN, the IETF, the ILO, the IPC, the ISO, ISOC, the ISTF, the ITU, the LAP, the OECD, TRUSTe, the UN, UNCITRAL, UNICTTF, the Ubuntu project, the VGT, the W3C, WGIG, WIPO, the WTO and the Wikimedia Foundation.
- In order to narrow this shortlist of forty down further, we will specify some more objective criteria drawn from earlier chapters, relating to the macroscopic issues of the organisation's role and structure. Such a list of criteria relating to the role of the organisation is as follows:

- Regime (whether the organisation fits within the Internet governance regime, or some quite separate regime, such as the FSC which exists within the regime of forest management);
- Sphere (whether the organisation predominantly practises in the sphere of standards development, technical coordination or public policy governance);
- Region (whether the organisation's primary focus is international, regional or local in scope);
- Operations (whether the organisation administers a substantive work programme of its own, outside of its governance functions; for example, capacity building or software development);
- Policy-setting (whether the organisation's role includes the development of public policy norms or technical standards, other than position statements simply intended for input into other governance fora);
- Audit (whether the body's functions include the oversight of another organisation or institution);
- Arbitration (whether the body performs any arbitral functions for its members or stakeholders);
- Coordination (whether the body is engaged in coordinating other institutional processes within its regime, which may include regional processes); and
- Regulation (whether the body is engaged in the development of rules of general application, other than internal administrative rules).[1]

The second set of criteria against which the shortlist of organisations will be assessed are those relating to their structure, namely:[2]

- Mechanism (whether the organisation governs principally through one of the mechanisms of rules, norms, markets, architecture or networks—granted that in some cases the nomination of a principal mechanism is somewhat subjective);
- Oversight (whether the organisation is responsible to some other body);
- Publicity (the extent to which the organisation is intergovernmental, governmental or otherwise linked to the international system);

---

[1] These last five criteria are drawn from the WGIG report: WGIG, Report of the Working Group on Internet Governance (as in n. 2 on page 29), 12.

[2] Compare Martens' much simpler categorisation of multi-stakeholder bodies into low, medium or high levels of institutionalisation: Martens (as in n. 103 on page 27), 23.

- Composition (whether the organisation is explicitly multi-stakeholder, open to all stakeholders but without classifying them into groups, or limited to particular stakeholder groups);
- Membership (whether membership is open—and if so whether it is also free—or whether it is closed or otherwise subject to significant restrictions other than cost);
- Representation (whether members participate in the organisation in a direct individual capacity or as representatives of their employers or affiliated organisations);
- Executive (how the organisation's council or other executive body is selected); and
- Secretariat (how the secretariat of the organisation, if any, is selected; for these purposes "hierarchical" appointment implies that the secretariat is appointed by the executive body).

The result of the application of these criteria to the forty shortlisted organisations is found in Appendix A. Before these results can be used to narrow down the shortlist into a final list of organisations most likely to hold lessons for the IGF, the same criteria noted above need to be applied one more: this time, to the IGF itself.

The IGF obviously falls within the Internet governance regime, in the sphere of public policy governance, and acts internationally. Its main operational role is that of capacity building,[3] and its main governance roles are those of policy-setting and coordination,[4] rather than audit,[5] arbitration or regulation. It acts as a governance network, under the oversight of the General Assembly of the United Nations, which also provides its link with the international system. It is multi-stakeholder in composition, with membership being open and free of charge, and held in an individual capacity. Its executive, if the Advisory Group can be described as such, and its Secretariat, are both appointed in a hierarchical fashion by the UN Secretary-General.

It is now possible to begin the final step in the process of narrowing down the shortlist of forty other organisations, by identifying a minimal set of key criteria that such organisations should share with the IGF to establish that they are close enough in role and structure to be meaningfully and usefully compared with it.

Although this is again a somewhat subjective task, enough ground has been covered already to make short work of it. In order to qualify as closely comparable to the IGF, an organisation should exercise the same

[3] WSIS, Tunis Agenda for the Information Society (as in n. 5 on page 2) paras 72(d), (e), (f), (h), and at some remove see para 72(k) which mandates the IGF to "[h]elp to find solutions to issues arising from the use and misuse of the Internet."

[4] Ibid. paras 72(a), (b), (c), (g) and (j)

[5] But see Ibid. para 72(i).

Table 6.1: Organisations comparable to the IGF

	Policy-setting	Coordination	Mechanism	Composition	Membership
APNIC	Yes	Yes	Rules[a]	Open	Open[b]
auDA	Yes	Yes	Rules[c]	Multi-stakeholder	Open
CGI.br	Yes	Yes	Networks	Multi-stakeholder	Democratic
GAID	No	Yes	Networks	Multi-stakeholder	Open, free
GKP	No	Yes	Networks	Multi-stakeholder	Open
gTLD-MoU	Yes	Yes	Networks	Open	Open, free
ICANN	Yes	Yes	Networks	Multi-stakeholder	Restricted[d]
UNICTTF	No	Yes	Networks	Multi-stakeholder	Open, free

[a] Although its policy processes are consensual, its control over IP addresses is hierarchical.

[b] Although not free, membership is not required to participate in its policy development process.

[c] The same argument expressed in footnote a. applies to auDA's control over domain names.

[d] Participation in the organisation is only possible indirectly through its ACs and SOs, which define static constituencies and provide varying levels of representation within the larger structure.

governance roles (policy-setting and coordination), should be of multi-stakeholder or open composition, should act as a governance network, and its membership should be open. There is no other existing organisation from the shortlist that meets each of these five criteria. However there are eight that meet at least four of the criteria:

Other than sharing similar attributes to the IGF according to the five key criteria, these eight organisations are highly diverse. National, regional and international organisations are all represented. Their executive bodies are constituted through the full range of consensual, consociational, democratic, and oligarchical means. Other than coordination, they do not even perform a common role, although they do fall into two identifiable clusters; those involved in technical coordination (along with policy governance in the case of CGI.br), and those (namely GAID, GKP and UNICTTF) involved in ICT for development.

These "exemplar organisations," as they will be referred to for convenience, therefore provide a usefully various, but also more comfortably delimited, set of case studies to which reference will periodically be made in the course of analysing the strengths and weaknesses of the IGF in its current form.

6.2 Role

The Tunis Agenda recognises "that there are many cross-cutting international public policy issues that require attention and are not adequately addressed by the current mechanisms."[6] The deficiencies of each of these current mechanisms were first noted in the introduction to this book.[7]

As far as governance by rules is concerned, international and domestic law each have their own shortcomings. Amongst those of international law are that it offers only weak mechanisms of enforcement (save in certain issue areas such as those within the WTO's remit), and that its development is prone to be democratically deficient.[8] Domestic law's main failing is that its extraterritorial effects, or lack thereof, tend either to defeat its purpose or to create spillover effects that transgress the democratic principle.[9]

Governance by norms, markets and architecture, whilst effective in some issue areas and less constricted by irrelevant national boundaries than governmental rules, in other areas also suffers from their lack of enforceability, and because the policy objectives furthered by these means are generally not developed in an accountable framework and may be in conflict with democratically expressed values. For example, markets tend to be a particularly poor mechanism of governance in issue areas that engage values not measurable in economic terms.[10]

This does not mean that there is no place for the use of each of these mechanisms of governance. Quite the contrary; the use of all of them in concert is likely to be necessary to achieve policy objectives in many issue areas.[11] But in order for their legitimacy and effectiveness to be maximised, they should be employed in a coordinated rather than an *ad hoc* manner, whereby not only the policy objectives to be achieved, but also the means by which they are to be achieved, are the subject of democratic deliberation amongst all affected stakeholders.

This is the essential advantage of the use of the mechanism of governance by network. Such a governance network does not so much incorporate all the other mechanisms of governance, as transform them, synergistically increasing both their legitimacy and effectiveness. They are endowed with greater legitimacy by being subjected to multi-stakeholder democratic oversight, and with greater effectiveness because they can be deployed through the network, either alone or in combination, in an adaptive manner.

Governance by network can thus be understood as a meta-mechanism, in that it provides the means by which for the use of other mechanisms of governance themselves to be governed. To put this in practical terms applicable to the case of the IGF:

---

[6]WSIS, Tunis Agenda for the Information Society (as in n. 5 on page 2), para 60

[7]See section 1.4 on page 18.

[8]See section 3.4 on page 147.

[9]See section 3.4 on page 160.

[10]See section 3.4 on page 151.

[11]See section 2.4 on page 91.

- If all stakeholder groups within the network reach consensus at the level of principle on a hierarchical approach to a particular issue of governance, governments can give effect to those collaboratively developed principles by coordinating their use of domestic and/or international legal rules (perhaps within other intergovernmental fora);

- Alternatively (or additionally), if it is considered appropriate to address an issue through the use of norms, the network can develop a soft law statement of those norms which civil society stakeholders can take the lead in disseminating through their own domestic and transnational networks;

- If an issue can be effectively addressed through the use of markets, the IGF's private sector members can create or enter such markets, whilst with all other stakeholders they monitor for any market failures that may need to be corrected by other mechanisms;[12] and

- If the use of architecture is considered an effective approach in a particular issue area, it will fall to all stakeholder groups to develop a statement of public policy principles to be transmitted to the relevant body (such as the IETF) responsible for the development of standards and protocols in reference to that framework of principle.

The roles that are inherent in the IGF's function as such a governance network are twofold, and have been described above as the organisational roles of policy-setting and coordination. The former role is that which allows its stakeholders to collaboratively decide upon the objectives to be achieved, and the latter includes the process of establishing how and by whom they are to be achieved.

As already noted, these two roles of policy-setting and coordination are found in the express mandate of the IGF in the Tunis Agenda. However as also noted, that document also arguably places some limitations upon the IGF's policy-setting role in established rather than "emerging" issue areas,[13] to which there has been only further accretion through the subsequent narrow interpretation of the IGF's mandate by the Advisory Group and Secretariat, which they have institutionalised in its structure.

The following two subsections will discuss what is involved in the roles of policy-setting and coordination in more detail, and will consider the extent to which the IGF's ability to carry out those roles, and thereby to fulfil its function as a multi-stakeholder governance network, is prejudiced by the limitations that have been placed upon it either constitutionally in the Tunis Agenda or institutionally by the Advisory Group and Secretariat.

[12]In principle, this is much like a domestic co-regulatory framework, only with a network rather than a government in the regulator's position.

[13]See section 5.2 on page 353.

But before moving on, it should also be noted that policy-setting and coordination are not the only two roles of the IGF noted in its mandate. The Tunis Agenda also assigns the IGF an operational role in contributing to capacity building,[14] and as the previous chapter illustrated, this has been very strongly emphasised by the Advisory Group and other Forum doves, at the expense of the IGF's policy-setting role. A third subsection will therefore address this role and consider whether it too constitutes a core function of a governance network that has somehow been overlooked until now.

Policy-setting

One of the fundamental issues about the role of the IGF that has divided the Forum hawks and doves is as to whether it has a decision-making role. Perhaps the strongest denunciation of this prospect has come from Nitin Desai himself, who said shortly before the inaugural meeting, "It's not a decision-making body. It cannot be a decision-making body. It does not have a membership, so who is going to author a decision? So there's no way it can ever become a decision-making body."[15]

To some extent, the division can be blamed on an unfortunate choice of terminology. Decision-making, after all, is a process, not an event. This process is sometimes divided into the separate acts of decision-shaping (or decision-recommending) and decision-taking, in recognition of the fact that these may involve quite different parties.[16]

If decision-making simply meant decision-taking, then Desai would be quite correct, as this phase of the process will often take place outside the IGF, depending on the mechanism of governance employed. In particular, governance by rules will continue to be centred in national parliaments and intergovernmental organisations, no matter how much weight they may give to the IGF's recommendations. To the extent that talk of a decision-making role for the IGF seems to imply otherwise, and particularly if it is also assumed that the decisions being spoken of are to be binding, the doves' objections are understandable.

However on closer analysis, the division between Forum hawks and doves on the role of the IGF is more than simply one over terminology. Many doves have been quite explicit that besides not taking decisions, the IGF should not even not make recommendations, and indeed should not be a forum for policy development at all, in spite of the express words of

[14]WSIS, Tunis Agenda for the Information Society (as in n. 5 on page 2), para 72(h)

[15]The speech in question is referred to at Waters (as in n. 533 on page 289), but Desai's actual words are misreported there. The words transcribed above, which are stronger than those reported in the article, are taken from the audio recording available at `http://kierenmccarthy.co.uk/mp3s/nominet-igf-9oct06/nitin-desai-combined.mp3`.

[16]G Smith, Taking Deliberation Seriously: Institutional Design and Green Politics, Environmental Politics 10:3 2001, 85

its mandate.[17] This goes far beyond a simple objection to the notion of the IGF making binding decisions (which, by definition, involves governance by rules), but would appear also to proscribe its participation in the development of norms and architecture and in the operation of markets. Indeed, in these cases, there is no real decision-taking phase of the decision-making process.

Even in the case of governance by rules, the division between decision-shaping and decision-taking (or between policy development and policy-setting) is quite an artificial one. Rather than separate acts, they are more of a continuum, along which power is apportioned between those endowed with formal authority and those from whom their authority is derived. At one end of the continuum (with APNIC providing a good example), the authority of the decision-taker is little more than formal, with its constituents retaining the substantive power to set policy. At the other end, those in authority reserve full discretion to disregard or override any recommendations made by the organisation's stakeholders.[18] Participatory democracy is usually taken to represent an intermediate position, in which the decision-taker is required or expected to demonstrate that the recommendations of stakeholders have been taken into account and given due weight in the final decision.[19]

Recommendations

What, then, is the appropriate point along that continuum for the IGF? The notion that it should be at the most restrictive extreme—that the IGF ought not make decisions or recommendations at all—is difficult to sustain, because the effect of this would be to deny its role in providing input to other institutions in the Internet governance regime, in outright contradiction of its express mandate in the Tunis Agenda.[20]

Moreover despite the ardour of the Forum doves on this point, the idea that the IGF ought not to make recommendations is quite a novel one. It was certainly not the view of WGIG, which saw the forum they proposed as one in which "all stakeholders will be represented and feel free to discuss and make recommendations."[21] Even WGIG, however, was unsure as

---

[17]Government of Canada, Questionnaire on the Convening the Internet Governance Forum (as in n. 141 on page 356), 1

[18]There is no good example of this from amongst the exemplar organisations, but the WTO is an example from the earlier shortlist of forty.

[19]See section 4.3 on page 243.

[20]WSIS, Tunis Agenda for the Information Society (as in n. 5 on page 2), para 72(c) (which calls upon the IGF to "[i]nterface with appropriate inter-governmental organizations and other institutions on matters under their purview"), and para 72(g) (which requires it to "[i]dentify emerging issues, bring them to the attention of the relevant bodies and the general public, and, where appropriate, make recommendations").

[21]Charles Sha'ban, *Reforming Internet Governance: Perspectives from the Working Group on Internet Governance (WGIG)* New York: UNICTTF, 2005, chap. Proposal for the Establishment of

to the exact point along the continuum of decision-recommendation and decision-taking that the IGF would occupy, saying:

> Whether such multistakeholderism can be extended beyond consultations, agenda setting, and technical operations into actual policy decision making, or into extant and exclusionary intergovernmental and private sector bodies, of course remain open questions. [22]

It has been speculated that the motive of the doves in seeking to disempower the IGF can be traced to the investment of these powerful actors in other, less open and transparent institutions and processes, such as the investments of stakeholders such as ISOC, the US government and its allies in the ICANN regime, and those of the private sector in the WIPO intellectual property regime.[23] But the politics behind the doves' position are of less relevance for present purposes than their arguments.[24]

As the previous chapter's detailed account of preparations for and follow-up from the first two IGF meetings illustrated, the arguments of the Forum doves for limiting the role of the IGF in making recommendations follow two recurrent themes:

- That delegates will not participate freely and frankly at the IGF if they are under pressure to make decisions.[25]
- That because the IGF has no fixed membership, it is not a body capable of making decisions.[26]

As to the first of these objections, it is true that strategic behaviour and backroom deals are a hallmark of the participation of governmental delegates in intergovernmental negotiation processes. WSIS is as good an example of this phenomenon as any, and there is no reason to think that it would not be replicated within the IGF if its decision-making apparatus were to be modelled on that of a traditional intergovernmental forum.

However, there are two answers to this objection: first, there is no reason that the IGF should make decisions in the manner of a traditional

an Internet Governance Forum, 235

[22]Drake, Reforming Internet Governance: Perspectives from the Working Group on Internet Governance (WGIG) (as in n. 14 on page 325), 251

[23]Milton Mueller, "A Funny Thing Happened on the Way to the Forum...": Multistakeholderism, International Institutions and Global Governance of the Internet ⟨URL: http://web.si.umich.edu/tprc/papers/2006/615/Multistakeholdersim.pdf⟩, 10

[24]Though see section 6.3 on page 464 for further analysis of their underlying motives.

[25]ICC, ICC/BASIS Feedback on First Internet Governance Forum (IGF) in Athens, Greece (as in n. 236 on page 381)

[26]Waters (as in n. 533 on page 289)

intergovernmental organisation; indeed, this is one suggestion that *nobody* has made. As Chapter 4 illustrated, there are techniques from the literature on deliberative democracy, and others from that on consensual decision-making, that are designed to avoid strategic decision-making in favour of the collaborative development of a rational consensus through a process of deliberation amongst equals. This is a matter that will fall for fuller discussion under the treatment of the IGF's processes, rather than that of its role.[27]

Second, it is difficult to see how the tendency of governmental (or indeed other) delegates to engage in dysfunctional behaviour, could possibly detract from the mandate of the IGF as expressed in the Tunis Agenda. It is doubtless that IGF meetings will proceed more smoothly without the requirement to adhere to that mandate, but if the smooth running of meetings were an overriding criterion, the mandate ought never to have been drafted to include a policy-setting role for the IGF in the first place. As William Drake pointedly observed during the afternoon of the first consultations on the convening of the IGF in February 2006, "Presumably, when governments carefully negotiated this text, they meant what they said."

In answer to the second objection of the Forum doves, that it is impossible for a body without a fixed membership to make decisions, this was also addressed in Chapter 4, when it was shown to flow from the misconception that democratic decision-making requires adherence to the principle of "one vote, one value."[28] In fact, it was shown that the democratic principle can also be legitimately and effectively institutionalised in alternative forms that do not require numerically proportional representation, so long as they engage all affected viewpoints and perspectives in a process of rational deliberation.[29] The difficulties of reconciling this theory with the hegemonic practices of governments have also already been acknowledged,[30] and will be revisited when considering questions of the IGF's structure below.[31]

---

[27]See section 6.4 on page 474.

[28]The objection also contradicts the experience of WSIS. Ralf Bendrath, from the University of Bremen and the Privacy Dynamic Coalition, pointed out at the February 2007 consultation:

> I wouldn't say just because we don't have a defined membership it's not possible to agree on anything. If I look back on the—to the WSIS process, where I participated in civil society, there was no clear membership on who was a member of civil society, who can decide and vote and whatever on our joint documents. But we still managed to come up with a lot of joint documents, a lot of joint statements, and even with two large, about 20 pages each, civil society declarations for the two summits. That was possible. And we just used maybe more innovative, more open, more tolerant mechanisms instead of the diplomatic negotiation mechanism. There are mechanisms like the IETF is using, rough consensus, things like that.

[29]See section 4.3 on page 257.

[30]See section 4.3 on page 289.

[31]See section 6.3 on page 442.

Although the two arguments most often expressed as to why the IGF ought not to make non-binding decisions or recommendations have thus been addressed, there is also a third argument that has not been so prominent. This is the fact that the Tunis Agenda makes mention of the IGF making recommendations only in respect of "emerging issues." Whilst the meaning of this phrase is not defined (in fact, no clear understanding of it had even emerged by the time of the Emerging Issues session in Athens), it can be taken to be narrower than the full gamut of public policy issues that the IGF is called upon to discuss.[32]

This apparent limitation of the IGF's decision-making role prompt two responses. The first is that the capacity to make recommendations in respect of other issues is inherent in other paragraphs of the IGF's mandate. In particular, the IGF is charged to "[d]iscuss public policy issues related to key elements of Internet governance," but not simply in the abstract; it is to do so "in order to foster the sustainability, robustness, security, stability and development of the Internet."[33]

This clearly envisages that the discussions that take place at the IGF will have a flow-on effect into existing Internet governance arrangements. Indeed, the mandate explicitly states as much, requiring the IGF to "[i]nterface with appropriate inter-governmental organizations and other institutions on matters under their purview."[34] Even Marcus Kummer has acknowledged that the IGF is to "prepare the decisions that will be taken into consideration by other organizations that do have the decision-making power."[35] However the IGF's discussions could not foster the objectives laid out in its mandate if they were to be left irresolute, and neither would there be any purpose in interfacing with other organisations if they were not to be provided with any tangible input.[36]

---

[32]WSIS, Tunis Agenda for the Information Society (as in n. 5 on page 2), para 72(g)

[33]Ibid., para 72(a), and see also paras 72(b) and 72(j) respectively regarding the discussion of issues not falling within the scope of any existing body, and of issues relating to critical Internet resources.

[34]Ibid., para 72(c)

[35]United Nations Office of the Secretary-General, Internet Governance Forum This Month Will Be Wide-Ranging, Says UN Official ⟨URL: http://www.un.org/apps/news/story.asp?NewsID=24520⟩

[36]Apparently against this view are two mechanisms by which a potential compromise has been suggested between those insisting that the IGF fulfil its mandate, and those uneasy with the pressure to develop concluded recommendations. The first of these was put forward by Wolfgang Kleinwächter, one of the Special Advisers to the Secretariat, during the February 2007 consultations (and was supported by Switzerland in May):

> The forum was established to send messages to the organizations involved in the process in Athens. So it means organizations like the ITU, like UNESCO, like ICANN, like IETF, and others, and to say, "This is what we discussed, and, here, this is an input for you. Please take this into consideration." And probably we can create a new, you know, form of this which we could call message, messages from the IGF. It is not a recommendation, it is not a resolution, it is not any declaration or something like that. This is just a message. And we can also send mixed messages, so that—say, "okay, one message is this, but we have to the

The second response is that the Tunis Agenda's omission to empower the IGF to make recommendations other than on emerging issues does not prevent it from doing so, as it is not from the Tunis Agenda that that power stems to begin with. For one thing, although the IGF is a multi-stakeholder network, the Tunis Agenda cannot fairly be described as a multi-stakeholder agreement. As Chapter 5 revealed, for all the claims of the WSIS process to incorporate "the full involvement of governments, the private sector, civil society, and international organizations,"[37] non-governmental stakeholders were permitted only very limited involvement in the process of drafting the output documents. As such, the Tunis Agenda can only be regarded as an intergovernmental agreement, which carries no legitimate authority over transnational non-state actors and networks.[38]

As for states, the WSIS outcome documents do draw from the supranational authority of UN bodies and agencies such as the General Assembly that have been charged with exercising oversight over their follow-up and implementation. However, the Tunis Agenda does not purport to limit states' power to make recommendations or other soft law in issue areas besides those specified in paragraph 72, either within the structure of the IGF, or indeed in any other venue of their choosing. In fact, the Declaration of Principles states explicitly that "[n]othing in this Declaration shall be construed as impairing, contradicting, restricting or derogating from … any other international instrument or national laws adopted in furtherance of these instruments."[39]

If the Tunis Agenda is not competent to limit the participation of non-state actors within the IGF, and is not intended to limit the autonomy of

---

> same issue also another message, but it's now up to you, to the decision-making body to consider these mixed messages and then to start the negotiation process" where you have an appropriate organization which has a mandate to negotiate a special issue.

However provided that the process of discussion that takes place within the IGF is structured in such a way as to facilitate the pursuit of consensus, Kleinwächter's approach does not necessarily conflict with this book, nor with the processes followed in other organisations that seek to make decisions by consensus. For example, a like approach has been seen in the IETF, when its members failed to reach consensus on which of the conflicting SPF and Sender ID specifications should become a standard (see section 2.2 on page 52). In that case, the IETF allowed the two specifications to be published as informational RFCs, thereby sending a "mixed message" to the technical community and allowing market forces to decide the winner.

The second compromise by which the IGF could produce outcomes short of actual recommendations was suggested by Alun Michael of the UK Parliament, during the Rio meeting's session on "Taking Stock and The Way Forward." His suggestion, later reiterated by Nitin Desai when summarising that session, was that the Secretariat should establish a space on its Web site for stakeholders to voluntarily make commitments arising out of the meeting. This again is not inconsistent with the role of the IGF as theorised here, only it is more limited in that the joint commitments made would not need to have been the outcome of a process of reasoned deliberation undertaken with the aim of reaching a consensus amongst all impacted stakeholders.

[37] WSIS, Geneva Declaration of Principles (as in n. 104 on page 27), para 48

[38] See section 3.4 on page 147.

[39] Ibid., para 18

states in pursuing parallel initiatives, then it can present no obstacle to all stakeholders collaborating within the IGF on the consensual development of public policy recommendations in any issue area they see fit. Naturally in practice, this will depend upon the willingness of states to engage in this process on an equal footing with other stakeholders, and on this point, more will be said at section 6.3 on page 442.

Transnational law

Making recommendations to other bodies is one aspect of policy-setting, but the IGF is also directed to "discuss issues that do not fall within the scope of any existing body."[40] What is to be the outcome of these discussions, where no appropriate organisation exists to receive any recommendations that may flow from them? Or, indeed, where there is an existing organisation to receive the IGF's output, does the making of recommendations to that body mark the end of the matter, even if those recommendations are ignored?

To answer these questions, it is necessary to more precisely place the IGF's position along the continuum from decision-shaping to decision-taking. In summary, it will be argued that:

- in respect of issues not falling within the scope of any existing body with a legitimate claim to exercise governance over them, the IGF should exercise essentially a decision-taking (or to be more accurate a policy-setting) role; and
- in other issue areas, the normative force of the IGF's recommendations will vary, as they must be balanced with the parallel policy-setting activities of one or more other bodies, which may also have a measure of legitimacy of their own.

It is the first case that is to be discussed here, with the second to be dealt with under the following heading.[41]

To state that the IGF should set policy on its own account in issue areas not being dealt with by other bodies is hardly a radical proposition. It implies nothing more than that as a governance network whose structure and processes are demonstrably legitimate for the performance of its assigned role (assuming this to be the case, for now), its policy recommendations carry normative force in their own right, and do not require the imprimatur of any other body. It does not mean that the IGF's recommendations will become formally authoritative (at least not in the short to medium

[40] WSIS, Tunis Agenda for the Information Society (as in n. 5 on page 2), para 72(b)

[41] See section 6.2 on page 431.

term); rather as Held argues, "it needs to be stressed that any global legislative institution should be conceived above all as a 'standard-setting' institution."[42]

Like other standards-setting institutions, those of the IGF that prove successful will tend to be adopted and promulgated at domestic and local levels using the mechanisms of rules, markets or architecture; indeed this may be necessary in some issue areas for their effective realisation. However the normative status of its recommendations is derived not from whether or how they have been adopted by stakeholders, but from the multi-stakeholder structure and democratic processes by which they were developed.

Although the success of the IGF's recommendations is not the source of their legitimacy, it does serve as a kind of "running code" test of their effectiveness[43] that could, in time, serve to further anchor the IGF and its free-floating norms in transnational society, in much the same way as the success of the Incoterms and the international commercial arbitration regime has consolidated the transnational legal force of the new law merchant.[44] The result could be the development of the IGF's recommendations from mere norms into an independent body of transnational law.[45]

To put this into context, consider if the IGF were to develop an Internet Bill of Rights by consensus amongst its stakeholders, without the intention that it be delivered to an intergovernmental body for formal signature and ratification. Such a document could still have effect as an instrument of governance by norms, to the extent that it informed the decentralised collective action of its stakeholders, who would tend to act in accordance with it or be judged by reference to it. After some time, it might be the Internet Bill of Rights had become sufficiently ubiquitous amongst stakeholders in Internet governance, perhaps even being referred to in legislative instruments in the same way that Internet standards are today,[46] that it could be described in its own right as an instrument that "people identify and treat through their social practices as law."[47] At this point, the Internet Bill of Rights would effectively have passed into transnational law, and the IGF become a transnational lawmaker.

In order to even commence along this path and thereby build up a track record of "running code," the authority of the IGF to develop transnational law must not only be formally legitimate, but must also be seen as such by all participants and stakeholders in the Internet governance regime.[48] As

---

[42]Held, *Models of Democracy* (as in n. 270 on page 240), 356

[43]See section 5.4 on page 410.

[44]See also section 4.2 on page 221.

[45]See section 3.5 on page 175.

[46]See section 3.3 on page 140.

[47]Tamanaha (as in n. 245 on page 143), 194

[48]See section 3.4 on page 145.

noted above, this in turn requires that the IGF possess a multi-stakeholder structure and democratic processes (for example, that its output is the product of open, reasoned deliberation, and that it incorporate mechanisms of democratic accountability and transparency). A further prerequisite of the IGF acting as an autonomous transnational lawmaker is that its legitimacy to set policy in a given issue area is not shared with any other body. If it is, then the development of transnational law will engage the IGF not only in its role of policy-setting, but also in the role of coordination with that other body.

Coordination

As described above, the IGF's role of coordination includes the process of establishing how and by whom the objectives that were determined during the policy-setting phase should be pursued.[49] For example, this may involve the IGF forwarding its recommendations to appropriate other bodies to be implemented through some other mechanism of governance such as rules, when they cannot be effectively implemented through the political and moral force of the IGF's self-developed norms.

If the IGF's independent policy-setting role has been controversial, then its coordination role has been accepted much more readily. For example, the opening remarks of the UN Secretary-General that were transmitted to the Athens meeting noted that "while the Forum is not designed to take decisions, it can identify issues that need to be tackled through formal intergovernmental processes."[50]

Apart from intergovernmental organisations, the IGF also has a role to play in coordinating with non-governmental actors; most notably the other specialised Internet governance institutions that preceded the IGF. Although only ICANN and the RIRs are referred to in the Tunis Agenda in this regard (and then only obliquely rather than by name), other notable organisations in this category are those involved in the standards development sphere, which has been largely isolated from any public policy oversight to date.

The role of coordination is also broader than the making of recommendations, particularly in that the Tunis Agenda makes it clear that the process is to be two-way; speaking of it in terms of "discourse between bodies," "engagement," and the need to "interface" and "exchange." Thus in appropriate cases, just as the IGF can forward its output to other organisations, so other organisations can provide material to the IGF as an impetus for or an

[49] Though in cases where policy-setting authority is shared with another body, the two phases overlap: see section 6.2 on page 436.

[50] United Nations Office of the Secretary-General, The Secretary-General's Message to the Internet Governance Forum ⟨URL: http://www.un.org/NewLinks/int_for.htm⟩; and see Vinton Cerf, Does the Internet Need to be Governed? ⟨URL: http://www.circleid.com/posts/does_the_internet_need_to_be_governed⟩.

input into multi-stakeholder deliberation. For example, the OECD could submit its Anti-Spam Toolkit[51] for multi-stakeholder endorsement by the IGF (which in fact it did, in a sense, by submitting it as a contribution to the Athens meeting).[52]

Whether the IGF makes a recommendation to another body on its own initiative, or in response to input submitted by that body, the case where only one such other body is involved will be discussed under the heading of subsidiarity below, because in both cases the purpose of coordination between the two organisations is to ensure that the relevant governance roles (such as that of policy-setting and rule-making) are taken at the most appropriate level.

A slightly more complex case is that in which the implementation of policy requires several stakeholders to engage in coordinated collective action. Since the stakeholders participating in such a programme thereby form a governance network in their own right, this case will be discussed below under the heading of network building.

It is also useful to distinguish a third aspect to the role of coordination, though it is inherent in the other two. It was determined above[53] that there is no reason why the IGF should be precluded from making recommendations in any issue area of Internet governance not already inhabited by an existing body of comparable democratic design and multi-stakeholder composition. However, the analysis of forty other organisations earlier in this chapter suggests that that proviso is likely to apply to few other organisations. This leaves the IGF at the centre of a network of other actors that make up the Internet governance regime, most of which cannot claim the same legitimacy as the IGF in dealing with public policy issues.

Does this mean that these other organisations present no limitation upon the IGF's legitimate policy-setting role? If so, how can this be reconciled with the political reality of those organisations' existence and claims of authority? These vexed questions will be discussed under the heading of meta-governance below.

Subsidiarity

The principle of subsidiarity reflects the facts that governance incorporates a number of distinct roles, including those of policy-setting, audit, arbitration, coordination and regulation that were used to categorise the organisations short-listed earlier in this chapter, and that different organ-

[51]OECD, Anti-Spam Toolkit ⟨URL: http://www.oecd.org/dataoecd/63/28/36494147.pdf⟩

[52]Unfortunately this fell rather flat, as the IGF had not developed the procedures necessary for it to deliberate upon or respond to the input.

[53]See section 6.2 on page 429.

isations may be more effective in performing certain of these roles than others.[54]

As well as being a key principle of transnational democracy,[55] EU law, and indeed the very concept of federalism, the principle of subsidiarity has also long been applied in Internet governance. Although decentralisation is the more general value around which the Internet architecture was designed, where hierarchy is found on the Internet, it tends to be qualified by subsidiarity. For example, in the sphere of technical coordination it is inherent in the structure of the DNS system, whereby each level of a domain name is separately administered. Similarly in standards development it has been observed that the IETF formally abnegated responsibility for the development of standards for the World Wide Web in favour of a more specialised body, the W3C.[56]

The principle applies in a similar manner to the public policy sphere of governance inhabited by the IGF. It is inherent in the Tunis Agenda's constitution of the IGF as "a neutral, non-duplicative and non-binding process"[57] that is to "have no involvement in day-to-day or technical operations of the Internet."[58] It also underlies the definition of the separate roles of stakeholders in the Geneva Principles,[59] and is one of six cross-cutting principles for effective Internet governance in the Asia-Pacific region as recommended by the UNDP-APDIP.[60]

This principle of subsidiarity will be engaged by recommendations of the IGF whenever another organisation can legitimately exercise one or more of the governance roles associated with the implementation of that recommendation more effectively than the IGF alone, either because it operates using another mechanism of governance (such as rules), in another sphere of governance (such as standards development), or at another level of governance (such as the domestic level).

This will likely be so in all cases other than those where norms alone are a sufficient mechanism for the implementation of the recommendation,[61] and where no other organisation is legitimately involved in the development or promulgation of norms in that issue area.

---

[54] Some may also be more legitimate than others; a question to be dealt with at section 6.2 on page 436.

[55] See section 4.3 on page 236.

[56] IETF, The "text/html" Media Type (as in n. 104 on page 56)

[57] WSIS, Tunis Agenda for the Information Society (as in n. 5 on page 2), para 77

[58] Ibid., paras 63 and 77.

[59] Although rather than focusing on which organisations should perform which roles, it simply attempts to allocate the roles between the stakeholder groups, whilst recognising that no individual stakeholder group is competent to assume overall responsibility for Internet governance: Idem, Geneva Declaration of Principles (as in n. 104 on page 27), paras 35 and 20.

[60] APDIP, *Internet Governance: Asia-Pacific Perspectives* New Delhi: Elsevier, 2005, chap. Internet Governance in the Asia-Pacific Region, 64

[61] Or at least, where consensus cannot be reached upon the need for any other mechanism to be employed.

The simplest cases in which the principle of subsidiarity is thus engaged will be those in which the IGF's recommendations require application at a level of governance beyond its competence (such as rules), and where there is only one legitimate body exercising authority at that level of governance in the issue area in question (such as ICANN or WIPO). In such cases, the effect of the IGF's mandate is that it should make recommendations to that other body so that it in turn can take the appropriate further action. This is how WGIG foresaw the IGF's role, with one of its members recording the view that:

> In the event that an issue may currently be addressed to an established entity, this fact shall not preclude the forum from discussing the issue in question and passing recommendations to the competent responsible entity.[62]

In other cases where there is no existing body to take the IGF's recommendations forward, the IGF may still exercise a coordinating role in accordance with the principle of subsidiarity by calling for action to be taken at an intergovernmental level. Thus WGIG expected that the IGF "may also invite—or recommend that the United Nations invites—member states to discuss a certain issue in an official capacity, or via a vote in the United Nations General Assembly."[63]

There are, of course, also more complex cases in which the application of the principle of subsidiarity raises greater practical difficulties than found above. These include the case in which there is more than one relevant existing body to which the IGF's recommendations might be addressed, and that in which the other existing body and the IGF both purport to exercise policy-setting authority in the same issue area. The first of those cases will be dealt with next, and the second under the following heading of meta-governance.

Network building

Where the effective governance of a particular issue requires the collaboration of multiple bodies, coordination between them requires more than the unilateral process of transmitting a recommendation or the bilateral process of dialogue; it requires multilateral interaction between stakeholders such as is only possible within a governance network incorporating deliberative democratic or consensual processes.

Since the IGF is (let us continue to assume for now) such a network, and is open to all stakeholders, the ideal case would be for all such bodies to participate in the processes by which the IGF builds consensus upon the

[62]Sha'ban (as in n. 21 on page 424), 236
[63]Ibid., 236

issues to be addressed and the means by which they are to be addressed. However, without preempting the discussion on the IGF's structure or processes, if this entails participation in plenary meetings, the overhead involved in developing the norms of trust and cooperation that a diverse plenary group requires to function may deter some stakeholders from participating. Thus the very open and consensual nature of the IGF may work against its effectiveness.

A possible solution to this is for the IGF to act in the coordinating role of facilitating the decentralised collective action of its members, through their own, self-organised smaller networks. Its particular mandate to do this is found in the call to "[f]acilitate discourse between bodies dealing with different cross-cutting international public policies regarding the Internet."[64] This is also the model of the GKP, whose motto is "Sharing Knowledge, Building Partnerships," and which has facilitated the formation of a number of smaller global and regional multi-stakeholder networks.[65]

Another example of an Internet governance issue around which which a smaller multi-stakeholder network has come together is that of private sector involvement in governmental Internet filtering and surveillance.[66] The IGF's contribution to debate on this issue occurred during the Openness panel in Athens, when panelists Fred Tipson from Microsoft and Art Reilly from Cisco Systems, and from the floor, Vinton Cerf of Google, were interrogated over their companies' participation in Internet content regulation in China.

Assuming that the IGF had the structural and procedural capacity to deliberate on public policy issues of any kind, the polarisation of the debate in Athens[67] demonstrated that this particular issue would likely be a very difficult one to begin with. Absent a strong culture of trust, equality and cooperation to provide a bedrock for deliberation, the likelihood of a consensus position being developed on it within the plenary forum could only have been described as remote.[68]

Thus the Athens meeting ended without any attempt having been made

---

[64] WSIS, Tunis Agenda for the Information Society (as in n. 5 on page 2), para 72(c)

[65] For example, the Youth Social Enterprise Initiative (YSEI); see http://www.ysei.org/.

[66] See sections 2.3 on page 79 and 4.3 on page 268.

[67] At one extreme, a Chinese government delegate, Yang Xiokun, denied that there even were any restrictions on access to Internet content in China, to the surprise of panelists who had been personally affected by such restrictions. At the other extreme, Amnesty International presented a petition of 50 000 signatures later that week containing a "call on governments to stop the unwarranted restriction of freedom of expression on the Internet—and on companies to stop helping them do it."

[68] See particularly sections 4.4 on page 316, 4.3 on page 245 and 4.2 on page 211, and also section 6.4 on page 474. This is one ground upon which the IGF was justified in focusing on less divisive issues first, in order to leave room to develop such norms and build the social capital upon which it would need to draw in tackling more contentious issues later: David Allen, The Role of Intellectual/Academic Work in a Policy Forum ⟨URL: http://davidallen.org/papers/Policy_Brains_Trust-A4.pdf⟩, 7.

at conciliation of the opposing views on this issue, let alone deliberation upon how they might be balanced in, say, a code of conduct on private sector involvement in national Internet regulation. And yet, less than three months later, it was announced that Microsoft, Google and Yahoo were amongst the members of a new multi-stakeholder network that aimed to produce just such a code.[69] Bringing together an academic initiative,[70] the work of private sector group Business for Social Responsibility and that of civil society's Centre for Democracy and Technology, the network has no affiliation with the IGF.

If more focused networks such as this can be formed in particular issue areas without reference to the IGF, does this make the latter superfluous? Certainly this was the view of the ITU prior to the IGF's formation, with the Director of its TSB, Houlin Zhao, stating in 2005 that "if ICANN, ITU, UNESCO and WIPO see each other as complementary and try to work together, we don't need to have a special agency."[71]

However, whilst there is nothing to prevent any stakeholders from forming their own networks, the IGF will retain a legitimate role in receiving and deliberating upon the output of any such networks that do not fulfil the same criteria of multi-stakeholder composition and democratic process as the IGF itself. This includes the (yet-unnamed) network described above, which apart from having no Chinese members, contains no governmental representatives either (other than a Special Representative to the UN Secretary-General).

The appropriate role for the IGF, then, in order to balance the flexibility and effectiveness of smaller networks with the legitimacy of a larger and more open group, is to foster the formation of networks between its members, but also to ensure that their output is subjected to multi-stakeholder deliberation, both within those smaller networks if possible, and finally within the IGF at large. One possible framework within which for this to be accomplished is through the IGF's dynamic coalitions, as will be discussed below.[72]

Meta-governance

It has been concluded that the legitimacy of the IGF's policy-setting role flows (or rather, should flow) from its multi-stakeholder structure and democratic processes. Many of the organisations and networks it must coordinate its activities with do not share those virtues, yet assume a role

[69] CDT, Companies, Human Rights Groups, Investors, Academics and Technology Leaders to Address International Free Expression and Privacy Challenges ⟨URL: `http://www.cdt.org/press/20070118press-humanrights.php`⟩

[70] The OpenNet Initiative; see `http://opennet.net/`.

[71] McCullagh, The UN Thinks About Tomorrow's Cyberspace (as in n. 4 on page 2), and see Zhao (as in n. 2 on page 1), 10

[72] See section 6.3 on page 457.

preeminent to that of the IGF. How is the IGF to relate to these other bodies and reconcile their governance programmes with its own?

Two possible answers to this question can be dismissed in short order. The first is that the claims of other institutions with lesser legitimacy than the IGF to exercise authority in Internet governance should be denied, and that the IGF should purport to act as the sole legitimate policy-setting body for the regime. This answer fails on three counts. First, it contradicts the Tunis Agenda, which prohibits the IGF from duplicating the work of any existing body. Second, were the IGF to make such an audacious claim, it could no longer expect the impugned institutions to continue to participate in the network. The third reason, which underlies the others, is that even in the new medieval age, formal authority still matters.

To elucidate, the IGF is a microcosm of the mythical greater public sphere in which democratic deliberation takes place. This public sphere does not take decisions on its own account, but must be linked with formal decision-making bodies such as parliaments and courts.[73] So it is too with the IGF, whose role it is to coordinate with bodies holding formal authority, such as domestic governments and international organisations, not in order to usurp their function, but in order to elevate them to greater levels of democratic legitimacy. Therefore they cannot be regarded merely as functional appendages to implement or enforce the IGF's recommendations, but rather as the formal policy-setting authorities that can give force to those recommendations in the international system.

To give an example, the IGF might seek that its recommendations in a particular issue area—say on the Internet Bill of Rights, to return to an earlier hypothetical case—be given force in the international system. In order for this to be achieved, it could petition the General Assembly to resolve that a new treaty or convention on this topic be drafted. States would, as always, formally take the leading role in this process, but there is no reason why they could not utilise a document prepared by the IGF as their first draft; indeed, they would have every reason to do so if they participated in the process by which it was prepared within the IGF. The IGF could also be consulted during the intergovernmental negotiation process (much as, imperfectly, civil society was consulted during the WSIS negotiations), with the result that the final treaty, although *de jure* intergovernmental, would *de facto* be a document of multi-stakeholder ownership.

Lest this example be thought far-fetched, it closely describes the process by which the Mine Ban Treaty, and more recently the Disability Convention,[74] were prepared largely at the initiation and with the integral involvement of civil society.[75]

---

[73] Habermas, *Between Facts and Norms: Contributions to a Discourse Theory of Law and Democracy* (as in n. 209 on page 227), 371

[74] *Convention on the Rights of Persons with Disabilities*, 6 Dec 2006, A/61/611 (not yet in force)

[75] Cameron (as in n. 140 on page 125); Janet E Lord, Mirror, Mirror on the Wall: Voice

If the first possible response of the IGF to the involvement of less legitimate bodies in Internet governance was to oppose their claims, and this response has been rejected, then the second and contrary response is to yield to those claims, and thereby for the IGF to allow its own recommendations to be accorded only the weight that other institutions would accord them. In this case, if WIPO should insist that it remain the sole venue for policy-setting in relation to intellectual property issues, and the WTO the only proper forum in which for the development of international trade policy, then the result would be the IGF's recommendations carrying little if any weight within those bodies.

This response is also clearly problematic, for two reasons. First, along the continuum between decision-shaping and decision-taking, whilst the IGF is not to act as a decision-taker in place of existing governance bodies that exercise that role, neither can it be relegated to the position of just another stakeholder submitting input into higher-level policy-setting processes.

To do so would be to deny the individual autonomy of its participants who have delegated to the IGF the function of expressing their collective interests. This makes its recommendations more than the expression of individual preferences such as would be received as input into a "participatory democracy-style" open consultation, and having a purely advisory status, but rather the culmination of a policy development process that is democratically legitimate in its own right.[76]

Second, it would significantly weaken the IGF's policy-setting role if its capacity to make recommendations and have them implemented were left to the whim of other bodies without regard to those bodies' legitimacy. Although the IGF is directed to be non-duplicative in its operation, this cannot be taken to be merely a reference to duplication of the substantive issues being addressed, but also that of the procedures by which they are addressed. Where the IGF's recommendations are developed through multi-stakeholder, democratic deliberation and those of another body addressing the same issues are developed through a less inclusive and legitimate process, it is not accurate to describe the IGF's activities as duplicative.

So if the IGF is not to reject the parallel claims of authority of less legitimate organisations, but nor to automatically accede to them, what is the IGF's responsibility when faced with a clash between existing bodies' authority and its own? The Tunis Agenda suggests the answer. It states that the IGF is to "[p]romote and assess, on an ongoing basis, the embodiment of WSIS principles in Internet governance processes."[77]

This means that in interfacing with "appropriate inter-governmental

Accountability and NGOs in Human Rights Standard Setting, Seton Hall Journal of Diplomacy and International Relations 2004 and see section 3.2 on page 124.

[76]See section 3.4 on page 152.

[77]WSIS, Tunis Agenda for the Information Society (as in n. 5 on page 2), para 72 (i)

organizations and other institutions on matters under their purview," the IGF is to assess the extent to which they satisfy the WSIS process criteria that "international management of the Internet should be multilateral, transparent and democratic, with the full involvement of governments, the private sector, civil society and international organizations."[78]

The result of this assessment will then inform the IGF's relationship with these other organisations. If an external body adequately fulfils the WSIS process criteria in its own right, then in order to remain non-duplicative, the IGF's role will be narrower than in the case of a body that does not fulfil those principles. In the latter case, the IGF's role of coordinating with that body will require it to provide an overarching multi-stakeholder democratic framework by which to augment the body's structures and processes so that the WSIS principles are fulfilled for that issue area within the governance regime as a whole. An implication of this is that the IGF is not precluded from participating in any area of Internet-related public policy unless the body by which such issues are already being dealt with is adequately democratic and multi-stakeholder in composition, such that the IGF's involvement would be redundant.

Interestingly, much the same view was aired during the plenary session on security of the Athens meeting of the IGF, in which the moderator Ken Cukier asked the panel whether the IGF had a role to play in putting forward technical standards designed to address public policy issues, into bodies such as the IETF. Gus Hosein of the London School of Economics was amongst those who responded that there was a legitimate role for the IGF here, but that it was at the level of establishing general principles that standards bodies and other organisations of Internet governance could take into consideration in their work, rather than in assuming responsibility for that work directly.[79]

Of course, the IGF has no authority to enforce its assessment of another body's compliance with the WSIS process criteria, but that is where its mandate to "promote" those principles comes in. One way in which to do so is for the IGF to hold bodies that do not adequately fulfil the process

[78]WSIS, Geneva Declaration of Principles (as in n. 104 on page 27), para 48

[79]This in turn reflected a suggestion contained in the written contribution of the Information Society Project of Yale Law School to the Athens meeting (Eddan Katz and Laura DeNardis, Best Practices for Internet Standards Governance ⟨URL: http://intgovforum.org/Substantive_1st_IGF/BestPracticesforInternetStandardsGovernance.pdf⟩, 5):

> One option for greater oversight, accountability, and legitimation in the Internet standards process is an IGF-administered system of accreditation for legitimating standards setting organizations based on adherence to best practices in standards setting. The IGF would not be involved in standards setting, but would provide legitimating accreditation of standards organizations based on these best practices. Multi-stakeholders, including governments and corporations, might endorse the efficacy of such a system to provide balance and consistency and to thwart the possibility of a single stakeholder gaining undue influence in the standards process.

criteria accountable for their implementation of the IGF's recommendations through a public follow-up process. Another is to discuss the structure and processes of other Internet governance organisations and to make recommendations for their reform. This could be done through the open forum sessions that made their debut at the Rio meeting,[80] if these were appropriately facilitated to achieve this end.

Thus the meta-governance role of the IGF is to promote, assess and where necessary provide, a common standard of governance for interconnected governance organisations, analogous to the common TCP/IP protocols by which Internet hosts are interconnected. This is a programme that would fulfil the transnational democratic ideal at its most ambitious: to extend the principles of democracy on a transnational basis across all applicable levels of governance.[81]

It is also, inevitably, a highly charged political process, and therefore one that the IGF has perhaps naturally been slow to embrace. For example, although ICANN purports to be a democratic and multi-stakeholder forum in its own right, because it is not yet adequately democratic according to the reckoning of this book, there remains a legitimate role for the IGF in setting policy for the management of critical Internet resources. Yet this is clearly not a role that ICANN will be inclined to accept, nor that the IGF has yet sought.[82]

As contentious as the process will be, the appropriate way forward is for the extent of the IGF's role in setting policy for critical Internet resource management, and other grey areas of the IGF's mandate such as the divide between public policy and technical issues in this area,[83] to be discussed between ICANN and the stakeholders of the IGF in an agenda-setting process that is itself conducted on a democratic, multi-stakeholder basis.[84]

[80] William J Drake, *The Power of Ideas: Internet Governance in a Global Multi-Stakeholder Environment* Berlin: Marketing für Deutschland, 2007, chap. Encouraging Implementation of the WSIS Principles on Internet Governance Procedures

[81] See section 4.3 on page 236.

[82] However in February 2008 the IGP suggested that it should do so, in putting to the NTIA "that a new external oversight arrangement for ICANN be set up by leveraging the innovation and experimentation of the Internet Governance Forum": IGP, Comments of the Internet Governance Project on The Continued Transition of the Technical Coordination and Management of the Internet's Domain Name and Addressing System: Midterm Review of the Joint Project Agreement ⟨URL: `http://internetgovernance.org/pdf/IGP-JPA-08-comments.pdf`⟩, 5.

[83] It is adequately clear that the IGF could provide recommendations to ICANN on, for example, the privacy implications of its WHOIS database, the ramifications of IPR and A2K policy on the UDRP, and the relevance of the WSIS principles to the introduction of multilingual domain names. But what about the introduction of new gTLDs into the global root—is this a purely administrative function, or, as the GAC would have it, one that engages public policy interests (see GAC, GAC Principles and Guidelines on Public Policy Issues Regarding the Implementation of New gTLDs ⟨URL: `http://gac.icann.org/web/meetings/mtg26/gTLDs_principles_on_public_policy_draft_17_oct_2006.doc`⟩)?

[84] Biegel (as in n. 60 on page 19), 223

Development

A number of paragraphs of the IGF's mandate in the Tunis Agenda require the IGF to directly engage in the promotion of development objectives such as capacity building. Thus it will be recalled that the IGF is directed to "[f]acilitate the exchange of information and best practices," to "[a]dvise all stakeholders in proposing ways and means to accelerate the availability and affordability of the Internet in the developing world," to strengthen the engagement of stakeholders particularly from developing countries "in existing and/or future Internet governance mechanisms," and to "[c]ontribute to capacity building for Internet governance in developing countries."[85]

The inclusion of these paragraphs on development in the IGF's mandate may be largely attributed to the forum's origin in WSIS, a summit which by the nature of its consensual process was strongly influenced by developing country interests.[86] What is most notable about these paragraphs is that unlike the balance of the IGF's mandate which requires it to perform the Internet governance functions of policy-setting and coordination across a range of substantive Internet governance issues, they entreat the IGF to address particular development-related Internet governance issues such as capacity building itself. In fact, only one of the development-related paragraphs in the IGF's mandate requires it to engage in any of the governance roles recognised in this chapter; namely the call to "strengthen and enhance the engagement of stakeholders in existing and/or future Internet governance mechanisms,"[87] which can be regarded as a coordination role.

Although these paragraphs do not specify roles of governance for the IGF to undertake in the procedural sense used in this chapter, this does not mean that they are not still appropriate functions for a democratic governance network to address. After all, the programme of substantive democracy is to ensure that all have an equal opportunity as well as an equal right to participate in governance, and it has already been noted the digital divide is one of the most significant impediments to this objective for the Internet governance regime.[88]

The inclusion of a development programme within the IGF's mandate also puts it in good company with other of the exemplar organisations, namely the GKP, GAID and UNICTTF, all of which are also linked with the WSIS process, and also with ISOC whose motto is "The Internet is for Everyone."

Even so, it is perhaps unfortunate that this programme, as important as it is to the development of a democratic transnational Internet governance

[85]WSIS, Tunis Agenda for the Information Society (as in n. 5 on page 2), paras 72(d), (e), (f) and (h)

[86]See section 5.1 on page 322.

[87]Ibid., paras 72(f)

[88]See sections 4.3 on page 285 and 4.3 on page 234.

regime, should be intermingled with the quite distinct procedural governance roles assigned to the IGF in the balance of its mandate, particularly since there are many other specific issues that are of equal importance to the development of a substantively democratic Internet governance regime, which the mandate omits to include.[89]

As the focus of this book is on procedural rather than substantive issues, no further attention will specifically be given to the operational roles in the IGF's mandate, which include those relating to development noted above, and also the mandate to "[h]elp to find solutions to the issues arising from the use and misuse of the Internet, of particular concern to everyday users."[90] The analysis that follows as to the effectiveness of the IGF's structure and processes to fulfil its mandate should therefore be understood as being subject to this limitation.

6.3 Structure

Having set out the specific roles of policy-setting and coordination that are inherent in the IGF's function as a governance network, as well as being mandated by the Tunis Agenda, it is now necessary to assess whether an appropriate institutional structure exists to support the fulfilment of those roles.

In making this assessment, both too little structure and too much structure are to be avoided. As will be seen, the case of too little structure bears much resemblance to the IGF in its present form, which is essentially that of an annual conference on Internet governance, and a banner under which stakeholders may engage in decentralised collective action through dynamic coalitions. The problem with such a lack of structure is that multistakeholder policy development does not "just happen" without a degree of institutionalisation:

> Without roles and rules for decision-making and resource mobilization, collective action becomes more difficult and thus less likely. Facilitating communication among persons, as well as resolving any conflicts that may arise among them, is likewise needed for getting and keeping people together to accomplish things that are beyond the capability of individuals who are seeking just their own well-being.[91]

[89]The most obvious example is the importance of upholding human rights, as appears to have been acknowledged by both the CS-IGC and A2K@IGF when they proposed during the May 2007 open consultations that human rights should join capacity building as a "cross-cutting priority" for the IGF (though this was blocked by China during the following meeting of the former Advisory Group).

[90]WSIS, Tunis Agenda for the Information Society (as in n. 5 on page 2), para 72(k)

[91]Uphoff (as in n. 196 on page 220), 228

On the other hand, worse still than a lack of structure is a surfeit, especially when the structure is ill-matched to the effective and legitimate fulfilment of the network's roles. This too can be seen in the IGF, for example in the juxtaposition of the hierarchical leadership of the Secretary-General of the United Nations and his Secretariat (at least in relation to questions of the IGF's role and structure) with what is notionally an open, consensual and multi-stakeholder network of equals.

Thankfully the deficiencies of the IGF's present structure are neither inevitable nor irremediable, since the IGF was expressly established to "have a lightweight and decentralised structure that would be subject to periodic review."[92] It is only to be expected that such review might entail a radical overhaul of the IGF's preliminary structure, which after all was established in a short space of time in accordance with the mandate of the Tunis Agenda, thereby limiting the practicality of extensive advance consultation and the development of adequately transparent processes for the convening of the inaugural meeting.

The longer such review is delayed or minimised, however, the more likely it is that structural inertia will set in and the IGF's preliminary structure will become calcified.[93] Kenneth Cukier writes:

> What is needed is more concentration on designing an organization that is capable of changing for new circumstances. It should have the seeds of its own diminishment or dissolution within it. It must have a separation of powers, and checks and balances—the one thing that every attempt at Internet governance, oddly, has lacked.[94]

These are the hallmarks of democratic forms of ordering, as discussed in detail in Chapter 4. In that chapter it was concluded that a democratic organisational form, in conjunction with a consensual deliberative process, provided a suitable balance between the poles of anarchistic ordering (which is decentralised and adaptable, but copes poorly with strategic behaviour and imbalances of power), and hierarchical design (which can be more effective, accountable and transparent, but is by definition non-consensual).

More specifically, it was suggested that a suitable such democratic structure for transnational Internet public policy governance would consist of a plenary body open to participation by all stakeholders, which would be

[92] WSIS, Tunis Agenda for the Information Society (as in n. 5 on page 2), para 73

[93] Massimo G Colombo and Marco Delmastro, The Determinants of Organizational Change and Structural Inertia: Technological and Organizational Factors, Journal of Economics & Management Strategy 11:4 2002

[94] Kenneth Neil Cukier, Slouching Towards Geneva: Ten Unappreciated Axioms of Internet Governance ⟨URL: `http://www.oii.ox.ac.uk/collaboration/specialevents/20050505_governance_position_papers.pdf`⟩, 5

responsible for building consensus on public policy issues, under the guidance of a multi-stakeholder executive council to which nominees would be appointed on the basis of merit through a consensual or democratic process, and which would have the responsibility of assessing and ratifying the consensus of the plenary body.

How does this ideal compare with the IGF as it exists, and what is required to reform its structure to accord with the ideal more closely? These are the questions to which this section is addressed. They will be addressed first in the context of the existing structures that have been developed for the IGF, before a broader view is taken that allows for more radical reforms to be considered.

Existing structures

The existing structures that are to be considered here are the annual plenary meetings of the IGF, the Secretariat, the Advisory Group, the open consultation meetings, the workshops and dynamic coalitions organised by stakeholders, and finally the open fora that were first held in Rio.

Plenary

The application of the democratic principle to the Internet governance regime requires that all stakeholders impacted in respect of a given issue should be empowered to participate in the policy development process. However exactly which stakeholders are so impacted will vary from one issue to another, and therefore the weight that should legitimately be accorded to the input of each of those stakeholders will vary accordingly.[95]

To manage this, there are two basic templates for designing a democratic Internet governance institution that relates the participation of stakeholders in policy development to how directly and how often their interests are engaged by the issues within its remit. These templates can be understood as being drawn from the theory of representative democracy and that of deliberative democracy respectively.

The representative democratic approach is to determine antecedently which stakeholders are impacted by the issues within the organisation's mandate and to what extent, to divide them into stakeholder groups on that basis, and to institutionalise the representation of those groups within the organisation in a fixed structure. An example of this approach is found in auDA, whose supply-side and demand-side members each vote only for representatives of their own stakeholder groups to serve on the body's board of directors, thus preserving a balance of the presumed different

[95]See section 4.3 on page 289.

interests of suppliers and consumers of domain names in fixed proportions within the organisation's decision-making organ. Other examples of the representative democratic approach from the exemplar organisations include CGI.br (with its governmental, private sector, civil society and technical stakeholder representatives) and ICANN (with its three Supporting Organisations and their various constituency groups).[96]

In addition to the more general shortcomings of representative democracy discussed at section 4.3 on page 231, such an approach suffers from the following problems:

- the determination of who will be impacted by the issues within the organisation's mandate, and their division into groups according to their (presumed or actual) interests in those issues, are themselves matters which ought to be determined through an inclusive and transparent democratic process rather than by what has been described as "top–down gerrymandering":[97] this presents a chicken-and-egg dilemma;[98] and
- such a structure is inflexible, in that novel issues may arise that impact upon stakeholders not already included within the organisation's defined constituencies, from whom it cannot easily receive formal input without being restructured. Or as in the IGF's case, there may be so many issues requiring of the input of different groupings of affected stakeholders, that it is impracticable for all of those groupings to be institutionalised in the organisation's structure.

The second, deliberative democratic approach overcomes these problems. Central to this approach is to structure the organisation's plenary decision-making body as an open forum to which all interested stakeholders have access,[99] and to determine the weight that particular stakeholders' input into that forum should be accorded subsequently rather than antecedently, by subjecting that input to a process of reasoned public deliberation.[100]

---

[96] Although not one of the exemplar organisations, an even clearer example of the representative democratic approach is given by the ILO, with its division between governmental, employer and worker representatives.

[97] Johnson and Crawford, What's Wrong With ICANN—And How to Fix It (as in n. 592 on page 304)

[98] The only exception is in the case where stakeholder groupings can be determined objectively, but the only common such case is that of geographical division. Even then, the determination can be incorrect or over-simplistic, as in ICANN's case: Centre for Global Studies, Enhancing Legitimacy in the Internet Corporation for Assigned Names and Numbers ⟨URL: http://www.markle.org/downloadable_assets/icann_enhancelegitemacy.pdf⟩, 4.

[99] This does not exclude the need for outreach to disadvantaged stakeholders, however: see section 4.3 on page 285.

[100] This does not mean that stakeholder groupings may not be used within the organisation, as such groupings serve more than one purpose. Their purpose for the IGF as theorised in this book is to ensure that the legitimacy of the organisation as a governance network is drawn from

On the surface, this may seem to suggest that the structure of the IGF's plenary body accords quite closely with the deliberative democratic ideal. It is open to all stakeholders, including—uniquely for a UN body—unaffiliated individuals. Stakeholder groups are not segregated. There is no cost to attend, other than travel and accommodation costs or the costs of obtaining Internet access through which to participate remotely.[101] However, where the plenary structure of the IGF falls down is in its disempowerment to perform its policy-setting roles, such as the making of recommendations.

This shortcoming is of course not the result of oversight, but design. Nitin Desai has consistently argued, as he did again at the open consultations in May 2007:

> If you are going to have agreed recommendations, who are the people who will have a right to sit at that table? To recite this [agreement]? Because we do not have a membership defined for IGF, because we only defined it as an event. And in a multi-stakeholder environment, there is a genuine problem in talking in terms of membership. Are you going to say all those who are present [decide]? Then let's be very realistic. With the under-representation that you will always have, [and] continue to have from developing countries, all those present will probably give you a geographically unbalanced mix. It will also vary depending on where the meeting is held.

The appropriate response to this line of argument depends on how strongly it is taken. In its strongest form, it implies not merely that the plenary body of the IGF cannot make recommendations in its present, imperfectly-constituted form, but that no open plenary body, however constituted, is capable of fulfilling a policy-setting role. This is an objection that goes to the heart of the IGF's mandate, and has been answered earlier in this chapter, when it was reiterated that although such a body may be unsuited as a representative democratic forum, it can be perfectly well suited for democratic deliberation, provided that the perspectives of all those significantly affected are able to be voiced during the discussion.[102]

If on the other hand the above argument is taken simply as pointing to the fact that many stakeholders who would otherwise participate in the IGF will be precluded by cost and distance from attending its annual plenary meetings in person, then it should be understood that this disadvantage impacts upon each of the roles in the IGF's mandate, not merely its policy-setting role. The appropriate response to this disadvantage is therefore not

---

a balance of each of the sources that the various stakeholder groups contribute. Importantly the IGF's plenary body, however, acts as an amalgam of all four groups.

[101] But see section 6.4 on page 504 regarding the limitations of the latter.

[102] See section 6.2 on page 424.

to disregard the most inconvenient paragraphs of the IGF's mandate, but rather to attempt to address the underlying causes of the problem. Indeed, this itself falls within the IGF's mandate to "[s]trengthen and enhance the engagement of stakeholders in existing and/or future Internet governance mechanisms, particularly those from developing countries."[103]

There are a number of specific strategies by which the disadvantage of those who cannot attend annual meetings of the IGF can and should be redressed, such as:

- Structuring the IGF less as a monolithic annual event, and more as a process made up of a number of coordinated events and activities including intersessional regional meetings and parallel fora for online participation.[104]

  APNIC provides a good model of such a structure, in that although it holds regular Open Policy Meetings for those with the capacity to attend in person, policy proposals put forward for decision at such a meeting must be tabled in advance on one of APNIC's open mailing lists, and if passed at the meeting (by rough consensus) may still be overturned by objections subsequently lodged online.[105]

  To compare this to the IGF, selecting one example only for now,[106] although a "plenary" mailing list was established for the use of IGF members at large, it has been near-dormant since then, largely because it was never advertised by the IGF Secretariat.[107] As for supportive regional meetings, whilst a handful have been convened through the decentralised action of stakeholders,[108] the Secretariat has neither coordinated nor promoted these *ad hoc* events.

- Online participation should be facilitated not only as a parallel process (whereby discussion and deliberation takes place in online fora that are separate from the annual offline meeting), but also as a channel for communication between the annual meeting and remote participants. This means both that the proceedings at the annual meeting should be accessible to remote participants, and also that the contributions of such participants should be received by the meeting much as they are received by those present in person.

[103] WSIS, Tunis Agenda for the Information Society (as in n. 5 on page 2), para 72(f)

[104] Both of these deficiencies have been well noted by stakeholders. The need for regional meetings was discussed at the February 2006 and 2007, and May 2007 open consultation meetings, and criticisms of the IGF's lack of support for online participation have been referred to at section 5.2 on page 381.

[105] See section 4.4 on page 307 and compare also the similar case of the IETF: Froomkin, Habermas@discourse.net: Toward a Critical Theory of Cyberspace (as in n. 40 on page 13), 803.

[106] But see also section 6.4 on page 504.

[107] See section 5.2 on page 377.

[108] See section 5.3 on page 395.

APNIC also provides a model of this, by using synchronous discussion software (Jabber chat) to transmit live transcripts of meeting sessions and to allow for the receipt of input from remote participants. A fuller assessment of how the IGF fares in comparison will await later treatment,[109] but for now it suffices to note that whilst, like APNIC, it provides video and audio webcasting of plenary meetings, its failure to provide an equivalent real-time transcript to APNIC's Jabber service excludes many participants from developing countries whose Internet access speed is limited.

- If it is taken as a given for now that full participation in the process of policy development within the IGF requires attendance at its annual plenary meetings, the fulfilment of the IGF's mandate will depend upon those from developing countries being provided with additional assistance to attend those meetings.

  APNIC once again provides a model of this, through the fellowships that it offers members from developing countries to attend its OPMs. A slightly different model is the establishment of a specialised bureau dedicated to ensuring that the interests of less well-resourced groups are represented, such as the Economic and Social Committee of the EU, or the Civil Society Bureau of WSIS. In comparison to these initiatives, the IGF, having been provided with no funding by the United Nations, relies upon its stakeholders to provide fellowships to disadvantaged stakeholders.[110]

In summary then, the basic structure of the IGF's plenary body as an open forum has been found to be well-suited to the fulfilment of its policy-setting roles through appropriate deliberative democratic processes,[111] and although the argument that it is improper for such a body to engage in policy development at all has been rejected, this argument has drawn attention to the need for the IGF to foster fuller participation by disadvantaged stakeholders, through a number of strategies including the development of regional and online fora that can be coordinated with the main plenary forum, the facilitation of dialogue between the plenary meeting and remote participants, and the provision of support to those who wish to participate in the plenary forum but are otherwise unable to do so.

Despite all this, it may still be that the IGF's plenary body ought not become its peak decision-making organ. Whilst it cannot be questioned that the IGF has a mandate to perform policy-setting roles, those roles might in practice be more effectively distributed between the open plenary body and more highly institutionalised organs of the IGF. It has already

---

[109] See section 6.4 on page 504.

[110] The largest of these has been Canada's contribution of $100 000 for fellowships for developing country experts announced during the May 2007 open consultation meeting. Japan also announced in September 2007 its contribution of 10 million yen for this and related purposes.

[111] The nature of which are to be discussed separately at section 6.4 on page 474.

been noted that, regardless of how sound the conceptual justification may be for policy development to be conducted by a body of indeterminate size and composition, governments will be loathe to concede any more than the weakest advisory authority to such a body,[112] and that a more substantial connection to the existing international system is likely to be required if the IGF is to progress any further along the continuum from decision-shaping to decision-taking.

Were the plenary body therefore to delegate the formal part of its policy-setting authority to some form of subcommittee with a more tightly defined membership, the balance of the plenary's own activities would draw it somewhat closer to the role espoused by the Forum doves: it would become less of an assembly, like the General Assembly of the United Nations, and more of a think tank or a public policy institute. Its principal function would remain to engage in democratic deliberation, with the aim of reaching consensus on issues of Internet-related public policy, but it would no longer be called upon to declare its own consensus, nor to draw the output of that discursive process together into an agreed form suitable for input into other organisations. Those functions would instead lie elsewhere.

The question then becomes, where? If the plenary meeting is not to act as the peak body for policy development within the IGF, who else is to do so: the Secretariat, the Advisory Group, or some other organ or organs altogether?

Secretariat

The suggestion that the Secretariat should take on these substantive functions, or a subset of them, may seem difficult to countenance of an institution that traditionally carries out only clerical duties, and in the case of the IGF, is appointed unilaterally by the Secretary-General of the United Nations rather than by a multi-stakeholder process.

But in fact it is naïve to imagine that the clerical duties of the Secretariat could be neatly separated from underlying substantive issues relating to the role of the IGF, its structure and processes, even if responsibility for those substantive issues were institutionalised in another body. Rather, just as in the regime of Internet governance public policy issues are often engaged in the notionally value-free spheres of technical coordination and standards development, so too the responsibilities of the IGF's Secretariat have engaged it in making deeply political decisions.

To illustrate this, consider three of the most visible functions the IGF Secretariat has performed for the Athens and Rio meetings:

[112] See sections 4.3 on page 289 and 5.4 on page 407.

- the preparation of synthesis papers and reports summarising the contributions and discussions of stakeholders;
- recommending appropriate structures and processes for the IGF to the UN Secretary-General based upon the views of stakeholders expressed during open consultation meetings; and
- the preparation of a draft agenda for IGF meetings.[113]

If it were even possible to perform such functions with neutrality as to the substantive content of the IGF's mandate, then it is far from clear that the IGF Secretariat has done so:

- Certain of the synthesis papers it has prepared have been criticised for their partiality in the views they record.[114]
- Similarly the Secretariat's assessment of the "emerging consensus" expressed by stakeholders has appeared to privilege certain interests, particularly those of governments, over others; as evidenced for example by the appointment of an Advisory Group far larger than any other stakeholders besides the G77 and China had suggested,[115] and in refusing to consider a reduction in the proportionate representation of governments within the group.[116]
- It also prepared a draft agenda for the Rio meeting that omitted to make provision for the discussion of Internet naming and numbering in a plenary session (once again, until demanded by China), in the face of strong and sustained criticism from numerous stakeholders over its omission from the Athens programme.

The Secretariat's apparent partiality should be understood in the context that Marcus Kummer and Nitin Desai are both veterans of WSIS. In fact their programme for the IGF can be seen as the continuation of that of WSIS: a development-focused summit at which civil society's proposal for an Internet Governance Forum, put forward through WGIG, was part of a political bargain struck to postpone the clash between developing countries and the US government over Internet naming and numbering.

It should not therefore be particularly surprising that the Secretariat may have its own (doubtless well-meant) agenda for the IGF, rather than being a neutral organ for the implementation of policy developed by stakeholders; indeed, this is almost a truism, as one commentator explains:

---

[113]This was done in conjunction with the Advisory Group for the Athens meeting, but for the Rio meeting there was no Advisory Group when the first draft agenda was prepared.

[114]For example, ETNO criticised the post-Rio synthesis paper as unbalanced at the February 2008 open consultations.

[115]See section 5.2 on page 358.

[116]See section 5.2 on page 394.

> a "real" or "pure" international bureaucracy, in the sense of being politically neutral, must be viewed as imaginary in many if not most of the various agencies of the United Nations system. The reality more closely approximates the highly politicized bureaucracies of most of the member-states. Just as it is often true that the national bureaucracies are viewed as bearing the responsibility of ensuring the continuation in power of the dominant political party or perhaps military faction, and not as ready to serve any other parties or factions that may be standing in the wings, it may equally be more "real" that, at best, international bureaucracies inevitably are intended to preserve the current political mandates of their organizations and thus inevitably are vulnerable to accusations of political partiality (as well as laziness, corruption, etc) by those elements of the membership opposed to the status quo.[117]

However as inevitable as it may be that the Secretariat should privately hold preferences of its own, it is unacceptable that it should be allowed to appear to shape the structure and processes of the IGF to favour particular substantive positions and thereby to influence the content and direction of the IGF's work programme. As a multi-stakeholder governance network, the task of setting the IGF's agenda, structure and processes can only legitimately be performed on a multi-stakeholder, democratic basis.

This has two implications for the IGF's Secretariat. First, regardless of whether its partiality is real or only apparent, its technical roles should be separated from its substantive roles. Indeed, there is no reason why both should be performed by the same body, and every reason why the latter should not be performed by a UN-appointed Secretariat unilaterally. While the Secretariat continues to be appointed by the UN, it should thus be limited to the role of a technical secretariat like that of WSIS, and deal only with organising meetings, coordinating stakeholders and the like, while a separate substantive secretariat carries out activities such as reviewing and synthesising contributions and drafting briefing documents to focus discussion.[118]

The second implication for the IGF Secretariat is that it must be made accountable to the stakeholders at large. Presently, its lack of accountability stems not only from its appointment solely by the UN Secretary-General, but from the fact that it has gone about its role with very little transparency, which has limited stakeholders' ability to supervise the Secretariat's activities.[119]

---

[117] Robert S Jordan, *Politics in the United Nations Systems* Durham, NC: Duke University Press, 1998, chap. "Truly" International Bureaucracies: Real or Imagined?, 438

[118] John Mathiason, The Distributed Secretariat: Making the Internet Governance Forum Work ⟨URL: `http://www.internetgovernance.org/pdf/distrib-sec.pdf`⟩, 1

[119] See section 6.4 on page 494.

One proposal to address the above concerns was made early on by the Internet Governance Project in a submission by which it suggested that "stakeholder groups, especially the academic community, should be considered part of a 'Distributed Secretariat' to the extent that they facilitate forum activities and are willing to undertake the substantive support functions."[120] Such a distributed secretariat would also offer the flexibility of allowing different configurations of stakeholders to support the IGF in different ways, much as different groupings of stakeholders come together in dynamic coalitions covering different issue areas.[121]

A limitation of the Distributed Secretariat proposal is that it does not solve, but in fact multiplies, the problems of ensuring the Secretariat's impartiality on substantive matters and its accountability. Even accepting the IGP's suggestion that the academic community is more likely to be politically neutral then other stakeholders (as well as being likely to be technically competent), it would not intrinsically be any more accountable for this neutrality than other stakeholders or the UN-appointed Secretariat.

The only effective way in which to ensure both the legitimacy and the accountability of a substantive secretariat is for it to be appointed by and accountable to the stakeholders; that is, the IGF at large. But this also raises practical difficulties, in that the plenary body of the IGF, as noted under the last preceding heading, has been designed without any decision-making capacity. The IGP's proposal is therefore for the Advisory Group to be entrusted with the role of approving applications from groups of stakeholders to act as nodes of a Distributed Secretariat. However this is not a satisfactory solution either, as it will be seen that the Advisory Group has significant problems of its own.

Advisory Group

The Advisory Group was established with a narrow mandate "to prepare the substantive agenda and programme for the first meeting of the Internet Governance Forum."[122] It might therefore reasonably be assumed, particularly given the group's size and multi-stakeholder structure, that it had effectively been established to act as a meritocratically-appointed programme committee for the IGF, as a number of stakeholders had suggested in the consultations prior to its formation.[123]

However following the completion of its mandate for the inaugural meeting, Nitin Desai made a decisive move to downplay the significance

---

[120] IGP, Building an Internet Governance Forum (as in n. 144 on page 357), 4

[121] Mathiason, The Distributed Secretariat: Making the Internet Governance Forum Work (as in n. 118 on the previous page), 4–5

[122] United Nations Office of the Secretary-General, Secretary-General Establishes Advisory Group to Assist Him in Convening Internet Governance Forum (as in n. 180 on page 365)

[123] See sections 5.2 on page 356 and 5.2 on page 358.

of the Advisory Group and to confine it to its formal role of advising the UN Secretary-General. At the May 2007 open consultation, he urged those present "to keep a sense of balance" about the Advisory Group's role, which he described as mere "fine tuning" of the structure and the parameters of the IGF's meetings. He asserted that:

> We could have done everything that we did without a formally constituted Advisory Group, simply by consulting those individuals individually as a UN secretariat. But we chose to constitute it as an Advisory Group precisely because we felt that it was important to get people involved in the process who were connected with the broader community from which they came.

In either case, the fundamental problem with the structure of the Advisory Group is that it lacks legitimacy.[124]

In the first case given above, where the Advisory Group is conceived as a meritocratically-selected executive committee for a multi-stakeholder governance network, its illegitimacy arises from the undemocratic manner in which it was convened. It will be recalled from Chapter 4 that the only legitimate means by which a meritocracy can be selected are consensual or democratic.[125] In no sense could the Secretariat's selection of candidates for the Advisory Group, in a closed process pursuant to criteria that were never published, be described as consensual or democratic.

Neither was this a shortcoming only of the initial selection process, as the same deficiencies were repeated in the Advisory Group's reappointment. At the open consultation in May 2007, Nitin Desai assured those present that "fairly extensive consultations have taken place, with missions, with stakeholder groups, before the Secretary-General takes a decision," but without identifying who had been consulted, by what means, or how those who were not fortunate enough to have been consulted could participate in the process or put their names forward for selection.

If on the other hand the Advisory Group is effectively powerless in its own right, merely serving as a focus group to be consulted for its opinions on the substantive agenda and programme of the IGF before the UN Secretary-General and the Secretariat make their own decisions independently, then the deficiencies of the process of its appointment become secondary, and the illegitimacy of the Advisory Group reflects that of the hierarchical power lying behind it.

Whilst the most accurate characterisation of the Advisory Group—whether as an empowered multi-stakeholder programme committee or

[124]There are also problems with the working processes of the Advisory Group, including its lack of accountability and transparency, but these will be dealt with separately at section 6.4 on page 474.

[125]See section 4.2 on page 204.

a weak instrument of the Secretary-General—is to some extent a matter of perspective, one factor tending to institutionalise it in the latter mould is its sheer size. In the absence of an effective deliberative process, this "empowers the Secretariat of the Forum, run by Markus Kummer and Nitin Desai; this group will be too large and diverse to do much on its own and will rely quite heavily on the Secretariat for organization, agenda-setting, and results."[126]

It is illegitimate for the United Nations thus to exercise leadership of a multi-stakeholder governance network, because the UN remains fundamentally an intergovernmental organisation, which allows for only limited participation in certain of its activities by civil society and the private sector, and is not accountable to them as it is to states.[127] It is for the same reason that it was argued above that the Secretariat should be limited to performing technical roles.

But an additional reason for excluding the UN from maintaining hierarchical control over the Advisory Group is that the Tunis Agenda itself appears to limit the Secretary-General's role to the establishment of that group, providing no warrant for the continuing role that he has assumed.[128] The only ongoing roles provided for the Secretary-General by the Tunis Agenda are to periodically report back upon the IGF's progress to the General Assembly, and to re-assess the IGF's mandate following its fifth meeting.[129]

Therefore, reform of the Advisory Group is necessary. The most pressing reforms are twofold. First, like the Secretariat, it must be appointed by multi-stakeholder, democratic means, though as also noted in respect of the Secretariat, this implies a parallel reform that would provide the means for the stakeholder groups each to nominate or appoint their own representatives to smaller committees of the IGF. Whilst this reform is yet to be discussed in detail,[130] it would hardly be much of an innovation, as it was in like manner that civil society's representatives were appointed to WGIG.[131]

At the September 2007 open consultation, Nitin Desai acknowledged this possibility for the first time, explaining the UN's current leadership of the IGF on the basis that

> the United Nations itself is not a player in Internet gover-

[126] Mueller, The Forum MAG: Who Are These People? (as in n. 178 on page 364)

[127] See section 3.4 on page 147.

[128] WSIS, Tunis Agenda for the Information Society (as in n. 5 on page 2) paras 72, 74, 78 and 82; Muguet (as in n. 252 on page 387), 5; IGP, Building an Internet Governance Forum (as in n. 144 on page 357), 5

[129] WSIS, Tunis Agenda for the Information Society (as in n. 5 on page 2) paras 75 and 76

[130] See section 6.3 on page 464.

[131] De la Chapelle, The World Summit on the Information Society: Moving from the Past into the Future (as in n. 53 on page 335), 281

> nance directly. And to that extent, the Secretary-General is a disinterested party. And to some extent I suppose somebody like me, who is his representative, is also seen as a disinterested party. Not a representative of any particular stakeholder group. But we have never thought of that as anything more than an interim measure till the thing stabilizes.

The second required reform is not so much one for the Advisory Group, as one that the limitations of the Advisory Group make necessary. It is the need for another body to take up functions that exceed the mandate of the Advisory Group and Secretariat. Some of these are functions that they have taken upon themselves regardless of this being in excess of their mandate; such as setting the structure and working methods of the IGF.[132] Others are functions that they have not attempted to address at all, such as facilitating the development of recommendations, as Brazil emphasised during the May 2007 open consultations in pressing for the establishment of an IGF bureau.[133]

Open consultations

Nitin Desai's response to the discussion of a bureau during those consultations was to argue that there was no need for another such body, because in addition to the purely supportive or facilitative role of the Advisory Group, the IGF already had another body whose function was to address the substantive preparatory process; namely, the open consultation meeting itself. Desai described this as "the most influential body" in defining "the structure and the parameters of the meeting, including the themes." Importantly, he also acknowledged the enhanced legitimacy lent to this process by the use of an open, multi-stakeholder group, in saying:

> The real role is of this large body which meets regularly. And that is why we always persisted with the process of this open consultation. ... We had it for the Working Group [on Internet Governance] and we always had it after that, because this is our substitute for the [bureau] process. In the [*scil* that] sense, this is what lends it a certain legitimacy and credibility.

What is interesting about this is that the large body of which Desai speaks is essentially indistinguishable from the IGF's plenary body: both are open, multi-stakeholder meetings, free to attend, unsegregated, and held in person with some (albeit limited) accessibility for those wishing to participate remotely. As the Greek delegate put it at the first open consultation in

[132] Muguet (as in n. 252 on page 387), 6
[133] See section 5.2 on page 385.

February 2006, "The cornerstone of the forum is basically everyone represented in this room. We are the forum."

In this light, Desai's acknowledgment of the legitimate authority of the open consultation meetings in shaping policy for the development of the IGF's structure and processes makes a striking contrast to his denial of the capacity of what is essentially the same plenary body to develop substantive recommendations when it convenes at annual meetings of the IGF.[134]

The distinction however is that the open consultation meetings have a hidden layer of hierarchical structure that the plenary meetings do not: the former, like meetings of the Advisory Group, in most cases generate a range of views, which it falls to the Secretariat to decide between or to forward in a report to the UN Secretary-General for his decision. Thus the consultation meetings, although open and bearing the trappings of participatory democracy, are not truly democratic, because ultimate decision-making authority is vested in those who are not democratically accountable.

Furthermore, the consultation meetings suffer from all of the other limitations of the plenary body of the IGF, and in some cases to an even greater extent. Thus, those who cannot afford to attend annual meetings of the IGF are also disadvantaged in their ability to attend open consultation meetings; but even more so, given that less funding is available to assist them. Similarly, the lack of attention that has been paid to the provision of online mechanisms to facilitate remote participation in the IGF's plenary meetings equally affects the open consultations.

Finally, whilst none have argued that the open consultations ought to be precluded from making recommendations on the structure and process of the IGF, these meetings are no better equipped than the plenary meetings with the procedural means of developing such recommendations. That is, the meetings are not designed to foster democratic deliberation.[135]

In summary then, the structure of the open consultation meetings lies somewhere in between that of the plenary body of the IGF and the Advisory Group. Like the IGF in plenary session, the greatest strength of the open consultation meetings is that their open and multi-stakeholder composition potentially provides them with greater legitimacy than the UN-appointed Advisory Group to shape decisions about the structure and processes of the IGF. However this potential is undermined by the subordination of the meeting's recommendations to the hierarchical power of the United Nations (much as in the case of the Advisory Group), and also by the failure of the meeting's chair to make use of deliberative democratic or consensual processes.

In addressing the shortcomings of the Advisory Group and Secretariat, it was suggested that another body should be formed to take up functions that

---

[134]Muguet (as in n. 252 on page 387), 7

[135]See sections 5.2 on page 358 and 6.4 on page 474.

exceed their mandate, with a more defined membership than the plenary body which would be appointed by democratic or consensual means. The existence of such a multi-stakeholder subcommittee of the IGF could also overcome the limitations of the open consultation meetings in their present form, were those meetings to make their recommendations to that body, rather than to the UN-appointed Secretariat or the Advisory Group. This in itself would be sufficient to constitute the open consultation meeting as a participatory democratic institution (or a deliberative democratic institution if its own processes were simultaneously reformed).

Alongside this reform, the disadvantage of those unable to attend open consultation meetings should be addressed by the same means as it was suggested above should be adopted to reform the plenary body of the IGF, including the facilitation of parallel regional and online processes that would also feed into the multi-stakeholder body's deliberations, the use of online mechanisms for remote participation, and the development of sources of financial support to those wishing to attend consultation meetings in person but unable to do so.[136]

Workshops and dynamic coalitions

Another important institutional structure of the IGF are its dynamic coalitions. These are to be treated here together with the IGF's workshops, because the group of stakeholders that comes together to organise a workshop can be regarded as a short-term dynamic coalition formed for that specific purpose, and a successful workshop can also serve as a precursor to the formation of a dynamic coalition with an ongoing work programme, just as in the IETF a successful BOF session is required before a new working group may be formed.[137]

Having said that, there is no need here to discuss the workshops themselves, as distinct from the groups that coordinate them, as these form part of the programme of the IGF's annual plenary meeting rather than part of its structure, and in that context will be discussed further in the section on the IGF's processes.

It was noted above that dynamic coalitions include three quite different types of group, which were described as networks, working groups and BOFs. Each of these serves a different purpose for the IGF as a governance network, and accordingly they are served differently by the existing institutionalisation of dynamic coalitions (or the lack thereof) within the IGF.

Taking them in turn, networks have the capacity to further the IGF's mandate of coordination. It is the network that may in fact have inspired the choice of the term "dynamic coalition," which was not known to scholars

---

[136] See section 6.3 on page 444.

[137] See section 2.2 on page 52.

before it was invented for the IGF, but which carries echoes of the concept of a "governing coalition"; an informal emergent form of "civic cooperation based on mutual self-interest between government and non-governmental actors."[138]

The second type of dynamic coalition, the working group, can conveniently be thought of as one which broadly meets the IETF's definition of that term:

> a group of people who work under a charter to achieve a certain goal. That goal may be the creation of an Informational document, the creation of a protocol specification, or the resolution of problems in the Internet. Most working groups have a finite lifetime. That is, once a working group has achieved its goal, it disbands.[139]

Similar bodies exist in most of the exemplar organisations.[140] Early on, it was anticipated by the Forum hawks, particularly those from civil society,[141] that the IGF too would form working groups that would provide reports or recommendations to the plenary body. However as the establishment of such groups as formal subcommittees of the IGF was strongly opposed by the Forum doves,[142] dynamic coalitions were the resulting compromise. Dynamic coalitions as working groups have the potential to serve the IGF's role of policy-setting.

Third and finally, dynamic coalitions as BOFs are those that do not yet have an explicit programme to contribute to the fulfilment of the IGF's mandate, but which may still provide a deliberative space within which interested stakeholders may discuss policy issues, thereby contributing indirectly to the IGF's policy-setting roles.

The lack of institutionalisation of dynamic coalitions within the IGF creates two problems, the first of which affects each of the three types of dynamic coalitions in much the same way, and the second of which is specific to working groups.

First, dynamic coalitions are entirely self-organised, with no procedure by which to be recognised or accredited so as to attain a formal affiliation to the IGF (save that they may informally request the Secretariat to list their contact details on its Web site). This contrasts with the case of workshops,

---

[138]Gordon MacLeod and Mark Goodwin, Restructuring an Urban and Regional Political Economy: On the State, Politics and Explanation, Political Geography 18 1999, 701

[139]IETF, Internet Users' Glossary (as in n. 10 on page 4)

[140]Including APNIC (as SIGs), auDA (as panels and committees), CGI.br, GAID (as Communities of Expertise or CoEs), the GKP (as Working Committees), and UNICTTF.

[141]IGP, Building an Internet Governance Forum (as in n. 144 on page 357), 6; Bertola, An Implementation Proposal for the Internet Governance Forum (as in n. 154 on page 358), 2

[142]See sections 5.2 on page 356, 5.2 on page 358 and 5.2 on page 379.

which are required to be approved by the Advisory Group and must comply with specific selection criteria directed to their relevance, capacity and multi-stakeholder structure.[143] It also contrasts with other organisations, including GAID whose Steering Committee is required to approve proposed CoEs by reference to an open set of criteria,[144] and ICANN's RALOs which approve the participation of their constituent At-Large Structures.

In consequence, there are no institutional checks and balances to ensure that the structure of a dynamic coalition is (and remains) multi-stakeholder and democratic, nor that its procedures are accountable and transparent. In the absence of such democratic safeguards, dynamic coalitions will tend towards oligarchy,[145] becoming narrow interest or advocacy groups,[146] inclined to fragment into competing coalitions in the same issue areas.[147] Whilst there is nothing wrong with stakeholders forming such groups, the problem is that without some criteria to distinguish them from more open and diverse deliberative fora, the plenary body of the IGF is to have no way of knowing whether to treat any recommendations that they might make as mere advocacy statements, or as the outcome of a deliberative democratic process.

The second significant problem from the under-institutionalisation of dynamic coalitions, which specifically affects working groups, is that there is no formal mechanism by which their reports or recommendations may be received by the IGF's plenary body as an input to its policy-setting role. In contrast the working groups of other organisations such as APNIC and UNICTTF[148] support and are coordinated with the programme of their plenary bodies; for example, an APNIC policy proposal that meets with consensus at the level of its originating SIG is then required to be tabled at a plenary Open Policy Meeting and reach consensus there also.[149]

---

[143]See section 5.2 on page 375.

[144]GAID, Business Plan for 2006–2007 ⟨URL: http://www.un-gaid.org/en/system/files/GAID+Business+Plan+07Dec2006.pdf⟩, Annex B

[145]See section 4.2 on page 198.

[146]As in the case of the A2K@IGF dynamic coalition, which includes only members with a programme of liberalisation of IPRs, and none with a balancing—even if reactionary—perspective such as Microsoft, the MPAA or WIPO. In contrast the Dynamic Coalition on Open Standards announced at its formation that "divergent viewpoints on topics of study are welcomed. Should the IGF DCOS not be able to reach a rough consensus, our goal will be to provide clarity around the argument, the divergence and its origins (who has different views and why) so that more informed decisions can be made": DCOS, IGF Dynamic Coalition on Open Standards ⟨URL: http://igf-dcos.org/wp-content/uploads/igf-general-statement-2006.odt⟩, 2.

[147]This does not mean that multiple dynamic coalitions in the same issue area should be prohibited, since this would exclude the potential benefits of regulatory competition (see section 3.4 on page 165). However only if competing recommendations are the output of equally multi-stakeholder and democratic processes can the plenary assess them on a level footing.

[148]UNICTTF, Strategic Plan ⟨URL: http://infolac.ucol.mx/eventos/reunion-varadero/strategic_plan.pdf⟩, 8

[149]With the superadded requirement of ratification by APNIC's Executive Council: see section 4.4 on page 307.

In contrast, the activities of the IGF's dynamic coalitions are quite divorced from those of the annual plenary meeting, with no occasion other than the brief daily "summing-up" (for Athens) or "reporting back" (for Rio) sessions available for them to informally present their output to the meeting, and no means for that meeting to deliberate upon the output in turn.

The effective outcome is that deliberation within dynamic coalitions, and the development of policy within the plenary body, flow in separate streams.[150] Thus following the Rio meeting, APC[151] and even the Swiss Government[152] were still calling for the convening of separate working groups of the IGF to develop policy recommendations.

Both of the problems noted above point to the need for stronger institutionalisation of the relationship between the IGF and its dynamic coalitions. This initially requires a mechanism for dynamic coalitions proposed by stakeholders to be recognised by their parent body, which would again most conveniently fall to a multi-stakeholder subcommittee of the IGF to be charged with that task. This was foreshadowed by the Internet Governance Project, amongst others, in proposing during the earliest open consultations in February 2006 that a multi-stakeholder bureau should approve the formation of working groups and appoint their facilitators, whilst consideration of their output would remain the responsibility of the plenary body:

> The Plenary has the following role:
>
> - It deliberates and discusses general issues and Working Group products, guided by the Chair and the Agenda;
> - Any accredited participant or group of them can petition the Bureau to create a Working Group
> - It reviews, discusses and approves or refuses to approve Working Group reports. Approval is based on "rough consensus" called by the Chair after sufficient deliberation. Approved reports are issued and publicized as IGF reports.[153]

By the date of the Rio meeting, this proposal had re-emerged in refined form, with support being widely expressed in the closing "Way Forward" session for the IGF's policy development function to be devolved to its

---

[150] Allen (as in n. 68 on page 435), 8

[151] APC, APC Statement on the Second Internet Governance Forum (as in n. 265 on page 391)

[152] Swiss Federal Office of Communication, Swiss Comments on the Second IGF Held in Rio de Janeiro in November 2007 and Recommendations for Future IGF Events ⟨URL: `http://www.intgovforum.org/images/20080208%20IGF%20swiss%20contribution.doc`⟩, 3

[153] IGP, Building an Internet Governance Forum (as in n. 144 on page 357); and see MMWG (as in n. 145 on page 357), 2.

specialist multi-stakeholder dynamic coalitions, much as the decentralised design of the Internet locates its intelligence at the edges of the network rather than at the centre. Ultimately however, the output of the dynamic coalitions must still be endowed with democratic legitimacy through the endorsement of the plenary body at large, and be cast in written form suitable for promulgation into other fora by a body such as the IGP's proposed bureau.

Whilst it is a given that such a bureau must be appointed by democratic or consensual means (as will be discussed under the following heading), its *operation* must also be democratic, which means that it must be accountable and transparent in the process by which it recognises new dynamic coalitions on the plenary's behalf. Central to this is that the process should be conducted by reference to a set of criteria that are cast in general terms, are public, not retrospective, are intelligible, not contradictory or impossible, relatively stable, and administered as proclaimed—in short, that fulfil Fuller's definition of the rule of law.[154]

In order for dynamic coalitions to legitimately contribute towards the fulfilment of the larger IGF's mandates of policy-setting and coordination, it is necessary that the criteria by which such coalitions are recognised include a minimal set of key principles mirroring those that apply to the IGF itself, including a subset of the structural criteria distilled at section 6.1 on page 417 along with some of the basic procedural principles that will be discussed at section 6.4 on page 474. These will include:

- multi-stakeholder (or open) composition;
- open membership;
- possibly a number of measures of accountability and transparency; and[155]
- a deliberative democratic or consensual decision-making process.

There is much room for more detailed criteria, consistent with these basic requirements, to be specified by multi-stakeholder, democratic or consensual means.[156]

[154]See section 4.3 on page 260.

[155]See section 6.4 on page 494.

[156]More broadly, Martens has suggested that the increasing importance of multi-stakeholder networks involving private sector actors, of which dynamic coalitions are an example, requires that "the United Nations should develop an effective regulatory and institutional framework for its relations to the private sector" which would include not only the positing of criteria for the formation of such networks, but also the appointment of a UN ombudsman as a contact point for complaints (Martens (as in n. 103 on page 27), 6). The establishment of the proposed UNMSP discussed at section 5.4 on page 407 could be one manner of eventually realising this recommendation.

Open fora

The final existing institutional structures of the IGF that are to be briefly examined are the open fora that made their debut in Rio.

One of the shortcomings of these open fora was that the subject organisations were not required to design them so as to support the fulfilment of the paragraphs of the IGF's mandate that had prompted the establishment of open fora in the first place. Specifically, the IGF is called upon to "[i]nterface with appropriate inter-governmental organizations and other institutions on matters under their purview,"[157] and to "assess, on an ongoing basis, the embodiment of WSIS principles in Internet governance processes."[158] These form part of the IGF's role of coordination, and in particular that of meta-governance.[159]

The fulfilment of this mandate will require more than a one-way channel of communication from the other organisation to the IGF, yet because that organisation alone currently determines the content of its open forum, and because there is no formal interface between its session and those of the plenary body, there are no means by which the IGF and the other organisation can engage in dialogue with the object of fulfilling the above paragraphs of the Tunis Agenda.

To address this, an open forum should be conducted not by a single stakeholder seeking to defend its position in the Internet governance regime, but by a multi-stakeholder panel similar to those that organise workshops, and accredited in a similar manner. If no such panel can be organised through the decentralised action of stakeholders, it is appropriate that one be appointed, just as the Advisory Group currently appoints panels of speakers for the plenary sessions.[160]

The working processes appropriate to an open forum, and to workshops more generally, are to be discussed below at section 6.4 on page 484.

Structural reform

Common to the reforms proposed above to the plenary body, Secretariat, Advisory Group, open consultation meetings and dynamic coalitions is the need for a new, democratically or consensually appointed multi-stakeholder body to exercise the following substantive functions:

---

[157] WSIS, Tunis Agenda for the Information Society (as in n. 5 on page 2), para 72(c)

[158] Ibid., para 72(i)

[159] See section 6.2 on page 436.

[160] Indeed, when the concept of the open forum was raised at the February 2007 consultations, it was accompanied by the suggestion that the IGF should be able to initiate its own workshops on key issues, rather than relying on individual stakeholders to do so: IT For Change, Taking Stock and the Way Forward (as in n. 237 on page 382), 2.

- approving the appointment of the Secretariat;[161]
- preparing documents for the use of the plenary body (a function currently performed by the Secretariat), including:
  - background briefing documents to inform discussion and foster the development of consensus at open consultation and plenary meetings; and
  - synthesis papers and reports summarising the contributions and discussions of stakeholders at such meetings;
- preparing the substantive agenda and programme for IGF meetings (that is, assuming the functions of the existing Advisory Group);
- creating multi-stakeholder democratic structures and processes for the IGF that incorporate any consensus of stakeholders expressed during open consultation meetings, including processes for:
  - the approval of workshops and recognition of dynamic coalitions;
  - the receipt of the output of workshops and dynamic coalitions as inputs to open consultation and plenary meetings;
  - policy development within the plenary forum; and
  - coordination with other existing bodies;
- appointing members to the panels of plenary sessions and (where necessary) open fora;
- assessing the consensus of open consultation and plenary meetings on substantive policy issues and the appropriate response to those issues; and
- preparing formal responses in the appropriate form based on the consensus of the plenary forum (such as recommendations for input into other organisations).

Such a body would essentially constitute the "effective and cost-efficient bureau" referred to in the Tunis Agenda and in early contributions from Forum hawks that preceded the formation of the Advisory Group.[162] Once it had become apparent, following the expiration of its initial mandate from the Secretary-General, that the Advisory Group possessed neither the capacity nor the legitimacy to fulfil the roles that the Tunis Agenda and the hawks demanded, some of the hawks began to renew their calls for a multi-stakeholder bureau,[163] and these are calls that would also be addressed by such a body as outlined above.

---

[161] Though while the IGF remains a UN-affiliated body, this will be on the nomination of the UN Secretary-General.

[162] Such as those of the IGP and MMWG referred to above: IGP, Building an Internet Governance Forum (as in n. 144 on page 357) and MMWG (as in n. 145 on page 357).

[163] See section 5.2 on page 385.

Consociationalism and the IGF

The establishment of a new multi-stakeholder bureau for the IGF will however have to be acceptable not only to the Forum hawks, but to the doves also, lest they withdraw from the governance network altogether.[164] This will require some thought to be given to their motivations for opposing an IGF with the structural capacity to fulfil its mandate to develop public policy recommendations, and to how those objections can be countered without compromising the democratic principle or the equality of all stakeholders within the network.

There is very little difficulty in explaining the doves' opposition in terms of the realist school of international relations theory.[165] From that perspective, it is a truism that the first priority of actors in the international system is to preserve their own political and economic power.[166] The status quo in Internet governance favours the forum doves, in that the United States holds authority over the global DNS root (with varying degrees of support from its allies), and has strongly supported the "private, bottom–up coordination"[167] of the Internet technical community, in which the private sector has heavily invested. *Ipso facto*, on the realist view, there is no reason for them to concede any ground to the Forum hawks who seek to disturb that status quo, particularly since the hawks—developing country governments and civil society—wield comparatively little political and economic power with which to do so.

Whilst the realist school has been found overall to offer a simplistic account of the status and motivations of international actors (particularly in understating the significance of non-state actors), it does plausibly explain the doves' opposition to the development of the IGF's capacity to make soft law through a consensus process, since such a process magnifies the power of minorities, as WSIS demonstrated.[168] Although allowing "rough consensus" addresses this to some extent, governments in particular are likely to be no more comfortable with rough consensus than they are with full consensus, since it may require them to accept politically unpopular concessions if they are left in a small minority; quite a far-fetched expectation if the US government's position on oversight of the global DNS root is taken as an example.

In designing a multi-stakeholder bureau for the IGF it will therefore be necessary to balance the need to ensure that the bureau is capable of effectively performing the roles outlined above, with the risk of overtly challenging the existing political and economic power of the Forum doves

[164] A prospect made most explicit by Chris Disspain of auDA in May 2007: see section 5.2 on page 385.

[165] This may be compared with the *stated* reasons for their opposition at section 6.2 on page 424.

[166] See section 3.1 on page 100.

[167] NTIA, Management of Internet Names and Addresses (as in n. 23 on page 36)

[168] See section 4.4 on page 316.

and thereby inducing them to leave or to undermine the IGF. A liberal institutionalist gloss upon the realist scholar's position would allow that even the Forum doves will have reason to support an empowered IGF if it will contribute towards a more sustainable international Internet governance regime for the long term, provided also that the soft power it exercises offers no significant threat to their own.

Such support from the doves would not be forthcoming for a multi-stakeholder bureau that acted by voting or rough consensus, because such a bureau might reach decisions that would challenge the authority of particular stakeholders or stakeholder groups; most obviously the sovereignty of governments. To continue the previous example, consider the (admittedly far-fetched) prospect of the bureau recommending the use of an alternate DNS root, if the only dissent to this recommendation came from the United States government and ICANN.

There can be nothing wrong with the IGF in plenary session reaching such a position through a process of democratic deliberation, even if only rough rather than full consensus on it is achieved in the end. Neither would (or could) the effect of the plenary's rough consensus be prevented from carrying its own normative resonance, which might independently influence the actions and shape the expectations of participants in the Internet governance regime. However, there are good reasons why the bureau ought not also in such a case elevate the plenary's rough consensus to the level of a formal recommendation of the IGF:

- It would not constitute governance by network, as in its pure form this is a process in which disparate stakeholders maintain their own authority and legitimacy in full measure, simply dipping into it to contribute towards the fulfilment of collaboratively agreed ends. Whilst governance by network may result in the realignment of power amongst transnational actors in the long term through processes such as regulatory competition, its purpose is not to facilitate the circumvention of the underlying authority of its members, which would be the effect of making a recommendation in defiance of the interests of significantly affected stakeholders.
- In any case, for the multi-stakeholder bureau to overrule the objections of significantly affected stakeholders or stakeholder groups would be futile, since the IGF is inherently a consensual body. The soft power that it possesses on its own account is unfit to overcome the political and economic power of its stakeholders; and that of governments least of all.[169] It is better for the structure of the IGF to

[169] Examples of this are given by the gTLD-MoU, over which the NTIA rode roughshod, and that of its successor the IFWP, which similarly at the hands of IANA and NSI "was ultimately bypassed and superseded by more powerful forces impatient with the transaction costs of an open, democratic process": Mueller, *Ruling the Root: Internet Governance and the Taming of Cyberspace* (as in n. 21 on page 35), 5.

overtly accommodate the autonomy of these more powerful forces in order to co-opt them as partners, than to stand against them, thereby inducing them to silently undermine its authority whenever its recommendations go against their interests.

Kenneth Cukier, moderator of two sessions at the Athens meeting, had also earlier written of the need for new multi-stakeholder structures not to reiterate old power struggles over Internet governance:

> The battle over the institutional design becomes a proxy for a much narrower interest one wants. In 1996 with the IAHC, this was for new TLDs by Internet entrepreneurs; in 1998 with ICANN it was for privately operated TLDs by NSI (now VeriSign); in 2005 with WSIS it is for more power by governments. As in previous cases, any arrangement that leaves other parties unsatisfied is bound not to endure long. Every party employs the term "multi-stakeholder" to mean that they will enjoy predominant power but leave a few, merely symbolic crumbs for others.[170]

The alternative is a structure which institutionalises the distinct but complementary authority of each of the stakeholder groups. Such a structure has already been described as a consociation. It will be recalled that the four attributes of a consociation in its ideal form are the sharing of power between the stakeholder groups within the organisation's decision-making organ or "grand coalition," their proportional election to that organ, the right of veto which they each hold over any proposal of mutual concern, and the preservation of their segmental autonomy over matters not of mutual concern.[171] Apart from procedural benefits to be discussed later,[172] the principal benefit of a consociational bureau which is segmented into stakeholder groups, over a bureau in which the stakeholders are required to make decisions only as a uniform entity, is that it formally and publicly institutionalises the equality of the stakeholder groups, thereby acting as a balance to the political and economic inequality of the stakeholder groups

[170] Cukier, Slouching Towards Geneva: Ten Unappreciated Axioms of Internet Governance (as in n. 94 on page 443), 4

[171] See section 4.4 on page 294.

The proposal of ENSTA and EUROLINC put forward in May 2007 for the formation of a "four components bureau" for the IGF is close to the consociational ideal: see EUROLINC (as in n. 252 on page 387) (and compare the proposal for three WSIS-style bureaus made by the G77 and China in February 2006: G77 (as in n. 166 on page 359)). Although the proposed four components bureau would only have a procedural mandate, it would be necessary for consensus to be reached not only within, but also between its four components, with much the same effect as granting them a power of mutual veto: Muguet (as in n. 252 on page 387), 20. The main distinction between these proposals and a consociational bureau is that the division of power between the stakeholder groups proposed here would not create separate bureaus, which defeats the essential purpose of the bureau as a forum for multi-stakeholder deliberation.

[172] See section 6.4 on page 475.

outside the IGF. This in turn fosters the value of deliberation between equals, which is one of the key requisites of deliberative democracy, and one of the most difficult to realise.[173]

To put this in context, whilst the power of mutual veto would allow governments to formally block a proposal supported by the other stakeholder groups (thus addressing their inability to abide the diminishment of their existing political and economic power), this only reflects their effective power to do so through domestic or intergovernmental rules in any case. However what is unique and valuable about the consociational structure is that this same power of veto is placed in the hands of the civil society and private sector members of the bureau, who could just as easily formally block a proposal supported by governments. This is a power that those groups lack within the present Advisory Group, since they sit in that group in their personal capacities and any balancing of stakeholder interests within it takes place informally and behind closed doors.

Nominating committee

Having concluded that a multi-stakeholder bureau is required, the next question that arises is how its members should be appointed. There are three basic alternatives. The first is for members to be appointed by the UN Secretary-General. This is the manner in which the Advisory Group is currently appointed, and is also the method of appointment of GAID's 60-member Strategy Council, and before that the 55 members and Panel of Advisors of UNICTTF.[174]

It might be thought that this alternative was strongly ruled out at section 6.3 on page 452, and indeed it was, except to the extent that it would be possible (and politic) during the term of the IGF's initial five-year mandate, for the bureau to continue to be officially appointed by the Secretary-General, but acting on the recommendations of the stakeholders. This however begs the question of how the stakeholders should make those recommendations.

In GAID's case, nominations for the private sector representatives were coordinated by the ICC, and those for the civil society representatives by CONGO through a volunteer nominating committee.[175] But to rely on external organisations to provide nominees simply shifts responsibility to them to ensure that the nominations are made in a democratically legitimate manner. Therefore the other two methods for the multi-stakeholder bureau's appointment (whether by the Secretary-General directly or by

[173] See section 4.3 on page 245.

[174] ECOSOC, Information and Communications Technology (ICT) Task Force ⟨URL: http://documents-dds-ny.un.org/doc/UNDOC/GEN/N01/260/47/pdf/N0126047.pdf?OpenElement⟩, 6

[175] Martens (as in n. 103 on page 27), 29 and see at 39 some other methods used by other UN-affiliated multi-stakeholder networks to nominate civil society and private sector representatives.

some peak body on behalf of an entire stakeholder group) must still be examined.

The second of them is voting. This is the method upon which APNIC, auDA and the GKP rely to elect their executive committees. However all of these organisations comprise a fixed body of members, whereas as Nitin Desai succinctly put it at the February 2007 consultation meeting, in the IGF's case "there's nobody who can elect a bureau, because there's no membership." A closer match for the IGF in this respect is ICANN, which of course attempted to hold elections for the At Large positions on its Board of Directors in 2000, but wrote the experiment off as a costly failure.[176]

The third possible method for the appointment of the IGF's multi-stakeholder bureau is to attempt to reach consensus on the appointments through democratic deliberation. After all, this is the process that was found to allow the IGF to fulfil its policy-setting functions despite its plenary body lacking a defined membership. However, it is not without reason that none of the other exemplar organisations utilise this time-consuming method of appointment, since it presents the risk that consensus might not be able to be reached.

Since none of these three basic alternative methods of appointment is appropriate, the answer lies in a hybrid approach, which includes elements of the hierarchical, democratic voting and consensual methods. A model for such a hybrid is found in the IETF's nominating committee (the Nomcom), which makes appointments to the IAB and to the IETF's IESG.[177]

The IETF Nomcom is a committee of at least fifteen, comprising a Chair, ten volunteers, three liaisons representing related organisations and an advisor.[178] The ten volunteers are chosen by random selection from an open pool of nominees, whose only qualification for membership is that they have attended three of the past five IETF meetings. The Chair is appointed by ISOC following a process of consultation with members of the IETF community and the board of ISOC.

The Nomcom's deliberations are to be "based on its understanding of the IETF community's consensus of the qualifications required," as well as being guided by criteria provided by the bodies to which candidates are to be appointed, though the final decision to put a candidate forward is put to a vote of the ten volunteers.

The Nomcom's recommendations are not final. Through a process described as "advice and consent," its recommendations must be ratified by ISOC's Board of Trustees in the case of appointments to the IAB, and by the IAB in the case of appointments to the IESG. When the confirming body withholds consent to a nomination, the confirming body and the Nomcom

---

[176]See section 5.4 on page 404.

[177]See section 2.2 on page 52.

[178]IETF, IAB and IESG Selection, Confirmation, and Recall Process: Operation of the Nominating and Recall Committees (as in n. 36 on page 40)

discuss the matter, and the Nomcom makes a new recommendation for any position left empty.

A similar process could be employed by the IGF for the appointment of its multi-stakeholder bureau. The main modification required to the structure of the nominating committee is that there should be an equal number of seats for each stakeholder group, and that whilst the committee would deliberate as a whole, only members from a given stakeholder group would select that group's nominees, in order to preserve its autonomy within the bureau. This equates to the system of proportional representation within the grand coalition that is one of the hallmarks of consociational ordering.

A second but related related reform to the IETF model is that each stakeholder group within the nominating committee should be empowered to employ consensual procedures for the nomination of its bureau members, rather than being limited to voting. In particular, it is typical that seats on the executive bodies of intergovernmental organisations (for example the ISO Council and Presidency of the EU) will be held by member governments in rotation, typically with one third (initially selected by lot) stepping down every year. There is no reason in the short term why governments ought not to be able to agree that this also ought to prevail within the multi-stakeholder bureau of the IGF.

Another consideration is that of diversity: both of the nominating committee itself, and of its nominees for the bureau. In this regard, there are a number of alternative models to inform the IGF's approach. The IETF goes no further than prohibiting more than two members with the same primary affiliation (for example, the same employer) from acting on the Nomcom, and imposes no requirements on the diversity of the nominees.

Other organisations utilising nominating committees have different procedures; ICANN for example is not concerned with the NomCom's own diversity, but requires its slate of nominees to exhibit diversity in geography, culture, skills, experience, and perspective.[179] The FSC upholds diversity at each level; requiring both its multi-stakeholder nominating committee and the candidates it nominates to include members from the North and South constituencies, and for those candidates also to reflect regional and gender balance.[180]

For the IGF, it is also appropriate that diversity be upheld at both levels, as a measure of redressing the impediments of disadvantaged groups in participating in the IGF's democratic processes on an equal footing, which is a substantive democratic value.[181] However as to exactly what measures of diversity should be institutionalised in the composition of the nominating committee and its slate of nominees, there is room for disagreement.

Whilst it is clear enough that the digital divide and its underlying

[179] ICANN, Bylaws (as in n. 39 on page 41), article VI, section 5.
[180] FSC (as in n. 561 on page 297), Articles 50–53.
[181] See section 4.3 on page 285.

economic divide impede universal participation in Internet governance, do issues such as gender and disability present similar obstacles that must be overcome in order to achieve substantive democratic equality within the IGF? As there is no *a priori* answer to this question, the criteria to be satisfied by candidates for the nominations committee and the bureau, and the appropriate size for those bodies to make them sufficiently diverse, should be determined in the first instance through a process of democratic deliberation in which all those potentially affected can discuss the issue in the light of relevant background material.

Since this presents a chicken-and-egg scenario (as it would normally be the bureau that would take a decision on such issues, drawing upon the deliberations at open consultation meetings), herein lies the place for an hierarchical hand in performing the following "bootstrapping" functions (which are analogous to, but narrower than, those performed by ISOC and the IAB for the IETF's nominating committee):

- establishing the initial size, term and selection criteria for the multi-stakeholder nominating committee;
- establishing the initial size, term and selection criteria for the multi-stakeholder bureau;
- determining whether any (and if so which) non-voting liaisons or advisors should be appointed to the first nominating committee in order to assist it with its deliberations; and
- appointing the first chair of the nominating committee.

It is suitable that these tasks fall to the UN Secretary-General, after having solicited recommendations from the IGF in plenary session at an annual or open consultation meeting. In future, they would fall to the bureau.

Thus in summary, the first significant structural reform that is required for the IGF is the establishment of a nominating committee comprising equal numbers from each of the stakeholder groups, who would periodically deliberate upon the appropriate composition of a multi-stakeholder bureau for the IGF, and then separately nominate candidates from their own stakeholder groups either by voting or through consensual means. This nominating committee would be chosen by random selection from an open pool of volunteers, subject only to the fulfilment of criteria designed to ensure that the process is also substantively democratic. The establishment of these criteria, along with similar criteria for the bureau, and the appointment of the nominating committee's non-voting chair, liaisons and advisors, would be performed in the first instance by the Secretary-General, and thereafter by the bureau itself, in both cases acting upon any consensus that may emerge during deliberation by the IGF's plenary body.

Multi-stakeholder bureau

The second significant reform is the establishment of the multi-stakeholder bureau itself. The broad parameters for the structure of this body have already been established above, when it was determined that it should be a hybrid between a standard deliberative democratic organ and a consociation:

- it is to include an equal number from each stakeholder group;[182]
- it is to pursue its operational programme through deliberation as a unitary body;[183] and
- each of the stakeholder groups should possess a power of veto over the bureau's output, even if it has already achieved rough consensus within both the bureau at large and the IGF in plenary session.

This immediately raises the question, how are those stakeholder groups to reach a coordinated view on when to exercise their right of veto? Whilst a more detailed answer will be given when considering the bureau's processes,[184] either consensual or democratic means may be used, and they may be tailored to the stakeholder group in question. This is another of the main benefits of the consociational form, which allows for the governmental group, for example, to require full rather than rough consensus to be reached on a recommendation if its veto is to be withheld. In fact, "there is no reason why a UN multi-stakeholder process should exclude an inner intergovernmental process, between governments, using existing UN rules, within [*scil* with] a defined membership."[185]

It follows that unlike in the present Advisory Group (but in common with all eight exemplar organisations, and almost all other UN bodies), members of the bureau will be appointed in a representative rather than a personal capacity, at least to the extent that the decisions they make will be for a particular stakeholder group. The importance of this is that stakeholders are appointed to the bureau not simply because of their personal merit, but because their participation provides a balanced base of legitimacy for the bureau that is drawn from the values of each stakeholder group.[186]

---

[182] The exact number should be determined in open consultation, balancing need for diversity against the fact that deliberation is easier in smaller groups: see section 4.3 on page 282.

[183] Including preparing briefing documents, meeting agenda and synthesis papers and reports, and reducing the consensus of the plenary body on substantive matters into draft recommendations, and on procedural matters into proposals for reform of the IGF's structures and processes.

[184] See section 6.4 on page 475.

[185] Muguet (as in n. 252 on page 387), 19

[186] That is, for governments the voice of their citizens as a sovereign nation, for the private sector the value of economic efficiency, and for civil society substantive public interests that cut across national boundaries or otherwise are inadequately represented by governments: see section 4.2 on page 204.

Two justifications have been given for the appointment of Advisory Group members in their personal rather than representative capacities. The first, that this allows for "more full and active participation of all members" (as claimed by ISOC at the February 2007 consultations), will arise for consideration in the following section on the IGF's processes. However there is a second, structural, justification which is that appointing members in representative capacities could risk "enshrining a fixed system of representation."[187]

This risk is minimised by the fact that each new bureau will be appointed by a new, randomly-appointed nominating committee. It is further reduced by appointing bureau members as representatives of stakeholder groups rather than of particular stakeholders, so that their mobility between employers, governments or organisational affiliations will not affect their seats. Appointing members to represent stakeholder groups also allows unaffiliated individuals to sit on the bureau within the stakeholder group that they are best qualified to represent (most likely civil society).

The next question of structure that has yet to be addressed relates to how the chair of the bureau should be appointed. Rather than being a policy-setting role, the appropriate role of the chair is simply to preside over meetings of the bureau, to coordinate its work programme, and to act as a point of contact for the IGF's Secretariat and other bodies with which the IGF is required to coordinate. Even so, it is inevitable that the substantive values of its incumbent will influence the manner in which the role is performed, as was found above to have been the case for the Secretariat and Advisory Group.

For this reason, a number of the earliest submissions on the appropriate structure and composition of a bureau for the IGF, even from Forum doves, stressed the importance of ensuring the diversity and accountability of the chair. ISOC, for example, suggested that rather than a single chair drawn from a given stakeholder group, there should be a panel of rotating co-chairs.[188] There is no example of this from amongst the exemplar organisations, but the appointment of co-chairs from different stakeholder groups has long been a practice of consultation panels in the Australian telecommunications regime.[189] Another instructive example is that of the CS-IGC, which although not a multi-stakeholder group, has two Coordinators who are elected for alternating two-year terms. Whilst the Advisory Group had two co-chairs for the Rio meeting, neither came from outside the governmental stakeholder groups.

---

[187]Government of Canada, Canadian Comment on First IGF ⟨URL: http://www.intgovforum.org/Feb_igf_meeting/Canadian_comment_on_first_IGF.DOC⟩, 2

[188]ISOC, ISOC Statement, Internet Governance Forum Meeting 17 February 2006 (as in n. 168 on page 360), 1. See also Government of Australia, Programme Committee—Internet Governance Forum ⟨URL: http://www.intgovforum.org/contributions/Au_govt_input_Program%20Committee.pdf⟩, 2.

[189]Such as Telstra's Consumer Consultative Council (TCCC) and the former Consumer Advisory Council (CAC) of what is now Communications Alliance.

Three best practices can be drawn out from these suggestions and examples:

- Rather than being appointed by the UN Secretary-General, the chair should be selected by democratic or consensual means by the bureau itself. Although a consensus decision should be allowed where possible, given that the bureau has a defined membership and therefore forms a convenient body of electors, it will be much more practical for it to vote for the chair from a pool of candidates drawn from its own number.
- The rotation of the candidates for chair among the stakeholder groups is necessary to ensure the bureau's legitimacy as the peak body of a multi-stakeholder governance network.[190]
- The election of co-chairs, as well as supporting the bureau's multi-stakeholder legitimacy, adds a layer of accountability to the bureau that is absent from the Advisory Group.[191]

In like manner, the bureau should be entitled to appoint its own advisors and liaisons, who would provide information to guide the bureau in its deliberations and act as a conduit for communication between the IGF and other participants in the Internet governance regime. Amongst the exemplar organisations, similar arrangements exist in ICANN (whose Advisory Committees each appoint a liaison to its board) and CGI.br (which includes a non-voting Internet expert), as well as the IETF's Nomcom (which contains three liaisons and an advisor) and even the IGF's Advisory Group (to which the Chairs have appointed their own Special Advisors).

Despite the fact that these positions would not participate in decision-making, due to their privileged position of influence upon the policy-setting process, the principle of subsidiarity indicates that ultimate responsibility for their establishment and appointment should rest in the bureau at large, though there is no reason why it could not delegate those tasks to the chair and even institutionalise that arrangement in standing rules that future bureaus could follow.

The same applies to the case of standing or *ad hoc* subcommittees that the bureau may wish to form, such as drafting committees (like those into which WGIG was divided), an appeals committee (such as that of the CS-IGC), and liaisons for appointment to other organisations. It is unnecessary for present purposes to be prescriptive about these internal structures, provided that the means by which they are established are themselves the product of multi-stakeholder democratic deliberation.

---

[190] Rotation between geographical regions, although not required as a matter of principle, could also be justified on substantive democratic grounds if it were to meet with the consensus of an open consultation meeting.

[191] Accountability will be discussed further at section 6.4 on page 498.

So in summary the multi-stakeholder bureau of the IGF is to be a balanced group of individuals appointed as representatives of their stakeholder groups, who are to deliberate on its operational programme together, but to exercise a power of veto of its formal recommendations within the stakeholder groups. Its chair, subcommittees, advisors and liaisons are to be appointed by the bureau itself. In the case of the chair, who exercises a special coordinating role, this should be done by voting, subject to the position's rotation through all of the stakeholder groups and the appointment of two co-chairs to provide continual stakeholder balance.

6.4 Processes

Although the establishment of a new multi-stakeholder nominating committee and bureau for the IGF, in place of the UN Secretary-General and his Advisory Group, would be a significant reform, it would not be nearly as revolutionary as the establishment of ICANN was for the management of critical Internet resources. In this context, it is laudable how much the Tunis Agenda and the IGF's Secretariat have gotten right: the open and multi-stakeholder composition of the plenary forum, the avoidance of inflexible representative structures, and the adherence to cultural values of the Internet such as decentralisation, openness, egalitarianism and cosmopolitanism, reflected for example in the bottom–up character of its dynamic coalitions.

Having said this, much of where the IGF falls short lies not in its structure but in its processes. Unless the theoretical openness of the plenary forum is matched with processes that actually render it reasonably accessible to all affected stakeholders, this not only defeats the openness of the structure, but can also obscure the need for reform. Such a gap between theory and practice has been observed in the case of ICANN,[192] and as a broader phenomenon, for example by Mathur and Skelcher who note that although an organisation's structure may appear democratic on the surface, this may easily be undermined in practice:

> For example, members of the public may have a right to attend meetings of the decision-making body, but notices drawing attention to the time and place of the meeting may be written and published in inaccessible ways, and the location of the meeting may constrain attendance by citizens. Sometimes the implementation gap between formal rules and actual practice will be a matter of lack of foresight or commitment by the organisation; other times it may be a deliberate strategy to limit democratic engagement.[193]

[192] Johnson and Crawford, The Idea of ICANN (as in n. 50 on page 192)
[193] Mathur and Skelcher (as in n. 395 on page 265), 9

An obvious example of this implementation gap in the case of the IGF is the holding of consultation meetings in Geneva, which privileges intergovernmental stakeholders and governments with permanent delegations in that city, and to a lesser extent the well-resourced private sector, over stakeholders from civil society and developing countries. Similarly, for the IGF's plenary meetings, the class of venue to which governments are accustomed may not be adequately accessible to civil society.

Further analysis of the procedural reforms required of the IGF in order for it to fulfil its potential as a democratic multi-stakeholder governance network requires a more thorough conceptual framework. This can be taken directly from Chapter 4, in which the basic principles of liberal democratic governance were discussed under the four headings of representation, consent, transparency and accountability, and inclusion. These will be considered again here in turn in their application to the IGF's processes.

Representation

If formal decisions of the IGF are not to be made directly by its plenary body but through the proposed multi-stakeholder bureau, then the IGF becomes closer to a representative than a direct democracy. However, the bureau does not represent the plenary in the same sense that the parliament of a liberal democratic state represents the *demos*. Specifically, there is no need for it to act as a filter for the plenary's views, since the plenary is itself to adopt a deliberative process. Rather, the fact that the bureau's recommendations are to reflect the plenary's deliberative consensus means that it acts strictly as a mirror of the plenary.[194] In fact if anything, the image of the plenary that is reflected in the bureau may be slightly biased towards the interests of the disadvantaged, by reason of the criteria employed by the nominating committee to ensure that the bureau's composition is substantively democratic and diverse.

Exactly what processes should such a multi-stakeholder bureau then employ in making its formal decisions? There is no close functioning model that conveniently answers this question. Francis Muguet describes the IGF as a UN multi-stakeholder process that

> is completely new at the UN and in International Public Law anywhere. There are no UN rules concerning a full, equal footing, multi-stakeholder process, only concerning intergovernmental processes, it is a simple as that ... For example, the very question concerning "observers" is meaningless because there are no "observers" since all stakeholders are on an equal footing. ... There is no need to bend existing UN rules, but to

[194]See section 4.3 on page 245.

find new ones, when none exist. UN multi-stakeholder rules of procedures and working methods are to be invented.[195]

The UN multi-stakeholder process

This does overstate the point slightly, in that the development of a multi-stakeholder process for the United Nations has been a concern of the organisation since at least the release of the Cardoso Report on UN–Civil Society relations that was released in 2004, which recommended that "[s]ince networked governance is clearly emerging as an important aspect of policy-making, the United Nations must embrace and support it more overtly if it is to remain at the forefront of global policy-making."[196] Moreover, there are precedents for the UN multi-stakeholder process in two of the other organisations addressed in this chapter: UNICTTF, and its successor GAID.[197]

Taking UNICTTF first, this was an example of a multi-stakeholder organisation, formed by intergovernmental agreement, with equal decision-making power distributed among all its members. Like the IGF, it was directed not "to take over or supersede other important processes in this area," being "not envisaged as an operational or executing agency," yet at the same time it was required to "submit an annual report to the Secretary-General which will focus on the major emerging issues, including recommendations thereon."[198]

The main difference between UNICTTF and the IGF in structural terms is that the former had a defined membership of 55 who were appointed in representative capacities, along with a Chair whom the body would elect itself.[199] In this respect therefore UNICTTF can be viewed as something of a hybrid between the IGF in plenary session and the multi-stakeholder bureau proposed here.[200]

Although the detail of its working processes was not the subject of UN resolution, in practice decisions of UNICTTF were made by "broad consensus" or "general agreement," as assessed by its Chair.[201]

GAID illustrates the evolution of the UN multi-stakeholder structure and process towards a post-WSIS model that is closer to that of its sister

[195] Muguet (as in n. 252 on page 387), 19

[196] Cardoso, Cardoso Report on Civil Society (as in n. 147 on page 126), 33

[197] Beyond those, see Martens (as in n. 103 on page 27).

[198] ECOSOC, Information and Communications Technology (ICT) Task Force (as in n. 174 on page 467), 4–6

[199] Ibid., 6; Martens (as in n. 103 on page 27), 28. Originally there were 37, then 40 members.

[200] Though UNICTTF additionally had its own bureau of six, as well as a Panel of Advisors of thirty; which was also known as its Advisory Group and was a precursor to that of the IGF.

[201] See UNICTTF, Summary of Conclusions and Decisions ⟨URL: `http://www.astrid-online.it/E-governme/United-Nat/UN-Task-Force-Geneva-13mar2003.pdf`⟩.

body, the IGF. Thus GAID, like the IGF and unlike UNICTTF, does not possess a fixed membership; being structured as a decentralised governance network that is open to all interested stakeholders.

With this looser structure has come a restriction of its policy-making capacity. GAID is described explicitly as a "channel for multi-stakeholder input to policy debate to be conducted in intergovernmental organs,"[202] which "will not have an operational, policy-making or negotiating function" in its own right.[203] Thus unlike the IGF and UNICTTF, the making of recommendations does not form part of GAID's formal mandate.

GAID's two decision-making organs are a multi-stakeholder Strategy Council and a Steering Committee, both of which are appointed by the Secretary-General. The Strategy Council of sixty is divided into equal numbers of governmental and non-governmental members, and pursuant to its terms of reference "[p]rovides overall strategic guidance and vision to the Alliance."[204]What few decisions the GAID Strategy Council has made pursuant to these very general terms of reference have been made by consensus, as assessed by the Chair of the Steering Committee and as reduced to writing by its Secretariat.[205]

The Steering Committee is a smaller group of twelve led by a Chair, who are appointed by the Secretary-General to act in their personal capacities. The Steering Committee has a more detailed terms of reference which includes the approval of applications for the establishment of Communities of Expertise (GAID's equivalent of working groups) and stakeholder networks, the review of progress reports from these bodies, the approval of recommendations from the Secretariat, and the delivery of "inputs" (not "recommendations") on ICT for development issues to the Secretary-General.[206] The Steering Committee's decisions are also made by consensus, as assessed by the Chairman and reported by the Secretariat.[207]

The evolution of the UN multi-stakeholder process from UNICTTF through to GAID and the IGF illustrates that as the openness and inclusiveness of the plenary body has been increased, so it has been disempowered, with decision-making authority instead being concentrated at the highest executive level; or in practice, in the organisations' UN appointed Chairs and Secretariats. The UNICTTF's defence is that "stakeholders involved in

[202]UNICTTF, Principles and elements of a Global Alliance for ICT and Development (Multi-stakeholder Forum) ⟨URL: http://www.unicttaskforce.org/perl/documents.pl?do=download;id=961⟩, 2

[203]Ibid., 4

[204]GAID, Terms of Reference—Strategy Council ⟨URL: http://www.un-gaid.org/en/council/tor⟩

[205]Idem, Strategy Council Meeting: Informal Summary ⟨URL: http://www.un-gaid.org/en/system/files/KL+StraC+summary+8jul2006.pdf⟩

[206]Idem, Terms of Reference—Steering Committee ⟨URL: http://www.un-gaid.org/en/steering/tor⟩

[207]Idem, Meeting of the Steering Committee of the GAID: Informal Summary ⟨URL: http://www.un-gaid.org/en/system/files/summary+SteerCom_23Mar07.pdf⟩

the ICT TF sometimes have competing or even conflicting aims. Organizations, including multilateral, bilateral and civil society groups are often competing for influence, leadership, support, and attention."[208]

Whilst this is undeniable, to accept it as a justification for the relegation of those stakeholders to a lowly advisory role flies in the face of UN rhetoric about the need for multi-stakeholder public policy governance, for which the proffered alternative of participatory democratic consultation is a poor substitute. The democratic principle, which specifies that governments must operate with the consent of the governed, and the principle of subsidiarity which requires that governance should be exercised at the lowest practical level, require more. So too, for that matter, does the Tunis Agenda.

A consociational multi-stakeholder process

How then, should the bureau produce its recommendations or other formal output, given that in doing so it is to act as a mirror of the plenary body, for which the United Nations multi-stakeholder process offers an inadequate model?

Referring back to section 6.3 on page 462, which listed seven substantive functions that it had been found such a bureau would need to perform, the process of making formal recommendations is made up of the last two functions: assessing the consensus of the plenary body as to the policy objectives to be achieved and the appropriate means of achieving them, and preparing any appropriate formal output for the IGF based on that consensus, such as recommendations for input into other organisations.

Since it has now been determined that the bureau should be consociational in form, it is also necessary that once draft recommendations or the like have been prepared, they must be separately approved by each stakeholder group within the bureau, by giving that group the opportunity to exercise its right of mutual veto.

These three phases, then—determining the consensus of the plenary body on a particular issue, drafting any applicable recommendation or statement that may be required in response, and then seeking the assent of each stakeholder group—form the core of the consociational multi-stakeholder process by which the bureau represents the views of the plenary body. The phases may also be iterative. That is, if a stakeholder group determines to exercise its veto, this may indicate that:

- the bureau's assessment of the consensus of the plenary body was imperfect, and should be carried out again (which may involve returning the issue to the plenary for further deliberation in light of the stakeholder group's veto);

[208] UNICTTF, Strategic Plan (as in n. 148 on page 459), 7

- the form in which the recommendation was drafted did not adequately conform to the consensus that had been assessed, which may require it to be brought back to the bureau for amendment until the veto can be overcome consistently with the plenary's consensus; or
- the policy objective upon which rough consensus was reached in the plenary forum is not capable of reaching full consensus within the multi-stakeholder bureau, in which case the plenary will be required to find another mechanism by which to pursue that objective (such as through the decentralised collective action of a dynamic coalition).[209]

The processes involved in the first phase outlined above, assessing the consensus of the plenary forum, will be considered under the following heading of consent, along with the analogous processes of assessing the consensus of workshops and dynamic coalitions.

As for the second phase, in which the bureau develops a formal expression of the public policy upon which the plenary forum has reached a consensus, the processes involved are simply those required to deliberatively develop an agreed text within a relatively small, multi-stakeholder group, much as WGIG did when producing its report. These processes will also be dealt with under the next heading, when considering the use of democratic deliberation within each of the IGF's organs. However two distinguishing features of these processes within the context of the multi-stakeholder bureau should be noted here:

- In many cases a proposed recommendation or statement may already have been drafted by a dynamic coalition (or perhaps by one or more stakeholders within the plenary body) around which a consensus of the plenary body has grown. In such cases, following the principle of subsidiarity, the role of the bureau will not be to draft the recommendation, but to endorse or reject it, much in the same manner as the Executive Council of APNIC is required to ratify policy proposals emanating from its SIGs.

  In other cases it will be necessary for the bureau itself to draft the text of a recommendation, either because there is no relevant dynamic coalition to do so, or because the dynamic coalition's draft does not accord with the consensus of the plenary body.
- Because, like the nominating committee, the bureau has a defined membership, the bureau could have recourse to voting in the event of being unable to reach consensus. For the bureau to consensually adopt such a voting procedure and to loosely institutionalise this in its standing rules would be to no stakeholder's disadvantage, given that any recommendation the bureau may develop during the second

[209]See section 6.2 on page 420.

phase in the decision-making process is subject to the consensus of all stakeholder groups during the third phase. However, for the process to remain deliberatively democratic, it should always aim towards consensus, even if that is not ultimately achieved.

The third phase in the bureau's decision-making process is that which provides each stakeholder group with the opportunity to veto any decision of the bureau at large that may have been reached during the second phase. Unlike the second phase which involves deliberation amongst the bureau's members as a multi-stakeholder entity, in the third phase of the process, the stakeholder groups decide whether to exercise their collective powers of veto separately.

Such separation of the stakeholder groups during the third phase carries two advantages, other than those already noted during the discussion of consociation and in considering the structural advantages of a consociational bureau.[210]

The first is that since the form of the consociational bureau is not prescriptive about how a stakeholder group should decide to exercise its power of veto, this phase allows for the different characteristic working methods of each stakeholder group to be accommodated.

So for example, governments may require a face-to-face meeting between diplomats to decide upon their exercise of the power of veto, while civil society may be accustomed to making such decisions by rough consensus using online tools, and the private sector representatives might even prefer to delegate the decision to a representative association such as the ICC. The segmentation between stakeholder groups in a consociation brings all of these modes of decision-making together within the bureau.[211]

The second benefit of each stakeholder group within the bureau sharing the power of mutual veto during the third phase of decision-making is that this will influence the shape of deliberations during the second phase; not only by reinforcing the equality of each group as previously noted, but also by streamlining the internal politics of the bureau. Avoiding the unwieldy need for a particular form of recommendation to be negotiated between fluid networks formed from amongst (say) forty individuals, instead it will be possible to move forward so long as the three stakeholder groups, who hold ultimate decision-taking power, are able to reach a rough accord between themselves. Collaboration and compromise between stakeholder groups then takes priority over power relations between the individuals who happen to constitute the bureau at any given time. As well as better meeting the deliberative democratic conditions of freedom and equality,[212]

[210]See sections 4.4 on page 294 and 6.3 on page 464.
[211]Compare Muguet (as in n. 252 on page 387), 20.
[212]See section 4.3 on page 282.

this also assists the bureau to overcome the concern noted by Kenneth Cukier that

> [t]he process of Internet governance fails because so far the notion of collaborative policy-making is completely missing—there are no ideological camps, no political parties or coalitions in which groups are forced to sublimate their ideal self-interest for a suitably acceptable compromise, in order to attain the benefits of the workable system as a whole.[213]

One possible criticism of a divided bureau is that the separation between stakeholder groups could create conflict and induce participants, cloistered in their fixed constituencies, to adopt entrenched positions. This in turn could limit the range of options and the perspectives surrounding a given issue from being fully considered, which works against the subsequent formation of consensus. This problem is an instance of the "silo effect" which produces conflict between separated organisational units,[214] and which in turn results from the phenomenon of groupthink that exists within such homogeneous units.[215]

Without necessarily accepting that the stakeholder groups in the present instance are particularly homogeneous, this potential weakness is overcome here by the fact that the third phase of decision-making, in which stakeholders deliberate separately upon the exercise of their right of mutual veto, is preceded by the second phase of full multi-stakeholder deliberation, which enables all perspectives to be aired at an early stage (not to mention that democratic deliberation has also already taken place within the plenary body when substantive consensus was reached).

A related criticism is that not only might the third stage of decision-making within a particular stakeholder group not be deliberative, it might not even be democratically accountable and transparent. Indeed if ICANN's GAC, or even the IGF's Advisory Group for that matter, is taken as a likely model upon which for the governmental stakeholder group to structure itself, this can be taken as a given. For now the same answer can be given to this as to the preceding criticism—that it is sufficient that the multi-stakeholder phase of deliberation within the bureau is open and transparent—though this criticism will also be further addressed below.[216]

A third possible criticism is that, in common with other consociational structures, the bureau will require a strong set of shared norms that inhibit

---

213 Cukier, Slouching Towards Geneva: Ten Unappreciated Axioms of Internet Governance (as in n. 94 on page 443), 5

214 Wyatt Warner Burke, *Organization Change: Theory and Practice* Thousand Oaks, CA: Sage Publications, 2002, 163

215 See section 4.4 on page 316.

216 See section 6.4 on page 494.

the use of the power of veto except where necessary to protect a stakeholder's core interests,[217] in order to mitigate the risk of consensus being blocked by a small minority during the third phase.[218]

In response to this, it should be noted that any recommendation that has passed the second phase is one which already carries the support of the majority of the bureau, as determined either by voting or rough consensus. Except where support for the recommendation falls strictly along stakeholder group lines (rather than, for example, between Forum hawks and Forum doves), this support is also likely to extend to some degree into each stakeholder group. It is therefore more likely that a proposal will fail at an earlier phase than that it will be vetoed out of hand once it reaches the third phase.

More importantly however, the process of democratic deliberation that resulted in a recommendation receiving majority support within the bureau will itself tend to induce the development of the group norms such as trust, cooperation and equality that are necessary to prevent the power of veto from being misused.[219] These norms will also be reinforced over time as the IGF's social capital is developed through its successful operation as a governance network.[220]

Consent

What has yet to be examined are the processes to be employed to ensure that the bureau's discussions actually are adequately deliberative, thereby fulfilling the democratic principle of consent which underlies its legitimacy. This is even more important in respect of the plenary body, for which the principle of consent cannot be fulfilled by making it proportionally representative.

A starting point is for the strengths and deficiencies of the IGF's existing processes for deliberation to be identified. Its strengths can be stated in three points, each of which relates back to earlier discussions of the features of deliberative democracy:[221]

- its structure is open to all members who wish to participate, and is free of either cost or coercion;
- it is relatively pluralistic in composition, displaying considerable diversity of opinion both within and across stakeholder groups; and

[217]Skelcher (as in n. 554 on page 295), 105

[218]See section 4.4 on page 316.

[219]Uphoff (as in n. 196 on page 220)

[220]See section 4.3 on page 240.

[221]See section 4.3 on page 245.

- it is publicly committed to the multi-stakeholder principle that holds that all members deliberate as equals.

The main deficiencies of the IGF as a forum for democratic deliberation can also be stated in three points:

- as noted at the commencement of this section, there is an implementation gap between the openness of its structure and its actual accessibility to all affected stakeholders, particularly those who are disadvantaged;[222]
- its lack of any structures or procedures for decision-making, particularly at the plenary level, effectively denies the IGF a policy-setting role, reducing it at best to a participatory democratic organ serving to inform external decision-makers, but disempowered from forming policy positions of its own; and
- even were it empowered to make recommendations, these would not be subjected to the test of public reason that characterises deliberative democratic discourse, because:
  - the fora within which discussion takes place, such as plenary sessions and workshops, are conducted in a seminar format that discourages participants from engaging with each other's perspectives and working towards a consensus in which all those perspectives are rationally reconciled; and
  - similarly, written contributions and submissions are prepared by stakeholders in isolation from one another, without the opportunity for their refinement through public analysis and debate to produce a balanced body of background material such as is employed in most institutional frameworks for democratic deliberation.[223]

The first two of these deficiencies have already arisen for consideration elsewhere. A summary of the strategies required to address the first deficiency, as to the IGF's capacity to capture the participation of all affected stakeholders, was given at section 6.3 on page 444 and will be revisited under the heading of inclusion below.[224] As to the second deficiency, the importance of the IGF's policy-setting role and the structures necessary to facilitate its performance were considered in the two preceding sections of this chapter.[225] This leaves the third deficiency, as to the IGF's incapacity to engage in deliberation towards the end of achieving a rational multi-stakeholder consensus, to be dealt with here.

---

[222]See section 6.4 on page 474.

[223]See section 4.3 on page 253.

[224]See section 6.4 on page 504.

[225]See sections 6.2 on page 420 and 6.3 on page 442.

Democratic deliberation

This last incapacity is illustrated by the fact that when the IGF or its dynamic coalitions have developed policy positions, these have tended to reflect the prevailing views of their dominant members, rather than emerging from a process of deliberation between equals in which the preferences of all stakeholders are considered and balanced.

This is evident at several levels, including those of the open consultation meetings, the Advisory Group, the annual plenary meetings and the workshops and dynamic coalitions:

- The views expressed by stakeholders in February 2006 as to the priority to be accorded to development issues became significantly stronger in May following the Secretariat's pronouncement that an emerging consensus on this point had been identified, although this was a consensus to which comparatively few had by then contributed;[226]

- The discussion papers prepared by Everton Lucero for the May 2007 meeting of the Advisory Group were not in fact discussed, and at a subsequent CS-IGC organised workshop on "Fulfilling the Mandate of the IGF" held in Rio, Lucero expressed the view that they had been deliberately ignored;

- Despite the strong statements of certain stakeholders leading up to the Rio meeting that new governance arrangements for Internet naming and numbering were required,[227] no voices putting this position were heard during the panel on critical Internet resources; and

- Most of the workshops and dynamic coalition meetings in Athens and Rio were dominated by presentations from panelists selected by the organisers, with little time being allocated for the presentation of alternative perspectives from the floor. Few meetings therefore presented a balanced account of the views of all affected stakeholders. As Milton Mueller put it at the February 2008 open consultation meeting:

  > Freedom expression advocates were in one workshop talking to each other. Advocates of stricter controls on content in the name of child protection were in another panel. Those people need to talk to each other, not past each other.

---

[226]See section 5.2 on page 358.

[227]Third World Network (as in n. 235 on page 381)

Instilling a more deliberative quality into the IGF's processes is therefore a project to be undertaken across multiple institutional layers. Furthermore, it is to extend within each of these layers from the earliest phase of discussion—that of agenda-setting—through to the final phase in which its output passes through to the next layer (or falls back to the previous one).

As will shortly be seen, the specific processes best suited for adoption at a given layer of governance within the IGF, or at a given phase within each layer, will differ. Processes will also differ markedly between those applicable to participants present in person, and those participating online.[228] But despite this variance in detail, the underlying features of most institutionalised frameworks for democratic deliberation, as examined in Chapter 4,[229] are common and relatively simple:

- deliberation takes place against a background of balanced briefing material, designed essentially to constitute the group as an informed public sphere in miniature; this material may take written form, or be presented in person by subject matter experts, or both;
- the group's discussions are guided by one or more impartial moderators or facilitators, who are to endeavour to maintain the conditions of democratic deliberation (such as equality and orientation towards consensus), and in the case where a group is divided into smaller units, to coordinate between these and the larger group; and
- the group, and any smaller units into which it is divided, are to be of pluralistic composition, in order to ensure that as many different perspectives as possible are represented in the deliberation, each of which is to be debated against the others on an equal footing without recourse to claims of external authority.

Any of the large-scale structures for democratic deliberation that incorporate these features, including the 21st Century Town Meeting, citizens' assembly, consensus conference and speed dialogue, have the potential to be applied directly to the IGF's plenary body. Since speed dialogues came close to being trialled for the Rio IGF meeting, and have been successfully employed by the ITU in an analogous context, these seem the most natural choice of method to improve the deliberative character of the IGF's plenary meetings.

As Henry Judy of the American Bar Association explained at the May 2007 open consultation meeting, the strengths of the speed dialogue format include the following:

[228] Though for present purposes, processes for online deliberation will be left aside, to be revisited under the heading of inclusion at section 6.4 on page 504.

[229] See section 4.3 on page 253 and compare section 4.4 on page 298.

> First, it introduces a large number of people to one another who might otherwise not have spoken to one another. It is a great networking tool, and it stimulates networking, and thus it would strengthen the multiparticipant orientation of the forum. Secondly, it is a great equalizer. The great and the small are at the same table and must listen to one another. Third, it forces people to speak crisply. You do not have time for the extended use of diplomatic code, euphemisms, and circumlocution. Fourth, it is useful for synthesizing the state of opinion and emotion in the group.

The reference here to "synthesizing the state of opinion" of the group is noteworthy. Ordinarily, speed dialogues are not used at the final stages of decision-making; unlike, for example, the 21st Century Town Meeting in which the closest to a rough consensus position that the groups achieves is put to a formal vote at the end of the meeting. However for the plenary body of the IGF, which as Nitin Desai is fond of noting has no defined membership, vote-taking is out of the question. Instead, it is for the bureau, with the assistance of the facilitators of the speed dialogue, to assess the state of the group's progress towards consensus following a speed dialogue session, as a preliminary stage to the deliberation and more formal decision-making phase that is to occur within the bureau. More will be said of this process of assessment under the following heading.

As originally scheduled for Rio, there was to have been an Athens-style moderated panel presentation and a speed dialogue session for each of the four main themes of the meeting, taking place one after the other. However, it was the speed dialogue session which was to have been held first, and the panel presentation second. More consistent with deliberative democratic principles would be for the order to be reversed, so that the panel presentation could provide the background of balanced briefing material upon which participants in the speed dialogue would begin their deliberations.

The panel presentations in turn should be built upon the written submissions contributed by stakeholders and dynamic coalitions in advance of the meeting, which provide a more diverse base of briefing material than that which can be provided by a necessarily limited group of panelists (around twelve for Athens, and six for Rio). Whereas the selection of briefing material is in most deliberative democratic models a matter for the group's facilitators in consultation with stakeholders, there is precedent in the case of the consensus conference for the partial devolution of this function to the group itself. This would also be so in the case of the IGF, in that whilst written submissions would be received and published without moderation (as is the case already), it would fall to the bureau to draft a synthesis paper summarising all of the contributed perspectives in a factually accurate and balanced manner.

This synthesis paper would then be translated and distributed to those attending the meeting, both by its advance publication on the IGF's Web site and by its inclusion in the materials received by each delegate upon registration. This did not occur for the Athens meeting, when the synthesis paper was published by the Secretariat only after many participants had already departed for the meeting, and in neither Athens nor Rio was the paper distributed with the registration materials or referred to during any of the plenary sessions.

Doubtless, there will be challenges in implementing speed dialogues at the IGF. As Henry Judy summarised the drawbacks of speed dialogues:

> First, it depends on each table having a reporter who can represent the views at the table in the summary in a skillful and disinterested manner. It is not easy to find a Markus Kummer for each table. Second, it requires a high degree of prior planning and instruction on the part of the organizers as well as a high degree of compliance on the part of the participants. Otherwise, it can become a confusing and unproductive exercise in herding cats, if I may use the English expression. I have heard it said that the likelihood that the technique will be successful is directly proportional to the tendency of the group to start its meetings on time. Third, it tends to work less well as the group becomes larger.

To some extent these difficulties, which largely accord with those discussed in Chapter 4,[230] may require the IGF to become better resourced so as to enable it to attract a skilled team of facilitators, along with sufficient translators for each of the round-table groups (though resourcing constraints were not given as a reason for speed dialogues being dropped from the Rio programme).

However they will also require the inculcation of shared norms such as trust, equality and cooperation that are necessary for the success of any consensual or deliberative democratic decision-making process.[231] Whilst these cannot be developed instantaneously, for a core of IGF participants (including many of the members of civil society's CS-IGC and the private sector's ICC/BASIS) such norms have been in the process of development since the first PrepCom of WSIS in 2002. Whilst this group is only a narrow segment of the present-day IGF, it could provide a catalyst for the development of a broader culture of cooperation through mimetic replication of its own norms.[232]

Beyond this, the development of shared norms to reinforce the deliberative process can only come from the initiation, repetition and refinement

---

[230] See sections 4.3 on page 282, 4.4 on page 311 and 4.4 on page 316.

[231] See sections 4.4 on page 316 and 4.3 on page 245.

[232] See section 1.3 on page 16.

of that process, as stakeholders within the group learn to understand and trust each other, and the group as a whole builds up its social capital.[233]

The use of speed dialogues as a framework for democratic deliberation has been put forward above only for the plenary body. For smaller groups within the IGF such as the multi-stakeholder bureau, dynamic coalitions and open fora, different techniques may be required. (For present purposes, the plenary body in open consultation can also be considered as one of these smaller groups, since the number of members in attendance is of approximately an order of magnitude smaller than at the annual plenary meeting.)

Provided that it incorporates at least the three main features of the deliberative democratic frameworks identified above—the use of background briefing, the guidance of a moderator or facilitator, and the pluralism and equality of the group—there is no need to be prescriptive of the precise method by which democratic deliberation is institutionalised within the IGF's smaller subcommittees.

In particular, insights from models of small group democracy such as that of Gastil,[234] those from the study of deliberative democracy such as the citizens' jury,[235] and those of consensus in small groups such as the Consensus Workshop,[236] are all potentially applicable. It is a feature of the latter that defining the process to be followed forms the group's first item of business; although to bootstrap the group into a form capable of deliberating upon its own processes (let alone anything else), these must at least initially be specified by hierarchical means, such as a constitutional document if one exists, or by its chair, or through standing rules previously established by the group.

Without detracting from this latitude on matters of detail, some broad guidance for the processes to be adopted by the open consultation meetings, the workshops and dynamic coalitions, the open fora and the multi-stakeholder bureau does flow from the findings already made, particularly given that the structural relationship between these bodies requires their deliberative procedures to be coordinated to some degree. Taking these in turn:

- The main role of the open consultation meetings is in shaping the structure and processes of the IGF and the agenda of its meetings, drawing on written submissions contributed by stakeholders and dynamic coalitions, and summarised in a synthesis paper prepared by the Secretariat. If that synthesis paper is to serve as a suitable input to democratic deliberation in accordance with the first of the three

[233]See section 4.3 on page 240.
[234]See section 4.3 on page 257.
[235]See section 4.3 on page 253.
[236]See section 4.4 on page 298.

features identified above, then as in the case of the annual plenary meetings it should be prepared by the bureau rather than the Secretariat. This is because substantive judgment is involved in ensuring that a diversity of views is presented and that obvious factual inaccuracies are corrected, which is a responsibility that mirrors that of the mass media in the model of deliberation in the public sphere.[237]

The second of the three main features of frameworks for deliberative democratic identified above—supportive moderation or facilitation—is also lacking in the case of the open consultation meetings, in that they are conducted in a format of round-robin presentations which is not conducive to engagement between stakeholders. Nitin Desai has acknowledged this deficiency, pleading with stakeholders (though largely in vain) in May 2007:

> I would strongly urge people to, if possible, to [*sic*] comment on suggestions which have come from others, also, so that I get a sense of where people are. ... because that will help us to move towards some form of [consensus on] what we will do with this forum.

However it is agreed by scholars of deliberative democracy and consensual decision-making that rather than simply expecting stakeholders to engage with each other spontaneously, it is the role of the moderator or facilitator to structure the discussion to specifically encourage this behaviour. For example, in the Consensus Workshop, an initial brainstorming session in which all input is welcomed, is followed by a period in which those ideas are grouped and named, and then finally discussed in turn with the objective of reaching consensus.[238] The adoption of a similar process for the open consultation meetings would promote the development of far more considered recommendations from the group at large upon which for the bureau to draw.

- Like considerations apply to the workshops and dynamic coalitions (specifically those recognised as working groups), which have a similar but more specialised role to play in providing reasoned, multi-stakeholder input for the plenary body and the bureau in specific substantive issue areas. It is only if a workshop or dynamic coalition has been able to effectively deliberate in a democratic and multi-stakeholder fashion that its output should carry any greater weight with the plenary body or bureau than the submissions of individual stakeholders.

  Criteria are already specified to ensure that workshops held at plenary meetings are of multi-stakeholder composition, but beyond that

[237] See section 4.3 on page 250.
[238] See section 4.4 on page 298.

they do not specify that its proceedings should be democratic or consensual, and do not extend to dynamic coalitions. Whilst it would be possible to expand the criteria that workshops must satisfy and to extend them to dynamic coalitions, it has been seen that there may be quite legitimate reasons for the formation of workshops and dynamic coalitions that are not deliberatively democratic, such as networks or BOFs, which unlike working groups are not designed to directly provide input for the plenary body or bureau.

Instead, whilst it remains necessary for the bureau to develop further criteria by which dynamic coalitions can be assessed for their compliance with democratic as well as multi-stakeholder principles,[239] it is quite possible for their compliance with certain of those criteria to be assessed *ex post facto*. In other words, rather than requiring them to document in advance how their decision-making processes will be deliberatively democratic or consensual as a condition of their approval by the bureau, a dynamic coalition, or for that matter a workshop, seeking to formally present its output to the plenary body could be required to submit to the bureau a report that documents the processes by which its recommendations were developed, and the extent of the consensus that was reached on them.[240]

- As far as open fora are concerned, the only additional consideration worthy of mention is the importance of the forum not being moderated by the chief executive of the organisation under consideration, but by an independent facilitator who would ensure that the forum addressed the role, structure and processes of the organisation in question with reference to the WSIS process criteria, along with the content of any relevant draft or final recommendations that the IGF had considered in plenary session.

- The final and most important subcommittee of the IGF whose processes fall for consideration is the multi-stakeholder bureau. The reports of workshops and dynamic coalitions effectively form part of the bureau's background briefing material as it deliberates on the IGF's formal output. So too does the input of any advisors and liaisons appointed to the bureau, along with the reports of any subcommittees established by the bureau, and indeed any consensus the plenary body itself may have reached either in open consultation or at its annual meeting.

  The bureau, then, does not lack for briefing material upon which to deliberate. What it does lack, or rather what its precursor, the Advisory Group, lacks, is the ability to act upon this input. In its present form, members of the Advisory Group discuss their views, but take only a very limited range of decisions on their own account.[241] This

[239] See section 6.3 on page 457.

[240] This option will be explored further under the following heading.

[241] See section 5.2 on page 364.

sits at odds with the object of democratic deliberation, which is a process not merely for dialogue but for decision-making.[242]

Reconstituted as the multi-stakeholder bureau, the group will have to become no longer a simple group of advisors to the UN Secretary-General (even though he remains as its figurehead), but a democratic executive committee in its own right, akin to the boards of directors of auDA and ICANN, or APNIC's Executive Council. The role of facilitating the group's adherence to deliberative democratic principles (perhaps following Gastil's guidelines for implementing small group democracy)[243] will fall naturally to its chairs.

Assessing consensus

One of the roles of the bureau that has received only cursory attention so far is that of assessing the consensus of the plenary body, along with that of dynamic coalitions or workshops submitting reports on their activities. Part of the difficulty of this endeavour lies in the lack of a universally accepted measure of consensus, given that even within the Internet governance regime, working definitions range from "general agreement" as in the case of APNIC,[244] to unanimity (though allowing for abstention) in the case of the W3C.[245]

For present purposes, the definition of consensus from Johnson and Crawford that was adopted in Chapter 4, and that is broadly consistent with deliberative democratic theory, will be accepted as appropriate for the IGF: that "opposition to a particular policy is limited in scope and intensity (or is unreasoned), and opposition does not stem from those specially impacted by the policy."[246]

It is noteworthy that the application of this definition to the IGF would not require full consensus or unanimity. This limits the capacity of individual stakeholders with limited interests in an issue to exercise disproportionate power over the decision-making process, whilst still preserving the rights of stakeholder groups to veto any measure that is against their interests as a whole, through the institutionalisation of this right within the bureau. At the same time, the definition looks not only to the number of stakeholders in dissent on a particular issue, but to the directness of their interest and the strength of the reasons for their position.

Although conceptually sound, the definition is very much a subjective one, which raises the prospect that the bureau might find consensus where

---

[242]See section 4.3 on page 245.

[243]See section 4.3 on page 257.

[244]See section 4.4 on page 307.

[245]See section 4.4 on page 309.

[246]Johnson and Crawford, Why Consensus Matters: The Theory Underlying ICANN's Mandate to Set Policy Standards for the Domain Name System (as in n. 541 on page 291)

it wishes to find it, and fail to find it where it does not. The appropriate response is to build in mechanisms of accountability to counteract this risk.[247] Some possible ways of doing so can be drawn from the experience of the use of consensus in other organisations of Internet governance. Two of those examined in Chapter 4 were ICANN and APNIC, which are also amongst this chapter's examples, and which will be revisited again here in turn.[248]

It will be recalled that ICANN assesses the consensus of the community upon proposed new policies by means of a formal Policy Development Process. Taken as a process intended to facilitate the formation of consensus, the PDP does not provide a successful model for the IGF to follow.[249] However what it has achieved, by requiring that the level of consensus upon any proposed new policy be fully documented, is to address criticisms that ICANN's board had previously ruled upon the existence of such consensus without any adequate factual basis for doing so.[250] The principle that may be drawn from ICANN's example is therefore that the most transparent and accountable way for the achievement of consensus to be assessed is through a process that is formally and openly documented.

An alternative and contrasting model is that of APNIC, which is a much more culturally homogeneous organisation than ICANN with a less tumultuous history. As described above, its process for establishing the achievement of consensus on a new policy is predicated upon the subjective judgment of the Chair of the Open Policy Meeting, but this is subject to various checks and balances: that the proposal first have been developed within the relevant SIG, then tabled four weeks ahead of the meeting, then achieved consensus at that meeting both amongst SIG members and in plenary session, then survived an eight week comment period, before finally receiving the majority approval of APNIC's Executive Council.

The most appropriate model for the assessment of consensus by the IGF's multi-stakeholder bureau is likely to be a hybrid of those of ICANN and APNIC. Like ICANN (only more so) the IGF is politically and culturally heterogeneous, and therefore the thorough documentation of any consensus claimed to have been achieved by its plenary body at an annual meeting or open consultation will avoid the same suggestions of partiality being made of the bureau that some have made of the Secretariat and Advisory Group.[251] The same applies to dynamic coalitions, who as noted above, ought in like manner to document the consensus that they have reached on any recommendations being forwarded to the bureau for presentation to the plenary body.

---

[247] See also section 6.4 on page 498 below.
[248] See section 4.4 on page 302.
[249] See section 4.4 on page 303.
[250] See section 2.1 on page 46.
[251] For example, by the Third World Network at the February and May 2007 consultations.

Furthermore, as in APNIC's case, it is also desirable for the achievement of consensus to be confirmed at more than one level. The procedures already put forward in this chapter ensure that this is so, as any consensus of the plenary body will be reconfirmed by consensus of the stakeholder groups within the bureau before it becomes a formal recommendation of the IGF. Similarly any consensus of a dynamic coalition (if accepted as such by the bureau) will have to be confirmed by the plenary body, before being reconfirmed by the bureau if it is to become part of the IGF's formal output.

The example of APNIC also teaches that any consensus reached at a plenary meeting should remain subject for a short period to the input of those who were unable to participate in that meeting. This practice will be discussed further when considering the ways in which to accommodate online participation in the IGF's processes.[252]

On this basis, a suitable initial process for the assessment of consensus by the multi-stakeholder bureau (subject, of course, to refinement through open consultation) would incorporate the following elements:

- if a proposed recommendation, statement or the like originated in a workshop or dynamic coalition, it must first have achieved the consensus of that body, as recorded in a written report to the bureau, before being presented to the plenary body for deliberation;
- in any case, a proposed recommendation or statement should be tabled in draft on the IGF's Web site ahead of the meeting at which it is intended that it be deliberated upon by the plenary body;
- if the bureau considers that consensus was reached by the plenary body, this should be recorded in its report of the meeting, along with the grounds for its conclusion that any opposition to the recommendation was limited in scope and intensity, was unreasoned, or did not stem from those specially impacted by it;
- the report of the meeting should be subject to an open comment period; and
- in deliberating upon the appropriate form in which to formalise a proposed recommendation or statement, the bureau should consider any comments received during the comment period and respond to them in the minutes of the meeting at which a decision is made.

Transparency and accountability

One example has just been given of a circumstance in which mechanisms of accountability are needed to guard against the subversion of democratic

[252] See section 6.4 on page 504.

processes by those in power; in that case, the bureau's power to influence the substantive programme of the IGF through its subjective assessment of the consensus of its plenary body. But numerous other examples can be given of circumstances in which transparency and accountability are as important as structure and process in ensuring that the IGF does not lapse into oligarchy.

Transparency

For instance, because the Advisory Group meets behind closed doors and utilises a secret mailing list, it was possible for one of its members to quietly insinuate that private sector support for the IGF and its Secretariat would be withdrawn if reforms unacceptable to that stakeholder group went ahead.[253] But for that communication being leaked, stakeholders at large might never have had as complete an explanation for the omission of those reforms from the IGF's agenda for Rio.

It is difficult to reconcile the Advisory Group's non-compliance with some of the most fundamental requirements of democratic transparency, such as the publication of agendas and minutes of its meetings, with the UN Secretary-General's promise at the outset that "the Advisory Group will carry out its work in an open, inclusive and transparent manner, and will seek to make the best possible use of electronic working methods, including online consultations."[254]

Although progress has been made in improving its transparency since the Rio meeting, the democratic transparency of a number of the other organisations to which the IGF has been compared in this chapter still far exceeds that of the Advisory Group, including in the case of ICANN's GNSO and ALAC, as well as CGI.br, the publication of full audio recordings of their meetings (omitting only the discussion of commercially or legal sensitive matters). ICANN also publishes an official blog as a less formal counterpart to the minutes of its board meetings.[255]

The Advisory Group's self-imposed seclusion, whilst incongruous, matches that of one other notable institution of Internet governance: ICANN's GAC. This is, of course, no coincidence, and points to the principal explanation for each body's lack of transparency: that governmental representatives are reticent about speaking freely and on the record during intergovernmental negotiations.

This is for at least two reasons. The first is to avoid the potential diplomatic embarrassment that they might cause in inadvertently speaking

---

[253]See section 5.2 on page 385.

[254]United Nations Office of the Secretary-General, Secretary-General Establishes Advisory Group to Assist Him in Convening Internet Governance Forum (as in n. 180 on page 365)

[255]See `http://blog.icann.org/`.

against domestic government policy. As one of the civil society delegates to WSIS put it:

> Governments are often well-disposed and willing to cooperate with us, but governmental delegates don't have the same flexibility as we do to propose, negotiate and adopt any proposal. Most of the time, they have to refer to their capitals for approval, whereas we are able to take decisions more quickly and defend our points of view.[256]

The second reason, which may also apply within other stakeholder groups, is that because decision-making within the Advisory Group could require stakeholders to compromise their publicly-stated positions, allowing them to do this privately minimises their potential loss of face. It is for the same reason that the grand coalition of a consociation normally convenes in private.[257]

Thus the democratic transparency of the Advisory Group has been traded off against the concerns of governments (and perhaps other stakeholders) to avoid the risk of diplomatic embarrassment and loss of face associated with an open democratic process. Whilst this can, perhaps, be justified on the pragmatic grounds that only by making such a trade-off will those stakeholders be persuaded to participate at all, in the absence of a conceptual justification, such a trade-off could only legitimately be agreed by multi-stakeholder, democratic means—which it has not been.

Having said that, the Secretariat has also attempted, though with limited success, to balance the concerns of governments with the need for transparency through the following measures:

- Following the example of WGIG, its meetings are held subject to the "Chatham House Rule,"[258] which allows the meeting's participants to use and disseminate any information received in the meeting so long as they do not reveal the identity of its source.[259] However whilst in theory this would allow the Advisory Group to open up its meetings at least to the media and to stakeholders who have agreed to abide by the Rule, in fact this has not occurred; leaving the group's effective transparency subject to the whim of the meeting's participants (and in practice, highly opaque).
- The appointment of members of the Advisory Group in their personal capacities might also have been thought to allow governmental

[256] Bloem (as in n. 13 on page 325), 101–102

[257] Skelcher (as in n. 554 on page 295), 105—though this is, deliberately, not true of the consociational multi-stakeholder bureau proposed here.

[258] IGF Secretariat, Multistakeholder Advisory Group Meeting Summary Report (as in n. 279 on page 395), 2

[259] See `http://www.chathamhouse.org.uk/about/chathamhouserule/`.

> representatives to speak freely without being taken to be stating government policy. However again, in practice this appears to have made no difference to the transparency of the Advisory Group in comparison to the GAC, whose members act in a representative capacity. Moreover, as already noted, the appointment of members as individuals dissociates them from the capacity in which they represent their stakeholder group, which defeats the purpose of appointing a multi-stakeholder body in the first place.[260]

The failure of these measures to be reflected in the level of the Advisory Group's transparency in practice indicates that a more radical approach to the problem of governmental participation is called for in the case of the proposed multi-stakeholder bureau.

This is provided by the consociational multi-stakeholder process developed above. This process, as it will be recalled, is divided into three phases: assessing the consensus of the plenary body, developing draft recommendations encapsulating that consensus, and then ratifying such draft recommendations by consensus between the stakeholder groups.

There are no reasonable grounds for contention over the need to maintain transparency during the first phase: whether the plenary body has reached consensus on a particular issue or not is a question of fact, which bears no necessary relation to the views of the stakeholder representatives within the bureau on that issue, nor calls for any negotiation on or compromise of those views.

The second phase is more problematic, in that the process of democratic deliberation during this phase will normally require governmental representatives to state, justify and negotiate positions. However, because no formal decision-making takes place in the second phase, these positions are only required to be provisional. This reduces the strength of governmental arguments against the maintenance of transparency during the second phase. Moreover, to the extent that those arguments still do carry, they may justify such compromise measures of transparency as are employed in the existing Advisory Group as outlined above, if agreed by multi-stakeholder, democratic means.[261]

---

[260] See section 6.3 on page 471.

[261] For example, in open consultation with all stakeholders, the bureau may agree to procedures (which could be enshrined in standing rules) by which private sessions may be held during the second phase on sensitive issues, or those issues discussed on a private mailing list, provided that the Chatham House Rule is applied.

It may also agree in like manner to a standing rule providing that the positions taken by governmental members are not those of the governments that appointed them, unless or until officially cleared. Alternatively, it could agree that only senior diplomats, authorised to make statements of policy in real time, should be eligible for appointment as governmental representatives; compare ICANN Governmental Advisory Committee (as in n. 41 on page 42), Principle 14.

It remains the case that some final negotiations (which on the experience of WSIS will most likely be between governments in private) may be required before recommendations can be formally agreed. But that is the express purpose of the third phase, in which each of the stakeholder groups deliberates in isolation (though not necessarily in seclusion) on whether to exercise its power of veto. Because the second and third stages of the consociational multi-stakeholder process are designed with the flexibility to be iterative, if the separate deliberation of a stakeholder group raises new issues not taken into account in the draft under consideration, the power of veto can be exercised and these issues brought back before the bureau as a whole for further deliberation.

Because each stakeholder group determines its own processes to employ during this final phase, they might not be transparent at all (and in the case of governments, probably will not be). Whilst this may make that phase of the process less democratic overall, this shortcoming is limited by the fact that the third phase is in many ways the least important, taking place as it does after multi-stakeholder deliberation has already resulted in democratic agreement on a draft recommendation, and provided a background of reasoned and balanced argument for the stakeholder groups to individually consider. Indeed, the third phase serves only to provide a mechanism for formal decision-taking that upholds the autonomy of each stakeholder group.

If consensus is reached upon a certain issue at both the plenary level and within the bureau as a whole, this is not nullified by the failure of one of the stakeholder groups to ratify a formal recommendation on that issue. Rather, this simply means that the IGF has no formal output to use in interfacing with other bodies acting in this issue area. The plenary's consensus may nonetheless possess normative weight with those other bodies, regardless of the bureau's recognition and ratification of it, particularly as the IGF consolidates its social capital and thereby its influence within the Internet governance regime over time.

Furthermore, the transparency of the processes adopted by a particular stakeholder group need not be taken as given over the longer term. The transnational democratic programme, which is reflected in the IGF's mandate to "[p]romote ... WSIS principles in Internet governance,"[262] seeks to further democratise all layers of governance, in order to preserve democratic freedoms in a new medieval world in which the authority of pluralistic public and private actors overlaps.[263]

[262]WSIS, Tunis Agenda for the Information Society (as in n. 5 on page 2), para 72(i)

[263]See section 4.3 on page 236.

Accountability

Chapter 4 discussed the difficulty of applying criteria of accountability specific to other contexts, such as liberal democratic states or domestic administrative agencies, to assess the performance of transnational governance networks such as the IGF.[264] In the absence of an appropriate general framework of accountability applicable to the IGF, it was concluded that a balance of bottom–up, top–down and peer-to-peer accountability should be constructed by reference to best practices observed elsewhere, assessing their overall adequacy by reference to general democratic principles. This can now be undertaken using the exemplar organisations as case studies where relevant.

Beginning with bottom–up accountability, this relates to the extent to which the actions of the IGF's decision-making organs can be demonstrated to fulfil the democratic principle by deriving from the consent of the stakeholders who make up its membership. In other contexts, bottom–up accountability may be provided by regular, free and fair democratic elections, or thorough the design of participatory democratic processes for soliciting public input into proposed policy-making.

In the case of the IGF, they are provided by the transcription of open consultation meetings and plenary sessions, and the publication of stakeholders' written contributions. These currently provide the only basis against which to assess the congruence of the actions and decisions of the Secretariat and Advisory Group with the consensus of the stakeholders at large.

The limitations of these documents are evident, however. First, as Nitin Desai admitted in the February 2007 open consultations, it is something of "a labor of love to go through that record ... we may have to do a little bit more to direct people in the right way, because saying that there's 15 hours of transcript is, I'm not sure enough." On the account given here, the preparation of a balanced report of the discussions of stakeholders at meetings, along with a synthesis of written contributions, is another of the responsibilities that properly falls to the multi-stakeholder bureau.[265]

A second limitation is that the Secretariat and Advisory Group have made no reference to the transcripts or synthesis papers to justify their decisions, but have simply asserted that "broad agreement" or an "emerging consensus" has existed to support the decisions made.[266] It is for this reason that it was proposed above that the multi-stakeholder bureau should, following ICANN's example, document its assessment of the consensus of the plenary body in much more exacting detail.[267]

[264]See section 4.3 on page 260.

[265]See section 6.3 on page 462.

[266]For example IGF Secretariat, The Substantive Agenda of the First Meeting of the Internet Governance Forum (as in n. 171 on page 361).

[267]See section 6.4 on page 491.

A third and final limitation on the existing mechanisms of bottom–up accountability for the IGF is that in the event that the decisions of the Secretariat or Advisory Group are found not to be in accord with the consensus of the plenary body, there is very little that can be done about it. The introduction of a randomly-selected, multi-stakeholder and democratic nominating committee, as proposed in this chapter, overcomes this problem, by making the proposed multi-stakeholder bureau—and through it, the Secretariat—accountable to the stakeholders on whose behalf they are required to act.

Moving on to top–down mechanisms of accountability, at present the IGF as a whole is subject to the supervision of the Secretary-General of the United Nations, who is required in turn to periodically report on the IGF's affairs to the General Assembly and to recommend whether it should continue after the fulfilment of its initial mandate.[268] As already noted, this is a conceptual anomaly. The IGF's status as a transnational governance network precludes its subjection to top–down supervision, since no other multi-stakeholder, democratic institution yet exists to which it could legitimately be made accountable.[269]

Therefore whilst the Secretary-General may retain his formal role of oversight at least in the short term for political reasons, it is desirable that the IGF meanwhile develop an additional and more legitimate layer of top–down accountability. Even without any appropriate transnational governance institutions to exercise such oversight, the IGF can design internal hierarchies (or networks) of its own to provide a structure for accountability,[270] much as the accountability of a liberal democratic state is furthered by the system of mutual checks and balances between its legislative, executive and judicial branches.

An example of this principle in practice is given by auDA.[271] One of the objects established in its constitution is "to develop and establish a policy framework for the development and administration of the .au ccTLD."[272] Formal responsibility for this role lies with the Board of Directors, but in doing so it acts upon the report of a specialised Advisory Panel, which is convened as required to conduct public consultations and to generate recommendations for the Board's consideration. The Chair of the Advisory Panel is appointed by and reports to the Board, and in turn appoints the

[268] WSIS, Tunis Agenda for the Information Society (as in n. 5 on page 2), paras 75 and 76

[269] But for the future, any multi-stakeholder arrangements that may yet be made for enhanced cooperation in Internet public policy making will be a likely candidate: see section 5.1 on page 344.

[270] See section 5.4 on page 410.

[271] A number of other ccTLD regulators and registries follow a similar model; for example Nominet appoints a multi-stakeholder Policy Advisory Board (PAB) to advise it on policy matters.

[272] auDA, Constitution ⟨URL: `http://www.auda.org.au/pdf/auda-constitution.pdf`⟩, clause 3.1(d)

panel's other members.[273]

The division within auDA between the site of formal policy-setting authority and the process of policy development, along with the fact that the Board does not directly appoint the members of the Advisory Panel, are both characteristic of the separation of legislative and executive powers that exists to varying degree in most liberal democracies.

Even so, a number of shortcomings in the accountability of auDA's policy development process have still been identified. First, the Advisory Panel is accountable to the Board for its output, but not for its processes, which are devised at its own discretion. Thus for example, because the Chair of the Advisory Panel is not accountable for the selection of Advisory Panel members, the transparency of that process has been criticised,[274] as has the process of building consensus within the Panel.[275] Leaving aside the merits of these specific complaints, scholar John Selby has concluded that

> greater transparency, procedural fairness, accountability and an appeals process would improve the decisions made by auDA's policy development committees without significantly impacting on flexibility.[276]

The second shortcoming is that when the Board of auDA elects to engage in policy development on its own account, there is no top–down accountability to constrain the process it employs. As a result, as former auDA board member Kim Davies writes:

> There have been some cases when operational changes or new policies have been implemented without advance notice to the general public, with no ability for public participation in the policy's formulation other than through indirect means such as lobbying auDA directors. As it has not been practice for board members to explain their deliberations in public, or canvas specific opinion on an issue prior to decision-making, this is not an effective mechanism to channel contributions into the board's considerations.[277]

---

[273] AuDA, Constitution (as in n. 272), clause 24.8

[274] John Selby, Submission to Review of the Structure and Operation of the .au Internet Domain Name ⟨URL: http://www.dbcde.gov.au/__data/assets/pdf_file/0009/55836/John_Selby_-_Macquarie_University.pdf⟩, 16

[275] Domain Industry Association, Domain Industry Submission to DCITA au Namespace Review ⟨URL: http://www.dbcde.gov.au/__data/assets/pdf_file/0004/56614/Domain_Industry_FINAL_WEB_COPY.pdf⟩, 5

[276] Selby (as in n. 274), 16

[277] Kim Davies, Contribution to the DCITA .au Review ⟨URL: http://www.dbcde.gov.au/__data/assets/pdf_file/0010/55837/Kim_Davies.pdf⟩, 6

How then can the IGF's processes incorporate top–down accountability whilst avoiding the errors drawn from the lesson of auDA? First, dynamic coalitions should be accountable to the bureau not only for their output, but also for their processes. As suggested above, this can be done by requiring them to document the processes by which their recommendations were reached, to ensure that they are multi-stakeholder and democratic.[278] For dynamic coalitions that operate online, mechanisms of accountability can also be built into online tools at an architectural level[279] (for example, by automatically creating public archives of discussions).

Second, there should be a clear separation between the formal decision-taking role of the bureau and the policy development role of the plenary body. Such a separation is enshrined in the structure and processes proposed in this chapter, whereby the bureau has no authority to make recommendations other than in accordance with its assessment of the consensus of the plenary body as a whole. An additional benefit of the separation of formal authority from the plenary body is that this is more conducive to free and open deliberation than the fusion of authority and deliberation, which tends to politicise discussion.[280]

A third recommendation for enshrining top–down accountability in the IGF, although only fleetingly suggested in the discussion of auDA above, is that there should be a power of review, such as that exercised by the judicial branch of government that balances the legislative and executive powers of the liberal state. This would allow for the multi-stakeholder bureau to be made accountable for the misuse of its power with more immediacy than through its ouster by the next nominating committee.

A better example of this is seen in ICANN. ICANN's bylaws make provision for the internal review ("reconsideration") of a decision of its Board by "any person or entity materially affected" on the grounds that the decision was made in contravention of policy or in disregard of material information (without fault of the complainant). It also provides for the independent review of any decisions of the Board that are alleged to have been made unconstitutionally.[281]

The grounds of review specified in the bylaws have been criticised as being quite limited in comparison to those available for the challenge of executive decisions under domestic administrative law,[282] such as denial of natural justice and impropriety of purpose.[283] Further reducing the grounds of challenge available at the suit of its constituents, ICANN amended its bylaws in 1999 to ensure that its at large members could not

[278] See section 6.4 on page 491.

[279] Rundle (as in n. 379 on page 262), 18

[280] See section 4.3 on page 250.

[281] ICANN, Bylaws (as in n. 39 on page 41), article IV, sections 2 and 3

[282] Weinberg, ICANN and the Problem of Legitimacy (as in n. 71 on page 49), 233

[283] *FAI Insurances Ltd v Winneke* (1982) 151 CLR 342; *The Queen v Toohey; Ex parte Northern Land Council* (1981) 151 CLR 170

bring a derivative action against the company under Californian corporations law.[284]

Moreover, of the applications for review that have been brought as of 2008, only one in seven requests for internal reconsideration has been determined in the complainant's favour,[285] and none of the pending requests for independent review have yet been heard. In fact, an Independent Review Panel (IRP) to hear such requests was not established until 2004, despite having been specified in ICANN's bylaws since its establishment,[286] creating the impression of a Board resistant to the imposition of top–down accountability.

The principal lesson for the IGF to be drawn from ICANN's processes of review, whilst not particularly novel, is clear: that accountability is best served by an adequate separation of powers between the IGF's formal decision-making organ and the body that reviews its decisions. Whilst it was suggested above in considering the structure of the bureau that it could form an appeals subcommittee from its own members,[287] this alone would not satisfy that criterion of independence.

A better model is provided by the CS-IGC, whose Appeals Team is appointed by a randomly-selected Nominations Committee. Since such a committee has already been proposed for the IGF to appoint the multi-stakeholder bureau, it would be straightforward for it to appoint an appeals committee for the IGF simultaneously. This is also consonant with the findings of a 2002 report on ICANN, which recommended that its reconsideration committee should not be composed of members of the current Board, though could include former members.[288]

The appeals committee would not have an extensive role. After all, since the IGF is a consensual governance network, the ultimate sanction for the abuse of power would simply be the withdrawal of stakeholders from that network. Thus the power of the appeals committee, like that of any constituent body of the IGF, would be to make recommendations only, and then strictly only on procedural matters involving the disregard of the multi-stakeholder, democratic processes that underlie the IGF's legitimacy; for example, that a decision of the bureau had been made in the absence of any evidence that consensus had been reached upon it by the plenary body.[289]

---

[284] A Michael Froomkin, ICANN and Individuals ⟨URL: http://osaka.law.miami.edu/~amf/individuals.htm⟩

[285] See http://www.icann.org/committees/reconsideration/. Of forty-two requests listed here dated between June 1999 and May 2006, six were decided for the complainant.

[286] Idem, Independent Review Panel Appointed After Years of Delay ⟨URL: http://www.icannwatch.org/article.pl?sid=04/04/23/1314207⟩

[287] See section 6.3 on page 471.

[288] Centre for Global Studies (as in n. 98 on page 445), 21

[289] The exact scope of its authority should be determined in open consultation with all stakeholders, balancing the need for the bureau's accountability with its operational efficiency,

The addition of such an appeals committee to the already proposed structures of nominating committee, bureau, plenary body and dynamic coalitions would complete the institutional framework required to constitute the IGF as a democratically accountable governance network both in bottom–up and top–down terms.

There is, however also a third and final level of accountability, which has been described as peer-to-peer, and which is created by situating the IGF in a network of cooperative (or competitive) governance institutions.[290] Just as it was explained that part of the IGF's mandate is to hold other bodies accountable for their adherence to the WSIS process criteria,[291] so too the IGF will, over the long term, be held accountable for its own effectiveness as a multi-stakeholder governance network by other actors in the Internet governance regime.

Little more need be said here of this final level of accountability, since the IGF has little direct control over it. However it has been stressed, particularly in Chapter 4,[292] that by reason of its inherently consensual nature, the power of a governance network is conditioned upon its ability to serve its stakeholders' ends. If they can achieve the same ends less expensively through some other mechanism of governance (or through another governance network), then there is nothing to prevent them from doing so.

In that sense, the ultimate accountability for the IGF is provided through the pressure of regulatory competition from other institutions in the market for governance solutions. This competition gives it cause to hold as closely as possible to multi-stakeholder democratic principles in order to provide

---

but could legitimately include the determination of complaints from affected stakeholders that a decision of the bureau had been made:

- without having been the subject of deliberation by the plenary body during an annual or an open consultation meeting;
- in breach of any other procedures that had been agreed by multi-stakeholder, democratic means to apply to the making of such a decision;
- in excess of its authority, for example because the decision purported to override the consensus of the plenary body;
- in excess of the mandate of the IGF as a whole accepted by all stakeholders, as initially set out in the Tunis Agenda;
- through a serious and manifest deviation from the multi-stakeholder, democratic process, such as making the decision at the behest of an external authority;
- by reason of fraud (for example, if the decision was made in reliance upon the report of a subcommittee that was found to have been falsified); or
- without any evidence that could justify the decision.

These are also amongst the grounds upon which the actions of a domestic administrative agency may be challenged by common law judicial review: see *Administrative Decisions (Judicial Review) Act 1977* (Cth), section 5.

[290] Mueller and Klein (as in n. 387 on page 263), 3

[291] See section 6.2 on page 436.

[292] See sections 4.2 on page 221, 4.4 on page 316 and 4.5 on page 319.

its stakeholders with ever greater reason to commit themselves to the network, thereby consolidating its social capital and fortifying its authority within the regime.

Inclusion

The annual meetings of the IGF have been attended by approximately one person for every million Internet users.[293] Whilst deliberative democracy does not require all impacted parties to be represented, so long as all relevant perspectives are,[294] such a low rate of participation casts doubt on just how diverse and inclusive the IGF really is. Neither is the low level of attendance at annual IGF meetings—which is easily explained by the cost of global travel—the only indication of its limited reach. In comparison to ICANN at an equivalent stage of its development, the IGF is also little known amongst Internet users, rarely the subject of media attention, and has prompted limited academic interest.

The IGF's limited mindshare reflects its failure to engage with the Internet community in its native element: that is, online. It is oddly anachronistic that the IGF, whilst seeking to become a key institution of Internet governance, was conceived from its genesis as an annual meeting held in person, with online tools as a mere adjunct. This contrasts with many of the institutions of Internet technical coordination and standards development reviewed in Chapter 2 (most obviously the IETF) for which online mechanisms are the primary mode of engagement. Indeed this is typical of decentralised transnational organisations of the Internet age, including a number of others examined throughout this book such as the ASF, APNIC, Debian and Wikipedia.

In Chapter 4, the use of online mechanisms in the manner employed by these organisations was highlighted as an important means of redressing the lack of democratic participation in transnational governance institutions and networks.[295] Indeed, it can be argued that the Internet is a vital enabling force for the mechanism of transnational governance by network, just as the printing press was for representative government before it:

> This multi-stakeholder governance approach is a major conceptual innovation. But it only became practicable at the global level because of the existence of online tools facilitating: access to information (Web sites without costs of paper duplication), remote participation (webcasts, blogs), iterative consul-

---

[293]Based on the approximate attendance at each meeting of 1300 as a proportion of the 2006 estimate of 1.13 billion global Internet users: ITU, ICT Statistics Database (as in n. 520 on page 287).

[294]See section 4.3 on page 245.

[295]See section 4.3 on page 276.

> tation processes (mailing lists and forums) and soon, collaborative drafting (wikis). Indeed, multi-stakeholder governance requires a combination of physical interactions and "intersessional" online collaboration that only the Internet itself allows to envisage.
>
> Internet Governance is therefore not only the governance "of" the Internet and "on" the Internet. It is also, in a certain way, governance "enabled by" the Internet, or in other terms, the embryo of a "Governance for the Internet Age." The global network demands a new type of governance; but it is also the tool that makes this new governance possible and shapes it in its own image: real-time, participatory and distributed.[296]

This subsection of the book will therefore focus on the use of online tools in advancing transnational participation in the processes of the IGF.[297]

In Chapter 4, a distinction was drawn between two conceptions of the democratising role of online processes.[298] The first, described (though not canonically) as e-democracy, is very much that which has informed the approach of the IGF Secretariat. In this conception, online participation serves essentially as an extension of the physical meeting. That is, it is largely concerned with providing a channel of communication (generally passive and one-way) between remote participants and those present in person at IGF meetings. It does not involve independent online deliberation, save in a form strictly secondary to, and tightly integrated with, that which takes place face-to-face.

Although the e-democratic model has its limitations, this is not to suggest that its programme is not important in its own right. On the contrary, given the prohibitive cost of international travel particularly for disadvantaged stakeholders, streamlining communications between physical meetings and remote participants is essential if those meetings are to be adequately inclusive and diverse.

However the second conception of online or digital democracy, termed Internet democracy in Chapter 4, is equally important in broadening participation in the fulfilment of the IGF's mandate, yet has been entirely neglected by the IGF's Secretariat. On this conception, parallel online processes should supplement rather than merely supporting the physical meetings, in order that they might redress some of the limitations inherent in the latter.

---

[296] Bertrand de la Chapelle, *Governing the Internet—Freedom and Regulation in the OSCE Region* Vienna: OSCE Representative on Freedom of the Media, 2007, chap. The Internet Governance Forum: How a United Nations Summit Produced a New Governance Paradigm for the Internet Age, 25

[297] It will not directly address the other democratic uses of online tools, such as the advancement of accountability and transparency, which have been already been dealt with above.

[298] See section 4.3 on page 266.

e-democracy

Even granted that its approach has been limited to the former conception, the IGF's implementation of e-democratic mechanisms has been as deficient from a deliberative democratic standpoint as its structure and processes are. The four categories of tools for online democratic deliberation discussed in Chapter 4 were those for synchronous and asynchronous discussion, document preparation and decision-making.[299] However since the IGF has been structured simply as a discussion forum, without the capacity to fulfil its policy-setting role, the only online mechanisms that have been put in place for the IGF have been those to facilitate discussion; that is, the first two of the above categories.

What passes for synchronous discussion is the transmission of the proceedings of the IGF's plenary sessions and workshops to remote participants via webcast, and the selective relaying of remote participants' input to the floor of plenary sessions by a moderator. However, this does not allow for an adequately interactive exchange; for example, it was typical in Athens for the input of remote participants to be delayed by as much as half an hour (if it was relayed to the meeting at all), by which time the face-to-face discussion had long moved on, and the introduction of the remote input became disruptive and irrelevant. In Rio, perhaps recalling this experience, fewer remote participants took the trouble to attempt to interject comments or questions. Others had trouble accessing the webcasts of the plenary meeting.

These problems could have been addressed if a more accessible technology than webcasting had been selected for use at the meeting, such as Jabber chat as used by APNIC.[300] Since a real-time transcription of proceedings at the plenary meeting is generated in any case for projection to the front of the main venue, this could easily also have been copied in real time to the chat forum to enable all users (including those without the high speed access required to access the webcast) to follow the meeting's progress instantaneously.

As a complement to this, comments from that chat forum could have been displayed on a large projection screen at the venue alongside the English transcription/translation, in near real-time (perhaps lightly moderated for obscenity and plainly irrelevant content). This would have afforded online participants a much more equal and interactive voice in the plenary discussions than they have yet enjoyed, but without interrupting the flow of the proceedings. Such a facility was in fact developed for the use of the Secretariat at the Rio meeting, but in the end was never utilised.

Moving on to asynchronous discussion tools, the extent of the IGF's use of these has largely been confined to the Secretariat's SMF Web forum,

[299]See section 4.3 on page 276.

[300]Or IRC as used by a number of online civil society organisations, such as EFA, for their general meetings.

which is limited by its fixed list of topics and unthreaded format.[301] There has also been no attempt to integrate its content into the discussions at plenary meetings, save that general reference was made to the messages posted in the Web forum in two of the synthesis papers.[302]

The risk of such a disconnect between online tools and the offline processes that they are intended to support was recognised at the outset by a number of stakeholders. At the first open consultation meeting in February 2006, Jovan Kurbalija of DiploFoundation noted, "there is a considerable difference between availability of online tools and their integration in working procedures. There is a gap that should be bridged in order to have proper integration of those online tools." During the same meeting, ICANN blogger and lawyer Brett Fausett put forward a solution:

> I would like to recommend that you appoint Internet rapporteurs or list managers to manage and steer the online discussions so they move forward productively. Unmanaged, open forums unread by the leadership of the IGF can quickly become black holes for public comment, creating the illusion of participation while providing no meaningful access to the IGF. These rapporteurs who would work with the Secretariat would participate in the online forums and help define areas of consensus and highlight areas of disagreement for further work or discussion.

Given the limitations of the Secretariat's official forum, the IGF Community Site, along with a number of independent blogs linked from that site, soon became the dominant fora for asynchronous online discussion around the Athens meeting. In principle, this distribution of online discussion is consistent both with deliberative democratic theory—in which the public sphere is constituted as an "associational network"[303]—and also with the value of decentralisation that is a persistent feature of Internet culture (and which is reflected in the IGP's proposal for a "Distributed Secretariat" for the IGF).[304]

On the other hand, on a practical level, the dispersal of asynchronous discussion across the Internet greatly complicates the task of integrating those discussions with those of the plenary body, particularly given the Secretariat's failure to support those other discussion fora by promoting them to participants or linking to them from its Web site, let alone by

[301] See section 5.2 on page 377.

[302] IGF Secretariat, Stock-taking Session Synthesis Paper (as in n. 233 on page 381), 1; Idem, IGF Second Meeting Synthesis Paper (as in n. 258 on page 389), 3

[303] Habermas, *Between Facts and Norms: Contributions to a Discourse Theory of Law and Democracy* (as in n. 209 on page 227), 359

[304] Mathiason, The Distributed Secretariat: Making the Internet Governance Forum Work (as in n. 118 on page 451)

appointing rapporteurs to participate in and report on those discussions. The multiplication of fora for discussion, as an example of decentralised collective action, also has the potential to reduce rather than to increase the transparency of the process.[305]

The need to draw distributed online discussion in to the mainstream of the IGF's processes has been acknowledged by the IGF's Secretariat. Nitin Desai remarked during the May 2006 consultations, "I'm sure there are NGOs who are reading this and typing away stuff on some blog or the other, commenting on this. But we are not getting that comment here, you see. So give some thought to ... how do we bring the outside in?"

One possible response is to maintain that just as it is a fundamental responsibility of the IGF's Secretariat to provide a venue for an annual plenary meeting at which all interested stakeholders can attend and collaborate, so too it can be characterised as its responsibility to provide an equivalent venue online. Thus scholar Mary Rundle has recommended that intergovernmental organisations involved in Internet governance should provide a "one-stop-shop web portal that ... offers online discussion tools," rather than requiring participants to proactively track numerous online fora in order to participate in online policy discussion.[306] The intent of the original IGF Community Site was to provide such a "one-stop shop" portal.

A weakness of this response is that whilst it recognises the importance of facilitating the integration of online discussion into the IGF's plenary processes, it downplays the desirability (and likely inevitability) that online participation will be decentralised. An alternative approach that balances the values of integration and decentralisation is the development of a loose framework for the aggregation of content from diverse sources under a single domain, through Internet standards such as RSS (Really Simple Syndication)[307] and the utilisation of metadata to tag related resources so that they can be automatically grouped together.[308] This has also been a project of the Online Collaboration Dynamic Coalition, though only partially realised in the second incarnation of the IGF Community Site.

Besides synchronous and asynchronous discussion, the other categories of online tools for democratic deliberation are those for authoring documents and making decisions. Since these are being considered here only for e-democratic purposes (that is, the support rather than the replacement of in-person deliberation), their application will be limited to the proposed multi-stakeholder bureau and to the dynamic coalitions, since it is not

---

[305] See section 4.1 on page 194.

[306] Rundle (as in n. 379 on page 262), 17

[307] Actually Atom, a variation on RSS, is the official IETF specification for content syndication: IETF, The Atom Syndication Format ⟨URL: http://www.ietf.org/rfc/rfc4287⟩.

[308] This is a small part of the W3C's larger semantic Web project; see generally Berners-Lee and Fischetti (as in n. 105 on page 56), chapter 13.

suggested that the plenary body should draft documents or take formal decisions at its annual meeting.

Presently, both the Advisory Group (as the prototype of the proposed multi-stakeholder bureau) and most dynamic coalitions operate electronic mailing lists on which texts and decisions are discussed, and a number of the dynamic coalitions also operate wiki sites for collaborative document drafting,[309] as previously WGIG also had, though with limited success.[310] Whilst a number of more sophisticated tools were examined in Chapter 4,[311] one of the main obstacles to the successful implementation of any online tools for democratic deliberation, as borne out by WGIG's experience, is the reluctance of governmental representatives to use them.[312]

If the purpose of these tools is only to support rather than to substitute for face-to-face processes in which governments do participate, and so long as the two parallel processes are adequately bridged or integrated by appointed or volunteer rapporteurs, then the disuse of e-democratic mechanisms by governments is not a problem in itself. Indeed, enabling multi-modal means of engagement encourages the broadest possible participation from those with a preference for the use of one mechanism over another.[313]

Where it can become a problem is where the disinterest of governments results in the provision of e-democratic mechanisms being neglected by the Secretariat, to the detriment of other, less well-resourced stakeholder groups. One strategy to address this, as suggested by Robert Guerra, now of ICANN's ALAC, at the May 2006 open consultations, is that "capacity-building focused towards governments on how to use these technologies could be part of the capacity-building exercise for the IGF."

Internet democracy

Another reason why governmental representatives should be encouraged in the use of online tools for democratic deliberation is that there are some purposes for which online tools can achieve what an annual face-to-face meeting cannot. Examples of circumstances in which online tools are either a better means, or even the only practical means of realising multi-stakeholder democratic participation in the activities of the IGF include:

---

[309] See those of the dynamic coalitions on Privacy and Online Collaboration at http://wiki.igf-online.net/.

[310] See section 5.1 on page 335.

[311] See section 4.3 on page 276.

[312] DiploFoundation (as in n. 102 on page 26), 3. One member of the IGF's Advisory Group has even remarked that "[r]arely if ever does a government representative from anywhere take part in online discussions of this group": IGF Secretariat, Advisory Group Discussion 11 to 17 March 2008 ⟨URL: http://intgovforum.org/AGD/AG%20emails%2010mar08.pdf⟩, 6.

[313] Rik Panganiban, Top-down, Middle Layer and Bottom-up E-democracy ⟨URL: http://www.rikomatic.com/blog/2006/10/my_talk_on_edem.html⟩

- Addressing complex and contentious issues, the resolution of which exceeds the capacity of the annual meeting but which could be addressed through a more sustained programme of intersessional activity. Lynn St Amour of ISOC stated in Athens, "I don't think people can come together for four days and have a discussion and believe we have addressed the technological, political, social, cultural ramifications of something that's so vast." Whilst this is undeniable, there is no such limitation on the scope of the issues upon which the IGF could deliberate through an ongoing process facilitated by Internet communications.

- The drafting of documents, which is at best an impractical undertaking for a large-scale plenary meeting (the WSIS output documents, for example, had been drafted during a long sequence of preparatory negotiations before the formal plenary sessions even opened). However it is a much more manageable undertaking for an extended process of deliberation managed using online tools.

  Although in some cases the drafting of such texts could be left to dynamic coalitions (which case was dealt with under the previous heading), this might not always be appropriate; for example, no relevant dynamic coalition might exist. Similarly the bureau itself cannot begin upon the preparation of a text before the plenary body has reached at least partial consensus as to what it should contain, and it is difficult to build such consensus without being able to develop a draft text for discussion. An open, democratically deliberative online process offers a better alternative in these cases.

- Face-to-face meetings tend to perpetuate divisions of status, race, gender and disability that are anathema to democratic deliberation, and which online discourse more easily and naturally overcomes. Whilst the dynamic of a face-to-face meeting (incorporating such subtleties as body language and inflection of voice) may be more difficult to convey by accessible means online, so too there is a dynamic to online discussions that cannot be replicated in face-to-face meetings. In such discussions, participants, represented by screen name or avatar, speak with a level of vigor, frankness and equality that is difficult to achieve in person.[314]

- Whilst the above observation applies to synchronous online discussion, asynchronous mechanisms also possess a unique dynamic of their own. For example, they allow for each respondent to take more time to consider his or her response than would be possible in a face-to-face meeting, and even easily allow for the pertinent points raised by a thread of previous messages to be referenced ("quoted") in the body of the respondent's contribution; indeed, this is commonplace in email and newsgroup discussions.

[314]See section 4.3 on page 272.

To give another example, wiki software automatically records the history of revisions to a document, thereby allowing any given revision to be easily placed in a precise temporal context. No matter how diligent the work of a rapporteur seeking to bridge online and offline discussions, it would be impossible for the subtlety of mechanisms such as these to be adequately represented in the face-to-face context.

In sum, it is a quixotic endeavour to seek to constitute the IGF's annual plenary meetings as the principal mode of engagement amongst its stakeholders for every purpose, when there are some purposes for which that meeting and the e-democratic processes set up to support it are not, and can never be adequately suited on their own. Rather, independent processes of Internet democracy are required to supplement (not merely to support) the IGF's face-to-face deliberations in order that the IGF's mandate may be fully and adequately addressed. Three such processes can be identified as possessing the highest priority.

The first is an analogue of the recommendation made above that the plenary meetings should be augmented with speed dialogue sessions that follow each of the panel sessions.[315] One way in which these speed dialogue sessions could benefit from the unique dynamic of online synchronous discussion is for the table groups present in person to be supplemented by "virtual" table groups. Each virtual group, convening using a synchronous discussion tool such as IRC, would be of a similar size to a face-to-face table group, and would be staffed by a moderator who would guide and focus the deliberation and summarise its output for presentation to the larger plenary body. The same practice could be applied within workshops seeking to produce output for introduction to the plenary body.

Second, online asynchronous discussion should be established as a parallel and complementary process to discussion in person at plenary meetings. Consequently, when preparing its summaries of the contributions and discussions of stakeholders, and when assessing the consensus of the plenary body, the bureau should be required to take into account the views emerging from democratic deliberation in the IGF's online fora on an equal footing with those expressed by participants deliberating in person.[316]

However, before online discussion groups can be taken as deliberative democratic fora in their own right, they will have to satisfy similar criteria

[315]See section 6.4 on page 484.

[316]A fine but important distinction exists between this and the narrower e-democratic conception of online discussion described above, whereby such discussion is taken simply as an input into the deliberations of the plenary body at annual meetings, rather than being equivalent to and potentially a substitute for face-to-face deliberation. On this broader view, it is not necessary for the output of a deliberative online discussion to be confirmed by the group attending the IGF's plenary meetings in person, as their deliberation on substantive issues possesses no greater legitimacy than that of the online participants (perhaps to the contrary, since those able to attend in person are likely to be a more privileged and less diverse group overall).

of multi-stakeholder, democratic structure and process as those that have been put forward for dynamic coalitions.[317] This means that a much narrower class of such fora will qualify to deliver their output to the bureau for direct consideration, than those which could interface with the plenary body under the e-democratic conception. In particular, it would be necessary to ensure that:

- the group is adequately diverse and of multi-stakeholder composition;
- the group's membership is open and its operation transparent (for example, discussions should not be silently moderated);
- the group's size may however be limited, and if necessary divided into sub-groups;[318]
- all relevant perspectives are represented within the group (including the use of the same background briefing material that is put before the plenary body meeting in person); and
- the services of moderators or facilitators are provided to ensure that the group adheres to a deliberative democratic process (for example, that its members acknowledge each other's equal capacity to contribute).

These rather stringent criteria do not necessarily preclude the operation of decentralised discussion fora organised from the grass-roots, in competition with any official fora established by the Secretariat. As an example of this, the IGP organised a Global Deliberative Dialogue on Internet Governance as an online analogue to PrepCom 3 of the Tunis phase of WSIS. Although it was open to all participants, the dialogue was distinguished by the participation of panelists from the Internet governance community, a facilitator who "encourages everyone to join in the conversation, ensures that all aspects of the topics are considered and keeps the conversation focused,"[319] and a summarizer who would draw together highlights of the discussion from each day.

But equally, there is no reason why a single forum that fulfills the above criteria could not meet the IGF's need for asynchronous online discussion, just as there is presently only one such forum for face-to-face discussion at the IGF's annual plenary meeting.[320]

---

[317]See section 6.3 on page 457.

[318]See section 4.3 on page 276.

[319]See `http://www.webdialogues.net/cs/dialogue-wgig-guidelines/view/di/70?x-t=guidelines.view`.

[320]Such a forum may still of course need to be sub-divided into groups of manageable size, as the speed dialogue sessions are to be subdivided into table groups.

A third new online process for the IGF, that is independent of and supplementary to those that can be realised offline, is a mechanism for collaborative drafting, such as a wiki or one of the other tools for collaborative authoring described at section 4.3 on page 276. This facility could be employed in at least two circumstances:

- where there is consensus within the plenary body that a statement, declaration, policy or other soft law document is called for, but not yet sufficient consensus as to its content for the bureau to begin to draft the document; and
- to enable diverse stakeholders to develop written contributions and submissions for the IGF collaboratively, rather than, as at present, doing so in isolation.

ICANN provides an example of such an online process in action, with its grass-roots developed ICANN Wiki, which hosts an experimental online Consensus Poll to develop an ICANN policy on gTLDs.[321] There is no reason why the Secretariat—or, as in ICANN's case, the community itself—could not provide similar facilities, as an adjunct to online deliberative discussion fora, for the development of texts at a grass-roots level within the IGF.

6.5 A new IGF

The Tunis Agenda indicates that the purpose of the IGF is to address the "many cross-cutting international public policy issues that require attention and are not adequately addressed by the current mechanisms."[322] It is notable that this does not imply that the public policy issues in question were not being addressed at all, because in many cases they were; however they were addressed either relatively ineffectively, illegitimately, or (most often) both.

Specifically, prior to the IGF's establishment, as described in Chapter 2, issues of Internet related public policy tended to be addressed only by the private sector and/or civil society (usually by their preferred mechanisms—markets, norms and architecture) to the exclusion of governments, or to be addressed by governments (generally through domestic regulation) to the exclusion of the other stakeholder groups. Even where governance did take place through networks, these were not multi-stakeholder but were dominated by one stakeholder group.[323]

[321] See section 4.4 on page 300.

[322] WSIS, Tunis Agenda for the Information Society (as in n. 5 on page 2), para 68

[323] For example, by the private sector in the case of the Global Business Dialogue on Electronic Commerce (GBDe), and governments in the case of the OECD. (As to the GBDe see `http:`

The unilateral policy decisions of these stakeholders have been undemocratic in that they have failed to consider the perspectives of all affected parties. For example, when governments have prohibited or restricted the use of Internet services within their borders (for example, many developing nations have outlawed the use of VoIP telephony),[324] there has been no representation for the interests of those affected by the transnational impacts of that decision.[325] But by the same token, civil society and the private sector have also exhibited a tendency to act unilaterally on matters of policy, without inviting the participation of governments; as seen for example in the case of the W3C's PICS initiative and the IETF's policy on wire-tapping.[326]

There are limited exceptions, in which governments have sought to involve certain private stakeholders in the policy development process. For example, Australia has by and large adopted a "light-touch" approach to Internet regulation, relying predominantly on industry self-regulation in the issue areas of spam, DNS management and content regulation. Even so, in this process civil society (let alone transnational civil society) has not been engaged as an equal stakeholder, but only as an interest group to be consulted in accordance with principles of participatory democracy.[327]

Since the establishment of the IGF, which provides an institutionalised framework for multi-stakeholder public policy development within the Internet governance regime, there is no longer any excuse for Internet-related public policy to be developed in such an unaccountable, parochial fashion as it has been to date. A good indication of the IGF's success might therefore be gauged by determining the extent to which actors in the Internet governance regime have begun to look to the multi-stakeholder process of the IGF to lubricate and legitimise their own policy processes.

There is scant evidence of this to date. Arguably the Council of Europe's 2007 Recommendation on promoting freedom of expression in the new information and communications environment, which emphasises the "importance that member states, the private sector and civil society develop various forms of multi-stakeholder co-operation and partnerships" to this end, is one of the early fruits of the IGF at an intergovernmental level.[328] However this did not represent the outcome of a multi-stakeholder

---

//www.gbd-e.org/ and Kleinwächter, Global Governance in the Information Age: GBDe and ICANN as "Pilot Projects" for Co-regulation and a New Trilateral Policy? (as in n. 106 on page 207), 17–21.)

[324]Phillippa Biggs, The Status of Voice over Internet Protocol (VoIP) Worldwide, 2006 ⟨URL: http://www.itu.int/osg/spu/ni/voice/papers/FoV-VoIP-Biggs-Draft.pdf⟩, 22–41

[325]This does not simply mean the interests of those outside the country's borders, because the transnational social entities that are affected by the decision may be partially located within the country.

[326]See section 2.2 on page 65.

[327]See also Biegel (as in n. 60 on page 19), 217.

[328]Council of Europe, Recommendation of the Committee of Ministers to Member States on Promoting Freedom of Expression and Information in the New Information and Commu-

consensus, judging by the strong opposition to the Recommendation that has emerged from civil society.[329]

On this basis, the IGF can not yet be judged a success, as all stakeholder groups have largely continued to act unilaterally in their activities in the Internet governance regime, even where public policy issues of transnational and cross-stakeholder impact are clearly engaged. For example:

- in 2005 governments intervened to prevent the addition of the xxx gTLD into the DNS root following its provisional approval by the ICANN board,[330] and have since drafted a policy that asserts the right for any GAC member government to do the same for any other proposed new gTLD;[331]
- as for the private sector, since 2007 copyright collecting agencies in countries such as Australia,[332] Japan,[333] France and the United Kingdom[334] have been seeking to secure the agreement of ISPs to voluntarily suspend or disconnect the Internet accounts of customers suspected of trading copyright material;
- even civil society has bypassed the IGF and the input of governments in working with the private sector towards the development of a code of practice on private sector involvement in national Internet regulation.[335]

Since the IGF exists to provide a forum for policy development in just such cases as these, why is it not being employed for that purpose? Whilst an obvious part of the explanation is that the IGF is still in its early days, two further possible answers will be suggested here. The first is that the IGF is not yet equipped to fulfil its appointed role, and unless significant reforms are made, it will never be. Instead, it has been fashioned by its Secretariat

nications Environment ⟨URL: https://wcd.coe.int/ViewDoc.jsp?Ref=CM/Rec(2007)11⟩. A subsequent recommendation falling into the same category is Council of Europe, Recommendation of the Committee of Ministers to Member States on Measures to Promote the Public Service Value of the Internet (as in n. 392 on page 172).

[329]European Digital Rights, New Council of Europe Recommendation Fails to Uphold Online Freedom of Expression ⟨URL: http://www.edri.org/coerec200711⟩

[330]McCullagh, Bush Administration Objects to .xxx Domains (as in n. 7 on page 3)

[331]GAC, GAC Principles Regarding New gTLDs ⟨URL: http://gac.icann.org/web/home/gTLD_principles.pdf⟩

[332]Sunday Mail, Music Pirates to be Cut Off ⟨URL: http://www.news.com.au/adelaidenow/story/0,22606,21557674-5006301,00.html⟩

[333]Yomiuri Shimbun

[334]Computer Business Review, Illegal Downloaders Could Lose Web Access ⟨URL: http://www.cbronline.com/article_news.asp?guid=DD68835B-505A-4AA1-B391-5382AD2EF499⟩

[335]See 6.2 on page 434, and compare calls for a similar code of conduct for bloggers (see BBC News, Call for Blogging Code of Conduct ⟨URL: http://news.bbc.co.uk/1/hi/technology/6502643.stm⟩) and for a bill of rights for the Social Web (see Joseph Smarr, A Bill of Rights for Users of the Social Web ⟨URL: http://opensocialweb.org/2007/09/05/bill-of-rights/⟩).

principally as a forum for the discussion of Internet issues, with a bias towards development.[336] In other words it is not, at present, an Internet governance forum at all, but simply an Internet issues forum.

The required characteristics of a new IGF capable of fulfilling its policy-setting role, rather than just its operational role for the promotion of capacity building and ICT development, has been described in some detail in this chapter. This new IGF will need to comprise:

- a Secretariat that is accountable to the IGF through its multi-stakeholder bureau, rather than merely to the UN Secretary-General, and which is no longer to carry out substantive functions such as the preparation of documents or the design of the IGF's structures and processes;
- a multi-stakeholder nominating committee, containing equal numbers of randomly-selected volunteers from each stakeholder group, to appoint members from that same stakeholder group to the IGF's multi-stakeholder bureau, as well as appointing an appeals committee for the IGF, in each case pursuant to criteria developed in open consultation with the IGF at large;
- a multi-stakeholder bureau which:
  - contains equal members from each stakeholder group acting as representatives of that group, and which although deliberating as a unitary body, ultimately gives each stakeholder group within the bureau a separate power of veto over its decisions;
  - appoints its own co-chairs (from different stakeholder groups on a rotating basis), and a chair for the nominating committee, along with any liaisons and advisors for either body;

[336]It is questionable whether it has succeeded even in this, as whilst the Secretariat, summarising the view of the Forum hawks, has stated that a focus on development issues for the IGF was seen as necessary to prevent it from "being captured by dominant political and business interests," (IGF Secretariat, Inaugural Meeting Background Report (as in n. 193 on page 367), 5) a contrary perspective is that this development focus may in fact have served the interests of the Forum doves in diverting attention away from the broader issues of Internet governance reform (not to mention the IGF's other governance roles): Mueller, "A Funny Thing Happened on the Way to the Forum...": Multistakeholderism, International Institutions and Global Governance of the Internet (as in n. 23 on page 425), 10.

Furthermore, even Nitin Desai has acknowledged the overreaching potential for the IGF's operational activities in the area of development, noting in the February 2007 consultation:

> we should also be careful that we do not end up duplicating the work on ICT for development which is being done in the WSIS follow-up. The WSIS follow-up is a very thick process with a lot of things happening, and I would urge that we do not sort of stray into areas like e-education or e-health which are being dealt with very thoroughly in the context of the WSIS follow-up, for instance.

See also to similar effect IGF Secretariat, The Substantive Agenda of the First Meeting of the Internet Governance Forum (as in n. 171 on page 361).

- also appoints moderators and panelists for plenary sessions and open fora, taking into account the IGF's mandate and the need for balanced representation of all stakeholder groups;
- is to assume the other functions of the existing Advisory Group and those taken from the Secretariat, in addition to functions that have yet been unassigned, such as assessing the consensus of the plenary body and preparing any soft law instruments required to give effect to that consensus; and
- conducts these functions independently of the UN Secretary-General, except in a strictly formal sense;[337]

- dynamic coalitions which satisfy criteria of multi-stakeholder composition and democratic process developed in open consultation with the IGF at large, and which may deliver recommendations that have demonstrably been made by consensus to the bureau for consideration by the plenary body; and

- a plenary body which:
  - at open consultation meetings instructs the bureau on the agenda to be set for plenary meetings and on the development of the structure and processes of the IGF according to multi-stakeholder, democratic principles;
  - at annual plenary meetings is empowered to engage in democratic deliberation towards the end of achieving a rational multi-stakeholder consensus, through mechanisms such as the speed dialogue; and
  - continues its work intersessionally through online mechanisms, particularly in respect of matters that are too complex or otherwise unsuited for resolution at an annual meeting.

Whilst these reforms are significant, they are both consistent with the Tunis Agenda, and also practically achievable; particularly in comparison to other proposals for the democratisation of Internet governance such as ICANN's 2000 At-Large elections.[338]

There is however more doubt as to whether they are yet politically achievable, and this constitutes the second reason why other actors in the Internet governance regime are not having recourse to the processes of the IGF: that the transaction costs of moving to an open, democratic and multi-stakeholder process are greater than those of bypassing the IGF and

[337] However after the five year initial mandate of the IGF expires, the IGF could be reconstituted as an international organisation in its own right, without even formal UN oversight.

[338] See section 5.4 on page 404.

continuing to act unilaterally or in narrower, less accountable governance networks.[339]

The transaction costs of acting through the IGF rather than in narrower private networks are likely to be highest for the regime's most powerful actors, the Forum doves; and to that extent this second reason for the failure of the IGF largely underlies the first, since it is at the behest of the Forum doves that the IGF has been structurally and procedurally disempowered since its formation was first proposed by WGIG and subsequently agreed at WSIS. Whereas the Tunis Agenda establishes a broad mandate for the IGF that unequivocally involves it in making substantive policy recommendations, the Forum doves have been resolute in downplaying the IGF's policy-setting role, as their submissions outlined in Chapter 5 demonstrate time and again.

This has been justified by some by pointing to the division between the IGF as a venue for multi-stakeholder discussion, and the government-led "enhanced cooperation" process as the locus of policy-setting authority.[340] But in fact there is no clear division between the role of the IGF and the process of enhanced cooperation in the Tunis Agenda; rather the former is treated as an integral component of the latter.[341] What can be taken from this is that whilst governments will continue to maintain sovereignty over the authoritative statement of public policy principles in international and domestic law, those principles are to be developed in a multi-stakeholder forum, the IGF (from where they may equally find implementation through other, non-legal mechanisms of governance).

Regardless of the terms of the Tunis Agenda however, the role of civil society in the enhanced cooperation process (and hence the role of the IGF) has been played down by governmental actors in Tunis' wake; for example in EU Commissioner Viviane Reding's description of it as a "process of enhanced cooperation between governments."[342] In any case, the disunity of states following WSIS on exactly what the content of a new model of enhanced cooperation should be seems effectively to have ground that broader process to a halt.[343] Thus the momentum of the programme of multi-stakeholder democratisation of Internet governance that began at WSIS has since been lost (or perhaps unmasked as expedient politics), leaving the IGF as its only extant remnant.

---

[339] Mueller describes the experience of the IFWP in much the same way: Mueller, *Ruling the Root: Internet Governance and the Taming of Cyberspace* (as in n. 21 on page 35), 5.

[340] Idem, "A Funny Thing Happened on the Way to the Forum...": Multistakeholderism, International Institutions and Global Governance of the Internet (as in n. 23 on page 425), 10

[341] See WSIS, Tunis Agenda for the Information Society (as in n. 5 on page 2), paras 67–72, in which the middle paragraphs on enhanced cooperation are sandwiched by those calling for the establishment of the IGF.

[342] European Commission, Internet Governance: Commission Welcomes Move Towards Full Private-Sector Management by 2009 ⟨URL: `http://europa.eu/rapid/pressReleasesAction.do?reference=IP/06/1297`⟩

[343] See section 5.1 on page 344.

This makes it all the more important that the role of the IGF in multi-stakeholder policy development is not forsaken. This in turn can only ultimately be assured through change at a political level. It must, in short, become more politically expensive for intransigent governments and other Forum doves to continue to bypass the IGF than for them to embrace it. This is, doubtless, quite a hope. As one commentator observed ahead of the Athens meeting, "There is no indication that rulers of China, Tunisia or Iran will take any notice of what is said in Athens, and no real hope that the Western governments will step back from their own campaigns to control, regulate and censor the net."[344]

Yet there are cases in which, as liberal institutionalism predicts, governments have been willing to restrain their authority in the interests of making longer term absolute gains through cooperation with other stakeholder groups. For example, governments have for the most part been content to leave ccTLD administration to private, bottom–up coordination, as in the cases of auDA, Nominet and SIDN amongst others. With slightly less universal contentment, they have also acquiesced in ICANN's administration of the global DNS root and IP addressing system.

WGIG is another prominent example of governments sharing responsibility for policy development with other stakeholder groups. Although this occurred in a somewhat more controlled environment than the IGF, it well illustrates the significant effect that a body without formal decision-making authority can nevertheless have on policy development at a higher, more authoritative level; after all, there would certainly be no IGF were it not for WGIG. Outside the Internet governance regime, a number of similar examples have already been given, including the processes by which the Mine Ban Treaty and Disability Convention were developed with the integral involvement of civil society.[345]

So whilst political change is required in order for the IGF to be allowed to take its place as the multi-stakeholder forum for policy development that the Tunis Agenda describes, provided that a good case can be made for such change, there is no cause to rule it out as utopian, particularly given the progress that has already been made towards the realisation of multi-stakeholder democratic Internet governance through WSIS, WGIG and the establishment of the IGF (for now) as a venue for freeform discussion.

This book has endeavoured to make that case, by demonstrating that performing public policy governance of the Internet through the mechanism of a democratic multi-stakeholder network (generally compatible with the model proposed for the IGF in the Tunis Agenda):

- is more legitimate than the use of hierarchical mechanisms of governance, because states do not even conceptually possess sole authority

[344] Bill Thompson, Everyone Talks, But No-One Listens ⟨URL: `http://news.bbc.co.uk/1/hi/technology/6091282.stm`⟩

[345] See section 6.2 on page 436.

over public policy issues that have substantially transnational rather than domestic effects;

- is also likely to be more effective than the use of rules, which is at odds with the architectural values of the Internet such as decentralisation, openness, egalitarianism and cosmopolitanism that continue to permeate its culture;

- does not however threaten the existing political and economic power of governments or other stakeholders, because of its inherently non-binding, consensual form, and even less so given the consociational structure for the bureau that has been devised in this book; and

- does not even detract from the need for states to exercise an independent policy-setting role, since when consensus cannot be achieved on a particular issue, it will fall through to be dealt with on a decentralised basis by other mechanisms, including rules.[346]

As strong as the case for reform of the IGF may be, its implications will not be self-executing. In none of the other cases referred to above in which international public policy-setting has been opened up to other stakeholders (the WSIS process and the Mine Ban and Disability treaties), did this occur without sustained pressure from civil society. Therefore it will be incumbent upon democracy activists and academics to catalyse the political change required for the IGF to undergo the reforms that this chapter has shown necessary, and for that new IGF to be accepted as legitimately filling the policy void referred to in the Tunis Agenda.[347]

Part of what this involves is refusing to accept the curtailment of the IGF's mandate by stealth. If the Forum doves are no longer willing to share their responsibility for policy development with other stakeholders through an empowered and effective IGF, this agenda should be unmasked and debated transparently rather than being quietly effected through the inaction of its Secretariat and Advisory Group and their imposition of inappropriate institutional strictures on the IGF.

This is not to downplay the significant achievement that has been made already, in attracting all stakeholder groups to share their perspectives on issues of Internet governance in an open and egalitarian discussion forum. This is an important foundation for the fuller implementation of multi-stakeholder governance in the future. Given time, the IGF might even evolve naturally into the body envisaged by the Tunis Agenda, as trust between stakeholders is earned and the social capital of the governance network develops. However, as the IGF has only five years to establish

[346]Similarly, when only a limited or partial consensus can be reached, this can narrow down the issues that would otherwise be at large for the policy maker: John Mathiason, The Road to Rio and Beyond: Results-based Management of the UN Internet Governance Forum ⟨URL: `http://www.internetgovernance.org/pdf/roadtorio.pdf`⟩, 2.

[347]WSIS, Tunis Agenda for the Information Society (as in n. 5 on page 2), para 60

itself before its existence is reviewed, it does not have the luxury of time. Further, structural inertia will make change more difficult the longer it is left.

If, on the other hand, the IGF does come to fulfil its potential, the implications of its success should resonate throughout the Internet governance regime, perhaps leading other Internet governance fora such as ICANN and the ITU to progressively develop their own structures and processes along similar multi-stakeholder lines.[348] In fact, there is no reason why the example of the IGF should not extend far beyond the regime of Internet governance. Conceptually, multi-stakeholder governance calls for application to many other issue areas of transnational public policy development, such as the environment, intellectual property, trade, peacekeeping and human rights. The IGF may therefore represent not only an innovation for Internet governance, but the vanguard of a new paradigm for the post-Westphalian age of international relations.

[348] De la Chapelle, Governing the Internet—Freedom and Regulation in the OSCE Region (as in n. 296 on page 505), 26

Appendix A

Comparison of other organisations

	APNIC	ASF	auDA	CA/Browser	CGI.br
Role					
Regime	Internet	Open source	Internet	Internet	Internet
Sphere	Coordination	Standards	Coordination	Standards	Various
Region	Asia Pacific	International	Australia	International	Brazil
Operations	Yes	Yes	Yes	Yes	Yes
Policy-setting	Yes	No	Yes	Yes	Yes
Audit	No	No	Yes	No	No
Arbitration	No	No	Yes	No	No
Coordination	Yes	Yes	Yes	Yes	Yes
Regulation	Yes	No	Yes	No	Yes
Structure					
Mechanism	Rules	Norms	Rules	Norms	Networks
Oversight	IANA	None	Government	None	Government
Publicity	None	None	Oversight	None	Oversight
Composition	Open	Open	M/stakeholder	Non-state	M/stakeholder
Membership	Open	Open, free	Open	Restricted	Democratic
Representation	Representative	Individual	Representative	Representative	Representative
Executive	Democratic	Meritocratic	Democratic	None	None
Secretariat	Hierarchical	Consensual	Hierarchical	None	Governmental

	CONGO	CS-IGC	CSB	Debian	ECOSOC
Role					
Regime	Various	Internet	Internet	Open source	Various
Sphere	Policy	Policy	Policy	Standards	Policy
Region	International	International	International	International	International
Operations	No	No	Yes	Yes	Yes
Policy-setting	No	No	No	No	Yes
Audit	No	No	No	No	No
Arbitration	No	No	No	Yes	No
Coordination	Yes	Yes	Yes	No	Yes
Regulation	No	No	No	No	No
Structure					
Mechanism	Networks	Norms	Norms	Norms	Networks
Oversight	None	None	CS Plenary	None	None
Publicity	None	None	None	None	Governmental
Composition	Civil society	Civil society	Civil society	Open	States
Membership	Open	Open, free	Open, free	Meritocratic	Democratic
Representation	Representative	Individual	Representative	Individual	Representative
Executive	Democratic	Democratic	Consensual	Democratic	Democratic
Secretariat	Hierarchical	None	Governmental	Consensual	Governmental

	EFF	EU	FSC	GAID	GKP
Role					
Regime	Internet	Various	Forestry	Internet	Internet
Sphere	Policy	Policy	Policy	Policy	Policy
Region	United States	Europe	International	International	International
Operations	Yes	Yes	Yes	No	Yes
Policy-setting	No	Yes	Yes	No	No
Audit	No	Yes	Yes	No	No
Arbitration	No	Yes	No	No	No
Coordination	No	Yes	Yes	Yes	Yes
Regulation	No	Yes	No	No	No
Structure					
Mechanism	Norms	Rules	Norms	Networks	Networks
Oversight	None	None	None	ECOSOC	No
Publicity	None	Governmental	None	Oversight	None
Composition	Open	States	Non-state	M/stakeholder	M/stakeholder
Membership	Open	Restricted	Open	Open, free	Open
Representation	Individual	Representative	Representative	Representative	Representative
Executive	Oligarchical	Consocional	Consocional	Hierarchical	Democratic
Secretariat	Hierarchical	Hierarchical	Hierarchical	Governmental	Hierarchical

	gTLD-MoU	IAB	ICANN	ICC	ICPEN
Role					
Regime	Internet	Internet	Internet	Commerce	Consumers
Sphere	Coordination	Coordination	Coordination	Policy	Policy
Region	International	International	International	International	International
Operations	Yes	Yes	Yes	Yes	Yes
Policy-setting	Yes	No	Yes	No	No
Audit	No	Yes	Yes	No	No
Arbitration	Yes	Yes	Yes	Yes	No
Coordination	Yes	Yes	Yes	Yes	Yes
Regulation	Yes	No	Yes	No	No
Structure					
Mechanism	Networks	Norms	Networks	Norms	Networks
Oversight	ISOC	ISOC	NTIA	None	Executive govt
Publicity	Weak via ITU	None	Oversight	None	Govt network
Composition	Open	Open	M/stakeholder	Private sector	Governmental
Membership	Open, free	Meritocratic	Restricted	Open	Restricted
Representation	Representative	Individual	Representative	Representative	Representative
Executive	Consocional	None	Oligarchical	Democratic	None
Secretariat	Hierarchical	None	Hierarchical	Hierarchical	Hierarchical

	IETF	ILO	IPC	ISO	ISOC
Role					
Regime	Internet	Labour	IPR	Standards	Internet
Sphere	Standards	Policy	Policy	Standards	Coordination
Region	International	International	International	International	International
Operations	No	Yes	Yes	No	Yes
Policy-setting	Yes	Yes	No	Yes	No
Audit	No	No	No	No	Yes
Arbitration	No	No	No	No	No
Coordination	No	No	No	Yes	Yes
Regulation	No	Yes	No	Yes	No
Structure					
Mechanism	Norms	Rules	Norms	Norms	Norms
Oversight	IAB	None	None	None	None
Publicity	None	Governmental	None	None	None
Composition	Open	M/stakeholder	Private sector	Open	Open
Membership	Open, free	Restricted	Restricted	Restricted	Open, free
Representation	Individual	Representative	Representative	Representative	Individual
Executive	Meritocratic	Consocional	None	Democratic	Democratic
Secretariat	Hierarchical	Hierarchical	Hierarchical	Hierarchical	Hierarchical

	ISTF	ITU	LAP	OECD	TRUSTe
Role					
Regime	Internet	Telecomms	Internet	Various	Internet
Sphere	Policy	Standards	Policy	Policy	Policy
Region	International	International	International	International	United States
Operations	No	Yes	No	Yes	Yes
Policy-setting	Yes	Yes	No	Yes	Yes
Audit	No	No	No	No	Yes
Arbitration	No	No	No	No	Yes
Coordination	No	Yes	Yes	Yes	No
Regulation	No	Yes	No	Yes	No
Structure					
Mechanism	Norms	Rules	Networks	Rules	Norms
Oversight	ISOC	None	None	None	None
Publicity	None	Governmental	Executive govt	Governmental	None
Composition	Open	Govt, private	Govt, private	States	Private sector
Membership	Open, free	Open	Restricted	Restricted	Open
Representation	Individual	Representative	Representative	Representative	Representative
Executive	None	Democratic	None	Democratic	Oligarchical
Secretariat	None	Hierarchical	None	Hierarchical	Hierarchical

	UN	UNCITRAL	UNICTTF	Ubuntu	VGT
Role					
Regime	Various	Trade	Internet	Open source	Crime
Sphere	Policy	Policy	Policy	Standards	Policy
Region	International	International	International	International	International
Operations	Yes	No	No	Yes	Yes
Policy-setting	Yes	Yes	No	No	No
Audit	Yes	No	No	No	No
Arbitration	Yes	No	No	No	No
Coordination	Yes	No	Yes	No	Yes
Regulation	Yes	Yes	No	No	No
Structure					
Mechanism	Rules	Rules	Networks	Norms	Networks
Oversight	None	UN	UN	None	Executive govt
Publicity	Governmental	Governmental	Oversight	None	Govt network
Composition	States	States	M/stakeholder	Open	Governmental
Membership	Restricted	Democratic	Open, free	Meritocratic	Restricted
Representation	Representative	Representative	Representative	Individual	Representative
Executive	Democratic	None	Hierarchical	Oligarchical	None
Secretariat	Hierarchical	Governmental	Governmental	Hierarchical	Hierarchical

	W3C	WGIG	WIPO	WTO	Wikimedia
Role					
Regime	Internet	Internet	IPR	Trade	Open content
Sphere	Standards	Policy	Policy	Policy	Standards
Region	International	International	International	International	International
Operations	No	No	No	No	Yes
Policy-setting	Yes	Yes	Yes	Yes	No
Audit	No	No	No	No	No
Arbitration	No	No	No	Yes	Yes
Coordination	No	No	No	No	No
Regulation	No	No	Yes	Yes	No
Structure					
Mechanism	Norms	Norms	Rules	Rules	Norms
Oversight	None	WSIS	None	None	None
Publicity	None	Oversight	Governmental	Governmental	None
Composition	Open	M/stakeholder	States	States	Open
Membership	Open	Closed	Restricted	Restricted	Open, free
Representation	Representative	Individual	Representative	Representative	Individual
Executive	Democratic	None	Democratic	Democratic	Meritocratic
Secretariat	Hierarchical	Governmental	Governmental	Governmental	Meritocratic

Bibliography

Electronic references were last accessed on 1 April 2008 unless otherwise specified.

Abbot, Kenneth W et al., The Concept of Legalization, International Organization 54:3 2000, p. 401.

ACA, Regulatory Issues Associated with Provision of Voice Services Using Internet Protocol in Australia Canberra: Australian Government Information Management Office, 2004.

Accuosto, Pablo, WSIS Wraps Up With Mixed Emotions ⟨URL: http://www.choike.org/nuevo_eng/informes/3730.html⟩.

ACICA, Arbitration Rules ⟨URL: http://www.acica.org.au/arbitration_rules.html⟩.

ACLU, Fahrenheit 451.2: Is Cyberspace Burning? ⟨URL: http://www.aclu.org/privacy/speech/15145pub20020317.html⟩.

Adams, John, The Political Writings of John Adams Washington, DC: Regnery Publishing, Inc, 2000.

AGIMO, Principles for ICT-enabled Citizen Engagement ⟨URL: http://www.agimo.gov.au/__data/assets/pdf_file/0008/55745/Principles.pdf⟩.

AGIMO, Australian Government Consultation Blog Discussion Paper ⟨URL: http://www.agimo.gov.au/__data/assets/pdf_file/0014/61601/Consultation_Blog_Discussion_Paper.pdf⟩.

Agrawal, Ruchika, Why is P3P Not a PET? ⟨URL: http://www.w3.org/2002/p3p-ws/pp/epic.pdf⟩.

Ahrens, Frank, Death by Wikipedia: The Kenneth Lay Chronicles ⟨URL: http://www.washingtonpost.com/wp-dyn/content/article/2006/07/08/AR2006070800135.html⟩.

Akehurst, Michael, A Modern Introduction to International Law, 2nd edition London: George Allen & Unwin, 1970.

Aktiv Demokrati, Partyprogram for Aktiv Demokrati ⟨URL: http://wse75376.web16.talkactive.net/ads%20websida/Party%20program.html⟩.

ALAC, Charter ⟨URL: http://icannwiki.org/ALAC_Charter⟩.

Ali Khan, L, A Theory of Universal Democracy: Beyond the End of History The Hague: Kluwer Law International, 2003.

Allen, David, The Role of Intellectual/Academic Work in a Policy Forum ⟨URL: http://davidallen.org/papers/Policy_Brains_Trust-A4.pdf⟩.

Alston, Philip, The Myopia of the Handmaidens: International Lawyers and Globalization, Eur J Int'l Law 8:3 1997, p. 435.

Anandarajan, M, Simmers, C and Igbaria, M, An Exploratory Investigation of the Antecedents and Impacts of Internet Usage: An Individual Perspective, Behaviour & Information Technology 19 2000, p. 69.

Annan, Kofi, In Larger Freedom: Towards Development, Security and Human Rights For All ⟨URL: http://documents-dds-ny.un.org/doc/UNDOC/GEN/N05/270/78/pdf/N0527078.pdf?OpenElement⟩.

APC, Internet Rights Charter ⟨URL: http://rights.apc.org/documents/APC_charter_EN.pdf⟩.

APC, Questionnaire on the Convening the Internet Governance Forum ⟨URL: http://www.intgovforum.org/contributions/apc-questionnaire.pdf⟩.

APC, APC Statement on the Second Internet Governance Forum ⟨URL: http://pakistanictpolicy.bytesforall.net/?q=node/104⟩.

APDIP, Internet Governance: Asia-Pacific Perspectives New Delhi: Elsevier, 2005, chap. Internet Governance in the Asia-Pacific Region, p. 37.

APEC, Recommendation by the APEC TELWG to SOM for an APEC Cybersecurity Strategy ⟨URL: http://www.apec.org/apec/apec_groups/working_groups/telecommunications_and_information.MedialibDownload.v1.html?url=/etc/medialib/apec_media_library/downloads/som/mtg/2002/word.Par.0204.File.v1.1⟩.

Arend, Anthony Clark, Legal Rules and International Society New York: Oxford University Press, 1999.

Aristotle, Politics Oxford: Clarendon Press, 1943.

Aristotle, Nicomachean Ethics Raleigh, N C: Alex Catalogue, 2000.

Arrow, Kenneth J, Social Choice and Individual Values, 2nd edition New Haven, CT: Yale University Press, 1963.

Arrow, Kenneth J and Debreu, Gerard, Existence of an Equilibrium for a Competitive Economy, Econometrica 22:3 1954, p. 265.

Aschendorff/Münster, The Westphalian Treaties from October 24th, 1648 ⟨URL: `http://www.pax-westphalica.de/`⟩.

ASF, How the ASF Works ⟨URL: `http://www.apache.org/foundation/how-it-works.html`⟩.

ASO, Memorandum of Understanding ⟨URL: `http://aso.icann.org/docs/aso-mou.html`⟩.

ASTA, Technology and Policy Proposal ⟨URL: `http://postmaster.info.aol.com/asta/proposal_adobe.pdf`⟩.

At-Large Study Committee, Final Report on ICANN At-Large Membership ⟨URL: `http://www.icann.org/at-large/final-report-05nov01.htm`⟩.

Auchard, Eric, Google Agrees to Censor Service to Enter China ⟨URL: `http://www.news.com/8301-10784_3-6030773-7.html`⟩.

auDA, .au Dispute Resolution Policy ⟨URL: `http://www.auda.org.au/policies/auda-2002-22/`⟩.

auDA, WHOIS Policy ⟨URL: `http://www.auda.org.au/policies/auda-2003-08/`⟩.

auDA, Constitution ⟨URL: `http://www.auda.org.au/pdf/auda-constitution.pdf`⟩.

Auerbach, Karl, Stakeholderism—The Wrong Road For Internet Governance ⟨URL: `http://www.cavebear.com/archive/rw/igf-democracy-in-internet-governance.pdf`⟩.

Austin, John, The Province of Jurisprudence Determined, and the Uses of the Study of Jurisprudence London: Widenfeld and Nicolson, 1954.

Avio, Kenneth L, Constitutional Contract and Discourse Ethics: The Agreement Theories of James Buchanan and Jürgen Habermas, Journal of Theoretical Politics 9:4 1997, p. 533.

Bacard, A, Electronic Democracy: Can We Retake Our Government?, Humanist 53:4 1993, p. 42.

Bakunin, Mikhail Aleksandrovich, God and the State New York: Courier Dover Publications, 1970.

Baldi, Stefano, The Internet for International Political and Social Protest: the Case of Seattle ⟨URL: http://baldi.diplomacy.edu/articles/protest.htm⟩.

Balnaves, Mark, Walsh, Lucas and Shoesmith, Brian, Participatory Technologies: The Use of the Internet in Civic Participation and Democratic Processes ⟨URL: http://www.public-policy.unimelb.edu.au/egovernance/papers/03_Balnaves.pdf⟩.

Barbrook, R and Cameron, A, The Californian Ideology, Science as Culture 26 1996, p. 44.

Barlow, John Perry, A Declaration of the Independence of Cyberspace ⟨URL: http://homes.eff.org/~barlow/Declaration-Final.html⟩.

Barquin, Ramon, The Ten Commandments of Computer Ethics ⟨URL: http://www.cpsr.org/issues/ethics/cei/⟩.

Barr, Michael S and Miller, Geoffrey P, Global Administrative Law: The View from Basel, EJIL 17:1 2006, p. 15.

BBC News, Call for Blogging Code of Conduct ⟨URL: http://news.bbc.co.uk/1/hi/technology/6502643.stm⟩.

Benkler, Yochai, Coase's Penguin, or, Linux and The Nature of the Firm, Yale LJ 112 2002, p. 369.

Berners-Lee, Tim and Fischetti, Mark, Weaving the Web London, United Kingdom: Orion Business Books, 1999.

Bertola, Vittorio, An Implementation Proposal for the Internet Governance Forum ⟨URL: http://www.intgovforum.org/contributions/An%20implementation%20proposal%20for%20the%20IGF.pdf⟩.

Bertola, Vittorio, An Introduction to Trusted Computing ⟨URL: http://www.intgovforum.org/Substantive_1st_IGF/An%20Introduction%20To%20Trusted%20Computing.doc⟩.

Biegel, Stuart, Beyond Our Control? Confronting the Limits of Our Legal System in the Age of Cyberspace Cambridge, MA: MIT Press, 2001.

Biggs, Phillippa, The Status of Voice over Internet Protocol (VoIP) Worldwide, 2006 ⟨URL: http://www.itu.int/osg/spu/ni/voice/papers/FoV-VoIP-Biggs-Draft.pdf⟩.

Bloem, Renate, The World Summit on the Information Society: Moving from the Past into the Future New York: UNICTTF, 2005, chap. Multi-Stakeholderism and Civil Society, p. 99.

Bobbio, Norberto, Cosmopolitan Democracy: An Agenda for a New World Order Cambridge: Polity Press, 1995, chap. Democracy and the International System, p. 17.

Brackertz, Nicola et al., Community Consultation and the Hard to Reach: Concepts and Practice in Victorian Local Government ⟨URL: `http://www.sisr.net/cag/docs/HardtoReach_main.pdf`⟩.

Braithwaite, John, Enforced Self-Regulation: A New Strategy for Corporate Crime Control, Mich LR 80 1982, p. 1466.

Brennan, Richard, E-vote a Virtual Cinch to Take Off, The Toronto Star Nov 16 2006.

Britannica, Encyclopædia, Fatally Flawed: Refuting the Recent Study on Encyclopedic Accuracy by the Journal Nature ⟨URL: `http://corporate.britannica.com/britannica_nature_response.pdf`⟩.

Bryan, Cathy, Tsagorousianou, Roza and Tambini, Damian, Cyberdemocracy London: Routledge, 1998, chap. Electronic Democracy and the Civic Networking Movement in Context, p. 1.

Bull, Hedley, The Anarchical Society, 2nd edition New York: Columbia University Press, 1977.

Burke, Wyatt Warner, Organization Change: Theory and Practice Thousand Oaks, CA: Sage Publications, 2002.

Burnstein, Matthew, Internet: Which Court Decides? Which Law Applies? The Hague: Kluwer Law International, 1998, chap. A Global Network in a Compartmentalised Legal Environment, p. 23.

Burr, J Beckwith, Media Advisory: Letter to ICANN ⟨URL: `http://www.ntia.doc.gov/ntiahome/press/icann102098.htm`⟩.

Butler, C T and Rothstein, Amy, On Conflict and Consensus: A Handbook on Formal Consensus Decisionmaking Tahoma Park, MD: Food Not Bombs Publishing, 2004.

Butt, Danny, Internet Governance: Asia-Pacific Perspectives New Delhi: Elsevier, 2005, chap. The Open Regional Dialogue on Internet Governance, p. 1.

Byfield, Bruce, Maintainer's Resignation Highlights Problems in Debian Project ⟨URL: `http://www.linux.com/articles/56883`⟩.

CAMDUN, Main Options for a UN Peoples' Assembly ⟨URL: `http://www.camdun-online.gn.apc.org/options.html`⟩.

Cameron, Maxwell A, Global Civil Society and the Ottawa Process: Lessons From the Movement to Ban Anti-Personnel Mines, Canadian Foreign Policy 7:1 1999, p. 85.

Campbell, K, A Net Conspiracy So Immense ⟨URL: http://w2.eff.org/legal/cases/Canter_Siegel/c-and-s_summary.article⟩.

Cardoso, Fernando Henrique, Civil Society and Global Governance ⟨URL: http://www.ngocongo.org/files/cardoso_paper1.doc⟩.

Cardoso, Fernando Henrique, Cardoso Report on Civil Society ⟨URL: http://www.capacity.undp.org/indexAction.cfm?module=Library&action=GetFile&DocumentAttachmentID=1236⟩.

Carroll, Archie B, Corporate Social Responsibility: Evolution of a Definitional Construct, Business & Society 38:3 1999, p. 268.

Carson, Lyn, Innovative Consultation Processes and the Changing Role of Activism, Third Sector Review 7:1 2001, p. 7.

Caslon Analytics, auDA Profile ⟨URL: http://www.caslon.com.au/audaprofile.htm⟩.

Caslon Analytics, Cyberspace Governance ⟨URL: http://www.caslon.com.au/governanceguide.htm⟩.

Cassavoy, Liane, Music Labels Declare War on File Swappers ⟨URL: http://www.pcworld.com/article/id,112364-page,1/article.html⟩.

Catinat, Michel and Vedel, Thierry, Digital Democracy London: Sage Publications, 2000, chap. Public Policies for Digital Democracy, pp. 184–208.

Cavanagh, John and Anderson, Sarah, Top 200. The Rise of Corporate Global Power ⟨URL: http://www.tni.org/archives/cavanagh/top200.pdf⟩.

CCBI and ICC, CCBI/ICC Questions and Further Input on the Internet Governance Forum ⟨URL: http://www.intgovforum.org/contributions/CCBI%20further%20input%20on%20IGF%206%20February%20FINAL.pdf⟩.

CDT, Companies, Human Rights Groups, Investors, Academics and Technology Leaders to Address International Free Expression and Privacy Challenges ⟨URL: http://www.cdt.org/press/20070118press-humanrights.php⟩.

Centre for Global Studies, Enhancing Legitimacy in the Internet Corporation for Assigned Names and Numbers ⟨URL: http://www.markle.org/downloadable_assets/icann_enhancelegitemacy.pdf⟩.

Cerf, Vinton, Does the Internet Need to be Governed? ⟨URL: http://www.circleid.com/posts/does_the_internet_need_to_be_governed⟩.

Chapelle, Bertrand de la, The World Summit on the Information Society: Moving from the Past into the Future New York: UNICTTF, 2005, chap. WSIS: The First Summit of the Internet Age?, p. 277.

Chapelle, Bertrand de la, Governing the Internet—Freedom and Regulation in the OSCE Region Vienna: OSCE Representative on Freedom of the Media, 2007, chap. The Internet Governance Forum: How a United Nations Summit Produced a New Governance Paradigm for the Internet Age, p. 19.

Charnovitz, Steve, Two Centuries of Participation, NGOs and International Governance, Mich J Int'l L 18 1997, p. 183.

Chen, Peter, e-lection 2004? New Media and the Campaign ⟨URL: http://eprints.infodiv.unimelb.edu.au/archive/00000772/01/e-lection_2004.pdf⟩.

Cheniti, Tarek, Reforming Internet Governance: Perspectives from the Working Group on Internet Governance (WGIG) New York: UNICTTF, 2005, chap. The WGIG Process: Lessons Learned and Thoughts for the Future, p. 31.

Cherry, Steven, The Net Effect ⟨URL: http://www.spectrum.ieee.org/jun05/1219⟩.

Chinkin, C M, The Challenge of Soft Law: Development and Change in International Law, ICLQ 38:4 1989, p. 850.

Cisco IOS Learning Services, The ABCs of IP Version 6 ⟨URL: http://www.sixxs.net/archive/docs/Cisco%20IPv6%20ABC.pdf⟩.

Civic Alliance to Rebuild Downtown New York, Listening to the City: Report of Proceedings ⟨URL: http://www.listeningtothecity.org/background/final_report_9_20.pdf⟩.

Civil Society Scientific Information Working Group, Substantive Contributions as Material to Synthesis Papers in View of the First Meeting of the Internet Governance Forum ⟨URL: http://intgovforum.org/Substantive_1st_IGF/si-synthesis-oa.pdf⟩.

Clark, Tim, Visa, Mastercard Try to Revive SET ⟨URL: http://www.news.com/2100-1017-225723.html⟩.

Clarke, Grenville and Sohn, Louis B, World Peace Through World Law Cambridge, MA: Harvard University Press, 1958.

Clarke, Joe, To Hell with WCAG 2 ⟨URL: http://www.alistapart.com/articles/tohellwithwcag2/⟩.

Clarke, Roger, Freedom of Information? The Internet as Harbinger of the New Dark Ages ⟨URL: http://firstmonday.org/issues/issue4_11/clarke/⟩.

Clarke, Roger, "Information Wants to be Free ..." ⟨URL: http://www.anu.edu.au/people/Roger.Clarke/II/IWtbF.html⟩.

Clarke, Roger, Meta-Brands ⟨URL: http://www.anu.edu.au/people/Roger.Clarke/DV/MetaBrands.html⟩.

Clarke, Roger, The Internet and Democracy ⟨URL: http://www.agimo.gov.au/publications/2004/05/egovt_challenges/community/democracy⟩.

Coase, R, The Problem of Social Cost, J L & Econ 3 1960, p. 1.

Cohen, Joshua, The Good Polity: Normative Analysis of the State New York: Basil Blackwell, 1989, chap. Deliberation and Democratic Legitimacy, p. 22.

Cohen, Joshua, Deliberative Democracy Cambridge: Cambridge University Press, 1998, chap. Democracy and Liberty, p. 185.

Coleman, J, Foundations of Social Theory Cambridge, MA: Harvard University Press, 1990.

Coleman, Stephen and Gøtze, John, Bowling Together: Online Public Engagement in Policy Deliberation ⟨URL: http://www.bowlingtogether.net/bowlingtogether.pdf⟩.

Colombo, Massimo G and Delmastro, Marco, The Determinants of Organizational Change and Structural Inertia: Technological and Organizational Factors, Journal of Economics & Management Strategy 11:4 2002, p. 595.

Committee, ICANN Government Advisory, Principles for Delegation and Administration of Country Code Top Level Domains ⟨URL: http://www.icann.org/committees/gac/gac-cctldprinciples-23feb00.htm⟩.

Commonwealth of Australia, Review of the Treaty Making Process ⟨URL: http://www.austlii.edu.au/au/other/dfat/reports/review_treaty_making.html⟩.

Computer Business Review, Illegal Downloaders Could Lose Web Access ⟨URL: http://www.cbronline.com/article_news.asp?guid=DD68835B-505A-4AA1-B391-5382AD2EF499⟩.

Conklin, Jeff, Dialogue Mapping: Building Shared Understanding of Wicked Problems Chichester: John Wiley and Sons Ltd, 2005.

Content & Themes, Civil Society Working Group on, Does Input lead to Impact? How Governments treated Civil Society Proposals in Drafting the 19 September 2003 Draft Plan of Action ⟨URL: http://www.worldsummit2003.de/download_en/does_input_lead_to_impact-action-plan.rtf⟩.

Cooter, Robert D, Structural Adjudication and the New Law Merchant: A Model of Decentralised Law, Int Rev Law & Econ 14 1994, p. 215.

Corbet, Jonathan, PHP Nuke Remains Vulnerable ⟨URL: http://lwn.net/2001/1011/security.php3⟩.

Corbet, Jonathan, Where Does Kernel Development Stand? ⟨URL: http://lwn.net/2001/1011/kernel.php3⟩.

Corbet, Jonathan, Debian and Mozilla—A Study in Trademarks ⟨URL: http://lwn.net/Articles/118268/⟩.

Council of Europe, Electronic Governance ("E-Governance") ⟨URL: http://www.coe.int/t/e/integrated_projects/democracy/02_activities/01_e%2Dgovernance/00_recommendation_and_explanatory_memorandum/⟩.

Council of Europe, Council of Europe Submission to the Internet Governance Forum ⟨URL: http://intgovforum.org/Substantive_1st_IGF/CoE%20submission%20to%20the%20IGF.pdf⟩.

Council of Europe, Building a Free and Safe Internet ⟨URL: http://www.intgovforum.org/Substantive_2nd_IGF/CoE_Building%20a%20free%20and%20safe%20Internet.pdf⟩.

Council of Europe, Recommendation of the Committee of Ministers to Member States on Measures to Promote the Public Service Value of the Internet ⟨URL: https://wcd.coe.int/ViewDoc.jsp?id=1207291⟩.

Council of Europe, Recommendation of the Committee of Ministers to Member States on Promoting Freedom of Expression and Information in the New Information and Communications Environment ⟨URL: https://wcd.coe.int/ViewDoc.jsp?Ref=CM/Rec(2007)11⟩.

Council of the European Union, Reply of the European Community and its Member States to the US Green Paper ⟨URL: http://jgate.ncsi.iisc.ernet.in/cyberspace/law/governance/eu/ReplytoUSGreenPaper.html⟩.

Cox, Christopher, Who Rules the Net? Internet Governance and Jurisdiction Washington, DC: Cato Institute, 2003, chap. Establishing Global Internet Freedom: Tear Down This Firewall, p. 3.

Cox, Gary W, Making Votes Count: Strategic Coordination in the World's Electoral Systems Cambridge: Cambridge University Press, 1997.

Cranor, Lorrie Faith, The Role of Data Protection Authorities in the Design and Deployment of the Platform for Privacy Preferences ⟨URL: http://lorrie.cranor.org/pubs/paris-talk0901.html⟩.

Crocker, D, Making Standards the IETF Way ⟨URL: http://www.isoc.org/internet/standards/papers/crocker-on-standards.shtml⟩.

CS-IGC, Initial Reactions to the WGIG Report ⟨URL: http://www.itu.int/wsis/docs2/pc3/contributions/co23.doc⟩.

CS-IGC, Charter ⟨URL: http://www.igcaucus.org/IGC-charter_final-061014.html⟩.

CS-IGC, Input into the Open Round of Consultations on 23 May 2007 to Discuss Program and Agenda for the Second Meeting of the IGF in Rio de Janeiro ⟨URL: http://www.intgovforum.org/May_contributions/IGC%27s%20contribution%20to%20Rio%20agenda%200507.pdf⟩.

Cukier, Kenneth Neil, Slouching Towards Geneva: Ten Unappreciated Axioms of Internet Governance ⟨URL: http://www.oii.ox.ac.uk/collaboration/specialevents/20050505_governance_position_papers.pdf⟩.

Cukier, Kenneth Neil, The World Summit on the Information Society: Moving from the Past into the Future New York: UNICTTF, 2005, chap. The WSIS Wars: An Analysis of the Politicization of the Internet, p. 156.

Curtin, Jennifer, A Digital Divide in Rural and Regional Australia? ⟨URL: http://www.aph.gov.au/library/pubs/cib/2001-02/02cib01.htm⟩.

Cutler, A Claire, Canadian Foreign Policy and International Economic Regimes Vancouver: University of British Columbia Press, 1992, chap. Canada and the Private International Trade Law Regime, p. 89.

Cutler, A Claire, The Emergence of Private Authority in Global Governance Cambridge: Cambridge University Press, 2002, chap. Private International Regimes and Interfirm Cooperation, p. 23.

Cutler, A Claire, Private Power and Global Authority: Transnational Merchant Law in the Global Political Economy Cambridge: Cambridge University Press, 2003.

Cutler, A Claire, Haufler, Virginia and Porter, Tony, Private Authority and International Affairs New York: SUNY Press, 1999, chap. Private Authority and International Affairs, p. 3.

Dahl, Robert, Who Governs?: Democracy and Power in the American City New Haven, CT: Yale University Press, 1961.

Dahl, Robert, Pluralist Democracy in the United States Chicago: Rand McNally, 1967.

Dahl, Robert, Democracy and its Critics New Haven, CT: Yale University Press, 1989.

Dahl, Robert, Democracy's Edges Cambridge: Cambridge University Press, 1999, chap. Can International Organizations be Democratic? A Skeptic's View, p. 19.

Dahl, Robert and Lindblom, Charles, Politics, Economics and Welfare New Brunswick, NJ: Transaction Publishers, 1991.

D'Amato, Anthony, The Neo-Positivist Concept of International Law, Am J Int'l Law 59 1965, p. 321.

D'Amato, Anthony and Engel, Kirsten, International Environmental Law Anthology Cincinatti: Andersen Publishing Company, 1996.

David Post, Michael Froomkin and Farber, David, Elusive Consensus ⟨URL: http://www.icannwatch.org/archive/elusive_consensus.htm⟩.

Davies, Kim, Contribution to the DCITA .au Review ⟨URL: http://www.dbcde.gov.au/__data/assets/pdf_file/0010/55837/Kim_Davies.pdf⟩.

Davies, Todd et al., An Online Environment for Democratic Deliberation: Motivations, Principles, and Design ⟨URL: http://www.stanford.edu/~davies/deme-principles.pdf⟩.

Davies, William, You Don't Know Me, But... Social Capital and Social Software ⟨URL: http://www.theworkfoundation.com/Assets/PDFs/you_dontknowme.pdf⟩.

Dawkins, R, The Selfish Gene Oxford: Oxford University Press, 1976.

DCITA, World Summit on the Information Society and Internet Governance Public Forums ⟨URL: http://www.dbcde.gov.au/__data/assets/pdf_file/0003/29775/World_Summit_on_the_Information_Society-WSIS_and_Internet_Governance_Forums_3_4_Aug_05.pdf⟩.

DCOS, IGF Dynamic Coalition on Open Standards ⟨URL: http://igf-dcos.org/wp-content/uploads/igf-general-statement-2006.odt⟩.

Deakin, Simon, Two Types of Regulatory Competition: Competitive Federalism Versus Reflexive Harmonisation. A Law and Economics Perspective on Centros, CYELS 1 1999, p. 231.

Debian Project, Debian Constitution ⟨URL: http://www.debian.org/devel/constitution⟩.

Deibert, Ronald J, Digital Democracy: Politics and Policy in the Wired World New York: Oxford University Press, 1998, chap. Altered Worlds: Social Forces in the Hypermedia Environment, p. 24.

Delbecq, Andre L, Ven, Andrew H Van de and Gustafson, David H, Group Techniques for Program Planning: A Guide to Nominal Group and Delphi Processes Glenview, IL: Scott Foresman, 1975.

Detter, Ingrid, The International Legal Order Aldershot, England: Dartmouth, 1994.

Dezalay, Yves and Garth, Bryant, Merchants of Law as Moral Entreprenuers: Constructing International Justice from the Competition for Transnational Business Disputes, Law & Soc Rev 29:1 1995, p. 27.

DiBona, Chris, Ockman, Sam and Stone, Mark, editors, Open Sources: Voices from the Open Source Revolution Sebastopol, CA: O'Reilly & Associates, 1999.

Dijk, Jan van, Digital Democracy London: Sage Publications, 2000, chap. Models of Democracy and Concepts of Communication, pp. 30–53.

DiploFoundation, The Malta Discussions on Internet Governance ⟨URL: `http://www.diplofoundation.org/Conferences/IG/presentations/Conference_Summary.pdf`⟩.

DNS.net, PRC Government Approves Chinese Character Internet Domain Names ⟨URL: `http://www.i-dns.net/newsroom/news/OL050427-01.html.en`⟩.

Domain Industry Association, Domain Industry Submission to DCITA au Namespace Review ⟨URL: `http://www.dbcde.gov.au/__data/assets/pdf_file/0004/56614/Domain_Industry_FINAL_WEB_COPY.pdf`⟩.

Doria, Avri, Reforming Internet Governance: Perspectives from the Working Group on Internet Governance (WGIG) New York: UNICTTF, 2005, chap. WSIS, WGIG, Technology and Technologists, p. 41.

Doria, Avri, The IETF as a Model for the IGF ⟨URL: `http://www.intgovforum.org/contributions/IETF-as-model.pdf`⟩.

DOT Force, Digital Opportunities for All: Meeting the Challenge ⟨URL: `http://www.g7.utoronto.ca/summit/2001genoa/dotforce1.html`⟩.

Downs, Anthony, An Economic Theory of Democracy New York: Harper & Row, 1957.

Doyle, Michael, Kant, Liberal Legacies, and Foreign Affairs, Philosophy and Public Affairs 12 1983, p. 205.

Drahos, Peter and Braithwaite, John, Who Owns the Knowledge Economy? Political Organising Behind TRIPS ⟨URL: http://www.thecornerhouse.org.uk/pdf/briefing/32trips.pdf⟩.

Drahozal, Christopher R, Commercial Norms, Commercial Codes, and International Commercial Arbitration, Vand JTL 33 2000, p. 79.

Drake, William J, Reforming Internet Governance: Perspectives from the Working Group on Internet Governance (WGIG) New York: UNICTTF, 2005, chap. Why the WGIG Process Mattered, p. 249.

Drake, William J, The Power of Ideas: Internet Governance in a Global Multi-Stakeholder Environment Berlin: Marketing für Deutschland, 2007, chap. Encouraging Implementation of the WSIS Principles on Internet Governance Procedures, p. 271.

Dryzek, John S, Deliberative Democracy and Beyond Oxford: Oxford University Press, 2002.

Dryzek, John S, Deliberative Democracy in Divided Societies: Alternatives to Agonism and Analgesia, Political Theory 33:2 2005, p. 218.

Dryzek, John S and List, Christian, Social Choice Theory and Deliberative Democracy: A Reconciliation, British Journal of Political Science 33 2003, p. 1.

Dubois, David and Rothwell, William, The Competency Toolkit Amherst, MA: HRD Press, 2000.

Dubrovsky, Vitaly J, Kiesler, Sara and Sethna, Beheruz N, The Equalization Phenomenon: Status Effects in Computer-Mediated and Face-to-Face Decision-Making Groups, Human-Computer Interaction 6:2 1991, p. 119.

Dworkin, R, Taking Rights Seriously London: Duckworth, 1977.

Dyson, Esther, Prepared Testimony ⟨URL: http://www.icann.org/correspondence/dyson-testimony-22jul99.htm⟩.

ECOSOC, Consultative Relationship Between the United Nations and Non-Governmental Organizations ⟨URL: http://www.un.org/documents/ecosoc/res/1996/eres1996-31.htm⟩.

ECOSOC, Report of the Special Rapporteur on the Protection and Promotion of the Right to Freedom of Opinion and Expression ⟨URL: http://www.unhchr.ch/huridocda/huridoca.nsf/(Symbol)/E.CN.4.1999.64.En?OpenDocument⟩.

ECOSOC, Information and Communications Technology (ICT) Task Force ⟨URL: http://documents-dds-ny.un.org/doc/UNDOC/GEN/N01/260/47/pdf/N0126047.pdf?OpenElement⟩.

Edwards, Lilian, From Child Porn to China, in one Cleanfeed ⟨URL: http://www.law.ed.ac.uk/ahrc/script-ed/vol3-3/editorial.pdf⟩.

Elias, Norbert, The Civilizing Process: State Formation and Civilization Oxford: Blackwell, 1982.

Engel, Christoph, Governing the Egalitarian Core of the Internet, IJCLP 10 2005, p. 1.

ENSTA and EUROLINC, Taking Stock and the Way Forward ⟨URL: http://www.intgovforum.org/ensta-eurolinc_form_igf.rtf⟩.

Erlanger, Leon, Should You Trust TrustE? 2004, ⟨URL: http://www.pcmag.com/article2/0,2704,1463331,00.asp⟩.

Ess, C, Philosophical Perspective on Computer-Mediated Communication Albany, NY: SUNY Press, 1996.

ETNO, ETNO Reflection Document in Reply to the Consultation "Preparing for the Second Meeting of the IGF" ⟨URL: http://www.intgovforum.org/Substantive_2nd_IGF/ETNO_Reply_to_the_preparing_consultation_for_Rio.pdf⟩.

Etzioni, Amitai, Leveraging Islam, The National Interest 83 2006, p. 101.

EU, Proposal for Addition to Chair's Paper Sub-Com A Internet Governance on Paragraph 5 "Follow-up and Possible Arrangements" ⟨URL: http://www.itu.int/wsis/docs2/pc3/working/dt21.pdf⟩.

EUROLINC, Thoughts for Rio: a Bureau for the IGF ⟨URL: http://www.intgovforum.org/May_contributions/Propositions-Rio-V10.3.F1.pdf⟩.

European Commission, Directive on the Protection of Individuals With Regard to the Processing of Personal Data and on the Free Movement of Such Data ⟨URL: http://eur-lex.europa.eu/LexUriServ/LexUriServ.do?uri=CELEX:32002L0058:EN:HTML⟩.

European Commission, Directive on the Protection of Consumers in Respect of Distance Contracts ⟨URL: http://eur-lex.europa.eu/LexUriServ/LexUriServ.do?uri=CELEX:31997L0007:EN:HTML⟩.

European Commission, Guide to the Implementation of Directives Based on the New Approach and the Global Approach ⟨URL: http://ec.europa.eu/enterprise/newapproach/legislation/guide/document/1999_1282_en.pdf⟩.

European Commission, Internet Network Issues ⟨URL: http://ec.europa.eu/information_society/topics/telecoms/international/itu/internet_traffic.pdf⟩.

European Commission, Directive Concerning the Distance Marketing of Consumer Financial Services ⟨URL: http://eur-lex.europa.eu/LexUriServ/LexUriServ.do?uri=CELEX:32002L0065:EN:HTML⟩.

European Commission, Directive on Privacy and Electronic Communications ⟨URL: http://eur-lex.europa.eu/LexUriServ/LexUriServ.do?uri=CELEX:32002L0058:EN:HTML⟩.

European Commission, European Countries Launch Joint Drive to Combat "Spam" ⟨URL: http://europa.eu/rapid/pressReleasesAction.do?reference=IP/05/146⟩.

European Commission, Internet Governance: Commission Welcomes Move Towards Full Private-Sector Management by 2009 ⟨URL: http://europa.eu/rapid/pressReleasesAction.do?reference=IP/06/1297⟩.

European Digital Rights, New Council of Europe Recommendation Fails to Uphold Online Freedom of Expression ⟨URL: http://www.edri.org/coerec200711⟩.

European Parliament, Resolution on the Reform of the United Nations ⟨URL: http://www.europarl.europa.eu/sides/getDoc.do;jsessionid=77601C56E1A79956D73972A5D4FA233C.node1?pubRef=-//EP//TEXT+TA+P6-TA-2005-0237+0+DOC+XML+V0//EN⟩.

European Parliament, European Parliament Resolution on the Second Internet Governance Forum, held in Rio de Janeiro from 12 to 15 November 2007 ⟨URL: http://www.europarl.europa.eu/sides/getDoc.do?type=MOTION&reference=B6-2008-0041&language=EN⟩.

Feller, Joseph and Fitzgerald, Brian, Understanding Open Source Software Development Harlow, England: Pearson Education, 2002.

Ferguson, Yale H and Mansbach, Richard W, Between Celebration and Despair: Constructive Suggestions for Future International Theory, International Studies Quarterly 35:4 1991, p. 363.

Festinger, L and Carlsmith, J M, Cognitive Consequences of Forced Compliance, Journal of Abnormal and Social Psychology 58 1959, pp. 203–210.

Fingerhut, Eric T and Singleton, P L Skip, The gTLD-MoU: a Yellow Flag for Trademark Owners on the Information Superhighway, IDEA 38 1998, p. 281.

Fishkin, J S, Deliberative Polling As a Model for ICANN Membership ⟨URL: http://cyber.law.harvard.edu/rcs/fish.html⟩.

Fishkin, J S, Virtual Democratic Possibilities: Prospects for Internet Democracy ⟨URL: http://cdd.stanford.edu/research/papers/2000/brazil_paper.pdf⟩.

Fishkin, J S, Consulting the Public Through Deliberative Polling, Journal of Policy Analysis and Management 22:1 2003, p. 128.

Fleischer, Peter, Call for Global Privacy Standards ⟨URL: http://googlepublicpolicy.blogspot.com/2007/09/call-for-global-privacy-standards.html⟩.

Ford, P S, Rekhter, Y and Braun, H W, Improving the Routing and Addressing of IP, IEEE Network 7:3 1993, p. 10.

Foster, W A, Coordinating the Internet Cambridge: MIT Press, 1997, chap. Registering the Domain Name System: An Exercise in Global Decision-Making, pp. 194–207.

Fox, Gregory H, Democratic Governance and International Law Cambridge: Cambridge University Press, 2000, chap. The Right to Political Participation in International Law, pp. 48–90.

Fox, Gregory H and Nolte, Georg, Democratic Governance and International Law Cambridge: Cambridge University Press, 2000, chap. Intolerant Democracies, pp. 389–435.

Fragoso, Heloisa, An Overview of Employee Empowerment: Do's And Don'ts ⟨URL: http://www.angelfire.com/nb/ba1199/lesson028/emp4.htm⟩.

Franck, T M, The Power of Legitimacy Among Nations Oxford: Oxford University Press, 1990.

Franck, T M, Fairness in International Law New York: Clarendon Press, 1995.

Franda, Marcus F, Governing the Internet: The Emergence of an International Regime Boulder: Lynne Rienner Publishers, 2001.

Fraser, Nancy, Rethinking the Public Sphere: A Contribution to the Critique of Actually Existing Democracy, Social Text 25/26 1990, p. 56.

Friedrichs, Jörg, Governance and International Legal Theory Leiden, The Netherlands: Martinus Nijhoff Publishers, 2004, chap. The Neomedieval Renaissance: Global Governance and International Law in the New Middle Ages, pp. 3–36.

Froomkin, A Michael, ICANN and Individuals ⟨URL: http://osaka.law.miami.edu/~amf/individuals.htm⟩.

Froomkin, A Michael, Wrong Turn in Cyberspace: Using ICANN to Route Around the APA and the Constitution, Duke LJ 50 2000, p. 17.

Froomkin, A Michael, Form and Substance in Cyberspace.

Froomkin, A Michael, ICANN's "Uniform Dispute Resolution Policy"—Causes and (Partial) Cures, Brook L Rev 67:3 2002, p. 608.

Froomkin, A Michael, Habermas@discourse.net: Toward a Critical Theory of Cyberspace, Harv LR 116 2003, p. 749.

Froomkin, A Michael, Independent Review Panel Appointed After Years of Delay ⟨URL: http://www.icannwatch.org/article.pl?sid=04/04/23/1314207⟩.

FSC, By-laws ⟨URL: http://www.fsc.org/keepout/en/content_areas/77/84/files/1_1_FSC_By_Laws_2006.pdf⟩.

FSF, GNU General Public License ⟨URL: http://www.gnu.org/licenses/gpl.html⟩.

FSF, GNU Free Documentation License ⟨URL: http://www.gnu.org/licenses/fdl.html⟩.

Fukuyama, Francis, The End of History?, The National Interest 1989, p. 3.

Fukuyama, Francis, America at the Crossroads: Democracy, Power, and the Neoconservative Legacy New Haven, CT: Yale University Press, 2006.

Fulk, Janet and DeSanctis, Gerardine, Electronic Communication and Changing Organizational Forms, Organization Science 6:4 1995, p. 337.

Fuller, Lon L, The Morality of Law New Haven, CT: Yale University Press, 1969.

Fung, Archon, Wright, Erik Olin and Abers, Rebecca, editors, Deepening Democracy: Institutional Innovations in Empowered Participatory Governance London: Verso, 2003.

G77, G77 & China Paper on the Proposed Internet Governance Forum ⟨URL: http://www.intgovforum.org/contributions/G77_9_March.pdf⟩.

GAC, Operating Principles ⟨URL: http://gac.icann.org/web/home/GAC_Operating_Principles.doc⟩.

GAC, GAC Principles and Guidelines on Public Policy Issues Regarding the Implementation of New gTLDs ⟨URL: http://gac.icann.org/web/meetings/mtg26/gTLDs_principles_on_public_policy_draft_17_oct_2006.doc⟩.

GAC, GAC Principles Regarding New gTLDs ⟨URL: http://gac.icann.org/web/home/gTLD_principles.pdf⟩.

GAID, Business Plan for 2006–2007 ⟨URL: http://www.un-gaid.org/en/system/files/GAID+Business+Plan+07Dec2006.pdf⟩.

GAID, Strategy Council Meeting: Informal Summary ⟨URL: http://www.un-gaid.org/en/system/files/KL+StraC+summary+8jul2006.pdf⟩.

GAID, Terms of Reference—Steering Committee ⟨URL: http://www.un-gaid.org/en/steering/tor⟩.

GAID, Terms of Reference—Strategy Council ⟨URL: http://www.un-gaid.org/en/council/tor⟩.

GAID, Meeting of the Steering Committee of the GAID: Informal Summary ⟨URL: http://www.un-gaid.org/en/system/files/summary+SteerCom_23Mar07.pdf⟩.

Galston, William A, The Internet in Public Life Lanham, MD: Rowman & Littlefield Publishers, 2004, chap. The Impact of the Internet on Civic Life: An Early Assessment, p. 59.

Garfinkel, Simpson L, The Web's Unelected Government ⟨URL: http://www.technologyreview.com/InfoTech/wtr_11776,258,p1.html⟩.

Garrett, Paula, What Can the Internet Do for You? Join the Revolution ⟨URL: http://www.csu.edu.au/special/online97/proceedings/onl203.htm⟩.

Gastil, John, Democracy in Small Groups Philadelphia: New Society Publishers, 1993.

Geist, Michael, Fair.com?: An Examination of the Allegations of Systemic Unfairness in the ICANN UDRP, Brook J Int'l Law 27:3 2002, p. 903.

Geist, Michael, Who Rules the Net? Internet Governance and Jurisdiction Washington, DC: Cato Institute, 2003, chap. The Shift Towards "Targeting" for Internet Jurisdiction, p. 91.

Geist, Michael, China and the Break-Up of the Net ⟨URL: http://news.bbc.co.uk/1/hi/technology/4779660.stm⟩.

General Assembly of the United Nations, Universal Declaration of Human Rights ⟨URL: http://www.un.org/Overview/rights.html⟩.

General Assembly of the United Nations, Uniting for Peace ⟨URL: http://www.un.org/Depts/dhl/landmark/pdf/ares377e.pdf⟩.

General Assembly of the United Nations, Guidelines for the Regulation of Computerized Personal Data Files ⟨URL: http://www.un.org/documents/ga/res/45/a45r095.htm⟩.

General Assembly of the United Nations, World Summit on the Information Society ⟨URL: http://www.itu.int/wsis/docs/background/resolutions/56_183_unga_2002.pdf⟩.

General Assembly of the United Nations, Creation of a Global Culture of Cybersecurity: Resolution ⟨URL: http://documents-dds-ny.un.org/doc/UNDOC/GEN/N02/555/22/pdf/N0255522.pdf⟩.

General Assembly of the United Nations, Combatting Defamation of Religions ⟨URL: http://documents-dds-ny.un.org/doc/UNDOC/GEN/N05/496/60/pdf/N0549660.pdf?OpenElement⟩.

Georgakopoulos, Nicholas L, Statistics of Legal Infrastructures: A Review of the Law and Finance Literature, Amer Law Econ Rev 8:1 2006, p. 62.

Gerlach, Luther, Waves of Protest: Social Movements Since the Sixties Lanham, MD: Rowman & Littlefield Publishers, 1999, chap. The Structure of Social Movements: Environmental Activism and Its Opponents, p. 85.

Ghosh, Rishab A, Cooking Pot Markets: An Economic Model for the Trade in Free Goods and Services on the Internet ⟨URL: http://www.firstmonday.dk/issues/issue3_3/ghosh/index.html⟩.

Ghosh, Rishab A, Perspectives on Free and Open Source Software Cambridge, MA: MIT Press, 2005, chap. Understanding Free Software Developers: Findings from the FLOSS Study, p. 23.

Gibson, Rachel, Elections Online: Assessing Internet Voting in Light of the Arizona Democratic Primary, Political Science Quarterly 116:4 2001, p. 561.

GIC, Declaration of Lima ⟨URL: http://www.alfa-redi.org/ar-dnt-documento.shtml?x=3499⟩.

Glasner, Joanna, Vote Swaps Revamped for 2004 ⟨URL: http://www.wired.com/techbiz/media/news/2004/09/64777⟩.

GNSO Council, New Rules of Procedure ⟨URL: http://gnso.icann.org/council/new-procedures.shtml⟩.

GNSO Council, Recent GNSO Policy Development Activities on WHOIS ⟨URL: http://gnso.icann.org/issues/whois-privacy/gnso-council-report-board-whois-15nov07.pdf⟩.

Godwin, M, The Electronic Frontier Foundation and Virtual Communities ⟨URL: http://w2.eff.org/Misc/EFF/?f=virtual_communities.eff.txt⟩.

Goldman, Berthold, Contemporary Problems in International Arbitration London: The Eastern Press, 1986, chap. The Applicable Law: General Principles of Law—The Lex Mercatoria, p. 113.

Goldman, Joe and Torres, Lars H, Approaches to Face-to-Face Deliberation in the US ⟨URL: http://www.deliberative-democracy.net/resources/library/f2f_matrix_030304.pdf⟩.

Goldsmith, Jack L, Who Rules the Net? Internet Governance and Jurisdiction Washington, DC: Cato Institute, 2003, chap. Against Cyberanarchy, p. 31.

Goldsmith, Jack L and Wu, Tim, Who Controls the Internet?: Illusions of a Borderless World Oxford: Oxford University Press, 2006.

Gordenker, Leon and Weiss, Thomas G, NGOs, the UN & Global Governance Boulder: Lynne Rienner Publishers, 1996, chap. Pluralizing Global Governance: Analytical Approaches and Dimensions, p. 17.

Gore, Al, Forging a New Athenian Age of Democracy, Intermedia 22:2 1995, p. 4.

Gould, Mark, Coordinating the Internet Cambridge, MA: MIT Press, 1997, chap. Governance of the Internet: a UK Perspective, p. 39.

Government of Australia, Programme Committee—Internet Governance Forum ⟨URL: http://www.intgovforum.org/contributions/Au_govt_input_Program%20Committee.pdf⟩.

Government of Australia, Response to Questionnaire on Internet Governance Forum ⟨URL: http://www.intgovforum.org/contributions/Au%20Govt%20response%20to%20IGF%20questionnaire%20060213.pdf⟩.

Government of Australia, Second Intervention by the Government of Australia ⟨URL: http://www.intgovforum.org/contributions/Au%202nd%20intervention%20060217.pdf⟩.

Government of Azerbaijan, Proposed Answers to the Questionnaire on the Convening the Internet Governance Forum ⟨URL: http://www.intgovforum.org/contributions/Azerbaijan_Q.pdf⟩.

Government of Brazil, Comments to the "Programme Outline" Document ⟨URL: http://www.intgovforum.org/Substantive_1st_IGF/Brazilian%20Position.doc⟩.

Government of Brazil, Discurso IGF Meeting Fev 2006 ⟨URL: http://www.intgovforum.org/contributions/Discurso%20IGF%20meeting%20fev-2006.doc⟩.

Government of Canada, Canadian Statement, IGF Consultations Feb 16 2006 ⟨URL: http://www.intgovforum.org/contributions/Canadian%20Statement%20IGF%20consults%20Feb%2016.pdf⟩.

Government of Canada, Questionnaire on the Convening the Internet Governance Forum ⟨URL: http://www.intgovforum.org/contributions/GOC_IGF%20Questionnaire%20Response%20.pdf⟩.

Government of Canada, Canadian Comment on First IGF ⟨URL: http://www.intgovforum.org/Feb_igf_meeting/Canadian_comment_on_first_IGF.DOC⟩.

Government of France, Lessons From the Inaugural Meeting of the IGF in Athens and Recommendations for the Second Annual Meeting ⟨URL: http://www.intgovforum.org/Feb_igf_meeting/IGF%20Stoktaking.doc⟩.

Government of Saudi Arabia, Response to Questionnaire on Convening the Internet Governance Forum ⟨URL: http://www.intgovforum.org/contributions/questionnaire%20Saudi.pdf⟩.

Government of Western Australia, A Voice For All: Strengthening Democracy ⟨URL: http://www.citizenscape.wa.gov.au/documents/citizenship_strategy.pdf⟩.

Government of Western Australia, e-Engagement: Guidelines For Community Engagement Using Information And Communications Technology (ICT) ⟨URL: http://www.citizenscape.wa.gov.au/documents/e_engagement.pdf⟩.

Graham, Gordon, The Internet: A Philosophical Enquiry London: Routledge, 1999.

Graham, Irene, Will PICS Torch Free Speech on the Internet?, Commmunications Law Bulletin 17:1 1998, p. 11.

Green, Donald and Shapiro, Ian, Pathologies of Rational Choice Theory: A Critique of Applications in Political Science New Haven, CT: Yale University Press, 1994.

Green-Armytage, James, Direct Democracy by Delegable Proxy ⟨URL: http://fc.antioch.edu/~james_green-armytage/vm/proxy.htm⟩.

Greenleaf, Graham et al., AustLII—Changing the Nature of Public Access to Law ⟨URL: http://austlii.edu.au/~graham/NZLLG/AustLII_NZLLG-AustLII.html⟩.

Gronlund, A, Emerging Infrastructures for E-Democracy: In Search of Strong Inscriptions, e-Service Journal 2:1 2003, p. 62.

Grossman, Lawrence, The Electronic Republic: Reshaping American Democracy for the Information Age New York: Penguin Books, 1996.

Guehenno, Jean-Marie, The End of the Nation-State Minneapolis: University of Minnesota Press, 1993.

Gunningham, Neil and Rees, Joseph, Industry Self-Regulation: An Institutional Perspective, Law & Policy 19:4 1997, p. 363.

Gurak, Laura J, Communities in Cyberspace London: Routledge, 1999, chap. The Promise and the Peril of Social Action in Cyberspace, p. 243.

Gutmann, Amy, Communitarian Critics of Liberalism, Philosophy & Public Affairs 14:3 1985, p. 308.

Habermas, Jürgen, The Theory of Communicative Action: Lifeworld and System: A Critique of Functionalist Reason, volume vol 2 Boston: Beacon Press, 1987.

Habermas, Jürgen, Between Facts and Norms: Contributions to a Discourse Theory of Law and Democracy Cambridge, MA: MIT Press, 1996.

Habermas, Jürgen, The Inclusion of the Other: Studies in Political Theory Cambridge, MA: MIT Press, 1998, chap. Three Normative Models of Democracy, p. 239.

Hacker, Kenneth L and Dijk, Jan van, Digital Democracy London: Sage Publications, 2000, chap. What is Digital Democracy?, pp. 1–9.

Hagen, Martin, Digital Democracy London: Sage Publications, 2000, chap. Digital Democracy and Political Systems, pp. 54–69.

Hague Conference on Private International Law, Preliminary Draft Convention on Jurisdiction and Foreign Judgments in Civil and Commercial Matters ⟨URL: `http://www.state.gov/www/global/legal_affairs/991030_forjudg.html`⟩.

Hague Conference on Private International Law, Some Reflections on the Present State of Negotiations on the Judgments Project in the Context of the Future Work Programme of the Conference ⟨URL: `http://www.cptech.org/ecom/hague/hague16feb2002-bureaurefects.rtf`⟩.

Hall, Rodney Bruce and Biersteker, Thomas J, The Emergence of Private Authority in Global Governance Cambridge: Cambridge University Press, 2002, chap. The Emergence of Private Authority in the International System, p. 3.

Hall, Rodney Bruce and Biersteker, Thomas J, The Emergence of Private Authority in Global Governance Cambridge: Cambridge University Press, 2002, chap. Private Authority as Global Governance, p. 203.

Halliday, Fred, Global Governance: Prospects and Problems, Citizenship Studies 4:1 2000, p. 19.

Halpin, Tony, Russia Shuts Down Allofmp3.com ⟨URL: http://www.timesonline.co.uk/tol/news/world/europe/article2016297.ece⟩.

Hamm, Steve, Linus Torvalds' Benevolent Dictatorship ⟨URL: http://www.businessweek.com/print/technology/content/aug2004/tc20040818_1593.htm?tc⟩.

Hancock, Douglas, An Assessment of ICANN's Mandatory Uniform Dispute Resolution Policy in Resolving Disputes Over Domain Names ⟨URL: http://www2.warwick.ac.uk/fac/soc/law/elj/jilt/2001_3/hancock⟩.

Hanna, K S, The Paradox of Participation and the Hidden Role of Information: a Case Study, Journal of the American Planning Association 66:4 2000, p. 398.

Hardin, Russell, The Good Polity: Normative Analysis of the State New York: Basil Blackwell, 1989, chap. Political Obligation, p. 103.

Hardy, Henry Edward, The History of the Net ⟨URL: http://www.eff.org/Net_culture/net.history.txt⟩.

Hart, H L A, Are There Any Natural Rights?, Philosophical Review 64 1955, p. 175.

Hart, H L A, The Concept of Law, 2nd edition Oxford: Clarendon Press, 1987.

Hasenpusch, Tina, Does an Economist's Dream Come True—The Internet as a Perfect Market? ⟨URL: http://citeseer.ist.psu.edu/hasenpusch00does.html⟩.

Hauben, Michael and Hauben, Ronda, Netizens: On the History and Impact of Usenet and the Internet ⟨URL: http://www.columbia.edu/~hauben/netbook/⟩.

Hayek, F A, The Road to Serfdom London: Routledge & Kegan Paul, 1976.

Heckscher, C, The Post-Bureaucratic Organization: New Perspectives on Organizational Change Thousand Oaks, CA: Sage Publications, 1994, chap. Defining the Post-Bureaucratic Type, p. 14.

Hedquist, Ulrika, WYSIWYG Guide to WSIS ⟨URL: http://computerworld.co.nz/news.nsf/news/467909CAE61A19A2CC2570C100678772⟩.

Heinrich-Böll Foundation, Negotiations Closer to Agreement: Consensus on Internet Governance Forum and—Almost—ICANN Oversight ⟨URL: http://www.worldsummit2005.de/en/web/825.htm⟩.

Hekman, Susan, Radical Plural Democracy: A New Theory For the Left? ⟨URL: http://www.datawranglers.com/negations/issues/96w/96w_hekman.html⟩.

Held, David, Cosmopolitan Democracy: An Agenda for a New World Order Cambridge: Polity Press, 1995, chap. Democracy and the New International Order, p. 96.

Held, David, Democracy and the Global Order: From the Modern State to Cosmopolitan Governance Cambridge: Polity Press, 1995.

Held, David, Models of Democracy, 2nd edition Cambridge: Polity Press, 1996.

Held, David, Law of States, Law of Peoples, Leg Th 8 2002, p. 1.

Held, David, The Political Philosophy of Cosmopolitanism Cambridge: Cambridge University Press, 2005, chap. Principles of Cosmopolitan Order, p. 10.

Idem and McGrew, Anthony, editors, The Global Transformations Reader: An Introduction to the Globalization Debate, 2nd edition Malden, MS: Polity Press, 2000.

Henkin, Louis, How Nations Behave: Law and Foreign Policy New York: Columbia University Press, 1979.

Herman, Edwards S and Chomsky, Noam, Manufacturing Consent: The Political Economy of the Mass Media London: Vintage, 1994.

Hertel, Guido, Niedner, Sven and Herrmann, Stefanie, Motivation of Software Developers in Open Source Projects: An Internet-based Survey of Contributors to the Linux Kernel ⟨URL: http://opensource.mit.edu/papers/rp-hertelniednerherrmann.pdf⟩.

Heylighen, Francis, Evolution of Memes on the Network: from Chain-Letters to the Global Brain ⟨URL: http://pespmc1.vub.ac.be/Papers/Memesis.html⟩.

Heywood, Lachlan, Onus on Providers to Clean Up Web Content ⟨URL: http://www.news.com.au/story/0,23599,22989028-421,00.html⟩.

Higgs, S, Applying Game Theory To The Domain Name Root System ⟨URL: http://www.higgs.com/archive/internet/drafts/draft-higgs-dns-game-theory-00.txt⟩.

Highsmith, J and Cockburn, A, Agile Software Development: The Business of Innovation, Computer 34:9 2001, p. 120.

Hilde, Thomas C, The Internet in Public Life Lanham, MD: Rowman & Littlefield Publishers, 2004, chap. The Cosmopolitan Project: Does the Internet Have a Global Public Face?, p. 113.

Hill, Benjamin Mako, Towards a Standard of Freedom: Creative Commons and the Free Software Movement ⟨URL: http://www.advogato.org/article/851.html⟩.

Hippel, Eric von, Democratizing Innovation Cambridge, MA: MIT Press, 2005.

Hobbes, Thomas, The Leviathan, edited by **Curley, Edwin** Indianapolis: Hackett Publishing Company, 1994.

Holck, Jesper and Jørgensen, Niels, Free/Open Source Software Development Hershey, PA: Idea Group Publishing, 2005, chap. Do Not Check In On Red: Control Meets Anarchy in Two Open Source Projects, p. 1.

Holden, B, Understanding Liberal Democracy Oxford: Philip Allen, 1998.

Holitscher, Marc, Internet Governance Revisited: Think Decentralization! ⟨URL: http://www.itu.int/osg/spu/forum/intgov04/contributions/holitscher-presentation.pdf⟩.

Honnold, John, The United Nations Commission on International Trade Law: Mission and Methods, Am J Comp Law 27 1979, p. 201.

Houtte, Hans van, The Law of International Trade London: Sweet & Maxwell, 1995.

Huntington, S P, The Clash of Civilizations?, Foreign Affairs 72 1993, p. 22.

Hurd, Ian, Legitimacy and Authority in International Politics, International Organization 53:2 1999, p. 379.

Huston, Geoff, ICANN, the ITU, WSIS, and Internet Governance, Internet Protocol Journal 8:1 2005, ⟨URL: http://www.cisco.com/web/about/ac123/ac147/archived_issues/ipj_8-1/internet_governance.html⟩, p. 15.

IANA, IANA Report on Request for Redelegation of the .au Top-Level Domain ⟨URL: http://www.iana.org/reports/2001/au-report-31aug01.html⟩.

ICANN, Staff Manager's Issues Report on UDRP Review ⟨URL: http://www.icann.org/gnso/issue-reports/udrp-review-report-01aug03.htm⟩.

ICANN, Membership Implementation Task Force: Call for Expressions of Interest ⟨URL: http://www.icann.org/committees/at-large/call-1dec99.htm⟩.

ICANN, Uniform Domain Name Dispute Resolution Policy ⟨URL: http://www.icann.org/dndr/udrp/policy.htm⟩.

ICANN, Evolution and Reform Committee's Final Implementation Report and Recommendations ⟨URL: http://www.icann.org/committees/evol-reform/final-implementation-report-02oct02.htm⟩.

ICANN, Bylaws ⟨URL: http://www.icann.org/general/bylaws.htm⟩.

ICANN, IDN Status Report ⟨URL: http://www.icann.org/announcements/announcement-28oct07.htm⟩.

ICANN, Milestone Agreement Reached Between ICANN, and F Root Server Operator, Internet Systems Consortium ⟨URL: http://www.icann.org/announcements/announcement-04jan08.htm⟩.

ICANN Governmental Advisory Committee, GAC Operating Principles ⟨URL: http://gac.icann.org/web/home/GAC_Operating_Principles.doc⟩.

ICC, ICC Policy Statement on "Spam" and Unsolicited Commercial Electronic Messages ⟨URL: http://intgovforum.org/Substantive_1st_IGF/spam.pdf⟩.

ICC, Global Business' Preliminary Input on WSIS Tunis Agenda Paragraphs 69-71 Regarding "Enhanced Cooperation" and Key Priorities Regarding Internet Governance Forum (IGF) 2006, ⟨URL: http://www.iccwbo.org/uploadedFiles/ICC/policy/e-business/pages/CCBI_ICC_enhanced_cooperation_preliminary_input_31March06.pdf⟩.

ICC, ICC/BASIS Feedback on First Internet Governance Forum (IGF) in Athens, Greece ⟨URL: http://www.iccwbo.org/uploadedFiles/BASIS/Documents/ICCBASIS_input_on_IGF_Athens_Final_12_01_07.pdf⟩.

IETF, Documentation Conventions ⟨URL: http://www.ietf.org/rfc/rfc3.txt⟩.

IETF, Host Software ⟨URL: http://www.ietf.org/rfc/rfc1.txt⟩.

IETF, Simple Mail Transport Protocol ⟨URL: http://www.ietf.org/rfc/rfc821.txt⟩.

IETF, IAB Official Protocol Standards ⟨URL: http://www.ietf.org/rfc/rfc1083.txt⟩.

IETF, IAB Recommended Policy on Distributing Internet Identifier Assignment ⟨URL: `http://www.ietf.org/rfc/rfc1174.txt`⟩.

IETF, The Internet Activities Board ⟨URL: `http://www.apps.ietf.org/rfc/rfc1160.html`⟩.

IETF, A Simple Network Management Protocol (SNMP) ⟨URL: `http://www.ietf.org/rfc/rfc1157.txt`⟩.

IETF, A Standard for the Transmission of IP Datagrams on Avian Carriers ⟨URL: `http://www.ietf.org/rfc/rfc1149.txt`⟩.

IETF, The Tao of IETF: A Novice's Guide to the Internet Engineering Task Force ⟨URL: `http://www.ietf.org/tao.html`⟩.

IETF, FYI on "What is the Internet?" ⟨URL: `http://www.ietf.org/rfc/rfc1462.txt`⟩.

IETF, Guidelines for Management of IP Address Space ⟨URL: `http://www.ietf.org/rfc/rfc1466.txt`⟩.

IETF, Internet Relay Chat Protocol ⟨URL: `http://www.ietf.org/rfc/rfc1459.txt`⟩.

IETF, Assigned Numbers ⟨URL: `http://www.ietf.org/rfc/rfc1700.txt`⟩.

IETF, Domain Name System Structure and Delegation ⟨URL: `http://www.ietf.org/rfc/rfc1591.txt`⟩

IETF, IETF Working Group Guidelines and Procedures ⟨URL: `http://www.ietf.org/rfc/rfc1603.txt`⟩.

IETF, Netiquette Guidelines ⟨URL: `http://www.ietf.org/rfc/rfc1855.txt`⟩.

IETF, Architectural Principles of the Internet ⟨URL: `http://www.ietf.org/rfc/rfc1958.txt`⟩.

IETF, The Internet Standards Process—Revision 3 ⟨URL: `http://www.ietf.org/rfc/rfc2026.txt`⟩.

IETF, Internet Users' Glossary ⟨URL: `http://www.ietf.org/rfc/rfc1983.txt`⟩.

IETF, A Means for Expressing Location Information in the Domain Name System ⟨URL: `http://www.ietf.org/rfc/rfc1876.txt`⟩.

IETF, The Organizations Involved in the IETF Standards Process ⟨URL: `http://www.ietf.org/rfc/rfc2028.txt`⟩.

IETF, Domain Name System Security Extensions ⟨URL: http://www.ietf.org/rfc/rfc2065.txt⟩.

IETF, Lightweight Directory Access Protocol (v3) ⟨URL: http://www.ietf.org/rfc/rfc2251.txt⟩.

IETF, Internet Protocol, Version 6 (IPv6) ⟨URL: http://www.ietf.org/rfc/rfc2460.txt⟩.

IETF, OpenPGP Message Format ⟨URL: http://www.ietf.org/rfc/rfc2440.txt⟩.

IETF, Domain Name System Security Extensions ⟨URL: http://www.ietf.org/rfc/rfc2535.txt⟩.

IETF, Charter of the Internet Architecture Board (IAB) ⟨URL: http://www.ietf.org/rfc/rfc2850.txt⟩.

IETF, E.164 Number and DNS ⟨URL: http://www.ietf.org/rfc/rfc2916.txt⟩.

IETF, IETF Policy on Wiretapping ⟨URL: http://www.ietf.org/rfc/rfc2804.txt⟩.

IETF, Internet Transparency ⟨URL: http://www.ietf.org/rfc/rfc2775.txt⟩.

IETF, Memorandum of Understanding Concerning the Technical Work of the Internet Assigned Numbers Authority ⟨URL: http://www.ietf.org/rfc/rfc2860.txt⟩.

IETF, The "text/html" Media Type ⟨URL: http://www.ietf.org/rfc/rfc2854.txt⟩.

IETF, Management Guidelines & Operational Requirements for the Address and Routing Parameter Area Domain ("arpa") ⟨URL: http://www.ietf.org/rfc/rfc3172.txt⟩.

IETF, Defining the IETF ⟨URL: http://www.ietf.org/rfc/rfc3233.txt⟩.

IETF, SIP: Session Initiation Protocol ⟨URL: http://www.ietf.org/rfc/rfc3261.txt⟩.

IETF, IAB and IESG Selection, Confirmation, and Recall Process: Operation of the Nominating and Recall Committees ⟨URL: http://www.ietf.org/rfc/rfc3777.txt⟩.

IETF, The IETF in the Large: Administration and Execution ⟨URL: http://www.ietf.org/rfc/rfc3716.txt⟩.

IETF, IETF Problem Statement ⟨URL: http://www.ietf.org/rfc/rfc3774.txt⟩.

IETF, The Rise of the Middle and the Future of End-to-End: Reflections on the Evolution of the Internet Architecture ⟨URL: http://www.ietf.org/rfc/rfc3724.txt⟩.

IETF, The Atom Syndication Format ⟨URL: http://www.ietf.org/rfc/rfc4287⟩.

IETF, DNS Security Introduction and Requirements ⟨URL: http://www.ietf.org/rfc/rfc4033.txt⟩.

IETF, Protocol Modifications for the DNS Security Extensions ⟨URL: http://www.ietf.org/rfc/rfc4035.txt⟩.

IETF, Resource Records for the DNS Security Extensions ⟨URL: http://www.ietf.org/rfc/rfc4034.txt⟩.

IETF, Sender ID: Authenticating E-Mail ⟨URL: http://tools.ietf.org/id/draft-lyon-senderid-core-01.txt⟩.

IETF, Sender Policy Framework (SPF) for Authorizing Use of Domains in E-MAIL ⟨URL: http://tools.ietf.org/html/draft-schlitt-spf-classic⟩.

IGF Secretariat, Inaugural Meeting Background Report ⟨URL: http://www.intgovforum.org/synth/E.doc⟩.

IGF Secretariat, The Inaugural Session of the Internet Governance Forum ⟨URL: http://www.intgovforum.org/Summary.Final.07.11.2006.htm⟩.

IGF Secretariat, The Substantive Agenda of the First Meeting of the Internet Governance Forum ⟨URL: http://www.intgovforum.org/Summary%20of%20discussions.htm⟩.

IGF Secretariat, Advisory Group Meeting Summary Report ⟨URL: http://www.intgovforum.org/Summary.AG.05.09.07.rtf⟩.

IGF Secretariat, Draft Programme Outline for the Second Meeting of the Internet Governance Forum ⟨URL: http://www.intgovforum.org/Rio_Meeting/DraftProgramme.24.09.2007.rtf⟩.

IGF Secretariat, IGF Second Meeting Synthesis Paper ⟨URL: http://www.intgovforum.org/Rio_Meeting/IGF.SynthesisPaper.24.09.2007.rtf⟩.

IGF Secretariat, Open Consultations Geneva, 23 May 2007: Summary of Contributions Prepared by the IGF Secretariat ⟨URL: http://www.intgovforum.org/May_contributions/SynthesisPaper.23.May.rtf⟩.

IGF Secretariat, Second Meeting of the Internet Governance Forum: Chairman's Summary ⟨URL: http://www.intgovforum.org/Rio_Meeting/Chairman%20Summary.FINAL.16.11.2007.pdf⟩.

IGF Secretariat, Stock-taking Session Synthesis Paper ⟨URL: http://www.intgovforum.org/Feb_igf_meeting/Synthesis.Paper.Feb.2007.rtf⟩.

IGF Secretariat, Advisory Group Discussion 11 to 17 March 2008 ⟨URL: http://intgovforum.org/AGD/AG%20emails%2010mar08.pdf⟩.

IGF Secretariat, Advisory Group Discussion 30 January to 3 February 2008 ⟨URL: http://intgovforum.org/AGD/AGdiscussion.30.01.-03.02.2008.pdf⟩.

IGF Secretariat, Advisory Group Discussion 6 December 2007 to 15 January 2008 ⟨URL: http://intgovforum.org/AGD/AG_Discussion_Thread.pdf⟩.

IGF Secretariat, Multistakeholder Advisory Group Meeting Summary Report ⟨URL: http://www.intgovforum.org/Feb_igf_meeting/MAG.Summary.28.02.2008.v2.pdf⟩.

IGF Secretariat, Synthesis Paper—Open Consultations, Geneva, 26 February 2008 2008, ⟨URL: http://www.intgovforum.org/rio_reports/Feb.synth.paper.rev.1.pdf⟩.

IGP, Building an Internet Governance Forum ⟨URL: http://dcc.syr.edu/miscarticles/IGP-Forum.pdf⟩.

IGP, Contribution to the Internet Governance Forum Athens Meeting ⟨URL: http://www.intgovforum.org/Substantive_1st_IGF/IGF-writtencontrib.doc⟩.

IGP, Comments of the Internet Governance Project on The Continued Transition of the Technical Coordination and Management of the Internet's Domain Name and Addressing System: Midterm Review of the Joint Project Agreement ⟨URL: http://internetgovernance.org/pdf/IGP-JPA-08-comments.pdf⟩.

IIA, Internet Industry Spam Code of Practice ⟨URL: http://www.iia.net.au/files/IIA/Codes%20of%20Practice/Spam/iia%20spam%20code.pdf⟩.

ILO, The ILO: What it is. What it Does. ⟨URL: http://www.ilo.org/public/english/bureau/inf/download/brochure/pdf/broch_0904.pdf⟩.

ILO, Representation of International Non-Governmental Organizations at the International Labour Conference and Other ILO Meetings ⟨URL: http://www3.ilo.org/public/english/standards/relm/ilc/pdf/note.pdf⟩.

Imhorst, Christian, Anarchy and Source Code—What Does the Free Software Movement Have to Do With Anarchism? ⟨URL: http://opensource.mit.edu/papers/imhorst.pdf⟩.

Immergut, Ellen M, The Theoretical Core of New Institutionalism, Politics and Society 26:1 1988, p. 5.

IMO, International Code of Signals ⟨URL: http://www.gyc.com/ICOSbook.pdf⟩.

Innes, Judith E and Booher, David E, Reframing Public Participation: Strategies for the 21st Century, Planning Theory & Practice 5:4 2004, p. 419.

Innis, Harold A, The Bias of Communication Toronto: University of Toronto Press, 1991.

International Bar Association, International Code of Ethics ⟨URL: http://www.ibanet.org/images/downloads/international_ethics.pdf⟩.

International Law Commission, Introduction—International Law Commission ⟨URL: http://untreaty.un.org/ilc/ilcintro.htm⟩.

Isenberg, D J, Group Polarization: A Critical Review and Meta-Analysis, Journal of Personality and Social Psychology 50:6 1986, p. 1141.

ISOC, Annual Report ⟨URL: http://www.isoc.org/isoc/reports/ar2004/index.php⟩.

ISOC, The Internet Society's contribution on the formation of the Internet Governance Forum ⟨URL: http://www.intgovforum.org/contributions/ISOC%20IGF%20CONTRIBUTION.pdf⟩.

ISOC, ISOC Statement, Internet Governance Forum Meeting 17 February 2006 ⟨URL: http://www.intgovforum.org/contributions/ISOC%20statement%20Feb%2017.pdf⟩.

ISOC, Contribution to the Internet Governance Forum Consultations May 2007 ⟨URL: http://www.intgovforum.org/May_contributions/ISOC%20IGF%20May%2007.pdf⟩.

ISOC, From Athens to Rio de Janeiro: Building on the Success of the First Internet Governance Forum ⟨URL: http://www.intgovforum.org/Feb_igf_meeting/ISOC%20IGF%20FEB%2007.pdf⟩.

Issues Deliberation Australia, Australia Deliberates: Muslims and Non-Muslims in Australia ⟨URL: http://ida.org.au/content.php?p=dpprelease⟩.

IT For Change, Four Critical Issues for the IGF, Rio, from a Southern Perspective ⟨URL: http://www.intgovforum.org/Substantive_2nd_IGF/IT%20for%20change_Four%20Critical%20Issues%20for%20the%20IGF%20Rio.pdf⟩.

IT For Change, Taking Stock and the Way Forward ⟨URL: http://www.intgovforum.org/ITfC%27s%20contribution%20to%20IGF%27s%20Stock%20Taking%20Meeting.doc⟩.

ITAA, ITAA IGF Comments ⟨URL: http://www.intgovforum.org/ITAA%20IGF%20-%20Feb%202%202007.pdf⟩.

Ito, Joichi, Emergent Democracy ⟨URL: http://joi.ito.com/joiwiki/EmergentDemocracyPaper⟩.

ITU, Management of Internet Domain Names and Addresses ⟨URL: http://www.itu.int/osg/spu/resolutions/2002/res102.html⟩.

ITU, ICT Statistics Database ⟨URL: http://www.itu.int/ITU-D/icteye/Indicators/Indicators.aspx⟩.

ITU, ITU-T Guide for Beginners ⟨URL: http://www.itu.int/itudoc/gs/promo/tsb/87029.pdf⟩.

ITU, TSB Director's Ad Hoc IPR Group Definition of "Open Standards" ⟨URL: http://www.itu.int/ITU-T/othergroups/ipr-adhoc/openstandards.html⟩.

ITU, ITU's Role With Regard to International Public Policy Issues Pertaining to the Internet and the Management of Internet Resources, Including Domain Names and Addresses ⟨URL: http://www.itu.int/osg/spu/resolutions/2006/final-acts-internet-extracts.pdf⟩.

ITU, Preliminary Response to the Questionnaire on the Convening of the Internet Governance Forum ⟨URL: http://www.intgovforum.org/contributions/IGF%20Questionnaire%20Response%20ITU.pdf⟩.

ITU, Report of Meeting of ITU Membership on Mechanisms for Cooperation on Cybersecurity and Combating Spam ⟨URL: http://intgovforum.org/Substantive_1st_IGF/13-IGF-ITU-D_Report_on_WTDC06_Resolution_45.doc⟩.

ITU, Study on the Participation of All Relevant Stakeholders in the Activities of the Union Related to the World Summit on the Information Society ⟨URL: http://www.itu.int/council/groups/pp06-plen7.html⟩.

ITU, Summary Report: Consultation Meeting of WSIS Action Line Facilitators/Moderators ⟨URL: http://www.itu.int/wsis/implementation/docs/consultations/feb2006/summary-report.pdf⟩.

ITU, Introduction to Action Line C5 Speed Exchanges ⟨URL: http://www.itu.int/osg/spu/cybersecurity/pgc/2007/events/docs/c5-speed-exchange-information-document-14-may-2007.pdf⟩.

ITU, World Information Society Report 2007 ⟨URL: http://www.itu.int/osg/spu/publications/worldinformationsociety/2006/wisr-web.pdf⟩.

James, Jeffrey, Bridging the Global Digital Divide Cheltenham, UK: Edward Elgar, 2003.

Janis, Mark W, Why Do We Continue to Distinguish Between Public and Private International Law?, Am Soc'y Int'l L Proc 79 1985, p. 352.

Jayakar, Roshni, What Stops Free Flow of Information is Dangerous ⟨URL: http://www.india-today.com/btoday/20001206/interview.html⟩.

Jensen, Darryn M, The Transformation of International Law, Policy 20:1 2004, p. 36.

Jessup, Philip, Transnational Law New Haven, CT: Yale University Press, 1956.

Johns, Fleur, The Invisibility of the Transnational Corporation: An Analysis of International Law and Legal Theory, Melb Univ L Rev 19 1994, p. 893.

Johnson, David R and Crawford, Susan P, What an ICANN Consensus Report Should Look Like ⟨URL: http://www.icannwatch.org/archive/what_icann_consensus_should_look_like.htm⟩.

Johnson, David R and Crawford, Susan P, What's Wrong With ICANN—And How to Fix It ⟨URL: http://www.icannwatch.org/archive/how2fixicann.htm⟩.

Johnson, David R and Crawford, Susan P, Why Consensus Matters: The Theory Underlying ICANN's Mandate to Set Policy Standards for the Domain Name System ⟨URL: http://www.icannwatch.org/archive/why_consensus_matters.htm⟩.

Johnson, David R and Crawford, Susan P, The Idea of ICANN ⟨URL: http://www.icannwatch.org/archive/the_idea_of_icann.htm⟩.

Johnson, David R and Post, David G, Law and Borders—the Rise of Law in Cyberspace, Stan LR 48 1996, ⟨URL: http://www.cli.org/X0025_LBFIN.html⟩, p. 1367.

Johnson, T J and Kaye, B K, It's Show Time! Media, Politics, and Popular Culture New York: Peter Lang, 2000, chap. Democracy's Rebirth or Demise? The Influence of the Internet on Political Attitude, p. 209.

Jordan, Robert S, Politics in the United Nations Systems Durham, NC: Duke University Press, 1998, chap. "Truly" International Bureaucracies: Real or Imagined?, p. 424.

Jordan, Tim, Cyberpower: The Culture and Politics of Cyberspace and the Internet London: Routledge, 1999.

Joss, S, Danish Consensus Conferences as a Model of Participatory Technology Assessment: An Impact Study of Consensus Conferences on Danish Parliament and Danish Public Debate, Science and Public Policy 25:1 1998, p. 2.

Kahler, Miles, Modeling Races to the Bottom ⟨URL: `http://irps.ucsd.edu/assets/014/6739.pdf`⟩.

Kaiser Family Foundation, See No Evil: How Internet Filters Affect the Search for Online Health Information ⟨URL: `http://www.kff.org/entmedia/3294-index.cfm`⟩.

Kant, I, Groundwork to the Metaphysics of Morals, volume Paton, H (trans) New York: Harper & Row, 1965.

Kant, Immanuel, Kant: Political Writings, edited by **Reiss, Hans**, 2nd edition Cambridge: Cambridge University Press, 1991.

Kapur, Akash, Internet Governance: A Primer New Delhi: Elsevier, 2005.

Katz, Eddan and DeNardis, Laura, Best Practices for Internet Standards Governance ⟨URL: `http://intgovforum.org/Substantive_1st_IGF/BestPracticesforInternetStandardsGovernance.pdf`⟩.

Katz, J, Birth of a Digital Nation, Wired US 5.04 1997, p. 49.

Katz, M L and Shapiro, C, Technology Adoption in the Presence of Network Externalities, Journal of Political Economy 94 1986, p. 822.

Kaufman, Michael and Dilla Alfonso, Haroldo, editors, Community Power and Grassroots Democracy: The Transformation of Social Life London: Zed Books, 1997.

Keane, John, Democracy and Civil Society London: Verso, 1988.

Keane, John, Global Civil Society? Cambridge: Cambridge University Press, 2003.

Keohane, Robert O, After Hegemony: Cooperation and Discord in the World Political Economy Princeton, NJ: Princeton University Press, 1984.

Keohane, Robert O, International Institutions and State Power Boulder: Westview Press, 1989, chap. Neoliberal Institutionalism: A Perspective on World Politics, p. 1.

Keohane, Robert O and Hoffmann, S, The New European Community: Decision-making and Institutional Change Boulder: Westview Press, 1991.

Keohane, Robert O and Nye, Joseph S, Governance in a Globalizing World Washington, DC: Brookings Institution Press, 2000, chap. The Club Model of Multilateral Cooperation and Problems of Democratic Legitimacy, p. 1.

Khan, Isha, Islamic Human Rights: Islamic Law and International Human Rights Standards, Appeal 5 1999, p. 74.

Kingsbury, Benedict, Krisch, Nico and Stewart, Richard, The Emergence of Global Administrative Law, L & CP 68 2005, p. 15.

Kinna, Ruth, Anarchism: A Beginner's Guide Oxford: Oneworld Publications, 2005.

Klasen, Norbert, Directory Services for Linux ⟨URL: `http://www.daasi.de/staff/norbert/thesis/html/thesis.html`⟩.

Kleinwächter, Wolfgang, Global Governance in the Information Age: GBDe and ICANN as "Pilot Projects" for Co-regulation and a New Trilateral Policy? ⟨URL: `http://www.cfi.au.dk/publikationer/cfi/003_kleinwachter`⟩.

Kleinwächter, Wolfgang, Reforming Internet Governance: Perspectives from the Working Group on Internet Governance (WGIG) New York: UNICTTF, 2005, chap. De-Mystification of the Internet Root: Do We Need Governmental Oversight?, p. 209.

Kleinwächter, Wolfgang, The World Summit on the Information Society: Moving from the Past into the Future New York: UNICTTF, 2005, chap. A New Diplomacy for the 21st Century? MultiStakeholder Approach and Bottom-Up Policy Development in the Information Society, p. 110.

Kleinwächter, Wolfgang and Stauffacher, Daniel, The World Summit on the Information Society: Moving from the Past into the Future New York: UNICTTF, 2005, chap. Introduction, p. 4.

Klotz, Robert J, The Politics of Internet Communication Lanham, MD: Rowman & Littlefield Publishers, 2004.

Knight, W Andy, Future Multilateralism: The Political and Social Framework Tokyo: United Nations University Press, 1999, chap. Engineering Space in Global Governance: the Emergence of Civil Society in Evolving "New" Multilateralism, p. 255.

Kobayashi, Bruce H and Ribstein, Larry E, Who Rules the Net? Internet Governance and Jurisdiction Washington, DC: Cato Institute, 2003, chap. Multijurisdictional Regulation of the Internet, p. 159.

Kobrin, Stephen J, The Emergence of Private Authority in Global Governance Cambridge: Cambridge University Press, 2002, chap. Economic Governance in Global Economy, p. 43.

Koh, Harold H, Transnational Legal Process, Neb LR 75 1996, p. 181.

Koh, Harold H, Why Do Nations Obey International Law, Yale LJ 106:8 1997, p. 2599.

Koh, Harold H, Transnational Legal Processes: Globalization and Power Disparities London: Butterworths, 2002, chap. Opening Remarks: Transnational Legal Process Illuminated, p. 327.

Koman, Richard, Karl Auerbach: ICANN "Out of Control" ⟨URL: `http://www.oreillynet.com/pub/a/policy/2002/12/05/karl.html`⟩.

Kooiman, Jan, Governing as Governance Thousand Oaks, CA: Sage Publications, 2003.

Krasner, Stephen D, Structural Causes and Regime Consequences: Regimes as Intervening Variables, International Organization 36 1982, p. 1.

Kronke, Herbert, Internet: Which Court Decides? Which Law Applies? The Hague: Kluwer Law International, 1998, chap. Applicable Law in Torts and Contracts in Cyberspace, p. 65.

Kuerbis, Brenden and Mueller, Milton, Securing the Root: A Proposal for Distributing Signing Authority ⟨URL: `http://www.internetgovernance.org/pdf/SecuringTheRoot.pdf`⟩.

Kummer, Markus, Reforming Internet Governance: Perspectives from the Working Group on Internet Governance (WGIG) New York: UNICTTF, 2005, chap. Introduction, p. 1.

Kunkel, J D and Richard, G, Recent Developments in Shrinkwrap, Clickwrap and Browsewrap Licenses in the United States, E LAW 9:3 2002, ⟨URL: `http://www.murdoch.edu.au/elaw/issues/v9n3/kunkel93_text.html`⟩.

Kurth, James, War, Peace and the Ideologies of the Twentieth Century, Current History 98:924 1999, p. 3.

Kuz, Ihor, Beyond HTTP: An Implementation of the Web in Globe ⟨URL: `http://www.nlnet.nl/project/sirs/200004-report/`⟩.

Kwa, Aileen, Cancun Preparatory Process: "Opaque, Exclusive and Rule-less", South Bulletin 59 2003, ⟨URL: `http://www.southcentre.org/info/southbulletin/bulletin59/bulletin59-04.htm`⟩, p. 9.

Kymlicka, W, Democracy's Edges Cambridge: Cambridge University Press, 1999, chap. Citizenship in an Era of Globalization, p. 112.

La Porta, R, Law and Finance, Journal of Political Economy 106 1998, p. 1113.

La Porta, R, The Quality of Government, Journal of Law, Economics, and Organization 15:1 1999, p. 222.

Lakhani, Karim R and Wolf, Robert G, Perspectives on Free and Open Source Software Cambridge, MA: MIT Press, 2005, chap. Why Hackers Do What They Do: Understanding Motivation and Effort in Free/Open Source Software Projects, p. 3.

Landley, Rob, A Modest Proposal—We Need a Patch Penguin ⟨URL: `http://www.cs.helsinki.fi/linux/linux-kernel/2002-04/0320.html`⟩.

Landwehr, Claudia, Rational Choice, Deliberative Democracy and Preference Transformation, Studies in Social and Political Thought 11 2005, p. 40.

Langille, Benjamin, It's "Instant Custom": How the Bush Doctrine Became Law After the Terrorist Attacks of September 11, 2001, B C Int'l & Comp L Rev 26:1 2001, p. 145.

Larmouth, John, Understanding OSI ⟨URL: `http://www.packetizer.com/osi/understandingosi/`⟩.

Lasswell, Harold D and McDougal, Myres S, Jurisprudence for a Free Society: Studies in Law, Science, and Policy New Haven, CT: New Haven Press, 1992.

Lawrence, David C, How to Create a New Usenet Newsgroup ⟨URL: `http://www.faqs.org/faqs/usenet/creating-newsgroups/part1/`⟩.

Leadbeater, Charles, Living on Thin Air: The New Economy London: Viking, 1999.

Lehmann, Christopher, Bail Reform in Ukraine: Transplanting Western Legal Concepts to Post-Soviet Legal Systems, Harv Hum Rts J 13 2000, p. 191.

Leiner, Barry M, A Brief History of the Internet ⟨URL: `http://www.isoc.org/internet/history/brief.shtml`⟩.

Lemley, Mark, The Law and Economics of Internet Norms, Chi-Kent L Rev 73 1998, p. 1257.

Lepard, Brian D, Rethinking Humanitarian Intervention: A Fresh Legal Approach Based on Fundamental Ethical Principles in International Law and World Religions University Park, PA: Pennsylvania State University Press, 2002.

Lerner, Josh and Tirole, Jean, The Economics of Technology Sharing: Open Source and Beyond ⟨URL: `http://opensource.mit.edu/papers/lernertirole3.pdf`⟩.

Lessig, Lawrence, The Zones of Cyberspace, Stan LR 48:5 1996, p. 1403.

Lessig, Lawrence, Code and Other Laws of Cyberspace New York: Basic Books, 1999.

Lessig, Lawrence, Free Culture New York: Penguin Books, 2004.

Leuf, Bo and Cunningham, Ward, The Wiki Way: Quick Collaboration on the Web Boston: Addison-Wesley Professional, 2001.

Levinson, Stephen C, Language and Conceptualization Cambridge: Cambridge University Press, 1997, chap. From Outer to Inner Space, p. 13.

Levy, Steven, Hackers: Heroes of the Computer Revolution London: Penguin Books, 2001.

Lijphart, Arend, Consociational Democracy, World Politics 21 1969, p. 207.

Lijphart, Arend, Democracy in Plural Societies: A Comparative Exploration New Haven, CT: Yale University Press, 1977.

Lijphart, Arend, Patterns of Democracy: Government Forms and Performance in Thirty-Six Countries New Haven, CT: Yale University Press, 1999.

Likert, Rensis and Likert, Jane Gibson, New Ways of Managing Conflict New York: McGraw-Hill, 1976.

Lipschutz, Ronnie D and Fogel, Cathleen, The Emergence of Private Authority in Global Governance Cambridge: Cambridge University Press, 2002, chap. "Regulation for the Rest of Us?" Global Civil Society and the Privatization of Transnational Regulation, p. 115.

Lipschutz, Ronnie D and Mayer, Judith, Global Civil Society and Global Environmental Governance New York: SUNY Press, 1996.

Locke, J, Two Treatises of Government, Revised edition New York: Cambridge University Press, 1963.

Loney, Matt, Microsoft Agrees to Passport Changes ⟨URL: `http://www.news.com/2100-1001-982790.html`⟩.

Lord, Janet E, Mirror, Mirror on the Wall: Voice Accountability and NGOs in Human Rights Standard Setting, Seton Hall Journal of Diplomacy and International Relations 2004, p. 93.

Lucero, Everton, Elements to be Considered for Structuring the IGF ⟨URL: http://www.intgovforum.org/EL_paper1_3Sept2007.doc⟩.

Lucero, Everton, A "Package" Deal for Rio ⟨URL: http://www.intgovforum.org/EL_paper2_3Sept2007.doc⟩.

Lukensmeyer, Carolyn J and Brigham, Steve, Taking Democracy to Scale: Creating a Town Hall Meeting for the Twenty-First Century, National Civic Review 91:4 2002, p. 351.

Luthiger, Benno, Fun and Software Development 2005, ⟨URL: https://www.foss.ethz.ch/people/lbenno/BLuthiger_Fun_SoftwareDevel_OSS2005.pdf⟩.

Lynn, Jonathan, Antigua Wins Modest Sanctions in US Gambling Case ⟨URL: http://www.reuters.com/article/politicsNews/idUSL2160157420071221⟩.

Lynn, M Stuart, President's Report: ICANN—The Case for Reform ⟨URL: http://www.icann.org/general/lynn-reform-proposal-24feb02.htm⟩.

Lyons, Michal, Smuts, Carin and Stephens, Anthea, Participation, Empowerment and Sustainability: (How) Do the Links Work?, Urban Studies 38:8 2001, p. 1233.

Ma, Herbert H P, Law and Morality: Some Reflections on the Chinese Experience Past and Present, Philosophy East and West 21:4 1971, p. 443.

Macartney, Jane, Dissident Jailed "After Yahoo Handed Evidence to Police" ⟨URL: http://www.timesonline.co.uk/tol/news/world/asia/article729210.ece⟩.

Macintosh, A, Electronic Democracy and Young People, Social Science Computer Review 21:1 2003, p. 43.

MacLean, Don, Reforming Internet Governance: Perspectives from the Working Group on Internet Governance (WGIG) New York: UNICTTF, 2005, chap. A Brief History of WGIG, p. 9.

MacLean, Don, Louder Voices: Strengthening Developing Country Participation in International ICT Decision-Making ⟨URL: http://www.panos.org.uk/download.php?id=59⟩.

MacLeod, Gordon and Goodwin, Mark, Restructuring an Urban and Regional Political Economy: On the State, Politics and Explanation, Political Geography 18 1999, p. 697.

Macpherson, C B, The Life and Times of Liberal Democracy London: Oxford University Press, 1977.

Malatesta, E, Anarchy London: Freedom Press, 1974.

Malcolm, Jeremy M, Do Corporations Have Rights? ⟨URL: http://www.malcolm.id.au/honours/⟩.

Malcolm, Jeremy M, Opinion: APRA v Telstra, Intellectual Property Forum 32 1998, p. 6.

Malcolm, Jeremy M, Who Owns .org.au? Where Domain Name Policy and Law Collide ⟨URL: http://www.ilaw.com.au/public/dnsarticle.html⟩.

Malcolm, Jeremy M, Australia's Stand on Spam ⟨URL: http://www.ilaw.com.au/public/spampaper.html⟩.

Malcolm, Jeremy M, Dark Shadows of the Australia-United States Free Trade Agreement ⟨URL: http://www.ilaw.com.au/public/ftaarticle.html⟩.

Malcolm, Jeremy M, Privacy Issues with VoIP Telephony, Privacy Law Bulletin 2:2 2005, p. 25.

Marks, Susan, Democratic Governance and International Law Cambridge: Cambridge University Press, 2000, chap. International Law, Democracy and the End of History, pp. 532–566.

Marshall, Garry, Internet and Memetics ⟨URL: http://pespmc1.vub.ac.be/Conf/MemePap/Marshall.html⟩.

Martens, Jens, Multistakeholder Partnerships: Future Models of Multilateralism? ⟨URL: http://globalpolicy.igc.org/eu/en/publ/martens_multistakeholder_partnerships_online_version.pdf⟩.

Marx, K and Engels, F, The Communist Manifesto New York: Signet Classic, 1998.

Maslow, Abraham, Motivation and Personality, 3rd edition New York: Harper & Row, 1987.

Mastanduno, Michael, International Order and the Future of World Politics Cambridge: Cambridge University Press, 1999, chap. An Institutionalist View: International Institutions and State Strategies, p. 19.

Mathiason, John, A Framework Convention: An Institutional Option for Internet Goverance ⟨URL: http://www.internetgovernance.org/pdf/igp-fc.pdf⟩.

Mathiason, John, The Distributed Secretariat: Making the Internet Governance Forum Work ⟨URL: http://www.internetgovernance.org/pdf/distrib-sec.pdf⟩.

Mathiason, John, The Road to Rio and Beyond: Results-based Management of the UN Internet Governance Forum ⟨URL: http://www.internetgovernance.org/pdf/roadtorio.pdf⟩.

Mathiason, John, Internet Governance: The State of Play ⟨URL: http://dcc.syr.edu/miscarticles/MainReport-final.pdf⟩.

Mathur, Navdeep and Skelcher, Chris, The Democratic Performance of Network Governance: Conceptual and Methodological Issues ⟨URL: http://www.inlogov.bham.ac.uk/research/pdfs/Democratic_performance.pdf⟩.

Matthews, Gerald, Deary, Ian J and Whiteman, Martha C, Personality Traits Cambridge: Cambridge University Press, 2003.

Matthews, Jessica T, Power Shift, Foreign Affairs Jan-Feb 1997, p. 50.

May, Timothy C, Crypto Anarchy, Cyberstates, and Pirate Utopias Cambridge, MA: MIT Press, 2001, chap. Crypto Anarchy and Virtual Communities, p. 65.

Mayer-Schoenberger, Viktor and Ziewitz, Malte, Jefferson Rebuffed: The United States and the Future of Internet Governance ⟨URL: http://ksgnotes1.harvard.edu/Research/wpaper.nsf/rwp/RWP06-018⟩.

McAdams, Richard H, The Origin, Development, and Regulation of Norms, Mich LR 96 1997, p. 338.

McCarthy, Kieren, 2005: The Year the US Government Undermined the Internet ⟨URL: http://www.theregister.co.uk/2005/12/29/us_undermines_internet/⟩.

McCarthy, Kieren, Read the Letter That Won the Internet Governance Battle ⟨URL: http://www.theregister.co.uk/2005/12/02/rice_eu_letter/⟩.

McCarthy, Kieren, US Government Told to Take Its Hands Off Internet ⟨URL: http://www.theregister.co.uk/2006/07/15/ntia_inquiry_results/⟩.

McCauley, Clark, The Nature of Social Influence in Groupthink: Compliance and Internalization, Journal of Personality and Social Psychology 57 1987, p. 250.

McCluskey, Alan, The Future of the Internet ⟨URL: http://www.connected.org/is/vint.html⟩.

McCorquodale, Robert, The New World Order: Sovereignty, Human Rights, and the Self-Determination of Peoples Oxford: Berg, 1996, chap. Human Rights and Self-Determination, p. 9.

McCullagh, Declan, Bush Administration Objects to .xxx Domains ⟨URL: http://www.news.com/Bush-administration-objects-to-.xxx-domains/2100-1028_3-5833764.html⟩.

McCullagh, Declan, Power Grab could Split the Net ⟨URL: http://www.news.com/Power-grab-could-split-the-Net/2010-1071_3-5886556.html?tag=nefd.ac⟩.

McCullagh, Declan, The UN Thinks About Tomorrow's Cyberspace ⟨URL: http://www.news.com/The-U.N.-thinks-about-tomorrows-cyberspace/2008-1028_3-5643972.html?tag=nefd.lede⟩.

McDougal, Myres S, Lasswell, Harold D and Reisman, W Michael, International Law Essays: A Supplement to International Law in Contemporary Practice New York: Foundation Press, 1981, chap. The World Constitutive Process of Authoritative Decision, p. 191.

McGlinchey, David, Pentagon Scraps Plan for Online Voting in 2004 Elections ⟨URL: http://www.govexec.com/dailyfed/0204/020504d2.htm⟩.

McGrew, Anthony, Democratic Theory Today: Challenges for the 21st Century Cambridge: Polity Press, 2002, chap. Transnational Democracy, p. 269.

McHenry, Robert, The Faith-Based Encyclopedia ⟨URL: http://www.tcsdaily.com/article.aspx?id=111504A⟩.

Michels, Robert, Political Parties: A Sociological Study of the Oligarchical Tendencies of Modern Democracy New York: Free Press, 1962.

Mill, John Stuart, Utilitarianism, 12th edition London: Routledge, 1895.

Mill, John Stuart, Considerations on Representative Government: Remarks on Bentham's Philosophy Cedar City, UT: Classic Books, 2000.

Miller, Jason, DOD to Allocate its IPv6 Addresses ⟨URL: http://www.gcn.com/print/26_03/43045-1.html⟩.

Milner, Helen, The Assumption of Anarchy in International Relations: A Critique, Review of International Studies 17:1 1991, p. 67.

Mishra, Ramesh, Globalisation and the Welfare State Cheltenham, UK: Edward Elgar, 1999.

MMWG, Internet Governance Forum Input Statement ⟨URL: http://www.intgovforum.org/contributions/Internet%20Governance%20Forum%20Input%20Statement1.pdf⟩.

Mockus, A, Fielding, R T and Herbsleb, J D, Two Case Studies of Open Source Software Development: Apache and Mozilla, ACM Transactions on Software Engineering and Methodology 11:3 2002, p. 309.

Montesquieu, Charles de, Montesquieu: The Spirit of the Laws, edited by **Cohler, Anne M., Miller, Basia Carolyn and Stone, Harold Samuel** Cambridge: Cambridge University Press, 1989.

Moravcsik, Andrew, Reassessing Legitimacy in the European Union, JCMS 40:4 2002, p. 603.

Moreira, Gilberto Passos Gil and Vimercati, Luigi, Joint Declaration on Internet Rights by the Minister of Culture of Brazil and the Undersecretary for Communications of Italy ⟨URL: http://internet-bill-of-rights.org/file/pdf/Joint%20Declaration%20Brazil-Italy.pdf⟩.

Morgenthau, Hans J, Politics Among Nations: The Struggle for Power and Peace, 5th edition New York: Alfred A Knopf, 1978.

Morrisett, Lloyd, Democracy and New Media (Media in Transition) Cambridge, MA: MIT Press, 2004, chap. Technologies of Freedom?, p. 21.

Moschovitis, Christos J P, History of the Internet: A Chronology, 1843 to the Present Santa Barbara: ABC-CLIO, Inc, 1999.

Mouffe, Chantal, Deliberative Democracy or Agonistic Pluralism ⟨URL: http://users.unimi.it/dikeius/pw_72.pdf⟩.

Mowshowitz, Abbe, Beyond Calculation: The Next Fifty Years of Computing New York: Springer-Verlag, 1997, chap. Virtual Feudalism, p. 213.

Mueller, Milton, ICANN and Internet Governance: Sorting through the Debris of Self-Regulation, Info 1 1999, p. 497.

Mueller, Milton, Rough Justice: An Analysis of ICANN's Dispute Resolution Policy (Version 2.1) ⟨URL: http://dcc.syr.edu/miscarticles/roughjustice.pdf⟩.

Mueller, Milton, Ruling the Root: Internet Governance and the Taming of Cyberspace Cambridge, MA: MIT Press, 2002.

Mueller, Milton, Success by Default: Domain Name Trademark Disputes Under ICANN's UDRP ⟨URL: http://dcc.syr.edu/markle/markle-report-final.pdf⟩.

Mueller, Milton, Competition in IPv6 Addressing: A Review of the Debate ⟨URL: http://internetgovernance.org/pdf/igp-v6.pdf⟩.

Mueller, Milton, "A Funny Thing Happened on the Way to the Forum...": Multistakeholderism, International Institutions and Global Governance of the Internet ⟨URL: http://web.si.umich.edu/tprc/papers/2006/615/Multistakeholdersim.pdf⟩.

Mueller, Milton, The Forum MAG: Who Are These People? ⟨URL: http://www.icannwatch.org/article.pl?sid=06/05/18/226205&mode=thread⟩.

Mueller, Milton, Net Neutrality as Global Principal for Internet Governance ⟨URL: http://www.internetgovernance.org/pdf/NetNeutralityGlobalPrinciple.pdf⟩.

Mueller, Milton and Klein, Hans, What to Do About ICANN: A Proposal for Structural Reform ⟨URL: http://internetgovernance.org/pdf/igp-icannreform.pdf⟩.

Mueller, Milton, Mathiason, John and Klein, Hans, The Internet and Global Governance: Principles and Norms for a New Regime, Global Governance 13:2 2007, p. 237.

Muguet, Francis, A Legal Analysis of the Internet Governance Forum Process ⟨URL: http://www.intgovforum.org/May_contributions/legal-igf.pdf⟩.

Muldoon Jr, James P, The Architecture of Global Governance: An Introduction to the Study of International Organizations Oxford: Westview Press, 2004.

Murphy, Sean D, Democratic Governance and International Law Cambridge: Cambridge University Press, 2000, chap. Democratic Legitimacy and the Recognition of States and Governments, pp. 123–154.

Mutua, Makau wa, Why Redrew the Map of Africa: A Moral and Legal Enquiry, Mich J Int'l L 16 1995, p. 1113.

Nadelmann, Ethan A, Global Prohibition Regimes: The Evolution of Norms in International Society, International Organization 44 1990, p. 479.

Netanel, Neil Weinstock, Cyberspace Self-Governance: A Skeptical View from Liberal Democratic Theory, Calif L Rev 88 2000, p. 395.

Nominet, Process Towards Enhanced Cooperation 2006, ⟨URL: http://www.nic.uk/digitalAssets/7716_060627_Enhanced_cooperation.pdf⟩.

Nominet, Questionnaire on the Convening the Internet Governance Forum ⟨URL: http://www.intgovforum.org/contributions/Nominet%20Questionnaire.pdf⟩.

Nonnecke, Blair and Preece, Jenny, Proceedings of the SIGCHI Conference on Human Factors in Computing Systems The Hague: ACM Press, 2000, chap. Lurker Demographics: Counting the Silent, p. 73.

Norris, Pippa, Governance in a Globalizing World Washington, DC: Brookings Institution Press, 2000, chap. Global Governance and Cosmopolitan Citizens, p. 155.

Noyes, Andrew, Biggest Threat to Internet Could Be a Massive Virtual Blackout ⟨URL: http://www.govexec.com/dailyfed/0407/040507tdpm2.htm⟩.

Nozick, Robert, Anarchy, State and Utopia New York: Basic Books, 1974.

NRO, Input on the Internet Governance Forum ⟨URL: http://www.intgovforum.org/contributions/nro-inputs-on-igf.pdf⟩.

NTIA, Request for Comments on the Registration and Administration of Internet Domain Names ⟨URL: http://www.ntia.doc.gov/ntiahome/domainname/DN5NOTIC.htm⟩.

NTIA, Management of Internet Names and Addresses ⟨URL: http://www.ntia.doc.gov/ntiahome/domainname/6_5_98dns.htm⟩.

NTIA, A Proposal to Improve Technical Management of Internet Names and Addresses ⟨URL: http://www.ntia.doc.gov/ntiahome/domainname/dnsdrft.htm⟩.

NTIA, US Principles on the Internet's Domain Name and Addressing System ⟨URL: http://www.ntia.doc.gov/ntiahome/domainname/USDNSprinciples_06302005.htm⟩.

Nye, Joseph S, Globalization's Democratic Deficit: How to Make International Institutions More Accountable, Foreign Affairs 80:4 2001, p. 2.

Nygh, P E, Conflict of Laws in Australia, 6th edition Sydney: Butterworths, 1995.

Ober, Josiah, Mass and Elite in Democratic Athens: Rhetoric, Ideology, and the Power of the People Princeton, NJ: Princeton University Press, 1991.

OECD, Guidelines for the Protection of Privacy and Transborder Flows of Personal Data ⟨URL: http://www.oecd.org/document/18/0,2340,en_2649_34255_1815186_1_1_1_1,00.html⟩.

OECD, OECD Guidelines for Consumer Protection in the Context of Electronic Commerce ⟨URL: http://www.oecd.org/dataoecd/18/13/34023235.pdf⟩.

OECD, Engaging Citizens in Policy-Making: Information, Consultation and Public Participation ⟨URL: http://www.oecd.org/dataoecd/24/34/2384040.pdf⟩.

OECD, OECD Guidelines for the Security of Information Systems and Networks: Towards a Culture of Security ⟨URL: http://www.oecd.org/dataoecd/16/22/15582260.pdf⟩.

OECD, OECD Guidelines for Protecting Consumers from Fraudulent and Deceptive Commercial Practices Across Borders ⟨URL: http://www.oecd.org/dataoecd/24/33/2956464.pdf⟩.

OECD, Anti-Spam Toolkit ⟨URL: http://www.oecd.org/dataoecd/63/28/36494147.pdf⟩.

OECD, Guidelines for Online Public Consultation ⟨URL: http://www.oecd.org/document/40/0,2340,en_2649_34495_37539752_1_1_1_1,00.html⟩.

Office of the Privacy Commissioner, Getting in on the Act: The Review of the Private Sector Provisions of the Privacy Act 1988 ⟨URL: http://www.privacy.gov.au/act/review/review2005.htm⟩.

OHCHR, The Right to Freedom of Opinion and Expression ⟨URL: http://www.unhchr.ch/huridocda/huridoca.nsf/(Symbol)/E.CN.4.RES.2002.48.En⟩.

Olsen, M, The Logic of Collective Action: Public Goods and the Theory of Groups Cambridge: Cambridge University Press, 1965.

Ota, Alan K, Disney in Washington: The Mouse That Roars ⟨URL: http://www2.cnn.com/ALLPOLITICS/1998/08/10/cq/disney.html⟩.

Ottaway, M, Corporatism Goes Global: International Organizations, Non-Governmental Organization Networks, and Transnational Business, Global Governance 7 2001, p. 265.

Page, A C, Self Regulation and Codes of Practice, Jnl of Bus L 1980, p. 24.

Pal, Leslie A, Virtual Policy Networks: The Internet as a Model of Contemporary Governance? ⟨URL: http://www.isoc.org/inet97/proceedings/G7/G7_1.HTM⟩.

Palfrey Jr, John G, The End of the Experiment: How ICANN's Foray into Global Internet Democracy Failed ⟨URL: http://cyber.law.harvard.edu/publications/2004/The_End_of_the_Experiment⟩.

Panganiban, Rik, Top-down, Middle Layer and Bottom-up E-democracy ⟨URL: http://www.rikomatic.com/blog/2006/10/my_talk_on_edem.html⟩.

Paré, Daniel J, Internet Governance in Transition: Who is Master of this Domain? Lanham, MD: Rowman & Littlefield Publishers, 2003.

Parker, Christine, The Open Corporation: Effective Self-Regulation and Democracy Cambridge: Cambridge University Press, 2002.

Parker, Martin, Post-modern Organizations or Postmodern Theory?, Organization Studies 13:1 1992, p. 1.

Patience, Nick, Internet Stumbles Towards Domain Name Consensus, Network Week Aug 15 1997.

Paulus, Andreas L, Governance and International Legal Theory Leiden, The Netherlands: Martinus Nijhoff Publishers, 2004, chap. From Territoriality to Functionality? Towards a Legal Methodology of Globalization, pp. 59–93.

People's Republic of China, Comments on the Draft Programme Outline for the Second Meeting of the Internet Governance Forum (IGF) ⟨URL: http://www.intgovforum.org/May_contributions/China%20Input.doc⟩.

Perens, Bruce, The Open Source Definition ⟨URL: http://www.opensource.org/docs/definition.php⟩.

Perritt Jr, Henry H, The Internet is Changing the Public International Legal System, Kentucky LJ 88 2000, p. 885.

Pettit, Philip, Debating Deliberative Democracy London: Routledge, 2003, chap. Deliberative Democracy, the Discursive Dilemma, and Republican Theory, pp. 138–162.

Pfaffenberger, Bryan, "If I Want It, It's OK": Usenet and the Outer Limits of Free Speech, The Information Society 12:4 1996, p. 365.

Picciotto, Sol, The Market or the Public Domain?: Global Governance and the Asymmetry of Power London: Routledge, 2001, chap. Democratizing Globalism, p. 335.

Planning & Infrastructure, Department for, Dialogue With the City—Final Report of Proceedings ⟨URL: http://www.dpi.wa.gov.au/mediaFiles/dialogue_finalproc.pdf⟩.

Poe, Marshall, The Hive ⟨URL: http://www.theatlantic.com/doc/200609/wikipedia⟩.

Posner, R, Utilitarianism, Economics and Legal Theory, JLS 8 1979, p. 103.

Post, David G, The "Unsettled Paradox": The Internet, the State, and the Consent of the Governed, Ind J Global Legal Stud 5 1998, p. 521.

Post, David G, ICANN and the Consensus of the Internet Community ⟨URL: http://www.icannwatch.org/archive/icann_and_the_consensus_of_the_community.htm⟩.

Post, David G, Who Rules the Net? Internet Governance and Jurisdiction Washington, DC: Cato Institute, 2003, chap. Against "Against Cyberanarchy", p. 71.

Postel, Jon, New Registries and the Delegation of International Top Level Domains ⟨URL: http://www.higgs.com/archive/internet/drafts/draft-postel-iana-itld-admin-02.txt⟩.

Poster, Mark, Virtual Politics: Identity and Community in Cyberspace Thousand Oaks, CA: Sage Publications, 1997, chap. Cyberdemocracy: The Internet and the Public Sphere, p. 212.

Poulantzas, Nicos, Political Power and Social Classes London: New Left Books, 1968.

Poundstone, William, Prisoner's Dilemma New York: Doubleday, 1992.

Productivity Commission, Standard Setting and Laboratory Accreditation ⟨URL: http://www.pc.gov.au/__data/assets/pdf_file/0012/11325/standards.pdf⟩.

Putnam, Robert D, Bowling Alone: America's Declining Social Capital, Journal of Democracy 6:1 1995, p. 65.

Rampell, Catherine, A Script for Every Surfer ⟨URL: http://www.washingtonpost.com/wp-dyn/content/article/2007/10/10/AR2007101002642.html⟩.

Rand, Ayn, The Virtue of Selfishness: A New Concept of Egoism New York: New American Library, 1964.

Ranson, Stewart and Stewart, John, Management for the Public Domain: Enabling the Learning Society Basingstoke: Macmillan, 1994.

Rawls, John, A Theory of Justice Cambridge, MA: Harvard University Press, 1971.

Rawls, John, Political Liberalism New York: Columbia University Press, 1993.

Raymond, Eric S, Goodbye, "Free Software"; Hello, "Open Source" ⟨URL: http://www.catb.org/~esr/open-source.html⟩.

Raymond, Eric S, The Cathedral and the Bazaar: Musings on Linux and Open Source by an Accidental Revolutionary, Revised edition Sebastopol, CA: O'Reilly & Associates, 2001.

Raymond, Eric S, The Jargon File ⟨URL: `http://www.catb.org/~esr/jargon/html/`⟩.

Reagle, Joseph, Why the Internet is Good: Community Governance That Works Well ⟨URL: `http://cyber.law.harvard.edu/people/reagle/regulation-19990326.html`⟩.

Reidenberg, Joel R, Governing Networks and Rule-Making in Cyberspace, Em LJ 45 1996, p. 911.

Reidenberg, Joel R, Lex Informatica: The Formulation of Information Policy Rules Through Technology, Tex LR 76 1998, p. 553.

Reidenberg, Joel R, States and Internet Enforcement, Uni Ottowa Law & Tech LJ 1 2003-2004, p. 213.

Reidenberg, Joel R, Technology and Internet Jurisdiction, Uni Penn LR 153 2005, p. 1951.

Resnick, Paul, The Value of Reputation on eBay: A Controlled Experiment, Experimental Economics 9:2 2006, p. 79.

Reynolds, Glenn, An Army of Davids: How Markets and Technology Empower Ordinary People to Beat Big Media, Big Government, and Other Goliaths Nashville, TN: Nelson Current, 2006.

Rheingold, H, The Virtual Community Reading, MA: Addison-Wesley Publishing, 1993.

Rheingold, H, High Noon on the Electronic Frontier Cambridge, MA: MIT Press, 1996, chap. A Slice of My Life in My Virtual Community, p. 413.

Rhodes, R A W, The New Governance: Governing Without Government, Political Studies 44 1996, pp. 652–667.

Risse, Thomas, Let's Argue!: Communicative Action in World Politics, International Organization 54 2000, p. 1.

Ritchie, Dennis M, The Evolution of the Unix Time-sharing System ⟨URL: `http://cm.bell-labs.com/cm/cs/who/dmr/hist.html`⟩.

Robert, Henry M and Robert, Sarah Corbin, Robert's Rules of Order Newly Revised Cambridge, MA: Perseus Books Group, 2000.

Roberts, N C, editor, The Transformative Power of Dialogue Amsterdam: JAI, an imprint of Elsevier Science, 2002.

Rocker, Rudolf, Anarcho-Syndicalism: Theory and Practice, 6th edition Edinburgh: AK Press, 2004.

Rony, Ellan and Rony, Peter, The Domain Name Handbook: High Stakes and Strategies in Cyberspace Lawrence: R&D Books, 1998.

Rose, Flemming, Why I Published Those Cartoons ⟨URL: http://www.washingtonpost.com/wp-dyn/content/article/2006/02/17/AR2006021702499.html⟩.

Rose, Greg G, The PGP Moose: Implementation and Experience ⟨URL: http://db.usenix.org/publications/library/proceedings/lisa96/full_papers/ggr/ggr.ps⟩.

Rosenau, James N, Governance Without Government: Order and Change in World Politics Cambridge: Cambridge University Press, 1992, chap. Governance, Order and Change in World Politics, p. 1.

Rosenau, James N, Governance Without Government: Order and Change in World Politics Cambridge: Cambridge University Press, 1992, chap. Citizenship in a Changing Global Order, p. 272.

Rosenau, James N, The Relocation of Authority in a Shrinking World, Comparative Politics 24:3 1992, p. 253.

Rossi, Sandra, Victoria the First to Cast E-Vote in a State Election ⟨URL: http://www.computerworld.com.au/index.php/id;1353237299;fp;16;fpid;1⟩.

Rossiter, Charles, editor, The Federalist Papers New York: Signet Classic, 2003.

Rowe, Michael C, The Transnational Law of International Commercial Transactions Deventer: Kluwer Law International, 1982, chap. The Contribution of the ICC to the Development of International Trade Law, p. 51.

Rundle, Mary, Beyond Internet Governance: The Emerging International Framework for Governing the Networked World ⟨URL: http://cyber.law.harvard.edu/publications/2005/Beyond_Internet_Governance⟩.

Rushkoff, Douglas, Open Source Democracy: How Online Communication is Changing Offline Politics ⟨URL: http://www.demos.co.uk/files/OpenSourceDemocracy.pdf⟩.

Russian Federation, Proposals of the Russian Federation to the Agenda of the Internet Governance Forum ⟨URL: http://intgovforum.org/Substantive_1st_IGF/Proposals_RF_Agenda_of_Internet_Governance%20Forum.pdf⟩.

Rutkowski, A, Regulate the Internet? Try If You Can., Communications Week International April 26 1999, p. 10.

Rutten, Andrew, Can Anarchy Save Us From Leviathan?, The Independent Review 3:4 1999, p. 581.

Sadowsky, G, Zambrano, R and Dandijinou, R, Internet Governance: a Discussion Document ⟨URL: http://pws.prserv.net/sadowsky/papers/unintgov.pdf⟩.

Saint, Steven and Lawson, James R, Rules for Reaching Consensus San Francisco, CA: Jossey-Bass/Pfeiffer, 1994.

Salzenberg, Chip, Spafford, Gene and Moraes, Mark, What is Usenet? ⟨URL: http://www.faqs.org/faqs/usenet/what-is/part1/⟩.

Samuelson, Pamela, Legally Speaking: Did MGM Really Win the Grokster Case?, Comm ACM 48:10 October 2005, p. 19.

Sandel, Michael, Morality and the Liberal Ideal, The New Republic 190:May 7 1984, p. 15.

Sandel, Michael, Liberalism and the Limits of Justice Cambridge: Cambridge University Press, 1998.

Sandoval, Greg, Visa Halts its Service for Allofmp3.com ⟨URL: http://www.news.com/Visa-halts-service-for-allofmp3.com/2100-1027_3-6127168.html⟩.

Sanger, Larry, Why Wikipedia Must Jettison Its Anti-Elitism ⟨URL: http://www.kuro5hin.org/story/2004/12/30/142458/25⟩.

Sassen, Saskia, Losing Control?: Sovereignty in the Age of Globalization New York: Columbia University Press, 1996.

Sassen, Saskia, The Emergence of Private Authority in Global Governance Cambridge: Cambridge University Press, 2002, chap. The State and Globalization, p. 91.

sayke, Liquid Democracy In Context or, An Infrastructuralist Manifesto ⟨URL: http://seed.sourceforge.net/ld_k5_article_004.html⟩.

Schach, S, Maintainability of the Linux Kernel, IEEE Proceedings—Software 149:1 2002, p. 18.

Schmidt, Eleonore, The Forest Stewardship Council: Using the Market to Promote Responsible Forestry, Yearbook of International Co-Operation on Environment and Development 1998/99, p. 23.

Schneider, S M, Creating a Democratic Public Sphere Through Political Discussion: A Case Study of Abortion Conversation on the Internet, Soc Sci Computer Rev 14 1996, p. 373.

Schoem, David and Hurtado, Sylvia, editors, Intergroup Dialogue: Deliberative Democracy in School, College, Community and Workplace Ann Arbor: University of Michigan Press, 2001.

Scholte, Jan Aart, Global Capitalism and the State, International Affairs 73:3 1997, pp. 427–452.

Schooley, Kimberley Younce, Cultural Sovereignty, Islam, and Human Rights—Towards a Communitarian Revision, Cumb LR 25 1995, p. 651.

Schuler, Doug, How Do We Institutionalize Democracy in the Electronic Age? ⟨URL: http://www.scn.org/ip/commnet/its98.html⟩.

Scott, Michael, The Tuna-Dolphin Controversy, Whalewatcher 30 1996, p. 16.

Scrutiny of Acts & Regulations Committee, Inquiry into Electronic Democracy: Final Report ⟨URL: http://www.parliament.vic.gov.au/SARC/E-Democracy/Final_Report/Final_Report.pdf⟩.

Security Council of the United Nations, Resolution 794 ⟨URL: http://documents-dds-ny.un.org/doc/UNDOC/GEN/N92/772/11/pdf/N9277211.pdf?OpenElement⟩.

Selby, John, Submission to Review of the Structure and Operation of the .au Internet Domain Name ⟨URL: http://www.dbcde.gov.au/__data/assets/pdf_file/0009/55836/John_Selby_-_Macquarie_University.pdf⟩.

Sell, Susan K, Private Power, Public Law: The Globalization of Intellectual Property Rights Cambridge: Cambridge University Press, 2003.

Sen, Amartya, Liberty and Social Choice, Journal of Philosophy 80:1 1983, p. 5.

Shaaban, H S, Commercial Transactions in the Middle East: Which Law Governs?, Law and Pol'y Int'l Bus 31:1 1999, p. 157.

Sha'ban, Charles, Reforming Internet Governance: Perspectives from the Working Group on Internet Governance (WGIG) New York: UNICTTF, 2005, chap. Proposal for the Establishment of an Internet Governance Forum, p. 235.

Shearer, Ivan, United Nations: Human Rights Committee: The Toonen Case, ALJ 69 1995, p. 600.

Shiva, Vandana, Doha: Saving WTO, Killing Democracy ⟨URL: http://www.globalpolicy.org/socecon/bwi-wto/wto/2001/1204dem.htm⟩.

Sinclair, Darren, Self-Regulation Versus Command and Control? Beyond False Dichotomies, Law & Policy 19:4 1997, p. 529.

Sinclair, Timothy J, Passing Judgment: Credit Rating Processes as Regulatory Mechanisms of Governance in the Emerging World Order, Review of International Political Economy 1:1 1994, p. 133.

Skelcher, Chris, Jurisdictional Integrity, Polycentrism, and the Design of Democratic Governance, Governance 18:1 2005, p. 89.

Skelcher, Chris, Mathur, Navdeep and Smith, Mike, The Public Governance of Collaborative Spaces: Discourse, Design and Democracy, Public Administration 83:3 2005, p. 573.

Slaughter, Annie-Marie, International Law in a World of Liberal States, Eur J Int' Law 6:4 1995, p. 1.

Slaughter, Annie-Marie, Democratic Governance and International Law Cambridge: Cambridge University Press, 2000, chap. Government Networks: the Heart of the Liberal Democratic Order, pp. 199–235.

Slaughter, Annie-Marie, The Role of Law in International Politics Oxford: Oxford University Press, 2000, chap. Governing the Global Economy through Government Networks, p. 177.

Smarr, Joseph, A Bill of Rights for Users of the Social Web ⟨URL: `http://opensocialweb.org/2007/09/05/bill-of-rights/`⟩.

Smith, Adam, The Wealth of Nations, volume IV Chicago: University of Chicago, 1976.

Smith, G, Taking Deliberation Seriously: Institutional Design and Green Politics, Environmental Politics 10:3 2001, p. 72.

Snider, J H, Citizens Assemblies: A Mechanism for Enhancing Legislative Transparency and Accountability ⟨URL: `http://www.w3.org/2007/06/eGov-dc/papers/NAS-eGovernmentPositionPaper.pdf`⟩.

Snyder, Monteze, Building Consensus: Conflict And Unity Richmond, IN: Earlham Press, 2001.

Souter, David G, Whose Information Society? Developing Country and Civil Society Voices in the World Summit on the Information Society ⟨URL: `http://rights.apc.org/documents/wsis_EN.pdf`⟩.

Spar, Debora L, Private Authority and International Affairs New York: SUNY Press, 1999, chap. Lost in (Cyber)space: The Private Rules of Online Commerce, p. 31.

Spencer, Laura, Winning Through Participation Dubuque, IA: Kendall/Hunt Publishing, 1989.

Sproull, L and Kiesler, S, Global Networks: Computers and International Communication Cambridge, MA: MIT Press, 1993, chap. Computers, Networks and Work, p. 105.

Stallman, Richard M, The Free Software Definition ⟨URL: `http://www.fsf.org/licensing/essays/free-sw.html`⟩.

Stauffacher, Daniel, The World Summit on the Information Society: Moving from the Past into the Future New York: UNICTTF, 2005, chap. A Tribute to Those Who Made it Happen, p. 79.

Stefferud, Einar, Image Online Design, Inc comments on the Registration and Administration of Internet Domain Names ⟨URL: http://www.ntia.doc.gov/ntiahome/domainname/not-emailed/imageonline.htm⟩.

Steiner, Jürg, Amicable Agreement Versus Majority Rule. Conflict Resolution in Switzerland, p. 77 Chapel Hill, NC: University of North Carolina Press, 1974.

Steiner, Jürg, Bächtiger, André and Spörndli, Markus, The Challenge of Cultural Pluralism Westport, CT: Praeger, 2002, chap. The Consociational Theory and Deliberative Politics. A Conceptual Framework for a Cross-National Analysis, p. 77.

Steiner, Peter, On the Internet, Nobody Knows You're a Dog, The New Yorker 69:20 1993, p. 61.

Stirling, Bruce, A Short History of the Internet ⟨URL: http://www.library.yale.edu/div/instruct/internet/history.htm⟩.

Stitt, Allan J, Mediation: A Practical Guide London: Routledge Cavendish, 2004.

Strange, Susan, The New Realisms: Perspectives on Multilateralism and World Order Tokyo: United Nations University Press, 1997, chap. Territory, State, Authority and Economy: A New Realist Political Ontology of Global Political Economy, p. 9.

Strauss, Andrew, Taking Democracy Global: Assessing the Benefits and Challenges of a Global Parliamentary Assembly ⟨URL: http://www.oneworldtrust.org/documents/taking%20democracy%20global.pdf⟩.

Strba, Fridrich, From TrainedMonkey to Google SoC Mentor ⟨URL: http://marketing.openoffice.org/ooocon2006/presentations/wednesday_c11.pdf⟩.

Stuckey, Kent D, Internet and Online Law New York: Law Journal Press, 1996.

Sugden, Robert, The Good Polity: Normative Analysis of the State New York: Basil Blackwell, 1989, chap. Maximizing Social Welfare: Is it the Government's Business?, p. 69.

Sunday Mail, Music Pirates to be Cut Off ⟨URL: http://www.news.com.au/adelaidenow/story/0,22606,21557674-5006301,00.html⟩.

Sunstein, Cass R, Republic.com Princeton, NJ: Princeton University Press, 2001.

Sunstein, Cass R, Debating Deliberative Democracy London: Routledge, 2003, chap. The Law of Group Polarization, pp. 80–101.

Susskind, L, The Consensus Building Handbook: A Comprehensive Guide to Reaching Agreement Thousand Oaks, CA: Sage Publications, 1999, chap. A Short Guide to Consensus Building. An Alternative to Robert's Rules of Order for Groups, Organizations, and Ad Hoc Assemblies that Want to Operate by Consensus, p. 3.

Suzuki, Eisuke, The New Haven School of International Law: An Invitation to a Policy-Oriented Jurisprudence, Yale Stud In World Pub Order 1 1974, p. 1.

Swiss Federal Office of Communication, Swiss Comments on the Second IGF Held in Rio de Janeiro in November 2007 and Recommendations for Future IGF Events ⟨URL: http://www.intgovforum.org/images/20080208%20IGF%20swiss%20contribution.doc⟩.

Swiss Internet User Group, Internet Quality Labels ⟨URL: http://www.intgovforum.org/Substantive_1st_IGF/SwissInternetUserGroup.txt⟩.

Tamanaha, Brian Z, A General Jurisprudence of Law and Society Oxford: Oxford University Press, 2001.

Teubner, Gunther, Global Law Without a State Brookfield: Dartmouth, 1997, chap. Global Bukowina: Legal Pluralism in the World Society, p. 3.

Thagirisa, Pavani, A Historial Perspective of the Sharia Project and a Cross-Cultural and Self-Determination Approach to Resolving the Sharia Project in Nigeria, Brook J Int'l Law 29:1 2003, p. 459.

The Pull, Confessions of a Hacktivist ⟨URL: http://www.hacktivismo.com/public/tfiles/confessionhacktivist.txt⟩.

Third World Network, Statement for the Preparatory Session for the Internet Governance Forum ⟨URL: http://www.intgovforum.org/Feb_igf_meeting/TWN.doc⟩.

Thompson, Bill, Everyone Talks, But No-One Listens ⟨URL: http://news.bbc.co.uk/1/hi/technology/6091282.stm⟩.

Thompson, Bill, Time To Led a Thousand Domains Bloom? ⟨URL: http://news.bbc.co.uk/1/hi/technology/6262386.stm⟩.

Thompson, Maryann Jones, Behind the Numbers: Browser Market Share ⟨URL: http://www.cnn.com/TECH/computing/9810/08/browser.idg/⟩.

Thurgood, J, How to Build Wikipedia ⟨URL: http://en.wikipedia.org/wiki/User:The_Cunctator/How_to_build_Wikipedia⟩.

Toffler, Alvin, The Third Wave New York: Bantam Books, 1981.

Torvalds, Linus and Diamond, David, Just For Fun: the Story of an Accidental Revolutionary New York: HarperCollins, 2001.

Trade & Industry, Department of, Points Raised at the Internet Governance Forum Consultation Meeting ⟨URL: http://www.intgovforum.org/contributions/igf.pdf⟩.

Tseng, Kuo-Hung, Using Online Nominal Group Technique to Implement Knowledge Transfer, Journal of Engineering Education 95:4 2006, p. 335.

Twining, William, Globalisation and Legal Theory London: Butterworths, 2000.

UNCITRAL, Arbitration Rules ⟨URL: http://www.uncitral.org/pdf/english/texts/arbitration/arb-rules/arb-rules.pdf⟩.

UNCITRAL, UNCITRAL Model Law on Electronic Commerce ⟨URL: http://www.uncitral.org/uncitral/en/uncitral_texts/electronic_commerce/1996Model.html⟩.

UNCITRAL, UNCITRAL Model Law on Electronic Signatures ⟨URL: http://www.uncitral.org/uncitral/en/uncitral_texts/electronic_commerce/2001Model_signatures.html⟩.

UNESCO, Recommendation Concerning the Promotion and Use of Multilingualism and Universal Access to Cyberspace ⟨URL: http://portal.unesco.org/ci/en/ev.php-URL_ID=13475&URL_DO=DO_TOPIC&URL_SECTION=201.html⟩.

UNICTTF, Strategic Plan ⟨URL: http://infolac.ucol.mx/eventos/reunion-varadero/strategic_plan.pdf⟩.

UNICTTF, Summary of Conclusions and Decisions ⟨URL: http://www.astrid-online.it/E-governme/United-Nat/UN-Task-Force-Geneva-13mar2003.pdf⟩.

UNICTTF, Principles and elements of a Global Alliance for ICT and Development (Multi-stakeholder Forum) ⟨URL: http://www.unicttaskforce.org/perl/documents.pl?do=download;id=961⟩.

UNIDROIT, UNIDROIT Principles of International Commercial Contracts ⟨URL: http://www.unidroit.org/english/principles/contracts/principles2004/blackletter2004.pdf⟩.

United Nations Non-Government Liaison Service, NGLS Roundup, November 1996 ⟨URL: http://www.un-ngls.org/documents/text/roundup/10NGOREV.TXT⟩.

United Nations Office of the Secretary-General, Global Alliance for Information Technologies and Development to be Launched ⟨URL: http://www.un.org/News/Press/docs/2006/dev2572.doc.htm⟩.

United Nations Office of the Secretary-General, Preparations Begin for Internet Governance Forum ⟨URL: http://www.un.org/News/Press/docs/2006/sgsm10366.doc.htm⟩.

United Nations Office of the Secretary-General, Secretary-General Establishes Advisory Group to Assist Him in Convening Internet Governance Forum ⟨URL: http://www.un.org/News/Press/docs/2006/sga1006.doc.htm⟩.

United Nations Office of the Secretary-General, The Secretary-General's Message to the Internet Governance Forum ⟨URL: http://www.un.org/NewLinks/int_for.htm⟩.

United Nations Office of the Secretary-General, Advisory Group to Prepare for Internet Governance Forum Meeting in Rio de Janeiro ⟨URL: http://www.un.org/News/Press/docs//2007/pi1791.doc.htm⟩.

United Nations Office of the Secretary-General, Internet Governance Forum This Month Will Be Wide-Ranging, Says UN Official ⟨URL: http://www.un.org/apps/news/story.asp?NewsID=24520⟩.

Updegrove, Andrew, The Role of Government in ICT Standardization ⟨URL: http://www.consortiuminfo.org/bulletins/feb07.php⟩.

Uphoff, N, Social Capital, A Multifaceted Perspective Washington, DC: The World Bank, 1999, chap. Understanding Social Capital: Learning from the Analysis and Experience of Participation, p. 215.

Urwin, Derek W, The Community of Europe: A History of European Integration since 1945, 2nd edition New York: Longman Publishing, 1995.

Utsumi, Yoshio, First Meeting of the Working Group on Internet Governance (WGIG) ⟨URL: http://www.wgig.org/docs/Utsumi.pdf⟩.

Utter, David A, Did Anti-Spam Gang Kill Russian Spammer? ⟨URL: http://www.webpronews.com/topnews/2005/07/25/did-antispam-gang-kill-russian-spammer⟩.

Van Alstyne, M and Brynjolfsson, E, Electronic Communities: Global Villages or Cyberbalkanization?, Proceedings of the International Conference on Information Systems 17 1996, p. 80.

Van Bogaert, E R C, Aspects of Space Law The Hague: Kluwer Law International, 1986.

Vaughan-Nichols, Steven J, Disgruntled Debian Developers Delay Etch ⟨URL: http://www.linux-watch.com/news/NS3128387759.html⟩.

Vedel, Thierry, Four Models for Internet Governance ⟨URL: http://www.oii.ox.ac.uk/collaboration/specialevents/20050505_governance_position_papers.pdf⟩.

W3C, Industry and Academia Join Forces to Develop Platform for Internet Content Selection (PICS) ⟨URL: http://www.w3.org/PICS/950911_Announce/pics-pr.html⟩.

W3C, Web Content Accessibility Guidelines 1.0 ⟨URL: http://www.w3.org/TR/WAI-WEBCONTENT/⟩.

W3C, Process Document ⟨URL: http://www.w3.org/2005/10/Process-20051014/⟩.

W3C, W3C Relaunches HTML Activity ⟨URL: http://www.w3.org/2007/03/html-pressrelease⟩.

Waclawsky, John G, Closed Architectures, Closed Systems And Closed Minds, Business Communications Review October 2004, p. 57.

Walker, R G, Australia's ASRB: A Case Study of Political Activity and Regulatory "Capture", Accounting and Business Research 17:67 1987, p. 269.

Walton, D, Appeal to Popular Opinion University Park, PA: Pennsylvania State University Press, 1999.

Ward, Colin, Anarchism as a Theory of Organization, Anarchy 52 1965, p. 171.

Warren, Mark E, Controlling Corruption Through Democratic Empowerment: Market-Style Accountability Revisited ⟨URL: http://www.politics.ubc.ca/fileadmin/template/main/images/departments/poli_sci/Faculty/warren/Market-Style_Accountability_Reconsidered_APSA_2006.pdf⟩.

Waters, Darren, Warning Over "Broken Up" Internet ⟨URL: http://news.bbc.co.uk/1/hi/technology/6037345.stm⟩.

Weale, Albert, The Good Polity: Normative Analysis of the State New York: Basil Blackwell, 1989, chap. The Limits of Democracy, p. 35.

Weber, Max, The Theory of Social and Economic Organization New York: Free Press, 1964.

Weber, Max, Economy and Society: An Outline of Interpretive Sociology, edited by **Roth, Guenther and Wittich, Claus** New York: Bedminster Press, 1968.

Weber, Max, The Protestant Ethic and the Spirit of Capitalism Mineola, NY: Dover Publications, 2003.

Weber, Rolf H, Regulatory Models for the Online World The Hague: Kluwer Law International, 2002.

Weinberg, Jonathan, ICANN and the Problem of Legitimacy, Duke LJ 50 2000, p. 187.

Weinberg, Jonathan, Geeks and Greeks, Info 3:4 2001, p. 313.

Weinstein, Lauren, PFIR Statement on Internet Policies, Regulations, and Control ⟨URL: http://www.pfir.org/statements/policies⟩.

Weiss, Thomas G, The Illusion of UN Security Council Reform, The Washington Quarterly 26:4 2003, p. 147.

Wellman, Barry and Gulia, Milena, Communities in Cyberspace London: Routledge, 1999, chap. Virtual Communities as Communities: Net Surfers Don't Ride Alone, p. 168.

WGIG, Background Report ⟨URL: http://www.wgig.org/docs/BackgroundReport.pdf⟩.

WGIG, Report of the Working Group on Internet Governance ⟨URL: http://www.wgig.org/docs/WGIGREPORT.pdf⟩.

WHATWG, The WHATWG and HTML 5 FAQ ⟨URL: http://wiki.whatwg.org/wiki/FAQ⟩.

White, Margaret, Equity—A General Principle of Law Recognised by Civilised Nations?, QUTLJJ 4 2004, p. 7.

Whorf, Benjamin Lee, Language, Thought and Reality Cambridge, MA: MIT Press, 1956.

Willets, Peter, "The Conscience of the World" The Influence of Non-Governmental Organisations in the UN System London: Hurst & Company, 1996, chap. Consultative Status for NGOs at the UN, p. 31.

Wilson, Matthew W, Ramsey, Kevin S and Nyerges, Timothy L, Design Considerations for Supporting Online, Analytic-Deliberative, Public Participation ⟨URL: http://www.online-deliberation.net/conf2005/viewpaper.php?id=37⟩.

WIPO, Joint Recommendation Concerning the Protection of Marks and Other Industrial Property Rights in Signs on the Internet ⟨URL: http://www.wipo.int/about-ip/en/development_iplaw/pdf/pub845.pdf⟩.

WIPO, Statement of the World Intellectual Property Organization ⟨URL: http://intgovforum.org/contributions/FINALSTAT%5B1%5D.doc⟩.

WIPO, Member States Adopt a Development Agenda for WIPO ⟨URL: http://www.wipo.int/pressroom/en/articles/2007/article_0071.html⟩.

Wired, The Wired Manifesto for the Digital Society, Wired UK 2.10 1996, p. 42.

Woods, Ngaire and Narlikar, Amrita, Governance and the Limits of Accountability: The WTO, the IMF, and the World Bank, International Social Science Journal 53:170 2001, p. 569.

Wright, Tom, EU Tries to Unblock Internet Impasse ⟨URL: http://www.nytimes.com/iht/2005/09/30/business/IHT-30net.html⟩.

WSIS, Geneva Declaration of Principles ⟨URL: http://www.itu.int/wsis/docs/geneva/official/dop.html⟩.

WSIS, Geneva Plan of Action ⟨URL: http://www.itu.int/wsis/docs/geneva/official/poa.html⟩.

WSIS, Tunis Agenda for the Information Society ⟨URL: http://www.itu.int/wsis/docs2/tunis/off/6rev1.html⟩.

WSIS, Tunis Commitment ⟨URL: http://www.itu.int/wsis/docs2/tunis/off/7.html⟩.

WSIS-SCT, Final Report on Prepcom-2 Activities of the Civil Society on Content and Themes ⟨URL: http://www.itu.int/wsis/docs/pcip/misc/cs_sct.pdf⟩.

WSIS Secretariat, Civil Society & NGO Open Ended Bureau Proposal ⟨URL: http://www.worldsummit2003.de/download_en/CS_Bureau_30Jan_ENG.doc⟩.

WSIS Secretariat, Final Report of PrepCom1 ⟨URL: http://www.itu.int/dms_pub/itu-s/md/02/wsispc1/doc/S02-WSISPC1-DOC-0011!R1!PDF-E.pdf⟩.

WSIS Secretariat, Compilation of Comments Received on the Report of the Working Group on Internet Governance ⟨URL: http://www.itu.int/wsis/docs2/pc3/working/dt7rev2.pdf⟩.

WTO, Guidelines for arrangements on relations with Non-Governmental Organizations ⟨URL: http://www.wto.org/english/forums_e/ngo_e/guide_e.htm⟩.

WTO, Understanding the WTO ⟨URL: http://www.wto.org/english/thewto_e/whatis_e/tif_e/understanding_text_e.pdf⟩.

Wu, Tim, The Power of Fun ⟨URL: http://www.slate.com/id/2138537/entry/2138647/⟩.

Wu, Tim, On the Future of Internet Governance ⟨URL: http://ssrn.com/abstract=992805⟩.

Wu, Timothy S, Cyberspace Sovereignty? The Internet And The International System, Harv J Law & Tech 10:647 1997.

Wyngaert, Christine Van den, International Criminal Law: A Collection of International & European Instruments Boston: Kluwer Law International, 2000.

Ye, Yunwen, Free/Open Source Software Development Hershey, PA: Idea Group Publishing, 2005, chap. The Co-Evolution of Systems and Communities in Free and Open Source Software Development, p. 59.

Yomiuri Shimbun, Winny Copyright Infringers "Should Be Identified" 2008, ⟨URL: http://www.yomiuri.co.jp/dy/national/20080328TDY02308.htm⟩.

Young, Iris Marion, Democracy and Difference Princeton, NJ: Princeton University Press, 1996, chap. Communication and the Other: Beyond Deliberative Democracy, p. 120.

Young, Michael D and Schafer, Mark, Is There Method in Our Madness? Ways of Assessing Cognition in International Relations, Mershon International Studies Review 42 1998, p. 63.

Young, Oran R, International Regimes: Problems of Concept Formation, World Politics 32:3 1980, p. 331.

Young, Oran R, Governance Without Government: Order and Change in World Politics Cambridge: Cambridge University Press, 1992, chap. The Effectiveness of International Institutions: Hard Cases and Critical Variables, p. 160.

Young, Oran R, Governance in World Affairs Ithaca: Cornell University Press, 1999.

Zakon, Robert H, Hobbes' Internet Timeline ⟨URL: http://www.zakon.org/robert/internet/timeline⟩.

Zamora, Stephen, Is There Customary International Economic Law?, German Yearbook of International Law 32 1989, p. 9.

Zeldman, Jeffrey, An Angry Fix ⟨URL: http://www.zeldman.com/2006/07/17/an-angry-fix/⟩.

Zhao, Houlin, ITU and Internet Governance ⟨URL: `http://www.itu.int/ITU-T/tsb-director/itut-wsis/files/zhao-netgov01.pdf`⟩.

Zimmerman, Joseph F, The Initiative: Citizen Law-Making Westport, CT: Praeger, 1999.

Zippay, Allison, The Politics of Empowerment, Social Work 40:2 1995, p. 263.

Zittrain, Jonathan, ICANN: Between the Public and the Private—Comments Before Congress, Berkeley Tech LJ 14 1999, p. 1071.

Zittrain, Jonathan, Who Rules the Net? Internet Governance and Jurisdiction Washington, DC: Cato Institute, 2003, chap. Be Careful What You Ask For: Reconciling a Global Internet and Local Law, p. 13.

Zumbansen, Peer, Globalization and the Law: Deciphering the Message of Transnational Human Rights Litigation, German LJ 5:12 2004, p. 1499.

Index